MCTS: Microsoft Office SharePoint Server 2007 Configuration Study Guide

Exam 70-630: MCTS: Microsoft Office SharePoint Configuring Objectives

D1490213

Sybex®
An Imprint of
WILEY

OBJECTIVE	CHAPTER
Managing Business Intelligence	
Configure Excel Services	12
Configure Report Center	12
Configure Filter Web Parts	8
Configure Business Data Catalog (BDC)	13
Manage Administration	
Manage Central Admin UI	1, 2, 3, 14
Manage the Shared Service Provider	2, 3, 14
Administrating Moss using STSADM	14
Configure Usage Analysis & Reporting	3, 14
Deploy/Upgrade Microsoft Office SharePoint Server 2007	
Manage CMS Assessment	16
Configure Shared Services	2, 3, 16
Manage Business Intelligence tools	16
Manage Portal and Site Migration	16
Finalize Upgrades	16

Exam objectives are subject to change at any time without prior notice and at Microsoft's sole discretion. Please visit Microsoft's website (www.microsoft.com/learning) for the most current listing of exam objectives.

Sybex®
An Imprint of
WILEY

MCTS:
Microsoft® Office SharePoint® Server 2007 Configuration
Study Guide (70-630)

MCTS:
Microsoft® Office
SharePoint® Server 2007
Configuration
Study Guide (70-630)

James Pyles

Wiley Publishing, Inc.

Acquisitions Editor: Jeff Kellum
Development Editor: Toni Zuccarini Ackley
Technical Editor: Randy Muller
Production Editor: Rachel Gunn
Copy Editor: Kim Wimpsett
Production Manager: Tim Tate
Vice President and Executive Group Publisher: Richard Swadley
Vice President and Executive Publisher: Joseph B. Wikert
Vice President and Publisher: Neil Edde
Media Associate Project Manager: Laura Atkinson
Media Assistant Producer: Josh Frank
Media Quality Assurance: Angie Denny
Book Designer: Judy Fung
Compositor: Craig Woods, Happenstance Type-O-Rama
Proofreader: Ian Golder
Indexer: Ted Laux
Cover Designer: Ryan Sneed

Library of Congress Cataloging-in-Publication Data

Pyles, James.
  MCTS : Microsoft Office Sharepoint Server 2007 configuration study guide (70-630) / James Pyles. — 1st ed.
    p. cm.
  ISBN 978-0-470-22663-6 (pbk. : CD-ROM)
 1. Microsoft SharePoint (Electronic resource) 2. Intranets (Computer networks) 3. Web servers. I. Title.
 TK5105.875.I6P95 2008
 004.6'82—dc22
                                    2008001408

10 9 8 7 6 5 4 3 2 1

Sybex®
An Imprint of
WILEY

Dear Reader

Thank you for choosing *MCTS: Microsoft Office SharePoint Server 2007 Configuration Study Guide (70-630)*. This book is part of a family of premium quality Sybex books, all written by outstanding authors who combine practical experience with a gift for teaching.

Sybex was founded in 1976. More than thirty years later, we're still committed to producing consistently exceptional books. With each of our titles we're working hard to set a new standard for the industry. From the the authors we work with, to paper we print on, our goal is to bring you the best books available.

I hope you see all that reflected in these pages. I'd be very interested to hear your comments and get your feedback on how we're doing. Feel free to let me know what you think about this or any other Sybex book by sending me an email at nedde@wiley.com, or if you think you've found a technical error in this book, please visit http://sybex.custhelp.com. Customer feedback is critical to our efforts at Sybex.

Best regards,

Neil Edde
Vice President and Publisher
Sybex, an Imprint of Wiley

To my parents, James and Barbara Pyles, who still believe the best in me, and to my children, Michael, David, and Jamie, whom my wife, Lin, and I will always love

Acknowledgments

I'd like to thank Jeff Kellum for having enough faith in me to ask me to write a second book for Sybex. I'd also like to thank Toni Zuccarini Ackley, who had to put up with me again and who has been very gracious and patient with me and my idiosyncrasies. Production editor Rachel Gunn has also been very good to work with, even when I told that her name reminded me of the old TV show detective Peter Gunn (a really cool jazz theme opens the show). Kim Wimpsett is one of the "unsung heroes" who edited my work and earned my respect, and technical editor Randy Muller kept me humble and on my toes at the same time.

My greatest thanks go to my wife, Lin, who has spent many a night and weekend patiently watching me pound away at the keyboard as I produced this book (when she wasn't reading, studying, working, taking classes, visiting the sick, and being the very active, involved, and caring person she has always been). I also want to acknowledge my children, who all make me see a different part of myself, as if I'm growing up all over again. To Michael, who continues to search for his dream and his place in a world filled with so many possibilities. To Jamie, who found her focus as an artist and writer a lot earlier in life than I did. To David, who found a courage I never had at his age and who is serving his country in Iraq as a United States Marine. To everyone in my family: I love you all very much.

About the Author

James Pyles (A+, Network+) is a freelance consultant and technical writer and is currently on contract as a lead technical writer for iAnywhere, a Sybase company. His most recent book is *SharePoint 2007: The Definitive Guide* (O'Reilly, 2007). He also authored *PC Technician Street Smarts* (Sybex, 2006) and has written numerous eLearning courses such as Wireless Networking Solutions, Small Business Servers and Networking, Securing Windows XP, and Senior Network Administrator Best Practices for hardware vendors such as HP, eMachines, and Gateway. James has worked as the SharePoint site administrator and technical writer for Micron Technology's Information Systems Support Operations Group, has been the technical writer for a software company developing a Linux-based server appliance, and has supported a usability lab for Hewlett-Packard, among other technical positions. He also writes book reviews on topics such as Linux, networking, programming, and web design for various publications including *Linux Pro* magazine. He is a regular contributor and moderator at www.certforums.co.uk, www.linux-tutorial .info, and www.mcseworld.com. James has bachelor's degrees in psychology and computer network support and a master's degree in counseling. He lives near Boise, Idaho.

Contents at a Glance

Contents

Table of Exercises

Introduction

Microsoft has recently changed its certification program to contain three primary series: Technology, Professional, and Architect. The Technology Series certifications are intended to allow candidates to target specific technologies and are the basis for obtaining the Professional Series and Architect Series of certifications. The certifications contained within the Technology Series consist of one to three exams, focusing on a specific technology, and do not include job-role skills. By contrast, the Professional Series of certifications focus on a job role and are not necessarily focused on a single technology but rather a comprehensive set of skills for performing the job role being tested. The Architect Series of certifications offered by Microsoft are premier certifications that consist of passing a review board consisting of previously certified architects. To apply for the Architect Series of certifications, you must have a minimum of 10 years of industry experience.

When obtaining a Technology Series certification, you are recognized as a Microsoft Certified Technology Specialist (MCTS) on the specific technology or technologies on which you have been tested. The Professional Series certifications include Microsoft Certified IT Professional (MCITP) and Microsoft Certified Professional Developer (MCPD). Passing the review board for an Architect Series certification will allow you to become a Microsoft Certified Architect (MCA).

MCTS: Microsoft Office SharePoint Server 2007 Configuration Study Guide (70-630) will help you organize and focus your studies and your skill sets so that you will be completely prepared to pass the Microsoft Office SharePoint Server 2007, Configuring (70-630) certification exam.

The Microsoft Certified Professional Program

Since the beginning of its certification program, Microsoft has certified more than 2 million people. As the computer network industry continues to increase in both size and complexity, this number is sure to grow—and the need for *proven* ability will also increase. Certifications can help companies verify the skills of prospective employees and contractors.

Microsoft has developed its Microsoft Certified Professional (MCP) program to give you credentials that verify your ability to work with Microsoft products effectively and professionally. Several levels of certification are available based on specific suites of exams. Microsoft has recently created a new generation of certification programs:

Microsoft Certified Technology Specialist (MCTS)   The MCTS can be considered the entry-level certification for the new generation of Microsoft certifications. The MCTS certification program targets specific technologies instead of specific job roles. You must take and pass one to three exams.

Microsoft Certified IT Professional (MCITP)   The MCITP certification is a Professional Series certification that tests network and systems administrators on job roles, rather than only on a specific technology. The MCITP generally consists of one to three exams, in addition to obtaining an MCTS-level certification.

Microsoft Certified Professional Developer (MCPD)   The MCPD certification is a Professional Series certification for application developers. Similar to the MCITP, the MCPD is focused on a job role rather than on a single technology. The MCPD generally consists of one to three exams, in addition to obtaining an MCTS-level certification.

Microsoft Certified Architect (MCA)   The MCA is Microsoft's premier certification series. Obtaining the MCA requires a minimum of 10 years of experience and requires the candidate to pass a review board consisting of peer architects.

How Do You Become Certified on Microsoft Office SharePoint Server 2007?

In the past, students have been able to acquire detailed exam information—even most of the exam questions—from online "brain dumps" and third-party "cram" books or software products. For that matter, many candidates who were "good students" and able to pass tests by memorizing information from textbooks passed Microsoft certification exams while having little or no practical experience in managing Windows systems. They sadly gave birth to the phrase *paper MCSE*. Those days are gone forever.

Microsoft has taken strong steps to protect the security and integrity of its new certification tracks. Now prospective candidates must complete a course of study that develops detailed knowledge about a wide range of topics. It supplies them with the true skills needed, derived from working with the technology being tested. Although no test maps to a set of skills with 100 percent fidelity, Microsoft is working to make its exam content and format measure, as closely as computer-administered exams can, the true abilities of the people taking the exams.

To that end, the new generation of Microsoft certification programs is heavily weighted toward hands-on skills and experience. It is recommended that candidates have troubleshooting skills acquired through hands-on experience and working knowledge.

Fortunately, if you are willing to dedicate the time and effort to learn the Microsoft technologies you want to master, you can prepare yourself well for the exams by using the proper tools. By working through this book, you can successfully meet the exam requirements to pass the SharePoint configuration exam.

This book is part of a complete series of Microsoft certification study guides, published by Sybex, that together cover the new MCTS, MCITP, and MCPD exams, as well as the core MCSA and MCSE operating system requirements. Please visit the Sybex website at www.sybex.com for complete program and product details.

MCTS Exam Requirements

Candidates for MCTS certification on Microsoft Office SharePoint Server (MOSS) 2007 for configuring must pass just a single exam. Other MCTS certifications may require up to three exams. For a more detailed description of the Microsoft certification programs, including a list of all the exams, visit the Microsoft Learning website at www.microsoft.com/learning/mcpexams/default.mspx.

The Microsoft Office SharePoint Server 2007, Configuring Exam

The Microsoft Office SharePoint Server 2007, Configuring exam covers concepts and skills related to installing, configuring, and managing SharePoint server farms, site collections, and interoperations with other Microsoft technologies. It emphasizes the following elements of design and administration:

- Configuring Microsoft Office SharePoint Server 2007 Portal
- Managing search
- Configuring content management
- Configuring business forms
- Managing business intelligence
- Managing administration
- Deploying and upgrading Microsoft Office SharePoint Server 2007

This exam is quite specific regarding SharePoint Server 2007 requirements and operational settings, and it can be particular about how administrative and configuration tasks are performed within SharePoint. It also focuses on fundamental concepts of SharePoint's operation and its interoperability with other Microsoft Office suite products, particularly other Office 2007 applications.

Microsoft provides exam objectives to give you a general overview of possible areas of coverage on the Microsoft exams. Keep in mind, however, that exam objectives are subject to change at any time without prior notice and at Microsoft's sole discretion. Please visit the Microsoft Learning website at www.microsoft.com/learning/default.mspx for the most current listing of exam objectives.

Types of Exam Questions

In an effort to both refine the testing process and protect the quality of its certifications, Microsoft has focused its newer certification exams on real experience and hands-on proficiency. There is a greater emphasis on your past working environments and responsibilities and less emphasis on how well you can memorize. In fact, Microsoft says that certification candidates should have hands-on experience before attempting to pass any certification exams.

Microsoft will accomplish its goal of protecting the integrity of its exams by regularly adding and removing exam questions, limiting the number of questions that any individual sees in a beta exam, limiting the number of questions delivered to an individual by using adaptive testing, and adding new exam elements.

Exam questions may be in a variety of formats: depending on which exam you take, you'll see multiple-choice questions, select-and-place questions, and prioritize-a-list questions. Simulations and case study–based formats are included as well. You may also find yourself taking what's called an *adaptive format exam*. Let's take a look at the types of exam questions and examine the adaptive testing technique so you'll be prepared for all the possibilities.

With the release of Windows 2000, Microsoft stopped providing a detailed score breakdown. This is mostly because of the various and complex question formats. Previously, each question focused on one objective. Recent exams, such as the Microsoft Office SharePoint Server 2007, Configuring exam, however, contain questions that may be tied to one or more objectives from one or more objective sets. Therefore, grading by objective is almost impossible. Also, Microsoft no longer offers a score. Now you will be told only whether you pass or fail. That's disappointing for those of us who quantify just about everything, but we can't have it all.

Multiple-Choice Questions

Multiple-choice questions come in two main forms. One is a straightforward question followed by several possible answers, of which one or more is correct. The other type of multiple-choice question is more complex and based on a specific scenario. The scenario may focus on several areas or objectives.

Select-and-Place Questions

Select-and-place exam questions involve graphical elements that you must manipulate to successfully answer the question. For example, you might see a diagram of a computer network. A typical diagram will show computers and other components next to boxes that contain the text "Place here." The labels for the boxes represent various computer roles on a network, such as a print server and a file server. Based on information given for each computer, you are asked to select each label and place it in the correct box. You need to place *all* the labels correctly. No credit is given for the question if you correctly label only some of the boxes.

In another select-and-place problem, you might be asked to put a series of steps in order by dragging items from boxes on the left to boxes on the right and placing them in the correct order. One other type requires that you drag an item from the left and place it under an item in a column on the right.

For more information on the various exam question types, go to www.microsoft.com/learning/mcpexams/policies/innovations.asp.

Simulations

Simulations are the kinds of questions that most closely represent actual situations and test the skills you use while working with Microsoft software interfaces. These exam questions include a mock interface on which you are asked to perform certain actions according to a given scenario.

Because of the number of possible errors that can be made on simulations, be sure to consider the following recommendations from Microsoft:

- Do not change any simulation settings that don't pertain to the solution directly.
- When related information has not been provided, assume that the default settings are used.
- Make sure your entries are spelled correctly.
- Close all the simulation application windows after completing the set of tasks in the simulation.

The best way to prepare for simulation questions is to spend time working with the graphical interface of the product on which you will be tested.

Case Study–Based Questions

Case study–based questions first appeared in the MCSD program. These questions present a scenario with a range of requirements. Based on the information provided, you answer a series of multiple-choice and select-and-place questions. The interface for case study–based questions has a number of tabs, each of which contains information about the scenario. Currently, this type of question appears only in most of the Design exams.

 Microsoft will regularly add and remove questions from the exams. This is called *item seeding*. It is part of the effort to make it more difficult for individuals to merely memorize exam questions that were passed along by previous test-takers.

Tips for Taking the SharePoint Server 2007 Configuration Exam

Here are some general tips for achieving success on your certification exam:

- Arrive early at the exam center so that you can relax and review your study materials. During this final review, you can look over tables and lists of exam-related information.
- Read the questions carefully. Don't be tempted to jump to an early conclusion. Make sure you know *exactly* what the question is asking.
- Answer all questions. If you are unsure about a question, then mark the question for review, and return to the question at a later time.
- On simulations, do not change settings that are not directly related to the question. Also, assume default settings if the question does not specify or imply which settings are used.

- For questions you're not sure about, use a process of elimination to get rid of the obviously incorrect answers first. Often there are one or two you can dismiss immediately, assuming you know the subject for which you are being tested. This improves your odds of selecting the correct answer when you need to make an educated guess.

Exam Registration

You can take the Microsoft exams at any of more than 1,000 Authorized Prometric Testing Centers (APTCs) and VUE Testing Centers around the world. For the location of a testing center near you, call Prometric at 800-755-EXAM (755-3926), or call VUE at 888-837-8616. Outside the United States and Canada, contact your local Prometric or VUE registration center.

Find out the number of the exam you want to take, and then register with the Prometric or VUE registration center nearest to you. At this point, you will be asked for advance payment for the exam. The exams are $125 each, and you must take them within one year of payment. You can schedule exams up to six weeks in advance or as late as one working day prior to the date of the exam. (The latter is generally but not universally true, so don't count on it.) You can cancel or reschedule your exam if you contact the center at least two working days prior to the exam. Same-day registration is available in some locations, subject to space availability. Where same-day registration is available, you must register a minimum of two hours before test time.

 You can also register for your exams online at www.prometric.com or www.vue.com.

When you schedule the exam, you will be provided with instructions regarding appointment and cancellation procedures, ID requirements, and information about the testing center location. In addition, you will receive a registration and payment confirmation letter from Prometric or VUE.

Microsoft requires certification candidates to accept the terms of a nondisclosure agreement before taking certification exams.

Who Should Read This Book

I suppose it goes without saying that the primary audience of this book is anyone who intends on taking the Microsoft 70-630 certification exam: Microsoft Office SharePoint Server 2007, Configuring. Of course, this could include people from several different backgrounds and could include people who aren't actually planning on taking the test:

- People who are currently administering SharePoint Server 2003 for an organization who are planning or at least considering upgrading to Microsoft Office SharePoint Server 2007 (MOSS 2007) should read this book, not only with the idea of becoming certified but also to learn about the many differences between the 2003 and 2007 versions of this application.

- People who are currently administering MOSS 2007 but who either think they need to know more or want to solidify their qualifications in managing this technology by earning the 70-630 certification should read this book.

- People who are interested in information and content management, multiteam collaboration in an enterprise environment, and large-scale project organization and tracking managed using a multipurpose, web browser–based interface and think SharePoint may be the answer to their dreams or at least their questions should read this book.

Installing, configuring, and managing a MOSS 2007 environment isn't an easy task. In fact, despite that I'm an experienced SharePoint site administrator and I use words for a living, I have difficulty describing exactly what MOSS 2007 is and what it does. I suppose that's because the range of activities and purposes served by SharePoint is really that vast and that varied. For that reason, if you are involved in administering SharePoint 2007, expect to be in the near future, or aspire to those roles, it's important to have resources that pull together all of the vital sources of information and organize them in a way that makes them accessible and easier to assimilate.

Although there are a number of fine books on the market on MOSS 2007 administration and development (I even cowrote one of them), none specifically addresses SharePoint from the point of view of the 70-630 exam. That makes the focus of this book unique. If you plan to take this certification exam, no other book will present the required information to you in the way you need it mapped out. Other books might contain some or all of the required subject matter, but they will make you work quite a bit harder to cull the gems you're looking for as you're studying. Here, the gems are gathered together in one place so all you have to do is open the book.

Like most people who work in a technical field, I tend to think and write in an organized and linear manner. Each chapter in this book builds on the last, so skipping around in the book won't be very helpful, at least not until you've gone through it at least once cover to cover. Alternately, you can skip around from chapter to chapter and follow only the steps of the individual chapters.

What's in the Book?

What makes a Sybex study guide the book of choice for hundreds of thousands of MCPs? We took into account not only what you need to know to pass the exam but also what you need to know to take what you've learned and apply it in the real world. Each book contains the following:

Objective-by-objective coverage of the topics you need to know   Each chapter lists the objectives covered in that chapter.

The topics covered in this study guide map directly to Microsoft's official exam objectives. Each exam objective is covered completely.

Assessment test   Directly following this introduction is an assessment test that you should take. It is designed to help you determine how much you already know about SharePoint Server 2007. Each question is tied to a topic discussed in the book. Using the results of the assessment test, you can figure out the areas where you need to focus your study. Of course, we do recommend you read the entire book.

Exam essentials   To highlight what you learn, you'll find a list of exam essentials at the end of each chapter. The "Exam Essentials" section briefly highlights the topics that need your particular attention as you prepare for the exam.

Glossary   Throughout each chapter, you will be introduced to important terms and concepts that you will need to know for the exam. At the end of the book, a detailed glossary gives definitions for these terms, as well as other general terms you should know.

Review questions, complete with detailed explanations   Each chapter is followed by a set of review questions that test what you learned in the chapter. The questions are written with the exam in mind, meaning they are designed to have the same look and feel as what you'll see on the exam. Question types are multiple choice. You'll find other question types such as exhibits and select-and-place on the actual exam.

Hands-on exercises   In each chapter, you'll find exercises designed to give you the important hands-on experience that is critical for your exam preparation. The exercises support the topics of the chapter, and they walk you through the steps necessary to perform a particular function.

Real-world scenarios   Because reading a book isn't enough for you to learn how to apply these topics in your everyday duties, we have provided real-world scenarios in special sidebars. These explain when and why a particular solution would make sense in a working environment you'd actually encounter.

Interactive CD   Every Sybex study guide comes with a CD complete with additional questions, flashcards for use with an interactive device, a Windows simulation program, and the book in electronic format. Details are in the following section.

What's on the CD?

With this new member of our best-selling Study Guide series, we are including quite an array of training resources. The CD offers numerous simulations, bonus exams, and flashcards to help you study for the exam. We have also included the complete contents of the study guide in electronic form. The CD's resources are described here:

The Sybex e-book for *MCTS: Microsoft Office SharePoint Server 2007 Configuration Study Guide*   Many people like the convenience of being able to carry their whole study guide on a CD. They also like being able to search the text via computer to find specific information quickly and easily. For these reasons, the entire contents of this study guide are supplied on the CD in PDF. We've also included Adobe Acrobat Reader, which provides the interface for the PDF contents as well as the search capabilities.

The Sybex test engine   This is a collection of multiple-choice questions that will help you prepare for your exam. There are four sets of questions:

- Two bonus exams designed to simulate the actual live exam.
- All the questions from the study guide, presented in a test engine for your review. You can review questions by chapter or by objective, or you can take a random test.
- The assessment test.

Sybex flashcards for PCs and handheld devices The flashcard-style of question offers an effective way to quickly and efficiently test your understanding of the fundamental concepts covered in the exam. The Sybex flashcards set consists of 150 questions presented in a special engine developed specifically for this study guide series.

Because of the high demand for a product that will run on handheld devices, we have also developed, in conjunction with Land-J Technologies, a version of the flashcard questions that you can take with you on your Palm OS PDA (including the PalmPilot and Handspring's Visor).

Contacts and Resources

To find out more about Microsoft Education and Certification materials and programs, to register with Prometric or VUE, or to obtain other useful certification information and additional study resources, check the following resources:

Microsoft Learning Home Page

www.microsoft.com/learning

This website provides information about the MCP program and exams. You can also order the latest Microsoft Roadmap to Education and Certification.

Microsoft TechNet Technical Information Network

www.microsoft.com/technet

800-344-2121

Use this website or phone number to contact support professionals and system administrators. Outside the United States and Canada, contact your local Microsoft subsidiary for information.

PalmPilot Training Product Development: Land-J

www.land-j.com

407-359-2217

Land-J Technologies is a consulting and programming business currently specializing in application development for the 3Com PalmPilot Personal Digital Assistant. Land-J developed the Palm version of the EdgeTests, which is included on the CD that accompanies this Study Guide.

Prometric

www.prometric.com

800-755-3936

Contact Prometric to register to take an MCP exam at any of more than 800 Prometric Testing Centers around the world.

Virtual University Enterprises (VUE)

www.vue.com

888-837-8616

Contact the VUE registration center to register to take an MCP exam at one of the VUE Testing Centers.

What Else You Will Need

You will need to practice using MOSS 2007 Enterprise Edition. Fortunately, you can download a trial version of this product that will allow you to use it free for 180 days. You must install SharePoint 2007 on a Windows Server 2003 machine, and you can obtain a trial version of this software from Microsoft. Although not absolutely necessary, it will be extremely helpful for you to have access to the Microsoft Office 2007 suite; you can download a trial version as Office Enterprise 2007 Win32 Trial. Here is where you'll need to go to download the various software packages:

- **Windows Server 2003 R2 with SP2 Trial Version**

  http://technet.microsoft.com/en-us/windowsserver/bb430831.aspx

- **SharePoint Server 2007 Trial Version**

  http://www.microsoft.com/downloads/details.aspx?FamilyId=2E6E5A9C-EBF6-4F7F-8467-F4DE6BD6B831&displaylang=en

- Microsoft Office Enterprise 2007

  Register for the product key here:
  http://technet.microsoft.com/en-us/bb736012.aspx

  Download the software here:

  http://www.microsoft.com/downloads/details.aspx?familyid=2D1189BF-D86A-4ACF-9DCC-4D61F500AD6D&displaylang=en

Hardware and Software Requirements

You should verify that your computer meets the minimum requirements for installing the required software packages. Each download site contains the relevant information you'll need. In addition, Chapter 2, "Installing and Deploying SharePoint 2007," contains detailed information about the hardware and software requirements, so it is highly recommended that you carefully review this entire chapter before installing the required software packages onto your computer.

The exercises in Chapter 2 will also guide you through the step-by-step process of installing MOSS 2007 as a stand-alone server deployment. SharePoint can be deployed on a single server computer or on a server farm in a data center. Although the book's content includes material relevant to managing SharePoint in a server farm environment, it's unlikely you'll have a data center tucked away in a back closet of your house or apartment, so the practical focus of installing and setting up SharePoint addresses using a single computer.

This book was written using the trial versions of MOSS 2007, Windows Server 2003, and Office Enterprise 2007 installed on a virtual machine in VMware Workstation 5.5 on a Windows XP Professional SP2 host computer.

The virtual machine was configured to use the following settings:

- *Memory*: 512MB

- *Hard disk*: (SCSI 0:0) 15GB (though I never used more than 2GB of hard drive space)

- *Virtual processors*: 1

- *Ethernet*: Bridged
- *USB controller*: Present

As you can see, I set the resources to be rather modest, and during the writing of this book I primarily had only the single virtual machine running. The virtual network was bridged to my actual home LAN so that SharePoint could have access to multiple virtual and actual host computers and to the Internet. The host Windows XP Professional SP2 computer's resources at the time of this writing were as follows:

- *Memory*: 1.25GB
- *Hard disk*: (IDE) 200GB
- *Processor*: Pentium 4 CPU 2.60GHz

If you have the resources to afford a more powerful computer on which to run SharePoint 2007, I recommend it. Although my virtual machine responded reasonably well, sometimes I had to wait when moving from one web page to the next or from one site to the next, so if patience isn't one of your virtues, buy more RAM.

How to Contact the Author

You never write a book alone. Sure, I'm the only author of this text, but there is a team of people who don't have their names on the cover who worked hard to make sure the book in your hands is the best it possibly can be. Every editor involved has taken a great deal of time and energy and provided me with invaluable feedback about how I could make the book better. That said, the one resource I don't have access to while writing is the reader. I can know what you think only after the book is available on the bookstore shelves and online.

I'd still like to hear what you think (be nice), and I do read and respond to my emails. You can reach me by writing to jmpyles@wiredwriter, and you can learn more about my work on my website at www.wiredwriter.net.

As I mentioned, the folks at Sybex work hard to keep you supplied with the latest tools and information you need for your work. Please check the website at www.sybex.com, where we'll post additional content and updates that supplement this book if the need arises. Enter *MCTS: Microsoft Office SharePoint Server 2007 Configuration Study Guide* in the Search box (or type the book's ISBN, which is 9780470226636), and click Go to go to the book's updates page.

Remember, studying for this exam is something you want to do, and you are learning about a subject you are really interested in. With that in mind, don't make it all work. Have fun. Play with the technology. See how far you can take the exercises, modify them, try different combinations of settings, and figure out all the different ways that SharePoint works and what it does. Really get to know it inside and out as you are working through the chapters, and by the time you schedule and take the exam, you'll be ready. Good luck.

Assessment Test

1. What are some of the collaboration tools supported in Microsoft Office SharePoint Server (MOSS) 2007?

   A. Blogs and wikis

   B. Indexing Service

   C. RSS feeds

   D. Office Outlook 2007 collaboration

2. What utility or application is required to create a new master page or modify page layouts in SharePoint?

   A. Office SharePoint Designer 2007

   B. Office FrontPage 2007

   C. Office Publisher 2007

   D. Office SharePoint Project 2007

3. What is the most basic container in architecting SharePoint 2007 design components?

   A. The server farm

   B. The shared services provider (SSP)

   C. The web application

   D. The site collection

4. You are going to install Office SharePoint Server 2007 on a Windows Server 2003 Standard Edition computer in order to evaluate SharePoint 2007 and develop a deployment plan for your company. To prepare Windows Server 2003 for the SharePoint installation, what pre-installation tasks do you need to perform? (Choose all that apply.)

   A. You must enable IIS 6.0.

   B. You must install the Microsoft .NET Framework 3.0 and then enable ASP.NET 2.0.

   C. You must install SQL Server 2005 Express Edition.

   D. You must install Windows Server 2003 Web Edition.

5. You are going to install Office SharePoint Server 2007 on a Windows Server 2003 Standard Edition computer in order to evaluate SharePoint 2007 and develop a deployment plan for your company. You are checking the official hardware requirements for the installation to make sure the physical server you have selected matches or exceeds those requirements. Of the following options, which meet Microsoft's recommended hardware requirements for installing SharePoint 2007 on a stand-alone computer? (Choose all that apply.)

   A. Dual processors that are each 2.5GHz or faster

   B. 2GB of RAM

   C. NTFS file system–formatted partition with 3GB of free space plus adequate free space for your websites

   D. 56Kbps or faster connection between the client computers and the server

6. You are in the process of installing SharePoint Server 2007 on a Windows Server 2003 machine. Rather than install SharePoint in the default file location, you want to specify your own location. Of the following options, which one is the correct way to accomplish this?

    A. On the Choose the Installation You Want page, click Basic, specify the location you want to install to, and finish the installation.

    B. On the Choose the Installation You Want page, click Advanced, and then on the File Location tab specify the location you want to install to, and finish the installation.

    C. On the Choose the Installation You Want page, click Basic, and then on the File Location tab, specify the location you want to install to, and finish the installation.

    D. On the Choose the Installation You Want page, click Advanced, specify the location you want to install to, and finish the installation.

7. You are the SharePoint administrator for your company. You have just finished installing SharePoint Server 2007 on a stand-alone server and have successfully run Configuring SharePoint Products and Technologies. You are now about to configure the incoming email settings. Of the following options, which one describes what you should do next?

    A. In Central Administration, click the Operations tab, and click Incoming Email Settings under Topology and Services.

    B. In Central Administration, click the Operations tab, and click Incoming Email Settings under Content Deployment.

    C. In Central Administration, click the Application Management tab, and click Incoming Email Settings under Topology and Services.

    D. In Central Administration, click the Application Management tab, and click Incoming Email Settings under Content Deployment.

8. You are the SharePoint administrator for your company. You want to make it possible to create email distribution lists in SharePoint Server 2007 rather than in Outlook. Of the following options, which one describes the service that needs to be enabled?

    A. The Content Management Service for incoming emails

    B. The Content Management Service for outgoing emails

    C. The Directory Management Service for incoming emails

    D. The Directory Management Service for outgoing emails

9. You are the SharePoint administrator for the Metis Commercial Real Estate Group. You have just created a SharePoint 2007 server farm for Metis and are currently editing the shared services provider (SSP) for the server farm. You are at the last step in the process. Of the following options, which is the last step you can take in editing the SSP before clicking OK?

    A. Editing the path for the index file location

    B. Choosing whether to enable SSL for Web Services

    C. Setting up SQL authentication by configuring an account name and password

    D. None of the above

10. You are the SharePoint administrator for your company. The manager of the public relations office for your firm wants you to set up a blog so she can have a venue to inform employees of upcoming events in the company intranet. Which one of the site templates presented will allow you to set up a blog site?

A. Collaboration

B. Enterprise

C. Meetings

D. Publishing

11. You are the SharePoint administrator for your company. The marketing department has a site under the company's main portal site, and the marketing manager wants you to set up a site beneath their main site for special projects. On the marketing department's site, what are the first steps you take to begin creating the subsite?

A. Click Site Actions and then Site Settings. In the Sites and Workspaces column, click Create Site.

B. Click Site Actions, and then click Create. On the Create page under Web Pages, click Sites and Workspaces.

C. Click Site Actions and then Site Settings. On the Site Settings page under Web Pages, click Sites and Workspaces

D. Click Site Actions, and then click Create. On the Create page under Sites and Workspaces, click Create Site.

12. The manager of the sales department has been granted rights to create sites under the main sales department site, but any sites he creates still require approval by you as the SharePoint site administrator. What are the first steps you must take to either approve or reject a newly created site?

A. From SharePoint Central Administration, click the Operations tab, and under the Site Operations column, click Approve/Reject Sites.

B. From the main portal site, click Site Actions, click Administration, and then click Site Administration.

C. From the submitted site, click Site Actions, and then click Approve/Reject.

D. From the Site Directory, click View All Site Contents, and under Lists click Sites. Then find the name of the submitted site, click to the right to open the menu, and then click Approve/Reject.

13. You are the SharePoint administrator for the Ango Corporation. The CTO has tasked you with adding a custom user profile property to the user profile store in the relevant SSP for the company's site collection. On the Add User Profile Property page under Property Settings, what actions must you take?

A. Type the name of the new user profile property in the Name field, and then type the name you want displayed for this property in the Display Name field.

B. Type the name of the new user profile property you want displayed in the Display Name field, and then type the name in the Name field.

C. Type the unique identifier for the new user profile property in the GUID field, and then type the name in the Name field.

D. Type the name of the new user profile property in the Name field, and then type the unique identifier in the GUID field.

14. You are the SharePoint administrator for your company. You want to create an audience made up of department managers and then target content to that audience relevant to that job role. To accomplish this task, after you create the audience, you must set up one or more rules that will apply, depending on your goal for the audience. You want the rule to apply to users so you select the User operand during the rule creation process. What operator selections must you now make? (Choose two.)

A. Member Of

B. Group Member

C. Belongs To

D. Reports Under

15. You are the junior SharePoint administrator for the Tycho Astronomical Association, a large nonprofit group that advocates for inclusion of astronomy classes in public and private schools across the country. The senior admin has tasked you with reviewing the default SharePoint site access groups and determining to which groups 10 new volunteers at Tycho should be assigned. Three of the volunteers are editors and you decide they will need to belong to the Quick Deploy Users group. Of the following options, which one best describes this group?

A. Users assigned to this group have the ability to control site performance.

B. Users assigned to this group are able to modify the structure of a site.

C. Users assigned to this group have the ability to quickly update content on the site.

D. Users assigned to this group have rights to read the Master Page Gallery and have read-only permissions to the Style Gallery.

16. You are the SharePoint administrator for your company, and you are planning an authentication scheme for SharePoint 2007. You are reviewing the requirements for the different authentication methods that you can configure in Central Administration. Some methods do not require any additional setup, but quite a few of them do. Of the subsequent options, which method requires that you configure a service principal name (SPN) for the domain user account that is used for the application pool identity and register the SPN for the domain user account in Active Directory?

A. Certificates

B. NTLM

C. Kerberos

D. Web SSO

17. You are the SharePoint administrator for your company. You have configured a single sign-on (SSO) environment in SharePoint so that users do not have to authenticate again when they want to access back-end and external data sources. There are a number of different reasons for needing to restore the SSO environment. Currently, you need to move the encryption-key server role from one server machine to another. In SharePoint Central Administration, what is the first step you must take to accomplish this task?

A. Disable the SSO Service on all servers in the server farm.

B. Disable the SSO Service on the current encryption-key server machine.

C. Enable the SSO service on the new encryption-key server machine.

D. Enable the SSO service on all servers in the server farm.

18. You are the SharePoint administrator for your company. You have configured a single sign-on (SSO) environment in SharePoint so that users do not have to authenticate again when they want to access back-end and external data sources. You need to set up a backup schedule for the SSO database server. Where would you go to best accomplish this task?

A. In SharePoint Central Administration on the Operations tab at the Manage SSO Database link

B. In Windows Server 2003 in the Computer Management box at Disk Management

C. In SharePoint Central Administration on the Applications Management tab at the SSO database backup link

D. Back up the SSO database as you would any other database server such as Microsoft SQL server

19. You are a site administrator for the technical documentation department's SharePoint website. As department manager, all of the writers on your staff must submit their work to you for approval. To facilitate this process on the SharePoint site, you have created several different workflow types on the site's document library. You've discovered that the default workflow types don't meet all of your needs, and you want to create several custom-made workflows. The company hires Robert, a consultant to work with you to accomplish this goal. Robert advises you that there are two main options that can be used to create a custom workflow. Which of the following options correctly identify these tools? (Choose two.)

A. Microsoft Visual Studio 2005

B. Microsoft Visual Basic

C. Office SharePoint Designer 2007

D. Microsoft Visual C#

20. You are a site member on your department's SharePoint website and are submitting a document you created to the site's document library. You realize that you need to add some information to the document, but when you try to edit it, you discover you are required to check the document out in the document library before you can open it in Microsoft Office Word. You are new to SharePoint and don't understand the process of checking a document out or into a library. You ask a more experienced coworker and learn a number of things about the process. Of the following options, which are true about the checkout and check-in process? (Choose all that apply.)

A. When a document is checked out, the author can save the document without checking it in.

B. When a document is checked out, it is saved in the user's My Documents folder in a subfolder named SharePoint Documents.

C. When a document is checked in after it has been edited, the author can write comments that describe the changes made to the document.

D. Users can check documents out, undo checkouts, and check documents in from Microsoft Office 2003 or higher application software.

21. You are the SharePoint site administrator for your department's SharePoint website. You have created a Contacts list of every member of the department and have made it visible on your department website's home page. The list is quite long, and Alison, a team lead in the research group, suggests filtering the list by workgroups so that each group can select a filtered view of only their team members. You are new to SharePoint and have to investigate exactly how to create filtered views to produce the desired result. You discover that you can create filtered views by information contained in which of the following?

A. Rows

B. Columns

C. Items

D. Records

22. You are the site administrator for your company's intranet site. You have just added several Links web parts to the sales department's web page, each presenting a different filtered view of the list. You want to designate a specific view as the default view for the list. Of the following options, which one correctly describes how to do this?

A. On the sales department's web page, click the arrow at the right of the list web part's title bar that you want to make the default view, click Modify Shared Web Part, and then use the Selected View drop-down arrow in the web part's toolbox to select Default View.

B. On the sales department's web page, click the name of the list in one of the list web part's title bars. Then on the list page, click Settings, and then click List Settings. Under Views, click the view you want to make default, and on the view's page, tick the Make This the Default View check box.

C. On the sales department's web page, click the name of the list in one of the list web part's title bars. Then on the list page, click Settings, and select the view you want to make default. When the view page appears, tick the Make This the Default View check box.

D. On the sales department's web page, click the arrow at the right of the list web part's title bar that you want to make the default view, and click Modify Shared Web Part. Then expand Appearance, and use the Selected View drop-down arrow in the web part's toolbox to select Default View.

23. You are the SharePoint site administrator for your company's intranet site. You are planning how web page content is to be published with your staff and going over the specific web page design elements you can use. Of the following options, which are valid SharePoint web page design elements? (Choose all that apply.)

A. Master pages

B. Content pages

C. Design pages

D. Style sheets

24. You are working with the SharePoint site administrator for your company's intranet site to design a new web part page. You have just been hired onto her staff, and she is showing you how SharePoint web parts work. She opens a Links list web part toolbox and shows you the different properties you can use to modify how the web part behaves. You notice there are four major areas in this web part's toolbox. Of the following options, which ones correctly name these areas? (Choose all that apply.)

A. Links Views

B. Appearance

C. Layout

D. Advanced

25. You are the SharePoint administrator for your company's site collection. You are in the process of planning how SharePoint search is going to function for different content sources. You previously administered the organization's SharePoint Portal Server 2003 environment before upgrading to MOSS 2007, and you notice that there have been improvements in SharePoint search included in this version. Of the following options, which are search features included in MOSS 2007 that were not available in previous versions? (Choose all that apply.)

A. The ability to crawl and index file shares

B. The ability to crawl and index the site collection

C. The ability to crawl and index Internet websites

D. The ability to crawl and index the SSP in a single content index

26. You are the SharePoint administrator for your company's site collection. You are planning to configure the crawl rules for SharePoint's search feature. Of the following options, which are true for configuring crawl rules? (Choose all that apply.)

A. You can use crawl rules to crawl links on the URL without crawling the URL itself.

B. You can enable crawl rules to crawl complex URLs such as ones containing special characters like question marks.

C. You can enable crawl rules to crawl SharePoint site content such as FTP pages.

D. You can specify crawl to use the default content access account, a different content access account, or a client certificate to use for crawling the specified URL.

27. You are the SharePoint administrator for your company's site collection. Brian, the site owner for the archives department's website, calls you saying that the navigation links have changed dramatically overnight. He logged onto the archives site this morning and noticed that in the Quick Launch menu on the left side of the page, all of the lists and libraries contained in the site are listed under Site Hierarchy, which is an item that didn't display when he left work yesterday. What is the most likely explanation for this change in navigation?

A. Someone added a series of navigational links to Quick Launch during a site maintenance task last night after business hours.

B. Someone enabled tree view navigation during a site maintenance task last night after business hours.

C. Someone added a series of link and library web parts to the site during a site maintenance task last night after business hours.

D. Someone hacked the site last night after business hours and corrupted the navigation links.

28. You are the SharePoint site collection administrator for your organization. You are planning document content flow in the site collection with the department heads, and you are describing different types of content flow. Of the following options, which one accurately describes a content flow that is driven by the needs of content authors, owners, and consumers, moving from one location to another depending on who needs to access, copy, modify, or retire a document?

   A. Automatic content flow

   B. Dynamic content flow

   C. Managed content flow

   D. Manual content flow

29. You are the SharePoint administrator for your company. You have been tasked with planning an information policy strategy for different content types to be used for your organization's business documents so you can manage tracking and expiration of those documents. There are a number of ways to associate policies to your documentation, but you need to use the method that is available when a library isn't configured to support multiple content types. Of the following options, which one is correct?

   A. You can associate the policy directly to the entire site collection and then export the policy to other site collections within the enterprise.

   B. You can set policy association directly to a particular content type prior to adding the content to a document library.

   C. You can associate the policy directly to the library.

   D. You can associate the policy to a particular site in the site collection and then export the policy to the other sites in the collection.

30. You want to apply an information management policy to a document library to prevent users who have access to that library from downloading and printing the documents it contains. Of the following options, which one describes the correct set of procedures to begin this process?

   A. On the Customize Shared Documents page under Permissions and Management, click Shared Document Management.

   B. On the Information Management Policy Settings page in the Content Type column, click Document.

   C. On the Information Management Policy Settings page, tick the Define a Document Policy check box.

   D. In the desired document library, click Settings ➤ Library Settings ➤ Information Management Policy Document Settings.

31. You are the SharePoint administrator for your company's site collection. Martin, one of the users in the sales department, wants to subscribe to the marketing department's RSS feed on its SharePoint site. You ask Martin what version of Outlook he has, and he tells you he uses Outlook 2003. What is your response to him?

   A. You tell him that he will be able to subscribe to the RSS feed.

   B. You tell him that he needs to have Outlook 2007 to subscribe to the RSS feed.

   C. You tell him that he will need to download and install the latest updates for Outlook 2003 in order to subscribe to the RSS feed.

   D. You tell him that he will be able to subscribe to an RSS feed only on a SharePoint site where he is a member.

32. You are the SharePoint administrator for your organization. You have been tasked by the CIO with enabling a SharePoint Records Center site to provide content management for the company's emails. One of the primary objectives of your mission is to ensure that the integrity of the email content in the Records Center remains intact. The company is facing a lawsuit brought by a competitor, and some of the company's emails will be used as evidence. The content of the emails must be the same when downloaded to be presented as evidence as they were when they were uploaded to the Records Center. Which Records Center feature will you use to ensure the content's integrity?

   A. The Information Management Policies feature

   B. The Record Collection Programmable Interface feature

   C. The Vault feature

   D. The Hold feature

33. You are the SharePoint administrator for your organization's site collection. Sarah, the manager of the HR department's site, wants to enable email support for her site's Announcements list, but she has never performed this task before. You talk her through the process, which is relatively straightforward. She asks about options that can be set when enabling email support in the list. Of the following options, which ones are valid? (Choose all that apply.)

   A. Configuring the list to save original emails in .eml format

   B. Configuring the list to save meeting invitations

   C. Configuring the list to save email attachments in the body of the email

   D. Configuring the list to accept email messages based on list permissions

34. You are the SharePoint administrator for your company. You are reviewing how Excel Services operates as part of SharePoint's business intelligence solution. A team lead in the research department is interested in how Excel Services might be used on their portal site but wants to know more about it. Of the following options, which one best describes Excel Services?

   A. Although data from an Excel workbook may be exposed in a web part, all the storage and calculation functions are managed on the server.

   B. Once Excel workbook data is exposed through a web interface, all the formulas and calculations are controlled from within the web interface.

   C. Excel workbook data being displayed in a SharePoint web part requires that the client computer viewing that data be running Office 2007.

   D. External data sources must be enabled to connect an Excel Web Access web part to workbook data so that Excel Services can present data.

35. You are the SharePoint administrator for your company, and you are planning to use external data sources as part of your business intelligence deployment. External data sources allow SharePoint users to access data sources both within and outside of SharePoint. Of the following options, which are valid external data sources? (Choose all that apply.)

   A. SAP

   B. Siebel

   C. SharePoint lists

   D. Reports library

36. You are the SharePoint administrator for your company, and you are currently modifying a key performance indicator to display the progress of the sales team toward meeting performance goals for this quarter. You want the various status colors (green for met or exceeded goals, yellow for warning, and red for danger) to accurately reflect the performance status of this team. How do you configure the KPI values to accomplish your task?

A. Use the Status Icon Rules drop-down menu to select either Better Values Are Higher or Lower, and then use the select buttons next to the green and yellow indicators to determine the specific values.

B. Use the Status Icon Rules drop-down menu next to the green, yellow, and red indicators to select ranges of values for each indicator.

C. In the Status Icon Rules fields next to the green and yellow indicators, type the acceptable values for each indicator. (The red indicator values are presumed to exist below the lowest value in the yellow indicator range.)

D. Use the select button next to the Indicator Value fiend to choose the cell addresses in the relevant Excel workbook that contain the acceptable values for the green, yellow, and red indicators.

37. You are the SharePoint administrator for your company and have recently enabled and configured InfoPath Forms Services for all your users. Bob, one of the managers in QA, was reviewing the document library for form templates on the QA portal site and asks that you activate several of the templates located in the Manage Form Templates page in Central Administration for the site collection so they can be available for use by his department staff. You make the appropriate selection to activate the CollectSignatures_Sign_1033.xsn template and receive an error message saying "This form template cannot be activated or deactivated." What is the most likely problem?

A. Form templates with the .xsn extension cannot be activated or deactivated for site collections and are available only in Central Administration. You must select templates with the .xml extension.

B. The form template is corrupted and will need to be deleted and replaced.

C. This particular template is part of a workflow and cannot be accessed directly outside of the workflow. You must select a different template that is not part of a workflow process.

D. The form template has been quiesced and is unavailable until restarted.

38. You are the SharePoint administrator for your company, and you are working with Bonnie, one of the designers in the content management department, to develop some standard business forms to be published to the Manage Form Templates page in Central Administration. You want to be able to control the use of and access to these forms by having the ability to activate or deactivate them for a site collection. Bonnie has designed these forms to the specifications provided by the management team, and they are now ready to be published into Central Administration. What instructions are you giving Bonnie so she can publish these form templates to the correct location?

A. You tell Bonnie to click File ➢ Publish on the InfoPath form, and in the wizard under Site Content Type, select Publish to Central Administration.

B. You tell Bonnie to click File ➢ Publish on the InfoPath form, and in the wizard under Location, type the URL to Central Administration in the available field.

C. You tell Bonnie to click File ➢ Publish on the InfoPath form, and in the wizard under Site Content type, select Administrator Approved Form Template (Advanced).

D. You tell Bonnie to click File ➢ Publish on the InfoPath form, and in the wizard click the Advanced button, and select Publish to Central Administration (Administrator Approved).

39. You are the SharePoint administrator for your organization. You are conducting an in-service training for the IT staff on SharePoint administration, and you are currently covering the onboard SharePoint Help service. You have accessed the root document library in Central Administration and are showing the group the files that make up the help system. Several days after the training, you get a call from Marc, one of the technicians in IT, who says he tried to access the same library to review those files but was denied access. What are the most likely causes? (Choose all that apply.)

   A. Marc used the incorrect URL to access Central Administration.

   B. Marc does not have access to Central Administration.

   C. Marc does not belong to the Help group, which is required to access this library.

   D. Marc is not on a network segment that has access to SharePoint Central Administration.

40. You are the SharePoint administrator for your organization. You are conducting an in-service training for the IT staff on SharePoint administration and are currently showing the group the Operations tab in Central Administration. This is a high-level training, and you are describing the general location of different administrative options. Of the following options, which would the group see on the Operations tab in CA? (Choose all that apply.)

   A. Services on Server

   B. Usage Analysis Processing

   C. Configure Session State

   D. Data Retrieval Service

41. You are the SharePoint administrator for your organization. You are conducting an in-service training for the IT staff on SharePoint administration and are currently showing the group the home page of the default SSP for the server farm. This is a very high-level training, and you are just showing the group the general administration options available on this page. Of the following options, which are valid options on the default SSP's home page? (Choose all that apply.)

   A. Services Enabled in This Farm

   B. Excel Services Settings

   C. Business Data Catalog

   D. User Profiles

42. You are the SharePoint administrator for your organization, and you've enabled the publishing portal site with multilanguage support. You have set up the English-language version of the portal as the source site and created labels for both Spanish and French. Now you want to add a web page to the source site and begin the workflow that will result in the content of that page being translated into those languages. During the creation of the page, after you give it a title and description, what option are you offered next?

   A. You are offered which master page to use.

   B. You are offered which layout page to use.

   C. You are offered which source page to use.

   D. You are offered which theme page to use.

43. You are the SharePoint administrator for your company. You are giving an in-service training to new employees on the role of SharePoint in the organization. You are currently discussing content management tools in SharePoint. Of the following options, which site do you say is the one used primarily for content management?

   A. The Collaboration Workspace

   B. The Publishing Portal

   C. The Records Center

   D. The Report Center

44. You are the SharePoint administrator for your company. You are giving an in-service training to new employees on the role of SharePoint in the organization. You are currently discussing content management tools in SharePoint including the Records Center. The Records Center contains a number of libraries and lists by default. Of the following choices, which Records Center features are lists? (Choose all that apply.)

   A. Holds

   B. Tasks

   C. Records Routing

   D. Unclassified Records

45. You are the SharePoint administrator for your organization. You have been responsible for managing the Windows SharePoint Services (WSS) 2.0 environment for your company but think an upgrade to WSS 3.0 would add significant functionality to your users. You sent your proposal to Bruce, the company's CTO, and you have just been notified that Bruce wants to have you consult with him and his staff. In the consultation meeting, Nigel, one of Bruce's staff, suggests directly upgrading from WSS 2.0 to MOSS 2007. You aren't even sure this is possible and, if it is, what path would have to be taken. You are tasked with researching this option and resubmitting your proposal with your research result included. What do you find out?

   A. There is no viable upgrade path from WSS 2.0 to MOSS through any means. To use MOSS 2007 in the organization, you would have to perform a clean install.

   B. The only viable upgrade path is to upgrade from WSS 2.0 to WSS 3.0 and then from WSS 3.0 to MOSS 2007.

   C. The only viable upgrade path is to upgrade from WSS 2.0 to SharePoint Portal Server 2003 and then to MOSS 2007.

   D. There is an option to migrate from WSS 2.0 to MOSS 2007; however, it's an advanced option that must use `stsadm` site transfers.

46. You are the SharePoint administrator for your organization. You have completed your upgrade migration of your SharePoint Portal Server 2003 environment to SharePoint Server 2007. Prior to the upgrade, you had modified a number of the sites in the site collection using FrontPage 2003 to alter their "look and feel." After you have finished the upgrade, you are getting complaints from the users of those sites that the upgrade process didn't occur and the sites are unchanged. What happened?

A. The SharePoint 2007 migration process doesn't "recognize" the FrontPage 2003 modifications, and although the migration was successful, the "look and feel" you created with FrontPage was retained.

B. The SharePoint 2007 migration process doesn't "recognize" the FrontPage 2003 modifications, so the migration process bypassed these sites and left them as SharePoint 2003 sites.

C. The SharePoint 2007 migration process doesn't "recognize" the FrontPage 2003 modifications resulting in the 2003 version of the sites being published to the URLs for the upgrade sites. The sites were upgraded, but temporary URLs were used for the upgraded sites. You will have to manually change the URL mappings so the users can access the 2007 version of the sites.

D. The users are viewing the older sites cached in their web browsers. They will need to clear their browser caches to view the upgraded sites.

Answers to Assessment Test

1. A, C, and D.   Options A, C, and D are all collaboration tools supported in MOSS 2007. Indexing Service is a service provided to web applications running in the SharePoint server farm by the shared services provider (SSP). For more information, see Chapter 1, "Getting Started with Microsoft Office SharePoint Server 2007."

2. A.   Office SharePoint Designer is the tool used for creating and customizing Microsoft SharePoint websites and building workflow-enabled applications based on SharePoint technologies. For more information, see Chapter 1, "Getting Started with Microsoft Office SharePoint Server 2007."

3. A.   The server farm is a logical construct in SharePoint 2007 design that contains all of the other logical components including shared services providers, web applications, SharePoint site collections, and subsites. For more information, see Chapter 1, "Getting Started with Microsoft Office SharePoint Server 2007."

4. A and B.   You must enable IIS 6.0 so Windows Server 2003 will act as a web server. You also must install Microsoft .NET Framework 3.0 and enable ASP.NET 2.0 to ensure proper functioning of web content, the Central Administration website, and other SharePoint features. SQL Server 2005 Express Edition is installed automatically during the setup of SharePoint Server 2007 on a stand-alone server, and you do not need to specifically use Windows Server 2003 Web Edition since SharePoint 2007 can be installed on all editions of this server operating system. See Chapter 2, "Installing and Deploying SharePoint 2007," for more information.

5. B, C, and D.   Microsoft's official recommended standard for processors is to run dual processors that are each 3GHz or faster. The minimum standard is a single processor with a speed of 2.5GHz. See Chapter 2, "Installing and Deploying SharePoint 2007," for more information.

6. B.   Clicking Basic will install SharePoint Server to the default location. You must click Advanced and then click the File location tab in order to specify a custom location for the installation. See Chapter 2, "Installing and Deploying SharePoint 2007," for more information.

7. A.   Option A correctly describes the starting steps to configuring incoming email services in SharePoint 2007. For more information, see Chapter 3, "Configuring SharePoint 2007."

8. C.   Option C correctly describes the service that you will need to enable in order to create distribution lists in SharePoint. For more information, see Chapter 3, "Configuring SharePoint 2007."

9. B.   The last possible step you can take is to choose whether to enable the SSL for Web Services option. (The default is not to enable this service.) For more information, see Chapter 3, "Configuring SharePoint 2007."

10. A.   When creating a site, you can click the Collaboration tab and select Blog Site to accomplish this goal. See Chapter 4, "Building Sites and Site Collections," for more information.

11. B.   The actions described in option B are the correct ones. The other options are bogus. See Chapter 4, "Building Sites and Site Collections," for more information.

12. D. You must use the Site Directory to access the correct location that allows you to approve or reject a submitted site. See Chapter 4, "Building Sites and Site Collections," for more information.

13. A. Option A describes the action you must take in this part of the process. The other options are bogus. See Chapter 5, "Managing Users and Groups," for more information.

14. A and D. The only two valid operators you can select after you select the Users operand are Member Of and Reports Under. See Chapter 5, "Managing Users and Groups," for more information.

15. C. Users assigned to this group have the ability to quickly update content on the site under circumstances where the site has different levels for creating content and then publishing that content to the site. Users in this group utilize SharePoint content deployment functionality, which is part of publishing and Web Content Management (WCM). See Chapter 5, "Managing Users and Groups," for more information.

16. C. Only Kerberos authentication has the additional configuration requirements listed here. See Chapter 6, "Configuring Authentication and Security," for more information.

17. A. You must disable the SSO service (SSOSrv) on all of the servers in the SharePoint server farm before you can proceed. See Chapter 6, "Configuring Authentication and Security," for more information.

18. D. The SSO database is no different from any other database running on a database server and can be backed up and restored using the same applications used to back up any server. See Chapter 6, "Configuring Authentication and Security," for more information.

19. A and C. You can create custom workflows using Microsoft Visual Studio 2005 or Office SharePoint Designer 2007. See Chapter 7, "Configuring and Maintaining Lists and Libraries," for more information.

20. A and C. When a document is checked out, it is saved in the user's My Documents folder in a subfolder named SharePoint Drafts. Also, you can use the Microsoft Office 2007 suite only to directly check documents into and out of SharePoint from within Office applications. See Chapter 7, "Configuring and Maintaining Lists and Libraries," for more information.

21. B. You can create a view by showing or hiding individual columns in a list. See Chapter 7, "Configuring and Maintaining Lists and Libraries," for more information.

22. B. Option B is the only correct answer. The other answers are bogus. For more information, see Chapter 8, "Configuring Web Part Pages, Web Parts, and Web Pages."

23. A, B, and D. SharePoint web page design elements are master pages, content pages, layout pages, style sheets, web parts, and field controls. For more information, see Chapter 8, "Configuring Web Part Pages, Web Parts, and Web Pages."

24. B, C, and D. Option A should say List Views rather than Links Views. For more information, see Chapter 8, "Configuring Web Part Pages, Web Parts, and Web Pages."

25. A, C, and D. SharePoint Server 2007 search is the first version of SharePoint that includes the ability to crawl and index content on external sources such as outside SharePoint server farms, outside websites, business information, file shares, and so on. One way that SharePoint Server 2007 is different from previous versions is that the service used for crawling and indexing content is part of a shared services provider (SSP) and all content crawled using the SSP is indexed to a single content index. For more information, see Chapter 9, "Managing SharePoint Navigation and Search."

26. A, B, and D. Crawl rules apply to the situations described in options A, B, and D. The answer in option C is bogus. For more information, see Chapter 9, "Managing SharePoint Navigation and Search."

27. B. Tree view adds the Site Hierarchy item to the Quick Launch navigation menu, which displays all of the SharePoint objects on or under the current site. For more information, see Chapter 9, "Managing SharePoint Navigation and Search."

28. B. Dynamic content flows are driven by the needs of content authors, owners, and consumers, moving from one location to another depending on who needs to access, copy, modify, or retire a document. This type of flow does not involve approvals or involves limited approvals for information transfers but maximizes the potential for information collaboration. Manual content flows require a workflow approval through every step of information transfer. Automatic and managed content flows are bogus answers. For more information, see Chapter 10, "Working with Microsoft Documents in SharePoint."

29. C. Option C is the correct selection and is rarely used. Options A and B are valid selections but do not fulfill the specified requirements. Option D is a bogus answer. For more information, see Chapter 10, "Working with Microsoft Documents in SharePoint."

30. B. Option B gives a correct description of this part of the process. The other options are bogus answers. For more information, see Chapter 10, "Working with Microsoft Documents in SharePoint."

31. B. You can use only Outlook 2007 to subscribe to a SharePoint RSS feed. See Chapter 11, "Working with Microsoft Outlook in SharePoint," for more information.

32. C. The Vault feature ensures content integrity. The other options are valid Records Center features but will not produce the desired results. See Chapter 11, "Working with Microsoft Outlook in SharePoint," for more information.

33. A, B, and D. All of the selections are correct except for option C. This would have been correct if it had said that the list could be configured to save email attachments. Although attachments can be saved, they cannot be saved in the body of the original email in the list. See Chapter 11, "Working with Microsoft Outlook in SharePoint," for more information.

34. A. Excel Services is basically an Excel workbook on a server. The storage and calculation of the workbook data occurs on the server, while the presentation is handled by the Excel Web Access web part. When workbook data is exposed in the web interface, the calculations and formulas are still secure in the server. External data sources do not need to be enabled unless you are accessing data outside of SharePoint and you do not need to be running Office 2007 to view workbook data in an Excel Web Access web part. See Chapter 12, "Using Excel Services and Business Intelligence," for more information.

35. A, B, and C.   SAP, Siebel, and SharePoint list data sources can all be external to the SharePoint site requiring the information they contain. However, the Reports library is contained directly within the Report Center, which is the core of SharePoint's business intelligence solution and thus not an external data source. See Chapter 12, "Using Excel Services and Business Intelligence," for more information.

36. A.   Option A is the only selection that correctly describes the process of configuring KPI values. All of the other answers are bogus. See Chapter 12, "Using Excel Services and Business Intelligence," for more information.

37. C.   Forms templates that are part of a workflow process cannot be activated or deactivated for a site collection. Either select a different template or have the required template designed in InfoPath. All templates have an .xsn extension, so this is not the problem. A corrupted template file would not display this type of error message, and although a form template can be quiesced (gradually taken offline), it would not display this type of message when you attempt to activate it. For more information, please see Chapter 13, "Using Business Forms and Business Intelligence."

38. C.   Options A, B, and D are all bogus answers. Only option C describes the correct process. For more information, please see Chapter 13, "Using Business Forms and Business Intelligence."

39. B and C.   It's unlikely that Marc has the wrong URL for CA or is on the wrong network segment. If he had the wrong URL, he would more likely get the wrong location or "location not found" error rather than an "access denied" error. Also, since he is part of the organization as all the other SharePoint users including admins, he should have a network connection to the server hosting CA. The most likely reasons are permissions issues. As an IT technician, he is unlikely to belong to the correct groups that would allow him access to CA in general or the HelpFold library specifically. For more information, please see Chapter 14, "Performing Advanced SharePoint Management."

40. A, B, and D.   Configure Session State can be found on the Application Management tab under Office SharePoint Server Shared Services. All of the other options are found on the Operations tab. For more information, please see Chapter 14, "Performing Advanced SharePoint Management."

41. B, C, and D.   Option A, Check Services Enabled in This Farm, can be found in Central Administration on the Application Management tab. All the other options are valid selections on the default SSP's home page. For more information, please see Chapter 14, "Performing Advanced SharePoint Management."

42. B.   Option A is incorrect because only one master page can be assigned to a site at one time. Option C is incorrect because the source page has already been defined. Option D is a bogus answer. For more information, see Chapter 15, "Working with Content Management."

43. B.   SharePoint content management functions are handled primarily by the Records Center since it can be configured as the repository for a variety of content types and has several document centers created with it by default. For more information, see Chapter 15, "Working with Content Management."

44. A, B, and C.   Holds, Tasks, and Records Routing are all list web parts. Unclassified Records is a document library. For more information, see Chapter 15, "Working with Content Management."

45. D. The only direct method of upgrading from WSS 2.0 to MOSS 2007 is to use an advanced `stsadm` option for site transfers. For more information, see Chapter 16, "Upgrading and Deploying Microsoft Office SharePoint Server 2007."

46. A. The SharePoint 2007 migration process doesn't recognize or understand the modifications created by FrontPage 2003, so although the modified sites were upgraded, their "look and feels" weren't altered. Options B, C, and D are bogus. For more information, see Chapter 16, "Upgrading and Deploying Microsoft Office SharePoint Server 2007."

Chapter

1

Getting Started with Microsoft Office SharePoint Server 2007

MICROSOFT EXAM OBJECTIVES COVERED IN THIS CHAPTER:

✓ **Configure Microsoft Office SharePoint Server 2007 Portal**

  ▪ Configure Site Management

✓ **Manage Administration**

  ▪ Manage Central Admin UI

If you picked up this book, it's because you're committed to using and administering Microsoft Office SharePoint Server (MOSS) 2007 in your organization, or at least that's your goal. Becoming certified in configuring MOSS 2007 will establish you as the human interface between your company and how SharePoint organizes and presents your company's information, tasks, and goals.

Before launching into the specific content areas involved in configuring MOSS 2007, it's important to take some time to review the basic features included in the latest version of SharePoint Portal Server. If you are familiar with SharePoint Portal Server 2003, you will have some advantages in learning MOSS 2007; however, there are quite a number of new features as well as a completely fresh look and feel to become familiar with.

Once you've gone through the overview of MOSS 2007 and before you actually install and configure SharePoint, you'll need to craft the server architecture that fits your organization's current and future needs. At this point, it's not too early to begin understanding the Central Administration interface of your soon-to-be-created portal site and review basic first tasks.

After you have established your architectural plan for SharePoint, you'll be ready to proceed to planning and implementing the actual installation of SharePoint 2007.

Introducing SharePoint Server 2007

SharePoint Server 2007 is more than just the tools and mechanisms required to organize corporate data content and business intelligence within web pages, lists, and libraries. MOSS 2007, like its predecessor SharePoint Portal Server 2003, is a portal technology.

A web portal is not just a website's index page. It represents a company's gateway into how information is collected, maintained, shared, presented, modified, and secured. A portal can lead into a highly varied environment involving one or multiple sites serving as an intranet to staff and management, an extranet to the customer base, an Internet site for the general public, or some combination of these sites.

The core technology of MOSS 2007 is Windows SharePoint Services (WSS) 3.0. This service is available at no cost for the Windows Server 2003 and Windows Small Business Server 2003 platforms; however, WSS 3.0 doesn't provide the full range of content management tools available in MOSS 2007.

SharePoint Server 2007 offers expanded functionality on top of the WSS 3.0 core including the Business Data Catalog (BDC), business intelligence (BI), Excel Services, Forms Services, and a new and more robust search engine.

Specific knowledge of WSS 3.0 as a stand-alone technology won't be included in the 70-630 exam. Microsoft maintains a separate certification for WSS 3.0 configuration—Exam 70-631: Windows SharePoint Services 3.0, Configuring.

What's New in SharePoint 2007?

Microsoft divides the capacities of SharePoint Server 2007 into six general areas:

- Business intelligence
- Business process and forms
- Collaboration
- Enterprise content management
- Enterprise search
- Portals

Each area contains updated or completely new features available in MOSS 2007.

Business Intelligence

Business intelligence was once the sole purview of the developer or consultant; however, MOSS 2007 puts this valuable capacity in the hands of the site administrator and content manager. Business intelligence is the term assigned to a collection of utilities designed to take a vast array of unstructured data and data types and present them as a chart, spreadsheet, or other organized form for the purpose of analysis. This includes the ability to pull raw data from numerous sources, including those external to SharePoint, and display them as reports or key indicators in order to track and evaluate specific, business-related trends. The following are the key Share-Point workspaces and web parts that collectively make up business intelligence:

Report Center site   This is a specific site within SharePoint, created as a central repository for storing reports, libraries, lists, and connections to data sources.

Excel Services   This solution is designed to manage and share Office Excel 2007 workbooks as interactive reports.

External data connections   SharePoint 2007 allows you to connect to external data sources such as SAP and Siebel and integrate information from those sources into lists, libraries, and web parts within SharePoint.

Key performance indicators (KPI)   Specialized lists and web parts in SharePoint let you visually track progress made toward specific business goals.

Dashboards   These are web part templates that you can use to collect information from a variety of data sources, such as charts, KPIs, metrics, and reports, and display the information in a single interface.

✓**Data filters**   Using filters, you can display only a subset of a data collection, designing the presentation for specific audiences that need to see only the information that's relevant to them.

✓**Business Data Catalog**   The BDC is a SharePoint shared service that accesses data from numerous back-end applications that exist outside SharePoint Server and combines that information into a single report or profile.

Business Process and Forms

Although we don't quite live in a paperless society, forms are now more commonly electronic than printed, and they maintain their place at the core of an organization's business process. Electronic forms are provided in SharePoint by InfoPath Forms Services, and they can help you collect and validate information that drives your business processes. The key to moving and tracking forms through your system is utilizing SharePoint's built-in workflow templates to automate the journey of business forms through your process.

Workflows provide a system of contact and review points as forms and other documents proceed from the beginning to the conclusion of a task. They also facilitate collaboration between team members and other partners in a particular project. The workflow process contains several decision points:

Approval   This workflow option directs a form, document, or item to an individual or group for approval.

Collect Feedback   This workflow option directs a form or document to an individual or group for feedback.

Collect Signatures   This workflow option directs a Microsoft Office document to a group to collect digital signatures.

Disposition Approval   This workflow option lets authorized personnel decide to retain or delete expired documents.

Group Approval   This workflow option allows you to choose workflow approvers from a hierarchical organizational chart and allow these approvers to use a stamp control instead of a signature.

Three-state   This workflow option is used to track and manage large volumes of business process forms, documents, or issues such as project tasks.

Translation Management   This workflow option creates copies of documents that need to be translated to other languages and assigns translation tasks to specified teams or team members.

Using web browser–based forms lets employees in your organization fill out forms without having to print hard copies from the browser. The forms are created by Office InfoPath 2007, which provides a central repository for all of the business forms your organization manages. As with all other documents and information in SharePoint, you can determine whether you want a form to be distributed just within your company's intranet or share it with customers, partners, or the general public using an extranet or Internet site.

Since you haven't installed SharePoint Server 2007 yet, the exercises in this chapter are designed to help you learn more about MOSS 2007 and related technologies and solutions. Exercise 1.1 will help you learn about using InfoPath within SharePoint.

EXERCISE 1.1

Learning More about InfoPath

1. Open a web browser, and go to `http://office.microsoft.com`.

2. Click the Products tab.

3. In the menu on the left under Servers, click SharePoint Server.

4. In the Microsoft Office SharePoint Server search field, type **InfoPath**, and press Enter.

5. In the search results list, click Export InfoPath Form Data from a Library to a Spreadsheet.

6. Review the tutorial on this page, and then add the web page to your Favorites list in your web browser. You'll need the information when you work with forms in Chapter 13, "Using Business Forms and Business Intelligence."

Collaboration

Collaboration is the one factor that comes to people's minds when they think of SharePoint. MOSS 2007 provides a specific set of utilities that allow project teams, departments, divisions, or entire companies to work together to attain a common goal. Site templates, blogs, wikis, and RSS feeds are all web parts that can be used for collaboration. Office Outlook 2007 can interact with elements in SharePoint. You can use Project Management to manage a set of tasks that can be accomplished using different web parts and web part configurations. Share-Point collaboration tools are how these jobs are created, managed, and completed within the MOSS framework.

Site templates   You no longer have to create a site from scratch; instead, you can use one of SharePoint's built-in site templates to suit your needs. Site templates are organized by function or purpose, so you can simply select the template that most closely meets your needs. For instance, you can select a Meeting Site template to manage the annual stockholder's meeting or a series of frequently recurring events such as a weekly staff meeting.

Blogs and wikis   A new feature in MOSS 2007 is support for both blogs and wikis. These information-sharing methods are common on the Web, and almost everyone has used them from time to time. Now you can leverage these data storage and sharing formats within your company by enabling them in SharePoint.

RSS feeds   Really Simple Syndication (RSS) technology is another well-known method of periodically receiving updated information on specific topics or subjects. Use RSS to subscribe to a blog in SharePoint and get the latest data updates.

Office Outlook 2007 collaboration   You can use Outlook to seamlessly share information back and forth between your email or calendar and SharePoint. For instance, you can add an item to a discussion group in SharePoint by sending an email to that group. You don't have to open Share-Point as a separate application but instead can add information to MOSS directly from Outlook.

Project Management   Never lose track of who is assigned to what project or how close to completion a task is again. Projects can be organized in lists or charts, such as a Gantt chart, to show you, at a glance, all of the details you need to manage job assignments.

Enterprise Content Management

Content management is more than just knowing which document library contains your author's contracts. Documents are not containers of static content anymore. After creation, content is subject to modification, versioning, and workflow. Addressing the needs of the enterprise, MOSS 2007 divides this arena into three distinct categories, all with multilingual publishing support. The categories are document management, records management, and web content management.

Document Management

Document management consists of the processes of creating, accessing, modifying, publishing, storing, and tracking documentation within your organization. Document management contains the following tools to enhance this content management form:

Document Center site template   The Document Center site template is one of the default site templates native to MOSS 2007. It provides document management for large-scale companies with functions including checkout and check-in for editing, versioning, auditing, and support for various document formats. Support for converting one document format to another is also available.

Translation Management library   In the realm of multinational corporations, you will likely need to manage documentation that can be translated into different languages. This library enables you to create, store, and provide workflow, as well as manage by document type all your multilingual documentation.

Microsoft Office 2007 integration   Not only can you control document management from within the SharePoint 2007 interface, but you can also create, manage, and initiate workflow directly from Microsoft Office client applications such as Word and Excel 2007.

Records Management

Records management may seem to be just document management renamed, but a company's official records represent the history, knowledge base, and legal documentation for the organization. As such, corporate records require specialized management based on the company's relevant policies as well as the regulations and laws that apply.

Records Center site template   The Records Center site template is the main utility within SharePoint for managing the maintenance and retention of business records; it provides a records collection interface, records routing, records vault capacities, and information policy management tools.

Information management policies   Just mentioned in conjunction with the Records Center site template, information management policies allow you to enforce compliance across the enterprise to all corporate policies and legal regulations that apply to records management.

Information rights management   This SharePoint capacity lets you limit what actions a person can take on a document that has been downloaded from SharePoint. Information rights management (IRM) encrypts documents that have been downloaded from MOSS libraries or lists so that what users can do with the documents depends on the permissions those users have. Limitations include whether a user can decrypt the files, print records, or copy text from records. IRM is built on top of a certificate-based infrastructure and allows users to restrict access to a document by both name and by certificate. This capacity focuses on what specific tasks users can perform when accessing content.

Microsoft Exchange Server 2007 integration   Emails are considered formal business documents, and although sometimes jokes or other personal content are transmitted across a company's email system, those emails are actually the property of the corporation. Not only can a user send an email directly to a Records Center site, but information management polices can be directly applied from SharePoint to managed email folders in Exchange.

Web Content Management

Web content management is an obvious capacity within SharePoint since MOSS uses a web interface to allow access to all its tools and information for Internet, intranet, and extranet sites. Although most people may think that the site administrator or webmaster governing the SharePoint site collection must be the person to add or modify content, content presentation, and content organization, in fact SharePoint users can access many tools to control the information for which they are directly responsible:

Office SharePoint Designer 2007   Office SharePoint Designer 2007 takes the place and performs the functions of Microsoft FrontPage for SharePoint Portal Server 2003; it is the primary web design tool for SharePoint Server 2007. Although SharePoint is very customizable, a number of elements cannot be modified with the tools native to SharePoint. You can use SharePoint Designer to create a new master page or modify page layouts without having to be a software engineer. The designer utilizes Cascading Style Sheets (CSS) technology to enable you to make changes across your entire MOSS site collection.

Default master pages and page layouts   You don't have to use Office SharePoint Designer to create the look and feel you want for your sites. The master page, page layouts, and content pages native to SharePoint 2007 are varied enough to suit almost anyone's needs. For example, you can select a particular content page such as a News Content page to specify how information is presented and modified.

SharePoint site templates   SharePoint 2007 contains a number of default site templates that you can choose based on the purpose and function of the site you want to create. These are the five general areas for site templates:

- Collaboration
- Custom
- Enterprise
- Meetings
- Publish

Each of these areas contains a variety of specific templates that serve particular requirements within that category. For instance, in the Publish category, the site templates are News Site, Publishing Site with Workflow, Collaboration Portal, and Publishing Portal.

Microsoft Office 2007 format integration   SharePoint Server 2007 has a Document Conversions feature that, when enabled, lets you convert Office 2007 documents such as Word documents to web pages. You can even convert Office InfoPath forms written in XML into web content.

HTML Content Editor   This utility allows you to access the underlying HTML markup language on any web page and modify the source. This is handy when you create page content in the What-You-See-Is-What-You-Get (WYSIWYG) window and how it renders is not quite how you want the content to appear.

Automatic site change adjustment   In SharePoint Server 2003, when you changed the web page structure of your site and moved a page to a different location, you needed to manually edit all the links that led to that page. MOSS 2007 automatically changes the site navigation links, correctly updating and renaming them.

Managing website variations   It's said that "one size fits all" is a myth, and it certainly is with websites including SharePoint site collections. In today's international business environment, websites often need to be presented in a variety of languages. SharePoint's Variations feature lets you publish your source site in a variety of languages including English, French, and Japanese. Additionally, the rendering of the source site can be modified for geographic region and browser device type (PC or mobile, for example).

Enterprise Search

Office SharePoint Server 2007 has vastly improved its search abilities over its predecessor. You can use Enterprise Search not only to locate the right document or piece of data but also to find the right person, such as a subject-matter expert to fill a particular need. MOSS 2007 search uses the following abilities:

Searching Center site   Like a lot of other SharePoint resources, search capacities are contained within a centralized site where you can initiate searches and filter results.

Finding documents and people   As mentioned previously, you can find both data and data experts using SharePoint search. Search queries will span across document libraries, information lists, and even user MySite sites to locate results matching your search string.

Searching enterprise applications   SharePoint search also has the ability to go through enterprise applications such as SAP, Siebel, or customized databases in its quest to provide the information you need.

Portals

Portals are gateways into a large organized repository of data and data management tools. SharePoint 2007 portal technology has advanced in providing greater personalization of its portal sites. For instance, individual users can now create personal MySite websites within SharePoint that act as a portal to any personal profiles, documents, graphics, lists, or other information directly relevant to them. This information is searchable by SharePoint Enterprise Search, and each time a user updates their MySite with information about training classes they've recently completed or a project they've just concluded, you can find them and access the person's expertise.

Any SharePoint solution you've reviewed in the "What's New in SharePoint 2007?" section of this chapter can be accessed through a dedicated portal site, meaning that you can create and manage gateways to each major piece of functionality provided by SharePoint as well as the site collection as a whole. Portals can be designed to fit your company's functional activities or along departmental lines. Each portal then operates like a large container for the information and activities it contains.

Understanding exactly which features are supported in various editions of WSS and SharePoint Server can be difficult to sort out. Exercise 1.2 will show you how to get the detailed information you need.

EXERCISE 1.2

Downloading the Microsoft Office SharePoint Server 2007 Products Comparison List

1. Open a web browser, and go to `http://office.microsoft.com/en-us/sharepointserver/HA101978031033.aspx`.

2. Click the download link that matches the version of Excel you have on your computer.

3. Select Save or Save to Disk.

4. Navigate to the folder on your computer where you want to save the products comparison worksheet, and click Save.

5. When the worksheet is saved to your computer, close your web browser.

Planning SharePoint 2007 Architecture

Before you start reaching for the SharePoint 2007 installation disk and slipping it in the server you plan to use to start building your site collection, you will need to develop a plan for the layout and deployment of SharePoint's architecture. This is a lot like saying before you build a house, you first have to draw up the blueprints, but it's not as simple as that. As the architect for your company's SharePoint implementation, you have several major tasks before you:

- Architecting with SharePoint components

- Architecting SharePoint server farms, shared services providers (SSPs), and topologies

- Architecting the SQL database infrastructure

Architecting with SharePoint Components

Just as you'd expect an architect designing your home to be familiar with the tools required to plan for and build your house, you will need to learn the components contained within SharePoint that you can use to build your organization's site collection. Although some design components are physical, such as the actual machine your SharePoint site collection will live in, many others are logical. For instance, SSPs are logical constructs that allow various services to move across numerous physical servers in a server farm. The following sections are a high-level view of SharePoint architecting components.

The Server Farm

At its most basic level, a *server farm* is a collection of physical server iron and logical servers grouped in a single location. This collection is also known as a *server cluster* or *data center*. The most common implementation of a server farm is a group of web servers utilized by a web hosting company or Internet service provider (ISP). Application software can be deployed on a server-by-server basis, or a single application can span numerous physical servers.

Although the server farm exists physically, as far as architecting SharePoint is concerned, the farm is administered logically as part of a single entity, which in this case will be all the components that will ultimately make up your site collection. The tool that SharePoint 2007 provides to administer the farm is called the SharePoint Central Administration tool.

This tool will be introduced later in this chapter in the section "Introducing the Central Administration Interface."

Utilizing a server farm on which to build your SharePoint infrastructure lets you provide centralized access and backup control as well as load balancing to manage many server requests. The logical server farm is a container for the following SharePoint design components.

Shared Services Providers

SSPs exist at the next level below the server farm. They are the logical environment that contains all of the particular services you want to make available across your web applications and SharePoint sites. Typically you would use only a single SSP in your server farm, but it is possible to create multiple SSPs. Multiple SSPs within the server farm are necessary if you need to create a security boundary between specific services. SSPs can contain the following services:

- Excel Calculation Services
- Index Services
- Search Services
- Web Services

Database Services

Database services are composed of the actual server that contains one or more databases for SharePoint. Within database services, SharePoint 2007 specifically uses SQL content databases to contain site collections, and a specific content database is created for each of the web applications operating in the server farm. Database services for SharePoint can be provided by a dedicated server running databases from other applications that provide SQL database functionality such as the following:

- Microsoft Identity Integration Server (MIIS)
- Microsoft Operations Manager (MOM)
- Systems Management Server (SMS)

In addition, SharePoint can also use SQL Server 2005 Express.

Web Applications

In general, a web application is any application accessed over a network using a web browser to provide a service. Common web applications include blogs, discussion forums, and wikis. Within the context of SharePoint and existing below the level of the SSP, web applications are the logical components that are physically associated with SharePoint's Internet Information Server (IIS) websites. Only one web application can be attached to an IIS website. Individual web applications are used to access a particular entry point in SharePoint and may use a content database created specifically for the application or an already existing database.

SharePoint Site Collections

A SharePoint site is an individual website that acts as a single container or point of access to web parts, libraries, lists, and other sites. A *site collection* is a grouping of SharePoint sites that are all associated with a root or top-level site. For example, you can have a top-level site called /bumblebee. Members of the /bumblebee site collection can include /bumblebee/hive, /bumblebee/honey, and /bumblebee/drones. Just as in any other website, a SharePoint site collection can drill down as deep as you want. For instance, you can create a site and subsite path such as /bumblebee/drones/sales/regions/northwest.

The top-level site exists directly under the level of the web applications. It is usually the portal site for your business or organization. Portal sites are also referred to as *root* or *root-level* sites since they occupy the "root" of the site "tree." Root-level sites are designated by a forward slash (/). Paths such as /bumblebee/honey or /bumblebee/drones/sales/regions/northwest are known as *managed paths* and are the locations where new sites or site collections can be created within a web application.

The lowest level within a site collection is the site content. Site content can be anything that is contained or displayed within an individual site such as web part pages, web parts, document libraries, link lists, and so on.

Architecting SharePoint Server Farms, SSPs, and Topologies

As mentioned earlier in this chapter, server farms are both physical collections of server iron and logical collections of servers. Your organizational plans may require one or several server farms to be designed and implemented. You not only will need to know how to determine how many farms you will need but how to design an individual farm.

Once you have determined the design for your farm, you will need to implement it using a particular design topology. The network and server topology you choose will usually follow the design of your server farm(s), which is based on the functional or organizational requirements of your business.

Designing SharePoint Server Farm Architectures

In addition to the specific SharePoint design components previously mentioned, a number of factors will determine whether you design a single server farm or multiple server farms. The following are the key issues you will need to consider when deciding on developing a single server farm or multiple server farms:

- Licensing
- Availability and service-level agreements
- Performance and scalability
- Organizational and security requirements

Licensing

You will need to purchase a license for each physical server on which you intend to install SharePoint Server 2007. Two types of MOSS 2007 licenses are available for purchase, but only one license type can be used on a single server or a single server farm:

Microsoft Office SharePoint Server 2007, Server License   This license is required to run Office SharePoint Server 2007 in client/server mode. You should use this license with the requisite number of Client Access Licenses (CALs) appropriate for your organizational needs. This license is used on servers and server farms that face your internal network and provide content to your organization. Remote employees can gain access to a server or server farm using this license over the Internet via a VPN as long as the appropriate number of CALs have been purchased.

Microsoft Office SharePoint Server 2007 for Internet Sites   You can use the software for Internet-facing websites only. All content, information, and applications must be accessible to nonemployees. This license has all the features of the Enterprise Edition of Office SharePoint Server. This is a per-server license that does not require the purchase of CALs.

If you intend on providing SharePoint 2007 sites and content both to an employee-oriented intranet and to customers on the Internet, you will need to design and deploy at least two server farms, one for each license type.

The issue of an extranet site for partners or customers has several licensing solutions:

- You can create an extranet site on the server farm that hosts the company intranet and uses the Server License. If you select this option, you'll need to purchase the required number of CALs. This option is more appropriate for partners than customers and is the best choice if you need to collaborate with a small number of partners.

- You can create an extranet site on the server farm that hosts your company's Internet site and uses the Internet Sites license. This option doesn't require you to purchase CALs for partners, customers, or internal employees working on collaborative projects with them. However, you will not be able to create sites in this server farm that only internal employees can access. This is the best choice if you need to communicate securely to a large number of partners or customers.

- You can deploy a server farm to be used for extranet sites servicing your partners and customers and use the Internet Sites license. This option doesn't require you to purchase CALs for partners, customers, or internal employees working on collaborative projects with them. However, you will not be able to create sites in this server farm that only internal employees can access. This is the best option if you need to collaborate with a large number of partners.

 Real World Scenario

Choosing the Correct Licensing Plan

You are a SharePoint administrator for a midsize university and you are developing a SharePoint Server site collection for the Economics department. In this case "Economics department" is the formal name of a department at our mythical university. This is a pilot project, and if it's successful, you will roll out SharePoint to all of the other university departments using the same licensing scheme. You need to find the right licensing plan for your organization and specifically for the current project.

The Economics department's classrooms, computer labs, and administrative offices have 350 desktop computers. You want a three-year license renewal plan with a renewal option for one to three years. You would prefer to buy from a Microsoft Authorized Large Account Reseller. To begin your investigation, you visit the office.microsoft.com website at the following URL: http://office.microsoft.com/en-us/products/FX101865111033.aspx.

You'll need to find out more about volume licensing plans, so click the link in the first bullet point on this web page, Find Out More About Volume Licensing. On the Microsoft Volume Licensing Programs page, click the first available link in the body of the page called Volume Licensing Programs in order to compare a list of volume licensing programs.

On the Buy or Renew Licenses Through Microsoft Volume Licensing Programs page, scroll down to Step 2: Review Microsoft Volume Licensing Programs, and review the specific information related to the four licensing plans presented in the four columns of the table. You should find that the Select License option best fits your needs.

Availability and Service-Level Agreements

Availability and service-level agreements are two related concepts that have to do with the level of accessibility you have regarding a service or data. In general, availability is defined as a ratio between the amount of time the service or data is accessible and the total amount of time measured. One hundred percent availability would mean that the service or data is available whenever the system (which is SharePoint in this case) is operational. Few systems, if any, are available 100 percent of the time, but the term *high availability* defines a system that is available 99.999 percent of the time (also known as the *five 9s*).

A service-level agreement (SLA) is usually defined in a contractual agreement between a network service provider and customer and specifies the types of services the network service provider will make available to the customer for a particular fee.

One hundred percent availability relative to SharePoint would be the most desirable but, as just mentioned, is a practical impossibility. In real life, not absolutely all information and services need to be available to all users or customers 24/7. As you design your SharePoint site collection around the needs of your company, you'll need to determine the level of availability necessary for the site collection as a whole and for the different services and information provided. In a high availability scenario where you are providing mission-critical data and services, your server farm design will likely need to include a number of systems to keep SharePoint available in the face of a disaster, such as a catastrophic server failure. The following is a brief discussion of such contingencies.

Develop a failover system so that in the event of a hard drive crash or other system failure, another system will immediately take over the original system's function until the failed component can be replaced. For instance, if you are using a storage area network (SAN) and your primary network path fails, a secondary path can be immediately implemented so there is no interruption of service. The failover should be transparent to the end user. This scenario is sometimes called a *hot server* scenario.

In any server farm or cluster, all of your information should be backed up. This is usually done by backing up server data onto tape on a rotating basis. The backup tapes are then transported to a remote site for storage. In the event of a server disaster, any failed hardware components can be replaced, and the data can be restored from the tape. This doesn't provide an immediate return to availability but will ensure that the information will again become available, most likely within a few hours. You can also restore taped data to a backup server so that, rather than repair the original server hardware, you can restore the data to another piece of hardware that will "step in" for the original. This scenario is sometimes called a *cold server* scenario.

A variation on these themes is *mirroring* or *replication*, which is where the primary server periodically copies its data to a backup server. In the event that the primary server fails, the backup server takes over, utilizing the data from the most recent replication. This scenario is sometimes called a *warm server* scenario.

The plans referenced so far are usually implemented in the same physical location; that is, all of these plans are typically executed within the same physical server farm or data center. In an extreme situation, when the services your company supplies absolutely must be available, you can create a plan that includes failover or recovery services at a completely different location.

As part of Microsoft's Software Assurance licensing program, free licenses are provided for servers implemented in the cold server scenario but are not available for the warm or hot server scenarios.

 It's not within the scope of this book to provide an exhaustive list of disaster recovery methods for SharePoint or for server farms in general. For more information, visit Microsoft's TechNet site at www.microsoft.com/technet/windowsserver/sharepoint/v2/reskit/c2861881x.mspx.

Although you can implement most of these recovery methods in a single server farm, you'll enjoy greater fault tolerance if you use more than one farm, even if you do so at the same physical location. The safest recovery implementation is to deploy two or more server farms in two or more physical locations. However, in any disaster recovery plan, you have to take into account the cost to your company for every minute your services and data are unavailable vs. the cost to your company to implement your disaster recovery plan. Most organizations don't have the financial capacity to implement the safest scenario. Practicality forces most businesses to deploy a compromise between availability and their budget. Another factor you must consider is to whom services and data must be available. This is where the service-level agreement comes into play.

You are unlikely to sign an SLA with company employees, but you will have such agreements with partners and customers. The SLA will define the specific parameters by which SharePoint 2007 services and information will be accessible and will include the level of availability you guarantee. Specific items addressed in a standard SLA can include the following:

- Level of availability
- Guaranteed number of simultaneous connections
- Advance notification for changes that may affect users
- Help desk response time
- Performance benchmarks
- Usage statistics

Although you can apply different SLAs on the same server farm, you may want to consider some of the following factors when you create your design.

If the SLA you signed with a customer includes a requirement for high-level security, you may want to implement their site collection on a separate server farm. This also gives you control over different authentication methods and access-control policies and results in separate content databases.

If you have agreed to provide a high level of web application performance, you may want to implement your SharePoint sites on a separate server farm.

Any agreement you sign that affects any significant aspect of the topology, configuration, and operations of the data center should most likely be implemented on a separate server farm.

Server farm topologies will be addressed in the "Designing Server Farm Topologies" section of this chapter.

Performance and Scalability

Performance is most commonly thought of as speed or responsiveness; that is, when accessing resources and traversing SharePoint sites, how quickly are you able to get where you're going and get what you want? Many factors affect overall performance, including network throughput, server processor speed, number of concurrent connections possible, and so on. Availability, as previously presented, can also be included in performance measurements.

The general definition of scalability is the ability of a piece of hardware or software to continue to function well when the size or capacity of the environment is changed to meet user requirements. As a rule, scalability almost always refers to upward scalability or the ability of a system to continue to function well when it is enlarged.

As far as SharePoint performance and scalability in server farm design are concerned, the primary factors affecting performance are application profile, software boundaries, and throughput.

Creating more than one server farm based on application profile is usually a good idea when you are working with enterprise-level production environments. Catalog the different web applications that you will be using, and create a separate server farm for those applications that will see the largest demands. You can also organize several web applications into the same farm when they will see similar usage demands. For example, let's say that applications A, B, and C will have similar usage to each other; D, E, and F will see similar usage to each other; and G, H, and I will see similar usage to each other. Organize A, B, and C in server farm 1; D, E, and F in server farm 2; and G, H, and I in server farm 3. As the number of users increases, application profiles may need to be altered. For instance, last year applications A, B, and C all had similar usage demands, but last month, your company created an entirely new department that equally needs to access applications A, B, and F. To properly scale, you'll need to rethink your server farm design in terms of application profiles.

You can think of software boundaries as a logical interface between a piece of software and either the users accessing it or the hardware on which it runs. Think of it as the requirements that SharePoint and SQL have as applications for optimal performance on server hardware. The software/hardware boundary differs depending on what application you need to operate, how you need the software to perform consistently, and how much usage it will be getting. If you are installing SharePoint 2007 on a single piece of server hardware running one dual-core Intel Xeon 2.8GHz 64-bit processor and 2GB RAM, the software/hardware boundary will be different than if you are implementing a large number of blade servers, each running four dual-core Intel Xeon 2.8GHz 64-bit processors and 32GB RAM.

You can think of throughput both in terms of individual servers and PCs and as a measure of network performance. In a piece of server hardware, throughput is the amount of work the device can accomplish in a given period of time. In terms of a network, throughput is the amount of traffic that can traverse a network segment in a given period of time. In addressing a server farm design, you will want to consider the actual hardware requirements for the server iron you are going to install, including CPU speed and RAM capacity. For network throughput, you will want to consider issues such as access-level, distribution-level, and core-level network speeds; the amount of traffic during normal usage; the amount of traffic at peak usage; and networking elements such as routers and switches in the topology. Especially in situations where a high level of network throughput is required, you may want to consider more than one server farm. As the number of users increases in your organization, resource demand will also increase, requiring you to either add more server hardware to your existing farm or create a new farm. Changing the data center topology by adding more high-capacity switches to accommodate more network traffic may also require either a redesign of the farm or the addition of a second farm.

As mentioned, usually performance and scalability needs to increase over time; however, if a company downsizes or sells significant portions of its holdings, the overall requirements may actually decrease. Also, a badly designed and bloated server farm may be costing the company more money to maintain than necessary. In either of these cases, a redesign of the server farm or farms to reduce the size and/or number of server farms would be required. Although everyone wants the biggest and baddest collection of server farms in existence, remember that they cost money to design, deploy, and maintain. The trick is to have just enough to satisfy requirements during optimal use without either causing horrible performance slowdowns or costing the company so much money that it has to come out of your paycheck.

Organizational and Security Requirements

Server farms are also designed based on how the company wants to organize resources, including services and data. Organization can be set up based on the company's hierarchy, functionality, geography, or just about any other criteria you can think of. For instance, size, location, and capacity of a particular server farm or farms can depend on funding sources, in other words, money. It's said that you get what you pay for, but you also have to be able to pay for what you want. The "perfect" server farm for your company's needs may be beyond your department's budget, so your design will have to reflect how much money you have to deploy and maintain it. Assuming (and it's a big assumption) that your budget will increase with the availability and performance requirements of the server farm, you may have the opportunity to expand an existing farm or to create additional farms over time; however, you will always have to balance performance, safety, and cost.

The structure of the company's organizational chart may also drive the design of your server farm and is the most common factor in how server farms are planned. This is especially true if your manufacturing plant is in Singapore but your software developers work in Boise. In this case, putting a single server farm in Phoenix (no earthquakes or hurricanes to worry about) will mean that everyone has to access SharePoint over a slow WAN link. It might make more sense to create a local server farm for each regional office and, if necessary, to back up to a separate, secure location that doesn't have to worry about many natural disasters.

If different divisions of your business or different regional offices have different security and authentication needs, you can create and deploy your server farms based on those requirements, and in fact, implementing security via isolation is the most straightforward method. In addition, government or corporate policies or contracts may require that security isolation be implemented physically rather than using software, even when physical isolation won't actually increase security. MOSS 2007 uses different software methods to allow you to isolate different applications running in the same server farm:

- Implement isolation at the process level with separate IIS application pools.
- Implement isolation at the application level with separate web applications.
- Implement isolation at the audience and content levels with separate SSPs.

Designing Shared Services Providers

As mentioned earlier in the chapter, an SSP is the logical organization of web applications and their associated SharePoint sites used to access a common set of services and information. While the server farm is the top-level logical container for all of the SharePoint design elements, the SSP is the next highest logical object, and MOSS 2007 will fail to function without at least one SSP being configured. In fact, once you have installed the server farm, creating the default SSP is one of the first tasks you must accomplish.

If you set up only one SSP, all of your web applications must be associated with that SSP. Any individual web application can be associated with only a single SSP, so if your server farm contains more than one SSP, select to which SSP you want any individual web application associated. Any sites and site collections within SharePoint that are contained within a particular web application will use the services provided by the SSP associated with that application. Services provided by an SSP can be enabled or disabled only at the application level, not the site or site collection level.

All SSPs provide the following generic set of services:

Business Data Catalog   This service provides a single unified schema for data stored in line-of-business applications.

Excel Services   This service provides shared worksheets and methods of analyzing business information from data connection libraries using dashboard reports.

Personalization Services   Personalization Services provides user profiles using information imported from directory services. This allows personal information about users located on their My Sites to be managed by privacy policies and shared by all users within the SSP.

Portal Usage Reporting   This service lets SSP administrators view aggregated information about site usage across the entire site hierarchy and enables site and site collection admins to view these reports.

SharePoint Server Search   This service creates a single index of all content, data, and metadata by crawling all SharePoint sites contained within the SSP's web applications.

At this point, it's important to note that a server farm can contain one or more SSPs, or the server farm can access services from an SSP contained in another server farm. This fact is critical to understand in terms of server farm design and implementation since a server farm accessing one or more SSPs on another farm does not have to contain any SSPs within its own farm. Think of this as the difference between hosting DNS services within your own domain and accessing DNS from an outside source. The caveat to using another farm's SSP is that sites within your farm will not be able to access Excel Services. If your site collection must provide Excel Services, your server farm must host SSP locally.

The most common deployment is to create a single SSP in a single server farm. A single SSP within your farm enables users to collaborate by sharing resources within your entire company. Enterprise-wide search is also available using a single SSP within the server farm. You will implement more than one SSP only if you have a specific need.

Creating more than one SSP within a server farm is more or less equal to creating an additional domain forest within Active Directory. It's a major undertaking with a great deal of additional administrative overhead attached. Although there are justifiable reasons for creating either more than one domain forest or more than one SSP, weigh the benefits and costs of that decision before going ahead.

The most outstanding need for creating multiple SSPs within a single server farm is security isolation. If you have more than one basic group of users accessing services within the farm and those different groups require different security for their content, develop an SSP for each group.

Previously, in the "Availability and Service-Level Agreements" section of this chapter, you read about how server farm design is affected by whether your consumers are employees accessing an intranet or customers and partners accessing an extranet. The differences between these consumers will also affect your SSP design since they all most likely will need different security levels. If you are planning to use a single server farm to service employees, partners, and customers, you will want to set up an SSP for each of these basic user types. Additionally, if you are going to allow the general public to access any portion of your SharePoint site collection via the Internet, you will need to create a separate SSP for that audience.

Most organizations create a separate web presence on the Internet for the general public that does not involve SharePoint access at all. Usually, web commerce involving the general public does not require potentially compromising SharePoint security. Best practices suggest allowing only preferred customers SharePoint access via an Internet-facing extranet requiring a logon.

Given the issues just stated, you should attempt to implement the smallest number of SSPs possible since each additional SSP that you deploy will reduce the overall performance of the server farm and thus SharePoint. Also keep in mind that security is not limited to just the server farm or SSP level. You can assign different users, departments, divisions, and so on, different levels of security access based on SharePoint groups.

Keep in mind that SharePoint group security implemented within a single SSP will prevent groups without the right privileges from accessing sites and site content, but content they can't access will still appear on the results page of a search.

Up until now, two or more SSPs have been treated like completely separate entities with no links between them, but it is possible to share information across different SSPs. This practice is discouraged for a number of reasons, not the least of which is that it defeats the purpose of creating more than one SSP in the first place. Shared content across multiple SSPs is not automatic and must be purposefully configured, such as adding the start address to an external content source to let one SSP crawl content on another SSP or using trusted MySite host locations to let users on one SSP view personalized information about users in another SSP. The bottom line is that if you don't absolutely need to enable this functionality, don't.

Designing Server Farm Topologies

The physical and logical topologies of a SharePoint Server 2007 server farm vary for a large number of reasons including security, customer requirements, and size. Topology designs can be created around the type of customer (intranet, extranet, and Internet) or based on the size of the server farm (small, medium, and large). Also, topologies for SharePoint 2007 can focus on either a single or multiple farm models. This section of the chapter will present topologies based on the most common examples of these design scenarios.

 This section of Chapter 1 is not meant to take the place of a basic book on server and network topology design. The book assumes you already possess these skills.

Small-Scale Server Farm

A small-scale server farm might not seem very "farm-like" based on Microsoft's recommendations and is composed of only two physical servers:

- One server running SQL Server 2000 or 2005
- One server running Microsoft Office SharePoint Server 2007 and IIS

Medium-Scale Server Farm

This level of server farm is typically used for small to medium-sized business environments and contains three to four servers:

- One or two front-end web servers running Office SharePoint Server 2007 and IIS
- One application server running Office SharePoint Server 2007
- One server running SQL Server 2000 or 2005

In this traditional layout, the application server provides indexing services and Excel Calculation Services, and the front-end web servers provide search queries and web content services.

Large-Scale Server Farm

This is the minimum server farm configuration suitable for an enterprise-level SharePoint environment:

- Several load-balanced front-end web servers running Office SharePoint Server 2007
- Two or more application servers running Office SharePoint Server 2007
- Two or more clustered database servers running SQL Server 2000 or 2005

In this traditional layout, each of the application servers provides specific SharePoint Server 2007 services such as Index Services or Excel Calculation Services, and the front-end servers provide web content services.

All of the servers in your server farm must be running the same server software, which in this case is Office SharePoint Server 2007. You cannot add a physical server to the farm that is running different server software such as Microsoft Office Forms Server 2007. If you need Office Forms Server 2007 to run in your server farm, you must install both MOSS 2007 and Office Forms Server 2007 on each of your web servers.

In addition to what is specifically required for an Office SharePoint Server 2007 server farm, you will also need to provide Active Directory and DNS services. Figure 1.1 shows a simple example of this.

As you can imagine based on the examples of server farm topologies previously discussed, you could take Figure 1.1 and simply add the appropriate number and type of servers to change it from small to medium to large scale. Let's take this basic structure and apply it to different design requirements.

FIGURE 1.1 A simple server farm

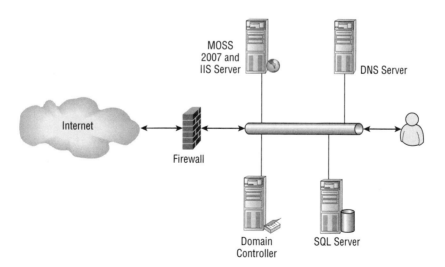

Intranet Server Farm Topologies

An intranet is the corporation's private SharePoint 2007 site collection. Ideally, the intranet is accessible only by company employees. Any information from the intranet that needs to be shared with partners or customers can be accessed via an extranet (see the following section). Intranet logical topologies consist of three general areas: the Internet, the perimeter network, and the corporate network. The intranet server farm exists in the corporate network. The Internet is the world's public network, which brings us to what stands in between the two—the perimeter network. This is often known as the *demilitarized zone* (DMZ) and is the portion of the overall business network that is facing the Internet.

In Figure 1.2 you can see a simple example of an intranet server farm topology.

FIGURE 1.2   Simple intranet server farm

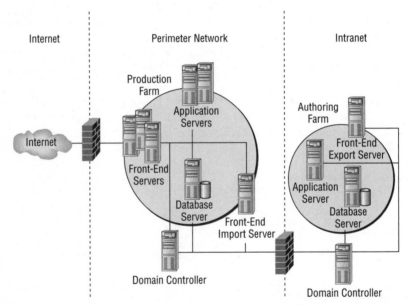

In this example, we assume that the intranet site is exclusively accessible from inside the corporate network and no component whatsoever can be accessed from the outside. In this case, the perimeter network exists as a barrier between the Internet and the corporate network to protect the intranet from intrusion. The safest way to do this of course would be to not connect the intranet to the Internet at all, but corporations often rely on Internet access to do research, send and receive email, conduct web conferences, and do other business-related activities. The perimeter network exists in this scenario because it's possible for the door to swing both ways. Without a barrier, an unscrupulous person would have a greater chance of getting unauthorized access to corporation data.

Although you can create an intranet server farm topology that serves only internal employees, it is more likely that you will want to allow at least some data and services to be accessed from the Internet. This should be limited to content you absolutely need to have be accessed from the outside. If you need to offer extensive information to and collaboration with customers and partners, use an extranet scenario. Your company's web presence to the Internet-at-large should be handled using a more conventional website scheme. That said, Figure 1.3 describes how you can use the classic three-tiered design to offer some services from the intranet to the Web while maintaining a secure environment.

FIGURE 1.3   Three-tiered design

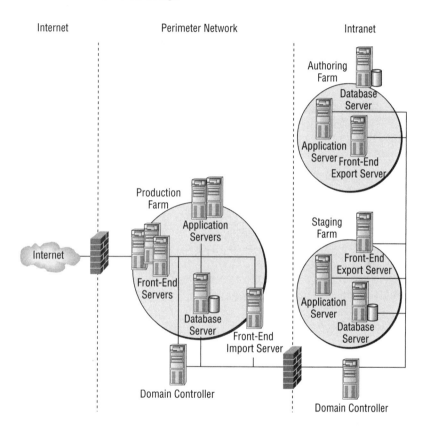

The following section will describe in more detail the server farm topology designs you would use to provide significant access to SharePoint content to the Web while protecting the internal intranet.

Extranet Server Farm Topologies

An extranet is a private network you allow specified users to access via the Internet. It is designed with the particular needs of specialized users such as partners and customers. An extranet site is an extension of the company's intranet site, but with its own security and identity. Content between the extranet and intranet can be separated so you share only the content from the intranet that is required by your extranet consumers.

Microsoft recommends a five-part plan for designing a SharePoint Server 2007 extranet:

The firewall plan   In every extranet topology, the firewall solution of choice is Microsoft Internet Security and Acceleration (ISA) server. Of course, you can use any firewall technology your company wants to support.

The authentication and logical architecture plan   An authentication and logical architecture plan must be established to allow external partners or customers to access restricted content on the extranet.

The domain trust relationships plan   The server farm for an extranet is usually located in a perimeter network between the Internet-facing firewall and the intranet firewall (sometimes known as the DMZ). Separate Active Directory domains are maintained for the extranet and intranet, and by default, these domains do not have a trust relationship; however, your plan may need to include developing a trust based on a particular scenario.

The availability plan   As presented earlier in this chapter, availability is the amount of time services are accessible on the system as related to the overall amount of time the system is in operation. Not all extranet consumers will need maximum availability, and this plan can include different levels.

The security hardening plan   Security plans can include specific firewall and router configurations such as the use of custom port numbers, domain trust relationships, communication paths between server types, and other factors.

Like intranets, extranet logical topologies consist of three areas: the Internet, the perimeter network, and the corporate network. The Internet needs no introduction. The perimeter network is the logical and physical home of the extranet. The corporate network is the company intranet. Each area is separated from the next by specifically configured firewalls or routers. Figure 1.4 shows the most typical extranet topology scenario.

FIGURE 1.4   Typical extranet topology

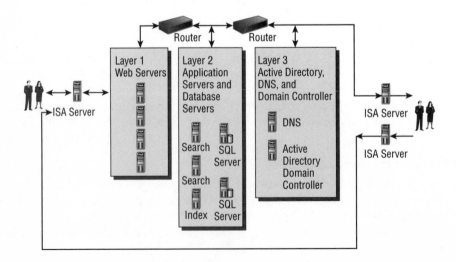

The interior of the perimeter network is separated into three layers:

- The Web Servers layer
- The Application and Database Servers layer
- The Active Directory, DNS, and Domain Controller layer

As you can see in Figure 1.4, each layer within the perimeter network is separated from the next by a router so that each layer can exist on a separate subnet or network segment. This allows you to make sure that only specific requests for data and services are allowed to traverse the different layers in the perimeter network. This also allows you to limit damage in the perimeter network to one layer if the extranet is compromised from the outside.

Both the physical and logical server farm topology of the extranet exist in the perimeter network, making it easier to share resources and reducing administrative overhead. DNS and Active Directory for the extranet are managed within the perimeter network, which both improves performance and protects the Active Directory domain of the corporate network. The only real disadvantage of this design is that it requires a significant network infrastructure built exclusively to support the extranet.

In the previous example, there are actually two separate server farms in operation—the extranet server farm in the perimeter network and the intranet server farm in the corporate network. It is also possible to use a single server farm to manage both the extranet and the intranet, as shown in Figure 1.5.

FIGURE 1.5   Split back-to-back topology

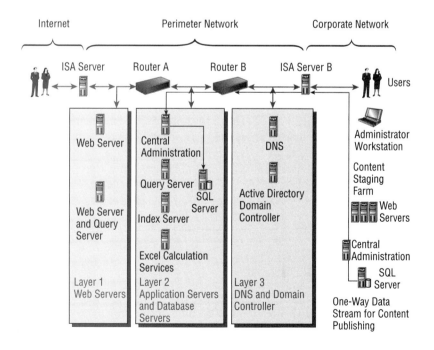

The overall topology is still composed of the Internet, the perimeter network, and the corporate network, but the perimeter and corporate networks exist in the same server farm and share resources. You'll notice in Figure 1.5 that the extranet and intranet areas of the server farm are separated by firewalls. Although web servers are located in the perimeter network and database servers are located in the corporate network, application servers can be placed in either realm. If you choose to place your application servers in the corporate network, you must also place a domain controller in the same network to provide Active Directory services.

This scenario requires that you establish a trust relationship between the domains for the extranet and intranet. Without this domain trust in place, the web servers (and application servers if located there) will not be able to connect to the database servers unless you use SQL authentication. If you choose to use SQL authentication, the domain trust relationship does not have to be put in place.

Architecting the SQL Database Infrastructure

A lot of people don't think databases are "sexy." By this I mean "attractive" or "exciting" or an interesting topic of discussion. This isn't a book on Microsoft's MCDBA certification, so maybe you don't think databases are sexy either. However, this often-overlooked topic in MOSS 2007 server farm design is absolutely vital to the smooth operation (or operation at all) of your server farm and your SharePoint sites. After all, everything you see and work with in SharePoint such as web parts, libraries, lists, and workspaces actually lives somewhere in a SQL database.

Although SharePoint Server 2007 can use SQL Server 2000 Standard Edition or Enterprise Edition (SP3a or newer) for database storage, Microsoft recommends using a version of SQL Server 2005 unless you have a compelling reason not to do so. Cost is the most likely reason to stick with SQL 2000, especially if you are upgrading from SharePoint Server 2003 to 2007 on a limited budget and are trying to leverage as much of your existing infrastructure as possible. This would occur if you were implementing a phased upgrade plan where you were moving to MOSS 2007 and planning to upgrade to SQL Server 2005 at a later time.

That said, there are a number of good reasons to choose SQL Server 2005 for your database needs. SQL Server 2005 is a completely redesigned version of SQL and offers many new features. Your organization may not need to take advantage of 2005, but it's a good idea to review what's new in this version before making that decision. Here's a brief summary:

- Database snapshots
- Instant file initialization
- Page checksum and page-level restore combination
- Partitioning
- Read-only filegroups on compressed drives
- Row-level versioning

Listing all of the new features offered in 2005 and their explanations would be a chapter unto itself. To review the complete list, go to the following URL: www.microsoft.com/sql/prodinfo/overview/whats-new-in-sqlserver2005.mspx.

It's common to have to make decisions about upgrading software and equipment while planning to deploy MOSS 2007. This can include upgrading SQL Server. As you learned earlier in this chapter, even if you have an adequate budget, you still need to choose the right license for your needs.

Since database design is its own specialty, this section of the book will be relatively brief. In a real-life scenario, you would likely either have a database design specialist in-house performing this function or hire a consultant to do the job.

In the physical storage design of the SQL Server 2005 database, Microsoft recommends the following five-step plan:

1. Characterize the I/O workload of the application.

2. Determine the reliability and performance requirements for the database system.

3. Determine the hardware required to support the decisions made in steps 1 and 2.

4. Configure SQL Server 2005 to take advantage of the hardware in step 3.

5. Track performance as workload changes.

As with your server farm in general, it's important to build a database design that is scalable. If anything in your organization can be said to grow explosively over time, it is information. Although the topology diagrams previously presented in this chapter have often shown only one or two physical database servers, remember that there isn't always a one-to-one relationship between the "map" and the "territory." In real life, you would have more hardware implemented for failover and redundancy purposes.

Imagine your new company is creating a SharePoint server farm for your company's customers. Now imagine you're Amazon.com. Within a relatively short period of time, you have millions and then hundreds of millions of customers. The necessity for designing highly scalable database storage is amazingly obvious. Scaling up database servers can involve a couple of different methods:

- Symmetric multiprocessing (SMP), which means adding processors, memory, disks, and network cards to individual servers

- Adding servers to the topology and then partitioning workload and database storage across the individual servers, sometimes called *database partitioning*

The first option assumes you will be using a single physical server for your database storage needs. Although this may practical in a small-to-medium-size server farm, you will (assuming your company and your company's database needs continue to grow) eventually hit the limit of how much you can physically upgrade an individual piece of hardware. Your one database server will become a bottleneck instead of a boon.

As you grow, you will find yourself adding database servers to your topology, or you may design multiple database server hardware into your topology from the beginning, depending on your organization's requirements. The second bullet will be the option of choice in that case, but there's a couple of different ways to deploy a multidatabase server plan:

- Deploy different elements of the overall database on different server hardware, such as putting a parts inventory on one server, your customer list on another server, and your shopping cart on yet another server.

- Deploy a single, large table across several physical servers.

In both cases, the partitioning of work and information should be transparent to your customers and to the applications accessing the database.

You can find a detailed paper on SQL Server scaling at the following URL: www.microsoft.com/technet/prodtechnol/sql/2005/scddrtng.mspx.

A few paragraphs back, you imagined that you were designing a database architecture in your server farm for Amazon.com. The idea is to imagine your company's database needs not only for today but for the future. That is, you need to plan for the rate of content growth in your database.

It's not enough to know that your information storage needs will grow. That's obvious. The trick is to estimate how much your database storage needs will grow over what period of time. Add too much storage capacity too fast, and you spend money you didn't have to spend. (You have a budget, just like every other department in the organization.) Add too little capacity or add it too slowly, and you bottleneck your system.

In general, server farm design starts small and grows as requests for data and services grow. Broken down to its basic limits, a small server farm will be able to manage the following:

- Up to 2,000 SharePoint users

- Up to 50,000 SharePoint site collections with up to 2,000 subsites per website

- Up to 10,000 documents in a document library with individual documents of up to 50MB in size

- Up to 100 web parts per web part page

The list is not exhaustive, so don't believe these are the only items you need to keep in mind. One way to keep a certain amount of control over growth is to implement size quotas for SharePoint users. Size quotas are a common tool used in server administration when you don't have infinite storage space (and who does?) and when you need to control how much data users store on the system. You can also monitor your database with specific utilities such as the Management Pack for MOM. Microsoft provides MOM packs that are optimized for a wide variety of their products including MOSS 2007 and SQL Server 2005.

You can find details about MOM for SharePoint Server 2007 at www.microsoft .com/downloads/details.aspx?FamilyID=247c06ba-c599-4b22-b2d3- 7bf88c4d7811&displaylang=en; you can find information about MOM for SQL Server 2005 at www.microsoft.com/downloads/details.aspx?FamilyId= 79F151C7-4D98-4C2B-BF72-EC2B4AE69191&displaylang=en.

Introducing the Central Administration Interface

Although you won't encounter the Central Administration interface until after you install SharePoint in Chapter 2, "Installing and Deploying SharePoint 2007," this advance look should give you an idea of the initial post-installation tasks you'll be facing. You'll get a more detailed look at the Central Administration interface and how it operates in Chapter 3, "Configuring SharePoint 2007." Right now, you're just getting what my grandfather used to call "the 10-cent tour."

As shown in Figure 1.6, when you are on the Home tab of the Central Administration page, you'll see a list of the top 10 ordered administrative tasks. There are actually more than 10, which you'll see in a minute, but these are the ones you'll want to visit first.

If you scroll to the bottom of the same page, you'll see a list of the services running on the server farm topology. As shown in Figure 1.7, this is a simple topology; in fact, all services, including database services, are running on a single server.

FIGURE 1.6   Central Administration page

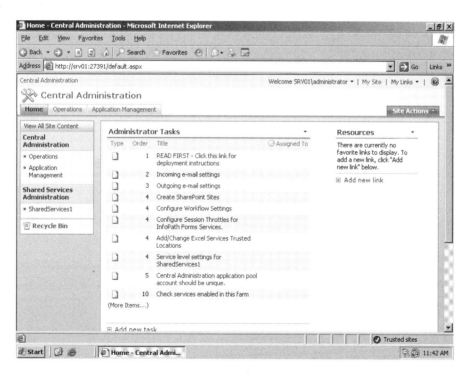

Although you can run WSS database services on the same physical server as MOSS 2007, this is recommended only for a single-server farm topology that would service a fairly small business platform.

FIGURE 1.7   Simple server farm topology services list

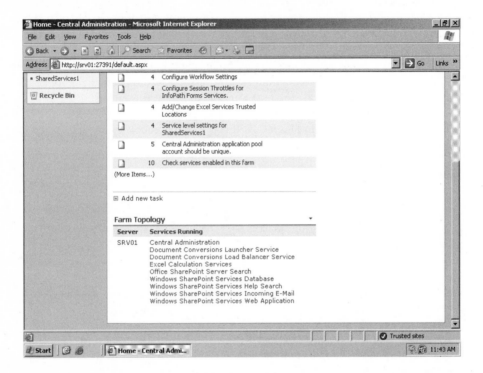

If you want to see the complete list of post-installation administrator tasks, click the More Items link just below the top 10 administrator tasks. You'll be able to see the remaining items, as shown in Figure 1.8.

This is what a typical SharePoint list looks like. The columns of information presented here are the default, but as in any SharePoint list, the columns can be manipulated and filtered. The default Administrator Tasks columns are as follows:

Type   The type of administrative task

Title   The name of the administrative task

FIGURE 1.8   Full Administrator Tasks list

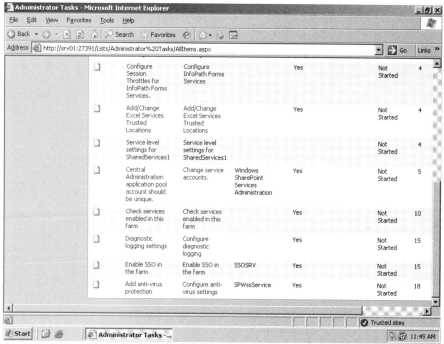

Action   What sort of action is required

Associated Service   The service (such as SMTP) associated with the task

System Task   Whether this is a system task (Yes or No)

Assigned To   To whom the task is assigned

Status   Whether the task has been started, is in progress, or has been completed

Order   The order or priority of the task

Due Date   When the task is expected to be completed

%Complete   The percentage of the task that has been completed

As you can see in Figure 1.9, when you click the title of one of the tasks, you are taken to a detailed page describing that specific task. This includes information on all of the columns that have just been described. Clicking the Edit Item button will let you update the information in any of the columns, as illustrated in Figure 1.10.

FIGURE 1.9 Administrator Tasks detail page

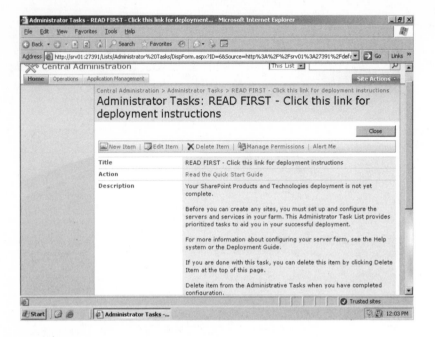

FIGURE 1.10 Administrator Tasks edit page

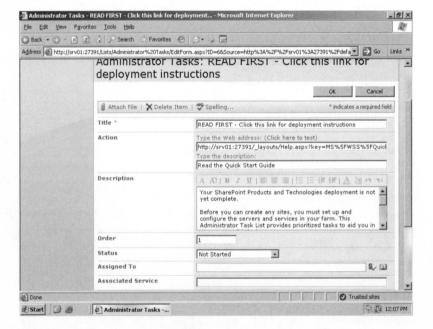

Summary

In this chapter, you were introduced to Microsoft Office SharePoint Server 2007 and learned the following topics:

- What's new in MOSS 2007 including the basic roles of business intelligence, business process and forms, collaboration, enterprise content management, Enterprise Search, and portals

- The primary elements in planning SharePoint 2007 architecture

- The components of architecting SharePoint including the server farm, shared services providers, database services, web applications, and SharePoint site collections

- The specific factors involved in architecting server farms including server farm design architectures, designing shared services providers, and designing server farm topologies

- Architecting of the SQL database infrastructure including physical storage design, database server scaling, and database content growth management

- Introduction to the Central Administration interface including post-installation administrator tasks and how they are organized

Exam Essentials

Understand how to manage administration.   Understand the basic tasks in administering SharePoint Server 2007 from the planning and design stages.

Know how to manage the Central Administration user interface.   Understand how to organize post-installation administrator tasks.

Review Questions

1. You are a consultant training a group of server administrators on the latest features of Microsoft Office SharePoint Server 2007. You are describing the services typically provided by the shared services provider (SSP). Which of the following services are you discussing? (Choose all that apply.)

   A. Database Services

   B. Excel Services

   C. Index Services

   D. Web Services

2. You are a SharePoint 2007 administrator for your company, and you have been tasked with designing a server farm for your organization's external partners and internal employees. You are told to create an environment where partners and employees can collaborate freely on mutual projects and does not require that the company purchase Client Access Licenses (CALs) for either the partner or employee users. Of the following options, which is the best choice?

   A. Create an intranet site on the server farm hosting the extranet, and purchase the Microsoft Office SharePoint Server 2007, Server License.

   B. Create an extranet site on the server farm hosting the intranet, and purchase the Microsoft Office SharePoint Server 2007, Server License.

   C. Create an extranet site on the server farm hosting the Internet, and purchase the Microsoft Office SharePoint Server 2007 for Internet Sites license.

   D. None of the above.

3. You are part of the design team that has been tasked with planning a SharePoint Server 2007 deployment for your business. Your company currently uses SQL Server 2000 SP2 for database services. You are required to determine whether this version of SQL Server will support MOSS 2007 and, if not, what upgrade option is available at the least financial and administrative cost. Of the following options, which choice best fits?

   A. SQL Server 2000 SP2 will support MOSS 2007.

   B. You must upgrade to SQL Server 2000 SP3a.

   C. You must upgrade to SQL Server 2005 SP1.

   D. You must upgrade to SQL Server 2005 SP2.

4. You are the SharePoint administrator for your company. The database content storage needs for your company's SharePoint 2007 server farm are growing rapidly, so you are working with your company's database administrator to determine the best scale-up plan for your SQL Server. You have SQL Server 2005 running on a single hardware server, and the processors and RAM have already been upgraded to their maximum limit. What options are available to scale up the database? (Choose all that apply.)

A. Deploy different elements of the overall database on several different servers.

B. Deploy a single, large table on a single SQL Server, and deploy a second server to provide mirroring services.

C. Deploy a single, large table across multiple SQL Server instances.

D. Run Windows SharePoint Services (WSS) database services on the same physical server as MOSS 2007.

5. You are the SharePoint administrator for your company. The CIO wants you to integrate Microsoft Office Project Server 2007 and Microsoft Office Forms Server 2007 into the Share-Point server farm. Of the following options, which one is the most viable solution?

A. Add two physical web servers to the server farm. Install Project Server on one of the hardware servers and Forms Server on the other hardware server.

B. Add one physical web server to the server farm, and install both Project Server and Forms Server on it.

C. Install Project Server and Forms Server on each one of the hardware web servers running MOSS 2007.

D. Install Project Server and Forms Server on just one of the hardware web servers running MOSS 2007.

6. Your company has just signed a service-level agreement (SLA) with one of its partners to provide a SharePoint extranet service for collaboration purposes. The agreement states that your company will guarantee high availability, and in the event of a service outage, you will return the extranet site to service within two hours of failure with a minimal loss of data. What fault-tolerant solution will come closest to meeting the terms of this agreement at the most economical cost?

A. Deploying a hot server solution

B. Deploying a warm server solution

C. Deploying a cold server solution

D. None of the above

7. You are a SharePoint 2007 consultant working with a customer's IT department staff on plans for an extranet server farm design. You are outlining Microsoft's recommended plan for extranets, and you are asked what part of the plan addresses custom port numbers and communication paths between server types. Of the following options, what is the best answer?

    A. The firewall plan

    B. The authentication and logical architecture plan

    C. The domain trust relationships plan

    D. The availability plan

    E. The security hardening plan

8. You are the SharePoint administrator for an enterprise-level software company. You have created a single server farm for the organization's employees. You have deployed five separate, custom-designed web applications in the farm that the software engineers you support need for development and testing purposes. You've noticed that two of the applications are used heavily while the other three are accessed with the same but much lighter frequency. This has caused a performance slowdown in the entire server farm. What is the best plan for improving performance based on the application profile?

    A. Create a second server farm, place the two web applications that are more heavily used in the second farm, and leave the other three on the first farm.

    B. Create a separate server farm for each custom-made web application.

    C. Upgrade the processing and memory capacity of the hardware server hosting the more heavily used applications, and add a second network interface card.

    D. Install a higher-speed switch in the data center to improve access speeds.

9. You are the SharePoint site administrator for a company called Applepaste, Inc. The site collection at Applepaste is organized by department. Brad, the manager of the engineering department, has asked you to create a subsite for his department called *projects*. He specifies that he needs a special projects site and that the first special project for his team is the Tantalis Project. This special project will need to contain a list of links entitled Plouto Research. Once you create this resource, Brad wants you to send him an email containing the managed path to the lowest-level resource. What is the path you will send him?

    A. /applepaste/engineering/projects/special_projects/tantalis_project/links/plouto_research

    B. /applepaste/engineering/projects/special_projects/tantalis_project/plouto_research

    C. /applepaste/engineering/projects/tantalis_project/plouto_research

    D. /applepaste/projects/special_projects/tantalis_project/plouto_research

    E. /engineering/projects/special_projects/tantalis_project/plouto_research

10. You are the SharePoint administrator for your company. You are working with Mary Jean, who is the security specialist in your company's IT department, to develop a new SharePoint site collection for the HR department. All of the content for the HR department must be kept separate from the rest of the company's SharePoint intranet sites. What form of security isolation would be most suitable?

    A. Process-level isolation

    B. Application-level isolation

    C. SSP isolation

    D. Database isolation

11. You are a consultant hired by the Magnotronics Corporation to upscale their SharePoint 2007 server farm. Magnotronics has seen extremely rapid growth in the past two years and has quickly outgrown its current server farm, based on a small-scale model. Currently, the farm has only two hardware servers, one running MOSS 2007 and IIS and the other running SQL Server 2005. You determine that its needs can be met by scaling up its server farm based on a large-scale model. Of the following options, what is your recommendation based on the minimal requirements for this model?

    A. Add several load-balanced front-end web servers running MOSS 2007, two application servers running MOSS 2007, and at least one more server running SQL Server 2005.

    B. Add several application servers running MOSS 2007, one load-balanced front-end web server running MOSS 2007, and two or more clustered database servers running SQL Server 2005.

    C. Add one load-balanced front-end web server running MOSS 2007, one application server running MOSS 2007, and one server running SQL Server 2005.

    D. Add five load-balanced front-end web server running MOSS 2007, three application servers running MOSS 2007, and three clustered database servers running SQL Server 2005.

12. You are the SharePoint administrator for your company. You have just finished installing MOSS 2007 and are on the Home tab of the Central Administration page. Under Administrator Tasks, you click the More Items link to view the entire list of post-installation tasks. What items are included on that list? (Choose all that apply.)

    A. Create SharePoint sites.

    B. Enable SSP in the farm.

    C. Configure workflow settings.

    D. Incoming Email Settings.

    E. Outgoing Email Settings.

13. You are the SharePoint administrator for your company. You have just finished installing MOSS 2007 and are on the Home tab of the Central Administration page. Under Administrator Tasks, you click the Incoming Email Settings link to open this task. You are going to assign this task to Mike. What do you have to do to add Mike's name to the Assigned To column?

    A. Click the New Item button.

    B. Click the Edit Item button.

    C. Click the Modify Item button.

    D. Click the Assigned To button.

14. You are the SharePoint administrator working at your company's main office in Seattle. You have been tasked with creating a SharePoint server farm topology for a new regional office in Nashville. You start by sketching a very simple intranet topology where only a firewall separates the Internet from the corporate network. This is usually an unrealistic design. In a production intranet model, what area would exist between the Internet and the corporate network?

    A. The parameter network

    B. The security network

    C. The perimeter network

    D. The distribution network

15. After you have finished the intranet design for the Nashville office, you are asked by your manager to design a simple extranet farm topology for a branch office in Oklahoma City. You present the design to Sue, the branch manager, and she asks you about the different layers in the perimeter network containing the extranet server farm. Of the following options, which one is the best explanation?

A. Layer 1 contains the web servers for the extranet, Layer 2 contains the application and database servers, and Layer 3 contains the DNS server and domain controller. ISA servers separate Layer 1 from the Internet and Layer 3 from the corporate network.

B. Layer 1 contains the web and application servers, Layer 2 contains database servers, and Layer 3 contains the DNS server and domain controller. ISA servers separate Layer 1 from the Internet and Layer 3 from the corporate network.

C. Layer 1 contains the web servers for the extranet, Layer 2 contains the application and database servers, and Layer 3 contains the DNS server and domain controller. ISA servers separate Layer 1 from the Internet, Layer 2 from Layer 3, and Layer 3 from the corporate network.

D. Layer 1 contains the web and application servers, Layer 2 contains the database servers and the domain controller, and Layer 3 contains the DNS and DHCP servers. ISA servers separate Layer 1 from the Internet and Layer 3 from the corporate network.

16. After you present your initial design to the Oklahoma City branch manager, she consults with her CIO and IT security specialist, and they ask you to modify your design and present an alternative topology. You create a split back-to-back topology with both the extranet and the intranet sharing database services located on a SQL Server in the corporate network. Since the perimeter and corporate networks exist inside different Active Directory domains, what options can you present that will allow the perimeter network to access the database server in the corporate network? (Choose all that apply.)

A. Establish a trust relationship between the domains for the extranet and intranet.

B. Use SQL authentication.

C. Use SSO authentication.

D. Place the extranet and the intranet in the same domain.

17. Once you have finished reviewing extranet topology designs for the Oklahoma City branch office, they ask you to take a look at their current intranet structure. Loren, the server administrator, tells you that recently their SharePoint sites have been experiencing some performance slowdowns. You discover that their intranet is based on a small server farm design. You review the logs and discover that there are areas where they have exceeded the limits of this design. Of the following options, which ones exceed small server farm limitations? (Choose all that apply.)

A. 3,000 SharePoint users

B. 10,111 site collections with an average of 1,500 subsites per website

C. 5,000 documents per document library with each document being an average of 20MB in size

D. An average of 150 web parts per web part page

18. In reviewing the extranet topology plans with Sue and Loren at your company's Oklahoma City branch office, they seem to be leaning toward a simple extranet design setup with Layer 1 containing the web servers for the extranet, Layer 2 containing the application and database servers, and Layer 3 containing the DNS server and domain controller. ISA servers separate Layer 1 from the Internet and Layer 3 from the corporate network. Of the following options, which ones describe the advantages of a simple extranet topology? (Choose all that apply.)

A. Ease in sharing resources between layers in the perimeter network

B. Improved performance

C. Separate domains for the perimeter and corporate networks

D. Significant network infrastructure for the perimeter network

19. Given the recent issues your company's Oklahoma City branch office has been having monitoring the growth of their intranet, you recommend that they implement the Microsoft Office SharePoint Server 2007 Management Pack in order to better keep tabs on critical events occurring on the system. You are asked to describe the advantages of using this tool. Of the following options, which are advantages to using Microsoft Operations Manager (MOM) for MOSS 2007? (Choose all that apply.)

A. Sends an alert when shared services provider (SSP) provisioning has failed

B. Monitors the available space in databases, configurable by percent or megabyte

C. Monitors the health of replication and sends an alert on failures

D. Sends an alert when the Central Administration site for the SSP is missing

E. Sends an alert when the Office Document Conversions Launcher service is not running

20. You are a SharePoint consultant and are giving a presentation on the advantages of deploying MOSS 2007 to the executives of the Minos Development Group. They are particularly interested in the Business Intelligence (BI) capacities of SharePoint and want to hear more details about this area. Nicole, the chief marketing manager, wants to hear about which BI features would help track progress made toward specific business goals. You mention that SharePoint BI uses specialized lists and web parts that let the user visually track these indicators. Which BI feature are you describing?

A. Key performance indicators (KPIs)

B. Dashboards

C. Business Data Catalog (BDC)

D. Report Center site

Answers to Review Questions

1. B, C, and D. A shared services provider is the logical environment that contains all of the particular services that you want to make available across your web applications and SharePoint sites. Those services include Excel Calculation Services, Index Services, Search Services, and Web Services. Database services are usually provided by some version of Microsoft SQL Server.

2. C. You can create an extranet site on the server farm that is hosting your company's Internet site and using the Internet Sites license. This option doesn't require you to purchase CALs for partners, customers, or internal employees working on collaborative projects. However, you will not be able to create sites in this server farm that are accessed only by internal employees.

3. B. Although options B, C, and D will all support MOSS 2007, option B will do so at the least financial and administrative cost.

4. A and C. Options A and C are the only two viable options. Although option B, installing another SQL server for mirroring, will provide a fault tolerance solution should the primary database server fail, it does nothing to solve the database storage problem. Although option D is a possibility if you are running MOSS 2007 in a single-server design, you cannot run WSS database services on the server hosting SharePoint and use a separate database server to increase storage capacity.

5. C. All of the servers in your SharePoint server farm must be running the same server software. You cannot add a physical server to the farm that is running different server software such as Project Server 2007 or Forms Server 2007. If you need Project Server or Forms Server to run in your server farm, you must install MOSS 2007, Project Server, and Forms Server on each of your web servers.

6. B. The warm server solution is the best option for restoring service within two hours and with a minimal loss of data since the warm server is almost immediately available and can restore data from the most recent period of replication. Although option A, the hot server solution, would return service nearly at once with no loss of data, it is not the most economical option, and the SLA did specify that some data loss was acceptable. Option C, the cold server solution, is not viable since two hours would not be enough time to repair or replace failed server hardware and restore data from a tape backup.

7. E. Option E, the security hardening plan, can include specific firewall and router configurations such as the use of custom port numbers, domain trust relationships, communication paths between server types, and other factors.

8. A. Options C and D would likely improve performance, but not based on the application profile that requires grouping applications in different server farms based on similar usage, as stated in Option A. Option B would likely improve performance but at a much greater administrative cost than option A.

9. B. Based on the stated requirements, option B is the correct answer. The root to the managed path is typically the company name, which is Applepaste. Since the SharePoint site collection for Applepaste is organized by department, engineering is the next level. Brad requested a subsite named *projects* and within projects another site named *special projects*. The first project in the special projects container is named Tantalis Project, and the links list is called Plouto Research. Links or any other list does not have to be located in a container such as *links* found in Option A.

10. C. To isolate the HR sites from the rest of the corporate intranet at the audience and content level, create a separate SSP for the HR department in the server farm.

11. A. The minimum configuration for the large-scale server farm model includes several load-balanced front-end web servers running Office SharePoint Server 2007, two or more application servers running Office SharePoint Server 2007, and two or more clustered database servers running SQL Server 2000 or 2005.

12. A, C, D, and E. All of the options are on the list except option B, which is bogus. If option B were Enable SSO (Single Sign-On) in the farm instead of Enable SSP (Shared Source Provider) in the farm, it would have been correct.

13. B. Click the Edit Item button to open the task for editing, and then type Mike's name into the Assigned To field. You would click the New Item button if you wanted to add a new task to the Administrator Task list. The other two options are bogus.

14. C. Generally, in any intranet or extranet scenario, you would place the perimeter network between the Internet and the corporate network, as in option C. The perimeter network is sometimes called the *demilitarized zone* (DMZ). Options A and B are bogus.

15. A. Option A describes a simple extranet design with three layers in the perimeter network. Although option C is also a valid extranet design, it is more security hardened than the simple topology you were asked to create. Options B and D are bogus.

16. A and B. By default, the extranet and intranet domains do not have a trust relationship, but as in option A, you can create this. You can also use SQL authentication as a viable solution as in option B. Option C, single sign-on authentication (SSO), would not apply in this case, and option D, placing the extranet and intranet in the same domain, would potentially give extranet users unauthorized access to intranet resources.

17. A and D. The small server farm design can support up to 2,000 SharePoint users only and 100 web parts per web part page.

18. A, B, and C. Both the physical and logical server farm topology of the extranet exist in the perimeter network, making it easier to share resources and reducing administrative overhead. DNS and Active Directory for the extranet are managed within the perimeter network, which both improves performance and protects the active directory domain of the corporate network. The only real disadvantage of this design is that it requires a significant network infrastructure built exclusively to support the extranet.

19. A, D, and E. Options A, D, and E are available on MOM for MOSS 2007. Options B and C are available on MOM for SQL Server 2005.

20. A. Key performance indicators (KPIs) use specialized lists and web parts in SharePoint that let you visually track progress made toward specific business goals.

Chapter

2

Installing and Deploying SharePoint 2007

MICROSOFT EXAM OBJECTIVES COVERED IN THIS CHAPTER

✓ **Configure Microsoft Office SharePoint Server 2007 Portal**

- Configure Site Management

✓ **Manage Administration**

- Manage Central Admin UI
- Manage the Shared Service Provider

✓ **Deploy/Upgrade Microsoft Office SharePoint Server 2007**

- Configure Shared Services

Now that you've been introduced to Microsoft Office Share-Point Server (MOSS) 2007 and its basic features, as well as learned the details of designing a SharePoint Server architecture, it's time to start actually working with SharePoint. The first task in this chapter is to plan for the installation of SharePoint. This includes learning about all of the hardware and software requirements.

The requirements for installing SharePoint can be tailored to either a stand-alone/single-server installation or a server farm installation. Since it is unlikely that the average candidate for this exam has access to a production-level server farm, many of the exercises will focus on the stand-alone installation model. Equal time will be given to the server farm installation model because it represents the actual environment in which you will be working.

Each installation model will present both the hardware and software requirements, but since both models are substantially different from one another, they will also have individual variables such as how database components and server role types are configured.

The chapter will conclude with brief introduction to some post-installation tasks.

Requirements for SharePoint Server 2007 Installation

There is a great deal of variance in the requirements for the stand-alone and server farm models. This chapter will present Microsoft's official minimum and recommended requirements for each installation model. For example, when you learn about the hardware and software requirements for a server farm in this chapter, you will learn how these requirements vary depending on how you want to optimize certain SharePoint features and services.

The hardware and software requirements discussed in this chapter apply to x32-bit and x64-bit systems; Itanium-based systems are not supported.

Stand-Alone Server Installation

Installing SharePoint Server 2007 in a single-server environment has a number of advantages. Installing SharePoint on a stand-alone server can let you quickly get up and running. The most likely scenarios for performing this kind of installation are to evaluate Share-Point 2007 as part of an upgrade or rollout plan or to make SharePoint available for testing, experimentation, and learning purposes.

See Chapter 16, "Upgrading and Deploying Microsoft Office SharePoint Server 2007," for more information about deploying a test environment for upgrading SharePoint.

As mentioned previously in this chapter, it's for the latter reason that many of the exercises in this chapter will focus on the stand-alone server installation model. In your pursuit of the 70-630 certification, you will need to have a great deal of hands-on practice with MOSS 2007. Even if you are an experienced administrator on SharePoint Server 2003, a number of differences in 2007 will not allow you to completely leverage your prior knowledge in learning this newer technology.

Besides using the stand-alone model as an evaluation or learning tool, a stand-alone installation is a valid production environment in its own right for smaller businesses. You can use just one piece of hardware to meet all the requirements for deploying a SharePoint 2007 site collection.

When you deploy MOSS 2007 on a single server and use the default settings, Microsoft SQL Server 2005 Express Edition is automatically installed for you and creates configuration and content databases for your sites. The default Setup program also creates a shared services provider (SSP), installs SharePoint Central Administration, and creates your first SharePoint site.

There is no direct upgrade from a stand-alone installation to a server farm installation. If you plan on using the stand-alone installation as an evaluation platform prior to deploying a full server farm, you will still need to perform the complete server farm installation.

Stand-Alone Installation Hardware Requirements

The following are the minimum and recommended hardware requirements for deploying Office SharePoint Server 2007, which includes the deployment of Microsoft SQL Server 2005 Express Edition, for a stand-alone installation:

Processors The minimum requirement is 2.5GHz, with dual processors at 3GHz or faster recommended.

Memory The minimum requirement is 1GB, with 2GB recommended.

Disk space and formatting The minimum is an NTFS-formatted partition with 3GB of free space; an NTFS-formatted partition with 3GB of free space and additional free space for websites is recommended.

Installation source The minimum requirement is a DVD drive; it is recommended you use either a DVD drive or the installation source copied to the hard drive or a network share.

Display The minimum requirement is a resolution of 1024×768; Microsoft recommends using the minimum or higher resolution.

Network speed   The minimum requirement is a 56Kbps connection between the server and client computers; again, Microsoft recommends the network speed to be the minimum or faster.

This book assumes you have the necessary skills to determine whether the computer you plan to use to install SharePoint 2007 in a stand-alone server deployment meets the necessary hardware requirements. You might be able to fudge a bit with the RAM, but you'll see noticeable performance slowdowns. I recommend that client computers and the server be placed on the same LAN segment if possible, leaving the 56Kbps network connection speeds a moot point.

Stand-Alone Installation Software Requirements

The software requirements for Windows SharePoint Services 3.0 (WSS 3.0) and SharePoint Server 2007 are the same since MOSS 2007 is built on top of WSS 3.0.

Operating System Platform

MOSS 2007 is designed to run on the following editions of Windows Server 2003 with SP1 or later:

- Windows Server 2003, Standard Edition
- Windows Server 2003, Enterprise Edition
- Windows Server 2003, Datacenter Edition
- Windows Server 2003, Web Edition

You can install SharePoint Server on all editions of Windows Server 2003 in either Basic or Advanced mode except for the Web Edition. A full-fledged edition of Microsoft SQL Server cannot be installed on Windows Server 2003 Web Edition because of licensing constraints. This limits your installation option for SharePoint on the Web Edition to Advanced mode. You will still be able to use SQL Server 2005 Express Edition or SQL Server 2000 Desktop Engine (Windows) (WMSDE).

The SharePoint Central Administration web interface requires that you use Microsoft Internet Explorer 6.0 with the most recent service packs or Internet Explorer 7.0.

If you do not have a full-fledged or evaluation copy of Windows Server 2003, you will need to acquire one before you can install SharePoint Server 2007. To download or order a copy, go to `http://technet.microsoft.com/en-us/windowsserver/bb430831.aspx#ELB`. If you do not have a Windows Live ID, you can acquire one at the following link: `https://accountservices.passport.net/ppnetworkhome.srf?vv=400&lc=1033`. Once you have installed Windows Server 2003 on the computer of your choice, make sure to apply all the critical updates before proceeding.

Required Pre-Installation Components

After installing Windows Server 2003 and applying all the critical updates, you will not be able to successfully install SharePoint Server 2007 until the following tasks have been completed:

Windows components   You must enable Internet Information Services (IIS) 6.0 so that your computer can function as a web server.

Microsoft .NET Framework   You must install the Microsoft .NET Framework 3.0 and then enable ASP.NET 2.0, which is necessary for Windows Workflow Foundation.

Once you install and configure the .NET Framework, make sure you apply all of the critical updates for ASP.NET.

Exercises later in this chapter will walk you through these processes in detail.

Database Services

When you install SharePoint Server 2007 in Basic mode, SQL Server 2005 Express Edition will automatically be installed. You can also use a full-fledged version of SQL Server on the same server. As previously mentioned, if you install SharePoint 2007 on Windows Server 2003 Web Edition, you must use Advanced mode to specify a database to use, and you cannot use a full-fledged version of SQL Server on the same server. You will still be able to use either SQL Server 2005 Express Edition or SQL Server 2000 Desktop Engine (WMSDE).

Networking

For the purposes of installing and running SharePoint Server 2007, you will need to not only be able to access the server interface directly but also to connect to SharePoint over a network using a client computer such as Windows XP. The typical network scenario for learning situations such as the one illustrated in this book is to have MOSS 2007 installed on one computer and Windows XP or another compatible client system installed on a separate PC.

The computers can be connected on a small LAN using an inexpensive switch. Internet access is required to install any of the critical updates required by the various applications already mentioned. Also, DNS services should be available for name-to-address resolution between network nodes (computers). If you have a typical home network setup, your DSL or cable modem will likely provide DNS services. Although servers typically have static rather than dynamically assigned IP addresses, for study purposes, you can allow your modem to act as a DHCP server and assign addresses to both your server and client computers.

Installing on a Stand-Alone Server

Now that you are aware of the hardware and software requirements for installing SharePoint Server 2007 as a stand-alone server, it's time to get to work. This part of the chapter assumes you already have either an evaluation copy or a full-fledged version of Windows Server 2003 installed on your computer or server hardware.

For the purposes of this chapter and the rest of the book, any PC that meets the hardware requirements already laid out will be sufficient. You also have the option of installing MOSS 2007 on a virtual Windows Server 2003 using software such as Microsoft Virtual PC or VMware Workstation. If you choose to go this route, you will be responsible for learning the additional hardware and software requirements of your virtualization application.

If you choose a virtual scenario, you can either use a virtual client computer to access SharePoint or use your host computer or other PC on the LAN to interact with SharePoint Server. Both devices, actual or virtual, must be on the same subnet or be connected via a router if on separate subnets.

If you uninstall Office SharePoint Server 2007 and then later install Office SharePoint Server 2007 on the same computer, the Setup program could fail when creating the configuration database, causing the entire installation process to fail. To prevent this, either delete all the existing Office SharePoint Server 2007 databases on the computer or create a new configuration database. You can create a new configuration database by running the following command:

```
psconfig -cmd configdb -create -database <uniquename>
```

Web Server Configuration

On your Windows Server 2003 device, before installing SharePoint Server 2007, you must configure the server as a web server. This involves installing and enabling IIS 6.0, installing the Microsoft .NET Framework version 3.0, and enabling ASP.NET 2.0.

IIS is not installed or enabled by default on Microsoft Windows Server 2003, so you are required to install and enable web services. Exercise 2.1 will take you through this process. You must be at your Windows Server 2003 device to complete this exercise.

EXERCISE 2.1

Installing and Configuring IIS

1. Click Start ➢ Administrative Tools ➢ Configure Your Server Wizard.

2. When the Welcome to the Configure Your Server Wizard dialog box appears, click Next.

3. On the Preliminary Steps page, click Next.

4. On the Server Role page, select Application Server (IIS, ASP.NET), and then click Next.

5. On the Application Server Options page, click Next.

6. On the Summary of Selections page, click Next.

7. Click Finish.

8. Click Start ➢ Administrative Tools ➢ Internet Information Services (IIS) Manager.

9. In the IIS Manager tree, click the plus sign (+) next to the server name to expand the options under the server. You should see folders for Applications Pools, Web Sites, and Web Services Extensions.

10. Right-click the Web Sites folder, and then click Properties.

11. In the Web Sites Properties dialog box, click the Service tab.

EXERCISE 2.1 *(continued)*

12. In the Isolation mode section, shown here, verify that the Run WWW Service in IIS 5.0 Isolation Mode check box is empty, and then click OK.

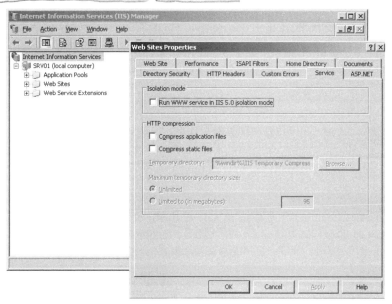

Installing Microsoft .NET Framework Version 3.0

Your next step is to install the Microsoft .NET Framework. This is a free download from Microsoft available at `http://go.microsoft.com/fwlink/?LinkID=72322&clcid=0x409`. Once you are on the Microsoft .NET Framework 3.0 Redistributable Package page, follow the instructions for downloading and installing the .NET Framework version 3.0. Packages for both x86- and x64-based computers are available, so make sure to choose the correct selection for your computer. Save the package to a folder on the computer on which you intend to install SharePoint Server 2007.

The Microsoft .NET Framework URL will result in the download of a 3MB installation file that is used to download a 54MB package.

Once the package has been downloaded, run the `dotnetfx3setup.exe` package, and follow the instructions in the installation wizard. When you have completed the wizard, the .NET Framework 3.0 will be installed.

After the .NET Framework is installed, you will need to enable ASP.NET 2.0. Exercise 2.2 will take you through the steps of this task.

EXERCISE 2.2

Enabling ASP.NET 2.0

1. Click Start ➢ Administrative Tools ➢ Internet Information Services (IIS) Manager.

2. In the IIS Manager tree, click the plus sign (+) next to the server name to expand the options under the server.

3. Click the Web Service Extensions folder to select it.

4. In the details pane, click ASP.NET v2.0.50727, and then click Allow. ASP.NET 2.0 will be enabled, as shown here.

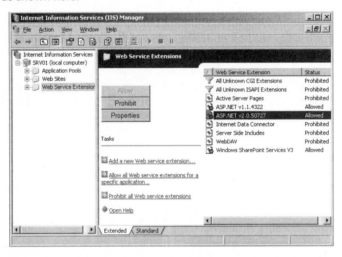

Before you proceed, go to the Windows Update site, and make sure all the critical updates for Windows Server 2003 and ASP.NET are applied. This process can take some time.

Installing SharePoint Server 2007

At this point, you'll need to have either a full-fledged version of MOSS 2007 or an evaluation copy. Evaluation copies are available for both 32-bit and 64-bit platforms:

- Find the evaluation copy for MOSS 2007 32-bit at `http://www.microsoft.com/downloads/details.aspx?FamilyId=2E6E5A9C-EBF6-4F7F-8467-F4DE6BD6B831&displaylang=en`.

- Find the evaluation copy for MOSS 2007 64-bit at `http://www.microsoft.com/downloads/details.aspx?FamilyId=3015FDE4-85F6-4CBC-812D-55701FBFB563&displaylang=en`.

You can also go to `http://office.microsoft.com`, click the Products tab, click Share-Point Server under Servers in the menu on the left, and then click the appropriate free trial link in the Try Office SharePoint Server 2007 box.

Before the actual download begins, you will be presented with product keys for both the Standard Edition and the Enterprise Edition of SharePoint Server. Make sure to write these down. Once the download begins, you will not be given the opportunity to record these keys. This is the only time they will be presented.

Once you have your copy of Office SharePoint Server 2007 available, launch the executable, and start following the instructions provided by the Setup program. Exercise 2.3 will show you how to begin the installation process by running the Setup program. Subsequent exercises will take you through the other steps leading to a completed installation of MOSS 2007.

In order to be able to participate in all of the exercises presented in this book, please install the Enterprise version of SharePoint 2007.

Installing MOSS 2007

EXERCISE 2.3

Running the Setup Program

1. If you are installing from a CD, run `Setup.exe`; if you are installing from a download, run `Officeserver.exe`.

2. On the Enter Your Product Key page, enter the product key in the available text field, and then click Continue.

   When you enter the product key you were previously provided with, Setup automatically places a green check mark next to the text field and enables the Continue button (assuming the key is correct). Also, depending on whether you use the Standard Edition or Enterprise Edition product key, that edition will be the one installed.

3. On the Read the Microsoft Software License Terms page, review the terms of the agreement, tick the I Accept the Terms of This Agreement check box, and then click Continue.

4. On the Choose the Installation You Want page, click Basic to install to the default location.

   You can install to a different location by clicking Advanced and then clicking the File Location tab to specify the location you want to install to and finish the installation. However, we will be using the default option in this step.

5. When the dialog box appears prompting you to finish the configuration of your server, tick the Run the SharePoint Products and Technologies Configuration Wizard Now check box.

6. Click Close to start the configuration wizard.

On the Welcome to SharePoint Products and Technologies page, when you click Next, a dialog box telling you that some services might need to be restarted or reset during configuration appears. Click Yes, and then click Finish on the Configuration Successful page. The basic Share-Point Server installation is complete when the default SharePoint portal site appears, as shown in Figure 2.1.

FIGURE 2.1   The default SharePoint portal site web page

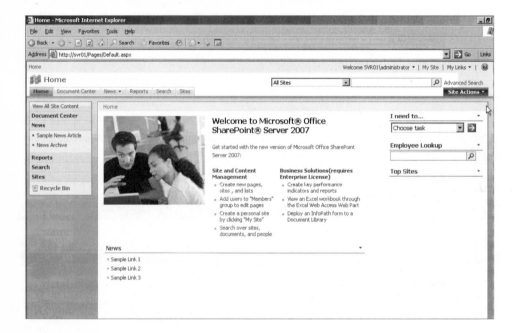

Initial Post-Installation Tasks

You may encounter one or two issues post-installation that will require your intervention before you continue:

- If you are prompted for a username and password after SharePoint Server installs, you may have to add the SharePoint site to the list of trusted sites and configure user authentication settings in Internet Explorer.

- If you get a proxy server error message after SharePoint Server installs, you may need to configure your proxy server settings so that local addresses bypass the proxy server.

Exercise 2.4 will walk you through the steps of adding your SharePoint site to the list of trusted sites in Internet Explorer. Exercise 2.5 will take you through the process of configuring proxy server settings to bypass your proxy server for local addresses.

EXERCISE 2.4

Adding Your SharePoint Site to the List of Trusted Sites

1. In an open Internet Explorer web browser, click Tools ➤ Internet Options.

2. Click the Security tab, and in the Select a Web Content Zone to Specify Its Security settings box, click Trusted Sites, and then click Sites.

3. Clear the Require Server Verification (https:) for All Sites in This Zone check box.

4. In the Add This Web Site to the Zone text field, type the URL to your site, and then click Add.

5. Click Close to close the Trusted Sites dialog box.

6. Click OK to close the Internet Options dialog box.

 If you need to use Internet Explorer on the server to access other web pages, you may need to use the procedure in Exercise 2.4 to add them to the list of trusted sites.

EXERCISE 2.5

Configuring Proxy Server Settings to Bypass the Proxy Server for Local Addresses   [I E 6]

1. In an open Internet Explorer web browser, click Tools ➤ Internet Options.

2. Click the Connections tab, and in the Local Area Network (LAN) Settings area, click LAN Settings.

3. In the Automatic Configuration section, clear the Automatically Detect Settings check box.

4. In the Proxy Server section, tick the Use a Proxy Server for Your LAN check box.

5. Type the address of the proxy server in the Address text field.

6. Type the port number of the proxy server in the Port field.

7. Tick the Bypass Proxy Server for Local Addresses check box.

8. Click OK to close the Local Area Network (LAN) Settings dialog box.

9. Click OK to close the Internet Options dialog box.

Site Management of SharePoint 2007

Now that SharePoint Server 2007 is installed as a stand-alone server, you are ready to begin the initial site management tasks using the Central Administration site you first visited in Chapter 1, "Getting Started with Microsoft Office SharePoint Server 2007." You will begin site management administration in detail starting in Chapter 3, "Configuring SharePoint 2007." To get ready to perform those tasks, click Start ➢ All Programs ➢ Microsoft Office Server ➢ SharePoint 3.0 Central Administration. The Central Administration home page will open. This is where you'll begin in Chapter 3.

Server Farm Installation

As you've seen in the stand-alone server installation, all of your server and application software is installed on one physical machine. In a server farm topology, you can install your software on multiple machines. Since you are dealing with different *server role types*, you will have different hardware and software requirements for each type. Three main server roles are contained within the server farm:

- Application server
- Database server
- Front-end web server

   As with the stand-alone server installation section, the hardware and software requirements in the following sections will present the minimum and recommended specifications for each server role type.

Application Server (IIS and ASP.NET)

The application server role contains all the functionality and other services for development, deployment, and runtime management of XML web services, web applications, and distributed applications. Services that run on the application server are IIS 6.0, COM+, and ASP.NET. In addition, SharePoint Server 2007 is installed on the application servers in the server farm.

Application Server Hardware Requirements

The following list illustrates Microsoft's minimum and recommended hardware requirements for an application server in a SharePoint 2007 server farm. Remember, these are the official guidelines; the practical requirements for your server farm may vary.

Processor   The minimum required CPU speed is 2.5GHz; processors of 2.5GHz or faster are recommended.

Memory   The minimum requirement is 2GB; 4GB is recommended.

Disk space and formatting   The minimum requirement is an NTFS partition with 3GB of free space; Microsoft recommends an NTFS partition with 3GB of free space plus additional space for data storage.

Installation source   The minimum is a DVD drive; the recommendation is for a DVD drive or installation source copied to either the hard drive or a network share.

Display   The minimum required resolution is 1024×768; the recommended resolution is the minimum or higher.

Network speed   The minimum requirements are a 56Kbps connection between the server and client computers and a 100Mbps connection between the computers and the server farm; the recommended speeds are a 56Kbps or faster connection between the server and client computers and a 1Gbps connection between the computers and the server farm.

Application Server Software Requirements

The software requirements for WSS 3.0 and SharePoint Server 2007 are the same since MOSS 2007 is built on top of WSS 3.0.

Operating System

MOSS 2007 is designed to run on the following editions of Windows Server 2003 with SP1 or later:

- Windows Server 2003, Standard Edition
- Windows Server 2003, Enterprise Edition
- Windows Server 2003, Datacenter Edition
- Windows Server 2003, Web Edition

The SharePoint Central Administration web interface requires that you use Microsoft Internet Explorer 6.0 with the most recent service packs or Internet Explorer 7.0.

Required Pre-installation Components

After installing Windows Server 2003 and applying all the critical updates, you will not be able to successfully install SharePoint Server 2007 until the following tasks have been completed:

Windows components   You must enable IIS 6.0 including Common Files, Simple Mail Transfer Protocol (SMTP), and WWW services so that your computer can function as a web server. When configuring IIS 6.0, you must specify an SMTP mail server to enable email alerts and notifications. You must also specify that the server is running in IIS 6.0 worker process isolation mode; however, this is the default configuration for new IIS 6.0 installations.

Microsoft .NET Framework   You must install the Microsoft .NET Framework 3.0 and then enable ASP.NET 2.0. The instructions for enabling ASP.NET 2.0 were shown previously in this chapter. If ASP.NET 2.0 is installed on the computer before IIS, you must enable ASP.NET 2.0 by running the command `aspnet_regiis -i.`

Database Server

Unless you are installing SharePoint as a stand-alone server, as we are in our example, you will require at least one database server for your SharePoint deployment. The following sections describe the hardware and software requirements for a database server installation.

Database Server Hardware Requirements

Table 2.1 lists the hardware requirements for the server. These are based on the SQL Server 2005 Standard Edition. To see a listing of the hardware requirements for all versions of SQL Server 2005, go to `http://www.microsoft.com/sql/prodinfo/sysreqs/default.mspx`.

TABLE 2.1   Database Server Hardware Requirements

Components	32-bit Bus	64-bit Bus	Itanium
CPU	The minimum required is a 600MHz Pentium III or compatible with a recommended processor of 1GHz or faster.	A 1GHz processor Pentium IV or compatible with EM64T support is recommended.	1GHz or faster Itanium processor.
Operating system	The minimum required OS can be Microsoft Windows 2000 Server with SP4 or newer, Windows 2000 Professional Edition with SP4 or newer, or Windows XP with SP2, with the recommended being Windows Server 2003 Enterprise, Standard, or Datacenter Edition with SP1 or newer or Windows Small Business Server 2003 with SP1 or newer.	The required OS can be Microsoft Windows Server 2003 Standard x64, Enterprise x64, or Datacenter x64 Edition with SP1 or newer or Windows XP Professional x64 Edition or newer.	The required OS is Microsoft Windows Server 2003 Enterprise or Datacenter Edition for Itanium-based systems with SP1 or newer.
Memory	512MB of RAM is the minimum requirement, with 1GB or more recommended.	512MB of RAM is the minimum requirement, with 1GB or more recommended.	512MB of RAM is the minimum requirement, with 1GB or more recommended.
Hard disk drive	350MB of available hard disk space is recommended for installation with 425MB of additional hard disk space for SQL Server Books Online, SQL Server Mobile Books Online, and the sample databases.	350MB of available hard disk space is recommended for installation with 425MB of additional hard disk space for SQL Server Books Online, SQL Server Mobile Books Online, and the sample databases.	350MB of available hard disk space is recommended for installation with 425MB of additional hard disk space for SQL Server Books Online, SQL Server Mobile Books Online, and the sample databases.
Optical drive	CD-ROM or DVD-ROM drive.	CD-ROM or DVD-ROM drive.	CD-ROM or DVD-ROM drive.
Display	Super VGA with 1,024×768 or higher resolution.	Super VGA with 1,024×768 or higher resolution.	Super VGA with 1,024×768 or higher resolution.

Database Services Software Requirements

The limitations of running SQL Server on Windows Server 2003 Web Edition previously mentioned continue to apply. All versions and platforms for SQL Server require that you use Internet Explorer 6.0 SP1 or newer.

For SQL Server 2005 Standard Edition for Reporting Services, you need IIS 5.0 or newer and ASP.NET 2.0 or newer on all platforms.

Front-End Web Server

Front-End Web Servers are the workhorse of a SharePoint 2007 deployment since they host the web applications required to support the user interface and access to the system as a whole.

Front-End Web Server Hardware Requirements

Table 2.2 displays Microsoft's minimum and recommended hardware requirements for running SharePoint Server 2007 on a front-end web server.

TABLE 2.2   Front-End Web Server Hardware Requirements

Components	Minimum Requirements	Recommended Requirements
CPU	2.5GHz	Dual 3GHz processors or faster
Memory	2GB of RAM	2GB of RAM or more
Hard disk drive	NTFS-formatted volume with 3GB of free space	NTFS-formatted volume with 3GB of free space or more plus additional space for your data storage requirements
Installation source	DVD drive	DVD drive or an installation source on the hard drive or on a network share
Display	1024×768 resolution	1024×768 or higher resolution
Network speed	56Kbps connection between client computers and the server and 100Mbps connection between the server and the server farm	56Kbps or faster connection between client computers and the server and 1Gbps or faster connection between the server and the server farm

Front-End Web Server Software Requirements

The software requirements for WSS 3.0 and SharePoint Server 2007 are the same since MOSS 2007 is built on top of WSS 3.0.

The operating system and required pre-installation components for the front-end web server are identical to the application server since the web server is a subset of the application server. Additional resources may be required on your web servers as demand increases.

Requirements for Server Farm Deployment

Hardware and software requirements for deploying a server farm go beyond planning for SharePoint Server 2007 running on a stand-alone server. There are hardware and design elements that affect availability, capacity, and performance that do not have to be taken into consideration when you are running a single-server environment. The following sections will illustrate the requirements for your server farm based on factors such as processors, bus architecture, and farm size.

System Architecture

Although SharePoint Server 2007 can run on a 32-bit system, Microsoft recommends, based on its testing of MOSS 2007, using 64 bit-platforms for your server farm. Here are some of the advantages of using 64-bit:

- 64-bit chipsets are faster and wider, passing more data to the cache and processor.

- The 64-bit architecture supports up to 64 processors and close to linear scalability with each additional processor.

- Windows Server 2003 SP1 running on a 64-bit system architecture supports up to 1,024GB of both physical and addressable memory as opposed to 32-bit systems, which can address only 4GB of addressable memory.

If you are planning to deploy your server farm on a mix of 32-bit and 64-bit architecture, you might want to prioritize the server role types in the following order, with those server roles higher on the list being given more consideration to being run on 64-bit platforms than those lower on the list:

1. Computers running SQL Server

2. Application servers

3. Front-end web servers

If you need to prioritize among application server roles which types are deployed on 64-bit systems, use the following list, with those types higher on the list being given more preference.

1. Index

2. Excel

3. Search

WARNING   You cannot mix 32-bit and 64-bit architectures within server type roles. For instance, all servers running the Query server role type must be using either a 32-bit or 64-bit architecture.

System Redundancy

In Chapter 1 you learned about system availability and redundancy in server farm architecture design. This section of Chapter 2 will expand on that knowledge. As you recall, availability is defined as the system's ability to respond to requests in a predictable manner; that is, availability is the way you expect the system to respond to service requests. You may also recall that the definition of high availability is that the system is accessible for 99.999 percent of the time it is in operation (also known as the *five 9s*). Table 2.3 illustrates in more detail availability metrics as defined by Microsoft.

TABLE 2.3   System Availability Metrics

Acceptable Uptime Percentage	Acceptable Downtime per Day	Acceptable Downtime per Month	Acceptable Downtime per Year
95	72 minutes	36 hours	18.26 days
99	14.40 minutes	7 hours	3.65 days
99.9	86.40 seconds	43 minutes	8.77 hours
99.99	8.64 seconds	4 minutes	52.60 minutes
99.999	0.86 seconds	26 seconds	5.26 minutes

Availability depends on a number of hardware components including hard disk drives, processors, RAM, and network cards. The greater the capacity and the more robust hardware components are, the greater the likelihood that system resources will be available when called upon. Of course, even the biggest, baddest, most resourceful server in the world may not be enough to meet demand if it is the only server in your farm. In that eventuality, you'll need to add more servers, but how many more?

The level of system availability you need to provide can be addressed by the level of redundancy built into your server deployment. The following sections will describe different server deployment scenarios and how they address availability and redundancy.

Physical Server Farm Topology

In Chapter 1 you learned a great deal about logical server farm topology. The following will present the differences between actual physical server farm designs including advantages, disadvantages, and how server role types are deployed on hardware.

Two-Server Farm

This design is generally not meant to be taken into production and is typically deployed for the following reasons:

- Deploying SharePoint Server 2007 for educational purposes
- Deploying SharePoint Server 2007 for evaluation purposes
- Deploying SharePoint Server 2007 for a limited environment (such as a single department within a company)
- Deploying SharePoint Server 2007 with only a subset of features (rather than all available features)
- Deploying Windows SharePoint Services 3.0 only

This minimal server farm requires only two physical servers, as illustrated in Figure 2.2:

- One physical server acting as a front-end web server and application server
- One physical server acting as a dedicated SQL server

FIGURE 2.2 Two-server farm

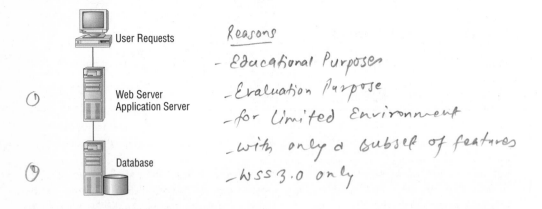

Reasons
- *Educational Purposes*
- *Evaluation Purpose*
- *for limited Environment*
- *with only a subset of features*
- *WSS 3.0 only*

Three-Server Farm

This design actually employs two different possible redundancy architectures, depending on your specific needs. Referring to the two-server farm design, you can add either a second front-end web server or a second dedicated SQL Server to create a clustered or mirrored SQL Server.

By adding a second web server, as shown in Figure 2.3, you create redundancy and improve the performance of the overall system, unfortunately at the cost of availability. This also does little or nothing for data redundancy, so deploy this particular scenario when system performance is more important than data redundancy. You have the option to install the Query and Index server roles on both web servers or install Query on one and Index on the other.

FIGURE 2.3   Three-server farm with web server redundancy

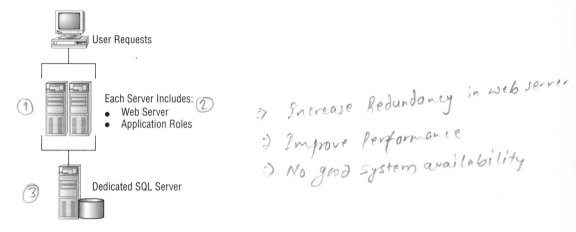

→ Increase Redundancy in web server
→ Improve Performance
→ No good system availability

On the other hand, if data redundancy is more important than performance in a small-scale scenario, add a second SQL server to create a mirrored or clustered database, as shown in Figure 2.4. This scenario also does nothing to enhance the availability of services.

FIGURE 2.4   Three-server farm with SQL Server redundancy

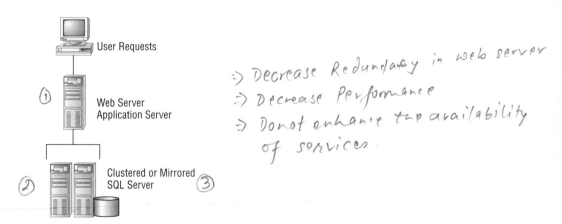

→ Decrease Redundancy in web server
→ Decrease Performance
→ Do not enhance the availability of services.

Four-Server Farm

This is the minimum server farm design that addresses system availability; it deploys two servers as front-end web servers and the other two as a SQL Server cluster, as shown in Figure 2.5. Although there is no variability as to where servers are placed, the Index and Query server roles are another story. In fact, performance will be impacted differently depending on which servers run Index and Query.

Index and Query installed on the same physical server   The Index server role will no longer propagate content indexes to external Query servers.

Index role installed on one of the physical web servers   You will not be able to host the Query role on both web servers.

Index role installed on the database server   This allows you to make the Query role available on both web servers, but the database server will take a performance hit.

Five-Server Farm

So far, all of the server farm designs have involved two levels, the web/application server level and the database server level. The five-server farm architecture adds a level by splitting out the web and application servers to their own areas, as shown in Figure 2.6.

This server farm topology is the most common design for SharePoint and allows you to install application server roles on dedicated physical hardware. The result of this action is improving the performance of the front-end web servers since the hardware doesn't have to pull double duty, processing both web and application server activity. This particular design can be tweaked for either performance or availability.

FIGURE 2.5   Four-server farm

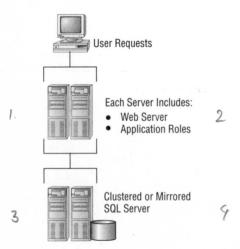

User Requests

Each Server Includes:
- Web Server
- Application Roles

Clustered or Mirrored
SQL Server

FIGURE 2.6   Five-server farm

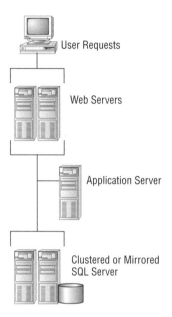

User Requests

Web Servers

Application Server

Clustered or Mirrored
SQL Server

To maximize performance, move Excel Services to one application server and the Query role to the other.

To maximize availability using redundancy, move the following application server roles to the application server hardware:

- Excel Calculation Services
- Query
- Microsoft Office Project Server 2007 (if in use)

NOTE   See the "Server Role Type Redundancy" section later in this chapter for more on this particular option.

Six-Server Farm

This is the design of choice for maximum redundancy and application server load balancing with the minimum number of physical servers. It is also the optimal design if maximizing availability of Excel Calculation Services and Office Project Server 2007 is your goal. The Query server role is installed on the web servers for redundancy of that role and provides for better overall performance of the server farm as a whole compared to the other topologies. You can see this design in Figure 2.7.

FIGURE 2.7 Six-server farm

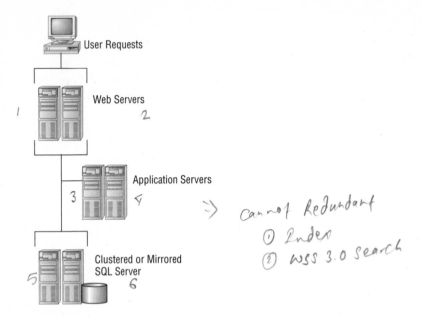

Server Role Type Redundancy

Not all application server roles can be made redundant in the server farm. In general, a server role can be made redundant if the application programming deployed on each physical server is identical to one another and no data is stored on the application servers. This provides for failover and load balancing. If one server containing a redundant role should fail, the other would continue responding to web server requests with no interruption of services and no loss of data.

Server roles that can be made redundant are as follows:

- Excel Calculation Services
- Query
- Office Project Server 2007

Application server roles that cannot be made redundant are those designed to crawl specific content and create content indexes. Although you can deploy these server role types on multiple physical application servers, the role on a particular server will crawl the data related only to that server. For example, if you deployed this role on two different physical servers, it would crawl the content on those two servers and thus generate two separate and conflicting indexes. When the content indexes are subsequently searched, erroneous results would occur.

Server roles that cannot be made redundant are as follows:

- Index
- Windows SharePoint Services 3.0 Search

Real World Scenario

Designing a Small Server Farm

You are the SharePoint administrator for a small company. For the past several months you have deployed and have been testing a small two-server server farm with one physical server running both web and application services and the other physical server running SQL Server 2005. You are now ready to deploy a small production server farm for SharePoint 2007. The results of your evaluation indicate that you should start by adding only one more physical server. Eventually you plan to execute a design that ensures both good performance and data redundancy. For now, your company's CTO has determined that performance is more important than optimizing availability or data redundancy. You decide to add a second web server to the farm to achieve these goals. The diagram shown here illustrates how to implement this.

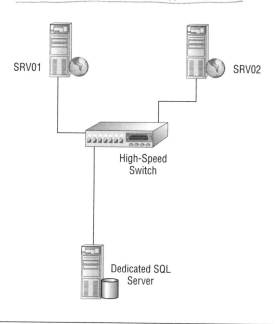

Two Servers Both Running Web and Application Services

Server Farm Installation Process

The process of installing all the applications on multiple pieces of hardware to create a production-level server farm is beyond the scope of both this book and exam 70-630, Microsoft Office Share-Point Server 2007, Configuring. This section will present the steps of installing SharePoint 2007 and creating a server farm:

1. If you are installing from CD, run `Setup.exe`; if you are installing from a download, run `Officeserver.exe`.

2. On the Enter Your Product Key page, enter the product key in the available text field, and then click Continue.

When you enter the product key you were previously provided with, Setup automatically places a green check mark next to the text field and enables the Continue button (assuming the key is correct).

3. On the Read the Microsoft Software License Terms page, review the terms of the agreement, tick the I Accept the Terms of This Agreement check box, and then click Continue.

4. On the Choose the Installation You Want page, click Advanced, click the Server Type tab, and select Complete. If you want to specify a different location for the installation files, click the File Location tab, and add the desired location.

5. When the dialog box appears prompting you to finish the configuration of your server, tick the Run the SharePoint Products and Technologies Configuration Wizard Now check box.

6. Click Close to start the configuration wizard.

7. On the Welcome to SharePoint Products and Technologies page, click Next.

8. When the dialog box notifying you that some services might need to be restarted or reset during configuration appears, click Yes.

9. On the Connect to a Server Farm page, click No, I Want to Create a New Server Farm. Then click Next. (Select Yes if you want to connect the new SharePoint Server you are installing to an already existing server farm.)

10. On the Specify Configuration Database Settings page, perform the following tasks:

   a. Type the name of the database server in the Database Server field.

   b. Type the name of the actual database in the Database Name field.

   c. Type the name of a valid user account in this server or a valid domain account in the Username field.

   d. Type the password for this account in the Password field.

   e. Click Next.

11. On the Configure SharePoint Central Administration Web Application page, either accept the default port number that the system chooses at random or tick the Specify Port Number check box and type a port number in the available field. The field will accept any number from 1 to 65535.

12. On the same page under Configure Security Settings, select either NTLM or Negotiate (Kerberos) as the authentication method for this web application, and then click Next. (Kerberos is the recommended method.)

The installation process will now proceed. This could take some time.

Initial Post-installation Tasks

After the installation is complete and the configuration specifications are committed to the database server, you will be taken to the Services configuration screen in Central Administration where you can continue to configure the server farm.

Summary

In this chapter, you learned about the installation and deployment methods for SharePoint Server 2007. I covered the following topics:

- The hardware and software requirements for installing SharePoint Server 2007 on a stand-alone physical server.

- The required pre-installation tasks before installing SharePoint 2007, including installing IIS 6.0 and Microsoft .NET Framework 3.0 and enabling ASP.NET 2.0.

- The step-by-step process of installing SharePoint 2007 on a single hardware server.

- The hardware and software requirements for installing SharePoint Server 2007 on a server farm. This includes information on the operating system requirements, database server requirements, web server requirements, and application server requirements.

- The server farm deployment requirements including the type of bus platform, system redundancy specifications, and physical server farm topologies.

- The server role types including Index, Query, and Windows SharePoint Services 3.0 Search, and which roles can be made redundant in the server farm.

- The step-by-step process of installing SharePoint 2007 and creating a server farm.

Exam Essentials

Understand how to manage administration. Understand the basic tasks in installing SharePoint Server 2007 from the planning and design stages to completing the installation and performing initial post-installation tasks, including the minimum and recommended hardware and software requirements of installation and operation. Also understand the requirements for installation and operation on a stand-alone server deployment vs. a server farm.

Know how to manage the Central Administration user interface. Understand how to organize post-installation administrator tasks using the Central Administration (CA) web application, including completing the basic administrator tasks listed on the CA home page and knowing the purposes of the Operations and Application Management tabs in CA.

Review Questions

1. You are the newly hired SharePoint administrator for your company. Your company's CIO has tasked you with developing a plan for installing Office SharePoint Server 2007 on a single stand-alone server. This server will be used to evaluate the product and develop a plan for eventual deployment across the enterprise. As part of your plan, you need to present the hardware requirements for installing SharePoint on a server. Of the following choices, which ones represent the minimum hardware requirements for installation? (Choose all that apply.)

   A. A 2.5GHz processor

   B. 2GB of RAM

   C. A DVD drive

   D. A display with a screen resolution of 1024×768

2. As part of your preparation for developing an installation plan for SharePoint Server 2007, you discover that you will need to install MOSS 2007 on a server running Windows Server 2003 SP1 or better. You plan to use SQL Server 2005 Standard Edition for SharePoint's database needs. Of the following options, which edition of Windows Server 2003 will you not be able to use for the installation?

   A. Windows Server 2003, Standard Edition

   B. Windows Server 2003, Enterprise Edition

   C. Windows Server 2003, Datacenter Edition

   D. Windows Server 2003, Web Edition

3. As you prepare your plan for installing SharePoint Server 2007 on a stand-alone server, you have specified your intent to use SQL Server 2005 for your database needs. You will be installing SharePoint 2007 on a Windows Server 2003 Standard Edition machine. How do you intend to use SQL Server 2005 for your database requirements?

   A. When you install SharePoint Server 2007 in Basic mode, SQL Server 2005 Standard Edition is automatically installed.

   B. When you install SharePoint Server 2007 in Advanced mode, SQL Server 2005 Standard Edition is automatically installed.

   C. Install SQL Server 2005 Standard Edition on the same physical server as SharePoint 2007.

   D. Install SQL Server 2005 Standard Edition on a separate physical server from SharePoint 2007.

4. As you continue to prepare your SharePoint Server 2007 stand-alone installation plan, you develop the networking specifications for single-server deployment. You refer to Microsoft's recommendations for this requirement. Of the following options, what are the officially recommended networking specifications?

   A. 56Kbps or faster connection between the client computers and the server

   B. 56Kbps connection between the client computers and the server

   C. 100Mbps connection between the client computers and the server

   D. 100Mbps or faster connection between the client computers and the server

5. You are the SharePoint administrator for your company. You have installed SharePoint Server 2007 on a single stand-alone server in order to evaluate this product and to develop a strategy for deploying MOSS 2007 across the enterprise. You are at the end of your evaluation period and are creating a plan for the production deployment. Of the following options, which is the correct upgrade path from a stand-alone server to a server farm?

   A. Add a separate physical server running SQL Server 2005.

   B. Add a separate server running IIS 6.0 and .NET Framework 3.0.

   C. Add a separate physical server running SQL Server 2005, and then rerun the Setup routine on the first server, selecting Advanced mode and choosing Complete instead of stand-alone.

   D. There is no direct upgrade from a stand-alone installation to a server farm installation.

6. You are the SharePoint administrator for the Wiredwriter Authoring and Publications Company. You are almost finished with the installation of their new server farm and are on the Configure SharePoint Central Administration Web Application page. You must configure a port number for the Central Administration site. Of the following options, which are viable solutions? (Choose all that apply.)

   A. Type 65535 in the available field.

   B. Tick the Specify Port Number check box, and type 26350 in the available field.

   C. Tick the Specify Port Number check box, and type 75000 in the available field.

   D. You do not need to configure the port number. The system will automatically select a number at random.

7. You are the SharePoint administrator for your company. You are in the process of preparing a Windows Server 2003 machine to serve as a test box for evaluating SharePoint Server 2007. You are at the stage of installing and configuring IIS 6.0 to enable web services. Of the following options, which ones represent actual steps in the installation and configuration process? (Choose all that apply.)

   A. In the IIS Manager tree, click the plus sign (+) next to the server name, and then right-click the Application Pools folder.

   B. In the IIS Manager tree, click the plus sign (+) next to the server name, and then right-click the Web Sites folder.

   C. In the Isolation mode section, verify that the Run WWW Service in IIS 5.0 Isolation Mode check box is ticked.

   D. In the Isolation mode section, verify that the Run WWW Service in IIS 5.0 Isolation Mode check box is clear.

8. You are the SharePoint administrator for your company. You are developing a SharePoint Server 2007 installation plan for a production server farm. You have been tasked by your CTO with developing different installation scenarios involving both 32-bit and 64-bit architectures. Of the following options, which are viable scenarios? (Choose all that apply.)

    A. Run your web and application servers on 32-bit platforms and your SQL servers on 64-bit platforms.

    B. Run your web servers on 32-bit platforms and your application servers on a mix of 32- and 64-bit platforms.

    C. Run your front-end web servers using Index server role types on 64-bit platforms, the web servers using Query server role types on 32- and 64-bit platforms, and your application and database on a mix of 32- and 64-bit platforms.

    D. Run your web servers on 32-bit platforms and your application and web servers on 64-bit platforms.

9. You have been tasked by your CIO to design a physical server farm topology that will maximize performance and redundancy. After doing some research, you present her with the topology that will best fit the request, along with the rationale for the design. Of the following options, which is the most optimal design and why?

    A. A five-server farm because it separates server roles into three levels—web server, application server, and database cluster—and then lets you move Excel Calculation Services, Query, and Microsoft Office Project Server to the application server hardware

    B. A four-server farm because it uses the minimum amount of server hardware to address system availability

    C. A six-server farm because it maximizes redundancy and application server load balancing with the minimum number of physical servers and is the optimal design for maximizing the availability of Excel Calculation Services and Office Project Server 2007

    D. A four-server farm because it allows you to install Index and Query server roles on the same physical server, maximizing query access to indexed data on application servers

10. As part of your design of a physical server farm, you must build in system and services redundancies. In the case of a server failure, you want services to continue to be provided to Share-Point consumers including company employees, partners, and customers. After doing your research, you determine that only some server role types can be made redundant. Of the following options, which can be redundant on application servers? (Choose all that apply.)

    A. Excel Calculation Services

    B. Index

    C. Office Project Server 2007

    D. Query

    E. Windows SharePoint Services 3.0 Search

11. You are the SharePoint administrator for your company. You are in the process of preparing a Windows Server 2003 machine to serve as a test box for evaluating SharePoint Server 2007. You are at the stage of enabling ASP.NET 2.0. Of the following options, which are valid steps in this process? (Choose all that apply.)

    A. Click the Web Service Extensions folder to select it.

    B. Right-click the Web Service Extensions folder, and then click Properties.

    C. In the details pane, click ASP.NET v2.0.50727, and then click Allow.

    D. In the details pane, right-click ASP.NET v2.0.50727, and then click Allow.

12. You are the SharePoint administrator for your company. You are meeting with the IT department staff to determine a plan for evaluating SharePoint Server 2007 prior to full-scale deployment. Brian, one of the system admins, believes that a single stand-alone server would be the best evaluation platform. You disagree, stating that a two-server server farm would offer more advantages. As part of your argument, you present these advantages. Of the following options, which one is valid?

    A. Your plan allows you to test a small server farm with a dedicated web server and dedicated application/database server.

    B. Your plan allows you to test a small server farm with a dedicated web/application server and a dedicated database server.

    C. Your plan allows you to test a small server farm with a dedicated web/database server and a dedicated application server.

    D. Your plan allows you to test a small server farm by deploying Windows SharePoint Services 3.0 only.

13. When presenting your plan to deploy a two-server server farm for SharePoint Server 2007 evaluation, you are discussing the hardware and networking requirements for this design with members of your company's IT department. You outline Microsoft's recommendations for client/server connections and server/server connections. Of the following options, which one represents the recommended network speeds for these connections?

    A. A 56Kbps or faster connection between the client computers and the servers and a 1Gbps connection between the servers

    B. A 56Kbps connection between the client computers and the servers and a 1Mbps connection between the servers

    C. A 1Mbps connection between the client computers and the servers and a 1Gbps connection between the servers

    D. A 128Kbps or faster connection between the client computers and the servers and a 1Gbps connection between the servers

14. You are the SharePoint administrator for your company. You are working on a service-level agreement (SLA) with your organization's newest partner. In terms of availability for the SharePoint extranet site you will provide them, they state the following system downtime limitations: downtime per day at 86.40 seconds, downtime per month at 43 minutes, and downtime per year at 8.77 hours. Of the following percentages, which one matches the partner's requirements?

   A. 99 percent

   B. 99.9 percent

   C. 99.99 percent

   D. 99.999 percent

15. You are designing the physical server farm topology for the SharePoint server farm you plan to deploy for your company. You would like to deploy the three primary server roles—web, application, and database—as three separate levels within the farm. Of the following selections, which server farm topology or topologies will allow this?

   A. Both four- and five-server farm topologies

   B. Both five- and six-server farm topologies

   C. Only the six-server farm topology

   D. The four-, five-, and six-server farm topologies

16. You have just finished installing SharePoint Server 2007 on a stand-alone server. Internet Explorer opens, but instead of showing the default index page of the SharePoint Server portal, you are prompted for your username and password. What is the most likely problem?

   A. You need to configure your proxy server settings so that local addresses bypass the proxy server.

   B. You need to set your privacy settings to Medium in Internet Explorer.

   C. You need to add the SharePoint site to the list of trusted sites in Internet Explorer.

   D. You need to clear your cookies from your Temporary Internet Files folder.

17. You are reviewing the database options available for the stand-alone server and server farm options in SharePoint Server 2007. You discover that both designs can use almost the identical database options with one exception. What is that exception?

   A. SQL Server 2000 Desktop Engine (Windows) (WMSDE)

   B. SQL Server 2005 Express Edition

   C. SQL Server 2005 Standard Edition

   D. SQL Server 2000 Standard Edition SP3a

18. You are installing SharePoint Server 2007 on a new server farm. As you go through the installation and configuration process, you arrive at the Specify Configuration Database Settings page. You are required to enter specific information on this page. Of the following options, which must you enter on this page? (Choose all that apply.)

   A. Database server name

   B. Database server IP address

   C. Username

   D. Password

19. As you continue the process of installing and configuring SharePoint Server 2007 on a new server farm, you arrive at the Configure SharePoint Central Administration Web Application page. You need to select a method of authentication under Configure Security Settings. With what options are you presented? (Choose all that apply.)

A. Internet Key Exchange

B. Kerberos

C. NTLM

D. SSL

20. You have just completed installing SharePoint Server 2007 on a new server farm. What screen or web page appears at this stage of the process?

A. Configuration status bar screen in the SPPT Wizard

B. Services administration screen in Central Administration

C. Search configuration screen in Central Administration

D. SSP management interface screen

Answers to Review Questions

1. A, C, and D. Options A, C, and D are all minimum hardware requirements for installation. Option B represents the recommended amount of RAM. The minimum requirement for RAM is 1GB.

2. D. A full-fledged edition of Microsoft SQL Server cannot be installed on Windows Server 2003 Web Edition because of licensing constraints. This limits your installation option for Share-Point on the Web Edition to Advanced mode so that you can select a database server. You will still be able to use SQL Server 2005 Express Edition or SQL Server 2000 Desktop Engine (Windows) (WMSDE).

3. C. Option C is the only possible answer. Options A and B are incorrect because SQL Server 2005 Express Edition is automatically installed when you use Basic mode. In Advanced mode, you can specify a database server to use, but installing Standard Edition is not automatic. You could install SQL Server on a separate physical server, but then you would not be using the stand-alone server model.

4. A. Microsoft's official hardware requirements for a stand-alone server installation include a network connection of 56Kbps or faster between the client computers and the server. The "or faster" option is easily accomplished on any LAN environment.

5. D. There is no direct upgrade path you can use to migrate from a stand-alone to a server farm installation. You will have to initiate a new installation process to install SharePoint 2007 and create a server farm.

6. B and D. If you want to specify a port number, you must tick the Specify Port Number check box and type a number between 1 and 65535 in the available text field. If you do not tick the check box, the system will assign an appropriate number automatically, selecting one at random.

7. B and D. Right-clicking the Web Sites folder and clicking Properties and then clicking the Service tab is the correct way to reach the Run WWW Service in ISS 5.0 Isolation Mode check box. This check box is not ticked by default in new IIS 6.0 installations. You would tick this check box only if you were upgrading from IIS 5.0 to IIS 6.0.

8. A and D. Server farms can run mixed 32-bit and 64-bit server platforms, but each server type must be run on the same platform. For that reason, Options A and D are the only correct answers.

9. C. The six-server farm design allows you to maximize performance and redundancy with the least number of physical servers.

10. A, C, and D. Server roles can be made redundant only if the application programming deployed on each physical server is identical to one another and no data is stored on the application servers. This provides for failover and load balancing. Application server roles cannot be made redundant if they are designed to crawl specific content and create content indexes such as Index and Search.

11. A and C. Clicking the Web Service Extensions folder lets the list of web service extensions become visible, including ASP.NET v2.0.50727. When you click ASP.NET v2.0.50727, you select it, and when it's selected, you can click the Allow button, enabling ASP.NET.

12. B. The two-server server farm model uses two dedicated hardware servers, one running web and application services and the other running SQL Server.

13. A. Option A is Microsoft's recommended network connection speeds for the previously stated connection types.

14. C. Option C matches the stated requirements.

15. B. Only the five- and six-server farm topologies will allow you to separate all three server roles into three separate levels in a server farm.

16. C. If you are prompted for a username and password after SharePoint Server installs, you may have to add the SharePoint site to the list of trusted sites and configure user authentication settings in Internet Explorer.

17. A. SQL Server 2000 Desktop Engine (Windows) (WMSDE) is only a database option for a single stand-alone server deployment.

18. C and D. You are required to enter the database server, the database name, a valid username, and the password for that account.

19. B and C. Kerberos and NTLM are the only two authentication options available for the Central Administration Web Application.

20. B. Once the installation process is complete, you are taken to the Services administration screen in the Central Administration Web Application.

Chapter

3

Configuring SharePoint 2007

MICROSOFT EXAM OBJECTIVES COVERED IN THIS CHAPTER:

✓ **Manage Administration**

- Manage Central Admin UI
- Manage the Shared Service Provider
- Configure Usage Analysis & Reporting

✓ **Deploy/Upgrade Microsoft Office SharePoint Server 2007**

- Configure Shared Services

Now that you have Microsoft Office SharePoint Server (MOSS) 2007 installed and running, it's time to get to work. As you'll recall from the previous two chapters, once the installation is complete, you still need to perform multiple configuration tasks for Share-Point to perform to its fullest capacity. To do this, your first stop on this journey is the SharePoint Central Administration site.

The SharePoint Central Administration site is the most important tool you'll use in configuring and managing MOSS 2007. It's run on a dedicated Internet Information Server (IIS) 6.0 virtual server and is accessible through a unique port number that you set up near the end of your installation routine in Chapter 2, "Installing and Deploying SharePoint 2007" (any number between 1 and 65535). When you install SharePoint in a server farm, Central Administration is installed on the first server created in the farm.

This chapter will begin with a tour of the Central Administration interface, which consists of three tabs: Home, Operations, and Application Management. Next, I'll talk about the Quick Start Guide for deploying Office SharePoint Server 2007 on a single server and complete each of the tasks for this server type. Finally, I'll cover the configuration tasks for Share-Point on a server farm.

The SharePoint Central Administration Web Application

To take the tour of the Central Administration (CA) site, you'll need to have SharePoint Server 2007 running on the Windows Server 2003 you set up in Chapter 2, "Installing and Deploying SharePoint 2007." To open the CA interface, click Start ➤ All Programs ➤ Microsoft Office Server ➤ SharePoint 3.0 Central Administration. If prompted, type your username and password in the dialog box, and press Enter. When Central Administration opens, you should be taken to the Home tab, as illustrated in Figure 3.1.

As mentioned, the CA interface has three tabs:

- The Home tab lists the initial administrative tasks you will need to perform subsequent to installing SharePoint. If you are working with a server farm, this tab will also list all the servers in your farm.

- The Operations tab allows you to manage a variety of critical activities including topology and services, security configuration, and global configuration. These tasks are the heart and soul of server and server farm management.

FIGURE 3.1   The Central Administration website Home tab

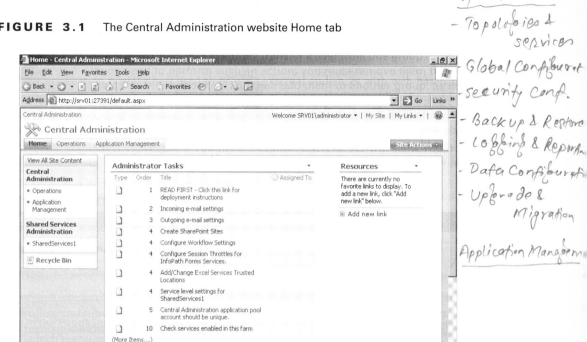

(handwritten margin notes:)

Operations Tab
- Topologies & services
- Global Configuration
- security conf.
- Backup & Restore
- Logging & Reports
- Data Configuration
- Upgrade & Migration

Application Management

- The Application Management tab is where you manage the web applications running in SharePoint Server 2007. Whereas the functions governed by the specific categories contained on the Operations tab are mostly transparent to the end user, the services managed on this tab are the very features your consumers will be using on a day-to-day basis. Items you can configure here include workflow, site collection creation, and search.

The Central Administration Home Tab

You'll recall that this is where we left off at the completion of your installation of SharePoint 2007 on a stand-alone server in Chapter 2. Before you and your customers can begin to use all of MOSS 2007's features and services, you have some work to do here. To do that, you have to understand more about what options are available to you on the Home tab.

Although you may not realize it yet, the Central Administration Home tab is organized like most SharePoint portal sites. The menu on the left offers you the option of viewing all site content and contains links to each web page that leads off this main page:

- Central Administration
  - Operations
  - Application Management

- Shared Services Administration
  - SharedServices1
- Recycle Bin

The top-right side of the page also contains links leading to various features and services:

- Welcome SRV01\administrator
- My Site
- My Links
- Site Actions

Let's take each area one at a time.

View All Site Content

When you click the View All Site Content link, you are taken to a web page containing links to all the containers of information and services related to this site. You can see an example of this page in Figure 3.2.

Here are the general areas contained on this page:

- Document libraries
- Picture libraries

FIGURE 3.2   All Site Content page

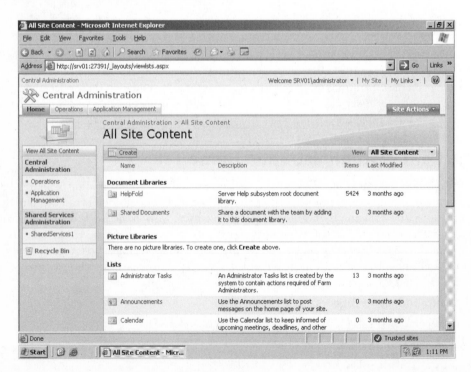

- Lists
- Discussion boards
- Surveys
- Sites and workspaces
- Recycle Bin

Although you may not make complete use of all the available options, these are SharePoint Server features that your customers will explore to their fullest on the sites they will access in SharePoint. Subsequent chapters will address the configuration and management of each of these services, although the Recycle Bin might not need a great deal of explaining.

The Central Administration, Operations, and Application Management links lead to the same content located on the main tabs at the top of Central Administration, so we'll skip those for now.

Shared Services Administration

When you click the Shared Services Administration link, you are taken to the default shared services provider (SSP) page shown in Figure 3.3. Here, you can configure and manage various aspects of SSP functionality.

FIGURE 3.3   Manage This Farm's Shared Services page

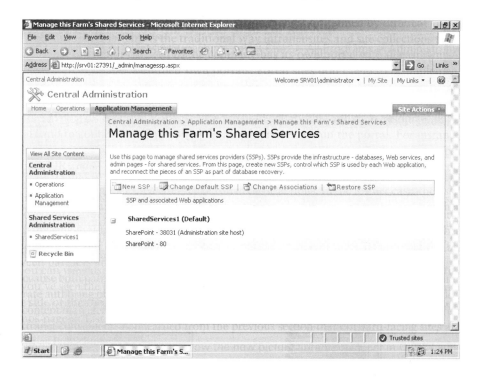

The two links under SharedServices1 (Default) are the web application representing the Central Administration site and the SharePoint Server site; those web applications are associated with this SSP. Clicking either of them takes you to the Web Application General Settings page for that site. There, you can manage a variety of services and features related to the web application including the following options: Default Time Zone, Default Quota Template, Maximum Upload Size, Alerts, and Web Page Security Validation. You can also click to the right of the SharedServices1 (Default) link and access the Edit Properties or Open Shared Services Admin Site link, as shown in Figure 3.4.

> The Delete option in the SharedServices1 (Default) link is grayed out because this SSP is the only one in existence. You can delete an SSP only if there is at least one more available for SharePoint for the stand-alone server or the server farm.

To create a new SSP, click the New SSP button. You can change the default SSP (assuming there is more than one) by clicking the Change Default SSP button. To move web applications between different SSPs, click the Change Associations button. You can rebuild an SSP from backup components by clicking the Restore SSP button.

FIGURE 3.4   SharedServices1 (Default) links

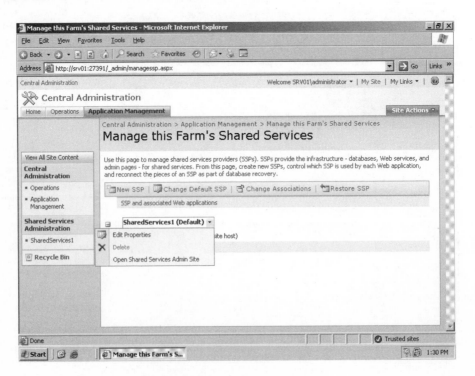

You will learn more about the SSP button operations later in this chapter.

If you take a look at the tabs at the top of the page, you'll see that you are no longer on the Home tab but are on the Application Management tab. Later, you will see how to get to this page directly from the Application Management tab.

SharedServices1

By clicking the SharedServices1 link, either in the menu to the left or in the main pane, you are taken to the Home tab of the Shared Services Administration page for this SSP. Here you can administer areas such as the following:

- User Profiles and My Sites
- Search
- Office SharePoint Usage Reporting
- Audiences
- Excel Services Settings
- Business Data Catalog

You can return to the Central Administration site by clicking Back to Central Administration or return to the Shared Services Administration page by clicking Shared Services Administration.

Welcome SRV01\administrator

On your computer, this will read as the name of the server and whoever is logged in to Central Administration. For the purpose of this illustration, it's the administrator of server SRV01. You can manage this user account by clicking just to the right of the name to show the drop-down menu items:

- My Settings
- Sign In as Different User
- Sign Out
- Personalize This Page ⟹ *Add, Edit, Delete WebParts*

In Central Administration, you will always log in as an administrator, but on many other SharePoint sites you'll take advantage of the Sign In as Different User option to work in SharePoint both as an admin and with your end user account.

My Sites

Clicking the My Sites link will initiate the process of creating a My Sites site for the user, if one does not yet exist. You'll learn more about My Sites in Chapter 4, "Building Sites and Site Collections," so we'll bypass this topic for now.

My Links

When you open the My Links menu, if no links have been configured for this user, you'll see just the Add to My Links and Manage Links menu items.

 Chapter 5, "Managing Users and Groups," will discuss My Links in the context of My Sites, and Chapter 7, "Configuring and Maintaining Lists and Libraries," will tell you more about Links lists.

Site Actions

Clicking Site Actions will give you access to different tools that you can use to manage this web page and the website. The menu items are as follows:

Create   Create will let you make a new library, list, or web page. Figure 3.5 shows a complete listing of what is available.

Edit Page   Edit Page will allow you to edit the contents of the current web page including the web parts.

Site Settings   Site Settings lets you configure the various properties of this website including the following categories:

- Users and Permissions
- Look and Feel
- Galleries
- Site Administration
- Site Collection Administration

Resources

This is an empty links list that you can use to add links to any resources that will help you in administering this site. You'll learn more about adding and managing links in Chapter 7, "Configuring and Maintaining Lists and Libraries"; however, you will be adding links to this list later in this chapter.

The Central Administration Operations Tab

When you click the Operations tab in Central Administration, you are taken to a list of links that allow you to manage every feature and aspect of server and server farm administration, as listed in the following categories and shown in Figure 3.6:

- Topology and Services
- Security Configuration
- Logging and Reporting
- Upgrade and Migration

- Global Configuration
- Backup and Restore
- Data Configuration
- Content Deployment

FIGURE 3.5   The Create page

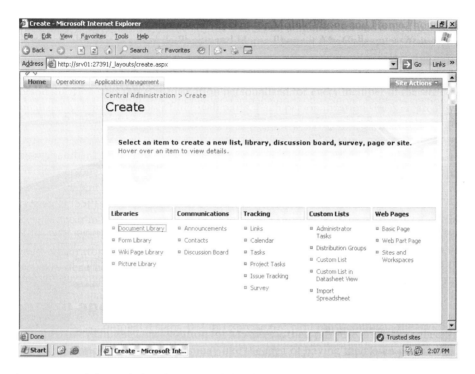

As we proceed through this chapter and the chapters that follow, we'll revisit this tab and delve into its contents in a lot more detail.

The Central Administration Application Management Tab

As you can see in the following list and Figure 3.7, the Application Management tab also contains a collection of links to tools that let you administer all of the applications and components installed in your server farm:

- SharePoint Web Application Management
- SharePoint Site Management
- Search
- InfoPath Forms Services

- Office SharePoint Server Shared Services
- Application Security
- External Service Connections
- Workflow Management

FIGURE 3.6   The Operations tab

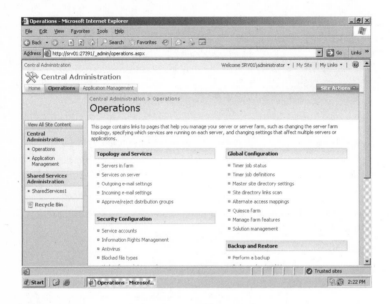

FIGURE 3.7   The Application Management tab

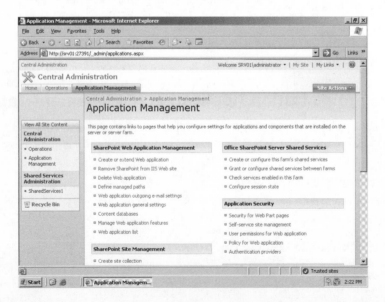

As with the Operations tab, I'll address the contents of the Application Management tab more completely as we progress through the rest of this book.

Troubleshooting Central Administration Access

You get the following error message when you try to connect to SharePoint Central Administration: "You are not authorized to view this page." None of your current documentation has any information about this issue, and you are certain you are using the correct username and password to log in. You suspect that your web browser is configured to use a proxy server, and the proxy server settings are blocking access to the Central Administration website; however, you need to do some checking to make sure.

You go to the Microsoft Office System page in TechNet at http://technet.microsoft.com/en-us/office/default.aspx and click the Support tab. Type **SharePoint Central Administration** in the search text field, and click Search. Click the Error Message When You Connect to the SharePoint Central... search result, which should be at the top of the search results list (you can also find it at http://support.microsoft.com/kb/829065).

Review the web page, and under Resolution, Method 2: Configure Proxy Server Settings for the Web Browser, follow the steps listed. This should resolve the problem and give you access to Central Administration.

Central Administration Post-Installation Tasks

Before you actually get down to the specific tasks you need to perform to get SharePoint 2007 up and running for your customers, you'll need to get organized. This means gathering your resources, assigning the first task, and managing task status. The next three sections will take you through these parts of the process.

Organizing Post-Installation Tasks

In Central Administration on the Home tab, click the READ FIRST – Click This Link for Deployment Instructions link under Administrator Tasks to begin configuring the newly created SharePoint server. Once on the Administrator Tasks: READ FIRST page, you will see a notice in the Description area stating that the SharePoint Products and Technologies deployment is not yet complete. The description refers you to the Administrator Tasks list.

Just above the Description area is the Action area, which contains a link called Read the Quick Start Guide. This is your first post-installation task. Exercise 3.1 will show you how to proceed.

EXERCISE 3.1 ·

Using the Quick Start Guide

1. Click the Read the Quick Start Guide link.

2. When the Quick Start Guide opens, read the first paragraph, and then click the Learn How to Deploy Office SharePoint Server 2007 on a Single Server link.

3. Review the following topics in this section:

   Configure Incoming Email Settings

   Configure Outgoing Email Settings

   Create SharePoint Sites

   Configure Diagnostic Logging Settings

   Configure Antivirus Protection Settings

4. Scroll back to the top of the page, and click the Find More Information about Office Share-Point Server 2007 Deployments link.

5. Record both the names and the URLs of the links you find there including Office SharePoint Server TechCenter, Office SharePoint Server Technical Library, and Office System Center. (You can copy and paste them into a Notepad document temporarily.)

6. Click the back arrow in your browser to return to Central Administration.

The topics displayed in the bulleted list in Exercise 3.1 will be the basis for the exercises that follow and will help you get SharePoint up and running quickly. Before you do that, in Exercise 3.2 you'll add the links you discovered in the Office SharePoint Server 2007 Deployments section of the Quick Start Guide to the Resources list on the Central Administration Home tab so that they'll be handy when you need them. You've already seen how useful these resources can be in the "Troubleshooting Central Administration Access" sidebar.

EXERCISE 3.2   ·

Adding Resource Links

1. On the Home tab of the Central Administration site, under the Resources web part, click Add New Link.

2. In the Type the Web Address field of the URL area, type or paste the URL to Office Share-Point Server TechCenter.

3. In the Type the Description field, type or paste **Office SharePoint Server TechCenter**.

4. Click OK to add the link.

5. Repeat steps 1 through 4 to add links to the Office SharePoint Server Technical Library and Office System Center.

You now have easy access to these resources from Central Administration. These web pages have a great deal of useful information about SharePoint 2007, so take a look when you get a moment.

When you first visit these sites from Central Administration, you will likely be prompted to add them to your trusted sites in Internet Explorer.

As previously mentioned, this section doesn't just cover doing post-install tasks, but tracking their status as well. Since you've just completed the READ FIRST task, you'll need to update its status. You could just delete it, but the information contained in the task might come in handy later. Exercise 3.3 will show you how to edit a task item.

EXERCISE 3.3

Managing Tasks

1. On the Home tab of Central Administration, click the READ FIRST – Click This Link for Deployment Instructions link.

2. Click the Edit Item button.

3. In the Status area, click the drop-down menu arrow, and select Completed.

4. In the Assigned To area, click the Browse icon to the right of the text field.

5. In the Find field of the Select People and Groups dialog box, type **administrator**, and click the Find magnifying lens icon.

6. When the list of matches appears, select the administrator for your server (which should be the account you are currently using), and click OK.

7. In the % Complete area, type **100** in the available field.

8. In the Start Date area, either type the starting date for this task or click the calendar to the right and select a date, and then click the hours and minutes arrows to select a time.

9. In the Due Date area, repeat the tasks you performed in step 8 to specify a date and time for the completion of this task. Your changes should look like the screen shown here.

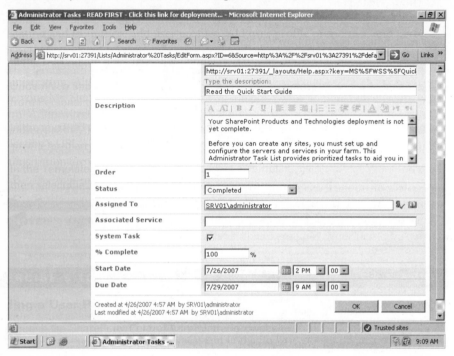

10. Click OK.

You are taken back to the Central Administration Home tab after you click OK, and you can see that the READ FIRST task no longer appears in the Administrator Tasks list. If you click the More Items link at the bottom of the list, you'll see that the READ FIRST task is still present and is marked Completed in the Status column.

Performing Post-Installation Tasks for a Stand-Alone Server

Now that you've become familiar with the Central Administration site and finished the preliminaries, it's time to get SharePoint 2007 configured and ready to use. As you'll recall from Exercise 3.1, when you were reviewing the Quick Start Guide, you saw a list of five tasks to perform in the Learn How to Deploy Office SharePoint Server 2007 on a Single Server section. Most of the items on that list are the next several exercises you will perform on your SharePoint server.

Installing SMTP Service in SharePoint Server 2007

The first task listed in the Quick Start Guide is Configure Incoming E-mail Settings; however, you won't be able to do this without access to a Simple Mail Transfer Protocol (SMTP) server. Although in a production environment, you would use Exchange Server, for the purposes of configuring email on a stand-alone computer, you can install the SMTP service on the same machine running SharePoint Server 2007.

The reason for installing SMTP on your server and performing the subsequent email-related tasks is to give SharePoint the ability to process emails and add email content to SharePoint elements such as lists and libraries. SharePoint can use its own built-in SMTP virtual server to perform these tasks and accept mail from other mail servers including those running Exchange. Since your users will likely be accessing their emails using the Microsoft Office Outlook email client, you will also be installing the Post Office Protocol (POP) 3 service. Exercise 3.4 will take you through the steps of installing the SMTP and POP 3 services. This activity cannot be performed in Central Administration; instead, you'll be installing these services on your Windows Server 2003 machine.

EXERCISE 3.4

Installing the SMTP and POP 3 Services on Windows Server 2003

1. Click Start ➢ Control Panel ➢ Add or Remove Programs.

2. Click the Add/Remove Windows Components button to the left of the Programs list. The Windows Components Wizard will appear.

3. Click Application Server to select it, as shown here, and then click the Details button (you don't have to tick the check box).

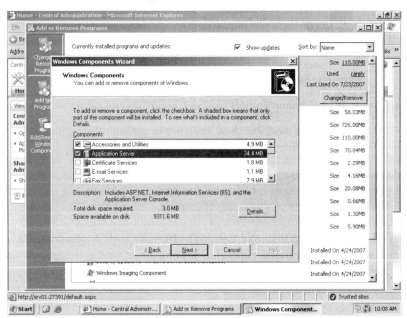

EXERCISE 3.4 *(continued)*

4. When the Application Server dialog box appears, click Internet Information Services (IIS) to select it, and then click the Details button. (Again, you don't have to tick the check box.)

5. Tick the SMTP Service check box, and click OK. Then click OK again in the Applications Server dialog box.

6. Click OK, and in the Windows Components Wizard dialog box, tick the E-mail Services check box. Then click the Details button.

7. Verify that both the POP 3 Service and the POP 3 Service Web Administration check boxes are ticked, and click OK.

8. In the Windows Components Wizard dialog box, click Next (insert your Windows Server 2003 installation CD if prompted to do so).

9. When the Completing the Windows Components Wizard dialog box appears, click Finish. (Remove the Windows Server 2003 installation CD if you previously inserted it.)

10. Close Add or Remove Programs.

Depending on your server's configuration, SMTP and POP 3 may already have been installed.

Configuring Incoming Email

Now that SMTP has been installed on your server, you'll be able to configure incoming emails for SharePoint. Once this feature has been enabled, SharePoint will be able to accept and archive emails and email discussions, save email messages, and display emailed meetings on SharePoint site calendars. If you enable SharePoint Directory Management Service, SharePoint will be able to provide email distribution list creation and management services.

SharePoint Directory Management Service can be enabled only on a Share-Point server that is a member of an Active Directory domain.

Exercise 3.5 will take you through the process of configuring SharePoint's incoming email settings.

EXERCISE 3.5

Configuring Incoming Email Settings

1. On the Central Administration site, click the Operations tab.

2. Under Topology and Services, click the Incoming Email Settings link.

3. Under Enable Sites on This Server to Receive Email, click Yes.

4. Under Settings, click Automatic to accept the default settings. (If you click Advanced, you have to specify an external mail server to provide SMTP services for SharePoint.)

5. Under Use the SharePoint Directory Management Service to Create Distribution Groups and Contacts, click No.

6. Under Email Server Display Address, the hostname for your server should already be populating the available text field. If not, type in the hostname for your server.

7. Click Accept Mail from All Email Servers. (If you click Accept Mail from These Safe Email Servers, you would have to add the IP addresses, one per line, of each email server from which to accept mail.)

8. Click OK. You are taken back to the Operations tab in Central Administration.

If you had clicked Yes in step 5 to use Directory Management Service, you would have been required to specify an Active Directory container where distribution groups and contact objects would be created in SharePoint. After clicking Yes, you would have gone through the following steps:

1. In the Directory Management Service URL box, type the URL of the SharePoint Directory Management Service.

2. In the E-mail Server Display address box, type the email server name, such as **mail.sharepoint.wiredwriter.net**.

3. Click either Yes or No next to Does the Directory Management Service Manage Distribution Lists?

4. Click either Yes or No next to Should Distribution Lists Accept Mail Only from Authenticated Senders?

5. In the Incoming Email Server Display Address section, type a display name for the email server, such as mail.wiredwriter.net, in the Email Server Display address box.

Once you have completed this task, it's a good idea to go back to the Administrator Tasks list on the Home tab and mark this job as completed and to continue this practice for all subsequent exercises. See Exercise 3.3 for the details.

Configuring Outgoing Email

When you configure outgoing email settings, you allow SharePoint's SMTP service to send email alerts and notifications to site administrators. Also, SharePoint users can receive email alerts from the system when they elect to be notified if there is a change in their SharePoint content. An example is a user named Mary receiving an email alert when one of her documents is approved or rejected in the workflow process.

Configuring outgoing emails can actually involve two processes: setting up the default outgoing email settings for SharePoint users and overriding the default settings for web applications. Exercise 3.6 will show you how to configure the default settings for outgoing emails.

EXERCISE 3.6

Configuring Outgoing Email Settings

1. If you aren't there already, click the Operations tab on the Central Administration website.

2. Under Topology and Services, click the Outgoing Email Settings link.

3. On the Outgoing Email Settings page under Outbound SMTP Server, type the hostname for the SMTP server managing outbound mail, such as **mail.wiredwriter.net**, in the text field.

4. Under From Address, type the email address you want to appear to email recipients.

5. Under Reply-to Address, type the email address to which you want email recipients to reply.

6. Under the Character Set menu, select the character set appropriate for your language (accept the default setting for English).

7. Click OK.

Setting the outgoing mail settings for SharePoint web applications is nearly identical to what's shown in Exercise 3.6. (You need to perform this task only if you want web applications to use different outgoing mail settings than those you configured in Exercise 3.6.) Simply click the Application Management tab on the Central Administration website, and under SharePoint Web Application Management, click the Web Application Outgoing E-mail Settings link. Then, perform steps 3 through 7 in Exercise 3.6, specifying the SMTP server, From Address, Reply-to Address, and Character Set options you want for outgoing web application emails.

The next task on the list is Create SharePoint Sites; however, since Chapter 4, "Building Sites and Site Collections," covers this activity in a great deal of detail, we'll step out of order and move on to configuring diagnostic logging. You'll have plenty of opportunities to create and manage SharePoint sites as we progress.

Configuring Diagnostic Logging

If something goes wrong, you will want to know about it, and your customers will want you to quickly fix any SharePoint service or feature that goes awry. Enabling diagnostic logging will allow you to use a number of troubleshooting tools on your server including event messages, trace logs, user-mode error messages, and Customer Experience Improvement Program events.

Exercise 3.7 will show you the steps in enabling this important server management feature.

EXERCISE 3.7

Configuring Diagnostic Logging

1. Click the Operations tab in the Central Administration website.

2. Under Logging and Reporting, click the Diagnostic logging link.

3. On the Diagnostic Logging page under Sign Up for the Customer Experience Improvement Program, click Yes, I Am Willing to Participate Anonymously in the Customer Experience Improvement Program (Recommended) if you want SharePoint users to have the option of reporting customer experience improvement program events to Microsoft.

4. Under Error Reporting, click Collect Error Reports, and then tick either or both of the check boxes below depending on your requirements. (Changing the computer's default error collection policy to send all reports by ticking the second check box will be very resource intensive.)

5. Under Event Throttling, use the Select a Category drop-down menu to choose a category of events on which you want to control throttling such as All, Administration, Communication, and so on.

6. Under Least Critical Event to Report to the Event Log, use the drop-down menu to choose an event type such as Information, Warning, Error, and so on.

7. Under Least Critical Event to Report to the Trace Log, use the drop-down menu to choose an event type such as Medium, High, Unexpected, and so on.

8. Under Trace Log in the Path field, either accept the default path or type the path where you want the trace log to be written.

9. Under Number of Log Files, type the maximum number of log files for the system to maintain, and under Number of Minutes to Use a Log File, type how long you want events to be captured to a single log file. Your screen should look like the one shown here.

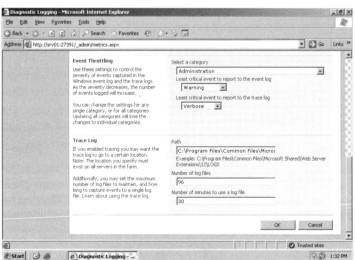

10. Click OK.

You can repeat steps 5 through 7 to individually configure separate event categories, or select All in step 5 and let the settings you made in steps 6 and 7 apply to all event categories.

Configuring Antivirus Protection

You must already have an antivirus application installed on your Windows Server 2003 machine to set up this feature, and the antivirus program must be designed to work with SharePoint Server 2007. Microsoft's TechNet site for SharePoint Server doesn't yield any information about which antivirus programs would work with SharePoint, but information under Beta 2 Updates and Compatibility at the following URL seems to indicate that one such program is Symantec's Norton AntiVirus scanner: http://www.microsoft.com/uk/office/preview/faq.mspx.

Configuring antivirus lets SharePoint scan documents for viruses on upload to and download from the system. If you don't have such an application installed on your Windows Server 2003 machine, you will not be able to successfully perform Exercise 3.8.

Configuring Antivirus Protection in SharePoint Server

1. If you aren't already there, click the Operations tab on the Central Administration website.

2. Under Security Configuration, click the Antivirus link.

3. Under Antivirus Settings, tick the Scan Documents on Upload check box if you want documents to be scanned before being uploaded into SharePoint.

4. Tick the Scan Documents on Download check box if you want documents to be scanned before being downloaded from SharePoint.

5. Tick the Allow Users to Download Infected Documents check box if you want SharePoint users to be able to perform this action. (You really don't want to allow users to be able to download infected documents. The only time this would be appropriate is if you need to recover the content, and the only way to do so is to download the infected document to an isolated machine and then delete the infection.)

6. Tick the Attempt to Clean Infected Documents check box if you want SharePoint to perform this action.

7. In the Time Out Duration (in Seconds) field, type the number of seconds you want the antivirus program to run before it times out. You should usually accept the default values unless the vendor of your antivirus solution has other recommended settings.

8. In the Number of Threads field, type the number of execution threads on the server that the virus scanner may use.

9. Click OK.

If you do not have an antivirus program running on your server, the options in steps 6 through 8 will not be available.

Configuring Usage Analysis and Reporting

Although this task wasn't on the list for stand-alone server configuration, it is one of the objectives for the certification exam and does tie in with the other tasks we've been performing. Exercise 3.9 will show you the steps to configure usage analysis and reporting.

EXERCISE 3.9

Configuring Usage Analysis and Reporting

1. In Central Administration, click the Operations tab.

2. Under Logging and Reporting, click the Usage Analysis Processing link.

3. On the Usage Analysis Processing page under Logging Settings, tick the Enable Logging check box.

4. In the Log File Location field, either specify a location where you want the log file to write or accept the default location.

5. In the Number of Log Files to Create box, specify the number of log files (between 1 and 30) you want to create.

6. Under Processing Settings, tick the Enable Usage Analysis Processing check box.

7. Under Run Processing Between These Times Daily, use the drop-down menus to choose a starting and ending time.

8. Click OK.

Performing Post-Installation Tasks for a Server Farm

Although you have finished most of the initial post-installation tasks for a stand-alone Share-Point server, there are still a number of additional jobs for SharePoint on a server farm. In a server farm configuration, SharePoint Server 2007 must be installed on all front-end web servers, and then the SharePoint Products and Technologies Configuration Wizard must be run on all of those servers. Once that is done, Microsoft recommends that the following post-installation tasks be performed:

- Configure the shared services provider.
- Configure services.
- Configure indexing.
- Create a web application and site collection.
- Start and configure Excel Calculation Services.
- Create alternate access mappings.
- Configure incoming email settings.
- Configure outgoing email settings.
- Configure diagnostic logging settings.
- Configure antivirus protection settings.

As you can see, you've already completed a number of these actions in the previous sections of this chapter. We'll address creating a web application and site collection in Chapter 4, "Building Sites and Site Collections," and starting and configuring Excel Calculation Services in Chapter 12, "Using Excel Services and Business Intelligence."

Configuring the Shared Services Provider

As you probably recall from Chapter 1, "Getting Started with Microsoft Office SharePoint Server 2007," unless you have a very good reason to do so, you should use just one SSP for your server farm. That said, you will also recall that there are a number of good reasons to create more than one SSP. In addition to creating SSPs, there are a number of other related tasks to perform:

- Create a new SSP.
- Restore an SSP.
- Edit SSP settings.
- Delete an SSP.
- Change the default SSP.
- Change SSP associations.

Most of the tasks in this list can't be performed if you are running only one SSP. You can't restore an SSP unless one was previously deleted or delete an SSP if you have only one running in the server farm. The same is true for changing the default SSP or changing web application associations to SSPs. The only task you would be likely to perform from the list on a single SSP running on a stand-alone server is editing its properties.

Editing SSP Settings

In terms of how your stand-alone server running SharePoint Server 2007 is set up, there is no practical reason to change the default SSP settings. However, walking through the properties of your current SSP will help you understand more about how it works:

1. In Central Administration, click the Application Management tab.

2. Under Office SharePoint Server Shared Services, click the Create or Configure This Farm's Shared Services link.

3. Use the drop-down arrow to the right of SharedServices1 (Default), and in the menu click Edit Properties. Not every property in your existing SSP will be available for modification.

    ▪ Under SSP Name in the SSP Name field, you can edit the name of your SSP, but you can't change the SSP Administration Site URL.

    ▪ Under My Site Location, you can't change the My Site Location URL.

    ▪ Under SSP Service Credentials, you can change the username and password in the available fields.

    ▪ Under SSP Database, you can't change the Database Server and Database Name as shown in Figure 3.8, but you can switch between Windows and SQL authentication and specify an account name and password.

    ▪ The same is true under Search Database.

    ▪ Under Index Server, you can't change the index server, but you can edit the path for the index file location. (You must use `stsadm` to actually move the index.)

 To learn more about the stsadm command line utility, see Chapter 14, "Performing Advanced SharePoint Management."

    ▪ Under SSL for Web Services, you can choose to enable SSL by selecting Yes. (The default is No.)

4. Click OK when you're done editing the SSP properties.

FIGURE 3.8   Edit Shared Services Provider page

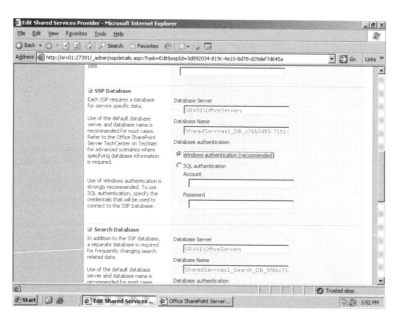

Creating a New SSP

Although a default SSP is created when you install SharePoint Server 2007 on a stand-alone server, this isn't necessarily the case when you install a server farm. It is possible at the end of the installation process to configure other features first. After Configuring SharePoint Products and Technologies wizard has run, you can start the SharePoint Server Search service, set up Search Configuration Administration, create a web application for the portal site, and create the first SSP. After that, you can create the first SharePoint portal.

The steps leading up to the creation of the SSP must be followed in the order presented, or it won't be possible to create the SSP. Only after all those steps including SSP creation are complete are you able to create the portal site:

1. In Central Administration, click the Application Management tab.

2. Under Office SharePoint Server Shared Services, click the Create or Configure This Farm's Shared Services link.

3. On the Manage this Farm's Shared Services page, click the New SSP button.

4. Under SSP Name, you can specify the name of the new SSP and the web application you want associated with the SSP, or if the web app doesn't exist, you can create it.

5. Under My Site Location, you can specify a web application, create a new web application, and specify a relative URL to the My Site location.

6. Under SSP Service Credentials, either type the name of an authorized account in the Username field and click the Check Names icon or click the Browse icon and search for an account name. Type the password in the Password field.

7. Under both SSP Database and Search Database, you can specify the database server, the database name, and the type of authentication to use to connect to the database.

8. The options under Index Server and SSL for Web Services are the same as when you edit SSP settings.

 You'll learn more about creating web applications as referenced in steps 4 and 5 in Chapter 4, "Building Sites and Site Collections."

Restoring an SSP

If your SSP becomes corrupt or is compromised, it will be necessary to restore it from the most recent backup. The following describes the restoration process:

1. On the Manage This Farm's Shared Services page, click Restore SSP.

2. Under the SSP Name section, in the SSP Name text field, type a name for the restored SSP.

3. On the Web Application menu, click a web application that will host an administration site for the restored SSP.

4. If you want to create a new web application to host an administration site for the restored SSP, click Create a New Web Application.

5. Under the SSP Service Credentials section, in the Username box and Password box, type the user name and password that will be used by SSP web services for communications between servers and the SSP timer service for running jobs.

6. Under the SSP Database section, in the Database Server text field, type the name of the database server.

7. In the Database Name text field, type the name of the database. (Using the default is recommended.)

8. Under Database Authentication, select one of the following:
   - Windows Authentication (recommended).
   - SQL Authentication. If you select SQL authentication, type the account credentials in the Account and Password boxes.

9. Under the Search Database section, in the Database Server text field, type the name of the database server.

10. In the Database Name text field, type the name of the search database. (Using the default is recommended.)

11. Under Database Authentication, select one of the following:
    - Windows Authentication (recommended).
    - SQL Authentication. If you select SQL authentication, type the account credentials in the Account and Password boxes.

12. Under the Index Server section, click an index server on the Index Server menu.

13. In the Path for Index File Location field, type the path of the index server that will be used by the restored SSP to crawl content. (You must use `stsadm` to actually move the index.)

14. The options under Index Server and SSL for Web Services are the same as when you edit SSP settings.

15. Click OK.

Deleting an SSP

If you delete an SSP, any web applications that are associated with that SSP become associated with the default SSP. You cannot delete the default SSP.

1. On the Manage This Farm's Shared Services page, select the SSP you want to delete, and click Delete.

2. Click OK in the message box confirming you want to delete the SSP.

Changing the Default SSP

Web applications are automatically associated with the default SSP when they are created to ensure they have access to necessary shared services. You can change which SSP is the default SSP by following these steps:

1. On the Manage This Farm's Shared Services page, click Change Default SSP.

2. On the Change Default Shared Services Provider page, on the SSP Name menu in the Shared Services Provider section, click the SSP you want to set as the default SSP.

3. Click OK. A Warning page will appear where you can read the implications of changing the default SSP.

4. If you want to change the default SSP, click OK.

Changing SSP Associations

Each web application is associated with a single SSP. More than one web application can be associated with the same SSP:

1. On the Manage This Farm's Shared Services page, click Change Associations.

2. On the Change Associations between Web Applications and SSPs page, in the SSP Name menu under the Shared Services Provider section, click the SSP with which you want to associate web applications.

3. Under the Web Applications section, tick the check boxes for each web application you want to be associated with the specified SSP. To select all of the web applications, tick the Select All check box.

4. Click OK.

Configuring Services

The primary service to configure in this section is Search, which will be covered in detail in Chapter 9, "Managing SharePoint Navigation and Search." The other major task in this area is to determine which services are hosted by which servers.

The following takes you through the process of enabling various services within the server farm:

1. In Central Administration, click the Operations tab.

2. Under Topology and Services, click the Services on Server link.

3. On the Services on Server for the current server under Server, click the down arrow next to the server name, and then click Change Server.

    The action in step 3 isn't necessary if you are already on the desired server.

4. Under Select Server Role to Display Services You Will Need to Start in the Table Below, you can select the role you want for the currently selected server. Your options are as follows:

   - Single Server or Web Server for Small Server Farms
   - Web Server for Medium Server Farms
   - Search Indexing
   - Excel Calculation
   - Custom

5. Next to View, click the down arrow, and select either All or Configurable to see a list of all the services running on the server or just a list of services that can be configured.

6. View the names of the running services in the list as well as their status (Started or Stopped) and an action (Stop or Start).

7. Click the When Finished, Return to the Central Administration Home Page link when you are done on this page.

If you walked through these steps on your stand-alone server, you probably noticed that all the selections in step 4 were unavailable and Single Server or Web Server for Small Server Farms was selected by default. If you suspect that one of the services on the server was stopped and you wanted to start it, this would be the appropriate place to visit.

Configuring Indexing

As you recall from Chapter 1, "Getting Started with Microsoft Office SharePoint Server 2007," Index is a service that crawls content in SharePoint and creates searchable index tables, allowing you to locate and access content more easily. For indexing to function, you need to configure the default content access account. To do so, follow these steps:

1. In Central Administration, click the Application Management tab.

2. Under Office SharePoint Server Shared Services, click the Create or Configure This Farm's Shared Services link.

3. On the Manage This Farm's Shared Services page, click the arrow to the right of SharedServices1 (Default) or the name of the desired SSP, and select Open Shared Services Admin Site.

4. On the Shared Services Administration Home page under Search, click the Search Settings link.

5. On the Configure Search Settings page under Crawl Settings, click the Default Content Access account link.

6. Under Default Content Access Account in the Account field, type a valid account name.

7. In the Password field, type the password for the specified account, and type it again in the Confirm Password field.

8. Click OK.

 For your stand-alone server, the account NT AUTHORITY\LOCAL SERVICE has already been set up for indexing.

9. To manage content sources, under Crawl Settings click the Content Sources and Crawl Schedules link.

10. Click the arrow to the right of Local Office SharePoint Server sites, and choose from among the following menu items:

   - Edit
   - View Crawl Log
   - Start Full Crawl
   - Start Incremental Crawl

11. Add a new content source by clicking the New Content Source button.

12. The status of the service, the next full crawl scheduled, and the next incremental crawl scheduled are also visible on this page.

13. Click the Shared Services Administration: SharedServices1 link in the upper left of the page to return to Shared Services Administration Home.

14. Click the Shared Services Administration link to return to the Manage This Farm's Shared Services page.

15. Click the Central Administration link to return to Central Administration's Home tab.

Chapter 9, "Managing SharePoint Navigation and Search" will cover indexing in more detail.

Creating Alternate Access Mappings

If you install and configure Office SharePoint Server 2007 on a single front-end web server and a user browses to your server, the server will render the content that is in your web application. However, if you add subsequent front-end web servers to your server farm, the newly added servers will not have alternate access mappings configured to your web application.

It would be as if you took your current setup and started adding more web servers. Right now, this task is unnecessary, but it becomes necessary if you try to grow your server farm.

Actually, as you recall, you can't directly upgrade a stand-alone server installation to a server farm installation.

To map newly added front-end web servers to your existing web application, you need to perform several different tasks, depending on your exact goal. To get started, go to Central Administration, and click the Operations tab. Then, under Global Configuration, click the Alternate Access Mappings link.

Editing an Internal URL

To edit an internal URL to create a mapping between a newly added front-end web server and a web application, follow these steps:

1. On the Alternate Access Mappings page, and click one of the internal URLs to open it.

2. In the URL Protocol, Host and Port box, edit the server name and port number, such as `http://svr01:27391`.

3. Use the Zone drop-down menu to select a zone type. Your options are as follows:

   - Default

   - Intranet

   - Internet

   - Custom

   - Extranet

4. Click OK.

Editing a Public URL

To create a mapping between a newly added web server and a web application on a public URL, follow these steps:

1. On the Alternate Access Mappings page, click the Edit Public URLs button.

2. If the mapping collection that you want to modify is not selected, on the Edit Public Zone URLs page, in the Alternate Access Mapping Collection section, click Change Alternate Access Mapping Collection on the Alternate Access Mapping Collection menu.

3. On the Select an Alternate Access Mapping Collection page, click a mapping collection.

4. In the Public URLs section, you may add new URLs or edit existing URLs in any of the following text boxes:

   - Default

   - Intranet

   - Extranet

   - Internet

   - Custom

5. Click Save.

Creating an External Resource Mapping

To create a mapping between a newly added web server and a web application that exists outside of the SharePoint server farm, follow these steps:

1. On the Alternate Access Mappings page, click the Map to External Resource button.

2. In the Resource Name field, type the name of the resource.

3. In the URL Protocol, Host and Port box, type the relevant information for the new source such as **http://svr01:27391**.

4. Click Save.

Adding an Internal URL

The following will show you how to add a new internal URL mapping to a newly added web server:

1. On the Alternate Access Mappings page, click the Add Internal URLs button.

2. If the mapping collection that you want to modify is not selected, on the Add Internal URLs page in the Alternate Access Mapping Collection section, select Change Alternate Access Mapping Collection from the Alternate Access Mapping Collection menu.

3. On the Select an Alternate Access Mapping Collection page, click a mapping collection.

4. In the Add Internal URL section, in the URL Protocol, Host and Port box, type the new internal URL, such as **http://svr01:27391**.

5. In the Zone list, click the zone for the internal URL.

6. Click Save.

Summary

In this chapter, you learned about how to use the SharePoint Central Administration web application to perform the initial configuration tasks for both a SharePoint stand-alone server and a server farm. The chapter covered the following topics:

- The features available on the Home, Operations, and Application Management tabs in Central Administration

- Organizing post-installation tasks including how to manage tasks, add resource links, and consult the Quick Start Guide

- Installing the SMTP and POP 3 services so that you can set up outgoing and incoming mail services in SharePoint

- Configuring incoming mail services so SharePoint can receive and archive email content and add it to lists and libraries

- Configuring outgoing mail services so that SharePoint administrators and users can receive email alerts and notifications

- Configuring diagnostic logging and Usage Analysis and Reporting so that SharePoint administrators can use these tools for management and troubleshooting in SharePoint

- Configuring antivirus protection so that documents can be scanned when being uploaded to or downloaded from SharePoint

- Setting up and editing SSPs

- Managing and editing services on a server or server farm

- Configuring the content access account so that the Indexing Service can crawl data in SharePoint and create a searchable index table

- Creating an alternate access mapping to allow for data crawling as you add front-end web servers

Exam Essentials

Know how to manage the Central Administration user interface.   When configuring features and services in SharePoint Server 2007, know which tasks must be performed first in both a stand-alone server installation and a server farm. Be familiar with what resources are available on the Home, Operations, and Application Management tabs. Know how to manage and track administrative tasks.

Know how to manage the shared services provider.   Know how to locate the Manage This Farm's Shared Services page from the Home and Operations tabs and what features are located on that page. Be able to locate the default SSP administration web page, and understand how to configure and manage shared services from this interface. Finally, know how to create, edit, and perform other tasks related to SSPs.

Understand how to configure Usage Analysis and Reporting and diagnostic logging.   Know how to configure diagnostic logging so that you can access troubleshooting tools such as event messages, trace logs, user-mode error messages, and Customer Experience Improvement Program events. Understand how to configure Usage Analysis and Reporting so you can enable logging, specify the number of log files you want created, and set a start and stop time for process logging.

Review Questions

1. You are the SharePoint administrator for your company. You have been tasked by your CTO with making several configuration changes in the SharePoint server farm in Central Administration. You use Remote Desktop to connect to a server and then click Start ➤ All Programs ➤ Microsoft Office Server ➤ SharePoint 3.0 Central Administration. What appears on the monitor?

   A. The Central Administration site at the Home tab

   B. The Central Administration site at the Operations tab

   C. The Central Administration site at the Application Management tab

   D. The Central Administration site at the Configuration tab

2. You are a SharePoint administrator, and you want to modify some of the site settings in the SharePoint Central Administration site. You know you can click Site Actions in the upper-right corner of the home tab and click Site Settings to begin your work. Is there any other location where you can find Site Actions in Central Administration?

   A. No, you can find only Site Actions on the Home tab.

   B. Yes, you can find Site Actions on the Operations tab.

   C. Yes, you can find Site Actions on the Application Management tab.

   D. Yes, you can find Site Actions on the Home, Operations, and Application Management tabs.

3. You are the SharePoint Server 2007 administrator for the Callisto Software Applications Company. In response to Callisto having recently purchased both Ananke Dynamics, Inc., and Elara Development Corp, you need to create an entirely new shared services provider (SSP) in your server farm to meet the changing requirements for SharePoint. You plan to delete the single existing SSP and create a new one. What are the first steps you must take?

   A. You must create a new SSP first before you can delete your only currently existing SSP in the server farm.

   B. On the Shared Services Admin Site under Manage Shared Services, click the Create and Delete link, and then click the Delete Current SSP button. The SSP will be deleted, and you'll automatically be taken to the Create a New SSP page.

   C. On the Manage this Farm's Shared Services page, click to the right of SharedServices1 (Default), and then click Delete. The default SSP will be deleted, and you'll be taken to the Create a New SSP page.

   D. You cannot create a second SSP in a server farm. You must either edit this SSP to meet your needs or create a new server farm with an SSP that meets your needs. Then you must connect the web applications in the original server farm to the SSP in the new server farm.

4. You are the SharePoint Server 2007 administrator for the Callisto Software Applications company. You have assigned the task of configuring diagnostic logging in the server farm to Jamie, a member of your staff. She has just sent you an email telling you that the task has been completed. You want to update the percentage of completion for this task in the Administrator Tasks list in Central Administration. What do you need to do?

  A. Click the task in the task list, click the Edit Item button, click the Status button, use the drop-down arrow, and select Completed.

  B. Click the task in the task list, click the Edit Item button, and in the % Complete area, type 100 in the available field.

  C. Click the task in the task list, click the Edit Item button, and in the % Complete area, use the drop-down arrow to select Completed.

  D. Click the task in the task list, click the Edit Item button, and in the % Complete area, use the drop-down arrow to select 100.

5. You are the SharePoint administrator for your company. You want to change the event throttling configuration for the Communication events category and switch the Under Least Critical Event to Report to the Event Log Setting from Warning to Error. Of the following options, which task allows you to do this?

  A. Configuring Usage Analysis and Reporting

  B. Configuring Logging and Reporting

  C. Configuring Diagnostic Logging

  D. Configuring Event Throttling

6. You are the SharePoint administrator for your company. You have just installed a SharePoint Server 2007 stand-alone server for evaluation purposes. You want to configure incoming mail services. What must you do before you are able to perform this task?

  A. Install SMTP services on SharePoint's Virtual SMTP Server.

  B. Install POP 3 services on Windows Server 2003.

  C. Install SMTP and POP 3 services on Windows Server 2003.

  D. None of the above.

7. You are the SharePoint administrator for your company, and you are configuring a newly installed SharePoint Server 2007 server farm. You are in the process of setting up incoming email services and want to enable SharePoint Directory Management so you can create email distribution lists in SharePoint. What services must be present for you to accomplish your goal? (Choose all that apply.)

  A. Active Directory

  B. Mail Services

  C. SNMP

  D. PHP

8. You are the SharePoint administrator for the Sinope Financial Group. Michael, a member of your staff, is working with you to develop the plans for installing both a stand-alone Share-Point server for evaluation and a full server farm that will subsequently be put into production. You are discussing the differences in services that must immediately be configured after installation in these two scenarios. You task Michael with creating a list of these services. Of the following options, which ones must be configured only on a server farm immediately after installation? (Choose all that apply.)

A. Configure diagnostic logging settings.

B. Configure antivirus protection settings.

C. Configure the shared services provider.

D. Configure indexing.

9. You are the SharePoint administrator for your company, and you have recently installed a Share-Point server farm. You are performing several post-installation tasks and are about to configure antivirus protection for SharePoint documents. Of the following options, what condition must be met for you to be able to configure antivirus? While both a stand-alone and server farm deployment require shared services, in a stand-alone installation, the shared services provider is created and given a default configuration automatically.

A. A suitable antivirus software scanner must be installed on your Windows Server 2003 servers.

B. A suitable antivirus software scanner must be installed in Office SharePoint Server 2007.

C. Symantec's Norton AntiVirus software scanner must be installed on your Windows Server 2003 servers.

D. Symantec's Norton Antivirus software scanner must be installed in Office SharePoint Server 2007.

10. You are a trainee being instructed by Lin, the SharePoint administrator at the Lysithea Sporting Goods Company. You are logged into SharePoint 2007 and are currently on the Home tab in Central Administration. You are currently touring the different services and features available and click the View All Site Content link. What are some of the categories you can see on this page? (Choose all that apply.)

A. Lists

B. Discussion Boards

C. Shared Services Administration

D. Recycle Bin

11. You are the SharePoint Server 2007 administrator for the Callisto Software Applications company. In response to Callisto having recently purchased both Ananke Dynamics, Inc., and Elara Development Corp, you need to edit some of the properties of the default SSP for your server farm. Of the following selections, which are options that you are able to edit in an SSP? (Choose all that apply.)

A. Under SSP Name, you can edit the name of your SSP in the SSP Name field.

B. Under SSP Name, you can change the SSP administration site URL.

C. Under SSL for Web Services, you can choose to enable SSL by selecting Yes.

D. Under Index Server, you can move the index from one server to another.

12. You have just configured the content access account for your SharePoint 2007 server farm in order to enable the indexing service. You want to perform a test by manually starting a full crawl. Of the following options, which one would you perform to do this?

A. On the Configure Search Settings page under Crawl Settings, click the Content Sources and Crawl Schedules link. Then click the arrow to the right of Local Office SharePoint Server sites, and click Start Full Crawl.

B. On the Manage This Farm's Shared Services page, click the arrow to the right of SharedServices1 (Default), and click Edit Properties. On the Service Settings Provider Administration page, click the Crawl Schedules link under Local Office SharePoint Server sites, and then click the Start Full Crawl button.

C. On the Configure Search Settings page under Crawl Settings, click the Content Sources and Crawl Schedules link. Then click the Local Office SharePoint Server Sites link, and click the Start Full Crawl button.

D. On the Configure Search Settings page under Crawl Settings, click the Content Sources and Crawl Schedules link. Then click the arrow to the right of Local Office SharePoint Server Sites, and select Edit Properties. Click to the right of the Schedule Properties link, and click Start Full Crawl.

13. You are the SharePoint administrator for your company, and after having installed a SharePoint stand-alone server, you are performing post-installation tasks. You want to restrict the mail servers that the SMTP server running on your server will accept. Of the following choices, which is the correct method of accomplishing this task?

A. Click Accept Mail from These Safe E-mail Servers, and add the IP addresses in the available text box one address per line.

B. Click Accept Mail from These Safe E-mail Servers, and add the IP addresses in the available text box using commas to separate addresses.

C. Click Accept Mail from the Following E-mail Servers Only, and add the IP addresses in the available text box one address per line.

D. Click Accept Mail from the Following E-mail Servers Only, and add the IP addresses in the available text box using commas to separate addresses.

14. You have recently added a number of new servers to your SharePoint 2007 server farm. As a result, you need to change the roles some of your servers play in the farm. You are on the Operations tab in the Central Administration site on a server named SRV03. Of the following options, which are available server roles for this server? (Choose all that apply.)

A. Single Server or Web Server for Small Server Farms

B. Web Server for Medium Server Farms

C. Web Server for Large Server Farms

D. Custom

15. You are the new SharePoint administrator for the Ganymede Import-Export Company. Ganymede has a preexisting SharePoint 2007 server farm, and you are currently familiarizing yourself with how it's set up. You want to take a look at the current User and Permissions settings for the Central Administration (CA) site. You are currently logged in to CA on the Home tab. What do you do next?

A. Click View All Site Content, and under Sites and Workplaces click the Security link. Then on the Security Properties page, you'll find the Users and Permissions category there.

B. Click the Operations tab, and Under Security Settings click Site Settings. You'll find the Users and Permissions category on that page.

C. Click Site Actions, and then click Site Settings. You'll find the Users and Permissions category on the Site Settings page.

D. Click View All Site Content. You'll find the Users and Permissions category on that page.

16. You have installed a new SharePoint Server 2007 server farm, and Configuring SharePoint Products and Technologies has just finished executing and committing the configuration to SQL Server 2005. Of the following options, which ones must be in place before a SharePoint portal site can be created? (Choose all that apply.)

A. Start the Office SharePoint Server Search service.

B. Start the Windows SharePoint Services Help Search service.

C. Create a web application for the portal site.

D. Create the first SSP.

17. You have just installed a SharePoint server farm and are performing post-installation tasks. Right now, you are about to set up outgoing mail services so SharePoint can send out alerts and notifications to administrators and users. You have decided to create a separate configuration for outgoing emails for web applications. To start this configuration process, what should you do first?

A. In Central Administration, click the Operations tab, and under Topology and Services click the Outgoing Email Settings link.

B. In Central Administration, click the Application Management tab, and under SharePoint Web Application Management click the Web Application Outgoing Email Settings link.

C. In Central Administration, click the Operations tab, and under Topology and Services click the Web Application Outgoing Email Settings link.

D. In Central Administration, click the Application Management tab, and under SharePoint Web Application Management click the Outgoing Email Settings link.

18. You are the new SharePoint administrator for the Ganymede Import-Export Company. You have familiarized yourself with how the server farm and the SharePoint site collection have been organized. You have several ideas for improving the site structure but want to check with the technical and content managers in the company to see what options they'd prefer. The relevant managers are located in a dozen offices around the world, and they all have access to SharePoint Central Administration. You decide to create a survey on the CA site to allow these managers to give input on the changes they'd like to see. Of the following options, which one represents the steps to start creating a survey?

A. In Central Administration on the Operations tab, locate the Surveys category.

B. In Central Administration on the Operations tab, under Sites and Workspaces, click Surveys.

C. In Central Administration on the Home tab, click View All Site Content, and locate the Surveys category.

D. In Central Administration on the Home tab, click View All Site Content, and under Sites and Workspaces click Surveys.

19. You want to enable SharePoint Directory Management Service in SharePoint so you can create email distribution lists. In one of the steps, you are required to specify a display name for the incoming server. Although the name can be anything, what is the proper expression of the host-name for an incoming mail server?

A. mail.adrastea.com

B. email.adrastea.com

C. exchange.adrastea.com

D. adrastea.mail.com

20. You have just finished restarting services on one of your web servers on the Services on Server page and want to return to the Central Administration Home tab. Of the following options, which one will accomplish this?

A. Clicking OK

B. Clicking Save

C. Clicking the When Finished, Return to the Central Administration Home Page link

D. Clicking the Save Work and Return to the Central Administration Home Page link

Answers to Review Questions

1. **A.** When you take the actions described in the question, you'll arrive on the Central Administration site at the Home tab. The tabs referred to in options B and C are valid, but neither is opened by default when you open Central Administration. The tab mentioned in option D is bogus.

2. **D.** Site Actions is a major feature on SharePoint sites including the Central Administration site and can be accessed from all three tabs.

3. **A.** You cannot delete an SSP if it is the only SSP for your server farm. You must first create a new SSP if you intend on deleting the original.

4. **B.** The steps presented in option B describe the correct way to update the percentage of completion for this task. You can also change the status of this task to Completed, but that is in a separate column.

5. **C.** Option C is the correct answer. When you configure Diagnostic Logging, you can select different event categories and determine the minimum critical event type to write to a log.

6. **D.** None of the solutions presented in options A, B, and C is correct. For you to be able to configure incoming mail services, you must install SMTP services on Windows Server 2003. POP 3 services are not necessary for incoming emails, and SMTP must be installed on the Windows Server 2003 machine, not in SharePoint. POP 3 is a protocol used to transfer mail on a mail server to a mail client such as Microsoft Office Outlook.

7. **A and B.** Distribution lists must be created in an Active Directory Organizational Unit (OU), so Active Directory must be available. Mail Services includes SMTP and POP 3, and SMTP is required for incoming mail. SNMP stands for Simple Network Management Protocol, and PHP stands for PHP Hypertext Preprocessor. Neither of these services is related to incoming mail, and they are not required.

8. **C and D.** Diagnostic logging and antivirus protection need to be set up in both stand-alone server and server farm environments soon after installation. Shared services provider and indexing configurations must be set up only in a server farm as initial post-installation tasks. While both a stand-alone and server farm deployment require shared services, in a stand-alone installation, the shared services provider is created and given a default configuration automatically.

9. **A.** You must install a software scanner application that is designed to work with SharePoint Server 2007 on all your Windows Server 2003 machines. Although Symantec's Norton Anti-Virus scanner is suitable, it is not the only program that can be used.

10. **A, B, and D.** Shared Services Administration is not a category on the View All Site Content page. The other answers are correct.

11. **A and C.** Under SSP Name, you can edit the text in the SSP Name field, but you can't change the SSP Administration Site URL. You can enable SSL under SSL for Web Services by choosing Yes. Under Index Server, you can't change the index server, but you can edit the path for the index file location. To move the index, you need to use the `stsadm` command-line utility.

12. A. Option A correctly describes the sequence that will manually start a full crawl. The other options are bogus.

13. A. After clicking Accept Mail from These Safe E-mail Servers, you must add the IP addresses of the desired servers in the available text box, one address per line.

14. A, B, and D. There is no option for a web server role on a large server farm. The roles listed are Single Server or Web Server for Small Server Farms, Web Server for Medium Server Farms, Search Indexing, Excel Calculation, and Custom.

15. C. You can get to the Users and Permissions category and the links under it by following the steps shown in option C.

16. A, C, and D. To create the first portal site in a SharePoint server farm, you need to start the Office SharePoint Server Search service, create a web application for the portal site, and create the first SSP if it doesn't yet exist. Then you can create the portal site.

17. B. Although the steps in setting up outgoing mail and outgoing mail for web applications are practically the same, outgoing mail is configured on the Operations tab, and outgoing mail for web applications is set up on the Application Management tab.

18. C. Option C is the correct process for beginning to create a survey in the Central Administration website. You can also click View All Site Content from any top-level site in SharePoint and follow the same instructions to create a survey on that site.

19. A. Typically, the hostname of a mail server is in the format mail.*domain*.com.

20. C. Rather than presenting the traditional OK or Save button to save changes and return you to a higher-level web page, you must click the link shown in option C to leave the Services on Servers page and return to the Home tab in Central Administration.

Chapter

4

Building Sites and Site Collections

MICROSOFT EXAM OBJECTIVES COVERED IN THIS CHAPTER:

✓ **Configure Microsoft Office SharePoint Server 2007 Portal**

  ▪ Configure Site Management

  ▪ Configure Personalization

Up to this point in the book, you've been introduced to Microsoft Office SharePoint Server (MOSS) 2007, you've learned how to plan for and install SharePoint Server in both a stand-alone and server farm setup, and you've learned how to perform the initial configuration tasks to get SharePoint up and running. However, right now you have SharePoint 2007 operating as a potential rather than a realized resource for your customers.

In this chapter, you will be introduced to the concept of sites and site collections and then take a tour of the default site templates. This will give you enough of a picture to move on to actually planning a site collection by type and purpose. You'll take a look at planning My Site sites as a special situation.

After you have made all of your planning decisions, you'll start the work of creating sites and site collections in SharePoint 2007, which includes using different site templates for different audiences and deploying your site collection plan into production.

This chapter will wrap up by showing you how to create a unique site and save it as a template. Although many of the routine site maintenance tasks will be covered in other chapters, you'll take a tour of the Site Directory and see many of the site administration tools.

SharePoint Site and Site Collection Overview

The concept of a website is fairly straightforward to people familiar with surfing the Web, and if you consider it for a moment, so is a site collection. If you open a web browser and go to www.microsoft.com, you'll be taken to the main page for the site. Clicking any of the links on the main page will take you to web pages that are underneath the main page. Unless Microsoft changes its main page between the time I'm writing this chapter and the time you get to read it, you should be able to look to the right side of the page and see a box called "All Microsoft Sites." That's right, Microsoft.com isn't a single, very big website but a collection of websites.

Let's take a look at this concept from the perspective of SharePoint. A site is the basic container for all content presented by SharePoint, from quarterly reports to pictures of the company picnic. SharePoint offers you the opportunity to organize all of your company's content in whatever structure best fits your corporate needs. It also lets you design and create different websites for different customers or purposes.

A single site is a container for various SharePoint elements such as libraries, lists, and other information containers. A site can also be designed for particular uses or users such as when creating a portal site, a team site, a document workspace site, and many others.

 You'll get a complete tour of SharePoint's default site templates later in this chapter.

All of this means you can create a main portal site within SharePoint for your business and create any number of special-purpose websites beneath the portal site to suit your needs. You can also use a hierarchy for site design, giving divisions, departments, and teams their own sites. Each website beneath the portal and top-level sites is considered a subsite, and all of the sites and subsites together make up the SharePoint site collection.

So, you can have a main portal site for your company, top-level sites for each major division or group, and then specific, purpose-driven sites beneath the top-level sites. You can continue to drill down the SharePoint site structure and create whatever subsites you need to fulfill your requirements.

This may seem very abstract, so let's take a more direct look at the specific building blocks of your site collection, the default site templates.

SharePoint Site Templates

In previous versions of SharePoint, if you wanted to create a site for a specific purpose, you had to take a basic template and heavily modify it to have it serve your needs. MOSS 2007 ships with a series of default site templates you have access to out of the box. Although you can modify any default template so that it meets your requirements, very often you won't have to do so. The tools offered by the templates available will be more than sufficient most of the time. Let's take a closer look.

The Portal Site

When you installed SharePoint 2007 in a stand-alone server configuration, the default portal site was automatically created, as you can see in Figure 4.1. The default portal site is not a template as such, but it is designed to provide a standard structure to present information and resources as the gateway site to your organization.

In Chapter 3, "Performing the Initial Site Management of SharePoint 2007," you had the opportunity to tour the SharePoint Central Administration (CA) site. The CA site uses the same basic structure and organization as any other SharePoint site. Using the CA site as a starting point, let's take a moment to compare the appearance and features of the portal with the Central Administration site on the Home tab.

FIGURE 4.1   The default portal site

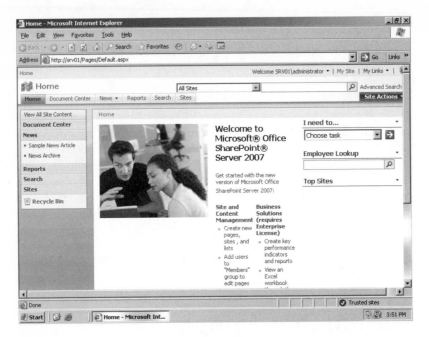

Both sites have tabs toward the top left of the page, and both sites, by default, open at the Home tab. There is a set of navigation links in a list on the left side of the page known as Quick Launch, and the top item in each list is View All Site Content. At the top right of each page is a link for the account logged into the site, a My Site link, and a My Links link. There is also a Site Actions link present on both sites.

Although there isn't an Administrator Tasks list on the portal page, there are a number of items suggesting what can be done to get started with SharePoint Server 2007 including creating sites, pages, lists, and users.

View All Site Content

When you click View All Site Content, you see a page such as the one shown in Figure 4.2.

It is somewhat, but not exactly, the same as the All Site Content page in SharePoint Central Administration. The specific categories and links underneath each one are shown in Table 4.1.

TABLE 4.1   Categories Under View All Site Content

Document Libraries	Lists
Documents	Contacts
Form Templates	Content and Structure Reports
Images	Events

TABLE 4.1   Categories Under View All Site Content *(continued)*

Pages	Links
Site Collection Documents	Reusable Content
Site Collection Images	Tasks
Style Library	Workflow Tasks
Picture Libraries	Discussion Boards
None (have to create)	Team Discussion
Sites and Workspaces	Surveys
Document Center	None (have to create)
News	
Reports	
Search	
Sites	

FIGURE 4.2   All Site Content page

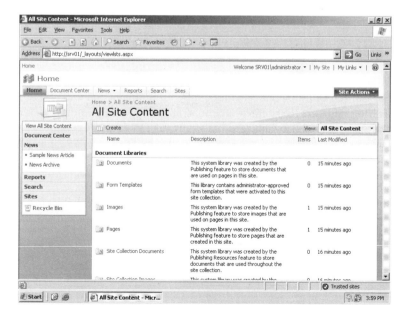

All of the same categories are present on the All Site Content pages for both the default portal and Central Administration sites, but there are more options under some of the categories for the portal page.

Tabs

Besides the Home tab, several other tabs are available on the portal site that aren't in Central Administration:

- Document Center
- News
- Reports
- Search
- Sites

You'll notice this list is identical to what appears under the Sites and Workspaces category on the All Site Content page. I will discuss these areas in more detail as we progress.

Other Site Links and Site Actions

The links at the top right of the page, Welcome SRV01\administrator, My Site, and My Links, respond the same way here as they do in CA; however, Site Actions offers additional menu items, as shown in Figure 4.3.

FIGURE 4.3 Site Actions menu

As you can see, in addition to the Create Page, Edit Page, and Site Settings options, several other selections appear.

The View All Site Content selection is just another link to the content I discussed previously. The View Reports and Site Settings options have other menu options underneath them. As we progress through this chapter and the rest of the book, you'll have a chance to learn more about them.

A few more options are available on this page:

I Need To... Use this drop-down menu to select a particular task. By default, the only task available when the portal site is first deployed is Setup MySite.

Employee Lookup You can quickly look up any employee who is a registered SharePoint user by typing their name in the available text field and clicking the Go Search button.

Top Sites Top Sites is a content query tool part and is designed to display a dynamic set of items based on a query you build using a web browser. You use the query to specify which items are displayed, and you can set presentation options to determine how those items are displayed on the finished page.

Site collections consist of portal sites, sites, and subsites. The building blocks for the sites in the collection under the main portal site are the default SharePoint Server site templates.

News Three sample links appear under News on the main page. These are bogus news items, but you can replace them with authentic news by binding the news page web part with an RSS feed. If you were to click one of the sample links, it would take you to a sample page on the News tab.

You'll learn more about web parts in Chapter 8, "Configuring Web Part Pages, Web Parts, and Web Pages."

Site Template Categories

There's a specific organization to SharePoint site templates. This makes it easier to identify a general purpose for the site you want to create and then look within that category for the particular site that best fits your intent. Later in this chapter, when you actually start to create sites, you'll see the procedures for how to find each template, but first, let's take a brief tour.

Each template contains different site and workspace elements, depending on the purpose of the site template. Some contain a top-level site, which is like the index page of a website. They can also contain subsites, which are like child sites to a main website. They can also contain specialized sites such as those configured with web parts and other design elements specifically for news sites, search sites, and other specialized elements. You'll learn the details about such elements as libraries and lists in Chapter 7, "Configuring and Maintaining Lists and Libraries," and web parts and web part pages in Chapter 8, "Configuring Web Part Pages, Web Parts, and Web Pages," that will help you understand many of these specifics.

Collaboration

This collection of site templates is available to help your business by providing a platform for sharing information and allowing collaborative efforts to be made by teams working together on common documents and resources. The default site templates in the Collaboration category are as follows:

Blank Site   A blank site for you to customize based on your requirements.

Document Workspace   A site for colleagues to work together on documents. It provides a document library for storing the primary documents and supporting files, a tasks list for assigning to-do items, and a links list to point to resources related to the documents.

Team Site   A site for a team to quickly organize, author, and share information. It provides a document library and lists for managing announcements, calendar items, tasks, and discussions.

Blog Site   A site for a person or team to post ideas, observations, and expertise that site visitors can comment on.

Wiki Site   A site for a community to brainstorm and share ideas. It provides web pages that can be quickly edited to record information and then linked together through keywords.

Enterprise

This collection of site templates provides features designed for use in enterprises, either because of their scale or because they provide features commonly used in large organizations. The default site templates in the Enterprise category include the following:

Document Center   A site to centrally manage documents in your enterprise.

My Site Host   A site used for hosting personal sites. The home page will always redirect to the user's My Site.

Records Center   A site designed for records management. Records managers can configure the routing table to direct incoming files to specific locations. The site prevents records from being modified after they are added to it.

Search Center   A site for delivering the Office SharePoint Server 2007 advanced search options including searching by information attributes such as file format, searching with Boolean logic, and searching by some or all words in the search string.

Search Center with Tabs   A site for delivering the search experience. The welcome page includes a search box with two tabs: one for general searches and another for searches for information about people. You can add and customize tabs to focus on other search scopes or result types.

Site Directory   A site for listing and categorizing other sites in your organization.

Meetings

This collection of site templates provides various site platforms that can be used to organize many types of business meetings, from a weekly staff meeting to an annual stockholders' report. The default site templates in the Meetings category are as follows:

Basic Meeting Workspace   A site to plan, organize, and capture the results of a meeting. It provides lists for managing the agenda, meeting attendees, and documents.

Blank Meeting Workspace   A blank meeting site for you to customize based on your requirements.

Decision Meeting Workspace   A site for meetings that track status or make decisions. It provides lists for creating tasks, storing documents, and recording decisions.

Multipage Meeting Workspace   A site to plan a meeting and to capture the meeting's decisions and other results. It provides lists for managing the meeting agenda and attendees, along with two blank pages for you to customize based on your requirements.

Social Meeting Workspace   A site to plan social occasions such as a birthday party or the company picnic.

Publishing

This is a collection of site templates used for presenting information to a large group. These templates include features that support creating and publishing pages based on page layouts. The templates available here are portal sites used to present information to Internet or intranet audiences. The default site templates in the Publishing category are as follows:

Collaboration portal   A starter site hierarchy for an intranet divisional portal. It includes a home page, a news site, a site directory, a document center, and a search center with tabs. Typically, this site has an equal number of contributors and readers. Collaboration portals often include subsites based on templates in the Collaboration category.

Publishing portal   A starter site hierarchy for an Internet-facing site or a large intranet portal. This site can be customized easily to supply distinctive branding. It includes a home page, a sample press releases subsite, a search center, and a login page. Typically, this site has many more readers than contributors.

This particular template category needs a bit more of an introduction since its role is so significant to large audiences. Both templates are designed to operate as portal sites in the same way as the default portal site. Portal sites are the entry point of an entire site collection to underlying content. Although the default portal is constructed to be a general gateway, the Collaboration and Publishing portals have more specific purposes.

The Collaboration portal contains the top-level site and four subsites, including a Document Center site, a News site, a Search site, and a Site Directory site. Site collection features include Collect Signatures Workflow, Disposition Approval Workflow, Office SharePoint Server Publishing Infrastructure, Office SharePoint Server Standard Site Collection Features, Reporting, Routing Workflows, and Translation Management Workflow.

The Publishing portal includes a top-level site and two subsites, which are a Press Releases site and a Search site. Site collection features include Collect Signatures Workflow, Disposition Approval Workflow, Office SharePoint Server Publishing Infrastructure, Routing Workflows, and Translation Management Workflow.

You can end up with multiple portal sites in your SharePoint site collection. The very top-level portal is the general gateway into your organization. Branching off, you can have a Collaboration portal for your internal employees and a Publishing portal for the general public or an extranet for customers or partners.

Planning a Site Collection Structure

A site collection is a grouping of websites with a number of common elements:

- A shared top-level website
- One or more subsites under the top-level site
- A common owner for the collection
- Shared administration settings
- A common navigation structure
- Other common features and elements

Based on what you learned in your tour of site templates, there are two primary areas where decisions need to be made about the SharePoint site collection structure—the portal site structure and the subsite structure.

Portal Sites

The following presents the different portal site decisions you can make based on your needs.

Collaboration

If you are deploying a MOSS 2007 site collection for the exclusive use of your company's staff, create a single Collaboration portal site. You can also accommodate interactions between partners and employees on a single portal site by controlling content access based on which privileges each group is assigned, or you can create two separate Collaboration sites, one for only employees and another for partner-employee common projects.

Publishing

If you are deploying a SharePoint site collection for an external audience such as customers or the general public, create one or more Publishing portal sites. A common scenario is to create a Publishing site collection as an extranet for customers and another as an Internet site for the general public. Of course, you can create links between the two sites, but customers will have to authenticate before accessing the extranet.

Since Publishing portals are outward-facing by design, SharePoint administrators often create the basic types such as production, authoring, and application:

- The production site is the one your customers and the public see and use for business.
- The authoring site is never viewable from the outside and is for the exclusive use of your internal designers and authors. Changes to the Publishing site are made and tested on the

authoring site. Once approved, those changes can be deployed to the production site. This gives SharePoint administrators and owners a chance to test and debug any changes before they are released to an external audience.

- The application portal site is used to provide external audiences with web-based access to business information based on Microsoft application solutions such as Project Server, Microsoft Excel Web Access, or some other business application. This type of portal is used to view schedules and processes. Shared spreadsheets can be made available that often include other business data from sources such as the data connection library, the business data catalog, or some other source such as a timecard reporting application.

Sites and Subsites

Site collections, sites, and subsites are usually built from the top down. You started at the top with your portal sites. The next step is to look at the site template level.

Templates

Referring to the earlier tour of SharePoint's default site templates, you have a lot of options in terms of site and subsite design elements. Once you've selected the required portal or portals, you can create sites and subsites beneath the portal to service the customer. Start by defining the site template category that best fits the needs of your audience.

For instance, let's say you've just deployed a Collaboration portal for your intranet. You have five departments, each of which needs its own sites beneath the portal, so you look in the Collaboration template category and use the Team Site template to create sites for each department. You can give each department its own blog and wiki sites for internal communication. You can also create multiple sites for a department using different site templates.

You can create a unique site out of different elements such as web parts and web part pages and save that site as a custom-made template. You'll learn more about this later in this chapter and in Chapter 8, "Configuring Web Part Pages, Web Parts, and Web Pages."

Users and Groups

Even though you've chosen an audience to serve with each of your portal site decisions, within a single general group such as company employees, there will be smaller groups such as divisions, departments, and teams that will need to have access to specific resources and will also need security restrictions so that one team's confidential data cannot be accessed by other groups.

You'll learn more about users and groups in Chapter 5, "Managing Users and Groups," and more about security in Chapter 6, "Configuring Authentication and Security."

Site Navigation

What websites and web pages a particular audience is aware of depends on their security settings. You may be surfing a site, whether on the company's intranet or on the Internet, and believe you are accessing all of its content, but your privileges on that site determine just how far you can go, or even how much you can see.

Site navigation can be configured to display a unique set of links in each part of your site's hierarchy that reflects the relationships among the sites and subsites in a site collection. This means you'll need to plan your navigation link structure at the same time as your site and subsite structure.

Search

Along with site navigation, site and subsite search can be configured so that only a subset of the entire site collection contents is presented in the results of a search run from a certain location in the collection. For example, you can specify that a particular subsite should never appear in search results run from another subsite.

> You'll learn more about navigation and search in Chapter 9, "Managing SharePoint Navigation and Search."

Site Layouts and Web Pages

You can further customize individual sites and web pages within a site by making unique layouts or master pages available in a subsite. You can also create a unique Welcome page and other pages for sites and subsites.

> You'll learn more about web part pages, web parts, and web pages in Chapter 8, "Configuring Web Part Pages, Web Parts, and Web Pages."

Planning Site Collection Implementation

Once you've decided which types of portals, sites, and subsites you need to fulfill your goals, you need to determine how to implement your decision across the site collection. Every site in your site collection exists in an overall, hierarchical structure, and they are stored in the same SQL Server. Often, sites within the collection will draw upon common resources such as document and graphics libraries, links lists, permissions, template galleries, and content types.

Site collection structure is usually planned from the top down, as previously mentioned. You've already made some portal site decisions based on the audience. The following are some ways to implement those decisions.

Implementing Portal Sites and Site Collections

The plan for portal sites is usually based on the scale and structure of your organization. Plan to create one portal site for an entire small organization or one for every division or project of 50 to 100 people within a medium to large organization. In large organizations, there might be several levels of portal sites, with each portal site focusing on the content created and managed at its level of the organization.

The scope of your portal sites depends on how you need to structure portals and the site collection as a whole. Much of the way you implement your portal site will drive how the site collection as a whole is deployed. The following are some options.

Rollup Portal Site

A *rollup portal site* type ignores the hierarchical structure of the company and presents information for the organization as a whole. Subsites are not structured by teams, departments, or divisions, but they can be mapped to divisional portals. The overall goal is to allow resources, information, and subject-matter experts to be accessible to all levels of the corporation. This portal site type is typically implemented for the intranet and is not accessible from the outside.

Hierarchical Portal Site

The structure for a *hierarchical portal site* is designed along organizational lines. This can be a reflection of the company's official organizational chart or defined by different company processes or functions. This is the traditional way intranet sites and site collections tend to be built. Often each major division of the company has its own portal with departments underneath each division also with their own portals. Portal sites don't tend to be implemented below the level of the department, but technically, each group and team in the company could have its own unique portal site and subsites.

Internal portal sites usually are deployed to both collaborate and share resources with other portals and to contain certain internal data and services within the portal. For instance, HR needs to cooperate with the IT department to develop network usage policies for employees, but both HR and IT perform tasks and operations that cannot be exposed to other parts of the company.

Extranet sites also tend to take on this structure with separate hierarchical portals being deployed for partners and customers. This allows internal employees to collaborate with other company stakeholders in separate site collections without compromising the barrier between corporate data and either partners or customers. Separate extranets also protect the barrier between partners and customers.

Because both partner and customer extranets are outward pointing, deploying and maintaining separate authoring portals is advisable. As you have already learned, this lets the internal designers and content managers develop and test content and resources prior to releasing any portal changes to extranet consumers. You learned from the previous section that outward-facing sites are also known as Publishing sites.

Application Portal Sites

This portal site type can be deployed for either internal or external customers; however, its structure is different because of the nature of the information presented. Application portals often include digital dashboards and other features for viewing and manipulating data related to the portal's purpose. The information presented in an application portal site usually comes from diverse sources, such as databases or other SharePoint sites.

All application portals are at least somewhat collaborative in that they are presenting business information to either employees or partners. For example, HR could design an application portal site to provide employees with general information such as employee handbooks and career opportunities. Also, corporate management could use an application portal to present the latest manufacturing, sales, and profit data to major investors.

Application portal design would have to include the specific types of information, the specific web parts, and other tools with which you intend to display that information and the databases and other sources you intend to access in order to create the display.

Business intelligence solutions used in application portals will be discussed more in Chapter 12, "Using Excel Services and Business Intelligence," and in Chapter 13, "Using Business Forms and Business Intelligence."

Web Presence Portal Sites

Web presence portal sites are Publication sites that are usually designed with a tightly controlled theme, branding, and appearance and contain the data, services, and links you want to publicly offer and have represent your company. Although many of the appearance elements remain stable over time, public sites are often very dynamic as to specific content in order to keep customers, partners, shareholders, and everyone else informed about and attracted to the company.

Because the company's web presence must be many things to many people, design elements can include those from application portals as well as blogs, wikis, newsfeeds, and many other data presentation elements. Like other public sites such as customer and partner extranets, it is common to keep an authoring site mirroring the production site to test any changes you plan to make before deploying them.

Security planning is also important for this portal since it is your most publicly accessible site.

You'll learn more about security in Chapter 6, "Configuring Authentication and Security."

Customization and Personalization

Depending on the audience and the function of your portal site and site collection, you can modify not only how everyone sees the collection but also how specific individuals and groups see it.

Customization is the modification of the theme, style, branding, layout, and other visible elements of a site collection. Often the customization of your company's web presence site is different from the corporate intranet site. Partner and customer extranet site collections may also have their own, unique appearances.

Personalization is customization for the individual. You can configure content filters that present only the information and features targeted to specific audiences based on their roles or interests. For instance, you can create a filtered view of the corporate portal site that presents only sales-related data and a separate filter aimed at the marketing staff. Each department in your organization can be presented with a somewhat different view of the portal based on their focus within the company.

 Real World Scenario

Setting a Quota for Site Collection Content

Amber, the CIO for your company, has expressed concern about how much storage the SharePoint site collection is occupying on the server farm. As the SharePoint site collection administrator, you investigate and discover that the majority of sites in the site collection are composed of an excessive number of subsites. Since no limitation was originally issued to corporate staff regarding how each department should construct their sites, many site owners have taken *carte blanche* and created sites with a great deal of excessive content. You inform Amber that the best course of action is to set a quota on the amount of content for each site in the collection. You develop a plan with your staff and have it approved by the CIO and the management staff. A policy is issued to all site owners informing them of the new quota limitations and requiring each department head to make sure that site content is reduced below the established quota.

Once you are informed that the department heads have complied with the new policy, you go through the process of establishing a new quota template to enforce policy. You accomplish this by creating a new quota template for the site collection. On the Quota Templates page under Template Name, you click Create a New Quota Template and accept the default of new blank template as the basis for the new quote template. Under Storage Limit Values, you set a value in megabytes to limit the maximum amount of storage for each site in the collection and set a slightly lesser value to trigger an email to be sent to any site owner whose site is approaching the maximum quota limit.

Planning My Sites

MOSS 2007 gives each SharePoint user the option of creating a personalized website for their individual use. This feature is enabled by default at the web application level, and users can create both public and private content on their My Site.

My Sites Overview

Before designing and implementing your My Site plan, let's take a look at the three default templates used to make up My Site sites.

Public Profile Page

This is the My Site page that is visible to anyone with access to the SharePoint site collection. The user can publish whatever information about themselves they want to be publicly available. The *public profile page* is also known as the My Site Public Page and is the public view of each user's User Profile and My Site. Anyone can access a user's public profile by clicking any link to a user within a portal site or site collection, including links in search results.

Each user can access their My Site by clicking the My Site link at the upper right of the SharePoint portal site page. If the user's My Site hasn't been created, clicking the link will initiate the creation process. A user's My Site contains the following elements.

- My Links
- Navigation Tabs
- Quick Launch menu
- As Seen By drop-down menu
- Site Actions

You'll recognize these elements as being the same as those shown on the Central Administration and default SharePoint portal site. This page also contains four web part zones. Users can edit their own public profiles on the My Profile link in their My Site. From their own public profile pages, users can return to the personal site by clicking My Home on the My Site top link bar. Users who view public profiles for other users will not see a My Site top link bar because they are not viewing pages in their own My Site.

Personal Site

This is the heart of the user's My Site and contains all of the content relevant to the user, including document libraries, picture libraries, and links. Anyone can use their personal site to collaborate with other users, but there's also a private home page only the user can access by default. This site functions as the user's My Site home page. Each user who has a personal site is an administrator of the site and can create and edit other pages, change the default layout or customize the page to personal taste, and change site settings.

The Quick Launch menu on the left side of the page has items you are familiar with, such as View All Site Content, but also contains the following links:

- My Profile
- Documents
- Pictures
- Lists
- Discussions

- Surveys
- Sites

The My Profile section contains links to details about your profile, your links list, your list of colleagues, and your memberships. Under Documents, you'll find links to both Personal and Shared Documents.

Personalization Site

A *personalization site* is actually owned by the SharePoint administrator and is used to disseminate targeted data to My Site users. For instance, if you wanted to publish a link to the HR department's Company Network Use Policy document to all SharePoint My Site users, you would use the personalization site to do so. Once published to My Site, users cannot modify or remove the link.

Personalization sites target information personalized for every member of the site by using personalized web parts and user filter web parts. Each personalization site is created by a site collection administrator or another user who has site creation permissions. Links to personalization sites can be added to the My Site top link bar by SSP administrators and can appear for every member of each site or can be targeted to specific audiences.

Links to personalization sites can also appear in the top navigation pane and the left pane of the All Site Content page of the main site. Personalization sites are registered by the shared services provider (SSP) so that personalization sites from all site collections that use the same shared service all appear in My Site, depending on the targeted audience of the personalization site link.

Individual users can add links to other personalization sites that have not been registered by an administrator, but those sites appear only on that user's My Site top link bar. Personalization sites can be branded by using either the main site logo or the My Site logo.

Planning and Implementing My Sites

The number-one planning consideration for My Sites is their purpose in the site collection and in your organization. Although users may like the idea of having their own personal sites in SharePoint, does this feature figure in to your overall design and to the goals the company has for SharePoint? Your plan may determine that only certain sites (and thus, certain groups of users) will benefit from having My Sites available. Although My Sites may be enabled by default, you as the SharePoint administrator can disable the My Site feature. If your decision is to disable the My Site feature for your site collection, your planning process ends here.

Beyond the decision of whether to disable My Site, the following are the key planning consideration points for this feature:

Purpose   What company goals does having My Site enabled across the site collection meet?

Scope   Should My Site be enabled for the entire site collection or only certain specific sites?

SSP scope   Should My Site be stored in a single SSP, or should they span multiple SSPs in the server farm (assuming more than one exists)?

Policies   Which policies will you apply to content appearing on user My Sites?

Personalization sites   Which personalization sites will be created, and who will own these sites?

Purpose and Scope

These two decision points are interrelated, so it's best to present them together. The primary purpose of the My Site feature is to let individual employees collaborate and share information and resources across team, departmental, or divisional boundaries. You can create a My Team site to let people working in the same team or department collaborate, but if you need people from diverse areas of your company to be able to find each other and interact, My Sites should be one of the business goals for your company's use of SharePoint.

Site collections that wouldn't benefit from the My Site feature would be those that primarily offer documentation or other data storage, with little or no need for collaboration between users. A Publication portal would be a good example of a site collection that doesn't need My Site functionality. Also, although My Site is a web application and doesn't typically affect Share-Point's performance by consuming a large amount of resources, if you have an unusually large number of SharePoint users or if the users intend to use their My Sites to store huge amounts of content, you will want to consider limiting the My Site feature's scope or disabling the feature.

SSP Scope and Personalization Sites

Personalization sites are modified within the SSP, so these two decision points are presented together. Any user who has permission to create sites within a site collection can select the personalization site template, but not all of these sites will be relevant for all users in the site collection, much less all users within the same SSP. Personalization sites that are relevant for users across the SSP can be added as links to the My Site top link bar. Every user who uses My Site will see links to all personalization sites that were linked by the SSP administrator, regardless of site collection, except for personalization site links that are targeted to specific audiences.

Personalization sites planned for initial deployment are important enough to add to the My Site link for the users who use the corresponding site collection, but not all users in the SSP will consider the same personalization sites to be relevant. My Site links to personalization sites can be targeted to specific audiences so they are seen only by relevant users.

For information that applies to everyone in an organization, such as human resources information, a My Site link to the personalization site might make sense for everyone. For a personalization site that shows personalized content to the sales team, it makes sense to target the My Site link so that it appears only for members of that team or for members of the sales site collection.

From the Shared Services Administration page, you can add more trusted personal site locations. This enables SSP administrators to select My Site locations from multiple sites. This is needed in any scenario that has more than one SSP, such as a global deployment that has geographically distributed sets of shared services, where each SSP contains a distinct set of users. By listing the trusted personal site locations for all other SSPs, you can ensure that My Sites are created in the correct location for each user. This also enables you to replicate user profiles across SSPs.

By default, My Sites are stored on the server that contains shared services. Public profiles are created and stored on the web application that contains the Shared Services Administration pages for the SSP; personal sites are stored on the default web application for the server. However, you can change the web application so that My Sites can be stored on the default web application, the web application for the SSP, or any other web application.

Personalization sites are created on individual site collections that can be on any farm that uses the same SSP. The settings for those sites are controlled by the administrators of those respective sites by using the same Site Settings pages that are available for any site.

Settings for personal sites are managed by the SSP administrator, who can manage settings that are unique for those sites. Personal site settings appear on the Manage Personal Sites page, which is available from the My Site settings link on the Shared Services Administration page.

Policies

When considering how to implement My Sites, you must consider how much control you want to give individual users over the visibility and presentation of their personal information and which policies you want to set for them based on the needs and policy decisions of your organization. There are three main decision points in terms of policy settings:

- Which users are allowed to create My Sites
- Which users are allowed to view and contribute to My Sites
- Which users do not have permission to access My Sites content

Permissions on all web applications including My Sites are enforced by policies. Policies for a web application are enforced regardless of permissions configured on individual sites or documents within the web application.

 You'll learn more about creating and working with My Sites and user and group policies in Chapter 5, "Managing Users and Groups."

Creating and Managing Site Collections

You can use a number of methods to create sites and site collections for the default portal site and for the Central Administration site. All of these methods require you to be the SharePoint administrator. Most divisions or departments in your company will likely want one of their staff to be the SharePoint site administrator for their group.

Enabling Self-Service Site Creation

To allow anyone besides the SharePoint administrator to create and manage sites, you'll first need to enable *self-service site creation* (see Exercise 4.1). Once enabled, you can delegate the creation of SharePoint sites to other SharePoint users. This service also lets you create sites and site collections from the Site Directory, as you'll see later in this chapter. You must be the administrator to enable this service, and it can be enabled only in SharePoint Central Administration.

Chapter 5, "Managing Users and Groups," and Chapter 6, "Configuring Authentication and Security," will cover groups and permissions including which groups are allowed to create sites in SharePoint.

EXERCISE 4.1

Enabling Self-Service Site Creation

1. Launch the Central Administration website.

2. Click the Application Management tab.

3. Under Application Security, click Self-Service Site Management.

4. Under Web Application, click the drop-down arrow, and then click Change Web Application.

5. Click SharePoint – 80 in the list.

6. Under Enable Self-Service Site Creation, click On.

7. Click OK.

If you had not changed the web application in step 4, you would have attempted to enable this service in Central Administration rather than on the SharePoint portal site, and you would have received an error.

After step 6, you could have optionally ticked the Require Secondary Contact check box if you wanted to require self-service site creation users to supply a secondary contact name on the sign-up page when creating a site. You can see this option displayed in Figure 4.4.

SharePoint users with the Use Self-Service Site Creation permission will now be able to create sites within specified URL namespaces. Once this service is enabled, an announcement will be added to the announcements list on top-level sites, providing a link to the site creation page.

Methods of Creating Site Collections

As an administrator, you can use several methods to create site collections:

- You can create a site collection in Central Administration.
- You can create a site collection using Site Actions on a top-level site.
- You can create a site collection using Site Actions on a subsite.
- You can create a site collection from the Site Directory.
- You can create a site and save it as a site template.

FIGURE 4.4 Enabling self-service site creation

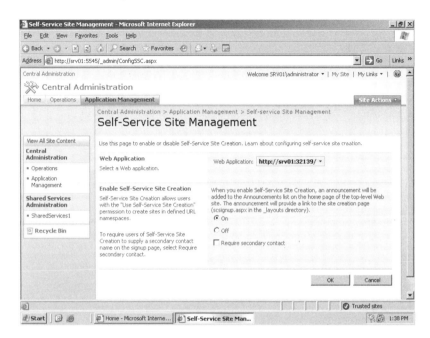

The following exercises will take you through each process. Also, each exercise will show you how to create a site collection using different site template categories.

Creating a Site Collection in Central Administration

This is the only method of site creation that requires you to use Central Administration to perform the task. Exercise 4.2 will get you started. You'll be using the Collaboration site template category in this exercise and the Team Site template to create the site.

EXERCISE 4.2

Creating a Site Collection from SharePoint Central Administration

1. Launch the Central Administration website.

2. Click the Application Management tab.

3. Under SharePoint Site Management, click Create Site Collection.

4. On the Create Site Collection page under Web Application, accept the default if it is the application where you want to create the collection.

EXERCISE 4.2 *(continued)*

If not, click the drop-down arrow, click Change Web Application, and select the desired web application from the list.

5.   Under Title and Description in the Title text field, type the title you want to give to your site collection.

6.   In the Description field, type an optional description of the site collection.

7.   Under Web Site Address, click the drop-down arrow in the URL, and change the setting from Personal to Sites.

8.   In the text field to the right of the drop-down arrow, type a unique name for your site collection's URL.

9.   In the Template Selection area under Select a Template, click the Collaboration tab, and then select the Team Site template, as shown here.

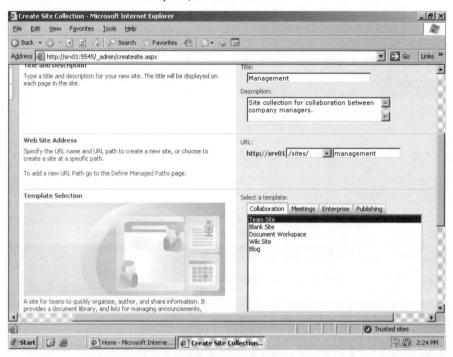

10. Under Primary Site Collection Administrator, choose a site administrator for the site collection, either by typing the name and clicking the Check Names icon or by clicking the Browse icon and browsing for a name.

11. If you want to specify a secondary site administrator, perform the same action as you did in step 10 under Secondary Site Collection Administrator.

12. Under Quota Template, use the drop-down arrow to select a *quota template* to limit resources used in the site collection, or accept the default of No Quota.

13. Click OK to create the new site collection.

The site creation process can take some time, but when it is completed, you are taken to the Top-Level Site Successfully Created page. You can either click the link `http://srv01/sites/management` to visit the new site collection or click OK to return to the Central Administration Application Management tab. You can see what the new team site looks like in Figure 4.5.

FIGURE 4.5   Collaboration team site

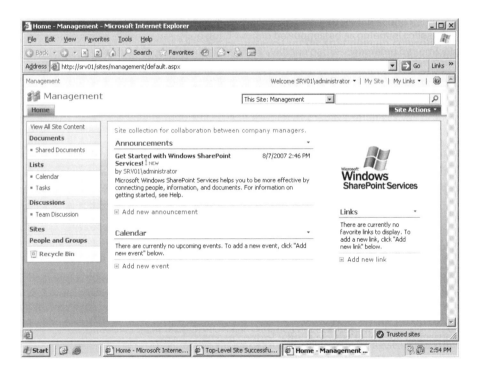

In step 12 of Exercise 4.2 you were asked to select a content quota template for the new site collection. The default is No Quota, and the only other selection you have by default is personal. If you wanted to set a different quota template for your new site collection, you'd have to create it as shown in Exercise 4.3.

EXERCISE 4.3

Creating a Site Collection Quota Template

1. On the Create Site Collection page under Quota Template, click the Manage Quota Templates link.

2. On the Quota Templates page under Template Name, click Create a New Quota Template. Under Template to Start From, accept the default of [new blank template].

3. Type a name for the new template in the New Template Name text field.

4. Under Storage Limit Values, if you want to limit the maximum amount of storage for the site, tick the Limit Site Storage to a Maximum Of check box, and specify a value in the MB field.

5. If you want to send an email warning when site storage reaches a particular amount, tick the Send Warning E-mail When Site Storage Reaches check box, and specify a value in the MB field.

6. Click OK.

When you are creating a new site collection as in Exercise 4.2 and you know in advance that you will want to create a new quota template, create the template before configuring the details for the new site. If you get to step 12 and then decide to create the quota template as in Exercise 4.3, when you click OK in step 6 and are taken to the Create Site Collection page, all of your settings will be gone.

Creating a Site Collection Using Site Actions on a Top-Level Site

As we go through the process of creating sites in different exercises, you'll notice that although each method starts from a different point, the process of site creation is pretty much the same. Exercise 4.4 will take you through creating a site using Site Actions. You must be at the top-level portal site for your SharePoint site collection. In this example, we'll create an enterprise-level document center site.

EXERCISE 4.4

Creating a Site Collection from the Site Actions Menu on a Top-Level Site

1. On the Home tab of your top-level portal site, click Site Actions near the upper-left corner of the page, and click Create Site (see Figure 4.3 earlier in the chapter).

2. On the New SharePoint Site page, in the Title text field, give your new site a name.

3. In the Description text field, give your site collection an optional description.

4. In the URL name field, complete the URL to this site. (The top-level server hostname is already populated.)

5. Under Select a Template, click the Enterprise tab, and select Document Center.

6. Under User Permissions, select Use Same Permissions as Parent Site.

7. In the Navigation Inheritance section under Use the Top Link Bar from the Parent Site, click Yes.

8. In the Site Categories section, tick the List This New Site in the Site Directory check box to display this site in the Site Directory.

9. In the same section under Division and Region, tick the check boxes that most closely describe the nature and locale of this site collection.

10. Click Create.

As you can see, the new document center has been created. Notice that it appears as a tab on the top navigation bar. This effectively makes the document center a subsite of your portal site; however, you will not be able to create a subsite under this one. To get to the portal site's main page, just click the Home tab.

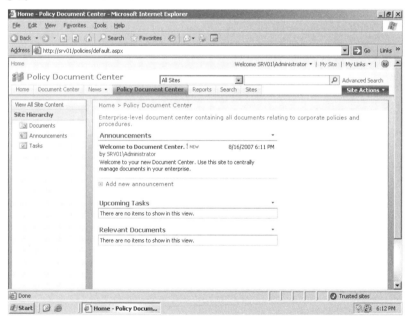

You may want to limit the number of sites you make available on the top navigation bar. Putting too many tabs there will make it appear cluttered, and it will be hard to find a specific tab.

Creating a Site Collection Using Site Actions on a Subsite

The process of creating a site collection from a subsite is only a little different from performing the same action from the portal site. For Exercise 4.5, you'll need to start from the management site you created in Exercise 4.2. In this exercise, we'll create a basic meeting site.

 Although the management site is a top-level site, it is still not a portal site. The Central Administration (CA) site is the portal for management, so management is considered a subsite to CA.

EXERCISE 4.5

Creating a Site Collection Using the Site Actions Menu on a Subsite

1. On the management site home page, click Site Actions, and then click Create.

2. On the Create Page under Web Pages, click Sites and Workspaces, as shown here.

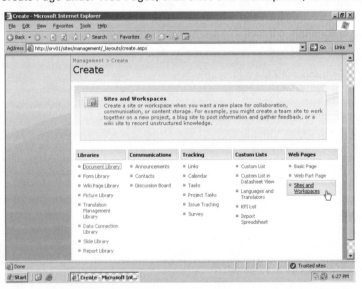

3. Perform steps 2 through 4 from Exercise 4.4 to give your new site a name and specify the URL.

4. Under Select a Template, click the Meetings tab, and then select Basic Meeting Workspace.

5. Under User Permissions, click Use Same Permissions as Parent Site.

6. In the Navigation section under Display This Site on the Quick Launch of the Parent Site, click Yes.

7. In the same section under Display This Site on the Top Link Bar of the Parent Site, click No.

8. In the Navigation Inheritance section under Use the Top Link Bar from the Parent Site, click Yes.

9. Click Create.

The navigation decisions you made in steps 6 through 8 are largely based on the navigation plan you have developed for your site collection. You'll read more about this in Chapter 9, "Managing SharePoint Navigation and Search."

Configuring Groups for a Meeting Workspace

Although it seems that the site creation should have been completed after step 9 of the previous exercise, in fact you know this isn't so. Clicking Create did create the site, but you still aren't finished. When you create a meeting site, you need to set up who can access it. Exercise 4.6 will show you how to do that. This exercise continues immediately after step 9 in the previous exercise.

EXERCISE 4.6

Configuring Group Access to a Meeting Workspace

1. On the Set Up Groups for This Site page, in the Visitors to This Site section click Use an Existing Group, and then click the drop-down menu to choose a group.

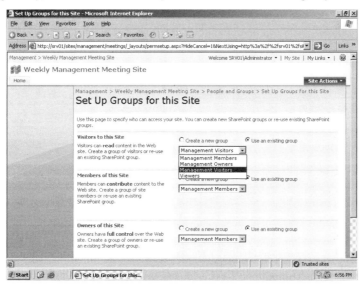

2. In the Members of This Site section, select Use an Existing Group, and click the drop-down menu to choose a group.

3. In the Owners of This Site section, select Use an Existing Group, and click the drop-down menu to choose a group.

4. Click OK.

If you had selected Create a New Group in steps 1, 2, or 3, you could have specified a name for the new group in the available text field and then either browsed for or input the names of the individual members of the group.

The new Weekly Management Meeting Site is now available. To return to the management home page, just click the Home tab. To access the Weekly Management Meeting site from the management home site, click the Weekly Management Meeting Site link under Sites in the Quick Launch menu on the left.

You'll learn more about configuring groups in Chapter 5, "Managing Users and Groups."

Creating a Site Collection from the Site Directory

The Site Directory is a catalog for the site collection and allows you to access different sites by division, region, or other selections. When we created the Policy Document Center in Exercise 4.4, I selected International under Region. I could use the Site Directory to view all sites in the collection that are International, as well as the Policy Document Center. The Policy Document Center is an enterprise-level document center containing all documents relating to corporate policies and procedure; it is included in the International region by default. You also have the ability to create additional site collections from the Site Directory.

The Site Directory is accessible either by clicking View All Site Content or Sites in Quick Launch or by clicking the Sites tab to open it. Exercise 4.7 will show you how to use the first method. In this example, I'll begin from the main portal page.

Creating a Site Collection from the Site Directory

1. In Quick Launch, click View All Site Content.

2. Scroll down until you can see the Sites and Workspaces section, and then click Sites.

3. On the Site Directory page, click the Create Site tab near the upper-right corner of the page.

4. Perform steps 2 through 4 from Exercise 4.4 to give your new site a name and specify the URL.

5. Under Select a Template, click the Publishing tab, and select Publishing Site.

6. Under User Permissions, click Use Unique Permissions.

EXERCISE 4.7 *(continued)*

7. Under Use the Top Link Bar from the Parent Site, click Yes.

8. Tick the List this New Site in the Site Directory check box.

9. Tick the appropriate check boxes under Division and Region, and then click Create.

Since you selected Use Unique Permissions in step 6, after you perform step 9, you will be taken to the Set Up Groups for This Site page for your new site. This is identical to the page you saw in Exercise 4.6.

Creating a Site and Saving It as a Template

Through the course of this chapter, you've seen how to access some of the default templates available in SharePoint Server 2007 and how to use them to create sites. If you need templates not available by default, you can create a unique site and then save it as a template. Once you've done that, you can use the new template to create additional sites. In this example, we'll create a simple site on which to base our template. Exercise 4.8 will start at the point where we've completed creating the site and are ready to save it.

EXERCISE 4.8

Saving a Site as a Template

1. On the site you want to save as a template, click Site Actions, and then click Site Settings.

2. On the Site Settings page in the Look and Feel column, click Save Site as Template.

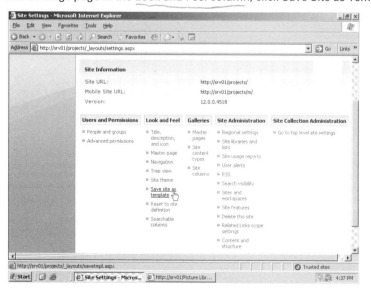

EXERCISE 4.8 *(continued)*

3. On the Save Site as Template page, give the template file a name in the File Name field.

4. In the Template Name field, type the name of the template.

5. In the Template Description field, type an optional description.

6. If you want to include the content on the site in the template, tick the Include Content check box.

7. Click OK.

8. On the Operation Completed Successfully page, either click Site Template Gallery to manage the template or click OK to return to the main site.

Now, when you go through the process of creating a new site, Under Select a Template, there is a new Tab named Custom. When you click it, you can see the new site template you just created as in Figure 4.6.

FIGURE 4.6   Custom Template tab

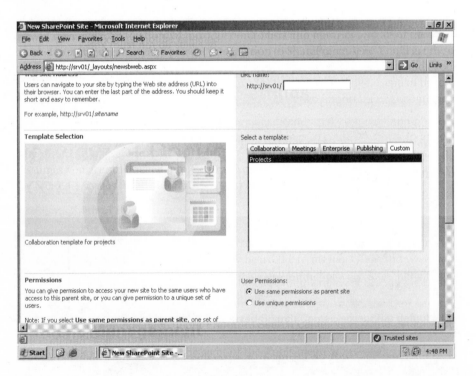

Touring the Site Directory

As previously mentioned, the Site Directory is your site toolbox, allowing you as the Share-Point administrator to access, view, and manage all of the sites in the site collection associated with the current portal site. You can view the portal's structure; view individual sites; and add, delete, approve, and reject sites. In this final portion of the chapter, we'll take a tour and perform a few site administration tasks from the Site Directory.

The easiest way to get to the Site Directory is from the portal site. Click the Sites tab across the top, and you'll immediately be taken to the Site Directory. Figure 4.7 shows you the default view of the Site Directory.

FIGURE 4.7   The Site Directory

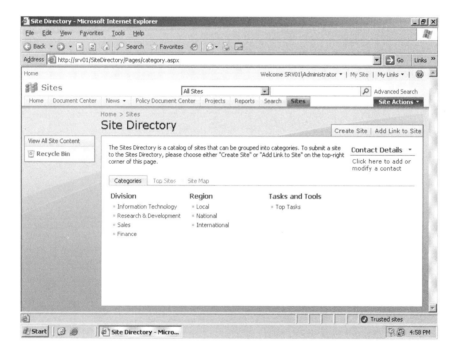

The Site Directory opens on the Categories tab by default. You can see the default categories available for selection when you create a new site. For instance, under Region, if you had ticked the Local check box when you created a site, clicking Local in the Site Directory will take you to a list of all sites in the collection you designated as Local. The same goes for any of the links under the Division column. Under Tasks and Tools, you can see the Top Tasks link. Clicking that link will take you to the Sites in Category page, where under Tasks and Tools: Top Tasks you can see a link called Setup MySite.

You'll set up My Sites in Chapter 5, "Managing Users and Groups."

At the upper right of the pane, you can see two tabs called Create Site and Add Link to Site. You've already used the Create Site tab in Exercise 4.6. Clicking Add Link to Site lets you add content to the Division, Region, and Tasks and Tools areas and the Top Sites tab. Figure 4.8 shows you the options available to you when you click Add Link to Site.

FIGURE 4.8 Add Link to Site page

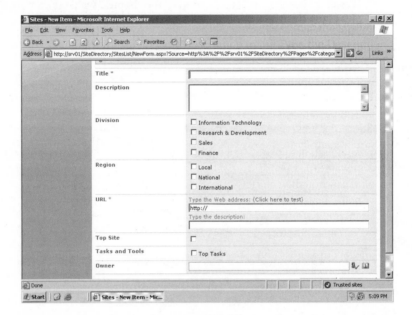

As your site collection grows, you could end up with hundreds or thousands of sites; however, there may be a much smaller group of sites that are the most frequently accessed or otherwise are more important. You can click Add Link to Site and tick the Top Site check box to designate a site as a top site. Exercise 4.9 will show you how to make a site a top site after it has been created.

EXERCISE 4.9

Making a Site a Top Site

1. In the Site Directory, click Site Actions, and then click View All Site Content.

2. On the View All Site Content page, find the Lists section, and click the Sites link.

3. Locate the site you want in the Title column, click to the right of the site name, and in the menu click Edit Item.

4. Under Tasks and Tools, tick the Top Sites check box, and then click OK.

Now in the Site Directory, if you click the Top Sites tab, the site you designated a Top Site will appear.

WARNING

When a site is created, it is not always immediately viewable until it's published. If you are the creator of a site that has not been published, you will not be able to make it a Top Site.

When a site is created, it enters the workflow process with the status of Pending and will be visible only to you as the administrator and to the creator of the site until it is either approved or rejected. If the administrator rejects the site, the site creator is advised, and the site remains unavailable. If it is approved, it becomes accessible in the site collection.

From the Site Directory, approving or rejecting a site takes very few steps, so I won't create an exercise for this task. Follow steps 1 through 3 from Exercise 4.9, but in the menu, instead of clicking Edit Item, click Approve/Reject. Then on the following page, select Approved, Rejected, or Pending. Add a statement in the Comment field if necessary, and then click OK. Back on the Sites page in the Approval Status column, the status will have changed from Pending to whatever option you selected. You can also delete a site by selecting Delete Item in the menu instead of Approve/Reject.

If you click the Site Map link, you are taken to the *site map* for the site collection. This functions the same way a site map does in any website, listing all of the contents in the site and providing links allowing you to jump to any location within the collection, as you can see in Figure 4.9.

FIGURE 4.9 The site map

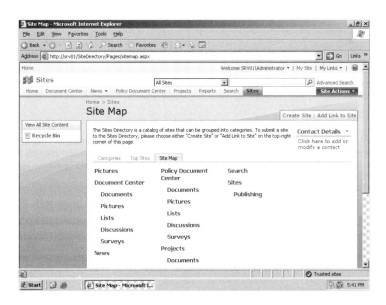

The final item in the Site Directory is Contact Details. You can add a list of contacts in your organization to the Site Directory. The most common list of names you can include would be site owners and administrators.

Summary

In this chapter, you learned a great deal about planning and implementing site collections in SharePoint Server 2007. I covered the following topics.

- I reviewed the structure of the main portal site.

- I introduced the default site templates including the Collaboration, Enterprise, Meetings, and Publishing site templates.

- I presented detailed elements of the planning and implementation of a site collection.

- I covered planning for My Sites including planning for the configuration of personalization.

- I covered creating site collections including enabling self-service site creation and the different methods of creating a site collection.

- I introduced the various features and services offered by the Site Directory as well as creating a site and saving it as a template.

Exam Essentials

Be familiar with the default site templates.   These are the basic building blocks for creating site collections. Each template has unique characteristics and features that serve specific purposes within an organization, and you must know how to create sites and site collections to meet your business goals.

Understand site collection planning and implementation.   SharePoint sites and site collections will not be utilized effectively if they are created in a haphazard manner. Before creating your first site under the Portal, you must develop a detailed plan for the structure and function of your sites. This includes planning for the My Sites to be used by SharePoint members and configuring personalization.

Know the different methods of site collection creation.   Site collections can be constructed in a number of different ways depending on who will be making sites and the purpose for those sites. You'll need to know how to use each method and what circumstances make one method of site creation preferred over another.

Know how to use the Site Directory.   The Site Directory is the central point that gives you the ability to create and administer any site or site collection under a given portal site. You must be familiar with all of the functions of the Site Directory and how to use it to manage SharePoint sites.

Review Questions

1. You are the SharePoint administrator for your company. The CTO has tasked you with putting together a justification for enabling the My Site feature for the organization's site collection. Of the following decision points, which is the first one you must consider?

   A. Policies: Which policies will you apply to content appearing on user My Sites?

   B. SSP scope: Should My Sites be stored in a single SSP, or should they span multiple SSPs in the server farm (assuming more than one exists)?

   C. Purpose: What company goals does having the My Site feature enabled across the site collection meet?

   D. Personalization sites: Which personalization sites will be created, and who will own these sites?

2. You are the SharePoint administrator for your company. You have been tasked by your supervisor to create a site for a series of meetings to be held by your organization's division managers. The division managers are in the process of determining the restructuring of the corporation, and they must be able to use the site to create tasks, store documents, and track status. Of the options presented, which one would best fit these requirements?

   A. Use a Meetings site template to create a Decision Meeting Workspace site.

   B. Use a Collaboration site template to create a Team Site site.

   C. Use a Publishing site template to create a Collaboration Portal site.

   D. Use an Enterprise site template to create a Records Center site.

3. You are the SharePoint administrator for your company. You must create a portal site that ignores the hierarchical structure of the company and presents information for the organization as a whole. The overall goal of this portal is to allow resources, information, and subject-matter experts to be accessible to all levels of the corporation. Of the following options, which portal site model best suits these requirements?

   A. Application portal site

   B. Hierarchical portal site

   C. Rollup portal site

   D. Web presence portal site

4. As the SharePoint administrator for your company, you have been assigned the task of creating a hierarchical Internet-facing site primarily to promote the company and present news releases and other information regarding new products and corporate growth. Some of the elements the site must include are a home page, a press releases subsite, and a search center. This site will attract mostly readers rather than contributors. Of the following selections, which default template most closely matches these requirements?

   A. An Enterprise site template Records Center site

   B. A Publishing site template Publishing portal site

   C. A Publishing site template Collaboration portal site

   D. An Enterprise site template Search Center site

5. You are the SharePoint administrator for your company, and you are creating a site collection from the Central Administration site. You want to limit the amount of data that can be stored on the new site. Of the following options, which one will allow you to set a customized quota limit?

A. On the Create Site Collection page, tick the Create a New Quota check box, and then type the desired value in the available text field.

B. On the Create Site Collection page, click Create a New Quota Template, accept the Default [new blank template], tick the Limit Site Storage to a Maximum Of check box, and specify a value in the MB field.

C. On the Quota Templates page, tick the Create a New Quota check box, and then type the desired value in the available text field.

D. On the Quota Templates page, click Create a New Quota Template, accept the Default [new blank template], tick the Limit Site Storage to a Maximum Of check box, and specify a value in the MB field.

6. You are a SharePoint user and are on the personal site of your My Site. You have just created your My Site, and this is your first opportunity to visit since you created it. You are surveying the links in the Quick Launch menu on the left side of the page. Of the following, what are the correct options in this list? (Choose all that apply.)

A. My Profile

B. Discussions

C. Surveys

D. Links

7. You are the SharePoint administrator for your company. At the request of the research and development division of your corporation, you have created a customized site based on their requirements. They want you to save this site as a template called RandD so that the different departments in that division will be able to build their own sites using that template. You have created the site and are now going to save it as a template. Of the following options, which are part of the process of saving a site as a template? (Choose all that apply.)

A. On the Site Settings page in the Look and Feel column, click Save Site as Template.

B. On the Site Settings page in the Sites and Workspaces column, click Save Site as Template.

C. On the Save Site as Template page, in the File Name field, give the template file a name.

D. On the Save Site as Template page, in the File Name field, either accept the default name or change the file name.

8. In the Site Directory, when you click Add Link to Site, you can perform numerous tasks. Of the following list, which actions can you perform? (Choose all that apply.)

A. Add links to Region.

B. Add links to Division.

C. Add tasks to Tasks and Tools.

D. Approve or reject a submitted site.

9. You are the SharePoint administrator for your company. The SharePoint portal for the company's intranet contains content relevant to each department in the organization. Department managers have complained that it's too difficult to find the information targeted just to their departments, so they task you with finding a solution. Of the following options, which is the appropriate solution?

A. You create sites for each department in your company, move the information relevant to each department from the portal to their departmental sites, and advise the managers to have their department employees access the site for their department.

B. You enable the My Site feature in the site collection and advise each department manager to have their subordinates create individual My Sites and personalize them with the information they want.

C. You create filtered view web parts for each department, place them on the portal site, and then label each web part by department so they know where on the portal to look for information relevant to them.

D. You create filtered views of the corporate portal site for each department so that when they visit the portal, they will see only the content targeted at them.

10. You are the SharePoint administrator for your company. Department managers and team leads want to be able to create their own sites in SharePoint. You determine the best way to allow this is to enable self-service site creation. You go to the Central Administration site and access the shared services provider (SSP) for the server farm. What next steps must you take in order to begin enabling self-service site creation?

A. Click the Application Management tab, and under Application Management click Self-Service Site Management.

B. Click the Application Management tab, and under Application Security click Self-Service Site Management.

C. Click the Application Management tab, and under Application Security click Self-Service Site Creation.

D. Click the Application Management tab, and under Application Management click Self-Service Site Creation.

11. You are the SharePoint administrator for your company. Typically, you use the default Site Directory that was created when the portal site was created to manage the site collection. Is there any method available for you to create another Site Directory for another site collection?

A. Only if you create another portal site first.

B. Yes, you can create a Site Directory from a subsite, but it will be able only to manage that subsite and any sites beneath it.

C. Yes, use the Enterprise site template to create a Site Directory.

D. No, there is only one default Site Directory for the server farm.

12. You are the SharePoint administrator for your company. You are currently planning the design, structure, and implementation of your organization's web presence site. Internet-facing websites are often called Publishing sites because information on them is mainly used to inform large audiences rather than for purposes of collaboration. As part of your plan, you intend to also create an authoring site. What is the purpose of doing this?

A. The authoring site will be a companion to the Publishing site that will give customers and partners the ability to collaborate on mutual projects.

B. The authoring site will allow partners to contribute additional content that you can then transfer to the Publishing site.

C. The authoring site is a mirror to the Publishing site and allows you to test any changes you plan to make to your web presence site before making them public.

D. The authoring site is a mirror to the Publishing site and serves as a backup for all your content and configuration information should anything happen to the Publishing site.

13. You are the SharePoint administrator for your company. Your organization's management team has been using a Decision Meeting Workspace site to administer a series of meetings they have been holding regarding a general restructuring of the corporation. The CTO has advised you that the scope of this workspace is too limited and that they need a site with the same capacities but more room. What is your solution?

A. Use an Enterprise site template, and create a Records Center site for the management team so they can have a greater ability to store and manage information related to their project.

B. Use a Meetings site template, and create a Multipage Meeting Workspace site that has the same capacities as the site they are currently working with and has additional blank web pages they can use.

C. Use a Publishing site template, and create a Collaboration portal that will provide the management team with a larger venue for them to continue managing their decisions and tasks.

D. Ask the management team to provide you with a list of elements and abilities they expect out of the site they need, and then create a customized site based on those requirements.

14. You are the SharePoint administrator for your company. You have been asked to create several custom-made sites and save them as site templates. The different divisions have very specific needs for their site collections that cannot be satisfied by the default templates. You have created templates called Management, Legal, Development, and Production. You now need to use these templates to start creating sites. On the New SharePoint Site page, where will you find these customized templates?

A. Under a new template tab called Custom.

B. When you saved the sites as templates, you were given the option of which template tab to use to save them.

C. By default, all sites saved as templates are located in the Collaboration tab.

D. Each site saved as a template has its own tab.

15. You have been working with the management team to determine whether there is a business need to enable My Sites in the corporate site collection. Management has determined that enabling My Sites will meet several business goals, and you are directed to proceed. What must you do to enable My Sites in SharePoint?

A. In the Site Directory, click Add Link to Site, tick the Enable My Sites check box, and click OK.

B. In SharePoint Central Administration, click the Application Management tab, and under Application Management click Enable My Sites.

C. From the Portal site, click Site Actions, click Site Settings, and on the Site Settings page under Sites and Workspaces click Enable My Sites.

D. My Sites are enabled in SharePoint by default at the web application level.

16. You are the SharePoint administrator for your company. You have been asked by the legal department to create a site for them that does not inherit permissions from the parent site. Because of the sensitivity of the information they work with, they need to have a customized set of permissions. You gather their requirements and begin creating their site collection from the Site Directory. Under User Permissions, you click Use Unique Permissions. What happens next?

A. A set of permission configuration check boxes and text fields appears that you can use to set the unique permissions for this site.

B. You are immediately taken to the Set Up Groups for This Site page where you can configure group permissions and then return to the site creation page and finish the steps to making the new site.

C. After you click Create, you are taken to the Set Up Groups for This Site page where you can configure group permissions for the new site.

D. After you click Create, the site is created. After it is created, you are taken to the site's main page where you click the Permissions link and configure group permissions on the Set Up Groups for This Site page.

17. You are the SharePoint administrator for your company. You want to create a new site collection using a process that will allow you to specifically select a primary and secondary site administrator. Of the following selections, which method requires this?

A. Creating a site collection in Central Administration

B. Creating a site collection using Site Actions on a top-level site

C. Creating a site collection using Site Actions on a subsite

D. Creating a site collection from the Site Directory

18. You own a consulting company that specializes in installing SharePoint Server 2007 for organizations, configuring SharePoint, and training staff on how to administer site collections. You are having your first meeting with the management team at Enceladus Enterprises and are giving them a basic explanation about SharePoint site collections. Of the following, which correctly describes the common elements in a site collection? (Choose all that apply.)

A. A shared top-level website

B. At least three subsites under the top-level site

C. A common owner for the collection

D. Shared administration settings

19. You own a consulting company that specializes in installing SharePoint Server 2007 for organizations, configuring SharePoint, and training staff on how to administer site collections. You are having your first meeting with the management team at Enceladus Enterprises and are showing them a demo site collection you have created by using your laptop to connect to it over the Internet. Currently, you are on the main portal site. You have just clicked View All Site Content and are showing them the available categories. Under the Lists category, which of the following options are available? (Choose all that apply.)

A. Contacts

B. Images

C. Pages

D. Reusable Content

20. You own a consulting company that specializes in installing SharePoint Server 2007 for organizations, configuring SharePoint, and training staff on how to administer site collections. You are having your first meeting with the management team at Enceladus Enterprises and are describing the features of My Site to your audience. Enceladus Enterprises is a vast corporation with offices in the United States, Europe, and Asia. The CTO is concerned that the vast scope of their organization will make My Site functionality too difficult to administer. What option do you offer that addresses this concern?

A. You explain that for very large companies the primary method of managing My Sites is to create a separate portal site and site collection for each major office and have My Sites administered in each local server farm.

B. You explain that you can use an Enterprise site template called My Site Host to host all personal My Sites for all employees in the enterprise.

C. You explain that you can set up a separate SQL Server database just to store all of the My Site accounts throughout the enterprise.

D. You explain that the My Site feature in SharePoint Server 2007 can host up to a million individual My Site sites and is completely able to manage their needs.

Answers to Review Questions

1. C. Prior to making any other decision, you must first define the business goals My Sites will satisfy.

2. A. Since the division managers are meeting to determine how to restructure the company and need to track those decisions, the features offered by the decision meeting workspace would best suit their needs.

3. C. A rollup portal site best fits these requirements. An application portal site is designed more for your internal and external customers and is somewhat structured. A hierarchical portal site would be inappropriate for obvious reasons, and a web presence portal site is your company's official Internet site.

4. B. A Publishing portal best fits the requirements since it is designed to be either a large-scale intranet- or Internet-facing site that publishes news and other informational items to an audience of mostly readers. It also includes elements such as a search center and home page.

5. D. You cannot set a custom storage quota for the new site collection from the Create Site Collection page. On the Quota Templates page, you must follow the procedure outlined in option D to be successful.

6. A, B, and C. The options in Quick Launch on the personal site of a My Site are My Profile, Documents, Pictures, Lists, Discussions, Surveys, and Sites.

7. A and C. Options A and C are the only valid selections in the list. Options B and D are bogus.

8. A, B, and C. You can perform all of the listed tasks except option D. To approve or reject a pending site from the Site Directory, you must click View All Site Content, click Sites under the Lists section, click next to the name of the site, and select Approve/Reject from the list.

9. D. Although a portal site can contain a great deal of information in a variety of forms, you can create filtered views for different audiences so that those audiences see only the information provided in the views targeted at them.

10. B. Option B is the only one that states the correct sequence of actions to begin enabling self-service site creation.

11. C. You can use the Enterprise site template to create a Site Directory.

12. C. Since your Publishing site is visible to everyone from the Internet, it's a good idea to test any changes you intend to make to it on an authoring site that mirrors your public site.

13. B. Since the management team needs a site very much like the one they are currently using but with expanded space, the Multipage Meeting Workspace template will satisfy their needs.

14. A. When you save a site as a template, a new site template tab called Custom is created, and all of the sites you have saved as templates will be found there.

15. D. Option D is the correct answer. All of the other procedures described in answers A, B, and C are bogus.

16. C. When you select Use Unique Permissions during site creation, you must finish configuring the site and click Create before you are taken to the Set Up Groups for This Site page, where you can set up the customized permissions.

17. A. Only when you create a site collection from Central Administration are you required to select a primary site administrator and also optionally choose a secondary site administrator.

18. A, C, and D. All of the answers in the list are correct except option B. A site collection must have one or more subsites under the top-level site. The minimum requirement is not three or more. A site collection also shares a common navigation structure.

19. A and D. Contacts and Reusable Content are found under Lists, whereas Images and Pages are found under Document Libraries.

20. B. You can use the Enterprise site template My Site Host to host all personal sites for the enterprise. Whenever a valid SharePoint user with a My Site visits the My Site Host, he or she is redirected to their own My Site personal site.

Chapter

5

Managing Users and Groups

MICROSOFT EXAM OBJECTIVES COVERED IN THIS CHAPTER

✓ **Configure Microsoft Office SharePoint Server 2007 Portal**

- Configure Site Management
- Configure Personalization
- Configure Users and Groups

If you've worked through this book from the beginning to this point, you now have a Microsoft Office SharePoint Server (MOSS) 2007 environment that includes a portal site and a few subsites. This is only the beginning of your site collection deployment and the full utilization of SharePoint's capacities, but before we continue setting up all of the features SharePoint has to offer, you need to start adding users and groups.

SharePoint Server 2007 is a terrific tool for data and service storage and for collaboration efforts, but without people, there will be no one to collaborate. Even if your ultimate goal is to create a publication site where little if any collaboration will occur, you still expect partners or customers to visit the site and access its content.

Unless you plan on developing a SharePoint site collection that will allow anonymous access to anyone who surfs in from the Internet, you will likely deploy the site so that not all content is available to all users. Although authentication and security is dealt with in more detail in Chapter 6, "Configuring Authentication and Security," how you create and configure your users and groups in SharePoint will go a long way toward determining who is served particular content and services.

The first stop on our journey through this chapter is an overview of the default user and group settings in SharePoint. Once that base is covered, you'll learn more about the issues involved in site personalization that we started to explore in Chapter 4, "Building Sites and Site Collections." We'll also learn how to actually add people to the SharePoint system, including adding users to both default and customized groups and controlling their permissions. With the system "populated," you'll learn how to create a personal My Site, set up and modify user profiles and create audiences, and then target content to those audiences based on user profiles.

SharePoint Users and Groups Overview

In a Windows Active Directory domain environment, the role of assigning users to groups and managing the access permissions for those groups has gone to the domain administrator. However, within the confines of SharePoint sites, additional permission groups are available by default.

The interaction between Active Directory and SharePoint will be covered later in this chapter and in Chapter 6, "Configuring Authentication and Security."

Default Site Permission Groups

When a site is created, three site permission groups are created by default:

Site Owner   This group has full control over all aspects of the site.

Site Members   This group can contribute and modify content on the site but cannot change access permissions.

Site Visitors   This group has read-only access to the site content.

In addition to each site having a designated owner, the entire site collection has an owner. For example, you may have 10 sites in your site collection with a different owner for each site. However, the site collection owner has full control of all the individual sites within the collection.

SharePoint Site Access Groups

SharePoint administrators, site collection owners, and site owners can use groups that allow very specific access rights to a site and then place users into those groups. That gives admins and owners the ability to assign very graduated rights to different users based on need. The available access rights include the following:

1. **Approvers**   Users assigned to this group are able to approve or reject pending documents or list items. Submitted content items are visible only to the creator and someone with Approvers rights until approved. Once approved, they become visible to both anonymous and restricted readers.

2. **Designers**   Users assigned to this group have the ability to control site performance and the "look and feel" of the site. Assign only a limited number of users to this group, such as web developers, so that only people who are authorized and have the skills to do so will be able to modify the overall site theme.

3. **Hierarchy Managers**   Users assigned to this group are able to modify the structure of a site or site collection, including moving or renaming sites.

4. **Home Members**   These users are also known as Site Members; this group has the same rights as the Site Members referenced in the previous section. They are able to contribute content to a site.

5. **Home Owners**   These users are also known as Site Owners; this group has full control rights on the site.

6. **Home Visitors**   These users are also known as Site Visitors; this group has read-only permissions on the site.

7. **Quick Deploy Users**   Users assigned to this group have the ability to quickly update content on the site when the site has different levels for creating content and then publishing that content to the site. Users in this group utilize SharePoint content deployment functionality, which is part of publishing and web content management (WCM).

8. **Restricted Readers**   Users assigned to this group have read-only permissions on the site.

Style Resource Readers   Users assigned to this group have the right to read the Master Page Gallery and have read-only permissions to the Style Gallery. By default, all authenticated users are assigned to this group.

Viewers   Users assigned to this group are restricted to viewing lists, pages, and documents in Server Rendering View.

Quick Deploy Users and WCM will be addressed more in detail in Chapter 15, "Working with Content Management."

All authenticated users should be removed from the Style Resource Readers group for security reasons. Place only those users who require these rights in this group.

In addition to the site access groups listed earlier, you can create customized access groups with unique permissions. You'll have an opportunity to create unique access groups in an exercise later in this chapter.

Personalization and Site Access Permissions

You'll recall from Chapter 4, "Building Sites and Site Collections," that personalization was defined as "customization for the individual." Let's review that topic before moving on to new territory because you'll need the information not only when we start creating My Sites but also for understanding how users access different resources in SharePoint in general.

Customization is the modification of the theme, style, branding, layout, and other visible elements of a site collection. Often the customization of your company's web presence site is different from the corporate intranet site. Partner and customer extranet site collections may also have their own, unique appearances.

Personalization is customization for the individual. Personalization allows you to make sure content published to SharePoint sites is relevant to the targeted groups of users. There are actually two different concepts in operation here—personalization and audiences.

Personalization is actually controlled by the user. Using SharePoint personalization features, users can customize their view of a site's content using filters provided by you, the administrator, so that only the content that is relevant to their needs will appear. Users have the ability to change that view using any of the available filters; if, for example, a user who works in sales wants to change their view using the filter you provided for marketing, they can do so. The user can also access the nonfiltered view and see all of the content presented on the site they have permission to see.

The audiences feature is under the control of the administrator and allows you to target different audience groups and publish information to only those groups. For example, let's say you have created audiences for sales, marketing, HR, management, and development, and you have been tasked with publishing the latest sales figures to the sales department. You can publish this information to the sales audience so that only members of that audience will be able to see that information. The audience has no control over whether they receive that information, and no other audience has the ability to access it.

Site Access Groups and Active Directory

Just a few pages back, you took a tour of SharePoint site access groups, and it seems reasonable to assume that the type of access you want a user to have to a site will depend on the access group in which you place them. If you are using MOSS 2007 in a small workgroup environment, this will be true; however, SharePoint 2007 was designed to operate in large enterprise environments using Active Directory.

Providing a detailed description of the features and services provided by Active Directory is beyond the scope of this book. This book will merely touch on Active Directory as it is relevant to SharePoint access issues. If you need to study up on Active Directory, there are many other fine books out there that will fit the bill, such as *MCSE: Windows Server 2003 Active Directory Planning, Implementation, and Maintenance Study Guide: Exam 70-294, 2nd Edition* by Robert Shimonski, James Chellis, and Anil Desai, published by Sybex.

Once a user logs onto an Active Directory (AD) domain, they have access to whatever AD objects and services their AD group has permissions to, which includes SharePoint sites. In smaller business environments, the SharePoint administrator can allow AD authenticated users specific SharePoint access rights by adding their names to a particular access group. You don't really want to use this method if you have more than a dozen users or so, because adding, removing, and moving users among SharePoint access groups one at a time is kind of boring and time-consuming.

It's better to add users to SharePoint access groups by their AD security groups rather than as individuals. This will require some coordination between the SharePoint administrator and the domain administrator so that there is a correct mapping between specific AD groups and specific SharePoint groups. However, once that gap has been bridged, the administrative cost of managing SharePoint access will be greatly reduced.

For instance, say your domain administrator has several AD security groups configured for the sales department:

- Sales Associates
- Sales Managers
- Sales Site Administrators

You could map those AD groups to SharePoint access groups, as in Table 5.1.

TABLE 5.1   AD Group to SharePoint Group Mappings

AD Security Groups	SharePoint Site Access Groups
Sales Partners $\longrightarrow$	Restricted Readers
Sales Associates $\longrightarrow$	Site Members
Sales Managers $\longrightarrow$	Approvers
Sales Site Administrators $\longrightarrow$	Site Owners

You many also elect to give the Sales Site Administrators group Designers permissions and reserve Site Owners permissions for SharePoint, web, or IT administrators for the organization.

Planning User Profiles and Profile Services

As part of implementing personalization in SharePoint, you have to plan how you will create or import information for SharePoint's *user profile database.* This database contains information, metadata, and properties for all SharePoint users. User profile information can include the following:

- Name
- Address
- Department
- Direct report
- Email address
- Employee ID Number
- Manager

Most of the time, user profile information for SharePoint users is imported from Active Directory since the user is an AD object in the domain and all of those properties are already defined. Information in the user profile database is used by SharePoint for both personalization and publishing content using audiences. In other words, you will not be able to use SharePoint's personalization and audiences features without the ability to add to and update user profiles.

User profile information can come from a number of Microsoft products and technologies besides Active Directory, such as Microsoft Exchange and Microsoft SQL Server. It can also come from industry standards for tracking people, such as Lightweight Directory Access Protocol (LDAP) as well as line-of-business applications, such as SAP. Utilizing these options allows you to bring all of the properties from these diverse data sources together to create unified and consistent user profiles across your corporation.

SharePoint Portal Server 2003 had the ability to natively import user profile data only from Active Directory. In addition to Active Directory, MOSS 2007 can natively import from the following:

- Business Data Catalog applications
- LDAP servers → *Lightweight Directory Access Protocol*
- User-defined properties

User profile information is not only necessary for the reasons previously stated but also allows for My Site functionality since My Sites is the primary platform for individual users to store and organize data and collaborate based on their user profile information stored in the user profile database. My Site allows users to maintain and update their personal profiles and display relevant information on their My Site public sites.

 NOTE User profiles are not absolutely necessary for deploying SharePoint 2007 in your organization, but they are necessary if you plan to use personalization and audiences as well as to allow users to have My Sites.

You can access user profiles and properties from the User Profiles and My Sites section of the Shared Services Administration page in SharePoint Central Administration. User profiles can be viewed by everyone else from the public profile page of each user's My Site.

 NOTE You'll see how this works in the "User Profile Properties" section later in this chapter.

Every site that uses the same shared services provider (SSP) accesses the same set of user profile properties and displays them in the site's user information list. SSP administrators can add additional properties to the user information list across all site collections that use the same SSP; however, administrators of each site collection cannot add properties to user profiles. They can add properties to the user information list for certain users, depending on their particular business needs.

The properties and data used for user profiles are managed by Profile Services. User profiles identify connections among users, and these relationships can be used to encourage more efficient collaboration with colleagues and across teams in the company. Collaboration includes the ability for users to find each other using SharePoint search to locate people by various profile items.

As previously mentioned, the User Profile properties are also used in the public page of My Site to display information about the relationships of each user to other users and content in your organization, including any documents and lists shared by each user and any policies that determine how that information is displayed and shared.

Each user's public profile contains elements that include the following data:

Documents This properties element includes all shared documents owned by a user, wherever they may be located in the site collection. The shared documents are organized on the user's My Site in tabs related to the sites where the documents are located.

Policies   As you learned in Chapter 4, "Building Sites and Site Collections" (specifically in the "Planning and Implementing My Sites" section), policies control what users are allowed to access and view in My Sites. Only administrators are able to view and edit policies, and policies can be set at the web application, site, or document level.

Private properties   Only SSP administrators can see and edit these user properties. Site collection administrators can see values of SSP-level properties in the user information list on the site collection but are unable to edit any part of the user profiles and their properties. They are only able to edit any site-level properties of user profiles.

Public properties   These are user properties that are visible on each user's public profile page on their My Site.

Good planning for user profile deployment consists of considering the best way to deploy Office SharePoint Server 2007 to effectively present all of this information. To create connections to data sources, the following information should be available:

- A list of the information sources for user profiles, including Active Directory, LDAP, SAP, and Siebel. In your list, include the location of the information, the authentication type, accounts, and any other information needed to connect Profile Services to each source.

- A list of the profile properties available from within user profiles, along with the policy setting, default access policy, and override and replication policies for each feature.

- A list of user profile properties managed by the SSP administrator and any associated policy information, including policies for features.

- A list of all the portal sites and site collections that are part of the user profile deployment.

- A list of who is planning the user information list properties for each site collection, including contact information.

- A record of user properties being configured at the site collection level vs. at the SSP level.

If the SSP administrator is planning user properties at the site collection level, record a list of properties and decide whether they are best stored in the user profile so they are available for site collections across the SSP or whether they are added later to the user information list for a site collection. The properties in user information lists in a site collection are based on replicated properties of user profiles but are not connected to user profiles. Properties added to the information list are not stored in the user profile. These properties are not imported, so you do not have to worry about planning property mappings.

Profile Services is used to connect user-profile properties data sources, such as Active Directory and LDAP, and is available from the SSP administration pages. From the Import Connections link on the User Profiles and Properties administration page in SharePoint Central Administration, you can connect directly to Active Directory or LDAP to import user profiles from those sources into SharePoint. Administrators can select the properties they desire from directory services to import to user profiles.

You can also add business data properties that contain information about users to existing user profiles by connecting to the Business Data Catalog, selecting a relevant entity from a registered business data application, and either mapping that entity to an existing profile property or adding it as a new property. These properties augment the existing profiles imported from directory services. You cannot create or import entirely new user profiles from the Business Data Catalog.

 You'll learn more about the Business Data Catalog in Chapter 12, "Using Excel Services and Business Intelligence," and in Chapter 13, "Using Business Forms and Business Intelligence."

You can import the properties from all of these sources into user profiles by connecting to the relevant service or database and mapping the unique identifier for each property in the shared service to the unique identifier of the corresponding property in the business application. These connections can be made regardless of the authentication method used by the business application.

The service maintains the connections with the relevant business applications and updates the properties of user profiles during regularly scheduled imports from all relevant data sources. Data is not exported, however, so the user profile database cannot overwrite the source databases.

Profile Services enables you to collect information about users in your organization across directory services and business applications so that consistent and timely information is always available. Information about users is synchronized across the deployment to all site collections that use the same SSP. This information can also be used by personalization features to increase the value of collaboration and relationships in your organization.

Planning Audiences

As you learned earlier, you can use the audiences features in SharePoint 2007 to target content to specific groups based on relevance. As an administrator, you can go into the Central Administration website, click the name of the relevant SSP such as SharedServices1, and under Audiences, click Audiences to access the Manage Audiences page. From there, you can create and manage up to 10,000 individual audiences for the site collection using that SSP. When planning audiences during initial deployment, you want to identify a small set of key audiences based on your evaluation of content needs, your information architecture planning, the structure of your site collections, and the users associated with each site collection.

You can use three audience types for planning:

Distribution lists and security groups   Various users in your organization have the ability to create distribution lists depending on whether you have configured policies to allow this action. This allows content to be targeted to users who are members of the particular distribution lists. The properties of distribution lists and security groups used for audiences must be imported from sources such as Microsoft Exchange Server, Active Directory services, and LDAP. When the user profile properties are imported, they include any existing distribution lists.

Global audiences   These are audiences based on the properties of the user profiles managed by the SSP administrator, and content targeted based on those properties.

SharePoint site access groups   As you've read previously in this chapter, site access groups are associated with a set of access permissions for a site or site collection. Also, in an Active Directory domain, AD security groups are mapped to site access groups so content that is targeted to a site access group is received by the members belonging to the AD security group mapped to it.

When you start planning for audiences in an initial deployment, you will record all distribution lists, SharePoint groups, and the central purpose for each site and site collection. Then, you consider how best to group all of that information to create a relatively small number of audiences that reflect the important groups within your organization based on all of these criteria.

Create specific SharePoint groups as related to the audiences to which you plan to target content. Each site collection will likely contain groups for which you will want to target content, so when planning, create customized SharePoint groups for each site and site collection that will contain specific audiences. Be sure to define each audience with a specific a set of criteria to ensure that you can accurately target the most appropriate content.

Audience planning can also identify potential improvements in planning for distribution lists, user profile properties, SharePoint groups, and reporting structure. If you want to target some users as a group and there are no existing SharePoint groups, distribution lists, or user profile properties, it is a good idea to plan for adding those groups, lists, or properties before proceeding.

Planning Audience Content Targeting

Once you create a plan for organizing and deploying specific audiences, you still need to develop methods of content targeting to avoid any irrelevant information being received by the various audiences in your site collection. You can use several methods as the basis for content targeting.

List Item or Web Part Targeting

One of the best ways to target content in site collection pages is by using the Content Query web part. The Content Query web part is provided by default for certain SharePoint template pages, such as portal site areas and team sites, and can target content in several ways:

- Displaying list items from multiple levels in the site hierarchy, which assists in better rendition of audience information

- Grouping results by options or audience, which is used to target both by web part and by list item

- Targeting particular list items to specific audiences by using the Content Query web part

My Site Navigation Bar Targeting

My Site links to personalization sites in the My Site navigation bar can be targeted to specific audiences. Links are added to the My Site navigation bar by SSP administrators. In many cases, a personalization site might be relevant for one group in your organization but not everyone. The SSP administrator can target links so they appear only for users for whom the personalized content in the site is relevant.

Trusted My Site Host Locations Targeting

In large, national, or multinational corporations, SharePoint users have access to more than one My Site host location. This occurs in a global SharePoint deployment with geographically distributed shared services. This requires that SSP administrators for each relevant SSP manage a list of Trusted My Site host locations across all SSPs in the organization. Each location must then be targeted to the user audiences who need to view those locations. Since Trusted My Site host locations are processed by priority within the list, users will see the personalized data most relevant to the My Site they are viewing at the moment. This allows personalization information to be available even when a particular SSP is not accessible at the time.

Web Part Filtering by Audience

Two web parts can be connected, and the information from the first web part can be filtered and displayed in the second web part, providing a unique view of the information based on specific properties. This data can be filtered by a number of criteria including by audience. This is part of SharePoint's Business Intelligence capacities, and it lets you target complex business analysis data to specific audiences using dashboards and sites such as the Report Center.

Web parts will be covered in Chapter 8, "Configuring Web Part Pages, Web Parts, and Web Pages," while business intelligence will be addressed in Chapter 12, "Using Excel Services and Business Intelligence," and in Chapter 13, "Using Business Forms and Business Intelligence."

Configuring Users and Groups in SharePoint

At this point, you won't be able to move forward in your work with SharePoint users and groups without actually being able to work with users and groups. You have yet to add any users to SharePoint, but you are about to get that opportunity. In the following sections of the chapter, you'll learn how to add a user to a group, how to create a new SharePoint group, how to edit the permissions of a group, and how to do related tasks.

Remember that any user you want to add to SharePoint must either be a domain user in Active Directory or, in a SharePoint stand-alone server installation, must be an authenticated user on the server.

Creating Users and Groups

Exercise 5.1 will get you started with your first users. In this exercise, you will add two users to the Home Members [Contribute] SharePoint site access group.

EXERCISE 5.1

Adding a User to a Default SharePoint Group

1. From the portal site, select Site Actions ➢ Site Settings ➢ People and Groups.

2. On the People and Groups: Home Members page, select New ➢ Add Users.

3. In the Add Users section in the Users/Groups field, type the names of the users you want to add, and then click the Check Names icon to verify their names.

4. Under Give Permission, select the Add Users to a SharePoint Group radio button, and use the drop-down list to select Home Members [Contribute], as shown here.

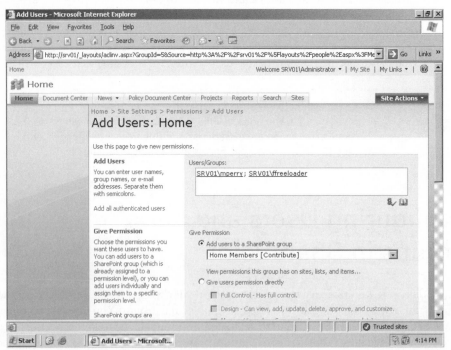

5. Under Send E-Mail, if you want to send the new members an email notifying them of their being added to this group, tick the Send Welcome E-mail to the New Users check box. If you do so, you can add a subject to the email in the Subject field and add a message in the Personal Message field.

6. Click OK.

The two new users are now added to the Home Members group. In step 4, the Home Members [Contribute] group is selected by default. If you had wanted to select a different group, you could have used the drop-down menu and made a selection from the list shown here.

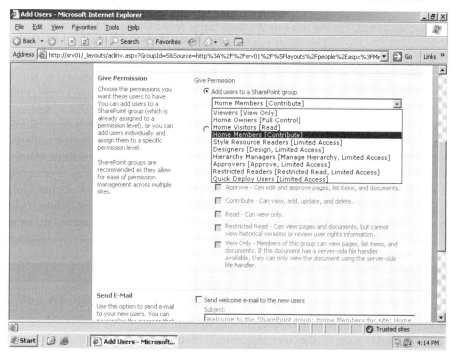

I recommend that you use the steps outlined in Exercise 5.1 to add users to several different SharePoint groups, choosing different groups using the different menu items shown earlier. That way, as you progress through the exercises, you can perform tasks as different users with different sets of permissions.

Earlier in this chapter, you learned about the default SharePoint groups available and the site access permissions each group possesses. You aren't limited to the default groups; you can create new groups with unique access permissions. Exercise 5.2 will take you through the steps of creating a new SharePoint group.

EXERCISE 5.2

Creating a New SharePoint Access Group

1. From the portal site, click Site Actions ➢ Site Settings ➢ People and Groups.

2. On the People and Groups: Home Members page, click New ➢ Add Group.

3. On the New Group page in the Name and About Me Description section, type the name of the new group in the Name field.

4. In the About Me text editor box, type a description of the new group using any of the text-editing tools to bold, italicize, or otherwise modify the text.

5. In the Owner section in the Group Owner field, either accept the default group owner (Administrator) or type the name of another SharePoint user and use the Check Names icon to verify.

6. In the Group Settings section under Who Can View the Membership of the Group, select either Group Members or Everyone.

7. Under Who Can Edit the Membership of the Group, select either Group Owner or Group Members.

8. In the Membership Requests section under Allow Requests to Join/Leave this Group, select either Yes or No. If you selected Yes, do the following:

   a. Under Auto-accept Requests, select either Yes or No.

   b. In the Send Membership Requests to the Following E-mail Address, type the email address where requests are to be sent.

9. In the Give Group Permission to This Site section, tick the check boxes for each of the permission types you want members of this group to possess.

10. Click Create.

The new group is created and ready for you to add users.

If you allow users to request membership to this group, the request will be sent to the email address specified in step 8b. If you allow auto-accept requests, users will be able to join the group at will and receive the permission levels associated with the group. Enabling this feature is highly discouraged.

Although enabling auto-accept requests is highly discouraged, you can give an individual user specific access permissions rather than adding the user to a default or customized group. Exercise 5.3 will show you how. The previous two exercises have been performed from the main portal site. This exercise will be done from a subsite.

There is no legitimate reason to give an individual user unique access rights to SharePoint sites or any other application or computer system.

EXERCISE 5.3

Giving an Individual User Unique Access Rights

1. Select Site Actions ➢ Site Settings.

2. In the Users and Permissions column, click People and Groups.

3. On the People and Groups: Home Members page, select New ➢ Add Users.

4. In the Add Users section in the Users/Groups field, type the name of the user, and click the Check Names icon to verify.

5. In the Give Permission section, select Give Users Permission Directly, and then tick the specific check boxes of the permissions you want to give the user.

6. Complete steps 5 through 7 from Exercise 5.1 to complete the email settings and give the new user unique access permissions.

The new user will now appear on the Permissions page along with the default and custom access groups listed for the site, as shown here.

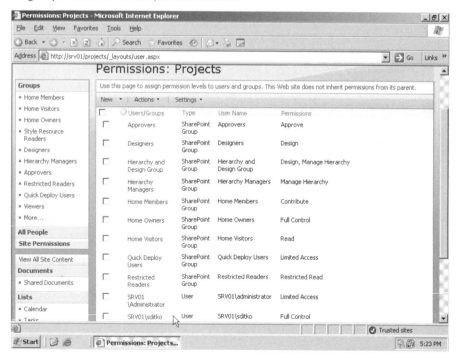

Users don't last forever in an organization. People are hired, are let go, quit, or are transferred on a regular basis. Although it's not difficult, it is important to know how to delete a user from the system. Exercise 5.4 will show you how. The action performed in this exercise is done from the portal site.

EXERCISE 5.4

Removing a User from a Group

1. Select Site Actions ➢ Site Settings ➢ People and Groups from the menu.

2. Select the specific group in the Quick Launch menu to the left, and then tick the check box by the desired user's name.

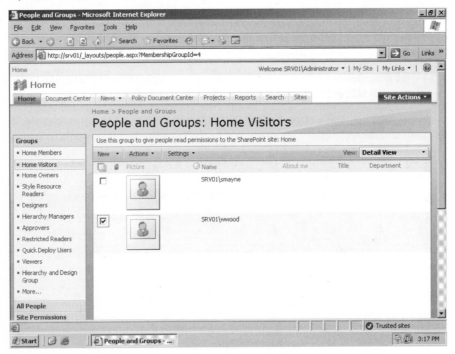

3. Click Actions ➢ Remove Users from Group.

4. When the confirmation dialog box appears, click OK.

When the page refreshes, the user's name will no longer appear in the list.

To perform this action from a subsite, click Site Action ➢ Site Settings, and in the Users and Permissions column on the Site Settings page, click People and Groups. Then follow steps 2 through 4 in the previous exercise to remove the user.

NOTE   There is no direct way to simply transfer a user from one group to another. If you need to perform such an action, you must remove them from one group, as in Exercise 5.4, and then add them to another group, as in Exercise 5.1.

You can modify either a default or custom-made group in SharePoint in a number of ways, and the next few exercises will show you those methods. Exercise 5.5 will show you how to modify a group's settings. This exercise will be done from a subsite, but the steps are the same if you perform them from the portal site.

EXERCISE 5.5

Changing a Group's Settings

1. Select Site Actions ➤ Site Settings.

2. In the Users and Permissions column, click People and Groups.

3. On the People and Groups page, click the name of the desired group from the Quick Launch menu, and then click Settings.

4. From the menu, click Group Settings.

5. On the Change Group Settings page, you can modify any of the settings you saw in steps 3 through 9 in Exercise 5.2 when you created a new SharePoint access group.

6. When you are done, click OK to save your changes.

You could also click Cancel to close the page without saving your changes or click Delete to delete the access group. (You would have to click OK when the confirmation dialog box appeared.)

If you plan on deleting an access group, make sure you have removed all the members first unless the members no longer need access to the site or belong to another site access group.

You can view but not edit a group's permissions by clicking Settings on the People and Groups page and then clicking View Group Permissions. This opens in a separate browser window. Just click OK when you're done and want to close the window.

The Groups Quick Launch menu can also be edited so that groups not currently appearing will display in the list or so that groups you don't want to appear will not be displayed. Find out how this works in Exercise 5.6.

EXERCISE 5.6

Editing the Group Quick Launch List

1. Select Site Actions ➤ Site Settings.

2. In the Users and Permissions column, click People and Groups.

3. On the People and Groups page, click Settings, and then click Edit Group Quick Launch.

4. On the Edit Group Quick Launch page in the Groups field, type one or more group names in the field, separated by semicolons, and then click the Check Names icon.

5. Click OK to finish.

You could also click the Browse icon and browse to and select the name of a group. The group must have already been created on the system in order for you to successfully perform this exercise. Also, to delete a group name, simply highlight the name, and press the Delete button on your keyboard.

You can add new groups to any site in the site collection directly from the People and Groups page. Exercise 5.7 outlines the steps.

EXERCISE 5.7

Setting Up a New Group for a Site

1. Click Site Actions ➤ Site Settings.

2. In the Users and Permissions column, click People and Groups.

3. On the People and Groups page, click Settings, and then click Set Up Groups.

4. On the Set Up Groups for This Site page under Visitors to This Site, select Use an Existing Group and accept the default of Home Visitors, or use the drop-down menu to select a different group.

5. Make the same selections under both Members of This Site and Owners of This Site.

6. Click OK to finish.

In any of those sections, you can also select Create a New Group instead of Use an Existing Group and then name and populate the new group for the site, as shown here.

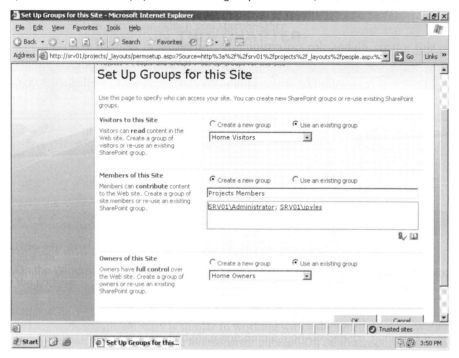

On the People and Groups page, you can click Actions, and then either click E-Mail Users or click Call/Message Selected Users to perform those actions. In the former case, the user must be associated with an email address; in the latter case, the user must be associated with an Session Initiation Protocol (SIP) address. If those aren't detected by the system when you attempt the actions, you will receive an error message. You must also select one or more users by ticking the check boxes by their names before you initiate either action.

You can view users on the People and Groups page in either Detail View or List View. So far, you've seen the page in Detail View. To change to List View, click the View button on the right side of the toolbar, and select the desired view. Figure 5.1 shows you the People and Groups page in List View.

FIGURE 5.1 The People and Groups page in List View

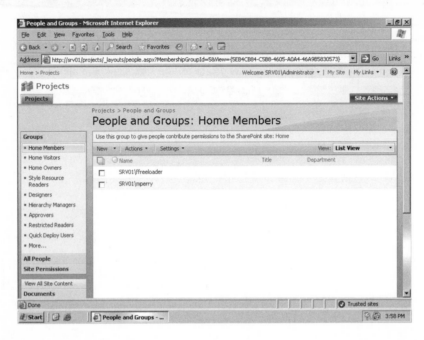

Also on this page, in the Quick Launch menu, you can click All People to view a list of all users on the site regardless of the group they belong to, and you can click Site Permissions to view a list of the site access groups associated with this site.

 Real World Scenario

Adding a User to a Group

Mindy is a new employee with the Tethys Financial Group. She has been hired as a web developer to design and deploy a new "look and feel" to the corporation's public and private websites including the company intranet, the extranet used by premium clients, and the public Internet site. You, as the SharePoint administrator for Tethys, have been tasked with adding her to the most appropriate site access group that will allow her to perform her job.

You determine that she needs to be added to the Designers group since users assigned to that group have the ability to control site performance and the look and feel of the site. You can add Mindy to the Designers group from the portal site by selecting Site Actions ➢ Site Settings and clicking People and Groups. From there, you can select the correct group and add her name to that group. You must be sure she is an authenticated user on the domain before you can complete this task.

Configuring User Profiles and My Sites

Now that you have a grasp of how to set up users and groups in SharePoint, it's time to move on and create the first My Site. Since My Sites are enabled by default, anytime a user wants to create their My Site, all they have to do is click the My Site link from the home page of a Share-Point site. The process can take a few minutes, but once it's done, you'll be taken to your My Site page on the My Home tab, as shown in Figure 5.2. Once there, under Get Started with My Site, you can perform a number of configuration tasks.

FIGURE 5.2   Your first look at My Site

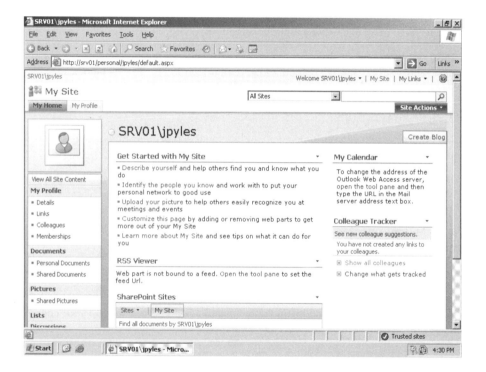

Setting Up a My Site

As you'll recall, user profile information can be imported into SharePoint from a variety of sources including Active Directory and LDAP. Since our working model of SharePoint Server 2007 is installed on a stand-alone server that does not belong to a domain, user profile data will need to be entered manually, as shown in Exercise 5.8.

EXERCISE 5.8

Describing Yourself to My Site

1. On your My Site page on the My Home tab, Under Get Started with My Site click Describe Yourself.

2. On the Edit Details page in the About Me text editor, type a brief description of yourself that will be meaningful to visitors.

3. Under Picture, click Choose Picture if you want to browse to and upload a photograph of yourself that will be displayed in your My Site.

4. In the Responsibilities field, type the projects you are or have been responsible for, your job description, and any other similar information.

5. In the Skills field, type any of your relevant skills such as programming languages, web design, and so on, that have helped you in meeting your job responsibilities.

6. In the Past Projects field, list any previous projects you've been responsible for or you've worked on.

7. Under Interests, you can optionally list any personal and professional activities and hobbies you are involved in.

8. In the Schools field, list any educational institutions you've attended.

9. Under Birthday, you can type your birth date in the available field.

10. In the Assistant field, you can type the name of your assistant (if any) and click Check Names to verify the name.

11. In the Mobile Phone, Fax, and Home Phone fields, you can choose to enter the relevant numbers in those fields.

12. Scroll back to the top of the page, and either click Save and Close to save your changes or click Cancel and Go Back to disregard your changes.

There are actually a number of other options beyond what the steps in Exercise 5.8 state. There's a Show To column toward the right of the Edit Details page that indicates who will be able to view each item you are configuring. The following items are able to be viewed by Everyone by default, and that view cannot be changed:

- Name
- About Me
- Picture
- Responsibilities
- Assistant
- Account Name

You can choose who can view the remainder of the items. Your choices are as follows:

- Only Me
- My Manager
- My Workgroup
- My Colleagues
- Everyone

The default value for all of those items except for Mobile Phone and Home Phone is Everyone. The default value for Mobile Phone and Home Phone is My Colleagues. You can see an example of these settings in Figure 5.3.

FIGURE 5.3   The Edit Details page

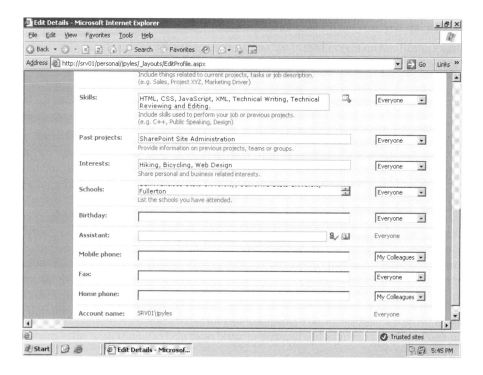

Back on your My Site page on the My Home tab, if you click Upload Your Picture, you will be taken to the Edit Details page you configured in Exercise 5.8 and will be able to upload a picture of yourself, as described in step 3 of that exercise.

Now that you've configured your new My Site with information about yourself, it's time to move on to the next task, which is to tell My Site about the people you work with. Remember, your My Site isn't just an area where you can collect all of the documents and lists relevant to you. It's also an area where you can collaborate with others. Exercise 5.9 will get you started.

EXERCISE 5.9

Identifying People You Work with in My Site

1. On your My Site page on the My Home tab, Under Get Started with My Site click Identify the People You Know.

2. On the My Colleagues page, click Add Colleagues.

3. On the Add Colleagues page, under Identify Colleagues in the Type Names field type the names of any colleagues you want to add, using a semicolon to separate the names, and then click the Check Names icon.

4. Under Privacy and Grouping, use the Show These Colleagues To drop-down menu to choose who will be able to see your Colleagues list. Your choices are as follows:

   Only Me

   My Manager

   My Workgroup

   My Colleagues

   Everyone

5. Select Yes under Add Colleagues to My Workgroup.

6. Under Grouping, either select Existing Group and accept the default option of General or click New Group and use the available field to give your new group a name, as shown here.

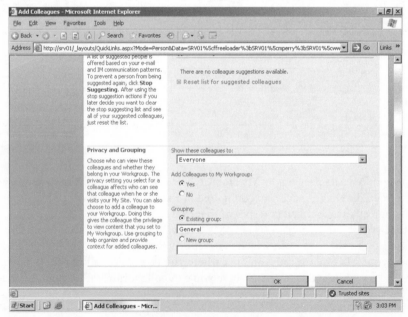

EXERCISE 5.9 *(continued)*

If you select Existing Group, the default options in the drop-down menu are General and Peers.

7. Click OK.

On the Add Colleagues page just below the Type Names field, you'll find the Suggested Colleagues list. This is a list of people who are most likely to be colleagues based on your email and instant messaging (IM) communication patterns. If you want the system to stop presenting a person as a suggested colleague, click Stop Suggesting by their name. To clear the Stop Suggesting list, click Reset list for suggested colleagues. If you have not received any email or IM messages, this area is likely to contain no names at all.

> You will not be able to add even authenticated SharePoint users to your Colleagues list if their names are not located in the user profile store. You will learn more about working with user profiles later in this chapter.

Navigating the My Home Tab

Clicking Customize on this page will open the page in Edit mode and allow you to add or modify the web parts and other elements on the page.

> You'll learn more about working with web parts and web part pages in Chapter 8, "Configuring Web Part Pages, Web Parts, and Web Pages."

Clicking Learn More About My Site opens the My Site help file in a separate browser window, as you can see in Figure 5.4.

Below the Get Started with My Site section is the RSS Viewer web part, which allows you to display an RSS feed on your My Home page. Beneath the RSS Viewer, you will find the SharePoint Sites web part, which displays links to any sites you want, and the Documents web part, which contains links to all of your documents.

Also on the page are the My Calendar web part and the Colleague Tracker web part.

On the left side of the page, Quick Launch displays the following options:

- My Profile
- Documents
- Pictures
- Lists
- Discussions
- Surveys
- Sites
- Recycle Bin

FIGURE 5.4   My Site Help File

Under My Profile, you'll find links for the following:

- Details
- Links
- Colleagues
- Memberships

Under Documents, you'll find links for Personal and Shared Documents.

When you click the My Profile tab, you can see all of the information you set up about yourself in Exercise 5.8. Much of the same information is available on your My Home tab; however, you can use the As Seen By menu near the upper-right corner of the page to determine which audience type can view which information on your public My Profile site:

- My Manager
- My Workgroup
- My Colleagues
- Everyone

Under Details on this page, anyone visiting can click the links representing your responsibilities, skills, and other profile items, which will take them to the Search Center where a list of other users who have that particularly quality in common with you will be displayed. Figure 5.5 shows how anyone can conduct a search from your My Profile page of all sites, of your My Site, or of people.

The view of a person's My Site is decidedly different depending on whether they are on their own My Site or someone else's. Figure 5.6 shows you an example of what it's like to visit someone else's My Site. In this case, user jpyles is visiting the My Site of user sditko.

FIGURE 5.5 Searching from the My Profile tab

FIGURE 5.6 Visiting another user's My Site

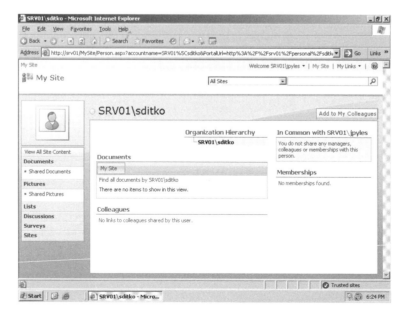

User Profile Properties

As you saw in Exercise 5.8, you can configure a number of standard user properties for your My Site including Responsibilities, Skills, Past Projects, and so on. However, the user profile store is not actually located in the My Site as such but in the SSP for the site collection. You can access the SSPs for your server farm from the SharePoint Central Administration web application and from there add user profiles, add user profile properties, and perform many other activities related to personalization and audiences.

We'll get started by adding a user profile to the user profile store for an SSP in Central Administration. Although you can be logged on as a SharePoint end user to create and configure your My Site, you must be logged in as someone with administrator rights to access Central Administration. Exercise 5.10 will get you started in this role by showing you how to add a user profile. This will seem similar to Exercise 5.8 where you, as the user, added your user profile property information in your My Site; however, the options available in Central Administration are expanded.

If you don't recall how to launch the Central Administration website, refer to Exercise 3.1 in Chapter 3.

EXERCISE 5.10

Adding a User Profile in Central Administration

1. Launch the SharePoint Central Administration website.

2. In Quick Launch, under Shared Services Administration click the name of the relevant SSP (which in this example is SharedServices1).

3. On the SharedServices1 home page in the User Profiles and My Sites column, click User Profiles and Properties.

4. On the User Profiles and Properties page, click Add User Profile. (You may have to scroll down depending on your screen resolution.)

5. On the Add User Profile page, type the user's account name in the Account Name field (the red asterisk next to the field indicates it's a required field), and then click the Check Names icon.

6. Add the appropriate user information in the First Name and Last Name fields, and then add the user's first and last name in the Name field.

7. Populate the Work Phone, Office (location), Department, and Title Required fields with the appropriate information for this user.

8. Type the account name of the user's supervisor in the Manager field, and then click the Check Names icon.

9. Type a brief description of the user in the About Me text editor using the desired text-editing tools.

10. Populate the Personal Site, Picture, Web Site, and Public Site Redirect fields with the appropriate URLs for each site or item.

11. If the user has a "dotted-line" manager or reports to a supervisor outside the usual chain of command, type that person's name in the Dotted-Line Manager field, and then click the Check Names icon.

12. Populate the Responsibilities, Skills, Past Projects, Interests, and Schools fields with the information appropriate to this user, as you did in Exercise 5.8, steps 4 through 8.

13. If this user will be accessing IM as part of their job duties, type their SIP address in the SIP Address field, and then populate the Birthday field.

14. To update this profile to the user's My Site, tick the My Site Upgrade check box.

15. Add any SharePoint user names you don't want to be suggested as potential colleagues on the user's My Site to the Don't Suggest List field, with the names separated by semicolons.

16. If appropriate, populate the Proxy addresses field with the relevant URLs.

17. Use the calendars next to the Hire Date and Last Colleague Added fields to add the correct values to those fields.

18. If the user accesses Outlook Web Access, add the correct URL to the Outlook Web Access URL field.

19. If the user has an assistant, type that person's name in the Assistant field, and then click the Check Names icon.

20. Add the user's email address to the required Work E-mail field.

21. Correctly populate the Mobile Phone, Fax, and Home Phone fields, as appropriate.

22. When finished, scroll to the top of the page, and click Save and Close.

As in Exercise 5.8, a number of these properties are visible to the Everyone group by default, and that selection cannot be changed. You can control who views the following properties:

- Skills
- Past Projects
- Interests
- Schools
- Birthday

- Hire Date
- Mobile Phone
- Fax
- Home Phone

The default values for those views are Everyone except for Mobile Phone and Home Phone. The default values for those two properties are My Colleagues.

Once you click Save and Close, you are taken back to the User Profiles and Properties page. To see the new user profile you just created along with the other profiles in this SSP's user profile store, click View User Profiles. As in Figure 5.7, you will be shown all of the user profiles created either here or in a user My Site. You can view profiles by account name here and search for users by account name, preferred name, or email address using the Find Users Whose drop-down menu and the Starts With field and then clicking Find.

FIGURE 5.7 View User Profiles page

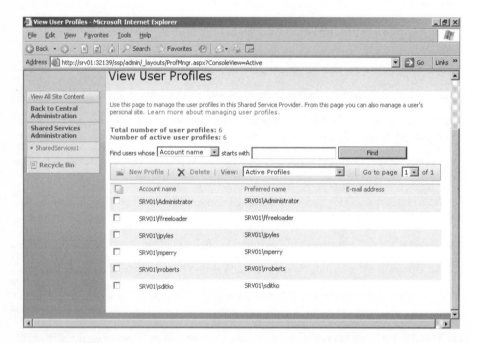

As you can see, you can tick the check boxes by user profile names and then click Delete to delete the accounts. You can also click New Profile to add a new user profile from here or use the View drop-down menu to view either Active Profiles or Profiles Missing from Import. Clicking Learn More About Managing User Profiles will open the Configure Profile Properties help file in a separate browser window. Click to the right of any name on this page to open a menu that will let you either edit or delete the profile or manage the user's personal site.

As you saw in Exercise 5.10, when you add a user role in Central Administration, a number of default user profile properties are available. If those properties are not sufficient for your needs, it's always possible to add more properties and configure them to access a wide variety of data types. Exercise 5.11 will show you how.

EXERCISE 5.11

Adding a User Profile Property

1. Launch the SharePoint Central Administration website.

2. In Quick Launch, under Shared Services Administration, click the name of the relevant SSP (which in this example is SharedServices1).

3. On the SharedServices1 home page in the User Profiles and My Sites column, click User Profiles and Properties.

4. On the User Profiles and Properties page, scroll down to the User Profile Properties section, and click Add Profile Property.

5. On the Add User Profile Property page, under Property Settings type the name of the new user profile property in the Name field, and then type the name you want displayed for this property in the Display Name field.

6. If you want to add a language that this property will be displayed in besides the default English language, click the Edit Languages button, and then click Add Language.

7. Accept the default string value in the Type drop-down menu. If you don't accept the default value of string, you can choose from the following options:

    big integer

    binary

    boolean

    date

    date no year

    date time

    E-mail

    float

    HTML

    integer

    person

EXERCISE 5.11 *(continued)*

string

unique identifier

URL

8. In the Length field, accept the default value of 25.

9. To allow multiple values to be added in the new property, tick the Allow Multiple Values check box, and when the Multivalue Separator drop-down menu appears, select the separator type (commas or semicolons) you want to use.

10. To allow a choice list for this new property, tick the Allow Choice List check box.

11. Under User Description in the Description field, type a description of this user property, and if you desire, click the Edit Languages button as you did in step 6.

12. Under Policy Settings, use the Policy Setting drop-down menu to select either Optional, Required, or Disabled.

13. Use the Default Privacy Setting drop-down menu to select the audience to whom you want the property to apply.

14. If you want users to have the ability to override the policy settings, tick the User Can Override check box.

15. Tick the Replicable check box if you want the property to display in the user info list for all sites. (This selection may not be available in a stand-alone server deployment.)

16. Under Edit Settings, select either Allow Users to Edit Values for This Property or Do Not Allow Users to Edit Values for this Property.

17. Under Display Settings, tick the Show in the Profile Properties Section of the User's Profile Page check box if you want the property displayed on the My Site profile page. (This selection may not be available in a stand-alone server deployment.)

18. Accept the default value of 10 in the Maximum Number of Values to Show Before Displaying Ellipsis drop-down menu.

19. Tick the Show on the Edit Details Page or the Show Changes in the Colleague Tracker Web Part check boxes to enable either of these features.

20. Under Search Settings, tick the Alias check box if you want the property to be considered equivalent to the username and account name when searching for items authored by a user. (This option may not be available if search is not configured.)

21. Tick the Indexed check box if you want the property to be crawled by the search engine and become part of the People search scope schema (recommended when the property is relevant to searches for people).

22. Under Property Import Mapping, use the Source Data Connection drop-down menu to select the field to map to this property when importing user profile data. (If there are no available sources, the only choice in the list will be Master Connection.)

23. Click OK.

After you click OK, you are taken back to the User Profiles and Properties page. Now when you add a user profile, as in Exercise 5.10, you will see the property you just added at the bottom of the page.

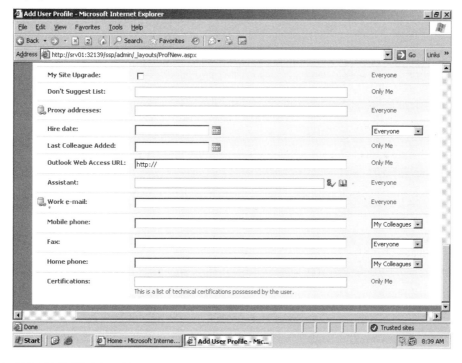

As you can tell, creating individual user profiles as you did in Exercise 5.10 can be a tedious task and would be totally impractical if you needed to accommodate hundreds or thousands of users. In any environment that contains more than a handful of users, it's much easier to import profiles from another source such as Active Directory or LDAP. Using Central Administration, you can not only configure a source for importing profiles but you can also create a schedule so that the process occurs automatically. Exercise 5.12 takes you through all the steps.

Exercise 5.12 assumes the source will be Active Directory. The steps will be slightly different depending on the actual connection type you choose.

EXERCISE 5.12

Automating User Profile Importing

Creating a New Connection

1. Launch the SharePoint Central Administration website.

2. In Quick Launch, under Shared Services Administration, click the name of the relevant SSP (which in this example is SharedServices1).

3. On the SharedServices1 home page in the User Profiles and My Sites column, click User Profiles and Properties.

4. On the User Profiles and Properties page, under Profile and Import Settings next to Import Source, click Specify Source.

5. On the Configure Profile Import page under Source, click View Import Connections.

6. On the View Import Connections page, click Create New Connection.

7. On the Add Connection page under Connection Settings, use the Type drop-down menu to select the type of connection, in this case Active Directory.

8. Type the domain name in the Domain Name field, and then select Auto Discover Domain Controller.

9. In the Port field, type the port number; if you are using SSL, tick the Use SSL-Secured Connection check box.

10. Accept the value of 120 in the Time Out (In Seconds) field, and allow the Enable Server Side Incremental check box to remain clear.

11. Type the distinguished name in the Username Attribute field (unless this feature is unavailable).

12. Under Search Settings you can click the Auto Fill Root Search Base button or type the distinguished name of the directory node in the Search Base field.

13. You can use the User Filter field to add new query clauses to the LDAP query that filters the user profiles that are imported.

14. Next to Scope, select either One Level or Subtree, and then accept the default value of 10 in the Page Size (In Number of Users) field and the default value of 120 in the Page Time Out (In Seconds) field.

EXERCISE 5.12 *(continued)*

15. Under Authentication Information, either select Use Default Account or select Specify Account, and then type the account name of someone with administrator rights to the domain controller in the Account Name field. (If you are using the default account, the Password and Confirm Password fields will already be populated.)

16. Click OK to create the connection.

Configuring the Import Schedule

1. On the Configure Profile Import page under Default Access Account, accept the default Use Default Content Access Account selection, and move to the next section.

2. Under Full Import Schedule, tick the Schedule Full Import check box, and then from the Start At drop-down menu select a time of day for the full import to begin.

3. Select either Every Day or Every Week On; if you select Every Week On, select a specific day of the week. (You can also select Every Month on This Date and then use the drop-down menu to choose a particular day of the month, such as 1, 2, 3, and so on.)

4. Under Incremental Import Schedule, use the same options to either schedule incremental imports every day at a certain time or specify a day in the week or a date in the month.

5. Click OK to finish.

On the User Profiles and Properties page under Profile and Import Settings, you can also click the links next to Import Schedule (Full) or Import Schedule (Incremental) to change those importing schedules. In the same section, click the link next to Last Import Errors to view the import errors log.

Editing User Profile Policies

As you read earlier in this chapter, planning and applying policies to site personalization is important if you as the administrator want to control what people can see and do relative to My Sites. Each user profile property has a policy available to be configured. As you can see, policies can be set as optional and disabled. Exercise 5.13 will show you how to edit a policy for one user profile property in Central Administration. This exercise assumes you are still logged into Central Administration as an administrator and you are on the Shared Services Administration: SharedServices1 home page.

EXERCISE 5.13

Editing a User Profile Property Policy

1. On the Shared Services Administration home page for the relevant SSP, in the User Profiles and My Sites column click Profile Services Policies.

EXERCISE 5.13 *(continued)*

---

2. On the Manage Policy page, click to the right of the user profile property you want, such as Links on My Site, and select Edit Policy.

3. Use the Policy Setting drop-down menu to select Enabled or Disabled.

4. Use the Default Privacy Setting drop-down menu to select the default audience who can view this setting.

5. If you want the My Site user to be able to override the default setting, tick the User Can Override check box.

6. Click OK.

Depending on the property you select, the options available for you to configure may be different. For example, if you select the Manager property, the Name option, Display Name option, Edit Languages button, Type option, and Policy Settings option appear on the page, but only the Display Name option and the Replicable check box are available to be configured.

 Tick the Replicable check box to replicate properties. For this to be effective, the default privacy must be set to Everyone and the User Can Override check box must not be selected.

Configuring Global My Site Settings

So far, your experience with the My Site feature has been based on the default SharePoint Server settings for this feature. You can alter these settings to cause My Sites to appear and operate differently. Exercise 5.14 will get you started configuring My Site settings. This exercise assumes you are still logged into Central Administration as an administrator and you are on the Shared Services Administration: SharedServices1 home page.

EXERCISE 5.14

Configuring My Site Settings

1. On the Shared Services Administration home page for the relevant SSP, in the User Profiles and My Sites column click My Site Settings.

2. On the My Site Settings page under Preferred Search Center, accept the default URL in the Preferred Search Center field.

3. Under Personal Site Services, accept the default URL in the Personal Site Provider field.

4. Under Personal Site Location, accept the default name of the location where personal My Sites are created in the Location field.

5. Under Site Naming Format, select either User Name (Do Not Resolve Conflicts), User Name (Resolve Conflicts By Using domain_username), or Domain and User Name (Will Not Have Conflicts) to choose the format to use to name new personal sites. User Name (Do Not Resolve Conflicts) is the default.

6. Under Language Options, tick the Allow User to Choose the Language of Their Personal Site check box if you want My Site users to have this ability (desirable for multinational companies).

7. Under Multiple Deployments, tick the Enable My Site to Support Global Deployments check box if you want to allow users whose My Site is hosted by a different Shared Service Provider to perform actions such as adding colleagues and links to their default My Site.

8. Under Default Reader Site Group, accept the default name of this group in the available field, and click OK.

As you'll recall from earlier in this chapter, if you allow My Sites functionality in a large enterprise environment using multiple SSPs, multiple My Site deployments can exist in the same environment, allowing specific users to have their My Site hosted by a different shared services provider. This is common with global deployments. When a user's My Site is hosted by a shared services provider other than this one, that user will be blocked from using My Site–related personalization features provided by this shared services provider.

Enabling My Site to support global deployments will allow a user whose My Site is hosted by a different shared services provider to perform all of the normal functions on their My Site such as adding links and My Colleagues. To associate specific users with different shared services providers, use the Trusted My Site hosts list.

It's important that you implement profile replication before enabling My Site to support global deployments. Without profile replication in place, users who have their My Site hosted on a different shared services provider than this one will have a disconnected user experience.

Earlier in this chapter you learned that in a global SharePoint deployment with geographically distributed shared services, SSP administrators for each relevant SSP need to manage a list of trusted My Site host locations across all SSPs in the organization. Each location must then be targeted to the user audiences who need to view those locations. Exercise 5.15 will show you how this is done. This exercise assumes you are still logged into Central Administration as an administrator and you are on the Shared Services Administration: SharedServices1 home page.

EXERCISE 5.15

Adding Trusted My Site Host Locations

1. On the Shared Services Administration home page for the relevant SSP, in the User Profiles and My Sites column click Trusted My Site Host Locations.

2. On the Trusted My Site Host Locations page, click New, and then click New Item.

3. Under URL in the Type the Web Address field, enter the URL of the site you want to add to this list, and then type an optional description in the Type the Description field.

4. In the Target Audiences field, type the name of the audience you want to target, and click the Check Names icon.

5. Click OK to finish adding the site to the Trusted My Site Host Locations list.

You can click the New button on the toolbar as in step 2 and also create a new folder and then collect lists of trusted sites by category using different folders. Clicking Actions on the toolbar lets you choose menu options such as Edit in Datasheet, Change Order, Export to Spreadsheet, View RSS Feed, and Alert Me. Clicking Settings on the toolbar lets you select the menu items Create Column, Create View, and List Settings.

 The default columns on the Trusted My Site Host Locations page are Edit, URL, Type, and Target Audiences.

You can click the button next to View to change the filter you want to use to view links on this page.

On the Shared Services Administration home page, you can also click Personalization Site Links and use the same process you saw in the previous exercise to add personalization site navigation links to the My Site horizontal navigation bar. Click Published Links to Office Client Applications to publish links to SharePoint sites and lists when opening and saving documents from Office client applications using the same process you just performed in the prior exercise.

Managing Audiences

Earlier you learned that you can target specific information to individual audiences. There is only one default audience in SharePoint (All Site Users); however, you can create and manage as many audiences as you need. Exercise 5.16 will get you started creating your first audience. This exercise assumes you are still logged into Central Administration as an administrator and you are on the Shared Services Administration: SharedServices1 home page.

EXERCISE 5.16

Creating a New Audience

1. On the Shared Services Administration home page for the relevant SSP in the Audiences column, click Audiences.

2. On the Manage Audiences page, click Create Audience, as shown here.

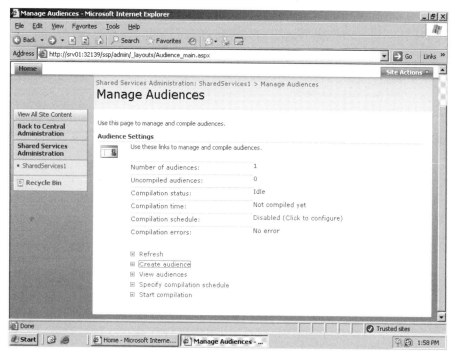

3. On the Create Audience page in the Name field, type the name of the audience.

4. In the Description field, type a brief, optional description of the audience.

5. In the Owner field, type the name of the user you want to own this audience, and then click the Check Names icon.

6. Under Include Users Who, select either Satisfy All of the Rules or Satisfy Any of the Rules.

7. Click OK to create the audience.

The audience has been created, but as you know if you completed step 7, the rules for the audience haven't been defined yet. After you completed step 7 in the previous exercise, you were taken to the Add Audience Rule page for this audience. Exercise 5.17 will pick up where Exercise 5.16 left off.

EXERCISE 5.17

Adding an Audience Rule

1. Under Operand, select either User or Property, depending on which you want the rule to apply.

2. If you selected Property, use the drop-down menu to select the specific user profile property to which the rule will apply.

3. Under Operator, use the Operator drop-down menu to select for the rule. If you selected Property in step 2, the options are Contains and Not Contains; if you selected User, the options are Reports Under or Member Of.

4. Under Value, type a relevant selection in the Value field.

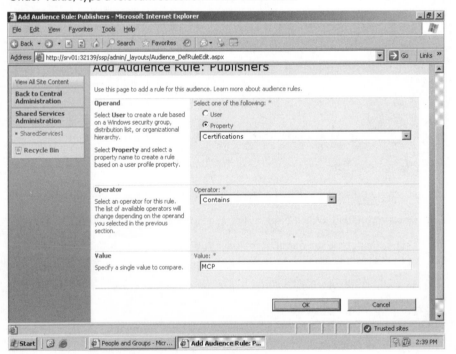

EXERCISE 5.17 *(continued)*

5. Click OK.

After you click OK in step 5, you are taken to the View Audience Properties page where you can see the new rule displayed under Audience Rules at the bottom of the page. To complete the job, click Compile Audience on the same page. You'll notice that the values for Create Time, Update Time, Compiled, Last Compilation, and Compilation Errors have been updated.

On the Manage Audiences page, you can click Specify Compilation Schedule and set up a schedule to automate audience compiling in the same way you set up schedules for importing user profiles in Exercise 5.12.

Configuring Audience Targeting

Now that you have created an audience and added an audience rule, it's time to benefit from your labors and send a targeted message to the audience.

 Even if you have a lot of experience administering SharePoint Portal Server 2003 including audience targeting, the process is quite different in SharePoint Server 2007.

In MOSS 2007, audience targeting is enabled at the library or list level; that is, if you want to target a particular document to an audience, you do so in a Document Library. Once audience targeting is enabled, you can use various web parts, including the Content Query web part, to display the content to the audience in question. Exercise 5.18 will show you the first part of this process. To follow along, you'll need to be on the portal site and logged in as an administrator.

EXERCISE 5.18

Enabling Audience Targeting in a Library

1. On the portal page, click View All Site Content in Quick Launch.

2. On the All Site Content page under Document Libraries, click Documents.

3. On the Documents page, click Settings, and then click Document Library Settings.

4. On the Customize Documents page, under General Settings click Audience Targeting Settings.

5. On the Modify List Audience Targeting Settings page, tick the Enable Audience Targeting check box, and then click OK.

6. On the Customize Documents page, click the Documents link to return to the Documents library.

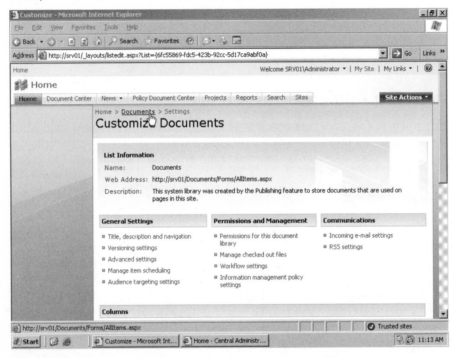

7. On the Documents page, click to the right of the document you want to use, and select Edit Properties from the list.

8. On the document's Edit Properties page, in the Title field, give a title to the document. (The required Name field should already be populated with the document's name.)

9. Next to the Target Audiences field, click the Browse button to browse for the desired audience.

10. Double-click the name of the desired audience to add it to the Add field, and click OK. The Find drop-down menu is set to look in Global Audiences by default. You can also click the drop-down arrow and select either Distribution/Security Groups or SharePoint Groups.

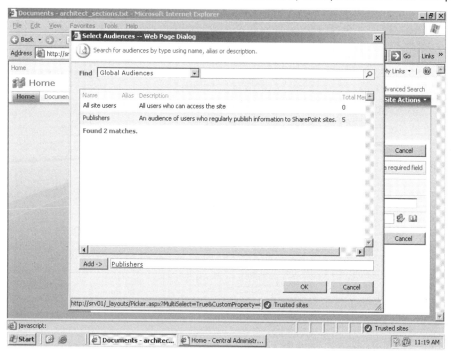

11. After the name of the audience is added to the Target Audiences field on the Edit Properties page, click OK.

Although the targeted item is visible to all users, only the targeted audience will be able to access the modified document.

The next part of the process is adding a Content Query web part to the appropriate page and then selecting the item configured in Exercise 5.18 so that when members of that audience visit the page with the Content Query web part, they will see the content targeted to them. Exercise 5.19 will show you how this works. You will need to be logged in as an administrator and on the portal page.

EXERCISE 5.19

Displaying Targeted Items in a Web Part

1. On the portal page, click Site Actions, and then click Edit Page.

2. Select a web part zone such as Right Zone, and click Add a Web Part.

3. Tick the check box next to Content Query Web Part (it should be at the top of the Suggested Web Parts for Right Zone list), and then click Add.

4. Click the Edit button to the right of the web part name. When the Content Query tool part appears, click Query.

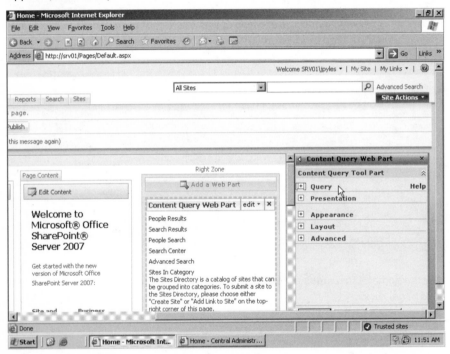

5. In the Query section under Source, select the Show Items from the Following List radio button.

6. Click the Browse button next to Show Items from the Following List, and browse to the desired content.

7. In the Select List or Library dialog box, select the document library you configured in Exercise 5.18.

8. In the Audience Targeting section, tick the Apply Audience Filtering check box to display these items to the audience you specified in the Exercise 5.18, and then click OK.

EXERCISE 5.19 *(continued)*

9. Check in the version of the page you are editing by selecting Page ➤ Check in. (This will allow your changes to be saved and others to view those changes.)

10. On the Check In page, select Major Version (Publish), and then click OK.

To verify that the process is working correctly, click to the right of the administrator's name near the top of the page, and select Sign in as Different User, then log in as a member of the target audience. You should see the document targeted for your audience in the Content Query web part.

The Content Query web part isn't the only web part you can target to an audience. In fact, you can configure any web part for audiences. Exercise 5.20, the final exercise in this chapter, will walk you through the process.

EXERCISE 5.20

Targeting a Web Part to an Audience

1. Click the drop-down arrow to the right of the web part's name, and select Modify Shared Web Part.

2. In the web part's tool part, expand Advanced, scroll to the bottom, and click the Browse button.

3. Double-click the name of the desired audience to add them to the Add field, and then click OK.

4. Click OK in the tool part to save your changes.

5. Check in the web page to save your changes, as described in steps 9 and 10 of Exercise 5.19.

Summary

In this chapter, you learned a great deal about SharePoint users and groups including the following:

- Default site groups and site access groups and their permissions
- Planning for user profiles including importing profiles from outside sources such as Active Directory
- Planning audiences including targeting content to audiences
- Creating groups, adding users to groups, and modifying different group properties

- Creating and configuring a My Site
- Creating and modifying user properties including how to add a new property
- Configuring global My Site settings and audience targeting

Exam Essentials

Be familiar with site groups and site access groups.   An important part of managing Share-Point users is being familiar with the default site groups and site access groups, including which groups have which default permissions, how to modify permissions, and how to allow and deny users access to site content.

Understand user profiles and profile services.   As you've seen, the ability to understand and manipulate different aspects of user profiles in SharePoint is the key to providing personalization and audience services in this environment. You must understand how to plan for and deploy user profiles including importing profiles from sources such as Active Directory and LDAP.

Know how to work with audiences and content targeting.   Even after you've acquired an understanding of the role of user profiles in SharePoint, developing and managing audiences and audience content targeting is still a complex issue. You must know how to create and configure an audience and the various methods used to target content to an audience.

Be able to create and configure My Sites.   A My Site is more than just a personal location for a SharePoint user to store their links and documents. It allows them to collaborate with other users and lets them choose what information about themselves they want other users to find. All of those abilities are controlled by policies you must be able to locate and set up for your My Sites deployment to be beneficial.

Review Questions

1. You are a junior SharePoint site administrator for your company, and you are reviewing the default site permission groups for your organization's SharePoint site. Of the following groups, which are default site permission groups? (Choose all that apply.)

    A. Site Owners

    B. Site Members

    C. Site Guests

    D. Site Visitors

2. You are a SharePoint user in the marketing department at Phoebe Studios, and you have just created your My Site. You are configuring your profile, and you notice that you can select who can view certain information about you. Of the following options, which groups can you select to restrict who can view your profile properties? (Choose all that apply.)

    A. Only Me

    B. My Manager

    C. My Domain

    D. My Colleagues

3. You are the SharePoint administrator for your company, and you are currently planning for the deployment of My Sites in your organization. You are reviewing the User Profile properties that are used to display user information on their My Sites public page. Of the following selections, which are valid public profile properties elements? (Choose all that apply.)

    A. Lists

    B. Policies

    C. Public Properties

    D. Private Properties

4. As part of your planning for My Site deployment on your company's SharePoint site collection, you are reviewing the types of user profile information sources you can make connections to from Central Administration. Which of the following sources can you use to import user profile data into SharePoint? (Choose all that apply.)

    A. Active Directory

    B. LDAP

    C. SAP

    D. Siebel

5. You are a SharePoint user in the marketing department at Phoebe Studios, and you have just created your My Site. While you are creating your public profile, you notice that a number of your user profile properties can be viewed by the Everyone group, and you cannot change the default group. Of the following selections, which properties can the Everyone group always see? (Choose all that apply.)

    A. Name

    B. Mobile Phone

    C. Manager

    D. Skills

6. You are the SharePoint administrator for the Hyperion Hydraulics company. You have created an audience called *technicians*, and you want to target web part information to the audience. Which web part must you use to accomplish this task?

    A. The Content Query web part

    B. The Content Editor web part

    C. The Page Viewer web part

    D. Any web part

7. As the SharePoint administrator for your company, you are planning your strategy for targeting different kinds of information to audiences in your organization. Of the following options, which represent items you can target to an audience? (Choose all that apply.)

    A. List items

    B. My Site Navigation Bar items

    C. Calendar items

    D. RSS feeds

8. You are a SharePoint user, and you've just finished setting up your My Site. You've configured different user profile properties to be seen by different groups, and you want to see how your public page looks to those groups. You click the As Seen By menu and review the available group options. Of the following options, which options should you be able to select? (Choose all that apply.)

    A. Only Me

    B. My Manager

    C. My Workgroup

    D. Everyone

9. You are the SharePoint administrator for your company, and you are creating a new audience in Central Administration. Under Include Users Who, you selected Satisfy Any of the Rules and clicked OK. What happens next?

    A. You are taken to the Shared Services Administration home page for the relevant SSP.

    B. You are taken to the Managed Audiences page.

    C. You are taken to the Add Audience Rule page.

    D. You are taken to the Create Audience page.

10. You are the SharePoint administrator for your company, and you are in the process of adding a new employee to the Home Members group for the portal site. From the portal site, you have just clicked Site Actions, Site Settings, and then People and Groups. What do you do next?

    A. On the People and Groups: Home Members page, click New, and then click Add Users.

    B. On the People and Groups: Home Members page, type the name of the new employee in the Name field, and then click the Check Names icon.

    C. In the Add Users section in the Users/Groups field, type the names of the users you want to add, and then click the Check Names icon to verify their names.

    D. Under Give Permission, tick the Add Users to a SharePoint Group radio button, and use the drop-down arrow to select Home Members [Contribute] from the list.

11. You are the SharePoint administrator for your company. You are enabling audience targeting in the sales department's document library so that the monthly sales reports in that library will appear in a web part on the sales department's home page. On the Customize Documents page under General Settings, you have just clicked Audience Targeting Settings and have been taken to the Modify List Audience Targeting Settings page. What actions can you perform on this page?

    A. Tick the Enable Audience Targeting check box, and then click OK.

    B. Tick the Enable Audience Targeting check box, and then click the Documents link to return to the Documents library.

    C. Click to the right of the document you want to use, and select Edit Properties from the list.

    D. None of these options are correct.

12. You are planning for user profile deployment in Office SharePoint Server 2007, and you want to effectively present user profile information. To create connections to data sources, you compile a list of the profile features available from within user profiles. What policy elements are available for each people feature? (Choose all that apply.)

    A. Default Access Policy

    B. Override and Replication Policies

    C. Restore Policies

    D. Mirroring Policies

13. You are a junior SharePoint site administrator for your company, and you have been tasked with adding a collection of new employees to a SharePoint site access group with the following characteristics: users assigned to this group are restricted to viewing lists, pages, and documents in Server Rendering View. Of the following options, which one was described in this question?

    A. Home Members

    B. Home Visitors

    C. Restricted Readers

    D. Viewers

14. You are the SSP administrator for your company's SharePoint site collection. You are planning the deployment of audiences in the site collection and are considering the most appropriate audience type to use. You want to create audiences based on the properties of the user profiles that you manage and have content targeted based on those properties. Of the following options, which one is correct?

A. Distribution Lists and Security Groups

B. Global Audiences

C. SharePoint Site Access Groups

D. Default Site Permission Groups

15. You are the SharePoint administrator for your company, and you are creating a new site access group. You have arrived at the step where you must specify the owner for the new group. Of the following options, what can you do? (Choose all that apply.)

A. Accept the default of Site Owner.

B. Accept the default of Administrator.

C. Type the name of another SharePoint user, and use the Check Names icon to verify.

D. Click the Browse icon, and browse for the name of a valid SharePoint user.

16. You are the SharePoint administrator for your company. You are in the process of adding a user profile using the Central Administration web application. What's the first action you should take once you arrive on the Add User Profile page?

A. Add the appropriate user information in the First Name and Last Name fields.

B. Type the user's account name in the Account Name field.

C. Type the user's full name in the Name field.

D. Use the Profile type drop-down list to select the correct profile type from the list.

17. You are a SharePoint user, and you have just finished adding your information to your user profile on your My Site. What actions can you take to exit from the current page? (Choose all that apply).

A. Click OK to save your changes.

B. Click Cancel to disregard your changes.

C. Scroll to the top, and click Save and Close.

D. Scroll to the bottom, and click Save and Close.

18. You are on your My Site, and you are trying to add someone to your My Colleagues list but can't. What are some likely reasons why you are having trouble? (Choose all that apply.)

A. The person is not an authenticated user on your domain.

B. Only people who are members of the same department can be added to the My Colleagues list.

C. The person's name is not located in the user profile store.

D. You have exceeded your quota of people you can add to My Colleagues.

19. You are the SharePoint administrator for your company. The new head of the marketing department wants to have unique access rights to the marketing site collection rather than be added to one of the site access groups. What is your most likely response?

A. You explain that this option is not available in SharePoint and that access is granted only through access groups.

B. You explain that this option is not available by default, but you can enable it by accessing the relevant SSP for the site collection.

C. You explain that this option is available, but for security reasons it is highly discouraged.

D. You explain that you can only do this by adding her to the Site Owner's group and giving her unique options once she's a member of that group.

20. You are the SharePoint administrator for your company, and you have just finished modifying a Content Query web part to display targeted content from a document library to a particular audience. You click OK in the Content Query tool part to save your changes, but now that the web page is not in Edit mode, you don't see any of the targeted content. You log in as a member of the audience, but you still can't see the content. What is the most likely problem?

A. You forgot to check in the web page.

B. The link to the Document library content is broken.

C. You can target list content only to a Content Query web part, not Document library content.

D. You forgot to refresh the web page.

Answers to Review Questions

1. A, B, and D. The default site permission groups are Site Owners, Site Members, and Site Visitors. Option C is bogus.

2. A, B, and D. The correct options are Only Me, My Manager, My Workgroup, My Colleagues, and Everyone.

3. B, C, and D. The correct list of public profile properties elements are Documents, Policies, Public Properties, and Private Properties.

4. A, B, C, and D. All of the listed data sources are able to be used to import user profile information into SharePoint.

5. A and C. By default, the Everyone group can always see your name and the name of your manager, but you can control which group sees your mobile phone number and your skills, including Only Me.

6. D. Although you must use the Content Query web part to display targeted information in a library or a list to an audience, you can also target any web part directly to an audience.

7. A and B. You can target list, library, and navigation bar items in My Sites and group results by options or audience.

8. B, C, and D. The correct options are My Manager, My Workgroup, My Colleagues, and Everyone.

9. C. After you click OK, you are taken to the Add Audience Rule page to create a rule for the new audience.

10. A. Option A is the correct selection. Option B is bogus, and options C and D occur later in the process.

11. A. The only action you can take on this page is to tick the Enable Audience Targeting check box, and then click OK to exit the page.

12. A and B. Options A and B are the only correct selections in this list. C and D are bogus.

13. D. The Viewers group meets the specified requirements. Home Members have the same rights as Site Members and are able to contribute content to a site. Home Visitors have read-only permissions on the site. Restricted Readers have read-only permissions on the site.

14. B. Global Audiences is the correct type and fulfills the stated requirements. Distribution Lists and Security Groups target content to audiences that contain users who are members of the particular distribution lists. SharePoint Site Access Groups are associated with a set of access permissions for a site or site collection. Option D is not a valid selection.

15. B, C, and D. You can select the name of a valid SharePoint user for the site owner by performing either C or D or accept the default in option B.

16. B. Option B is the first step in the process and adding the user's account name is required. Option A takes place later in the process. Options C and D are bogus.

17. B and C. Options B and C are the only valid actions you can take.

18. A and C. A person must be an authenticated user in the domain, or if SharePoint is on a stand-alone server, the person must be an authenticated user on the server. Even if the person is an authenticated user, they must also be in the user profile store. Options B and D are bogus.

19. C. The option to give an individual unique site access rights is available but is usually discouraged.

20. A. Whenever you modify a web page, it automatically is checked out so that no one else can modify the page at the same time you are working on it. You changes won't be saved, however, unless you check the page back in.

Chapter

6

Configuring Authentication and Security

MICROSOFT EXAM OBJECTIVES COVERED IN THIS CHAPTER

✓ **Configure Microsoft Office SharePoint Server 2007 Portal**

- ▪ Configure Users and Groups
- ▪ Configure Single Sign-On (SSO)

Although security is an important issue in any computing and networking environment, including SharePoint, the 70-630 exam objectives don't require that you become a security expert. Also, it's beyond the scope of this book to provide an extensive tutorial on network security, server hardening, firewall configuration, and the like.

That said, you will still be responsible for understanding how to configure single sign-on (SSO) in SharePoint. Also, lest you think Chapter 5, "Managing Users and Groups," taught you everything you need to know about user authentication and permissions, this chapter will drill down a bit deeper into both areas, including different authentication schemes for SharePoint.

This chapter will start with a general treatment of authentication and security issues, cover more information regarding permissions in SharePoint, and end up hitting the specifics of SSO. By the time you are finished here, you will be well able to manage authentication and access issues in MOSS 2007.

Planning for Authentication

How do you prove who you are? When I write a check at the grocery store, I'm asked for some form of identification, which is usually my driver's license. I'm also asked for my photo ID when I go through airport security before boarding my flight. When I go to work, I have to pass my security badge across a sensor to prove I have permission to enter the building. That usually brings me to sitting down at my desk and proving I have permission to access my computer and the resources on the network.

Authentication is providing a set of credentials (username and password) that establish that you have permission to access resources on the system. Exactly what rights you have depends on the security or SharePoint access groups to which you belong. The average end user usually isn't even aware that they are seeing only what they have permission to see and that other resources are either not accessible to them or not even visible.

SharePoint 2007 supports several methods of authentication including those types based on the Windows operating system. Let's take a brief look at those methods in the following summary. You may be surprised at what's "under the hood."

ASP.NET forms   SharePoint 2007 supports identity management systems that are not based on *Windows authentication* by using the *ASP.NET forms* authentication system. ASP.NET authentication enables SharePoint to work with identity management systems that utilize the Membership Provider interface. Using ASP.NET forms means you don't have to reinvent security administration pages or manage shadow Active Directory accounts. ASP.NET forms authentication allows you to use Lightweight Directory Access Protocol (LDAP) or Microsoft SQL authentication solutions.

Single sign-on   This is more formally known as web single sign-on (web SSO). Web SSO enables SSO in environments that include various authentication services running on a wide variety of platforms outside of standard Windows authentication such as Active Directory Federation Services (ADFS).

Windows authentication   This is the standard IIS Windows authentication, and it supports Anonymous, Basic, Certificates, Digest, Kerberos, and NTLM methods.

Configuring Authentication

As you recall from Chapter 2, "Installing and Deploying SharePoint 2007," when you installed SharePoint Server 2007, you set up a default authentication method based on Windows authentication (Kerberos or NTLM). Since then, you probably haven't given much thought to your authentication selection, how it works, or whether you should further manage SharePoint authentication. While Windows-based authentication is a pretty straightforward affair, configuring ASP.NET forms and SSO authentication requires a few more skills, particularly in the planning stage.

SharePoint authentication is set up at the web application level, which means that different site collections in the same server farm can use different authentication methods. When you originally installed and configured authentication for the web application for your current site collection, you probably selected either Kerberos or NTLM. (You could have also allowed anonymous authentication if you were creating a publicly accessible Internet site.)

Now that your site collection is up and running, as an administrator you can launch the SharePoint Central Administration (CA) web application and access a wider range of authentication types. Although you won't actually set up SSO until later in this chapter, Exercise 6.1 will show you how to get to the Edit Authentication page and have a look around.

EXERCISE 6.1

Accessing the Edit Authentication Page

1. Launch the Central Administration web application, and click the Application Management tab.

2. In the Application Security area, click Authentication Providers. Then next to Web Application, click the drop-down arrow, and select Change Web Application.

3. On the Select Web Application page, select the web application you desire, such as SharePoint – 80.

4. Under Zone, click Default (the only choice available at this time).

5. Review the selections on the Edit Authentication page, as shown here, and then click Cancel to return to the Authentication Providers page.

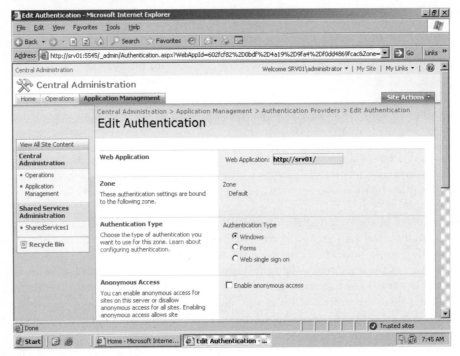

6. Click the Home tab to return to the Central Administration home page.

The different authentication methods available may require additional configuration, so it's not a matter of just selecting ASP.NET forms, SSO, or Windows on the Edit Authentication page and clicking OK. Although some authentication methods require no additional configuration or specialized roles, many do. The following is a guide to assist in your authentication planning:

- Anonymous authentication requires no additional configuration actions.

- Basic authentication requires no additional configuration actions.

- Certificates requires the following additional configuration steps:

  - You must select Windows authentication in Central Administration.

  - You must configure IIS for certificate authentication.

  - You must enable Secure Sockets Layer (SSL).

- You must obtain and configure certificates from a certification authority.
- You must be a Windows Server 2003 administrator to obtain and configure certificates.
- Digest authentication requires that you configure it directly in IIS.
- NTLM requires no additional configuration actions.
- Kerberos requires the following additional steps:
    - You must configure the web application to use Kerberos authentication.
    - You must configure a service principal name (SPN) for the domain user account that is used for the application pool identity (application pool process account).
    - You must register the SPN for the domain user account in Active Directory.
    - You must be an IIS administrator.
- ASP.NET forms authentication requires the following:
    - You must register the membership provider in the `Web.config` file for the SharePoint web application and the Central Administration site.
    - You can optionally register the role manager in the `Web.config` file for the SharePoint web application.
    - You must be an ASP.NET developer and an administrator of the identity management system to which you are connecting.
- SSO requires the following:
    - In addition to configuration steps required for ASP.NET forms authentication, you must register an HTTP module for the web SSO provider.
    - You must be an ASP.NET developer and an administrator of the identity management system to which you are connecting.

 Real World Scenario

Selecting an Authentication Method

You are the SharePoint administrator for your company, and your CIO has tasked you with configuring a specific authentication scheme for SharePoint 2007. You must set up an authentication method that supports identity management systems, but not one based on Windows authentication. Instead, this method will authenticate against an LDAP server.

You determine that the necessary method is ASP.NET forms since it has this capacity. You log in to the SharePoint Central Administration web application, click the Application management tab, and begin the process of setting up ASP.NET forms authentication on the Edit Authentication page.

Introduction to Single Sign-On (SSO) Authentication

The big advantage of using SSO in SharePoint Server 2007 is that you can allow your users to access back-end or external data sources from within SharePoint without having to authenticate to the outside source. This includes users having the ability to view, create, and modify information on these sources based on the mapping between the user credentials to the external sources.

SSO requires you to be using Windows credentials for user accounts in SharePoint. In environments where SSO is used to authenticate user accounts, SSO can be utilized only if the current thread that is invoking SSO application programming interfaces (APIs) has a Windows identity associated with it. The advantages to using SSO besides those mentioned thus far include the following:

- All user credentials are managed securely.

- User permission levels configured on external data sources are strictly enforced.

- MOSS 2007 has the ability to connect to multiple external data systems regardless of platform and authentication scheme.

The Single Sign-On Service

Applications or features on a computerized system are usually provided by services or daemons. SSO in SharePoint 2007 is provided by the single sign-on service (called SSOSrv). Implementing SSOSrv in SharePoint requires a certain set of actions to take place in sequence, as described here:

1. The SSO encryption-key server is the first server on which SSOSrv is enabled, which causes it to be assigned the encryption-key server role. The encryption-key server generates and stores the encryption key used to encrypt and decrypt credentials that are stored in the SSO database. The encryption-key server should be an application server such as the index server.

2. The single sign-on service must be installed on all web servers in the SharePoint server farm. Also, SSOSrv must be installed on any computers that host the Excel Services application server role. If a business data catalog (BDC) search is used, SSOSrv must be installed on the index server as well.

3. The SSO database is created when you configure SSO server settings in the Central Administration site, and by default it will be installed on the database server that hosts the configuration database. If Microsoft SQL Server is installed, the SSO database is a SQL Server database. If SQL Server is not installed, the single sign-on service uses SQL Server 2005 Express Edition. In either case, the SSO database stores the encrypted credentials.

If you are upgrading from SharePoint Portal Server 2003 or some other version of SharePoint Server, you will have to re-create the SSOSrv environment. There is no direct upgrade path for SSOSrv.

Backing Up and Restoring SSO

The SSO environment is not backed up during normal server backups in the server farm because SSO isn't composed of data in the conventional sense and because the regular backup procedures don't really lend themselves to how SSO operates. To back up SSO, you must back up two things, the encryption key and the SSO database.

Backing Up the Encryption Key

You should back up the encryption key after you initially set up SSO and then back it up again each time it is regenerated. It is absolutely necessary to perform the backup function on the local machine containing the encryption key since this process cannot be performed over a remote link.

Unlike normal data backups, you do not have to schedule a backup of the encryption key to occur on a regular basis, such as daily or weekly. The encryption key should not change unless it is regenerated. You should back up the key each time you regenerate it, however, to preserve the latest version.

Only members of the SSO administrator account have permissions to back up the encryption key, and it can be backed up only to removable storage such as an external USB drive. Backing up the encryption key must be performed from the Manage Encryption Key page in the Central Administration web application.

Backing Up the SSO Database

You should back up the SSO database for the first time after you create it and then each time the credentials are encrypted. Unlike the encryption key, you will benefit from regularly backing up the SSO database, since database content changes with daily use. You should also initiate an immediate backup of the database each time you make a major change or update.

Methods of Restoring the SSO

To back up the SSO, you need to back up both the encryption key and the SSO database, but the process of restoring the SSO depends on a variety of circumstances. It isn't always necessary to restore both the encryption key and the SSO database. Sometimes you will restore only the encryption key, sometimes you will restore only the SSO database, and sometimes you must restore both.

Although backing up the SSO requires backing up both the encryption key and the database, restoring the SSO isn't necessarily the reverse process. As previously mentioned, you may have to restore only the key, only the database, or sometimes both.

For instance, the encryption key is stored on only one server in the server farm. That server plays the encryption-key server role. There are several reasons why you might need to move that server role from one machine in the server farm to another. Examples include moving the server role to a machine with a larger storage capacity, more memory, or a faster CPU. In this situation, you must back up the encryption key after its most recent regeneration.

Once the backup is accomplished, disable SSOSrv on all servers in the server farm. Log on with an account that has SSO administer rights to the server you want to assign the encryption-key server role, configure SSO server farm–level settings in the Central Administration web application, and specify the existing SSO database. Restore the encryption key, and then start SSOSrv on all the web servers in the server farm.

Another example of why you would need to restore the encryption key is to change the SSOSrv account's security identifier (SID). This is used as part of the formula when you encrypt the SSO credentials. If you suspect that the SID has been discovered by an unauthorized party or have other security-based reasons to do this, you should change the SID.

This requires that you reconfigure the SSOSrv service on all the servers in the server farm using the new service account. You then must reconfigure the SSO server farm–level settings in the Central Administration web application with the new account and point it to the location of the SSO database. Once you have accomplished those tasks, restore the encryption key with the most recent backup.

Typically, you will restore the SSO database if it has been corrupted or had a hardware failure or other similar incident. Restoring the SSO database requires the same set of steps as restoring any SQL server database, so I won't outline the details here. Consult the relevant documentation for your database for the procedure.

SharePoint 2007 Security Planning

Before we take on the nuts and bolts of configuring the SSO environment in SharePoint 2007, we'll cover a little more ground about general security, specifically, permissions. Some of this material might seem like it belongs in Chapter 5, "Managing Users and Groups," but it's important to remember that you can't separate security issues from people, and particularly from end users. Although the hacker outside your network is certainly a threat, your biggest security vulnerability comes from within.

Access Permissions Planning

At this stage, it's helpful to go over a little old territory and introduce something new in terms of security elements:

Access groups These are also known as *site access groups* in SharePoint and are usually either a collection of users in an Active Directory security group mapped to a SharePoint access group or a collection of users in an access group. Each group grants the users it contains specific access to SharePoint site content. A group can be either a default SharePoint group with predefined permissions or a custom-made group with a unique set of permissions assigned by an administrator.

Anyone assigned a permission level that includes the Create Groups permission can create and modify access groups.

Permission level   These are the basic levels that assign particular degrees of access. Default permission levels are Limited Access, Read, Contribute, Design, and Full Control. Permissions can be included in multiple permission levels. Permission levels can be customized by anyone assigned to a permission level that includes the Manage Permissions permission.

Securable object   In SharePoint, *securable objects* can include lists, libraries, sites, documents, and other SharePoint elements. By default, permissions for a list, library, folder, document, or item are inherited from the parent site or parent list or library. A user with a permission level for a specific securable object that includes the Manage Permissions permission can change the permissions for that securable object. Permissions are controlled at the site level by default, with all lists and libraries inheriting those permissions from that level. You can use list-level, folder-level, and item-level permissions to further control which users can view or interact with the site content.

You can assign an individual user or group specific access permissions to specific securable objects such as sites, lists, or documents. For instance, the company's sales associates group can have one set of permissions to access the sales site and different permissions to access other sites within the company or different libraries, lists, and documents within the sales site.

 Remember that it is highly preferable to assign users to groups with the permissions you want the users to have rather than assigning individual users permissions directly. Also, assign users to a group that grants them the minimum level of permissions that allows them to perform their job functions rather than allowing them "excess" access rights.

Previously, you looked at site access permission in terms of which groups allow which kinds of access. Now you'll look at permissions from the perspective of roles and what each role can do.

Creating groups and assigning overall permissions for groups in a site can be performed by those who are site administrators, who belong to the Site Owners group, or who have Manage Web Site permissions in their permission level.

Modifying access permissions to lists and libraries, including allowing or denying access by a user or group, can be done by list or library administrators or people with the Manage Lists permission in their permission level.

Modifying access permissions at the document or item level, including allowing or denying access by a user or group, can be done by item or document creators.

 Security access at the document or item level wasn't possible with SharePoint Portal Server 2003.

Access permissions in SharePoint 2007 can be assigned to the following levels:

Site   This controls access to the site as a whole.

List or library   This controls access to a specific list or library including everything it contains.

Folder   This controls access to a folder contained within a list or library and the contents of that folder.

Document or item   This controls access to a specific document or item.

> An item is a single entry in a list. For example, a hyperlink to Microsoft's TechNet site in a list of links would be considered an item.

As you can guess, if you don't have access to a site, you don't have access to its contents. If you have access to a site, you still may be denied access or have limited access to a list or library. Even if you can access the list or library, you may be denied access to any of the folders, documents, or items it contains.

By default, permissions of the higher-level objects are inherited by the lower-level objects; however, it doesn't have to be this way. As the previous paragraph outlined, you can set highly granular permissions for greater security control of all securable objects within SharePoint.

It is easiest to manage permissions when there is a clear hierarchy of permissions and inherited permissions. It gets more difficult when some lists within a site have highly granular permissions applied and when others have some subsites with unique permissions and other subsites with inherited permissions. As much as possible, arrange sites and subsites and lists and libraries so they can share most permissions. Separate sensitive data into their own lists, libraries, or subsites.

Figure 6.1 shows you a simple example of how permissions and permission inheritance can be planned. The top-level or portal site always has a unique set of permissions because there are no sites above from which to inherit. As you can see in Figure 6.1, the company intranet and all of the items within it inherit permissions from the home site. The HR department's site, however, needs a different level of security access to prevent most company employees from gaining access so that site and its contents are configured with unique permissions not inherited from the parent site.

Administrative Groups

I've discussed different types of administrators in the past and most often referred to the SharePoint administrator. When you installed SharePoint 2007, you naturally gained control over every aspect of SharePoint, including the server farm or stand-alone server and all the site collections and their contents. There are actually three general types of administrators that should be at least briefly addressed:

Farm administrators   This administrator account has permissions to manage server farm settings in the Central Administration web application. The scope of authority for this account is at the server farm–level, and farm administrators are unable to access or modify content at the website level. If you want a person with Farm administrators permissions to access site-level content, you must add them to the Site Collection administrators group.

Site Collection administrators   This administrator account has full control permissions over all websites contained in the SharePoint site collection. You usually define who is assigned this administrator role when you first create the site collection.

FIGURE 6.1   Site permissions inheritance example

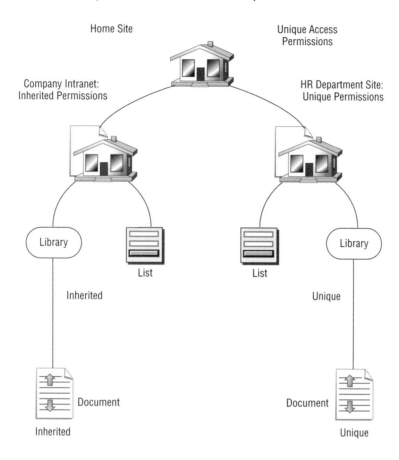

Home Site

Unique Access
Permissions

Company Intranet:
Inherited Permissions

HR Department Site:
Unique Permissions

Library

List

List

Library

Inherited

Unique

Document

Document

Inherited

Unique

Local Server administrators   This administrator account has the same permissions as the Farm Administrators account as well as permissions on each individual server, allowing them to create new web applications and new websites.

Selecting Security Groups

You learned in Chapter 5, "Managing Users and Groups," that you can map Active Directory security groups to SharePoint site access groups. In Active Directory, you can use the following two groups:

Distribution group   This group is used only for email distribution and is not security enabled. Distribution groups cannot be listed in discretionary access control lists (DACLs) used to define permissions on resources and objects.

Security group   This group can be listed in DACLs used to define permissions on resources and objects. A security group can also be used as an email entity.

You can use security groups to control permissions for your site by directly adding the security group and granting the entire group permissions. You cannot use distribution groups in this way; however, you can expand a distribution list and add the individual users to a SharePoint group. If you use this method, you must manage the process of keeping the SharePoint group synchronized with the distribution group. If you use security groups, you do not need to manage the individual users in the SharePoint application. Because you included the security group itself and not the individual members of the group, Active Directory manages the users for you.

If you want all users within your domain to be able to view content on your site, you can grant access to all authenticated users using the Domain Users Windows security group. This special group allows all members of your domain to access a website using the permission level you want, without you having to enable anonymous access.

You can enable anonymous access to allow users to view pages anonymously. Most Internet websites allow anonymous viewing of the site but might ask for authentication when someone wants to edit the site, such as on Wikipedia, or buy an item on a shopping site, such as on Amazon. Anonymous access must be granted at the web application level at the time that the web application is created. If anonymous access is allowed for the web application, then site administrators can decide whether to grant anonymous access to a site, grant anonymous access only to lists and libraries, or block anonymous access to a site altogether.

Anonymous access relies on the anonymous user account on the web server. This account is created and maintained by Microsoft Internet Information Services (IIS), not your SharePoint site. By default in IIS, the anonymous user account is IUSR_ComputerName. When you enable anonymous access, you are granting that account access to the SharePoint site. Allowing access to a site, or to lists and libraries, grants the View Items permission to the anonymous user account.

The 70-630 exam does not focus heavily on overall SharePoint Server 2007 security, so the security section here is not exhaustive.

Configuring Single Sign-On (SSO)

I'm tempted to say "And now the moment you've all been waiting for (drumroll, please)," but I digress. As you've already learned, using SSO functionality enables SharePoint users to authenticate only once when they access applications through the portal site, and obtain information from other business applications and systems including third-party applications and back-end systems such as enterprise resource planning (ERP) and customer relations management (CRM) systems.

You can configure Excel Calculation Services to retrieve authentication credentials from an SSO store. To enable SSO functionality for SharePoint Server 2007, you need to start the single sign-on service and then manage SSO settings in the SharePoint Central Administration web application. The single sign-on service (SSOSrv) must be installed on all Microsoft Windows front-end web servers in the server farm. SSOSrv must also be installed on all servers running Excel Services. If the business data catalog search is used, SSOSrv must also be installed on the index server.

The following conditions must be satisfied in order to proceed with the following exercise:

- Your server must belong to an Active Directory domain and be connected to a domain controller.

- You must use a domain user account and not just a group account.

- You must use a SharePoint Server farm account.

- You must be a member of the local Administrators group on the encryption-key server, which is the first server on which you start SSOSrv.

- You must be a member of the Security Administrators role and db_creator role on the computer running Microsoft SQL Server.

- You must belong to the single sign-on administrator account group.

 If you are the administrator who installed SharePoint Server on a stand-alone server, you will have the authority to perform the following exercise.

Exercise 6.2 will get you started configuring and starting SSOSrv.

EXERCISE 6.2

Setting Up and Starting the Single Sign-On Service

1. On the Windows Server 2003 machine, select Start ➢ All Programs ➢ Administrative Tools ➢ Computer Management.

2. Expand Services and Applications, and then click Services.

3. Scroll down the list until you find Microsoft Single Sign-On Service, right-click it, and select Properties, as shown here.

EXERCISE 6.2 *(continued)*

---

4. On the General tab of the Microsoft Single Sign-on Service Properties box, click the Startup Type menu arrow, and select Automatic.

5. On the same tab under Service status, click the Start button.

6. When the service has started, click OK to close the Properties box.

You will need to perform this task on every relevant server in your server farm.

Once the SSO service is started on each of the Windows Server 2003 machines, you will need to configure the SSO service within SharePoint. This needs to be done in the CA web application, which means you'll need to have administrator privileges. Exercise 6.3 will walk you through this process.

> Your server will need to be a part of an Active Directory domain for you to successfully complete the remainder of the exercises in this chapter.

EXERCISE 6.3

Configuring SharePoint SSO in Central Administration

1. Launch the Central Administration web application.

2. Click the Operations tab, and Under Security Configuration click Manage Settings for Single Sign-On.

3. On the Manage Settings for Single Sign-On page under Server Settings, click Manage Server Settings, as shown here.

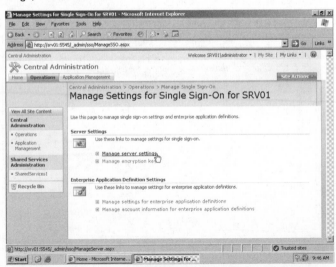

4. On the Manage Server Settings for Single Sign-On page under Single Sign-On Administrator Account, type the Single Sign-On administrator account name by using the form *domain/group* or *domain/username* in the Account Name field. The group or user you specify must possess all of the following:

    ▪ They must be either a Windows global group or an individual user account and cannot be a domain local group account or a distribution list.

    ▪ They must belong to the same account as the SSO service account, if a user is specified. If a group is specified, the SSO service account must be a member of that group.

    ▪ They must belong to the same account as the configuration account for SSO, if a user is specified. If a group is specified, the configuration account for SSO must be a member of that group.

    ▪ They must be a member of the Farm Administrators group on Central Administration.

5. Under Enterprise Application Definition Administrator Account in the Account Name field, type the account name of the group or user who can set up and manage enterprise application definitions, using the form *domain/group* or *domain/username*. The user or group you identify here must be either a Windows global group or an individual user account and a member of the Reader SharePoint group on Central Administration.

6. Under the Database Settings section, type the NetBIOS name of the single sign-on database server in the Server Name field. (In this case, this field is already populated with the current server name, SRV01\OfficeServers.)

7. In the Database Name field, type the name of the single sign-on database (which in this case is SSO). For steps 6 and 7 you should accept the default settings unless you are pre-creating databases.

8. Under Time Out Settings, type a value in the Ticket Time Out (In Minutes) field for how many minutes should pass before a single sign-on ticket expires. (The default is 2.)

9. In the Delete Audit Log Records Older Than (In Days) field, type a value for how many days the audit log holds records before deleting them. (The default is 10.)

10. Click OK to complete the operation.

Members of the single sign-on administrator account can create, delete, or modify application definitions. Members can also back up the encryption key.

The enterprise application definition administrator account you configured in step 5 of Exercise 6.3 can manage credentials of an enterprise application definition, including changing the password of a group enterprise application definition and changing or deleting credentials for an individual enterprise application definition.

As previously mentioned, the first server you enable SSOSrv on becomes the encryption-key server, which generates and stores the encryption key. The encryption key is used to encrypt and decrypt the credentials that are stored in the SSO database. Since the encryption key protects security credentials, you should create a new encryption key on a regular basis, such as every 60 to 90 days. You should also create a new encryption key if you suspect that account credentials have been compromised.

The encryption key must be backed up each time a new key is created. The only other time you need to back up the encryption key is when you are moving the encryption-key server role from one server to another. You must back up the encryption key from the encryption-key server locally since the key cannot be backed up remotely.

Managing the encryption key is done in Central Administration on the Operations tab from the Manage Settings for Single Sign-On page, where you initiated Exercise 6.3. The next three exercises will show you different aspects of managing the encryption key. Exercise 6.4 starts you out with creating a new encryption key. The exercise assumes you are still on the Manage Settings for Single Sign-On page where you were at after step 10 in Exercise 6.3.

EXERCISE 6.4

Creating an Encryption Key

1. On the Manage Settings for Single Sign-On page under Server Settings, click Manage Encryption Key.

2. On the Manage Encryption Key page under Encryption Key, click Create Encryption Key.

3. On the Create Encryption Key page, tick the New Encryption Key check box to reencrypt all credentials, and then click OK.

Reencrypting the existing credentials with the new encryption key prevents users from having to retype their credentials for individual application definitions and prevents administrators from having to retype group credentials for group application definitions.

Earlier in this chapter, you learned the rationale behind backing up the encryption key. Exercise 6.5 will show you how to do this. To successfully perform this exercise, you must first attach some form of removable storage media to your server computer, such as a USB drive.

EXERCISE 6.5

Backing Up the Encryption Key

1. On the Manage Settings for Single Sign-On page under the Server Settings section, click Manage Encryption Key.

2. On the Manage Encryption Key page in the Drive List in the Encryption Key Backup section, click the removable media drive on which you want to store the encryption key backup.

3. Click Back Up to initiate the process.

You should always back up the encryption key when you back up the SSO database, because the database is useless without the encryption key. Also, before you replace an encryption-key server, make sure to back up the encryption key so that it can be restored on the new encryption-key server.

Now that you've backed up the encryption key, it's time to perform the restore process. You'll see how to do this in Exercise 6.6. To successfully perform this exercise, you must attach the removable storage media to the server computer that contains the backed-up encryption key.

EXERCISE 6.6

Restoring the Encryption Key

1. On the Manage Settings for Single Sign-On page under the Server Settings section, click Manage Encryption Key.

2. On the Manage Encryption Key page in the Drive List in the Encryption Key Restore section, click the removable media drive from which you want to restore the encryption key backup.

3. Click Restore.

In the SSO environment, the back-end external data sources and systems are referred to as *enterprise applications*. For each enterprise application that SharePoint 2007 connects to, a corresponding enterprise application definition needs to be configured. On the Manage Settings for Single Sign-On page under Enterprise Application Definition Settings, you most likely saw two links relevant to managing the settings for enterprise application definitions. Exercise 6.7 will show you how to configure an enterprise application definition.

After you have completed steps 1–3 in Exercise 6.7, you must complete the process and configure account information for the enterprise application definition. If you are using a group to connect to the enterprise application, you'll need to provide account credentials for the group to use. If individual users are connecting directly to the enterprise application, you can either preset or reset user passwords, or you can delete users from the enterprise application definition.

EXERCISE 6.7

Configuring Account Information for an Enterprise Application Definition

1. On the Central Administration web application, click the Operations tab.

2. On the Operations page under Security Configuration, click Manage Settings for Single Sign-On.

3. On the Manage Settings for Single Sign-On page, click Manage Settings for Enterprise Application Definitions.

4.   Return to the Operations tab. Under Security Configuration, click Manage Settings for Single Sign-On.

5.   On the Manage Settings for Single Sign-On page under Enterprise Application Definition Settings, click Manage Account Information for Enterprise Application Definitions.

6.   On the Manage Account Information for an Enterprise Application Definition page in the Enterprise Application Definition list under Account Information, click the application definition for which you want to manage account information.

7.   In the Group Account Name field, type the name of the group that is allowed access to the enterprise application.

8.   In the Enterprise Application Definition area, make the desired selection. You have several options you can select, depending on your goal:

Select Update Account Information to enter credentials for the first time or update the credentials used to connect to the enterprise application.

Select Delete Stored Credentials for This Account from This Enterprise Application Definition to delete the credentials currently used to connect to the enterprise application.

Select Delete Stored Credentials for This Account from All Enterprise Application Definitions to delete the credentials currently used to connect the selected enterprise application from all enterprise application definitions. Deleting stored credentials deletes credentials only for individual accounts; it does not delete credentials for group accounts.

If you selected the Update account information option, you will need to complete the following steps:

a.   Click Set.

b.   On the Provide Account Information page under Logon Information, type the username and password of the account that will be used to connect to the enterprise application.

c.   Click OK.

9.   Click Done when you've completed your configuration.

Summary

In this chapter, you learned more about SharePoint site access groups, security measures, and authentication, including the following topics:

- General planning for and configuring of authentication
- Planning for single sign-on authentication
- Managing SSO including backing up and restoring the elements of the SSO service (SSOSrv)
- Planning for access permissions
- Setting up administrative and security groups
- Enabling and configuring an SSO environment

Exam Essentials

Plan for access group permissions.   It's important to fully understand the nature of how site access group permissions work, including configuring granular access configuration that will give a user or group access to content in a site at one level but not at all levels.

Understand administrative and security groups.   Associated with the concept of access groups are Active Directory security groups and distribution groups, since both can be used to import user profile data and map to SharePoint access groups. Also, you must have a grasp of which administrator type is capable of which SharePoint tasks.

Know how to plan single sign-on authentication.   Before you can implement a single sign-on environment in SharePoint, you must know the concepts behind SSO and the other forms of authentication in MOSS 2007 and the single sign-on service (SSOSrv), which is the underlying service behind this process.

Know how to configure single sign-on authentication.   After you've mastered the principles behind SSO, you still need to know how to enable the service in Windows Server 2003 and configure SSO from the SharePoint Central Administration web application. Relevant tasks are configuring SSO in general; generating, backing up, and restoring an authentication key; and configuring enterprise application definitions.

Review Questions

1. You are the SharePoint administrator for your company. You have been tasked with configuring a single sign-on (SSO) environment for your organization's site collection so that users can access several back-end and third-party databases without having to authenticate again after logging onto the SharePoint portal. In Central Administration on the Application Management tab, you follow the correct steps to get to the Select Web Application page. Under Zone on that page, which option must you choose to accomplish your goal?

   A. Web SSO

   B. SSO

   C. Single Sign-On

   D. Default

2. You are the SharePoint administrator for your company. You have been tasked with configuring a single sign-on (SSO) environment for your organization's site collection so that users can access several back-end and third-party databases without having to authenticate again after logging onto the SharePoint portal. Of the following selections, which one must you perform first to start the SSO service?

   A. On the Windows Server 2003 machine, select Start ➢ All Programs ➢ Administrative Tools ➢ Computer Management.

   B. On the Windows Server 2003 machine, select Start ➢ All Programs ➢ Administrative Tools ➢ Server Management.

   C. Click the Operations tab, and Under Security Configuration click Manage Settings for Single Sign-on.

   D. Click the Application Management tab, and Under Security Configuration click Manage Settings for Single Sign-on.

3. You are the SharePoint administrator for your company and have been charged with enabling and configuring an SSO environment within your organization's SharePoint site collection. You know that there are several tasks that must be performed in sequence in order to accomplish this goal. Of the following options, which is the first task?

   A. The SSO encryption-key server is the first server on which SSOSrv is enabled, and it becomes the encryption-key server.

   B. Single sign-on service must be installed on all web servers in the SharePoint server farm.

   C. The SSO database is created when you configure SSO server settings in the Central Administration site in MOSS 2007 on the database server that hosts the configuration database.

   D. None of the above.

4. You are the SharePoint administrator for your company and have been charged with enabling and configuring an SSO environment within your organization's SharePoint site collection. For you to accomplish this task, you must possess several different roles and permissions. Of the following selections, which ones must you possess? (Choose all that apply.)

A. You must use a SharePoint Server farm account.

B. You must be a member of the local Administrators group on the encryption key server.

C. You must use a group account.

D. You must be a member of the Security Administrators role and db_creator role on the computer running Microsoft SQL Server.

5. You are the SharePoint administrator for your company and have been charged with enabling and configuring an SSO environment within your organization's SharePoint site collection. You are in the Central Administration web application going through the steps of performing the initial configuration of SSO. Under Database Settings, what actions should you take?

A. Your only options are to type the NetBIOS name of the single sign-on database server in the Server Name field and type the name of the database in the Database field.

B. Accept the default values in the Server Name field and the database field unless you are precreating databases.

C. Type the fully qualified domain name (FQDN) of the single sign-on database server in the Server Name field and type the name of the database in the Database field.

D. Accept the default values in the Server Name field and the Database field unless you are not using Microsoft SQL Server for the SSO database.

6. You are the SharePoint administrator for your company. You are in the process of planning your access permissions strategy for your organization's site collection. You are aware that you can set access permissions on a variety of levels within SharePoint. Of the following options, to which ones can access permissions be assigned? (Choose all that apply.)

A. Site access

B. List and library access

C. Folder access

D. Document access

7. You are the SharePoint administrator for your company, and you are in the process of performing the initial configuration for the SSO environment. You are on the Manage Server Settings for Single Sign-On page and are designating a user for the single sign-on Administrator account. Of the following options, which ones must this Administrator account possess? (Choose all that apply.)

A. They must be a member of the Farm Administrators group on Central Administration.

B. They must be either a Windows global group or a domain local group account.

C. They must belong to the same account as the single sign-on service account, if a user is specified.

D. They must belong to the same account as the configuration account for single sign-on, if a user is specified.

8. You are the SharePoint administrator for your company. Over the weekend, the SharePoint server farm suffered a major failure requiring that you rebuild the system from backups. You are at the point of planning to restore the entire SSO environment. Of the following options, which action should you take first?

A. Set up and configure SSO as if you were configuring a new SSO environment.

B. Restore the encryption key to the new SSO environment.

C. Restore the SSO database to the database server.

D. Restart the SSO service on the SSO database server.

9. You are the SharePoint administrator for your organization. You are setting up site access permissions for your company's intranet site. The site and all of its contents are meant to be accessible to all company employees, so you want to assign all users to a group that will allow this. Of the following options, which special group allows all members of your domain to access the website?

A. The Authenticated Users security group

B. The Authenticated Domain Users security group

C. The Domain Members Windows security group

D. The Domain Users Windows security group

10. You are the SharePoint administrator for your company. SharePoint Server 2007 has suffered a security breach. You have investigated and found that it isn't serious, but you must take steps to resecure the SSO environment. Of the following options, which ones include the proper tasks? (Choose all that apply.)

A. Stop the SSO Service to prevent further intrusion while implementing the other steps.

B. Regenerate the encryption key.

C. Reencrypt the credentials in the SSO database using the new encryption key.

D. Change passwords for enterprise applications if the passwords might be compromised.

11. You are the SharePoint administrator for your company and are responding to a severe security breach of the SSO environment. You've already stopped the SSO service to prevent further compromise. Of the following options, which ones represent some of your next steps? (Choose all that apply.)

A. Restore the SSO environment to an isolated server.

B. Regenerate the encryption key.

C. Reencrypt the credentials in the SSO database.

D. Restore the SSO environment from the most recent backup.

12. You are the SharePoint administrator for your company and are performing the initial configuration of the SSO environment. You are identifying the user accounts for the single sign-on Administrator account and the Enterprise Application Definition Administrator account. Of the following selections, which ones are the correct format to use to type in the appropriate fields? (Choose two.)

A. Domain/username

B. Domain/group

C. Workgroup/username

D. Workgroup/group

13. You are the SharePoint administrator for your company, and you are reviewing plans to implement SSO authentication for your site collection. You are discussing the plan with the organization's IT department and explaining the requirements for SSO. Of the following options, which ones are requirements of SSO? (Choose two.)

A. SSO requires that you are using Windows credentials for user accounts in SharePoint.

B. SSO requires that you enable SSO services on the SSO database server first.

C. SSO requires that the current thread invoking SSO application programming interfaces (APIs) has a Windows identity associated with it.

D. SSO requires that the SSO Service be installed on the first domain controller in the domain first.

14. You are the SharePoint administrator for your company. You have successfully created and configured the SSO environment and have just backed up the encryption key after creating it for the first time. You have developed a schedule whereby the encryption key will be re-created every 90 days. What is the best schedule for you to use for backing up the encryption key?

A. Back up the encryption key every 30 days.

B. Back up the encryption key on a daily basis, just like how you back up your SSO database server.

C. Back up the encryption key whenever it is regenerated.

D. Back up the encryption key through a remote server every week.

15. You are the SharePoint administrator for your company, and you are performing the initial configuration of the SSO environment. You are creating a new encryption key for the first time in Central Administration. You are currently on the Manage Encryption Key page, and under Encryption Key you click Create Encryption Key. Of the following options, which one will you perform next?

A. Once the new encryption key process has completed, click OK.

B. Tick the New Encryption Key check box, and then click OK.

C. Click the Encryption Key drop-down arrow, select Create from the menu, and then click OK.

D. Select the Create radio button, and then click OK.

16. You are the SharePoint administrator for your company, and you are going to back up the encryption key because you want to move the encryption-key server role from one machine to another. Of the following options, which represents the correct method of backing up the encryption key?

A. Attach an external USB drive to the encryption-key server machine, and begin the backup from Central Administration.

B. Use a Remote Desktop connection to connect to the encryption-key server, and back up the encryption key across the network to the new encryption-key server machine.

C. Back up the encryption key by backing up all the data on that server machine to a backup tape the way you usually back up the rest of your servers.

D. From Central Administration, select a network mapped drive from the menu, and back up the encryption key to that drive.

17. You are the SharePoint administrator for your company, and you are planning an authentication scheme for SharePoint 2007. You are reviewing the requirements for the different authentication methods you can configure in Central Administration. Some methods do not require any additional setup, but quite a few of them do. Of the subsequent options, which method requires that you configure it directly in IIS as the only additional part of the setup?

A. Anonymous

B. Basic

C. Certificates

D. Digest

18. You are the SharePoint administrator for your company, and you are planning an authentication scheme for SharePoint 2007. You are reviewing the requirements for the different authentication methods that you can configure in Central Administration. You decide to go with Windows authentication since it supports a number of standard methods you can use. Of the following options, which ones are associated with Windows authentication? (Choose all that apply.)

A. Digest

B. Kerberos

C. Certificates

D. Web SSO

19. You are the SharePoint administrator for your company. You have just moved the SSO encryption-key server role to a new server machine and are going to restore the encryption key. You have the server machine connected to the media containing the key and are on the Manage Encryption Key page in Central Administration. Where must you select the media that contains the backed up encryption key so you can begin the restore process?

A. The Drive list

B. The Key list

C. The Media list

D. The Restore list

20. You are the SharePoint administrator for your site, and you are reviewing the different administrative roles in SharePoint Server 2007. You are considering who to assign to these roles so you can distribute administrative tasks rather than fulfill all these roles yourself. You are currently deciding who you will assign to be members of the Site Collection administrator group. Of the selections that follow, which ones describe qualities possessed by this group? (Choose all that apply.)

A. They can audit all site content.

B. They can create new web applications and new IIS websites.

C. They can designate one or more users as primary and secondary site collection administrators.

D. They have full control of all sites within the site collection.

Answers to Review Questions

1. D. On the Select Web Application page, after you have selected the desired web application, such as SharePoint – 80, the only choice available under Zones is Default. Once you make that selection, you are taken to a page where you can continue to configure the authentication method.

2. A. You must start the SSO service on the relevant Windows Server 2003 machines as described in option A before taking any other actions.

3. A. The first server you enable the SSO service (SSOSrv) on becomes the encryption key server. After you have enabled SSOSrv on the first server, you can enable the service on all the other web servers in the server farm and then create the SSO database.

4. A, B, and D. You must use a domain user account and not just a group account.

5. B. Although you can manually enter the database server name and database name as described in option A, it is not your only option, and in fact you should accept the default values as recommended in option B unless you are precreating databases.

6. A, B, C, and D. All of the options are correct. You can set access permissions at the level of the site, list, library, folder, document, and item.

7. A, C, and D. They must be either a Windows global group or an individual user account and cannot be a domain local group account or a distribution list.

8. C. Your first step would be to restore the SSO database, followed by setting up and configuring SSO as if you were configuring a new environment and finally restoring the encryption key.

9. D. If you want all users within your domain to be able to view content on your site, you can grant access to all authenticated users using the Domain Users Windows security group. This special group allows all members of your domain to access a website using the permission level you want, without you having to enable anonymous access.

10. B, C, and D. Although immediately stopping the SSO service (SSOSrv) is necessary in a severe security breach where unauthorized access is currently a risk, it is not a standard step in a non-emergency. The other options are appropriate steps.

11. A, B, and C. Rather than restoring the SSO environment from the most recent backup, after reencrypting the credentials in the SSO database, you should back up the SSO environment and then restore it to the current MOSS 2007 server farm.

12. A and B. SSO can be enabled only in an Active Directory environment, so usernames and groups must be identified by their domain name.

13. A and C. Options A and C are valid requirements. The other selections are bogus.

14. C. The encryption key must be backed up each time a new key is created. The only other time you need to back up the encryption key is when you are moving the encryption-key server role from one server to another. You must back up the encryption key from the local encryption-key server since the key cannot be backed up remotely.

15. B. Option B is the only correct answer.

16. A. The encryption key cannot be backed up across a network connection and must be backed up locally, as described in option A. Also, you must back up the encryption key to a removable storage media from Central Administration, not as part of a routine data backup to tape media.

17. D. Digest authentication requires that you configure it directly in IIS. Anonymous and Basic require no additional configuration, and Certificates requires an additional setup including configuring IIS for certificate authentication and several other steps.

18. A, B, and C. Windows authentication supports Anonymous, Basic, Certificates, Digest, Kerberos, and NTLM, but it does not support web SSO.

19. A. You must select the removable media drive in the Drive list under Encryption Key Restore.

20. A, C, and D. Site collection administrators cannot create new web applications and new IIS websites. This ability is reserved to the Local Server administrators group.

Chapter

7

Configuring and Maintaining Lists and Libraries

MICROSOFT EXAM OBJECTIVES COVERED IN THIS CHAPTER

✓ **Configure Microsoft Office SharePoint Server 2007 Portal**

- Configure Alerts

✓ **Configure Content Management**

- Configure Document Management
- Configure Records Management
- Configure Workflow

One of the major strengths of Microsoft Office SharePoint Server 2007 is its ability to store and organize a wide variety of information and data sources to allow easy access to that information by local or geographically diverse teams. SharePoint content can be acted on for the purposes of collaboration in the corporate environment in pursuit of common business goals. This chapter will focus on two related methods of managing information: lists and libraries.

You've had some introduction to these concepts in previous chapters. It's difficult to write about SharePoint without mentioning lists and libraries. This chapter will hone in on the details of adding lists and libraries to websites in SharePoint, adding information to them, configuring versioning of their contents, and filtering their contents.

Although Chapter 10, "Working with Microsoft Documents in SharePoint," will address document management and Chapter 15, "Working with Content Management," will deal with content management, this chapter will start by introducing those concepts as they relate to planning list and library deployment. Planning workflows and versioning will also be presented, as will the concepts of workflow approval and checking content into and out of SharePoint.

We will then move on to a formal introduction to lists and libraries and all of the ways they can be used to store, organize, and present information to SharePoint users. You'll get the opportunity to set up your own workflows and work with approval and rejection firsthand. You'll see how you can be notified when content changes in a list or library, and by the end of the chapter, you will be well on your way to mastering the use of these two important data containers.

Overview of Document and Records Management

As previously mentioned, document and records management will be covered in depth in subsequent chapters of this book, but it is difficult to discuss how lists and libraries operate without discussing management issues. You've probably heard the terms *workflow* and *governance* before, but perhaps you aren't sure of what they mean within the context of SharePoint 2007. The following sections in this chapter will make these concepts clearer.

Document Management

A *document management* system is implemented to control the flow of documents in your organization, including how documents are created, reviewed, published, and read, as well as how they are ultimately disposed of or retained. Because nearly all documentation within your organization will include these activities, expect to plan a document management system. Document management planning considerations include how content will be organized in document libraries, the metadata used to define each type of content, the workflows that will be required during the content's life cycle, and the policies to apply to the content.

Records Management

A *record* is a document or other physical or electronic entity in an organization that serves as evidence of an activity or transaction performed by the organization. *Records management* is the process used by the organization to determine which type of information constitutes a record, how to manage records through retention periods, and how to ultimately destroy or archive them. SharePoint 2007 includes features that help organizations implement records management processes. Most organizations have procedural, policy, and legal requirements they must meet relative to records management.

Workflows

Workflows implement business processes on documents, list items, and websites in SharePoint. For example, a workflow can route a document for review, track an issue through its various stages of resolution, or guide a contract through an approval process. SharePoint includes default workflow types that address primary content management needs, such as reviewing or approving documents for publication, along with specialized workflows for tracking issues, managing multiple language translations of content, and managing other processes. You can create custom workflows using Microsoft Visual Studio 2005 or Office SharePoint Designer 2007.

Governance and Scheduling

In addition to planning how much control you want users to have over modifying the appearance of a SharePoint website, you also need to plan how much governance you want content contributors to have over your site content within a site. *Governance* refers to the rules and processes that you want to establish for your site content. For example, you may want SharePoint to impose restrictions and functionality when authors create content. You have the option of giving authors no control, simple moderation, or the ability to start a workflow after they submit content. You can also plan restrictions on where and what type of content an author can place in certain areas of your site.

Scheduling is the ability of users to determine when content is to appear on a site. This feature is available only if versioning in a library is set to create both major and minor versions of content. The scheduled start times and dates are initiated by a timer service that has a one-minute lag time. It runs on a 24-hour clock, and it continually checks for pages and items in the document library or image library that are ready for publishing.

Versioning

Versioning is the method by which successive iterations of a document are numbered and saved. SharePoint has three versioning options:

None   Specifies that no previous versions of documents are saved. When no versioning is used, previous versions of documents are not retrievable, and document history is lost because comments that accompany each iteration of a document aren't saved. Only select this option for document libraries containing unimportant content or content that will never change.

Major Versions Only   Specifies that numbered versions of documents are retained using a simple versioning scheme (such as 1, 2, 3, and so on). To control the effect on storage space, you can specify how many previous versions to keep, counting back from the current version. In major versioning, each time a new version of a document is saved, all users with permissions to the document library will be able to view the content. Use this option when you do not want to differentiate between draft versions of documents and published versions.

Major and Minor Versions   Specifies that numbered versions of documents are retained by using a major and minor versioning scheme (such as 1.0, 1.1, 1.2, 2.0, 2.1, and so on). Versions ending with .0 are major versions, and versions ending with nonzero numerals are minor versions. Previous major and minor versions of documents are saved along with current versions. To control the effect on storage space, you can specify how many previous major and minor versions to keep, counting back from the current version.

In major and minor versioning, any user with read permissions can view major versions of documents. You can specify which users can view minor versions. Typically, you would grant users who can edit items permissions to view and work with minor versions, and you would restrict users with read permissions to viewing only major versions. Use major and minor versioning when you want to differentiate between published content that can be viewed by an audience and draft content that is not yet ready for publication.

Content Approval

Content approval is the method used by site members with approver permissions to control the publication of content. A document draft waiting for content approval is in the Pending state. When an approver reviews the document and approves the content, it becomes available for viewing by site users with read permissions. A document library owner can enable content approval for a document library and can optionally associate a workflow with the library to run the approval process.

Use content approval to formalize and control the process of making content available to an audience. For example, an enterprise that publishes content as one of its products or services might require a supervisory review and approval before publishing the content. The way that documents are submitted for approval varies depending on the versioning settings in the document library:

None   If versioning is not enabled and changes to a document are saved, the document's status becomes Pending. SharePoint keeps the previous version of the document so users with read permissions can still view it. After the pending changes have been approved, the new version of the document is made available for viewing by users with read permissions, and the previous version is overwritten. If you are not using versioning and a new document is uploaded to the document library, it is added to the library in the Pending state and is not viewable by users with read permissions until it is approved.

Major Versions Only   If major versioning is in use and changes to a document are saved, the document's state becomes Pending, and the previous major version of the document is made available for viewing by users with read permissions. After the changes to the document are approved, a new major version of the document is created and made available to site users with read permissions, and the previous version is saved to the document's history list. If major versioning is being used and a new document is uploaded to the document library, it is added to the library in the Pending state and is not viewable by users with read permissions until it is approved as version 1.

Major and Minor Versions   If major and minor versioning is enabled and changes to a document are saved, the author has the choice of saving a new minor version of the document as a draft or creating a new major version, which changes the document's status to Pending. After the changes to the document are approved, a new major version of the document is created and made available to site users with read permissions. In major and minor versioning, both major and minor versions of documents are kept in a document's history list. If major and minor versioning is in use and a new document is uploaded to the document library, it can be added to the library in the Draft state as version 0.1, or the author can immediately request approval. In the latter case, the document's status becomes Pending.

Checkout and Check-In

You can require that users check documents out of a document library before they can edit them and then check the documents back in when they are done. I recommend you always do this. The benefits of requiring checking in and out include the following:

- You have better control over when document versions are created. When a document is checked out, the author can save the document without checking it in. Other users of the document library will not be able to see these changes, and a new version is not created. A new version that is visible to other users is created only when an author checks in a document. This gives the author more flexibility and control.

- You can better capture metadata. When a document is checked in, the author can add comments describing the changes made to the document. This allows the author to create an ongoing history of the changes made to the document.

- Users can check documents out, undo checkouts, and check documents back in to SharePoint directly from a Microsoft Office 2007 application. It isn't necessary for the user to toggle back and forth between, say, a document open in Microsoft Word 2007 and a SharePoint document library.

- When a document is checked out, it is saved in the user's My Documents folder in a subfolder named SharePoint Drafts. This folder can be seen in Microsoft Office Outlook 2007. As long as the document is checked out, the user can save edits only to this local folder. When the user is ready to check the document in, the document is saved to the SharePoint site document library.

Introducing Lists and Libraries

Up until now, I've discussed lists and libraries as components within Microsoft Office Share-Point Server (MOSS) 2007 that store, organize, and filter information; however, SharePoint treats just about everything as a list. Lists can contain a wide variety of information, from your colleagues' contact information to links to external websites to collections of diverse data sources presented in one spot. Although a list may seem like a column of links, structurally it is put together more like a spreadsheet or a database, in rows and columns. These rows and columns are specific list elements that are particularly defined, as you will soon see.

Like lists, libraries are also a bit deceptive in their nature. It's tempting to think of a library as something like a shared folder on the network. You can have a shared folder containing all your business documents and another folder holding all the art department's graphics. You also have document and picture libraries in SharePoint, so what's the difference? In reality, a library is capable of so much more than a shared drive, including controlling document versions and like lists and filtering to show different views.

As you progress through this part of the chapter, you'll be presented with the basic structure and function of lists and libraries.

Understanding Lists

As previously mentioned, at its core a list is just a series of rows and columns that can be manipulated to present information in a variety of ways, depending on your needs. That said, rows and columns in the list grid structure have specific names and functions, as follows:

Items   Items are also known as records and are the "rows" in the list grid structure. An item contains the different property information for a single entry, such as an individual colleague, a link to a specific website, or other information. You may recall from Chapter 6, "Configuring Authentication and Security," that access security can be set at the item level, so if you have a collection of items in a list, access to each item for a particular user can be different.

Fields   If items are the "rows" in a list, then fields are the "columns" in the list grid structure. Fields are also known as *metadata* and are thought of as categories of information. Examples of fields are names, titles, last modified, and so on. Each field defines the different properties of a particular item.

Views   Views are a way of limiting the presentation of items and fields so that the person looking at a particular view sees only a subset of the information. For instance, let's say a list contains all of the names of employees for your company in every department. You can create different views that are defined by department name and then apply a particular view so that users in the sales department see the names of only those employees working in sales, rather than all items in the list.

There are other methods of modifying the presentation of lists besides views, which I'll address in a moment; however, the three previously listed elements are the core of what makes up a list.

You can create a view by showing or hiding individual fields (columns) in a list. You can also sort by the information in any two columns so that SharePoint will sort first by one column and then by another. Filtering is when you display information based on what field data you want to have seen. For instance, you can use the Show the Items When Column drop-down menu to select Title, use the next drop-down menu to select Is Equal To, and use the available field below to enter **Manager** (assuming you created a Manager field when you created the list). Once you've saved your changes, this particular view in the list will display only Manager items.

You'll get a chance to create and filter your own lists later in this chapter.

If a list has audience targeting enabled, as you read about in Chapter 5, "Managing Users and Groups," information contained in specific fields will automatically be added to the targeted audience view of the list.

SharePoint contains a number of list default templates, just as it does default site templates. Default list templates are as follows:

- Announcements
- Calendars
- Contacts
- Discussion Boards
- Links
- Project Tasks
- Surveys
- Tasks

You can also create custom lists if one of the default list templates doesn't quite fit your needs. Creating a list from a template allows you to select from a wide variety of field types. For instance, when you create a list from the Links default template, two default fields are created with the list: URL and Notes. The URL field is required and can't be modified or deleted.

You can add fields to the list with field attributes (for this particular template) organized in two basic categories; the first one is Name and Type, and the second is Optional Settings for the Column.

The options you are presented with under Name and Type are as follows:

- Column Name
- Single Line of Text
- Multiple Lines of Text
- Choice (menu to choose from)

- Number (1, 1.0, 100)
- Currency
- Date and Time
- Lookup (information already on this site)
- Yes/No (check box)
- Hyperlink or Picture
- Calculated (calculation based on other columns)

The options you are presented with under Optional Settings for the Column are as follows:

- Description
- Require That This Column Contains Information
- Maximum Number of Characters
- Default Value
- Add to Default View

The Column Name field under Name and Type is always blank, and you can name your column anything; however, the default option for the rest of the properties in this section is Single Line of Text. You can select only one of these options, and depending on which one you choose, the items under Optional Settings for the Column will change.

The options you are presented with when you want to add fields will be different depending on which list template you selected or whether you chose to create a custom list. This means the selections you just read may be different depending on what list template you choose.

Understanding Libraries

A library is a location within a SharePoint site where you can create, collect, update, and manage files with members of your work team or department or with other colleagues. Each library displays a list of files and key information about the files, which helps SharePoint users collaborate more effectively.

Just as with lists, you can customize libraries in many different ways depending on your needs. You can control how documents are viewed, tracked, managed, and created. You can track versions, including how many and which type of versions, and you can limit who can see documents before they are approved. You can use workflows to collaborate on documents in libraries, and you can specify information management policies to manage the handling and expiration of documents within libraries.

There's a temptation to think of libraries in SharePoint as being able to contain and act upon only documents or pictures, but SharePoint Server 2007 has a greater variety of library options than earlier versions of SharePoint:

Data Connection library This document library type is new to SharePoint 2007. Organizations can use it to centrally publish connection files and make it easy for users to find and use the data sources they need. Data connection files are easy to create and update, and solution designers can easily access them from within Microsoft Office 2007 client applications.

Document library This library can store many file types, including documents and spreadsheets. You can store other kinds of files in a document library, although some file types can be blocked for security reasons. When you work with programs that are compatible with Microsoft Windows SharePoint Services (WSS), you can create those files from the library. For example, your marketing team may have its own library for planning materials, news releases, and publications.

Form library If you need to manage a group of XML-based business forms, use a form library. For example, your organization may want to use a form library for expense reports. Setting up a form library requires an XML editor or XML design program that is compatible with Microsoft Office InfoPath.

Picture library To share a collection of digital pictures or graphics, use a picture library. Although pictures can be stored in other types of SharePoint libraries, picture libraries have several advantages. For instance, from a picture library you can view pictures in a slide show, download pictures to your computer, and edit pictures with a graphics program. Consider creating a picture library if you use a large number of graphics, such as business logos and other corporate images.

Reports library The reports library helps organizations create, manage, and share information contained in business data web parts, key performance indicator (KPI) web parts, and Excel web access web parts, which are used for business intelligence analytics. The Records Center site template mentioned in Chapter 4, "Building Sites and Site Collections," contains a reports library by default, but anyone who can create document libraries within a site collection can create a report library. The reports library includes a version history for each report and archives previous versions. Users can create new versions of reports for special events and later revert to a previous report.

Slide library Slide libraries allow Microsoft Office PowerPoint 2007 users to share individual slides from a presentation, reuse slides, track the history of a slide, compile individual slides into a presentation, and receive alerts when a slide in a presentation has been changed. Users can publish slides to a slide library directly from PowerPoint 2007 or upload slides to the library from their computer.

Translation Management library Translation management libraries help organizations create, store, and manage translated documents by providing both views and specific features that assist in the process of manual document translation. The translation management library is designed to store documents and their translations. The library tracks the relationship between a source document and the translations and groups all of these documents together for easy accessibility. The library can also be configured with a special translation management workflow that is designed to manage the process of manual document translation.

Wiki page library   This library is used to create a collection of connected wiki pages. A wiki enables multiple users to collect routine information in a format that is easily created and modified. You can add pages that contain pictures, tables, hyperlinks, and internal links to your wiki page library.

List and Library Content Types

SharePoint 2007 lists and libraries can store different documents based on content type. This allows you to tailor-make libraries for specific types of content such as proposals, legal contracts, statements of work, and product design specifications. Even though all of these different content types might be stored in the same location, you can still set security at the document level so that, for example, all of HR's documents can be read only by the HR staff. Also, you can create, use, share, and retain documents in different ways depending on content type.

Content types provide organizations with a way to manage and organize content consistently across different lists and libraries in a site collection. They also make it possible for a single list or library to contain multiple item types or document types.

MOSS 2007 defines a content type as a group of reusable settings used to describe the shared behaviors for a specific type of content. Content types can be defined for any item type, including documents, list items, and folders. You can specify a content type by the following:

- The columns (metadata) you want to assign to items of this type
- The document template on which to base new items of this type (document content types only)
- The custom New, Edit, and Display forms to use with this content type
- The workflows available for items of this content type
- The custom solutions or features associated with items of this content type
- The information management policies associated with items of this content type
- The Document Information panel, which is available in compatible Microsoft Office applications for items of this content type

Working with Lists

For the rest of this chapter, we will be working on a collaboration team subsite that has been previously created. As you'll notice in Figure 7.1, the subsite has several empty lists displayed on the home page that we will be using.

The default lists on this page are Announcements, Calendar, and Links. You can see some additional lists in the Quick Launch area to the left including Tasks and Team Discussion. We'll be working with these in the next several exercises. Exercise 7.1 will start you off with adding an announcement to the already created Announcements list.

FIGURE 7.1   Collaboration team subsite

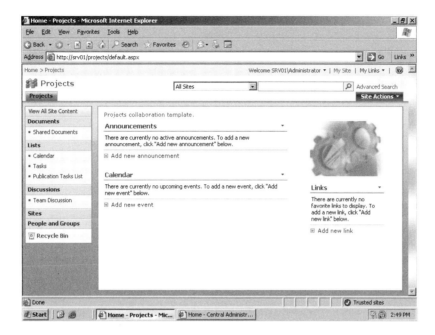

EXERCISE 7.1

Adding an Announcement

1. Just beneath the Announcements list, click Add New Announcement.

2. On the Announcements: New Item page, type a title for your announcement in the mandatory Title field.

3. Under Body in the text editor, type a paragraph announcing that the Projects site is now live and available to team members.

4. Create a hyperlink to the portal site by clicking the hyperlink symbol. When the Insert Hyperlink dialog box appears, type the text you want to appear for the link in the Text to Display field, type the URL of the site in the Address field, and then click OK. (Feel free to modify the text in this field using other text editor features.)

5. Click the calendar applet next to the Expires field, and select a month and day when this announcement will expire and no longer appear in the Announcements list.

6. When finished, click OK.

Notice in Figure 7.2 that the announcement now appears in the list, but you can't see the entire announcement.

To read the entire announcement, click the title of the announcement. When you are taken to the page for this particular announcement, if you have site administrator permissions or are the creator of the announcement, you can modify it by clicking Edit Item, or you can delete the announcement by clicking Delete Item, as shown in Figure 7.3. You can also add a completely new announcement to the list from here by clicking New Item.

FIGURE 7.2   An announcement displayed in the list

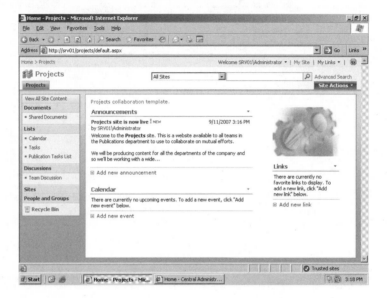

FIGURE 7.3   Viewing a full announcement

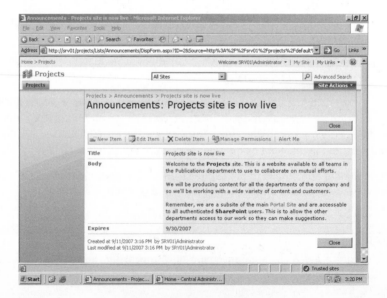

Now that you've created an announcement, it's time to learn how to manage it. Exercise 7.2 will show you how.

EXERCISE 7.2

Managing an Announcement

1. If you haven't already done so, click the title of the announcement you created in Exercise 7.1.

2. On the Announcements page, click Edit Item.

3. When the announcement opens for editing, modify something in the text editor field, such as adding or deleting a line of text, and then click Spelling in the toolbar.

4. When the Spell Checker dialog box opens, if any spelling errors appear, click the appropriate buttons (Correct, Ignore, and so on). When the spell-checking is done, click OK to close the dialog box.

5. Click OK to exit edit mode and return to the subsite's main page.

6. Click the title of the announcement again, and then click Manage Permissions.

7. On the Permissions page, when you see the list of default permissions, click Actions in the toolbar, and select Manage Permissions of Parent. (Click OK when the warning dialog box appears to proceed.)

8. On this page, you can click New to add a new user or a new group.

9. Tick one or more check boxes next to a default user or group, and click Actions to either remove or edit user permissions.

10. Select Actions ➢ Inherit Permissions to again inherit permissions from the parent site. (Clicking Manage Permissions of Parent in step 7 stopped permission inheritance and allowed you to start creating unique access permissions for this list item.)

11. Select Settings ➢ Access Requests. If you want users to be able to request access to this list item, tick the Allow Requests for Access check box, type the email address of those people you want to receive notifications in the Send All Requests for Access to the Following E-mail Address field, and then click OK.

12. Select Settings ➢ Permission Levels ➢ Edit Permissions Levels to create a custom access group for this list item. (You'll need to click OK in the warning dialog box to continue.) You can also click Delete Selected Permission Levels or Delete Selected Permission Levels at This Location to perform those actions.

13. Navigate to the Announcements page, and click Alert Me.

14. On the New Alert page, accept the default text in the Alert Title field, and accept the default username (which should be yours) in the Send Alerts To field. (You can add more names by typing them in the field separated by semicolons and then clicking the Check Names icon.)

EXERCISE 7.2 *(continued)*

15. Under Send Alerts for These Changes, make a selection such as Send Me an Alert When Anything Changes. Under When to Send Alerts, select Send a Daily Summary, and use the drop-down menu to select a time of day when you want to receive the alert. (If you had selected Send a Weekly Summary, the day of the week drop-down menu would have become active, and you could have selected the day in the week when you wanted the summary to be sent to your email address.)

16. Click OK.

Exercise 7.2 was fairly long, but it did give you a good chance to explore most of the ways you can manage an announcement item. As you work with other list types, you'll notice that most of the options you worked with here are similar to or the same as the options available in those other lists. Also, to see a complete list of all announcements, click Announcements at the head of the web part.

You've learned quite a lot just modifying an entry in an announcement. Exercise 7.3 continues the process of working with lists by adding an entry to a calendar in SharePoint 2007. The exercise assumes you are on the home page of the subsite we are using for this set of exercises.

EXERCISE 7.3

Adding an Entry to a Calendar

1. Under Calendar, click Add New Event.

2. When the Calendar: New Item page opens, as shown here, give the event a title in the mandatory Title field.

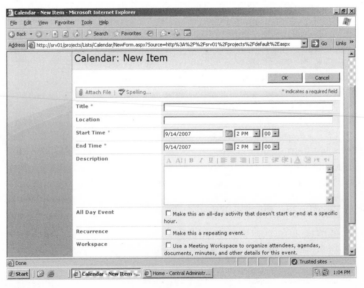

3. In the Location field, indicate a location for the event, if relevant.

EXERCISE 7.3 *(continued)*

4. Under Start Time, use the calendar applet to select a date for the event, and then use the drop-down menus to select a start time.

5. Under End Time, use the calendar applet to select a date for the ending of the event, and then use the drop-down menus to select an ending time.

6. In the Description text editor, type an optional description of the event, such as a meeting agenda.

7. Under All Day Event, tick the available check box if this event will last all day and does not have a specific start or end time.

8. Under Recurrence, tick the available check box if this is a recurring event such as a weekly staff meeting.

9. Under Workspace, if you want to create a Meeting Workspace for this event, tick the available check box.

10. Click OK when you're done.

Depending on what selections you made, you will find that other options are presented to you. For example, let's say that in step 7 you indicated that this will be an all-day event. When you tick the appropriate check box, the page refreshes, and the start and end time options are no longer available. If you tick the check box in step 8 indicating that this is a recurring event, additional options become available, as you can see here.

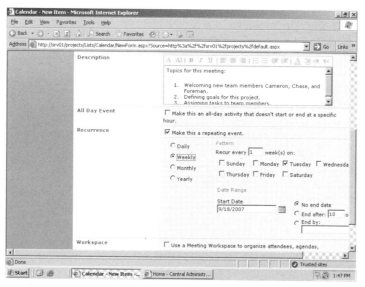

Exercise 7.4 will cover the additional steps that occur when you tick the Workspace check box mentioned in step 9 of Exercise 7.3. The first step in this exercise starts with the Workspace

check box on the Calendar: New Item page. The exercise assumes you've created a repeating meeting that occurs every Tuesday.

EXERCISE 7.4

Creating a Meeting Workspace by Scheduling an Event

1. Tick the available check box under Workspace on the Calendar: New Event page.

2. Click OK.

3. When the New Meeting Workspace page appears, verify that the name of the workspace in the Title field is what you desire. (The name of the event you created in Exercise 7.3 automatically populates this field.)

4. Type an optional description of the Workspace in the Description field.

5. Under Web Site Address, verify that the URL populating the URL Name field is the one you desire, and edit the URL if it is not.

6. Under Permissions, select either Use Same Permissions as Parent Site or Use Unique Permissions, and click OK.

7. When the Template Selection page appears, select Basic Meeting Workspace in the Template list, and click OK.

As you can see, you are taken to the newly created meeting workspace you created from the recurring meeting you set up in the calendar.

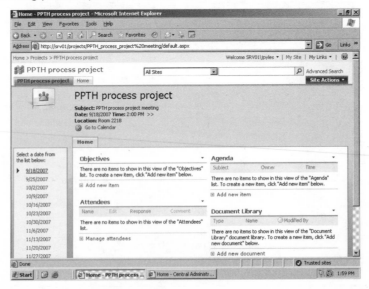

To return to the calendar, click the Go to Calendar link under the notations for Subject, Date, and Location for the originally scheduled meeting.

You worked with site and workspace creation in Chapter 4, "Building Sites and Site Collections," and you will work with this newly created workspace both in this chapter and in Chapter 8, "Configuring Web Part Pages, Web Parts, and Web Pages."

On the Calendar page, scroll down to view how each Tuesday on the calendar displays your recurring meeting. When you go to the home page of your subsite, you will see the error we introduced in the process (it was on purpose...honest). The calendar web part on the page displays a long list of the scheduled meetings, and the agenda we created for the first meeting is displayed for each weekly meeting. Exercise 7.5 will show you how to fix this.

EXERCISE 7.5

Creating a View in a Calendar List

1. On the site home page, click Calendar (the name of the web part, not any of the actual events).

2. When the calendar appears, click the View arrow; in the list that appears, click Create View.

3. Under Start from an Existing View, click Current Events.

4. Under Name in the View Name field, give the view a name such as This Week.

5. Tick the Make This the Default View check box to make this view the one everyone sees when they visit the home page.

6. Scroll down, and expand Item Limit.

7. In the Number of Items to Display field, enter **1**, and then select Limit the Total Number of Items Returned to the Specified Amount.

8. Click OK.

9. Return to the home page, click to the right of Calendar, and then click Modify Shared Web Part.

10. In the Calendar web part toolbox, click the Selected View drop-down menu, and select the This Week view. (Depending on your screen resolution, you may have to scroll right to see the toolbox.)

11. When the warning dialog box appears, click OK.

EXERCISE 7.5 *(continued)*

As you can see, although this is a recurring meeting; only the event information for this week's meeting is displayed in the current view.

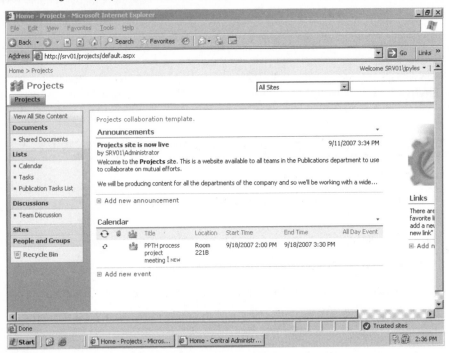

 Real World Scenario

Creating a View for a List

One of the site owners of a subsite in your company's site collection has created a links list for her home page. She calls you to say that the list contains more than 100 links and she doesn't want them all visible to every user in the department. She has links that are more relevant to different types of site members such as sales associates, managers, and marketing staff. You decide that the best course of action would be to create different views for each group and then have each group select the view containing the links they use most often. Although users in each group can select different views including viewing all the links, they will most likely use the view constructed for them since they won't have to scroll through a long collection of links, and their view of the home page will be more manageable.

One of the more interesting lists used in SharePoint to promote collaboration is the discussion board. You can create as many discussion boards as you want, but SharePoint 2007 creates a single default board called Team Discussion. You can use this ready-made board just the way it is or rename it to something more suitable. Exercise 7.6 will introduce you to how to begin a conversation in a discussion board.

EXERCISE 7.6

Beginning a Conversation in a Discussion Board

1. On the site home page, click the Team Discussion link under Discussions in Quick Launch.

2. On the Team Discussion page, select New ➢ Discussion.

3. On the Team Discussion: New Item page in the mandatory Subject field, type a subject name for the discussion.

4. In the Body text editor, create a message that you want the other site members to see and respond to.

5. When you are finished with your message, click OK.

You are returned to the Team Discussion page, and the new message is displayed by Subject, Created By, and Last Updated. There is also a Replies column, but until someone replies, the value in that column will be zero (0). To read the message, just click the subject title on the forum page, and it will be displayed, as shown here.

While you're viewing the message, responding is as easy as clicking Reply and typing your response in the Body field. When you are done, click OK. Once you do, you are returned to the message, and the response you added will appear beneath the original posting. On the Team Discussion page, the value under Replies will increment by one.

On the Team Discussion page, there is only one view, by default, for presenting posted discussions, the Subject view. As with any list, you can create additional views as you did in Exercise 7.5 with the calendar.

Within an actual discussion thread, there are two default views—Flat, which is the default, and Threaded. There's little difference between the two graphically; however, creating a threaded view for the Team Discussion page will significantly alter the way message topics are presented.

 You can create additional threaded views to alter the presentation of information from within a particular discussion, but to create a threaded view of all discussions seen from the Team Discussion page, you must modify the existing Subject view.

Exercise 7.7 will take you through the process of creating a threaded view. The exercise assumes you are beginning on the Team Discussion page.

EXERCISE 7.7

Creating a Threaded View for a Discussion Group

1. On the Team Discussion page, click the View drop-down menu, and select Modify View.

2. On the Edit View: Team Discussion page under Columns, tick the Threading (threaded) check box, and use the drop-down arrow next to this item to select 1. (The values of the other column items that have been selected by default will change automatically.)

3. Under Sort, use the First Sort By the Column drop-down menu to select Threading (threaded).

4. Accept the rest of the default settings, and click OK.

Changing the default Subject view to a threaded view will display not only the title of each discussion on the Team Discussion page but will also display the content of the first post to a thread. As you can see, although this view gives you more information about the contents of the threads, it also takes up a lot of space. You can reverse this view by repeating the steps in Exercise 7.8, unticking the check box next to Threading (threaded) in step 2, and using the drop-down Sort menu in step 3 to select Subject.

Another list in SharePoint 2007 that you might not think of as actually being a list is Tasks. Of course, as previously stated, SharePoint treats just about everything as a list, so the structure of many of SharePoint's content management containers isn't always as it appears. Since we've constructed a fictional Projects group that is assigned to create and manage documentation for different divisions, departments, and external customers (including the PPTH project), let's continue the process by assigning tasks to the team. Exercise 7.8 will walk you through the steps. You'll be starting from the home page of the subsite we've been using for these exercises.

EXERCISE 7.8

Assigning a Task

1. In Quick Launch, click Tasks.

2. On the Tasks page, select New ➤ New Item.

3. On the Tasks: New Item page in the mandatory Title field, give the task a name.

4. Under Priority, use the drop-down menu to select a priority for the task: (1) High, (2) Normal, or (3) Low.

5. Under Status, use the drop-down menu to select a status type for the task: Not Started, In Progress, Completed, Deferred, or Waiting on Someone Else.

6. Under % Complete, type a value in the % field to indicate how much of the project has been completed.

7. In the Assigned To field, type the name of the person the task is assigned to, and click the Check Names icon.

8. In the Description text editor, type a description of the task that will assist the person assigned to complete it.

9. Under Start Date, use the calendar to select a date for the beginning of the task.

10. Under End Date, use the calendar to select a projected date for the end of the task.

11. Click OK.

As you can see, the new task appears in the list on the Tasks page. (I've added several other tasks so you can get a better idea of what the page looks like populated.)

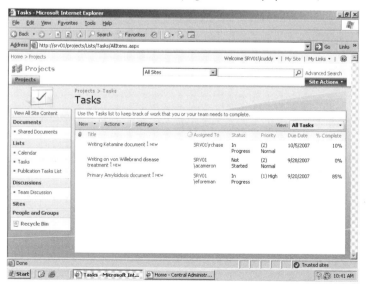

In the previous graphic, you can see the default columns displayed on the page and that the default view of All Tasks is being used. Like any other list, you can change the columns that are displayed either by modifying the default view or by creating additional views.

NOTE   You learned how to add links to a Links web part in Chapter 3, "Configuring SharePoint 2007," and since it is a fairly simple task, there won't be an exercise illustrating the process. I've added some links to our sample page just to flesh it out; you might want to do the same.

If you go to the workspace you created in Exercise 7.4, you'll see some additional list types. The easiest way to get to the meeting workspace is from the home page of the sample site. Under Calendar, click the title of the meeting, and then on the meeting page under Workspace, click the name of the workspace.

Objectives, Agenda, and Attendees are all SharePoint 2007 lists, and items can be added, edited, and filtered in them, just as in any other list. The document library by definition isn't a list, but we will be addressing libraries later in this chapter. Since working with these particular lists is substantially similar to the lists you've worked with so far, there won't be any exercises involving the lists in this workspace. Feel free to add items to this workspace since you'll be working on it later in this chapter and in subsequent chapters.

TIP   To add users to the Attendees list, each user must have an email address associated with their SharePoint user account.

There are a few more exercises in this section of the chapter that are generic to most Share-Point lists. You've already had some practice with modifying list behavior and presentation in previous exercises in this chapter.

If you navigate to the Tasks page you previously saw in Exercise 7.8, click Actions to view the following menu items:

- Edit in Datasheet
- Export to Spreadsheet
- View in RSS Feed
- Alert Me

When you click List Settings, you will see the following menu items:

- Create Column
- Create View
- List Settings

Click to the right of any list item title to view the following menu items:

- View Item
- Edit Item
- Manage Permissions

- Delete Item
- Alert Me

Clicking Edit Item in the toolbar on the Tasks page will provide the following options that you can apply to any item in the list:

- Attach File
- Delete Item
- Spelling

Click to the right of any item title, and then click View Item to view the following options:

- New Item
- Edit Item
- Delete Item
- Manage Permissions
- Alert Me

Select Manage Permissions to view the Manage Permissions page. On this page, click Actions to view the menu items Manage Permissions of Parent and Edit Permissions.

You can click the title of any column on any of these pages to change the order of the items displayed in the column. On the Tasks page, you can click the View drop-down menu and see the menu items:

- All Tasks (the default view)
- Active Tasks
- By Assigned To
- By My Groups
- Due Today
- My Tasks
- Modify this View
- Create View

The Edit in Datasheet and Export to Spreadsheet menu options mentioned earlier require that you have a spreadsheet application such as Microsoft Office Excel installed on the computer you are using to view this page. The Edit in Datasheet option also requires that Active X support be installed and enabled in your web browser.

Clicking the List Settings menu item takes you to the Customize page for the list. On that page you can modify any of these components:

- General Settings
- Permissions and Management
- Communications
- Columns
- Views

Clicking any of the links in a section will take you to a page where you can modify the properties of that list element. Whenever you create a new list, you have the opportunity to configure each of these list elements so that the list will display and behave as you desire.

Working with Libraries

Libraries are the other major container of content in SharePoint 2007. As you read about earlier in this chapter, you can work with a number of different libraries; to start, we'll use the two most common libraries, document and picture. In Exercise 7.9, you'll work in the default Shared Documents library. The exercise assumes you'll be starting on the home page of the sample site we've been using in this chapter. You should also be connected to the SharePoint Server 2007 site from a computer that already has Microsoft Office Word documents available. You must also have Word installed on your computer if you plan to open and edit these documents.

EXERCISE 7.9

Adding a Document to a Library

1. From the subsite home page, in Quick Launch, click Documents.

2. On the All Site Content page under Document Libraries, select Shared Documents.

3. On the Shared Documents page, click the Upload drop-down menu, and select Upload Document.

4. Click the Browse button, and browse your computer until you locate the document you want to upload to the Shared Documents library (which can include any shared files and folders on the network).

5. Tick the Overwrite Existing Files check box if you want this file to overwrite any earlier versions of the document.

6. Click OK.

The document is uploaded into the Shared Documents library. Now anyone who has access to the site and library will be able to read the document. You could also have clicked New and selected New Document to have created a new Word document directly in the library. Remember, though, this option is available only if you are working on a computer that has Word installed. If you are working directly from the server, this is highly unlikely.

Clicking New will also give you the Create Folder option. You can create folders and then move different categories of documents inside the folders.

I find working with SharePoint's document folders rather clumsy, so I tend to avoid them. I suggest either creating separate document libraries for different documents and setting security on each library based on intended audience or creating a single document library and creating multiple views based on the intended audience.

You can also use drag-and-drop functionality to add documents to a document library, as you'll see in Exercise 7.10. This exercise assumes you are still in the document library as you were at the end of Exercise 7.9.

EXERCISE 7.10

Dragging and Dropping a Document into a Library

1. In the Shared Documents library, select Actions ➢ Open in Windows Explorer.

2. On your computer, select Start ➢ My Documents, or browse to the location where you have a document you want to upload into the library.

3. Right-click the desired document, and select Copy.

4. In the Windows Explorer view of the Shared Documents library, right-click in any empty space, and select Paste.

5. Close the Explorer view of the library.

As you can see, the two documents you just added in the previous two exercises appear in the library.

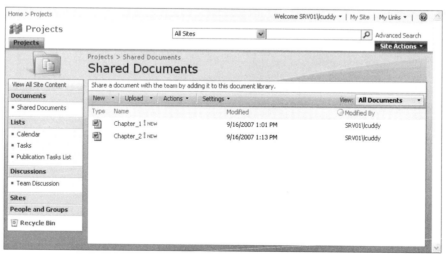

For the next several exercises, you'll need to work with the document library on the meeting workspace you created in Exercise 7.4. To get to the sample meeting workspace, on the home page under Calendar, click the name of the meeting. Then on the Calendar Item page under Workspace, click the workspace name. Exercise 7.11 and the exercises that follow will require you to have added several documents to the document library on that page; you can do so by following the steps in either Exercise 7.9 or Exercise 7.10. This exercise will show you how to check out and edit a document in a library.

EXERCISE 7.11

Checking Out and Modifying a Document in a Library

1. On the meeting workspace, click Document Library.

2. Click to the right of the desired document, and select View Properties from the menu.

3. On the subsequent page, click Check Out in the toolbar.

4. Click to the right of the desired document again, and select Edit in Microsoft Office Word.

5. When the File Open dialog box appears, click OK.

6. When the document opens in Word, perform any editing you require, save your changes, and close the document.

7. In the document library, click to the right of the desired document, and then click Check In.

8. On the Check In page under Document Check In, select Yes if you want to keep the document checked out after you check in this version, or select No to check in the document.

9. Under Comments, type optional comments about your edits.

10. Click OK.

Checking a document out before editing it prevents another user from making edits to the document at the same time. Once the document is checked out, if anyone tries to access it, the document will be unavailable until it is checked back in. If you had selected Yes in Step 8, you would have checked in the version of the document as it is to date, but you would still have the document checked out for further edits. This means that if you make errors in your checked-out version, you can discard it and use the checked-in version in the library you saved.

Two important features in libraries are versioning and workflow. Versioning allows you to save multiple versions of a document, which is handy if you need to review the steps in the development of a document. Workflow is used when you want to create an approval or tracking process for submitted content. Exercise 7.12 will show you how to enable versioning. Exercise 7.13 will continue by showing you how to set up a workflow for the library.

EXERCISE 7.12

Enabling Versioning in a Document Library

1. In the document library, click Settings ➤ Document Library Settings.

2. Under General Settings, select Versioning Settings.

3. On the Document Library Versioning Settings page under Content Approval, select Yes to require versioning or No if you do not require versioning.

4. Under Document Version History, select Create Major and Minor (Draft) Versions. (Your other options are No Versioning and Create Major Versions.)

5. If you want to limit the number of versions to retain, tick the Keep the Following Number of Major Versions check box and/or the Keep Drafts for the Following Number of Major Versions check box.

6. Under Draft Item Security, if you elected to keep minor versions in step 4, select either Any User Who Can Read Items or Only Users Who Can Edit Items to determine who can see the draft versions.

7. Under Require Check Out, select Yes, and click OK to finish.

You are taken back to the Customize Document Library page. Document versioning is now set up for all documents in this library.

EXERCISE 7.13

Enabling Workflow for a Document Library

1. On the Customize Document Library page under Permissions and Management, select Workflow Settings.

2. Under Workflow, select the type of workflow you want to apply—Approval, Collect Feedback, Collect Signatures, or Disposition Approval.

3. In the Name field, give the workflow a unique name.

4. Under Task List, accept the default selection of Tasks (New), and under History List, accept the default selection of Workflow History (New).

5. Under Start Options, tick one or more of the check boxes, depending on your requirements, and click Next.

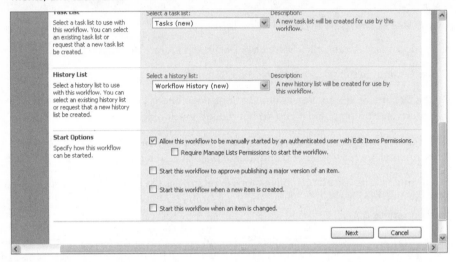

6. On the Customize Workflow: Submitted documents approval page under Workflow Tasks, next to Assign Tasks To, select either All Participants Simultaneously (Parallel) or One Participant at a Time (Serial).

7. Next to Allow Workflow Participants To, you can tick the Reassign the Task to Another Person and/or Request a Change Before Completing the Task check boxes.

8. Under Default Workflow Start Values in the Approvers field, type the name or names of users you want to be approvers, and then click the Check Names button.

9. You can tick the Assign a Single Task to Each Group Entered (Do Not Expand Groups) and/or the Allow Changes to the Participant List When This Workflow Is Started check boxes and then type a message to include with your request in the available field.

10. If you selected All Participants Simultaneously (Parallel) in step 6, under Due Date you would use the Calendar button to populate the Tasks Are Due By (Parallel) field.

11. In the Give Each Person the Following Amount of Time to Finish Their Task (Serial) field, type a value in the available field, and then use the drop-down menu to select either Days or Weeks.

12. If you want to notify anyone else besides approvers when a document is submitted, type their name or names in the Notify Others field, and then click the Check Names button.

13. Under Complete the Workflow, if you selected All Participants Simultaneously (Parallel) in step 6, you could tick the Complete This Workflow When check box.

EXERCISE 7.13 *(continued)*

14. Next to Cancel This Workflow When The, tick the Document Is Rejected and/or Document Is Changed check boxes.

15. Under Post-completion Workflow Activities, you can tick the Update the Approval Status (use this workflow to control content approval) check box next to After the Workflow Is Completed.

16. Click OK.

You will be taken to the Change Workflow Settings: Document Library page, where you can see the newly created workflow.

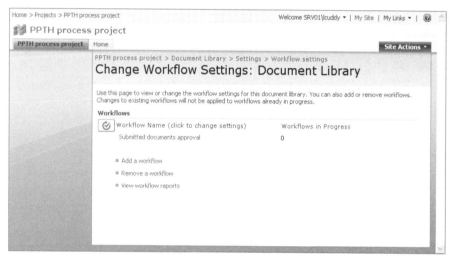

As you can tell, the exact process for setting up a workflow depends on which type of workflow you choose in step 2 of the previous exercise. Here is a list of those options again and how they're defined:

Approval   Routes a document for approval. Approvers can approve or reject the document, reassign the approval task, or request changes to the document.

Collect Feedback   Routes a document for review. Reviewers can provide feedback, which is compiled and sent to the document owner when the workflow has completed.

Collect Signatures   Gathers signatures needed to complete a Microsoft Office document. This workflow can be started only from within an Office client.

Disposition Approval   Manages document expiration and retention by allowing participants to decide whether to retain or delete expired documents.

If, in our current example, you submit a document to the library as a user who is not an approver, when you upload the document to the library and check it in, you will see in the column for the approval workflow the notation In Progress by your document.

Sign in to the site as a user who is an approver and click In Progress. You are taken to the Workflow Status page. Under Tasks, you will see that the workflow task has been assigned to an approver, and under Workflow History, you'll see when the workflow was started and when the approval task was created, as in Figure 7.4.

FIGURE 7.4   Workflow status and task

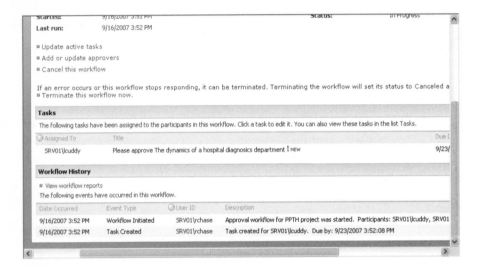

Clicking the name of the task will take the approver to the Approval Requested task page, where the approver can type a notation in the Type Comments to Include with Your Response field and then click Approve, Reject, or Cancel. In our example, the approver will click Approve.

> If the task is assigned to one approver and another approver attempts to manage the workflow by approving or rejecting the document, the system will return an error; however, this is true only if you selected One Participant at a Time (Serial) in step 6 of Exercise 7.13.

You can also click to the right of the document name in the document library and select Publish Major Version to publish the document as a major version.

The options for modifying a library are similar to those available for a list. On the document library page you've already seen what options are available when you click the New and Upload buttons in the toolbar. When you click Actions, the menu options are as follows:

- Edit in Datasheet
- Open with Windows Explorer

- Export to Spreadsheet
- View RSS Feed
- Alert Me
- All Meetings

You've already seen most of these options. When you click Settings in the toolbar, your options on the menu are as follows:

- Create Column
- Create View
- Document Library Settings

When you click the View drop-down menu, your menu options are as follows:

- All Documents
- Explorer View
- Modify this View
- Create View

This list should also seem familiar to you.

When you click to the right of any document name in the library, you receive the following menu options:

- View Properties
- Edit Properties
- Manage Permissions
- Edit in Microsoft Office Word
- Delete
- Send To
- Check Out
- Unpublish this Version
- Version History
- Workflows
- Alert Me

A submenu appears with these options if you hover over Send To:

- Other Location
- E-mail a Link
- Create Document Workspace
- Download a Copy

The ability to configure document libraries for content types is a new feature in MOSS 2007; it enables organizations to more efficiently organize and centrally manage content across a site collection. You can define content types for specific kinds of documents. Content types can be defined in a list as well as in a library and can consist of multiple items or document types. This is useful for enabling document libraries and lists to accept multiple document and item types.

As you previously learned, you can enter a document library, click the New button on the toolbar, and create a new document. The major advantage of configuring and using document types is that you can create different documents after clicking New based on the unique document properties and policies that are specific to that document type. Content types can be associated with a workflow so when a user creates a new document from a content type, a workflow is automatically initiated.

Exercise 7.14 will show you how to set a library to accept multiple content types. For this exercise, you will need to be back on the home page of the sample site we've been using.

EXERCISE 7.14

Configuring a Document Library for Multiple Content Types

1. On the home page in Quick Launch, click Documents.

2. On the Documents page, click Shared Documents.

3. Select Settings ➢ Document Library Settings.

4. Under General Settings, click Advanced Settings.

5. In the Content Type section under Allow Management of Content Types, select Yes.

6. Click OK.

    You cannot enable multiple content types on a wiki page library.

Now that you've enabled the library to accept different content types, you can add a content type to the library. Exercise 7.15 will show you the process. You will be starting out in the Shared Documents library.

EXERCISE 7.15

Adding a Content Type to a Library

1. Select Settings ➢ Document Library Settings.

2. Under Content Types, select Add from Existing Site Content Types.

3. On the Add Content Types page, accept the default selection of All Groups in the Select Site Content Types From drop-down menu.

EXERCISE 7.15 *(continued)*

4. Select one or more content types in the Available Site Content Types area, and click Add to move your selections to the Content Types to Add area, as shown here.

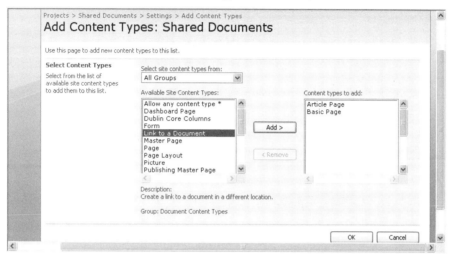

5. Click OK.

Now the additional content types can be added to the Shared Documents library.

Working with a picture library is similar to working with a document library. We'll take a quick look at how picture libraries are like document libraries. You'll start out in Exercise 7.16 at the home page of the sample site we're using.

EXERCISE 7.16

Creating a Picture Library

1. On the home page in Quick Launch, click View All Site Content.

2. Click Create in the toolbar on the View All Site Content page.

3. On the Create page under Libraries, click Picture Library.

4. On the New page under Name and Description, give your picture library a name in the Name field and an optional description in the Description field.

5. Under Navigation, click Yes to allow the new picture library to appear in Quick Launch.

6. Under Incoming E-Mail, click No so that the picture library cannot receive content by email.

EXERCISE 7.16 *(continued)*

7. Under Picture Version History, click Yes to allow a version of a picture to be created each time a picture is edited.

8. Click Create.

Once the picture library has been created, you are taken to the Picture Library page. It looks and acts just like a document library. The New, Upload, Actions, and Settings buttons on the toolbar provide the same menu options as in a document library. You can upload and manage all of the site's pictures here.

The process of updating and managing pictures is just a bit different from in a document library. The final exercise demonstrates this process: Exercise 7.17 will show you how to upload a picture.

EXERCISE 7.17

Uploading a Picture to a Picture Library

1. In the picture library, click Upload.

2. On the Add Picture page, browse to where the desired picture is located, and click OK.

3. On the picture page, either accept the default in the mandatory Name field or edit the name you want to give to the picture. (You will see a preview of the picture in the Preview area just beneath.)

4. Give the picture a title in the Title field, and under Date Picture Taken, use the calendar and drop-down menus to indicate the date and time the picture was taken.

5. Give the picture an optional description in the Description field.

6. To better allow search to locate the picture, type identifying keywords in the Keywords field.

7. Click OK.

If you click a specific picture in the library, the buttons in the toolbar will allow you to edit the item, delete the item, manage permissions, manage copies, check out the picture, manage versions of the picture, or send an alert when the item changes. If you check out the picture, you will not be able to actually edit the graphic unless you are on a computer with the appropriate software.

If you click Actions in the library, you can view the library contents as a slide show that opens in a separate browser window.

Slide libraries are almost the same as picture libraries except that they are designed to contain and manage PowerPoint slide files. Other library types such as data connection form, report, translation management, and wiki libraries will be addressed in Chapters 10, 11, 12, and 15.

On the Upload a Document or Upload a Picture page, rather than browsing for a single item, you can click Upload Multiple Files and then select several items you want to upload to the library all at once.

Summary

In this chapter, you learned a great deal about creating and managing lists and libraries, including the following topics:

- An overview of document and records management, including workflows, governance, scheduling, versioning, content approval, and checkouts
- Lists and libraries, including the basic features of each
- How to add content to the different types of lists, how lists can be used to create workspaces, and how to assign and manage tasks in lists
- How libraries work, using document and picture libraries as examples
- How to configure and use versioning and workflows, as well as how to enable and add content types

Exam Essentials

Know how to configure alerts.   By configuring alerts, you can be notified whenever an item or task belonging to you is created or changed. For example, if you are a document approver in a document library workflow, you can be alerted when a new approval task has been assigned to you. You can also be notified when changes have been made on a document on which you are collaborating with your team.

Understand document management.   This is a key administrative task in SharePoint, and you will need to know how to add content to a document library and how to impose workflow, versioning, and content type in the library.

Understand content management.   For this content area, you will need to understand how to manage different content types in a SharePoint site including documents, pictures, and a wide variety of lists. You also will need to know how to add content types to document libraries.

Know how to configure workflow.   You will need to know how to create workflow in a document library, set up its parameters including designating approvers and selecting the specific workflow type, add a document to the workflow, and understand how to approve or reject the document.

Review Questions

1. You are a site owner for your company's sales department site. You want to understand more about lists since you will be adding announcements, links, and calendar event items to your newly created site. You have also heard that you can set different access permissions to the site, to the lists, and even to items. In exploring how lists are constructed, what elements in a list's grid structure correspond to an item?

    A. Rows

    B. Columns

    C. Cells

    D. Fields

2. You are one of the site owners for your company's Creative Projects site and one of several approvers for workflow in the document library. Robert, one of the contributors, has completed a document for the PPTH project. You have reviewed the document and want to approve it, but when you try, you receive an error. Of the following options, which one is the most likely cause of the problem?

    A. Robert submitted an earlier version of the document than the one currently in the library, causing an error when you tried to approve it.

    B. You are not logged onto the system, and as an anonymous user, you do not have permissions to approve documents in the workflow.

    C. The approval task was assigned to another approver in the system besides you, and you are not able to finish a task assigned to someone else.

    D. Robert did not designate the assigned task of writing the document as completed before submitting the document to the library.

3. You are the site administrator for your company's special projects department. Your department is responsible for receiving customer requests for generating specialized documentation, researching, and submitting that content. You want to create a workflow process for your site's document library that will route submitted documents for review and allow reviewers to add comments and suggestions regarding the submission. Of the following options, which workflow type should you create?

    A. Approval

    B. Collect Feedback

    C. Collect Signatures

    D. Disposition Approval

4. You are a site administrator for a content management site in your company's site collection. You have already created and configured standard document and picture libraries for your site, but in order to facilitate collaboration between your department and the other departments in the corporation, you need a special library that you can use to centrally publish files and make it easy for company users to find and use the data sources they need. Of the following options, which library type will best suit your needs?

   A. Data connection library

   B. Form library

   C. Reports library

   D. Translation management library

5. You are the SharePoint administrator for your company. You are teaching a class for new site owners in the organization to help them better understand and administer the SharePoint sites for their departments. Right now, you are explaining what a content type is and what characteristics content types possess. Of the following options, which ones can you specify a content type by? (Choose all that apply.)

   A. The workflows available for items of this content type

   B. The custom solutions or features associated with items of this content type

   C. The information management policies associated with items of this content type

   D. The rows (metadata) you want to assign to items of this type

6. You are a site member on the document management site for your department. You have just updated a document on the treatment of congenital heart defects for the PPTH project, one of your department's customers. Rather than uploading it from your computer into the document library, you'd rather use a drag-and-drop process. You have the folder containing the document open on your desktop and a browser window open showing the document library. What do you do next?

   A. Click Actions, and then click Windows Explorer.

   B. Click Actions, and then click Drag and Drop.

   C. Click Actions, and then click Open in Windows Explorer.

   D. Click Actions, and then click Folder View.

7. You are the SharePoint administrator for your company. You are teaching a class for new site owners in the organization to help them better understand and administer the SharePoint sites for their departments. You are currently explaining the concept of lists in SharePoint 2007. Although the site owners could create customized lists for their sites, a number of default site templates should meet most of their needs. Of the following options, which ones are default list templates? (Choose all that apply.)

   A. Calendars

   B. Colleagues

   C. Tasks

   D. Project Tasks

8. You are a site owner for your company's new SharePoint public relations site. You want to create a general announcement on the site stating that the site is now available for use and briefly describing what it offers. You click Add New Announcement and on the subsequent page give the announcement a name. Where do you create the text for the announcement?

    A. Under Announcement in the text editor field

    B. Under Body in the text editor field

    C. Under Text in the text editor field

    D. Under Text Editor in the text editor field

9. You are a site owner for your department's special projects site. A new site member named Chase wants to view a list of tasks that you assigned to him in SharePoint, but he is new to the system and isn't sure how to do this. You instruct him to open a web browser on his computer and log into the department's SharePoint site. You then tell him how to open the Tasks page to view tasks. What view does Chase see by default when he opens Tasks?

    A. All Tasks

    B. Active Tasks

    C. Due Today

    D. My Tasks

10. You are the site owner for your department's SharePoint site. You have just created announcements in the Announcements list for the site, but only you receive an alert when an announcement is added or changed. There are two other site owners who should also be receiving alerts. What do you have to do to make sure they start receiving alerts as well?

    A. On the Alert page in the Alert Title field, add the other site owners' names to your own, separating them with semicolons.

    B. On the Alert page in the Send Alerts To field, add the other site owners' names to your own, separating them with semicolons.

    C. On the Edit Alert page in the People Receiving Alerts field, add the other site owners' names to your own, separating them with semicolons.

    D. On the Edit Alert page in the Sending Alerts To field, add the other site owners' names to your own, separating them with semicolons.

11. You are the site owner for your department's SharePoint site, and you are on the Calendar page setting up the weekly staff meeting as a recurring event. You are just about to finish, but need to make sure the calendar treats this event as regularly occurring. What step should you take from the following options?

    A. Under Reoccurring, tick the Weekly check box.

    B. Under Reoccurring, tick the Available check box.

    C. Under Recurrence, tick the Weekly check box.

    D. Under Recurrence, tick the Available check box.

12. You are a site owner for your company's document management site, and you are currently configuring the document library for versioning. You have made sure that both major and minor versions will be tracked, but you want to make sure that the library will retain only a certain number of versions to avoid wasting space. Of the following options, what step should you take to accomplish this?

A. If you want to limit the number of versions to retain, tick the Keep the Following Number of Major Versions check box and/or the Keep Drafts for the Following Number of Major Versions check box.

B. If you want to limit the number of versions to retain, tick the Keep the Following Number of Major and Minor Versions check box.

C. If you want to limit the number of versions to retain, type the correct value in the Limit the Number of Major Versions To field, and type the correct value in the Limit the Number of Minor Versions To field.

D. If you want to limit the number of versions to retain, add the correct values to the Limit the Number Of Major and Minor Versions field, separating the values with a semicolon.

13. You are one of the site owners for your company's public relations site. Currently, you are adding an announcement stating that your organization has just acquired three new companies, and you want to add hyperlinks to the websites of those companies to your announcement. What do you have to do in the text editor?

A. Create a hyperlink by clicking the hyperlink symbol; when the Insert Hyperlink dialog box appears, type the URL of the site in the URL field, and type the name you want to appear in the Hyperlink Name field.

B. Create a hyperlink by clicking the hyperlink symbol; when the Insert Hyperlink dialog box appears, type the text you want to appear in the link in the Text to Display field and the URL of the site in the Address field.

C. Create a hyperlink by clicking the hyperlink symbol; when the Insert Hyperlink dialog box appears, type the name you want to give the hyperlink in the Link Text field and the URL of the site in the Link Address field.

D. Hyperlinks can be added to the body of an announcement in the text editor only by writing them in HTML.

14. You are a site member on your department's SharePoint site. Last Friday, you started a discussion on the site's team discussion board regarding the current procedure for adding documents to a document library. You wanted to query the rest of the staff about whether the current workflow being applied is the most effective. On Monday, you come into the office and log in to the department's site. To your surprise, the text of your post to the discussion board and the text of those who've responded is visible in the Discussion Group web part on the site's home page. You had expected only to see the title of the discussion. What happened?

A. Someone has changed the view of the team discussion board from threaded to flat.

B. Someone has changed the view of the team discussion board from flat to threaded.

C. Someone has changed the view of the discussion you created from threaded to flat.

D. Someone has changed the view of the discussion you created from flat to threaded.

15. You are the site owner of your company's special projects site, which is responsible for providing specialized documentation for external customers. The PPTH project has just received a new assignment to create a document on recent improvements in the diagnosis of hereditary angioedema. You decide to assign this task to Foreman, one of your medical writers. This is a rush job and needs to be ready one week from today. When you assign the task to Foreman, what ways can you indicate the urgency of the task? (Choose all that apply.)

   A. Under Priority, use the drop-down menu to select (1) High for the priority.

   B. Under % Complete, type 0 in the % field to indicate that the project has not yet begun and must be started as soon as possible.

   C. Under Start Date, use the calendar to select today's date for the beginning of the task.

   D. Under End Date, use the calendar to select the date one week from today.

16. You are the site owner for your company's document management department. You are logged into the server and want to review some of the documents that have recently been added to the document library by your staff. You go through the procedure of logging out a document, but when you try to open it for editing, you receive an error. What is the most likely problem under these circumstances?

   A. You are logged in using your member credentials rather than your site owner credentials.

   B. The document has already been checked out by another SharePoint user, and you will have to wait until the user checks it back in to edit it.

   C. The computer you are on does not have the appropriate word-processing application installed on it.

   D. The document has been submitted to the document library but not yet approved.

17. You the site owner for your department's SharePoint site, and you are currently creating an additional workflow for the document library. You notice that there is a single drop-down menu under Task List and another drop-down list under History List. When you click them, they present only their default options, with no other selections being available. Of the following options, which are the correct options? (Choose two.)

   A. Under Task List, the default selection is Tasks (new).

   B. Under History List, the default selection is Workflow History (new).

   C. Under Task List, the default selection is All Tasks (new).

   D. Under History List, the default selection is Task History (new).

18. You are the site owner for your company's special projects SharePoint site. You want to schedule a special meeting about the type and level of documents your team will be requested to produce for the PPTH project, one of your top external customers. Rather than create a meeting work-space after you schedule the event, you want to create the workspace at the same time you create the event in the calendar on your site's home page. Of the following options, which is part of the correct procedure?

    A. Tick the available check box under Workspace on the Calendar: New Event page, and click OK to be taken to the New Meeting Workspace page.

    B. Tick the Create Workspace check box under Workspace on the Calendar: New Event page, and click OK to be taken to the New Meeting Workspace page.

    C. Use the drop-down menu to select Create Meeting Workspace under Workspace on the Calendar: New Event page, and click OK to be taken to the New Meeting Workspace page.

    D. Use the drop-down menu to select New under Meeting Workspace on the Calendar, and click OK to be taken to the New Meeting Workspace page.

19. You are the site owner for your company's special projects SharePoint site, and you are in the process of creating a meeting workspace while creating an event in the site's calendar. Since the meeting workspace is actually a subsite of your department's SharePoint site, you can deter-mine where it will be created by specifying the URL. Of the following options, which one will accomplish this task?

    A. Under Web Site Address, type the desired URL in the URL Name field, and accept the default suffix of the address.

    B. Under Web Site Address, use the URL Name drop-down menu to select a URL.

    C. Under Web Site Address, tick the Create URL check box to create a URL.

    D. Under Web Site Address, accept the default URL populating the URL name field.

20. You are a site member on your company's special projects site, and you have just submitted a document to the document library. The document library has an approval workflow applied so your submission will not be complete until someone with approver status either approves or rejects your document. A few hours have passed, and you haven't received an alert stating that any action was taken on your submission. You decide to check the document library any-way, and looking in the Status column, you see that it is unchanged. What is the status you see on a document that has been submitted but not approved or rejected?

    A. Pending

    B. Submitted

    C. In Progress

    D. Waiting

Answers to Review Questions

1. A. Items are also known as records and are the "rows" in the list grid structure. An item contains the different property information for a single entry such as an individual colleague, a link to a specific website, or other information. Columns, cells, and fields do not perform this function.

2. C. If approval tasks were set up to be serial when the workflow was created, then approval tasks are assigned to only one approver. If you are not the approver assigned and you attempt to approve or reject the document, you will receive an error.

3. B. The Collect Feedback workflow routes a document for review. Reviewers can provide feedback, which is compiled and sent to the document owner when the workflow has completed.

4. A. This is a document library type new to SharePoint 2007 that organizations can use to centrally publish connection files and make it easy for users to find and use the data sources they need. Data connection files are easy to create and update, and solution designers can easily reuse them from within Microsoft Office 2007 client applications.

5. A, B, and C. For option D to be correct, it would have to state columns (metadata) instead of rows (metadata).

6. C. Option C allows you to open the document library in a separate browser in Windows Explorer. From here, you can either drag the document from one Explorer window to another or do a copy and paste action.

7. A, C, and D. Option B would be correct if it said Contacts instead of Colleagues. All of the other options are valid default list templates.

8. B. You type the body of the announcement in the Body section in the text editor field.

9. A. The default view for the Tasks page is All Tasks. Other options on the View list are Active Tasks, By Assigned To, By My Groups, Due Today, My Tasks, Modify This View, and Create View.

10. B. Option B is the only correct answer. Although your name should appear in the Alert Title field as the default username, you cannot add names in that field. The other options are bogus.

11. D. Only option D is correct. You set up the times, dates, and frequencies of a recurring meeting at other steps in the process of creating an event.

12. A. Only option A is correct. The other options presented are bogus.

13. B. Option B describes the correct method of adding a hyperlink to the body of an announcement in the text editor. The methods described in the other options are bogus.

14. B. Although it's not uncommon to change the view of an individual discussion between flat and threaded, when you impose a threaded view on the Team Discussion page, the title and text of discussions will be displayed in the Team Discussion web part.

15. A and D. Indicating a high priority as in option A and selecting a due date of one week from today as in option B are the best ways to communicate the urgency of the task. Indicating that 0 percent of the task has been done and that today is the task's start date will not communicate this effectively.

16. C. If you are logged into the SharePoint site directly from the server, it's likely you can't open the document because the server does not have the appropriate word-processing application installed such as Microsoft Office Word. Your regular user account should reflect your rights as site owner, so option A is not valid. If the document had already been checked out, you would not have been able to check it out, so option B is not valid. Whether the document has been approved in the workflow should not affect your ability to open it as in option D.

17. A and B. Only options A and B are correct. The other two options are bogus.

18. A. Option A describes the correct procedure. The answers in the other options are bogus.

19. D. The URL Name field is populated with a valid location for the meeting workspace you are creating by default. You can specify a different location as suggested in option A, but there is no default suffix. The answers presented in options B and C are bogus.

20. C. The status of a document in this circumstance is In Progress.

Chapter

8

Configuring Web Part Pages, Web Parts, and Web Pages

MICROSOFT EXAM OBJECTIVES COVERED IN THIS CHAPTER

✓ **Configure Content Management**

- ▪ Configure Web Content Management

✓ **Managing Business Intelligence**

- ▪ Configure Filter Web Parts

In Chapter 7, "Configuring and Maintaining Lists and Libraries," I talked about lists and libraries as basic components for containing and displaying information on a SharePoint 2007 website. However, there is a more basic element that SharePoint web pages use to contain lists, libraries, and just about everything else you see in the browser on a SharePoint site: the web part.

You can think of web parts as the building blocks of a web page. There are many default web parts you can use to display and moderate different aspects of a web page from adding Announcements and Links web parts to Form, Image, and Page Viewer web parts. If none of the default web parts suits your needs, you can create a custom-made web part with ASP.NET (assuming you have the skills).

The 70-630 exam doesn't require that you have the developer skills to create customized web parts, but you will still need to know how to work with the default versions.

Of course, web parts are only half the story. Each site you create in SharePoint contains web part pages. These are pages configured with web part zones. Each site template has its web part zones positioned in different ways. You can also create a web part page and specify how the zones are to be positioned based on a default list.

This chapter will begin with SharePoint web pages as concepts and planning elements, move on to the default construction of web part pages and then to web parts, and finally take you through a series of exercises to help you learn how to put what you're learning into practice.

You've already worked with some web parts, perhaps not realizing what they were, and subsequent chapters will show you how to work with very specialized web parts such as those that apply to business intelligence (BI). This chapter will start you out with the basics.

Overview of Web Pages

SharePoint web page planning addresses how published content is presented and how to determine where site members and other contributors can add content to web pages. It also involves determining which content-authoring features you allow contributors to use. Developing an effective plan helps you make sure that each type of content published on your company's websites is designed and presented in a manner that meets your organization's business goals.

The sections that follow will help you understand how to best develop a plan and will present the following design elements:

- Master pages
- Content pages
- Layout pages
- Style sheets
- Web parts
- Field controls

Web Page Design Elements

When you visit any web page on a SharePoint 2007 site, the page displays in a particular way based on a set of elements that have been individually planned and deployed on the page. Considering each design element as a separate component of the whole helps you "mix and match" these elements to produce the desired effect.

This means that site elements such as search, navigation, branding, and themes can all be considered and developed as completely different tasks than web page design tasks. Share-Point as an entity has been created so that a number of subject-matter experts can each take a portion of site collection design and focus on that specialty. The specialists can then collaborate to create the overall effect of the site without any one designer having to "do it all."

This also means that site and page design are both separate from adding and modifying the actual content to web pages. We saw in Chapter 7, "Configuring and Maintaining Lists and Libraries," how contributors added list items and documents to a site without needing to understand how the overall site or web part pages were created and configured.

A SharePoint web page is an .aspx (Active Server Pages) page and is dynamically rendered out of its constituent parts. Web page elements can include the following content types:

- Title
- Image
- Body
- Date
- Page layout

Let's take a closer look at the different design elements, starting with the master page.

Master Page

The *master page* defines the framework of the web page. It contains the elements that you want all of your web pages in the site to have in common, and it provides a single location where you can control all the design elements. Typically, a SharePoint site uses a single site master page; however, very large websites can use more than one. One reason to use more than one master page is if you want the sites for different departments or divisions in your organization to be presented differently or if you want to brand each of your products in a unique fashion.

Master pages come in two varieties:

Site master pages This master page type is applied to all published web pages in a site and is the page that is viewed when accessed by any authenticated and anonymous user.

System master pages This is the master page type that provides the general layout of all web pages accessed and modified by any contributors such as page designers. It is also the page type used by some of the SharePoint site templates such as the Document Workspace template.

You can locate all master pages for the site collection in the Master Page Gallery. This gallery can be accessed at the top-level site for a site collection in SharePoint. The conditions and rules that apply to the Master Page Gallery are the same as those for any other SharePoint library. You can apply processes to this gallery such as versioning and workflow. A master page contains the same shared page elements:

- Shared branding
- Shared Cascading Style Sheets (CSS)
- Shared help and search
- Shared navigation

The publishing site templates in SharePoint include site master pages that you can use to start your page design. You can also customize an existing master page or create a new one using Microsoft Office SharePoint Designer 2007 or Microsoft Visual Studio.

Content Pages

Each *content page* in SharePoint consists of text, images, and other content stored as an entry in a Pages library. Each item in a Pages library represents an individual web page. The Pages library is just like the master pages or any other library, and because of that, content pages are subject to auditing, versioning, workflow, the checkout and check-in process, and content approval, just like any other library object. Although all pages in a site are in a single Pages library, specialized sites such as intranet portal sites and Internet presence sites consist of a tree of sites, each with its own separate Pages library. Creating and editing web pages in SharePoint is done either by using the SharePoint web interface or by converting a document into an HTML page.

Using the web interface on the portal main page, you can click Site Actions and then select either Edit Page or Create Page. From a subsite, you can click Site Actions and then click Create. On the Create page under Web Pages, you can select either Basic Page or Web Part Page. Either process will allow you to create one or more content pages using SharePoint's web interface. You can also use an application such as Microsoft Office Word to create web content and then convert the .docx or .docm formatted file to HTML.

Layout Pages

Layout pages define the layout for a content page. When you open a SharePoint web page in a browser, the layout page for that web page is combined with the master page for the site or portion of the site. After that, the contents of the page are supplied to the field controls on the layout page. The layout page must be designed for a particular content type since the field controls vary among content types. For instance, an article page content type would have several field controls, including a Page Content field control to hold the contents of the Page Content column and a Page Image field control to hold the image displayed on the page as a result of being linked to its location in a picture library.

Although a layout page must be designed for a single content type, content pages can be associated with multiple content types. Continuing with the example of the article page, it is associated with two different layout pages. One layout page displays an image on the left side of the page, and the other displays an image on the right. A layout page can also contain the following:

- Cascading Style Sheet links
- Server controls
- Web parts
- Web part zones

Cascading Style Sheets (CSS)

Cascading Style Sheets (CSS) is a style sheet language that is applied to an HTML page to provide styling to the web page. The styling can include the color of any page element including background, body, text, and so on. CSS can also provide font size and style, positioning of elements on the page, appearance of links, how graphics are displayed, and many more style choices. Style sheets make it possible for multiple web pages in a site to all display uniform styling by linking to a single CSS file rather than have styling applied to each individual web page.

You can find SharePoint 2007's default CSS files on the web server at `Local Drive:\Program Files\Common Files\Microsoft Shared\web server extensions\12\TEMPLATE\ LAYOUTS\1033\STYLES`. You can find any additional styles in the publishing feature at `Local Drive:\Program Files\Common Files\Microsoft Shared\web server extensions\12\ TEMPLATE\FEATURES\PublishingLayouts\en-us`.

 An excellent resource for learning more about SharePoint and CSS is a CSS Reference Chart for SharePoint 2007 published at `http://www.heathersolomon .com/content/sp07cssreference.htm`.

Field Controls

Field controls are actually part of page layouts and are simple Microsoft ASP.NET 2.0 controls that are bound to Windows SharePoint Services (WSS) data contained on the page. They have a small amount of code to display the two modes of the controls: one for render time and one for edit time. WSS 3.0 and Microsoft Office SharePoint Server (MOSS) 2007 provide several default field controls that you can use in your pages. All field controls you use in a SharePoint Server 2007 site are derived from a base class in WSS 3.0 called `FormComponent`. You can use any of the default field controls or write a field control by deriving from the `BaseRichField` class to suit your own specific needs.

As was previously mentioned, the 70-630 exam doesn't require you to have developer skills, so you will not be expected to answer detailed questions about extending or writing field controls. However, so that you have an understanding of this element, some programmatic information is included in this part of the chapter.

By opening your site in Microsoft Office SharePoint Designer 2007 or Microsoft Visual Studio 2005, you can edit the tags associated with field controls to restrict the types of Share-Point 2007 authoring features writers can use when editing pages in the browser window.

I didn't forget that web parts and web part pages are design elements. That information will be covered later in the chapter.

Planning Web Page Authoring

Earlier in this chapter, you learned that you can edit a SharePoint site web page either through controls accessible through the web interface or through document conversion. The following sections will briefly address the planning issues regarding web page authoring. Each method has its positive and negative aspects, which you'll need to be aware of when choosing how to modify a web page.

Web Page Authoring with the Web Interface

To determine whether this method is correct for your needs, review the following basic characteristics:

- Allows you to edit the web page directly from the page in a browser
- Uses document library management features such as versioning, approval, workflows, and check-in and checkout
- Unlike the document conversion method, does not require two workflow approval processes, both of the original document and of the converted document
- Unable to use available templates in third-party authoring applications
- Requires familiarity with SharePoint web page–authoring tools

To modify the portal page using the web interface, click Site Actions, and then click Edit Page. Figure 8.1 shows you the result.

As you can see when you look toward the upper-left area of the page, there are several page-editing menus and quick access buttons available. Figure 8.2 shows you the options available in the Page, Workflow, and Tools menus.

The two quick access buttons to the right of the Tools menu allow you to check in a draft and to publish the page. When you check in a draft, you can view how the page will appear without making any permanent changes to the current portal page. Clicking the Publish button will allow the edited page to become the permanent page that everyone can see.

FIGURE 8.1   The portal page in Edit mode

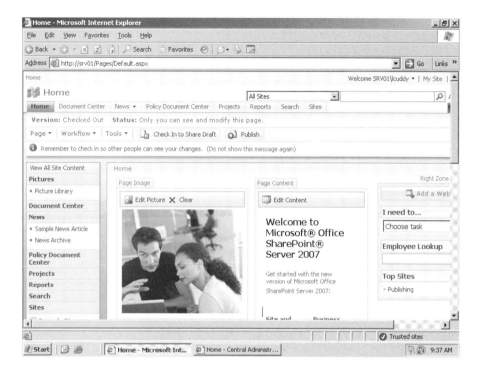

FIGURE 8.2   From left to right: Page menu options, Workflow menu options, Tools menu options

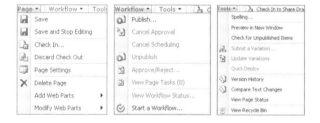

Web Page Authoring with Document Conversion

This method is also known as *smart-client authoring* and is essentially where a web page content contributor uses a software application outside the SharePoint framework to create content that will be transferred into acceptable content within SharePoint. SharePoint's native converters can create web page content from Microsoft Office Word and Microsoft Office InfoPath 2007 documents. SharePoint can also use a generic Extensible Stylesheet Language Transformation (XSLT) converter that enables users to apply an XSL transformation to an XML document.

You can also develop and install converters for other document formats.

For smart-client authoring to be effective, the document library containing the source documents and the library containing the converted web pages must be in the same site collection.

To more tightly control the appearance of web pages on your site, you can configure the SharePoint 2007 Word-to-HTML converter to remove the extracted set of CSS style definitions and not store them with converted web pages. The converter will still insert class references in converted web pages. To resolve those class references, you can define a set of CSS style definitions and associate them with layout pages or master pages in which the converted web pages will be displayed.

The SharePoint Word-to-HTML converter cannot remove inline CSS styles generated for inline formatting in the source document. To prevent inline styles from overriding your CSS style definitions, prohibit authors from using inline formatting in their source documents. Also, Word-to-HTML converters cannot convert inline images into images in the output web pages, and inline images in source documents will be missing from the converted web pages. To avoid this, web page contributors should store their images in a picture library in the site collection and insert images into their source documents as hyperlinks to the stored images.

Web Parts and Web Part Pages

As mentioned at the beginning of this chapter, web parts aren't particularly useful unless you have web part pages with web part zones available to accept the web parts. When you create a site using different site templates, each template uses certain web part page structures by default. You can also create your own web part page. From a subsite, it's as easy as clicking Site Actions and then clicking Create. Figure 8.3 shows you an example of the different web part zone configurations you can select when you create a web part page.

You can also create a basic web page, which is just about as plain vanilla as you can get in SharePoint, or you can create a site or workspace with predetermined web part page zone configurations.

Understanding Web Parts and Web Part Pages

Although the specific organization of web part page zones varies, there are really only three basic zone types:

- Header zones, as you can imagine, contain web parts that present the different information you would typically find in a web page's header. This includes your company or department logo, company or department name, and other identifying or introductory information.

FIGURE 8.3   Web part page choices

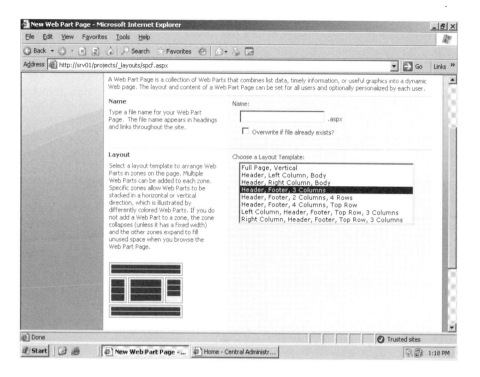

- Middle zones are used to contain web parts that present the "body" content of the page, and for that reason, the widest variety of web parts are presented in these zones. You've already seen examples of such web parts including Announcements, Calendars, and Links. You can also add graphics, libraries, or any other web part that will add meaningful content to the web page.

- Footer zones are again self-explanatory and can contain navigation links as well as Contact Us or About Us links.

The list of default web parts is extremely lengthy, and you won't have the opportunity to work with all of them in this chapter. When you elect to add a web part to a web part page, the Add Web Parts page, which opens in a separate browser window, organizes web parts by the following categories:

- Lists and Libraries
- Business Data
- Content Rollup
- Dashboard
- Default
- Filters

- Miscellaneous
- Outlook Web Access
- Search
- Site Directory

Only the Lists and Libraries category is presented by default when you open the Add Web Parts page, but by expanding All Web Parts, you can see the entire list. You can also click the Advanced Web Part Gallery and Options link on the Add Web Parts page to open the Add Web Parts toolbox directly on the web page, as shown in Figure 8.4.

FIGURE 8.4   Add Web Parts toolbox

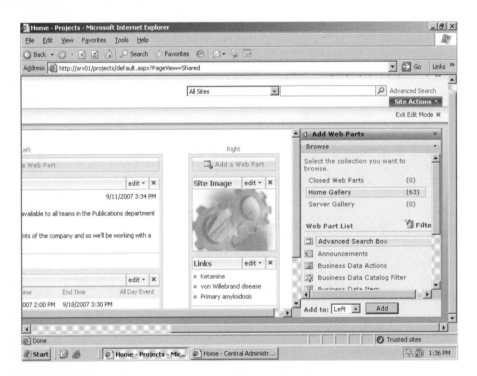

You can manipulate web parts in different ways when a web page is in Edit mode, as shown in Figure 8.4. You can add a web part to a web part zone, drag web parts from one zone to another, change the properties of a web part to affect its appearance and performance, and export a web part so that it's available to be used on more than one web page.

If you can export a web part, you can also import one. If a developer has created a customized web part for your use, you can browse to where it's located, such as on a network share. This doesn't mean you just drag and drop a web part that you want to import, though. You'll need to use the import function to successfully accomplish your goal.

If you are not familiar with the entire list of web parts available, you can perform a search based on all or part of the web part's name by clicking the arrow to the right of Browse at the top of the Add Web Parts toolbox and then selecting Search from the list. Browse and Import are the other menu options.

The appearance and functioning of a web part can be altered using the web part's toolbox. The toolbox can be opened in several ways, and when it is, it gives you access to the controls to change the web part's properties. Although each web part is used for a different purpose, the property controls in all web part toolboxes are the same. To view a web part's toolbox, just click the arrow to the right of the web part, and select Modify Shared Web Part from the list.

Each toolbox has four general sections. The top section varies depending on which web part type you're working with. For the sake of example, we'll use a Links web part here. The four sections of a Links web part are as follows:

- List Views

- Appearance

- Layout

- Advanced

List Views is the only section displayed by default. The other three sections are collapsed. List Views, or the corresponding section in other web parts, generally controls how content is displayed and can include options to select different filtered views. By default, the Links web part has a Current view and an All Links view, which are the same in this case. If additional views were created, they'd be displayed in the menu when you clicked the Selected View drop-down arrow. In this section, you can also click the Toolbar Type drop-down menu and select Full Toolbar, Summary Toolbar, or No Toolbar, with Summary Toolbar being the default.

When you expand the Appearance section, you can change the title of the web part by changing the text in the Title field. You can also control the height and width of the web part manually in a variety of measurement types including pixels, inches, millimeters, and points. There are also controls to select the chrome state between normal and Minimized and the chrome type between the default, None, Title and Border, Title Only, and Border Only options.

Chrome State determines whether the whole web part appears on the page when opened in the web part page or only in the title bar. Chrome Type determines whether the title bar and border of the web part frame are displayed.

The Layout section lets you tick a check box if you want the web part to be hidden and lets you select the direction of the web part zone (left to right or right to left), the zone you want (in this case left or right), and the zone index or order in which the web part appears in the zone (1 for top, 2 for second from the top, and so on).

The Advanced section, when expanded, offers a lot of different options. There are six check boxes that are ticked by default that you can accept or clear:

- Allow Minimize

- Allow Close

- Allow Hide

- Allow Zone Change

- Allow Connections

- Allow Editing in Personal View

  After the check boxes, there are additional configuration options:

- Title URL

- Description

- Help URL (which is blank by default)

- Help Mode Modal (which is a drop-down menu with the options Modeless and Navigate, which is the default)

- Catalog Icon Image URL (which is blank)

- Title Icon Image URL (which is blank)

- Import Error Message (which displays the text Cannot Import This Web Part)

- Target Audiences

 You learned about targeting content to specific audiences in Chapter 5, "Managing Users and Groups."

At the bottom of the toolbox, you can click OK, Cancel, or Apply, which are very familiar options to anyone who has worked with Microsoft applications.

The examples in the next section of this chapter will give you the opportunity to work with some of these web part toolbox options and give you experience in web parts and web part pages in general.

Working with Web Parts and Web Part Pages

The following series of exercises will take you through the process of creating and manipulating web parts and web part pages. The first few exercises may seem simple, but they are necessary to lay the foundation for the following tasks. Exercise 8.1 will start you out by adding a web part to a web part page. For this exercise, you should be on the sample website used in Chapter 7, "Configuring and Maintaining Lists and Libraries."

EXERCISE 8.1

Adding a Web Part to a Web Part Page

1. Click Site Actions, and then click Edit Page to open the page in Edit mode.

2. Just above the Announcements web part in the Left zone, click Add a Web Part.

3. When the Add Web Parts to Left browser window opens, scroll down to Miscellaneous, tick the Content Editor web part, and then click Add.

4. After the page refreshes and the web part is added, click Exit Edit Mode under Site Actions.

The Content Editor web part is added to the page, as shown here.

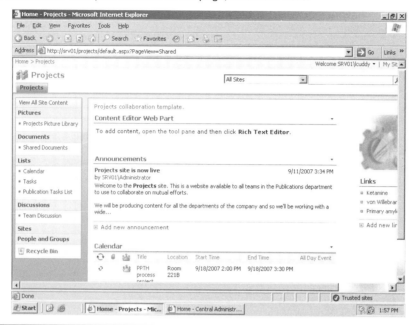

Notice that, by default, the new web part was added to the top of the web part zone. On this page, there are only two web part zones, left and right. Web parts in each zone are stacked on one another like building blocks. You can reorder the web parts as easily as adding one, as you'll find out in Exercise 8.2.

Moving a Web Part on a Web Part Page

1. Click Site Actions, and then click Edit Page to open the page in Edit mode.

2. Place your cursor over the title bar of the Content Editor web part until the four directional arrows appear.

3. Click the title bar, drag the title bar down until the bar appears just above the Calendar web part, and then release the mouse button.

4. Perform the same action on the Content Editor web part as you did in step 2, click it and drag it from the left to right zone, and drop it just above the Links web part.

EXERCISE 8.2 *(continued)*

5. Perform the same action again, and return it to its original location on top of the Announcements web part.

6. Under Site Actions, click Exit Edit Mode.

Obviously, this was only for practice since the net result of Exercise 8.2 didn't change anything. You did see, however, just how easy it is to move web parts around within a zone and between zones, so you can significantly change the appearance of a web page just by moving web parts.

Although the process of adding and modifying content within a web part is highly variable depending on the web part type, Exercise 8.3 will act as a simple example. You'll be using the Content Editor web part that you added to the page in Exercise 8.1. Since the Content Editor web part edits HTML, you'll either need to write a simple HTML document or copy and paste content into the editor.

> You could also use the Rich Text Editor option in the Content Editor web part to add content in text format rather than HTML.

EXERCISE 8.3

Adding Content to a Web Part

1. Click the arrow at the right of the Content Editor web part title bar, and then click Modify Shared Web Part to open the web part's toolbox. You may have to scroll to the right to see it after it's open, as shown here.

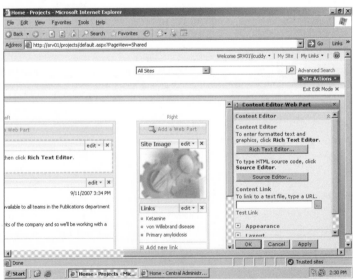

EXERCISE 8.3 *(continued)*

2. Click the Source Editor button under Content Editor.

3. When the Text Entry Web Page dialog box opens, add some HTML content to the page, and then click Save.

4. When the page refreshes, scroll down the web part toolbox, and expand Appearance.

5. Under Appearance in the Title field, either highlight the Content Editor Web Part text or click the Builder button to the right of the field and then highlight the text.

6. Replace the deleted text with a suitable title for your content in the web part, and then click OK.

As you can see, the HTML content that you added is displayed in the web part, and the title of the web part has changed to whatever you named it.

The next exercise will show you how to create a web part page. Creating a web part page isn't really difficult, but you will have to decide which type of web part page to create, what its purpose is, and what web parts you will want to add. The example this book will use is a page dedicated to a fundraising event to add a new pediatric wing to a hospital. Feel free to design your own content and theme. Exercise 8.4 will start on the same sample page you worked on in Chapter 7, "Configuring and Maintaining Lists and Libraries."

EXERCISE 8.4

Creating a Web Part Page

1. Click Site Actions, and then click Create.

2. On the Create page under Web Pages, click Web Part Page.

3. On the New Web Part Page under Name, type the name of the new web part page in the Name field. When you give the new web part page a name, it becomes part of the URL to the page. It will become a subsite of the site from which it was created and, like all SharePoint page URLs, will have an .aspx extension.

4. If the page already exists and you want to overwrite it, tick the Overwrite If File Already Exists check box.

5. Under Layout, choose the specific layout you want for the web part page in the Choose a Layout Template box. Notice that a preview of the layout appears to the left.

6. Under Save Location, use the Document Library drop-down menu to choose a location (which is the only menu available by default). The only option available in the drop-down menu is Shared Documents.

7. Click Create.

As you can see in Figure 8.5, when the web part page is created, it is just the bare bones and needs a lot of work to be useful. You'll also notice that it is automatically opened in Edit mode.

The next series of exercises will be used to modify this new page and turn it into something purposeful. I've created a web part page with a header, footer, and left, center, and right web part zones. The header will display a logo for Casino Night and the title of the fundraiser. The footer will contain typical Contact Us and About Us information. The left web part zone will hold web parts listing donors, sponsors, and so on, while the right web part zone will hold a series of images regarding the event. The center web part zone will contain information on the specifics of the event.

You are free to create whatever theme or event you desire as long as it will (more or less) fit in with the exercises provided. Some of the activities may seem like ones you've completed before, but this will give you the experience of web part page creation and configuration.

It probably would have been easier to accomplish my task of creating a fundraiser event page by using the Meetings template's Social Meeting workspace since it comes with a number of appropriate web parts already available, but the point of the following series of exercises is to create a complete page from scratch using SharePoint's available web part design elements.

Exercise 8.5 requires that you have several drawings or photographs uploaded into the sample site's picture library for use as a logo and other graphics you intend on displaying on your web part page in Image web parts. You'll also need to have the URLs to each picture. To get them, double-click the image in the picture library to open the preview, and double-click the preview to open the graphic. Copy the URL of each picture from the browser window where the picture is open.

FIGURE 8.5 New web part page

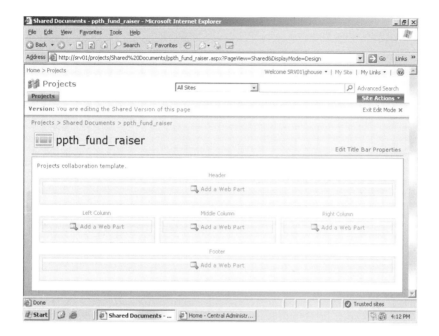

 Once you are done working with the picture library, to get back to the web part page, open Shared Documents to find it.

EXERCISE 8.5

Editing the Header on a Web Part Page

1. On the web parts page, click Edit Title Bar Properties.

2. In the Web Part Page Title Bar toolbox, type the title in the Title field that you want to appear on this page.

3. In the Caption field, type a descriptive caption you want to appear in the header.

4. Type an optional description in the Description field.

EXERCISE 8.5 *(continued)*

5. In the Image Link field, replace the current path with the URL to the logo you want displayed, as shown here.

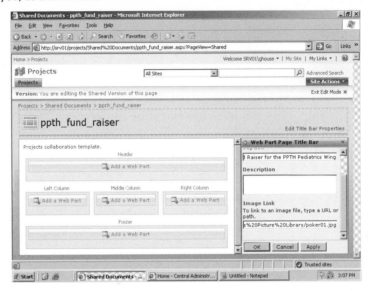

6. Click OK.

As you can see, after you click OK, the changes you made appear in the web part page title bar.

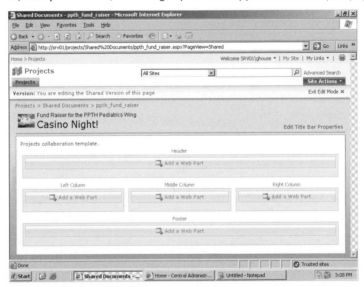

Exercise 8.6 will be similar in that you'll be adding images to the web part page, but this time, you'll be doing it using specific web parts. Since you will be adding a series of images in a column, you may want to edit them so that they are at least the same width if not the same width and height. Make note of the dimensions of the images and in what units they are being measured, such as pixels or inches.

 Real World Scenario

Managing Graphics on a Customized Web Part Page

James, one of the directors for your company's cinematography division, wants a new site built for his group including new themes, logos, and branding. Greg, one of his department heads, has submitted a graphic that he thinks would be good for the division's new logo. You consult with the graphics department, and they think it'll take some work to get the proposed logo to work on the site's top-level web page.

Once the graphics department has resized and modified the color scheme of the logo, you take a look at the result and tell them that it still doesn't meet the size limitation for the logo. Although the logo could be any size, if it's too large, it will overwhelm the web page's title bar and inappropriately dominate the rest of the page's content. You refer the graphic artist tasked with resizing the logo to the default logo on the new web part page. She takes a look at the default logo's properties, determines the correct size from it, and then resizes Greg's submitted image.

You review the logo a second time and decide it meets the necessary specifications. You then upload it to the picture library for the site and edit the title bar properties to link to the logo in the library. Finally, you take the web part page out of Edit mode and determine that it is displaying correctly.

EXERCISE 8.6

Adding Images to a Web Part Page

1. On the web part page under Right Column, click Add a Web Part.

2. On the Add Web Parts to Right Column page, expand All Web Parts if necessary. Under Miscellaneous, tick the Image Web Part check box, and then click Add.

3. Repeat step 2 as many times as necessary until you have the number of Image web parts added to the column that you need to display all of your graphics.

4. In the body of the Image web part, click open the tool pane.

5. When the toolbox opens, in the Image Link field add the URL to the image you want displayed.

6. In the Alternate Text field, add whatever alternate text you want for this image, and then click OK.

7. Repeat steps 4 through 6 with the remaining Image web parts so that all of the images you want are added to the web part page.

8. Click the Edit arrow at the right of each Image web part, and click Modify Shared Web Part.

9. Expand Appearance, and in the Title field give the web part a title matching the picture it contains. Repeat this step for all the Image web parts.

10. In the Appearance section under Width, select Yes. In the field to the right, type the value for the width of the image, and use the drop-down arrow to select the unit of measurement such as pixels. Repeat this step for all the Image web parts.

11. After you've made the adjustments in each Image web part's toolbox, click OK to save your changes.

The web part page should display the image as a part of the web page without any apparent border.

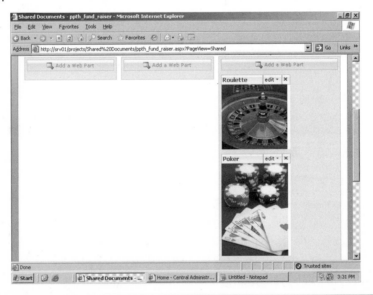

At this point, the appearance of the web part page may not seem ideal; however, you won't actually know what the final product will look like until all of the elements are in place. If you were to exit Edit mode at this point, the graphics you just added would all appear on the left side of the web part page, as if the left and middle web part zones didn't exist.

In Chapter 7, "Configuring and Maintaining Lists and Libraries," you added a series of hyperlinks to the Links web part on the sample website. The next task is to add links of contributors and sponsors of the mythical fundraiser to the left column web part, but if you added the Links web part to that area, it would display the same links as are on the sample page.

The only two options would be to add the contributors and sponsors links to that one web part and then create different views so that different information would be displayed in the different views. The other option would be to create a new Links web part specifically for this page. Exercise 8.7 will do the latter. You will need to perform this action from the sample page used in Chapter 7, "Configuring and Maintaining Lists and Libraries."

 Chapter 7, "Configuring and Maintaining Lists and Libraries," showed you how to create views and filter them in a single Links web part depending on purpose and audience, so this set of exercises will not repeat that information.

EXERCISE 8.7

Creating a New Links List Web Part and Configuring Views

1. Click View All Site Content in Quick Launch.

2. On the All Site Content page, click Create.

3. Under Tracking, click Links.

4. On the New page, give your links list a name in the Name field, give an optional description in the Description field, and click No under Navigation to indicate that this list will not appear in Quick Launch.

5. Click Create.

6. On the empty links page, click New, and then click New Item.

7. On the New Item page, add the URL you desire to the URL field, type the name you want to appear in the list in the Description field, type an identifying name for the view this item will belong to in the Notes field, and then click OK.

8. Repeat steps 6 and 7 to add the number of links you want in this web part.

9. Once you have added all your links, click Settings, and then click Create View.

10. On the Create View page, click Standard View.

EXERCISE 8.7 *(continued)*

11. Under Name, type a name of the view in the View Name field, and then tick the Make This the Default View check box.

12. Under Audience, select Create a Public View.

13. Under Columns, in the Display column, clear all the check boxes except the URL check box.

14. Scroll down to the Filter section, and select Show Items Only When the Following Is True.

15. Use the Show the Items When Column drop-down menu to select Notes.

16. Click the drop-down menu just below, and select Contains.

17. In the blank field, type the identifier for the view you added in Notes when you created the links, as shown here.

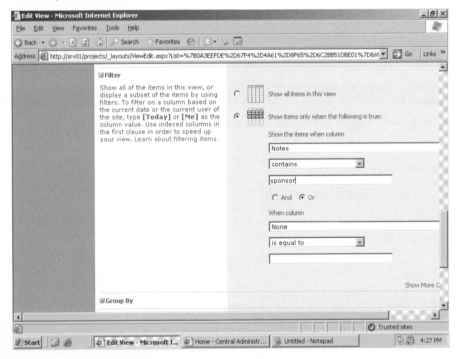

18. Scroll down, and click OK.

19. Repeat steps 9 through 17 to create as many views as you need (except for making the view the default view).

Exercise 8.8 will continue working with the web part page by adding Lists web parts to the left column web part zone. In the example used in the book, two Lists web parts will be added to the left column zone, but you may add more for your situation.

Adding List Web Parts to a Web Part Page

1. Under Left Column, click Add a Web Part.

2. On the Add Web Parts to Left Column page under Lists and Libraries, tick the check box next to the name of the links list you created in Exercise 8.7, and then click Add.

3. Repeat step 2 as many times as necessary for the number of views of this list you plan to present.

4. To the right of the first Lists web part, click the Edit arrow, and select Modify Shared Web Part.

5. Using the Selected View drop-down menu, select one of the views you want to display. Click OK when the warning dialog box appears.

6. Expand Appearance, and in the Title field give the web part title bar an appropriate name.

7. Click OK.

The web part page should look something like this.

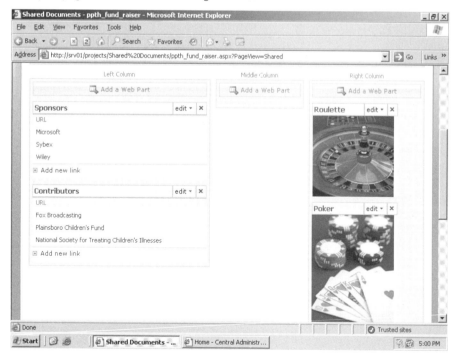

Referring to Exercise 8.3, add a Content Editor web page to the middle column web part and zone, and then add HTML content to the web part. The result will appear something like Figure 8.6.

FIGURE 8.6   Adding content to the body of the web part page

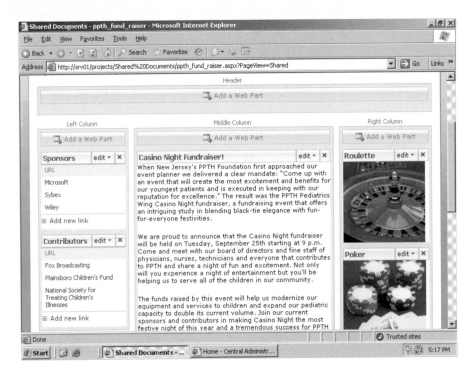

For the header, add a graphic that will appear as a banner for the page. You can refer to Exercise 8.6 and follow those steps; however, you don't want a title bar to appear for this graphic, so in the Image web part toolbox under Appearance, use the Chrome Type drop-down menu to select None. You can also add a Content Editor web part to the footer and add some appropriate text. In my example, I edited the graphics in the right column to be of a more manageable size and uploaded them to the picture library, overwriting the prior versions. The results appear in Figure 8.7.

Now that you've constructed a full-fledged web part page from scratch, the subsequent two exercises will address exporting and importing web parts. As mentioned earlier in this chapter, you might create a web part that you will want to export to another site because it will be useful there. Also, you may find a web part on another site that you want to use on your site. Exercise 8.9 will address the first situation.

FIGURE 8.7   Finalized version of the web part page

EXERCISE 8.9

Exporting a Web Part

1. On the page containing the web part you want to export, click Site Actions, and then click Edit Page.

2. Click the Edit arrow to the right of the desired web part, and click Export.

3. When the File Download dialog box appears, click Save.

4. In the Save As dialog box, browse to the location where you want to save the web part as a .dwp file, and then click Save.

5. Once the Download Complete dialog box appears, click Close.

The web part is now saved in the desired location and is ready to be imported by another SharePoint site.

Exercise 8.10 will show you how to import a web part. You will need to be on the web page where you want to import the web part to, and you must have access to where you saved the web part in Exercise 8.9.

EXERCISE 8.10

Importing a Web Part

1.   Click Site Actions, and then click Edit Page.

2.   In the web part zone where you want to import the web part, click Add a Web Part.

3.   On the Add Web Parts page, in the lower-right corner, click Advanced Web Part Gallery and Options.

4.   When the Add Web Parts toolbox opens on the far right of the page, click the drop-down arrow next to Browse, and then click Import.

5.   Click the Browse button, and browse the computer or the network until you find and select the desired web part and then click Open.

6.   Click Upload. When the imported web part is added under Uploaded Web Part in the tool-box, use the Add To drop-down arrow to select which web part zone to add the imported web part, and then click Import.

The imported web part is added to the selected web part zone. You can drag it up and down the web part zone column or to a different web part zone as required.

This is only the beginning of learning how to add and configure web parts. Future chapters in this book will show you how to use specialized web parts to achieve specific tasks. The information presented in this chapter instructs you in the basics.

Summary

In this chapter, you learned about working with web pages, web parts, and web part pages including the following topics:

- Using web page design elements including master pages, content pages, layout pages, style sheets, web parts, and field controls
- Planning web page authoring including authoring in the web interface and using document conversion
- Understanding the different categories of default web parts
- Working with web parts by adding and moving web parts in web part page zones

- Creating a web part page and adding and configuring web parts to create a completely new web page
- Importing and exporting web parts

Exam Essentials

Know how to configure web parts.   Adding and configuring web parts to a web part page is a vital part of configuring and adding web content in SharePoint. This is the basis for web content management as well as working with Filter web parts in SharePoint business intelligence.

Understand how to configure web content.   Along with web parts and web part pages, planning for web pages and web page design elements allows you to control a wide variety of content management, business intelligence, and other types of information control, modification, and presentation in SharePoint web pages and sites.

Review Questions

1. You are the site designer for your company's marketing department's intranet site. The site administrator of the company's sales department site has developed a web part you'd like to incorporate on your site. The sales site admin agrees to export the web part to a shared folder on the network where you can access it. Of the following options, which ones are part of the import process? (Choose all that apply.)

   A. You must be in Edit mode.

   B. You must click Add a Web Part in the web part zone on the page where you want to import the web part.

   C. You must browse to where the desired web part is located.

   D. You must import it to the Shared Web Parts Gallery so you can add it to the web part page.

2. You are the site administrator for your company's intranet site. You are creating a web part page for a special event and are adding web parts to a new web part page. You want to give the title bar of a new web part a different name besides the default name. How do you do this using the web part's toolbox?

   A. Expand Layout, and add the new title name in the Title field.

   B. Expand Appearance, and add the new title name in the Title field.

   C. Expand Content Editor, and add the new title name in the Title field.

   D. Under Home, which is expanded by default, add the new title name in the Title field.

3. You are a SharePoint site designer, and you are working with field controls on a web page for the distribution department's site. You know that all field controls you use in a SharePoint site are derived from a base class in WSS 3.0. You don't want to use any of the default field controls and would prefer to write a field control yourself. What class must you derive from to accomplish your task?

   A. FormComponent

   B. BaseRichField

   C. FormRichField

   D. BaseRichComponent

4. You are the site administrator for the Projects group in your company. Your team is responsible for providing specialized documentation for internal and external customers. You have been working for the Projects group only for a couple of weeks and are still putting together all of the web pages they've requested. Lisa, the group manager, has asked that you create a web part page to promote a special fundraising event for their top customer, PPTH. She specifies what she wants the web page to look like, and you make the appropriate selection when creating the new web part page. You know, though, that regardless of the specific layout of web part zones on the page, in general web part pages have only three basic zone components. Of the following, which are the correct zone elements? (Choose three.)

   A. Title bar zones

   B. Header zones

   C. Middle zones

   D. Footer zones

5. You are the site administrator for the Projects group in your company. Your team is responsible for providing specialized documentation for internal and external customers. You have been working for the Projects group only for a couple of weeks and are still putting together all of the web pages they've requested. Lisa, the group manager, has asked that you create a web part page to promote a special fundraising event for their top customer, PPTH. She wants specific graphics to be placed on the site that have been provided by Greg, one of the department heads. You'll need to edit the graphics for size and upload them to the picture library for the site. Once you link the necessary Image web parts on the web page with the graphics, you'll need to specify the size of the graphics measured in pixels in the each web part toolbox. Of the following selections, where in the toolbox will you be able to specify the image width?

   A. List Views

   B. Appearance

   C. Layout

   D. Advanced

6. You are the site administrator for your company's graphics department website. The graphics department has undergone a recent change in styling and branding, and the department manager has tasked you with editing all of the web pages on the site to match the department's new image. You decide the easiest way to implement the changes is using authoring through the web interface. You review the procedures about web page authoring using a browser and discover which of the following to be true? (Choose all that apply.)

   A. This process allows you to edit the web page directly from the page in a browser.

   B. This process uses document library management features such as versioning, approval, workflows, and check-in and checkout.

   C. This process requires two workflow approvals, one when the original page is submitted and the second when it's published.

   D. This process is able to use available templates in client authoring applications.

7. You are the SharePoint site administrator for the company's intranet. The board of directors wants you to change the basic design of the site's master page. You discuss their specific requirements with them, and they ask what elements the master page shares with all of the web pages of the site. Of the following selections, which ones are correct? (Choose all that apply.)

   A. Shared Cascading Style Sheets (CSS)

   B. Shared images

   C. Shared help and search

   D. Shared navigation

8. You are the site administrator for your company's intranet site. You've tasked Cameron, a member of your staff, to add some specific web parts to several web part pages on the Projects group's site. Cameron is having trouble locating the proper web parts and is confused about the number of web part categories she can choose from. You understand because there are quite a number of them. Right now, Cameron needs to select a Content Editor web part. Under which category would she find it?

A. Business Data

B. Content Rollup

C. Default

D. Miscellaneous

9. Chase, one of the site designers for the Projects group's site, has been tasked by one of the directors with adding several new web pages to the site. He has chosen to write the pages in Microsoft Word and use the Word-to-HTML converter to render them as web pages. As the SharePoint site administrator for the company's entire intranet, you warn him of several of the drawbacks in using the Word-to-HTML converter. Of the following options, which ones are valid drawbacks? (Choose all that apply.)

A. They cannot remove inline Cascading Style Sheets styles generated for inline formatting in the source document.

B. They cannot convert inline images into images in the output web pages.

C. Using converters will result in inline images in source documents being missing from the converted web pages.

D. Web page contributors will be unable to store their images in a picture library in the site collection and insert images into their source documents as hyperlinks to the stored images.

10. Foreman, one of the site designers for the Projects group's site, has just finished creating a new web part page for the site and configuring it with several web parts. He wants to prevent any of the other site designers or admins from casually moving web parts around to different zones. How should he accomplish his task?

A. In the web part toolbox under Advanced, clear the Allow Zone Change check box.

B. In the web part toolbox under Layout, clear the Allow Zone Change check box.

C. In the web part toolbox under Advanced, use the Configure drop-down menu to select Prevent Zone Change.

D. In the web part toolbox under Layout, use the Configure drop-down menu to select Prevent Zone Change.

11. You are the site designer for the Projects group's website. A fundraising event for their top customer, PPTH, was held last week, and you have been tasked with posting some photos of the event to their fundraising page. You upload the photos to the picture library after they were edited for size and composition and added some Image web parts to the web part page. How can you cause the images to be displayed in the Image web parts?

   A. Open the Image web part's toolbox, and in the Image Link field add the URL to where the image is located in the picture library.

   B. Open the Image web part's toolbox, expand Appearance, and in the Image Link field add the URL to where the image is located in the picture library.

   C. Open the Image web part's toolbox, expand Layout, and in the Image Link field add the URL to where the image is located in the picture library.

   D. Open the Image web part's toolbox, and in the URL field add the URL to where the image is located in the picture library.

12. You are one of the site administrators for the Projects group, a special documentation provider for both internal and external company customers. You are creating a list of sponsors, contributors, and special guests for an upcoming event hosted by PPTH, one of your group's top customers. You want to create one list of links but filter the list so you can display names by different groups. Of the following options, which one allows you to create a filtered view for the sponsors group?

   A. In the Filter section, select Show Items Only When the Following Is True, use the drop-down menu to select Is Equal To, and use the field below to type in sponsors.

   B. In the Filter section, select Show Items Only When the Following Is True, use the drop-down menu to select Contains, and use the field below to type in sponsors.

   C. In the Filter section, select Show Items Only When the Following Is True, use the drop-down menu to select When Present, and use the field below to type in sponsors.

   D. In the Filter section, select Show Items Only When the Following Is True, use the drop-down menu to select Column, and use the field below to type in sponsors.

13. You are a site administrator for the Projects group's website. You have added several Links web parts to a special events web page. You have created a single list of links, but three different views so that different categories of links can be displayed in different Links web parts. You add the web parts to a web part zone column, but they all display all of the links in the list, which is the default view. How do you change the view?

   A. Open the web part toolbox, and under Selected View use the List Views drop-down menu to choose the desired view name.

   B. Open the web part toolbox, and under Views use the Links Views drop-down menu to choose the desired view.

   C. Open the web part toolbox, and under List Views use the Selected View drop-down menu to choose the desired view name.

   D. Open the web part toolbox, and under Links Views use the Selected View drop-down menu to choose the desired view name.

14. You are the site administrator for your company's marketing website. You have created a web part that Alison, the site administrator of sales, would like to use on her site. You agree to export the specified web part so that Alison can access it and import it to her site. Of the following options, which one describes how you would go about exporting a web part?

    A. On the web page containing the desired web part, click the edit arrow to the right of the web part, click Modify Shared Web Part, expand Advanced in the toolbox, and use the Actions drop-down arrow to select Export.

    B. On the web page containing the desired web part, click the edit arrow to the right of the web part, click Modify Shared Web Part, expand Layout, and use the Export Mode drop-down arrow to select Export.

    C. On the web page containing the desired web part, click the edit arrow to the right of the web part, and click Export.

    D. On the web page containing the desired web part, click the edit arrow to the right of the web part, and click Export Web Part.

15. You are the site administrator for the Projects group's website. The Projects group is a special team of content providers and editors within your company that provides high-level technical and medical documentation for internal and external customers. You have been tasked by Erik, one of your supervisors, with creating a web page for PPTH, one of your group's top customers. You must add a series of links to the new web page in the left column web part zone. You open the Add a Web Part to Left page, tick the Links web part, and then click Add. To your surprise, when the Links web part is added, it already has a collection of links in the list. You had expected a blank Links list. What is the most likely explanation for this occurrence?

    A. The Links list web part was imported from another site where a series of links had already been added.

    B. You accidentally selected the Web Links list web part, which contains a default list of links rather than the empty Links web part.

    C. The Links list web part contains a group of bogus hyperlinks by default, and you simply need to delete the bogus links and add ones of your own.

    D. You had used the default Links list web part on the Project group's main page and populated it with hyperlinks. Adding the same web part to a different page will still display the links you originally added.

16. You are the site administrator for the Projects group's website. The Projects group is a special team of content providers and editors within your company that provides high-level technical and medical documentation for internal and external customers. You have been tasked by Edward, one of your supervisors, with creating a web page for PPTH, one of your group's top customers. Part of the task is to add a series of graphics to the right column web part zone of a new web part page. The graphics department directs you to the appropriate drawings and photos in the picture library, and you link them to several Image web parts you've added to the right column. You exit Edit mode to better view the results and are surprised to see all of the graphics at the far-left side of the page since the web part page also has left and middle web part zones. What is the most likely explanation for the change from right to left?

A. The left and middle web part zones aren't populated with web parts yet. When they are, the Image web parts in the right zone will appear at the right of the page when you exit Edit mode.

B. You neglected to modify the settings in the Image web parts toolboxes to specify the alignment to the right.

C. You have to open the toolboxes for all of the Image web parts and, under Appearance, adjust the width so that the images will appear at the right of the page.

D. You inadvertently added the web parts from the Add Web Parts to Left page rather than from the Add Web Parts to Right page.

17. You are the site administrator for your company's intranet site. You are training a new staff member named Michael to assist you in managing some of the web pages on the site. You are reviewing relevant information about content pages in a SharePoint site, and he asks where individual web pages are stored in SharePoint. What is the correct answer to give him?

A. Content Pages library

B. Pages library

C. Site Pages library

D. Web Pages library

18. You are the site administrator for your company's SharePoint intranet site. You are explaining the function of master pages to your trainee Michael. You mention to him that typically a site will use only a single master page to share the web page framework to all the web pages on the site. He asks whether there is any justification for using more than one master page. Of the following options, which are valid answers to Michael's question? (Choose all that apply.)

A. You can use more than one master page if you want web pages representing different product lines your company sells to be presented differently.

B. You can use more than one master page only if you have more than one SharePoint subsite in your organization.

C. You can use more than one master page if you want different departments or divisions in your organization to be presented differently.

D. You can use more than one master page if you have a very large website since a master page can be applied only to 1,000 web pages in SharePoint.

19. You have tasked your trainee Michael with adding a Content Editor web part to a newly created web part page. Shortly after you've assigned him this task, he comes back to you and says that the web part doesn't exist in the Add Web Part page. You know that this web part is one of the default web parts that come with SharePoint so it must exist. What is the most likely explanation for Michael's problem?

A. Michael tried to add the Content Editor to the left column web part zone, but only the middle column web part zone page offers an option to add the Content Editor web part.

B. The Content Editor web part is in the Default section of the Add Web Part page, which is not expanded by default. Michael needs to expand that section.

C. The Content Editor web part was exported from the web part library and no longer is in the list. Michael needs to import the web part again to use it.

D. The Content Editor web part is in the Miscellaneous section of the Add Web Part page, which is not expanded by default. Michael needs to expand that section.

20. On the Add Web Part page, your trainee Michael clicks Advanced Web Part Gallery and Options. When the Add Web Parts toolbox appears, he clicks the drop-down arrow next to Browse. What options is he presented with? (Choose all that apply.)

A. Browse

B. Search

C. Import

D. Export

Answers to Review Questions

1. A, B, and C. The imported web part is added under Uploaded Web Part in the Add Web Parts toolbox, not in the Shared Web Parts Gallery.

2. B. The Title field can be found when you expand Appearance in the web part's toolbox.

3. B. You can write a field control by deriving one from the `BaseRichField` class to suit your own specific needs. SharePoint default field controls are derived from a base class in WSS 3.0 called `FormComponent`.

4. B, C, and D. Although a web part page has a title bar, it is not considered a web part zone. The other options are the correct answers.

5. B. You can specify the height and width of an image in the Image web part's toolbox in the Appearance section.

6. A and B. Unlike the document conversion method, authoring does not require two workflow approval processes—for both the original document and the converted document. Also, this process is unable to use available templates in client authoring applications.

7. A, C, and D. Option B should read shared branding instead of shared images.

8. D. The Content Editor web part is found in the Miscellaneous section of the Add Web Part page.

9. A, B, and C. The SharePoint Word-to-HTML converter cannot remove inline Cascading Style Sheets styles generated for inline formatting in the source document. To prevent inline styles from overriding your Cascading Style Sheets style definitions, prohibit authors from using inline formatting in their source documents. Also, Word-to-HTML converters cannot convert inline images into images in the output web pages, and inline images in source documents will be missing from the converted web pages. To avoid this, web page contributors should store their images in a picture library in the site collection and insert images into their source documents as hyperlinks to the stored images.

10. A. The Advanced section in a web part toolbox contains a number of check boxes that determine how the web part can be used and manipulated, including whether the web part can change zones.

11. A. The Image Link field is available near the top of the Image web part's toolbox without expanding any of the sections.

12. B. You must select the Contains option using the drop-down menu to specify a text "value" in the field below.

13. C. Option C describes the correct procedure.

14. C. Option C describes the correct method of starting the process of exporting a web part.

15. D. The default Links list web part is empty by default, but once you add content to the list, if you add that web part to any other page, the same links will appear. Your options are to add the other links to the same web part and then create filtered views to allow you to select which links will display or create a custom-made links list and add the content you desire.

16. A. With the left and middle web part zones empty, when you exit Edit mode, the only available content on the page will default to the far left. Modifying settings in the Image web part toolboxes would not have this effect, and adding web parts to the left or the right is determined by which web part zone you selected when you clicked Add a Web Part at the top of the column.

17. B. Each content page in SharePoint consists of text, images, and other content stored as an entry in a Pages library. Each item in a Pages library represents an individual web page.

18. A and C. You can use more than one master page if you have a very large site and want to either present different sections of the site in a different manner or different product lines produced by different divisions in your organization in a different manner. Master pages are not limited to a certain number of web pages or subsites.

19. D. Only the Lists and Libraries section of the Add Web Part page is expanded by default. Michael needs to expand the Miscellaneous section by expanding All Web Parts to see the section where the Content Editor web part is contained.

20. A, B, and C. There is no Export option in that menu. All of the other options are correct.

Chapter

9

Managing SharePoint Navigation and Search

MICROSOFT EXAM OBJECTIVES COVERED IN THIS CHAPTER

✓ **Manage Search**

▪ Configure Search Center

▪ Configure Search Settings

▪ Monitor Search Activity

Thus far in this book, you have learned a great deal about how to create, upload, store, and filter information; however, SharePoint Server 2007 has a vast capacity for information storage and manipulation. If you were managing only a few sites, browsing through those sites might be sufficient to help you find what you're looking for, but in a large corporate or enterprise environment with hundreds or even thousands of sites, if you are looking for a single piece of data, how are you going to find it? Just as on any other website, there are two primary methods of locating information: navigation and search.

SharePoint site navigation is the primary interface for site users to move around in the sites, subsites, and web pages that make up your Internet or intranet portal site. SharePoint 2007 includes a set of customizable and extensible navigation features that help orient users of your portal site and enable them to move among its sites and pages.

SharePoint 2007's search capacities let users locate any stored content within the site collection as well as content stored outside SharePoint such as on network file shares. SharePoint Portal Server 2003 pioneered exceptional search abilities within the web-based collaboration environment, and SharePoint Server 2007 builds on those capacities, giving the user much greater power in locating SharePoint objects including documents, list items, and SharePoint members.

This chapter will begin with an overview of SharePoint search and its vast capacities and move on to how best to plan for search optimization. Planning for and enhancing SharePoint site collection navigation will follow. In the latter part of the chapter, I'll cover the actual tasks of setting up navigation and search.

Overview of Search

MOSS 2007 search is based on the search capacities of the Windows SharePoint Services 3.0 (WSS 3.0) search service but then adds enhancements that allow search to be effective in an enterprise site collection environment. SharePoint Server 2007 search isn't optimized just for size or capacity but also for the complexity of data and data indexing found in the enterprise. Enhancements for SharePoint search include the following:

- The ability to search a wider scope of content types
- Customizable search query and search results
- The ability to define content scopes on both the site and global level
- Highlighting in search results
- Suggested corrections for misspelled search strings

- Improved ability to return more relevant search results
- Advanced search options from within team collaborative sites
- Enhanced search abilities for user profile search

SharePoint Server 2007 search is managed from the Central Administration web application and specifically from the search settings utility within the shared services provider (SSP) for your stand-alone installation or SharePoint server farm.

Prior to taking actions to administer search, it's important to develop a plan for search in SharePoint Server 2007 so that the SharePoint Server search service is optimized for your corporate environment. If you take the time to plan how search is implemented, you can save time in the future by not having to reconfigure search based on user feedback of its effectiveness or lack thereof.

Carefully planning for search can prepare you for an initial limited deployment. You can continue to refine your search implementation, such as adding crawled content to the content index. Using an effective planning process can help make your search solution more effective, even if you implement the solution in stages or your needs continue to evolve after initial deployment.

When we deployed SharePoint Server 2007 initially, it was as a limited deployment, especially since our model is based on a stand-alone server rather than a server farm. This is the ideal opportunity to plan search from the beginning and build on the foundation you initially created.

Briefly, there are two basic search functions within SharePoint, and you are likely familiar with both if you've used any website's search functions:

- Basic search is the typical search query where the user enters a simple search string made up of keywords or phrases that are then used to locate relevant results of site or Internet content.

- Advanced search provides a more detailed set of filters based on the various properties of the content being searched including keywords and phrases, the order of words, the type of document, an exact phrase, and so on.

Planning Search

Planning SharePoint search is one of the more complex tasks involved in establishing and setting up a SharePoint service and is composed of multiple feature configurations. Elements in planning search include crawling, content sources, farm-level search settings, and the end user search experience.

Planning Content Crawling

SharePoint Server 2007 search is the first version of SharePoint that includes the ability to crawl and index content on external sources such as outside SharePoint server farms, outside websites, business information sources, file shares, and so on. One way that SharePoint Server 2007 is different from previous versions is that the service used for crawling and indexing content is part of an SSP and all content crawled using the SSP is indexed to a single content index. In most organizations, only one SSP is used to crawl and query all content, so these settings apply to all content sources in the organization. This applies to our situation since, by default, our SharePoint deployment uses a single SSP.

During deployment, you create one or more SSPs as needed and then create content sources for each SSP as we did during our installation. Best practices for planning search involve planning content sources prior to SharePoint 2007 deployment. This is particularly helpful in the minority of cases where more than one SSP is needed for isolating highly sensitive content. Planning content sources in advance can help identify the need for multiple SSPs.

Before using SharePoint search in an enterprise environment, you must first crawl the content that you want to make available to search queries. Crawling content is the process by which the system accesses and parses content and its properties to build a content index from which search queries can be serviced. SSP administrators create content sources that specify what type of content is crawled, what URLs to crawl, and how deep and when to crawl. After a content source is created, an SSP administrator can use the content source to crawl the content specified in the content source.

It's difficult to separate crawling planning from content planning since the two are interwoven; however, we will cover the various aspects of crawling first and then go back and plan for the content that will be crawled.

Planning Crawl Settings

You can plan your crawl settings for how extensively you need to crawl the start addresses in various content sources. The options you can select from within the content properties vary depending on the type of content source involved. There are five primary content types. The following lists those content types and their crawl settings options:

Business data Crawl setting options include either crawling the entire business data catalog (BDC) or crawling only selected applications within the BDC.

Exchange Public folder Crawl setting options include either crawling all folders and subfolders for each start address or crawling only the folder for the start address.

File shares Crawl setting options include either crawling all folders and subfolders for each start address or only crawling the folder for each start address.

SharePoint sites Crawl setting options include either crawling all content under the host name for each start address or crawling only the SharePoint website for each start address.

Websites Crawl setting options include crawling only within the server for each start address, crawling only the first page of each start address, or using a custom crawl setting to crawl a specified page depth and number of server hops.

The default crawl setting for page depth and server hops is unlimited.

You can bias your crawl settings to favor either SharePoint sites or SharePoint web pages to get the best search results in each environment.

For SharePoint sites, if only the content on the site itself is likely to be relevant and content on linked sites is unlikely to be relevant, set crawling to only the SharePoint site for each start address. If the links on the start address tend to point to relevant content, crawl everything under the hostname of each start address.

For other websites, if the content available on linked sites is not likely to be relevant and the content on the site itself is relevant, crawl only within the server of each start address. If you want to limit how deep to crawl the links on the start addresses, use the custom option to specify the number of pages deep and number of server hops to crawl.

Planning Crawl Schedules

As a SharePoint SSP administrator, you have the ability to set up crawl schedules for each content source you want to be able to search. Crawl schedules are configured in two scheduling routines, full and incremental. Whenever you initially configure a content source, you must perform one full crawl before scheduling any incremental crawls so you have indexed all the necessary elements of the content source. Subsequent incremental crawls will pick up only the information that has changed since the last full crawl.

Factors to consider when planning a crawl schedule are the availability of the server to be crawled, the availability of a network connection to the server, and the impact the crawl will have on the server.

Full crawls do not have to be performed very frequently. The initial full crawl will index all of the information you require, and the subsequent incremental crawls will note only the changes. For that reason, best practice suggests scheduling full crawls on a weekly basis and incremental crawls on a daily basis. Crawls should be scheduled at times when the server hosting the information is not being heavily used, such as late at night or at least after regular business hours.

The SharePoint SSP administrator can configure the crawl schedules independently for each content source. You can specify a time to do full crawls and a separate time to do incremental crawls for each source. A full crawl must run for a particular content source before incremental crawls can be run. You should plan crawl schedules based on the availability, performance, and bandwidth considerations of the servers running the search service and the servers hosting the crawled content.

You can also schedule crawls in a staggered format so that you access only a certain number of servers at any given point and not put an undue load on all of the servers in your server farm at one time. Grouping the start addresses of content sources so that they are available at the same time will also help avoid the overuse of server resources.

Planning Crawler Impact Rules

Crawler impact rules are particularly important when crawling external content sources because crawling uses resources on the crawled servers. *Crawler impact rules* enable administrators to manage the impact your crawler has on the servers being crawled. For each crawler impact rule, you can specify a single URL or use wildcard characters in the URL path to include a block of URLs to which the rule applies. You can then specify how many simultaneous requests for pages will be made to the specified URL or choose to request only one document at a time and wait a specified number of seconds between requests.

You can create a crawler impact rule for *.com that applies to all Internet sites whose addresses end in .com. For example, an administrator of a portal might add a content source for `examples.microsoft.com`. The rule for *.com applies to this site unless you add a crawler impact rule specifically for `examples.microsoft.com`. (The *.com example is overly broad and used for demonstration purposes only.)

For content within your organization that other administrators are crawling, you can coordinate with those administrators to set crawler impact rules based on the performance and capacity of the servers. For most external sites, this coordination is not possible. Requesting too much content on external servers or making requests too frequently can cause administrators of those sites to limit your future access if your crawls are using too many resources or too much bandwidth. The best practice is to crawl too little rather than crawl too much. In this way, you can mitigate the risk that you will lose access to crawl the relevant content.

Planning Crawl Rules

You can configure *crawl rules* for any individual source in order to customize how crawls will be applied to the source content and server. This is usually done by identifying sources by their URLs and using wildcard characters to specify relevant content and bypass content you do not desire. This lets you crawl only certain web pages or sources by their URLs rather than having to crawl the entire site, indexing data that is not useful.

For example, you may want to crawl some but not all information at `www.microsoft.com`. Your interests might be limited to `sharepoint.microsoft.com` *or* `office.microsoft.com`. This not only avoids taking excessive time to crawl web pages and sites that are useless to you but also aids in narrowing down search results so that users can find the information they want more quickly.

Some URLs are not as simple as the examples I just gave (which were bogus for the most part). You've probably encountered URLs that are extremely long and contain special characters such as question marks and equal signs. SharePoint crawling features allow you to crawl such complex URLs if necessary. Please keep in mind, though, that you should use this feature only if you are sure the data you need actually resides on such sites.

SharePoint crawl can let you crawl sites that sit behind a firewall or are otherwise restricted by crawling them as HTTP pages. Although SharePoint is configured with a default content access account, you may need to edit this account to give you access to information that requires a different set of credentials or a client certificate.

Planning Content Sources

SharePoint Server 2007 uses *content sources* to crawl content in your site collections or on related external sites or business data applications. Other search features filter or modify content after it has been crawled. Effective planning for content sources can help you build search capability during your initial deployment that enables you to configure and manage content across your organization based on specific subsets of content and data, content and data external to SharePoint 2007, or content and data external to your organization.

The system automatically adds the top-level web address of each site collection that is served by the SSP to the default content source. This is done so that all content served by the SSP is available to search after the initial crawl that uses the content source is performed. In our case, the top-level web address is http://srv01.

You may consider creating additional content sources for each of your site collections in each of your web applications. To manage and schedule crawls independently, you can create content sources for crawling a subset of content throughout the SSP. This is useful when you need to crawl high-priority or quickly changing content more frequently without needing to crawl all content again.

Planning the Default Content Access Account

The *default content access account* is the account that is used when crawling content sources. This account is selected by the SSP administrator during the post-setup configuration. The default content access account must have read access to all content that is crawled, or the content will not be crawled and will not be available during search queries. For individual URLs in a content source, you can use crawl rules to specify a different content access account to use when crawling those URLs.

I recommend you select a default content access account that has the broadest access to most of your crawled content and that you use other content access accounts only when security considerations require this action. For each content source you plan, identify the start addresses that cannot be accessed by the default content access account, and plan to add content access accounts for those start addresses. Administrators can configure additional content access accounts in crawl rules for the relevant start addresses.

Planning for External Content Sources

Two broad categories of external content are useful to plan for in your content search. The first is content that exists within a web application that uses a different SSP than that serving your site collection and that you want to crawl. The second is Internet or extranet content that is not under your administrative control and not controlled in any way by your organization.

Best practice states that you should use only one SSP to crawl all content for your organization. Typically, if content on a web application that uses a separate SSP is relevant enough to be included in a content source for your SSP, the web application should use the same SSP as the web applications that are crawled using your SSP. However, there are valid reasons to use more than one SSP for crawling content, such as a situation where you might want some content in a separate content index for security reasons or you might want to crawl content in separate geographical regions. Keep in mind that you can use one SSP to crawl content on servers in separate geographical regions; however, performance may suffer depending upon the bandwidth of your Internet link.

In some cases, you may be tempted to include a subset of content in your organization from a web application that uses a different SSP. Avoid this by carefully planning your information architecture, SSPs, and site structure. If you must crawl content on a web application that uses a different SSP, make sure the user account used to crawl the content has read permission to either the default content access account or a different content access account defined by a crawl rule. Then try to group the start address in a content source with other content available at similar times or with other content that is conceptually related.

Planning Content Sources for Business Data

Business data content sources require that the applications hosting the data are first registered in the BDC and that the properties are mapped to managed properties that are consistent with your search schema. Business data start addresses cannot be combined with start addresses for other content, so you must separately manage business data content sources.

Often, the people who plan for integration of business data into your site collections will not be the same people involved in the overall content-planning process. Include business application administrators in your content planning teams so that they can advise you how to integrate their data into your other content and effectively present it on your site collections.

Planning for Server Farm–Level Search Settings

Although the focus on search settings configuration will be on the SSP level throughout the majority of this chapter, there is also the option to configure some search settings at the server farm level to impact how content is crawled. There are four relevant areas to be considered:

- Crawling content affects the resources of the servers that are being crawled. Before you can crawl content, you must provide in the configuration settings the email address of the person in your organization who administrators can contact in the event that the crawl adversely affects their servers. This email address appears in logs for administrators of the servers being crawled so that they can contact someone if crawling causes too great an impact on their performance and bandwidth or if other issues occur.

- The contact email address should belong to a person who has the necessary expertise and availability to quickly respond to requests. Alternatively, you can use a closely monitored distribution list alias as the contact email address. Regardless of whether the content crawled is stored internally to the organization, quick response time is important in order to preserve your access to the data you want to crawl.

- You can choose whether to use proxy server settings when crawling content depending upon the topology of your SharePoint Server 2007 deployment and the architecture of other servers in your organization.

- The Secure Sockets Layer (SSL) setting determines whether the SSL certificate must exactly match crawl content. Also, timeout settings are used to limit the time that the search server waits while connecting to other services.

Planning How the End User Experiences Search

Search administrators can improve the relevance and presentation of search results by carefully planning the end user search experience. The goal of this planning is to create a search experience that enables users to quickly find the information they need. To effectively plan for the configuration choices that help you realize your goal, first consider what end users see in the user interface.

The User Search Interface

As you might imagine, the user interface for search is pretty straightforward. The focus of the user interface is a search box where users can enter search queries. A search box is provided on all nonadministrative pages in the site collection and also in the Search Center.

As you can see in Figure 9.1, the search interface on a typical SharePoint site is what you'd expect. Using the available drop-down menu or search scope, you can choose to search the current website, all sites in the site collection, or people in the site collection.

FIGURE 9.1   Search menu options

Clicking Advanced Search will take you to the Search Center, which contains the Advanced Search page shown in Figure 9.2. This page is applicable for searching all sites. You can also click the People tab and be taken to the People tab shown in Figure 9.3. Click Search Options to open the fields shown in Figure 9.2. If you are performing a search from within a list or library, the search scope will offer you a fourth option as This List or This Library, depending on where you are located when initiating the search.

FIGURE 9.2   Advanced Search page

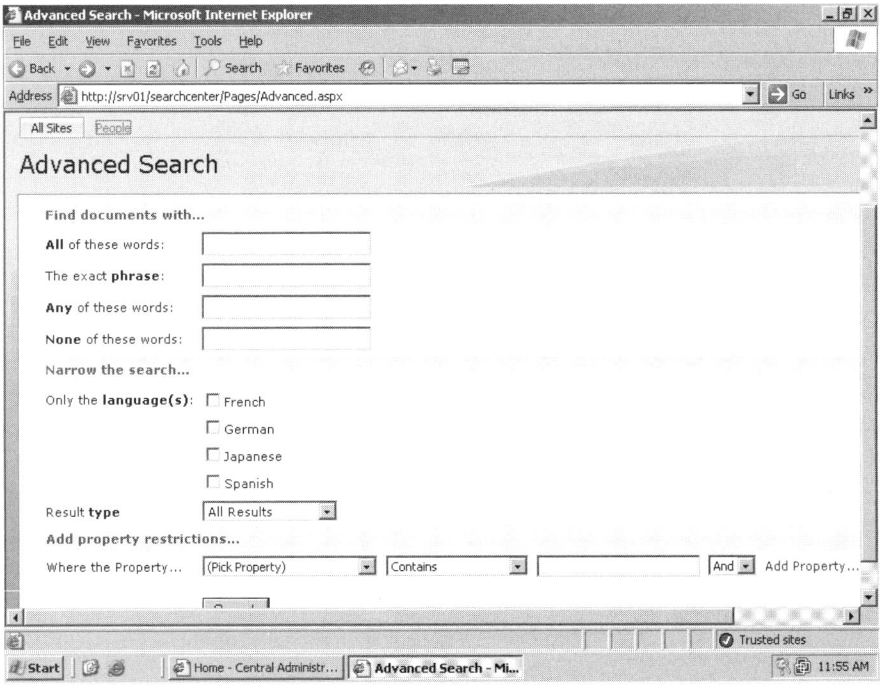

FIGURE 9.3   Advanced Search People tab

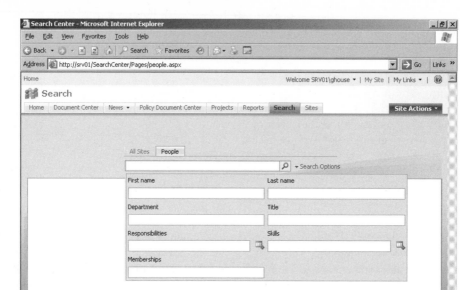

Planning Search Scopes

You may need to customize the user's search experience for more than just the default scopes presented thus far. You can use custom scopes with scope rules to group certain content in the index into individually searchable pieces of content. For instance, you can make it possible to search a specific set of websites, all Excel documents that were authored by a particular person or were authored during a specific period of time, or any combination of the presented parameters.

Scopes that you create at the SSP level are called *shared scopes* because they are shared with all site collections that use that SSP. Site collection administrators decide which shared scopes to use and how to display them.

You can also create custom scopes at the site collection level, which makes the custom scopes available only to the site collection on which they were created. Scopes created at this level are sometimes called *site collection–level scopes*.

The SSP administrator manages shared scopes for all sites that use the SSP. SSP administrators can perform tasks such as creating and editing shared scopes, adding scope rules to shared scopes, deleting shared scopes, and refreshing changes made to scopes. Shared scopes are visible and available for use by administrators for all site collections that are using the same set of shared services. As shown in Figures 9.2 and 9.3, the shared scopes of All Sites and People are available in the Search Center.

While planning search scopes for site collections, each site collection administrator will want to base their scopes on the information architecture within the site. They can choose to create new scopes, make a copy of shared scopes that becomes a site collection level scope, or both. For example, site collection administrators can add scopes by selecting shared scopes that are useful for people accessing the site collection and then supplementing those scopes by creating scopes for the site collection.

Planning for display groups provides a way to assign scopes to a particular search box. Site collection administrators have several options for configuring the existing display groups, or they can choose to create new display groups. Typically, a site owner identifies a particular need for a display group. For example, users of a particular team site might frequently need to search for content that is scattered across multiple document libraries.

To narrow the body of content to be searched, users currently have to either perform separate searches in different search boxes or construct an advanced query to filter the search results. To provide users with an easier way to perform this frequent search, a site collection administrator can create a display group and assign the appropriate scope to that group. Site owners can then associate this display group with a particular search box, such as a search box on a custom search page on the site. The default display groups are the search scope drop-down menu displayed in Figure 9.1 and the All Sites and People search scope items in the Search Center shown in Figures 9.2 and 9.3.

You can plan scope rules to define additional rules for the scope. Scope rules define what content to associate and not associate with the scope. Scope rules added to a particular scope define the extent of the scope. Each scope rule is based upon a particular scope rule type that defines the properties, locations, and sources of content.

Planning User Search Results

SharePoint 2007 provides a number of settings that enable SSP and site collection administrators to control what users see in search results pages. Although you can control the search results in different ways, the most common methods of managing user search results are as follows:

Keywords   *Keywords*, sometimes called *keyword phrases*, are the words that users type into a search box when constructing a query. When users perform a simple keyword search, such as entering a word in the search box and clicking the Go Search button, SharePoint 2007 displays the search results of all content in the selected scope that contains that keyword. Share-Point 2007 enables site collection administrators to create an entity called a *keyword* that is directly related to keyword phrases of the same name that are in the index. A site collection administrator can create a keyword using a single word, such as "LOA," or a group of words that must be typed in a particular order, such as "leave of absence."

Relevance of search results   The greater the body of content that is being searched, the more likely it will return several pages of search results for a particular query. This is especially true when basic keyword queries instead of advanced queries are used. To ease the end user search experience, ensure that links to the most relevant content are displayed as early as possible on the search results pages. SharePoint 2007 enables SSP administrators to assign relevance settings to indexed web pages. Each relevance setting, which is associated with a particular web page, determines how early on the search results page the link to a particular page appears.

Pages that are assigned a relevance setting are known as *authoritative pages*. Authoritative page settings are one factor in prioritizing search results and do not outweigh all other factors such as keywords managed by site collection administrators, managed properties that are managed by the SSP administrator, or the automatic weighting applied to content by the search technology.

Appearance of links   SSP administrators can use server name mappings to change how particular URLs or ranges of URLs are displayed in search results. Server name mappings are set at the SSP level for all content that is crawled by that SSP and are applied whenever queries are performed.

Search-based alerts   An SSP administrator can decide whether search-based alerts will be activated for a particular SSP. If search-based alerts are activated and the server is configured to send emails, end users can click the Alert Me link at the top of the search results pages and specify what kind of changes they want to be alerted to and how frequently they want to receive an email alert. When you allow search-based alerts, your system uses additional resources on mail servers and increases the load on query servers because queries for each search-based alert run every time a search-based alert is processed. When planning the initial deployment, consider the resources available for alerts and the likelihood that people using your sites will use alerts productively. Search-based alerts are enabled by default.

Planning Navigation

Navigation planning includes planning the user experience you want to create in your Internet or intranet portal site and deciding whether contributors will be able to insert navigation elements directly onto the web pages they create.

Planning User Navigation

Your navigation decisions are closely related to your decisions about the structure of sites and subsites in your site hierarchy. For each site in your site hierarchy, you can choose to inherit the global or current navigation from its parent site, or you can plan unique settings. There are two general navigational planning elements to consider:

Global navigation   *Global navigation* is the navigation scheme that appears consistently for all web pages in the site collection. Determine whether the site has unique global navigation settings or inherits its global navigation from its parent. If the site has unique global navigation, specify which subsites and additional sites to display.

Current navigation   *Current navigation* is a relative navigation scheme that has a much more limited scope, such as for one website or a few related websites. Determine whether the site has unique current navigation settings or inherits its current navigation from its parent. If the site has unique current navigation, specify whether to display its subsites, its peer sites, or additional sites. Also specify whether to include links to the site's web pages.

The decisions you make about your portal site's navigation will reflect its unique purpose and structure. When you plan navigation, consider the trade-off between having too many navigation links, which could make your site confusing or clumsy, and having too few, which could make it hard for site users to locate critical information.

Keep in mind that inheriting the parent site's navigation can place the current site in a larger context. In an intranet site, this can help information workers use the other sites in the site collection to accomplish their tasks. On the other hand, if users of a site do not have to go to other sites to complete their tasks, consider defining a unique global navigation at the site so that site users are not distracted by irrelevant global navigation links.

Planning Navigation on Master Pages

In Chapter 4, "Building Sites and Site Collections," and Chapter 8, "Configuring Web Part Pages, Web Parts, and Web Pages," you read the basics about master pages in SharePoint, what they are used for, and how they function. You may not be aware that you must plan a navigation scheme for your master pages as well. Since a master page contains a number of design elements that are replicated on all the web pages in your site collection that depend on it, you will want to create any special navigation design you need before deploying the site collection for general use. This plan needs to include both global and current navigation.

If you find it necessary to modify the menu type navigation controls found in a master page, you will need to use Microsoft Office SharePoint Designer or Microsoft Visual Studio to accomplish the task.

Planning Global Navigation

As previously mentioned, global navigation is the navigation scheme that's shared across all of the sites in the site collection that depends on a particular master page. As you look at any SharePoint web page, you can find the global navigation links on the horizontal navigation bar near the top of the page. Keeping this navigation link scheme consistent across sites and subsites allows users to more freely navigate between the top-level site and all of the related subsites without having to "backtrack" through locations they have previously visited.

By default, all subsites that exist one level below the top level are automatically added to global navigation. If you add subsites below the first level, they will not appear in global navigation unless you manually add them. You can also remove a site from global navigation on the Site Navigation Settings page and modify these links in any manner you choose.

Planning Current Navigation

As previously mentioned, current navigation represents a more limited navigation scheme, usually spanning the scope of only the individual site or the site and its subsites. You will find these navigation links located in the Quick Launch menu at the left of the web page.

This navigation setup makes it easy for users to quickly access web pages and sites that are specifically related to the site they are currently visiting. If necessary, you as a site administrator can modify the current navigation scheme to inherit the scheme from upper-level sites as well.

Planning Breadcrumb Navigation

Breadcrumb navigation sounds like something Hansel and Gretel would use, but it's actually a series of links that appears at the top of a web page that displays a linear path describing how deeply you have navigated into a website structure. For instance, you might see breadcrumb navigation expressed as the following:

Home > Department subsite > Projects site > Special projects site

If you were currently at the Special projects site and wanted to return to the Home site, you could just click the Home link to be immediately taken to that page. You could also click any of the intervening links to revisit those pages.

Breadcrumb navigation controls are located on the master page for the relevant sites in the site collection. There are actually two breadcrumb navigation controls, a global breadcrumb and a content breadcrumb. The global breadcrumb control encompasses only site content, while the content breadcrumb control manages both site and page content.

If you find it necessary to edit these controls, you will need to use either SharePoint Designer or Visual Studio.

Planning Navigation on Layout Pages

A layout page defines a layout for a web page by providing Microsoft ASP.NET controls in which the contents of pages are displayed. To customize a layout page, use Microsoft Office SharePoint Designer 2007 or Microsoft Visual Studio. You can add navigation controls to a layout page to support navigation links in web pages.

When a navigation control is inserted on a layout page, web pages using that layout page will display the control along with the page's contents. For example, you can define a layout page that includes a Summary Links navigation control so that a set of links to relevant pages and sites always appears when a page is displayed. SharePoint 2007 provides three major navigation controls that can be added to layout pages, as follows:

Content query Content query is used to control links to websites, web pages, or other web-accessible items displayed in a query page. Using a content query control on a website, you can present data that is specifically relevant to the content or theme of the site by specifying which content locations in the site collection to query. The data from those sources will be accessed and displayed in the content query control. Adding the content query to a layout page will display the query results on all the web pages dependent on the layout page. If you want to apply the content query uniquely to a single web page, you have the option of adding it as a web part to a web part page.

Summary links Summary links controls allow you to add a specific set of links to any web page in the SharePoint site collection. Just as with content query controls, you can add summary links controls to any layout page so that web pages dependent on the layout page will display the same set of links. Also, this control can be added uniquely to an individual web part page as a web part.

Table of contents This control lets you add a table of contents to one or a collection of web pages or websites. As with the previously mentioned controls, you can add a table of contents control directly to a layout page so that all of the web pages dependent on the layout page will display the same table of contents. This control shares the same controller as both global and navigation controls and can be used to display all of the links to the site collection or only the ones you specify. As with the previously mentioned controls, you have the option of uniquely adding the table of contents control to a web part page as a web part.

Planning Navigational Web Parts

As you learned in Chapter 8, "Configuring Web Part Pages, Web Parts, and Web Pages," a web part is a control that contributors can insert into a web part zone on a web part page and configure the properties. The summary links, table of contents, and content query controls each have web part counterparts that contributors can insert into web part zones. The web parts have the same configuration features and the same functionality as their related controls but are configurable when the contributor inserts them on the page rather than when the site designer inserts them on the page's layout. To make navigation web parts available for page contributors to insert on a page, you must include one or more web part zones on the page's layout page.

If you allow contributors to insert navigation web parts onto pages, you reduce the control you have over your portal site's navigation because those contributors can then control part of the navigation experience of site users. This might be appropriate in a loosely controlled environment such as a collaboration site within an organization, where individuals need the ability to point peers to content related to their work. You will want greater control in a more tightly controlled environment such as an Internet presence site, in which the navigation experience is planned and implemented in a consistent, controlled way by the site's designers and planners.

You have the ability to change permissions on layout pages to prevent users who have authorization to contribute to web part pages from being able to add any of the navigation web parts mentioned in this section. As administrator, you will retain the ability to add these web parts yourself on both web part pages and layout pages.

Using SharePoint Search

Now that I've gone through a rather lengthy explanation of search and navigation from a conceptual point of view, it's time to get some practical experience using these features. This section of the chapter will focus on how to use and modify SharePoint search. You can conduct your search from anywhere, but this book will begin with the sample site we've been using for the past few chapters. Try a basic search for a particular document in a document library now to test the process. Then try an advanced search to locate the same document.

You could have either opened the document in Microsoft Word on your computer or downloaded the document and saved it on your computer's hard drive. In this case, the point of trying the advanced search is to illustrate that it can locate a document not only by using keywords but also by using the document type.

The first exercise will involve searching for people. Before you go on to Exercise 9.1, take a few minutes and create a My Site site for at least one of the members of this site if you haven't already. When you actually conduct the search, you should log in as a different user than the one you are searching for.

Searching for People

1. On the site's home page, use the search scope drop-down menu, and select People.

2. In the search string field, type the username of the person you want to locate, and then click Go Search.

3. On the search results page in the Search Center, if there is an exact match, as shown here, click that result.

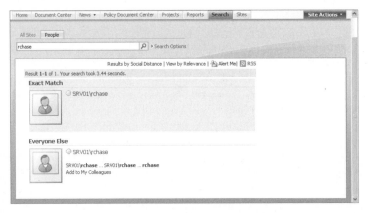

4. After the My Site page for the person you searched for opens, notice any information on that page that connects the user you are logged in as and this person, as shown here, and then return to the site's home page.

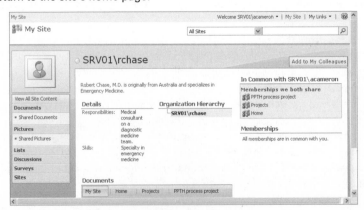

In the search results you see in the previous graphic, you will notice that the list is very limited. If you were working in a production environment with thousands of SharePoint users (perhaps some with similar names), you might have one result that is an exact match and several other results that would be similar but not the same person.

It's interesting to note in the previous graphic that the My Site page of the person you searched for is being viewed through the context of the person who has done the searching. This result would be the same if you had directly navigated to the user's My Site rather than searching for it, but this does illustrate SharePoint's ability to present information not as a static entity but in terms of relationships.

On the Advanced Search page of the Search Center, each of the search options available is considered an information property. The following are the default information properties available:

- Author
- Description
- Name
- Size
- URL
- Created Date
- Last Modified Date
- Created By
- Last Modified By

You most likely recognize that these properties map to columns in a typical SharePoint list. You may want to have additional properties available by which you can conduct searches. SharePoint allows you to create customized properties to use for advanced searches.

Exercise 9.2 will show you how to start. For this task, you'll need to be at the top-level site in the site collection, so leave the sample site we've been using and navigate to the portal site.

EXERCISE 9.2

Creating a New Property List and Column

1. On the home page of the top-level site, click View All Site Content in Quick Launch.

2. On the All Site Content page, click Create.

3. In the Custom Lists column, click Custom List.

4. On the New page, type the name of the new property in the Name field and an optional description of the property in the Description field.

5. Under Navigation, click No so the property list won't appear in Quick Launch.

6. Click Create.

EXERCISE 9.2 *(continued)*

7. On the List page, click New, and then click New Item to add an item to the list.

8. Perform step 7 again to add another item.

9. Click Site Actions ➤ Site Settings ➤ Modify All Site Settings.

10. On the Site Setting page in the Galleries column, click Site Columns.

11. On the Site Column Gallery page, click Create.

12. On the New Site Column: Home page, in the Column Name field, give the column the same name you gave the list in step 4.

13. In The Type of Information in This Column Is, select Lookup (information already on this site).

14. Under Group, select New Group, and type **Global Properties** in the available field.

15. Under Additional Column Settings, type a description of the property in the Description field.

16. Use the Get Information From drop-down menu, and select the name of the list you created as in step 4.

17. Use the In This Column drop-down menu to select Title.

18. Click OK.

Once you click OK in step 18 of the previous exercise, return to the portal site. This task isn't actually completed, and you'll need to go through Exercise 9.3 to continue setting up the new property for the Advanced Search page.

EXERCISE 9.3

Creating a New Advanced Search Managed Property

1. On the top-level site, click View All Site Content in Quick Launch.

2. On the All Site Contents page under Document Libraries, click Documents.

3. On the Documents page, click Settings, and then click Document Libraries Settings.

4. Under Columns, click Add from Existing Site Columns. (You may have to scroll down the page to see this option.)

EXERCISE 9.3 *(continued)*

5. On the Add Columns from Site Columns: Documents page in the Available Site Columns box, select the column you created in Exercise 9.2, and click Add to add it to the Columns to Add box.

6. Click OK.

7. Logged in as an administrator, launch the Central Administration (CA) web application.

8. In Quick Launch on the CA home page, click Shared Services Administration (SSA), and on the SSA page, click the name of the relevant SSP.

9. On the SSP's home page under Search, click Search Settings.

10. On the Configure Search Settings page, click Content Sources and Crawl Schedules.

11. On the Manage Content Sources page, move the cursor just to the right of Local Office SharePoint Server Sites, open the drop-down menu, select Start Incremental Crawl, and wait for the crawl process to complete.

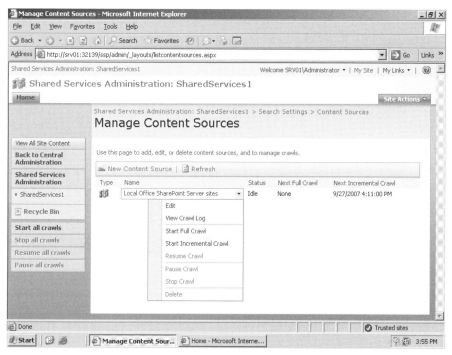

12. Return to the Search Settings page, and click Metadata Property Mappings.

EXERCISE 9.3 *(continued)*

13. On the Metadata Property Mappings page, click New Managed Property.

14. On the New Managed Property page, in the Name field, give the property the same name you gave the list in step 4 of Exercise 9.2.

15. Type a brief description of the property in the Description field.

16. Under The Type of Information in This Property, select Text.

17. Under Mappings to Crawled Properties, select Include Values from All Crawled Properties Mapped.

18. To the right of the Crawled Properties Mapped to This Managed Property field, click Add Mapping.

19. When the Crawled Property Selection box appears, in the Crawled Property Name field, type the name you gave the list in step 4 of Exercise 9.2, and then click Find.

20. In the Select a Crawled Property box, select ows_*name_of_crawled_property* (text) where *name_of_crawled_property* is the name you typed in the field in step 19.

21. Click OK to close the box.

22. On the New Managed Property page, tick the Allow This Property to Be Used in Scopes check box, and then click OK.

The name of the new managed property will appear in the list on the Metadata Property Mappings page.

Now that you've created the new managed property, you still need to add it to the Advanced Search web part. Exercise 9.4 will take you through the steps of this process. This exercise must be started on the top-level site.

EXERCISE 9.4

Adding a Managed Property on the Advanced Search Page

1. On the portal site's home page, click Advanced Search to open the Search Center.

2. On the Advanced Search page, click Site Actions ➢ Edit Page.

3. Click Edit ➢ Modify Shared Web Part

4. In the Advanced Search Box toolbox, expand Properties.

5. Select the Properties text field, and then on the right, click the Expansion button to open the Text Entry dialog box.

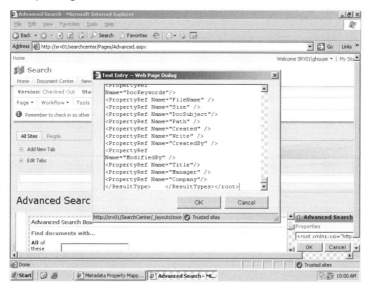

6. In the Text Entry box, locate the <PropertyDefs> tag, and place the following line directly after the tag: **<PropertyDef Name="name_of_property" DataType="text" DisplayName=" name_ of_property" />** where *name_of_property* is the name you gave the property.

7. Locate the line <ResultTypes><ResultType DisplayName="All Results" Name="Default"><Query /> and immediately after that line, type **<PropertyRef Name="*name_of_property*" />** where *name_of_property* is the name you assigned to the property.

8. Click OK to close the Text Entry box, and then click OK to close the Advanced Search Box toolbox.

9. Click Publish to publish your changes to this page.

10. Return to the relevant SSP's home page as you did in Exercise 9.5, steps 7 through 9, and under Search click Search Settings.

11. On the Configure Search Settings page, click Metadata Property Mappings.

12. On the Manage Content Sources page, click to the right of Local Office SharePoint Server sites, and select Start Full Crawl.

After the full crawl operation has completed, return to the top-level site, and click Advanced Search. You should see the new property as a drop-down menu. When you click the menu, you will see the items you added to the list in Exercise 9.2, steps 7 and 8.

The next several exercises will take place on the Central Administration web application on the SSP home page. As you've seen in the previous exercises, you can perform a number of search-related administrative tasks there. Now you'll get the experience of performing those tasks, starting with creating a content source in Exercise 9.5. Begin logged into the CA web application. In this particular example, we are going to configure an external website as the content source.

Creating a Content Source

1. On the CA home page in Quick Launch, click Shared Services Administration, and then click the name of the relevant SSP such as SharedServices1 (Default).

2. Under Search, click Search Settings.

3. On the Configure Search Settings page, click Content Sources and Crawl Schedules.

4. On the Manage Content Sources page, click New Source Content.

5. On the Add Content Source page, give your new content source a mandatory name in the Name field.

6. Under Content Source Type in the Select the Type of Content to Be Crawled list, select Web Sites.

7. In the Type Start Addresses Below (One Per Line) box, type the URL of the website or websites you want to have the system crawl.

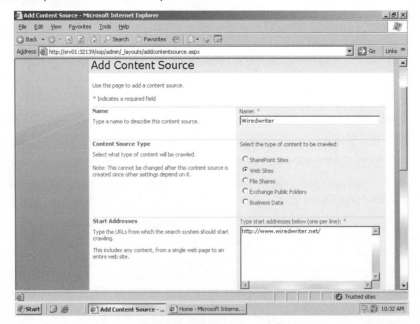

8. Under Crawl Settings, select Only Crawl Within the Server of Each Start Address.

9. Under Crawl Schedules, just beneath the Full Crawl drop-down menu, click Create Schedule.

10. When the Manage Schedules Web page Dialog box opens, under Type, select Weekly.

11. Under Settings, in the Weeks field, leave the default value of 1, and tick the day of the week check box for the day when you want to run the full crawl. Use the Starting Time drop-down menu to select a time to start the crawl.

12. If you want a crawl to occur more than once in a single day, tick the Repeat Within the Day check box, and add values in minutes for the Every and For fields.

13. When finished, click OK.

14. Under the Incremental Crawl drop-down menu, click Create Schedule.

15. Follow steps 10 through 13, except in step 10 select Daily and in step 11 leave the default value of 1 for days. Then use the drop-down menu to select a different starting time for this crawl than you did for the full crawl.

EXERCISE 9.5 *(continued)*

16. Under Start Full Crawl, if you want a full crawl of the content source to begin immediately after creating this new content source, tick the Start Full Crawl of This Content Source check box.

17. Click OK.

As you can see, the new external content source has been added to the Manage Content Sources page complete with schedules for the next full and incremental crawls.

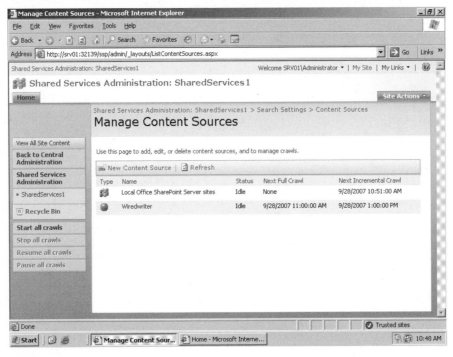

As you saw, you can create content sources from the following categories:

- SharePoint sites
- Web sites
- File shares
- Exchange Public folders
- Business data

Once you create a content source and SharePoint search has crawled that source, you will be able to use search in SharePoint to locate data contained in that source, including the locations listed earlier.

Steps 9 through 15 in Exercise 9.5 showed you how to set up full and incremental crawl schedules for a content source. If you want to edit those schedules, on the Manage Content Sources page, click the desired content source; instead of clicking Create Schedule as in steps 9 and 14 in Exercise 9.5, click Edit Schedule and proceed to modify the crawl schedules as you require.

🌐 Real World Scenario

Creating a Content Source

Lisa, the director of your company's Projects group, wants to make it easier for their top customer, the PPTH Project, to be able to search the Projects website for content Lisa's staff is producing for them. Currently, PPTH is searching the default content source, which is Local Office SharePoint Server sites, since that is the only content source available. Lisa says that she is receiving complains of excessive, irrelevant search results and wants to improve the performance of search so that PPTH can find their content more easily.

You decide that creating an additional content source would ease the burden and decide to make the Projects site a separate source. You go to the SSA page for the relevant SSP and open the Search settings page, click Content Sources and Crawl Schedules, and then click New Content Source. On the Add Content Source page, you name the new content source Projects and select SharePoint Sites in the Select the Type of Content to Be Crawled list. You add the path to the Projects site in the Start Addresses field and create a crawl schedule for full and incremental crawls. Before finishing, you make sure a full crawl will be started right after you create the new content source so it will be available for search as soon as possible.

As shown previously, you can also manually start a full or incremental crawl on the Manage Content Sources page by opening the menu to the right of the desired content source and clicking Start Full Crawl or Start Incremental Crawl. On the same page, you can go to Quick Launch on the left and click one of the following to manage crawls:

- Start All Crawls
- Stop All Crawls
- Resume All Crawls
- Pause All Crawls

Some options may not be available depending on the status of crawls on the content sources when you view this page.

You learned earlier in this chapter that crawl rules allow you to set separate rules for crawling different content sources to avoid crawling irrelevant content. Exercise 9.6 will take you through the basics of setting up a crawl rule. The exercise assumes you are on the Configure Search Settings page.

EXERCISE 9.6

Setting Crawl Rules

1. On the Configure Search Settings page, click Crawl Rules.

2. On the Manage Crawl Rules page, click New Crawl Rule.

3. On the Add Crawl Rule page, type the path or URL to the content source location you want to apply the rule to in the required Path field.

4. Under Crawl Configuration, select either Exclude All Items in This Path or Include All Items in This Path.

5. If you selected Include All Items in This Path in step 4, you can tick one or more of the check boxes for the options shown here.

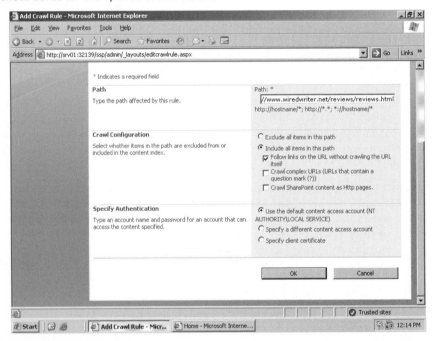

6. If you selected Include All Items in This Path in step 4, under Specify Authentication, you can select one of the three options in that section as shown earlier.

7. Click OK.

8. On the Manage Crawl Rules page, type the URL or path in the Type a URL field, and click Test to find out whether it matches a rule field. Then click Test to verify that the rule has been successfully applied.

EXERCISE 9.6 *(continued)*

You can see the result of performing step 8 here.

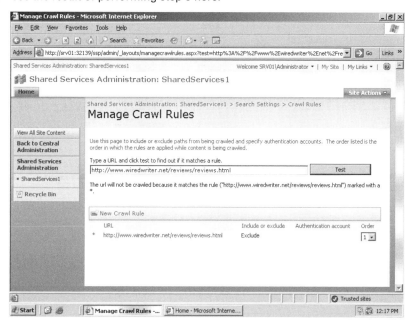

In an advanced search, you can specify a wide variety of file types to search for, but not every file type possible is included. Exercise 9.7 will show you how to add a file type. This exercise assumes you are on the Configure Search Settings page.

EXERCISE 9.7

Adding a File Type to Search

1. On the Configure Search Settings page, click File Types.

2. On the Manage File Types page, click New File Type.

3. On the Add File Type page, add a new file type extension such as pdf in the File Extension field.

4. Click OK.

The file extension will be added to the list on the Manage File Types page. Click to the right of any extension on this page to open the drop-down menu. The only item in this menu by default is Delete.

You may want to review how successfully content crawling is operating, and SharePoint provides this option. Exercise 9.8 will show you how to view the crawl logs for a particular content source. As with the previous exercises, you will be starting out on the Configure Search Settings page.

EXERCISE 9.8

Viewing Crawl Logs

1. On the Configure Search Settings page, click Crawl Logs.

2. When the Crawl Log page appears, you can view the crawl statistics by the Hostname, Successfully Crawled, Warnings, Errors, and Total columns. Click a hostname to view crawl log details.

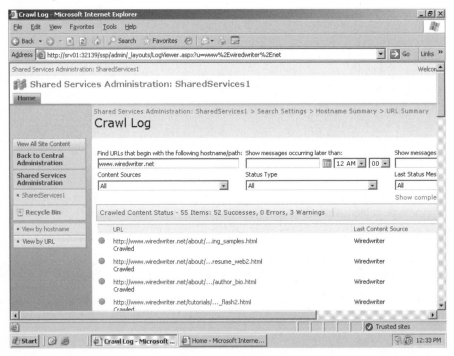

3. Click the Successfully Crawled, Warnings, and Errors logs for a particular content source to view the content.

4. Return to the Configure Search Settings page when finished.

On the Search Settings page, you can click Default Content Access Account to change the default account used for crawling content. The default account is NT AUTHORITY\LOCAL SERVICE, and it is advised that you do not change the default unless you need to use a different account that has read access to a specific target server.

WARNING   The default content access account should not be an administrator on the target server being crawled.

A number of other options are available on the Configure Search Settings page under Crawl Settings, but most of them are pretty straightforward. Here's the rundown.

You've already worked with metadata property mappings in Exercise 9.3, so there won't be an exercise duplicating that task. Server Name Mappings allow you to override how SharePoint Portal Server displays search results or how users access content after you crawl some documents. By default, no mappings exist. The Search Based Alerts page can be used only to activate or deactivate this feature, which is activated by default. Search Based Removal allows you to specify URLs that you do not want to appear in search results. This can be handy if you have SharePoint web content you want to keep private and not have it inadvertently show up in a user's search results. When you specify a URL to be excluded, a crawl rule will be written that will exclude the URL in future crawls. The Reset All Crawled Content option lets you erase the content index. If you select this option, content will not be available for search results until a new set of crawls have been completed.

If you scroll down the page, you'll see two other sections, Scopes and Authoritative Pages. As you already know, Scopes are limitations to the content to be searched such as All Sites, People, and the content on the current website. You have the ability to view and to create new scopes on the Configure Search Settings page. Exercise 9.9 will show you how.

EXERCISE 9.9

Creating a Search Scope

1. On the Configure Search Settings page under Scopes, click View Scopes.

2. On the View Scopes page, click New Scope.

3. On the Create Scope page, give your new scope a name in the required Title field, and give it a description in the Description field.

4. Under Target Results Page, select Use the Default Search Results Page.

5. Click OK.

6. On the View Scopes page, in the Update Status column next to the new scope, click Add Rules.

7. On the Add Scope Rule page, under Scope Rule Type, select Web Address, Property Query (Author = John Doe), Content Source, or All Content. (Each selection will produce a different result on the page. This exercise will use Web Address as the selection.)

EXERCISE 9.9 *(continued)*

8. Under Web Address, select Folder, Hostname, or Domain or Subdomain, and then type the relevant URL or path in the available field.

9. Under Behavior, select Include, Require, or Exclude, and then click OK.

The new scope will not be ready until after the next content crawl. The notation under Update Status will tell you when the next crawl in scheduled.

You can use the Authoritative Pages option to specify web pages that link to the most relevant information. Search uses this list to calculate the rank of every page in the index. There might be many authoritative web pages in your environment. Type the most significant in the topmost text box. You also have the option of specifying second- and third-level authorities in the lower text boxes. You can also specify Non-authoritative Sites, which are ranked lower than all other sites in the site collection or in all sites that are listed as content sources, both internal and external.

When you perform a search, whether within SharePoint or using an available search engine on the Internet, you usually type a keyword into the search field, click the Search button, and then await the search results. The keyword used represents the topic or information you are looking for. Using a search engine on the Internet doesn't allow you to view behind the scenes and see how that search engine is configured to handle keywords; however, you can create that keyword configuration within SharePoint. Exercise 9.10 will take you through the process of creating a keyword. This exercise assumes you are on the portal site's home page. You must be logged in as the SharePoint administrator to successfully complete this exercise.

EXERCISE 9.10

Creating a Keyword and Best Bet for Search

1. On the portal site's home page, click Site Actions ➢ Site Settings ➢ Modify All Site Settings.

2. In the Site Collection Administration column, click Search Keywords.

3. On the Manage Keywords page, click Add Keyword.

4. On the Add Keyword page, under Keyword Information, type the new keyword in the required Keyword Phrase field.

5. In the Synonyms field, type one or more words that are synonyms to the keyword, separating each word in this field by semicolons.

6. Under Best Bets, click Add Best Bet.

7. When the Add Best Bet Web page dialog box appears, type the URL that is the best bet for the keyword in the required URL field.

8. Type the title that is a best bet for the keyword in the required Title field.

9. Type a description in the Description field, and click OK to close the Add Best Bet web page dialog box.

10. Use the Keyword Definition text editor to add a description of the new keyword.

11. In the Contact field, type the name of the person to inform when the keyword is past its review date, and then click Check Names.

12. Under Publishing, Use the Start Date, End Date, and Review Date fields to indicate when you want the keyword to begin appearing in search results, when you want it to stop appearing, and when you want the keyword to be reviewed for relevancy.

13. Click OK.

The new keyword will appear on the Manage Keywords page with the entries you configured for the keyword in the Best Bets, Synonyms, Contact, and Expiry Date columns.

Using SharePoint Navigation

We've spent a considerable amount of time on search, and it's now time to switch to navigation as the other method of locating content within sites. Anyone who has accessed web-based content has experienced site navigation. In SharePoint, navigation is expressed using two methods: tree view and the breadcrumb trail.

Tree view allows you to see the entire site hierarchy expressed in Quick Launch so that all of the site's contents are immediately available using navigation links. Breadcrumb navigation displays a linear path describing how deeply you have navigated into a website structure. You can use a sufficiently long breadcrumb trail to click back and forth to various pages along the "trail"; this form of navigation makes it easy to return to your original location after navigating deep into a site's web page structure.

There are a few ways you can modify navigation. Exercise 9.11 starts you off at the home page of the portal site.

Modifying Navigation from the Portal Site

1. On the home page of the Portal site, click Site Actions ➢ Site Settings ➢ Modify Navigation.

2. On the Site Navigation Settings page, under Subsites and Pages, you can tick or clear the Show Subsites and Show Pages check boxes to show or hide navigation to these locations.

3. Under Sorting, select either Sort Automatically or Sort Manually. If you select Sort Manually, you can also tick the Sort Pages Automatically check box.

4. Use the Navigation Editing and Sorting box, and click Add Heading to add a navigation heading or click Add Link to add a link to the navigation tree.

5. In the same section, click a link, and then click the Move Up or Move Down buttons to change the order the link appears in the tree.

6. Click OK when finished.

You can click Picture Library and then click the Edit button to edit the title of the item and the URL to the library. You can't do this with any of the other items in Figure 9.4.

At the bottom of the Site Navigation Settings page in the Selected Item section, you can see details about an item selected in the Navigation Editing and Sorting box.

You can configure subsites to inherit the navigation scheme of their parent site, as you'll discover in Exercise 9.12. For this exercise, go to a subsite of the top-level portal site.

FIGURE 9.4   Site Navigations Settings page

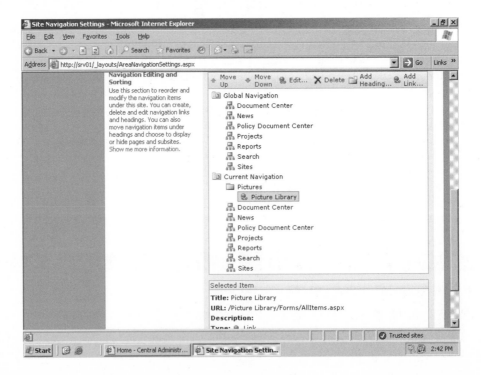

EXERCISE 9.12

Configuring a Subsite to Inherit Navigation from the Parent Site

1. On the desired subsite, click Site Actions ➢ Site Settings.

2. In the Look and Feel column, click Navigation.

3. On the Site Navigation Settings page, you can see sections for Subsites and Pages and Sorting that function just as their counterparts did in Exercise 9.11 in steps 2 and 3.

4. Under Global Navigation, select either Display the Same Navigation Items as the Parent Site or Display the Navigation Items Below the Current Site.

5. Under Current Navigation, select Display the Same Navigation Items as the Parent Site, Display the Current Site, the Navigation Items Below the Current Site, and the Current Site's Siblings; or select Display Only the Navigation Items Below the Current Site, depending on your requirements.

6. The Navigation Editing and Sorting box operates just as the one you saw in Exercise 9.11 in steps 4 and 5, and it includes the same Selected Item box.

7. Click OK when finished.

On the Site Settings page in the Look and Feel column, you can also click Tree View, and on the Tree View page you can tick or clear the Enable Quick Launch and Enable Tree View check boxes and then click OK. Figure 9.5 shows what navigation looks like on a website where both Quick Launch and tree view are enabled.

FIGURE 9.5   Quick Launch and tree view navigation

Summary

In this chapter, you learned how SharePoint uses search and navigation to locate information and people, including the following:

- The differences between basic and advanced searches
- How to plan for content crawling, content sources, and the user search experience
- How to plan for navigation including navigation on master pages, layout pages, and navigation web parts
- The different methods of configuring search including crawl schedules, rules, content sources, and search scopes
- How to modify navigation from the portal site and set up navigation inheritance

Exam Essentials

Configure the Search Center. You need to know how advanced search operates in the Search Center, including how to configure a search using different properties such as file type and content keywords. You also are expected to understand how to add a custom-made property to the Search Center.

Configure content sources. Know the default content sources available in SharePoint search and how to add a content source. This includes adding different types of content sources such as SharePoint sites, external websites, file shares, exchange public folders, and business data. You also need to know how to create search scopes and keywords.

Configure crawl settings. You need to understand the differences between a full and incremental crawl, how to set up crawl schedules for content sources, and how to set up crawl rules so that the crawl treats different sources in different ways.

View search settings. Know how to view crawl logs including monitoring successful crawls, warnings, and errors.

Review Questions

1. You are the administrator for the shared services provider (SSP) used by your company's SharePoint site collection. You are configuring the default content access account, which is the account that is used by default when search crawls content sources. Of the following options, which action should you not take when configuring this account?

   A. The account should never be set as NT AUTHORITY\LOCAL SERVICE.

   B. You should not click Default Content Access Account to change the default account.

   C. This account should not be an administrator on the target server being crawled.

   D. The default content access account must not have read access to all content that is crawled.

2. You are the shared services provider (SSP) administrator for your company's SharePoint site collection, and you are planning the management of shared search scopes in SharePoint. Of the following options, which represent your responsibilities in configuring search scopes? (Choose all that apply.)

   A. Creating shared scopes

   B. Editing shared scopes

   C. Deleting shared scopes

   D. Modifying shared scopes at the web page level

3. You are the SharePoint shared services provider (SSP) administrator for your company's site collection, and you've just created a new content source. You are setting up the crawl schedules for the new content source. Of the subsequent options, which do you know are true about configuring content crawling? (Choose all that apply.)

   A. After the initial full crawl of content, schedule full crawls more frequently than incremental crawls.

   B. Stagger crawl schedules so that server load balancing is utilized across the entire server farm.

   C. Schedule incremental crawls for each content source during times when the servers hosting that content type are available but the demand on the resources of the server are low, such as after business hours.

   D. Group start addresses in content sources based on similar availability and with acceptable overall resource usage for the servers that host the content.

4. You are the SSP administrator for your company's SharePoint site collection. Staff members in the purchasing department have repeatedly complained that they are getting too many results when they do an All Sites search for products on their top vendor's website and have asked whether there's anything you can do about it. You determine that the best course of action would be to create a new search scope limited to the contents of the site in question. Of the subsequent selections, which one will produce the desired result?

   A. On the Add Scope Rule page, under Scope Rule Type, select Web Address (Author = John Doe).

   B. Under Web Address, select Folder, and then type the path to the site in the available field.

   C. Under Web Address, select Domain or Subdomain, and then type the relevant URL in the available field.

   D. On the Add Scope Rule page, under Scope Rule Type, select Web Address (URL = domainname).

5. You are the SharePoint administrator for your company's SharePoint Intranet site. The CIO has tasked you with modifying navigation on the portal site's home page and all subsites of the portal. She gives you the specifics of her plan, and you proceed to make the changes. Of the following options, which are you able to perform? (Choose all that apply.)

   A. Edit the title and URL to the Sites navigation link under Global Navigation.

   B. Move the Sites navigation link higher on the list under Current Navigation.

   C. Edit the title and URL to the Picture Library under Current Navigation.

   D. Move the Document Center link lower on the list under Global Navigation.

6. You are the SharePoint site administrator for your company's intranet. You are providing an in-service training for the site owners of each of the major departments in your local division. Currently, the topic is on the capacities of MOSS 2007 and how they're enhanced compared to the Windows SharePoint Services 3.0 (WSS 3.0) search service. Of the subsequent selections, which are true about SharePoint Server 2007 search? (Choose all that apply.)

   A. MOSS 2007 search has the ability to search a wider scope of content types.

   B. MOSS 2007 search has the ability to define content scopes on the site level, while WSS 3.0 can define scopes on the global level.

   C. MOSS 2007 provides advanced search options from within team collaborative sites.

   D. MOSS 2007 search provides suggested corrections for misspelled search strings.

7. You are the SharePoint site administrator for your company's intranet. You are providing an in-service training for the site owners of each of the major departments in your local division. One of the department heads has asked about any limitations in configuring an external content source for SharePoint search. Of the following options, which options are true for external content sources? (Choose all that apply.)

   A. A web application that uses a different SSP than your site collection

   B. Internet content not under your administrative control

   C. Extranet content not under your administrative control

   D. A web application that uses a different SSP in your site collection than the default

8. You are the SharePoint site administrator for your company's intranet. You are providing in-service training for the site owners of each of the major departments in your local division. You are discussing different ways that site navigation can be presented. Of the subsequent choices, which are valid navigational options? (Choose all that apply.)

   A. Breadcrumb navigation

   B. Tree view

   C. Global navigation

   D. Local navigation

9. You are the SharePoint site administrator for your company's intranet. You are providing in-service training for the site owners of each of the major departments in your local division. You are discussing different ways that site navigation can be presented. Phil, the site owner of the public relations department, asks about the different ways breadcrumb navigation is controlled. Of the following options, which are correct about breadcrumb navigation? (Choose all that apply.)

A. The default master page displays form and view pages and includes a breadcrumb control that displays only sites.

B. The default master page displays form and view pages and includes a breadcrumb control that contains sites and the current page.

C. The default master page displays form and view pages and includes a breadcrumb control that contains only the current page.

D. The Team Site template includes one breadcrumb control on all web pages.

10. You are the SSP administrator for your company's SharePoint intranet site collection. Leah, the CIO, has tasked you with using server name mappings to change how particular URLs or ranges of URLs are displayed in search results. You understand that server name mappings are set at the SSP level for all content that is crawled by that SSP and are applied whenever queries are performed. Of the following selections, which one accurately describes the required task?

A. Appearance of links

B. Keywords

C. Relevance of search results

D. Search-based alerts

11. You are the SSP administrator for your company's SharePoint site collection. The marketing department has been complaining that when they are searching for a specific set of customer data, the relevancy of the search results isn't particularly helpful. They give you the names of the sites, listing them from most to least authoritative. You know that you can use the Authoritative Pages option to specify web pages that link to the most relevant information. Where must you configure this option?

A. On the Search Settings page, click Specify Authoritative Pages, and add the most authoritative page URL to the Most Authoritative Pages field. You can also add URLs to the Second-Level Authoritative Pages and Third-Level Authoritative Pages fields.

B. On the Search Settings page under Authoritative Pages, click Specify Authoritative Pages, and add the most authoritative page URL to the Most Authoritative Pages field. You can also add URLs to the Second-Level Authoritative Pages and Third-Level Authoritative Pages fields.

C. On the Search Settings page, click Specify Authoritative Pages, and add the most authoritative page URL to the Most Authoritative Pages field. You can also add URLs to the Mid-Authoritative Pages and Least Authoritative Pages fields.

D. On the Search Settings page under Authoritative Pages, click Specify Authoritative Pages, and add the most authoritative page URL to the Most Authoritative Pages field. You can also add URLs to the Mid Authoritative Pages and Least Authoritative Pages fields.

12. You are the SSP administrator for your company's SharePoint site collection. Dale, the head of research, has been receiving complaints from his staff that site navigation does not let them locate resources as easily as they'd like. They would like top-level navigation to give them access to resources in the entire site collection but have navigation in Quick Launch focus on resources specific to their subsite including any child sites they create for themselves. What must you do to give them the navigation options they need? (Choose all that apply.)

    A. Under Global Navigation, select Display the Same Navigation Items as the Parent Site and Display the Current Site Navigation Items for Current Navigation.

    B. Under Global Navigation, select Display the Same Navigation Items as the Parent Site.

    C. Under Current Navigation, select Display the Current Site, the Navigation Items Below the Current Site, and the Current Site's Siblings.

    D. Under Current Navigation, select Display Only the Navigation Items Below the Current Site.

13. You are the SSP administrator for your company's SharePoint site collection. The CTO has tasked you with creating a new custom-made property and adding it to the Advanced Search page in the Search Center specifically to enable searching for information by the regional office. You have created a new property list and column and created a new advanced search managed property on the SSA for the relevant SSP. Now you want to add the managed property to the Advanced Search page. You open the Advanced Search toolbox and open the Text Entry dialog box. What is the first tag you need to identify?

    A. <DataType>

    B. <PropertyDefs>

    C. <ResultTypes>

    D. <Query>

14. You are the SharePoint administrator for your company's site collection. You get a call from Ken, the manager of R&D, complaining about a navigation issue. He is the site owner of the R&D department's site, which is one of six departmental sites that exist just one level below the company portal site. Ken has created a site right below the R&D site for his engineering team. This morning he logged into SharePoint and launched the portal site's home page in his web browser. He looked at the Global Navigation bar, and while he saw a link to the R&D site, he didn't see the link to the engineering site he had created the day before. Of the following choices, which one is the most likely problem?

    A. Ken hasn't waited long enough for the link to appear. As soon as the next incremental crawl has occurred, the link will show up on the portal site's home page.

    B. Ken forgot to publish the changes he made when he created the new engineering subsite, so navigational links to that site won't appear on the portal site's home page.

    C. Ken didn't realize that by default only subsites one level below the top-level site of a portal site, such as the R&D site, are added to the global navigation. The engineering site is under R&D and thus two levels below, so it won't appear in the portal site's Global Navigation.

    D. Ken must request that a link to the engineering subsite be added to the Global Navigation bar on the portal site by the site owner or administrator since no navigational links appear there automatically.

15. You are the SSP administrator for your company's SharePoint site collection. You are planning for a site collection–wide deployment of search scopes and are collecting information relevant to your planning process. You have recruited Cassandra, Christina, and Dwayne, members of your staff, to assist you in this process. Currently, you are discussing search scope management. Of the following options, which are true about search scopes? (Choose all that apply.)

A. Scopes that the SSP administrator creates at the SSP level are called *shared scopes*.

B. SSP administrators can create custom scopes at the site collection level, which makes the custom scopes available to all the site collections.

C. The SSP administrator manages shared scopes for only the top-level sites that use the SSP.

D. The SSP administrator can make a copy of shared scopes that becomes a site collection–level scope.

16. You are the SSP administrator for your company's SharePoint site collection. You have been tasked by Dorothy, the manager of sales, to create a file share as a new content source that will then become searchable by her staff. You are in the process of configuring the crawl schedules and want to schedule full crawls to occur on a weekly basis. What do you have to enter in the Weeks field on the Add Content Source page to cause this to occur?

A. Type **1** in the Weeks field.

B. Type **one** in the Weeks field.

C. 1 is in the Weeks field by default, so you don't have to do anything there.

D. There is no Weeks field. You must tick the Weekly check box to accomplish your task.

17. You are the SharePoint administrator for your company's site collection. You are working with Cyndy, the SSP administrator, to plan deployment of navigation controls in the site's layout pages. Cyndy states that several customized controls will need to be added. Of the options that follow, which can you use to provide the required custom controls? (Choose all that apply.)

A. Microsoft Office SharePoint Designer 2007

B. Microsoft ASP.NET navigation control web parts

C. Microsoft Visual Studio

D. Microsoft .NET 3.5 Framework

18. You are the SSP administrator for your company's SharePoint site collection. Stan, the manager of the shipping department, says that the default properties available on the Advanced Search page in the Search Center aren't sufficient to allow his staff to adequately search for the parts descriptions they require to locate items in inventory. You review the default properties and think they are sufficient, but Stan insists that you add a custom-made property. Of the following selections, which one is not a default property in advanced search and is more likely to be a custom-made property?

A. Description

B. Name

C. Size

D. Type

19. You are the SSP administrator for your company's SharePoint site collection. You are in the midst of planning navigation for layout pages in the site. You want to insert a navigation control so that new informational articles produced by the Projects group are highlighted on their site's main page. Of the following options, which one is the navigation control that will best accomplish the task?

   A. Content query

   B. Navigation response

   C. Summary links

   D. Table of contents

20. You are the SSP administrator for your company's SharePoint site collection. Darlene, the CIO, states she is concerned about the possible impact of allowing search-based alerts to continue to operate by default in the site collection. She tasks you with researching which server and network elements in the company infrastructure could potentially have issues while the search-based alerts feature is enabled. Of the following choices, which are valid concerns? (Choose all that apply.)

   A. There can be an increased load on mail servers.

   B. There can be an increased load on web servers.

   C. There can be an increased load on query servers.

   D. There can be an increased load on database servers.

Answers to Review Questions

1. C. The default content access account is NT AUTHORITY\LOCAL SERVICE, so option A is not correct. You must click the Default Content Access Account to change the default account, so option B is not correct. The default content access account must have read access to all content being crawled, so option D is not correct.

2. A, B, and C. The SSP administrator can create, edit, and delete search scopes and refresh changes to scopes. Option D is bogus.

3. B, C, and D. After the initial full crawl of content, you should schedule full crawls less frequently than incremental crawls.

4. C. Option C represents the correct step in the process of creating a search scope that allows you to specify an external website.

5. B, C, and D. You can edit only the title and URL of the picture library, not of the other navigational links. You can move all navigational links up or down the list under both global and current navigation. You can also delete any link, add a heading, or add a link.

6. A, C, and D. MOSS 2007 search has the ability to define content scopes on both the global and site level.

7. A, B, and C. Options A, B, and C all correctly define an external content source. Option D is a bogus answer.

8. A, B, and C. Option D would have to be current navigation to be correct. The other choices represent different presentations of SharePoint navigation.

9. A and B. The default master page, which displays form and view pages, includes two breadcrumb controls: a global breadcrumb, which contains sites only; and a content breadcrumb, which contains sites and the current page. Some collaboration site templates, such as the Team Site template, also include two breadcrumbs on all web pages.

10. A. SharePoint 2007 provides a number of settings that enable SSP and site collection administrators to control what users see in search results pages. Although you can control the search results in different ways, the most common method of managing user search results is by the appearance of links. SSP administrators can use server name mappings to change how particular URLs or ranges of URLs are displayed in search results. Server name mappings are set at the SSP level for all content that is crawled by that SSP and are applied whenever queries are performed.

11. B. Option B describes the correct set of steps to take to accomplish the task. The other choices are bogus.

12. B and C. Option B will allow the top-level navigation bar to inherit the navigation links from the parent site, and option C will allow Quick Launch to display navigation links for the current site and any subsites it contains.

13. B. In the Text Entry box, locate the <PropertyDefs> tag, and place the following line directly after the tag: **<PropertyDef Name="name_of_property" DataType="text" DisplayName="**_name_of_ property_**" />**, where _name_of_property_ is the name you gave the property.

14. C. By default, all subsites one level below the top-level site of a portal site automatically are added to the global navigation. In option A, content crawling wouldn't affect the appearance of the link to the site Ken created unless he was using search to attempt to locate the site and the search results didn't display a link to the site. In option B, even if Ken didn't publish the site, because he created the changes, he would be able to see those changes on his page. Option D is a bogus answer.

15. A and D. SSP administrators can create custom scopes at the site collection level, which makes the custom scopes available only to the site collection on which they were created. The SSP administrator manages shared scopes for all sites that use the SSP.

16. C. Under Settings, in the Weeks field, leave the default value of 1. Tick the day of the Week check box for the day when you want to run the full crawl, and use the Starting Time drop-down menu to select a time to start the crawl.

17. A and C. A layout page defines a layout for a web page by providing Microsoft ASP.NET controls in which the contents of pages are displayed. To customize layout pages, use Microsoft Office SharePoint Designer 2007 or Microsoft Visual Studio.

18. D. The default properties in advanced search are Author, Description, Name, Size, Type, URL, Created Date, Last Modified Date, Created By, and Last Modified By.

19. A. You can use a content query control to link to pages or other items that are displayed based on a query you design. For example, if you are presenting articles in an online news site, you could add a content query control to your site's Welcome Page layout so that new articles are highlighted on that page. Summary links and table of contents are other navigation controls used with layout pages. Navigation response is a bogus option.

20. A and C. When you allow search-based alerts, your system uses additional resources on mail servers and increases the load on query servers because queries for each search-based alert run every time a search-based alert is processed.

Chapter 10

Working with Microsoft Documents in SharePoint

MICROSOFT EXAM OBJECTIVES COVERED IN THIS CHAPTER

✓ **Configure Content Management**

- Configure Document Management
- Configure Records Management
- Managing Policies and Compliance

Although it may seem that working with Microsoft documents in SharePoint would focus sharply on Microsoft Word documents in a document library, there is a much larger issue to consider. This chapter addresses several aspects of SharePoint content management including document and record management, policies and compliance with regard to document creation and access, and more information on workflow.

Once you've delved into the conceptual areas of content management, you'll get a chance to put what you've learned into practice, primarily using SharePoint features but also using Word. You'll learn how to perform standard management of Word documents and other document types in libraries and document centers. You'll also learn how to impose specific rules regarding how those documents are created, accessed, and processed.

You'll have a small opportunity to see how Word interoperates with SharePoint, including how to create content in SharePoint, such as a blog entry, directly from within Word. You'll also learn some of the differences between how Word 2003 and Word 2007 interact with SharePoint. Finally, you'll be introduced to SharePoint's Document Center and Records Center.

Document Management Overview

Document management is more than just administering how documents are created, uploaded, and secured in SharePoint. This dynamic flow controls the entire lifetime of any SharePoint document, regardless of its format. This process includes how documents are created, reviewed, published, accessed, retained, archived, and finally replaced or eliminated. Document management also reflects the collaborative nature of SharePoint and includes how documents are located and shared within and between teams.

This system treats documents not only as information sources but as business, policy, and legal records as well. Managing these records involves imposing corporate policy regarding how records are published and how you can and must access them. Since reviewing and versioning is so important with official documentation, SharePoint provides the tools necessary to ensure that company policy and legal requirements are adhered to in the treatment of these documents.

Document Management Planning

In Chapter 7, "Configuring and Maintaining Lists and Libraries," you were introduced to lists and libraries including document libraries. This section of the chapter will give you a more in-depth look at document libraries, specifically how to plan for them and just how many document libraries are available in SharePoint. The following list outlines the library types and how they are used:

Document Center library   This library type is designed for large-scale access from the enterprise and so may contain documents available to numerous offices with a multinational scope. This library can also be used as the archive for all historical records of a company including those that must be retained for a certain period of time because of legal requirements.

Portal Site library   Although this library doesn't have the vast scope of a Document Center library, the content is intended to be accessed by a company-wide audience from any site in the site collection.

Records Repository library   This library type has the specific purpose of containing formal company documentation such as legal, policy, and other similar records that represent the organization's official identity and relationship with other legal entities including other corporations and governmental agencies.

Slide library   This library type is designed to contain and manage Microsoft PowerPoint slides.

Team Site library   The scope of this library type is limited to within an individual team site and is used to manage content specific to this particular audience.

Transition Management library   This library type is designed for managing documents that require translating into other languages and supports a multinational, enterprise audience. Workflow processes are optimized to display multiple language versioning of individual documents.

In general, document libraries are repositories of files based on a variety of format and content types. Documents within the libraries are intended to be acted on not just by the document owner or creator but rather by a select or wide audience, based on their purpose.

Document libraries should be selected by the content they will encompass and who will require access. Access needs should determine where the libraries will be placed and what level of security will be imposed. The scope of content containment can be as limited as within a single site or as broad as the entire enterprise, with documents being accessed from multiple sites by a worldwide audience. Specific documents can also be contained within more than one library, such as documents that are authored, edited, and approved within the corporate intranet but published for a general audience on an Internet site.

Content Type Planning

A document content type is defined by the set of attributes possessed by the document. These attributes can include any properties associated with the document, but they can also include properties that are imposed on the document by different SharePoint features. For instance, a document content type can be defined by the workflow type, policies, document template type, or other features imposed by SharePoint.

Document libraries can be configured to contain specific content types. The advantage is that documents of the specified content type can be created directly within the library rather than created outside and then uploaded.

In Chapter 7, "Configuring and Maintaining Lists and Libraries," you learned how to associate a document content type to a document library.

Associating multiple document content types with a specific library lets you store different document types together related to the information they contain. For instance, you can write a Word document for a team presentation where relevant information is also contained in Microsoft Excel, PowerPoint, and graphics files. Configuring a single library for these content types allows you to store all of them in one location.

Document content type planning starts with knowing which content types you will need to include. If you are planning content types to be contained in a specific library, that library will have a core or parent content type by default; however, it is unlikely that you will use only the default content type since the real advantage of this feature is to collect a set of content types that are in some way related to a single document library.

Content types are also defined by various other attributes, as previously mentioned. To plan with these attributes in mind, you must determine the specific document templates, the types of workflows you will use with each type, and the policies that will be applied to the different content types. For some documents, you'll also need to take into account document conversions. This applies when you create a document in one format and then convert it to a different format. Examples of this are converting .doc-formatted documents to .pdf or .html.

Content Flow Planning

Content flow is the movement of documents from one location to another inside and outside the site collection, depending on the needs of the content creators and consumers. Content flow planning exists to ensure that the movement of content is predictable and orderly and requires the least number of moves to accomplish its goals. It also should include content security such that the movement of any particular document does not include a destination that is less secure than required. For example, you would not want a sensitive internal memo to be posted to a document library accessible by customers or the general public from the Internet.

Content flows can be configured to be manual or dynamic. A manual content flow requires specific human intervention at each stage of the flow so that the document is not copied or moved to the next location without a review and approval. Approval workflows are often used in these instances. This is something like a registered parcel moving through the postal service and requiring a signature at each point of transfer.

Dynamic content flows are driven by the needs of content authors, owners, and consumers, moving from one location to another depending on who needs to access, copy, modify, or retire a document. This type of flow either does not involve approvals or involves limited approvals for information transfers but maximizes the potential for information collaboration. Dynamic content flows operate by an automated system based on the collaborative needs of users, as opposed to traditional, manually driven workflows where each point in the movement of content through the system is predetermined and must be either approved or rejected by an individual.

To prevent multiple different versions of a single document from existing at different points in the system, copies can be linked to their source so that any changes made to the source document are automatically reflected in the copies in the other repositories. This content can span a range from a single Word document to an entire website, with the website being authored and edited in a secure location and then published to the corporate intranet or the Internet.

Content flow planning recognizes three general locations for corporate content: within specific SharePoint sites; within the corporate records repository; and for public consumption, which can be the corporate intranet, the customer extranet, or the Internet.

Ideally, all content authoring occurs within secure sites in the SharePoint site collection. After the content is initially authored, there should be some sort of workflow imposed, even if it's one review and approval step between the author and the author's supervisor or manager. Depending on the purpose of the document and the intended audience for the content, workflow can be a much more involved process.

Content can remain within a specific site, as in a document library within a team site and accessed only by that team, or it can be shared with other teams or sites within the collection as needed. Security can be set at the library or the document level to ensure that only those parties authorized to access the content will be able to open and read it.

Once created and approved, content can also be published to the portal-level document library so that all site members within the site collection can access the information. Often general company policies, announcements, and public relations information are published in this manner.

Assuming your company has a web presence, a great deal of content will be generated for general public consumption, such as information about newly released products, financial announcements, and other promotional data.

A great deal of content generated by any business involves the current and past history of official documentation such as contracts, policies, procedures, and a large number of other professional and legal documents. This information is usually enterprise-wide and warrants its own repository, which is the third major location in your company's content flow: the Enterprise Records Repository.

 You'll learn more about the Enterprise Records Repository and how it is used in content management in Chapter 15, "Working with Content Management."

Information Policy Planning

SharePoint allows you to set policies for documentation based on content type. This is a particularly important feature since often the management of different types of documents is determined by legal, procedural, or other standards that are set outside your organization and to which your organization must comply. For instance, legal statutes may require that your company archive certain business records for a specific number of years and make them available in an easily accessible location and format pursuant to an audit. Information policies can allow you to treat documents consistently with such standards with a minimum of administrative effort.

You can associate an *information policy* with your documentation in a number of ways. First, you can associate the policy directly to the entire site collection and then export the policy to other site collections within the enterprise. You also can set policy association directly to a particular content type prior to adding the content to a document library, or you can associate the policy directly to the library. The latter option should be used only if the library isn't configured to support multiple content types and this policy type is rarely used.

Information policy planning is a top-down process. First you must consider the documentation policies that impact the entire enterprise. Generally, legal standards applying to business documentation will fall in this category. Also, if your organization is multinational, you will need to set policies to comply with the different requirements of each country where you do business. There may be standards at the state or county level that will also require different treatment depending on where your offices are located.

Different departments and thus different sites and site collections may require different policy definitions. For instance, your legal department may face different standards for its documentation than sales or marketing. Human resource documentation also requires specific handling based on that department's role in your corporation.

Documentation types will also require different policy handling, although there is a lot of overlap between document type and which department or other business entity owns and manages the document (the legal department and contract document types, for example).

The following features in SharePoint are specific to setting information policy:

Auditing   This feature records any changes or actions made to a document and writes those changes to a log. You can configure the auditing feature to record when a document is viewed, edited, checked out, and checked in; when document permissions are changed; and when the document is deleted.

Barcode   This policy feature creates a unique identifier value for a given document and then inserts that value as a barcode image in the document.

Expiration   You can apply this policy feature to document types that must have a specific disposal date based on when they were created or how long they've existed. For instance, if a particular document type must expire after seven years, you can set the policy so that expiration will occur seven years from its initial creation date.

Form conversion for archiving   This policy feature does not directly archive any of your business forms but instead creates an image of a completed form that you can then archive as required. If you associate this policy with a library, the library will generate images of all the forms it contains each time you create a new form so these images will be automatically available when you need to archive them.

Labeling   This policy feature allows you to associate specific text-based properties to document types that are searchable, allowing you to easily locate documents possessing an assigned label. A label can be any text such as a name, part number, procedure number, or other identifier. If you print the document, the label will be included on the hard copy for reference and in lists and libraries; you can create filtered views based on labels.

Planning Information Rights Management (IRM)

SharePoint 2007 lets you manage how individual documents are treated by utilizing *information rights management* (IRM). IRM actually allows SharePoint to integrate with platforms such as Windows Server 2003's Rights Management Services (RMS) and allows you to determine how a SharePoint document can be handled, even if it is downloaded onto a local computer.

Although you can deny specific groups of users access to information based on site-level, library-level, and document-level permissions, if a user is able to access a document and, particularly, if the user can make the document available offline, you have lost control of what happens to that document next. It can be printed or sent to any other party as an email attachment.

🌐 Real World Scenario

Configuring an Expiration Policy for a Content Type

You are the site administrator for the sales department's SharePoint website. Greg, your manager, wants you to publish the department's quarterly profit figures in the site's document library but wants the document available for only 30 days. Greg suggests that after the allotted time, you just go back into the library and delete the document. You realize that it will be much easier to set a policy for the document's content type that will cause it to expire after 30 days. You have already created a content type and called it *temporary reports*. After you are given access to the quarterly profit content, you create the appropriate document. Next, you need to configure the content type using the expiration policy.

The library containing the document has already been configured for this content type. On the sales department's website, you click Site Actions and then Site Settings. On the Site Settings page under Galleries, you click Site Content Types. On the Site Content Type Gallery page, you locate the desired content type, and in the Source column, you click the source name for the content type. This makes the names of the content types clickable links. You click the name of the desired content type and on the Content Type page, you select Information Management Policy Settings. On the Information Management Policy Settings page, you select Define a Policy and then click OK. On the Edit Policy page, you tick the Enable Expiration check box. Under The Retention Period Is, select a time period based on the item's properties. You leave the default value of Created in the first drop-down menu. In the field to the right of that menu, you type the value **30**, and in the drop-down menu to the right of that field, you select Days. Under When the Item Expires, select Perform This Action, and use the drop-down menu to select Delete. To finish, click OK.

Even if the particular user is allowed access, you aren't always sure they won't make the document available to someone who isn't authorized to view the information.

IRM provides an additional layer of access control on your documentation, giving you even greater control over documents, regardless of which library they are located in or who accesses them. When IRM is implemented in SharePoint, you can specify exactly how a document is handled by a user. For instance, you can determine whether the document, even if it is downloaded on the user's computer and available offline, can be printed, copied, forwarded, or will allow a copy-and-paste operation. You can even set a specific date for the document after which the document will not be able to be opened.

The IRM feature is not available by default. To use this capacity, you must have the Windows Rights Management (WRM) service client installed on all your front-end web servers and allow them to connect to the server providing RMS to the server farm. You must also either specify the location of the RMS server or ensure that it is available as an Active Directory object so its location is defined by default.

Working with Document Management

Now that you've learned about the planning aspects of document management within Share-Point 2007 and some of the abilities you have at your disposal, it's time to get some practice working in this realm. Since the previous section finished off with IRM and how that works, let's start the practical exercises in the same area.

Information Rights Management and Policy Rights in SharePoint

Setting up IRM in SharePoint is a multistep process, so several of the exercises will be focused on these tasks. As you previously learned, IRM is not enabled by default in SharePoint and in fact is not available at all unless you have a server in the system that is acting as the RMS server.

> Installing and configuring a Windows RMS server is beyond the scope of this book and the 70-630 exam. Learn more about Windows Rights Management Services at http://www.microsoft.com/windowsserver2003/technologies/rightsmgmt/default.mspx.

The following set of exercises assumes you have installed and configured an RMS server in the server farm including the management of certificates, licenses, and client deployment. RMS server management would likely not be within the realm of duties for a SharePoint administrator but instead would fall to an IT admin responsible for server management in the infrastructure. The set of tasks presented here will begin with IRM integration with MOSS 2007.

Beyond the prerequisites already stated, you will need to add the RMS server to the MOSS server's trusted sites list, add the SharePoint server to the RMS server's trusted sites list, and install the RMS 1.0 with SP2 client software on all SharePoint front-end web servers.

> Download Windows Rights Management Services 1.0 Service Pack 2 (SP2) from https://www.microsoft.com/downloads/details.aspx?FamilyId=5794538F-E572-4542-A5BD-901B2720F068&displaylang=en.

> You must be logged in as a domain administrator in order to install the RMS 1.0 SP2 client software.

Exercise 10.1 will show you how to enable IRM in SharePoint 2007 after the RMS client is installed. You must be logged in as someone with administrative privileges to perform the following tasks.

EXERCISE 10.1

Enabling IRM in MOSS 2007

1. Launch the Central Administration web application.

2. Click the Operations tab, and then under Security Configuration, click Information Rights Management.

3. On the Information Management Rights page, if your SharePoint server is part of an Active Directory domain, select Use the Default RMS Server Specified in Active Directory; otherwise, select Use This RMS Server, and add the path to the server in the available field.

4. Click OK.

If you had not installed the RMS 1.0 SP2 client software, on the Information Management Rights page you would have seen a warning notice such as the one displayed in Figure 10.1.

FIGURE 10.1   Information Management Rights page

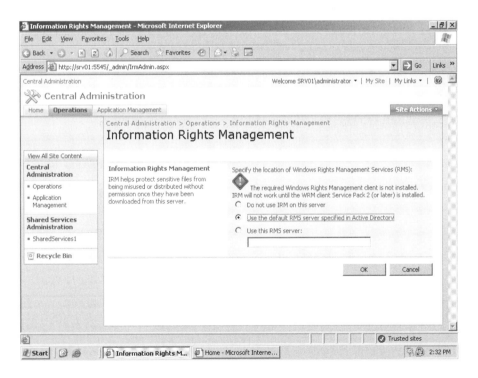

Now that IRM is enabled in SharePoint, the service still can't be used until you create an IRM permissions policy on a relevant library or list (Exercise 10.2). Keep this in mind because it means that documents and items in the libraries and lists in your site collection will have IRM policies applied only if you specifically configure such policies in each library or list where you want to have them enabled.

EXERCISE 10.2

Creating an IRM Permissions Policy

1. On the site containing the document library where you want the IRM permissions policy applied, open the relevant library.

2. In the library, select Settings ➤ Document Library Settings.

3. On the Customize Shared Documents page under Permissions and Management, click Information Rights Management.

4. On the Information Rights Management page, tick the Restrict Permission to Documents in This Library on Download check box.

5. Give the permission policy a title in the Permission Policy Title field, and add a description of the policy in the Permission Policy Description field.

6. Tick any of the following check boxes, depending on how you want this policy to apply to documents in this library:

   Allow Users to Print Documents

   Allow Users to Access Content Programmatically

   Users Must Verify Their Credentials Every (add a value in days to indicate the frequency of verification)

   Do Not Allow Users to Upload Documents That Do Not Support IRM

   Stop Restricting Permission to Documents in This Library On (use the calendar to include the date when you want policy permissions to stop being applied)

7. Click OK.

Adding a description for the policy, as in step 5 of Exercise 10.2, is important because it describes the behavior the policy is supposed to apply to the documents in the library. You may think that once you set a policy or some other configuration setting in SharePoint that you'll never forget what you did and why you did it, but after months or years of administering SharePoint (or anything else), you'll find that you need these reminders. Also, you may not be the SharePoint administrator forever, and your successor will be equally glad that you made such an effort.

You can also apply an information policy to a document library in a similar manner, as Exercise 10.3 describes.

EXERCISE 10.3

Applying an Information Policy to a Library

1. On the website containing the desired document library, proceed through steps 1 and 2 in Exercise 10.2.

2. On the Customize Shared Documents page under Permissions and Management, click Information Management Policy Settings.

3. On the Information Management Policy Settings: Shared Documents page in the Content Type column, click either Document, Article Page, or Basic Page. (For this exercise, click Document.)

4. On the Information Management Policy Settings: Document page under Specify the Policy, select Define a Policy, as shown here, and click OK.

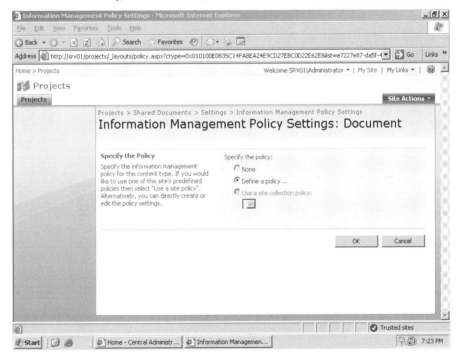

5. On the Edit Policy: Document page, in the Administrative Description field, add a description of the policy that managers will be able to view when configuring policies for the library.

6. In the Policy Statement field, add a statement explaining the function of this policy to end users who open documents in this library.

7. Tick any of the following check boxes: Enable Labels, Enable Auditing, Enable Expiration, and Enable Barcodes. (For this exercise, tick Enable Labels.)

8. Tick the Prompt Users to Insert a Label Before Saving or Printing and/or the Prevent Changes to Labels After They Are Added check box, which are shown here.

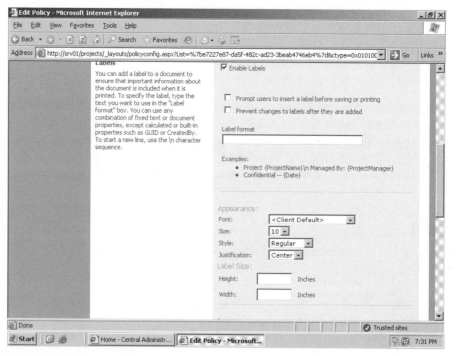

9. In the Label Format field, type the text for the label.

10. Under Appearance, use the Font, Size, Style, and Justification drop-down menus to configure the appearance of the label text.

11. Under Label Size, add values in inches to the Height and Width fields, and click the Refresh button to see what the label will look like in the Preview field.

12. Click OK.

Back on the Information Management Policy Settings: Shared Documents page, in the Policy column next to Documents, the column item is shown as Custom Policy, and in the Description column, the text you added in step 6 appears.

Naturally, this is only one possible method of setting a management policy for a document. First of all, in step 3, you could also have selected Article Page or Basic Page and not set a policy on documents at all. Also, in step 7, you could have chosen to apply the auditing, expiration, and barcode management policy features.

In Chapter 7, you had the opportunity to configure a document library to accept multiple content types and then add a content type to a library. Earlier in this chapter, you saw how important it was to carefully plan content types in order to optimize content management. The next set of exercises will delve deeper into content type management.

A content type is a collection of attributes identifying a specific document or item. The attributes can include name, description, group type, or another unique quality. A content type can also possess properties such as columns, policies, templates, and workflow.

SharePoint contains parent content types; so that these can be used throughout the site collection, they are stored in the content type gallery for the top-level site. If you create any new content types that you want used throughout the site collection, they must also be contained within this gallery.

If you create multiple new content types based on the same parent content type, filtering will be passed down to all of the content types that are based on that parent. This allows you to control the appearance and behavior of multiple content types with a minimum of administrative cost, but you must carefully plan ahead if you intend to use such parent-to-child filtering.

Content Type Management in SharePoint

Although you've already added a content type to a library, Exercise 10.4 will show you how to create an entirely new content type. For this example, let's say your company's legal department needs a standard method of managing contracts to be used when entering into partnership agreements with other companies. This exercise will illustrate how to create the bare bones for this new content type for legal contracts. You must be on the top-level site of your site collection to begin this exercise.

Creating a New Content Type

1. From the top-level site, select Site Actions ➢ Site Settings ➢ Modify All Site Settings.

2. Under Galleries, click Site Content Types.

3.   On the Site Content Type Gallery page, shown here, click Create.

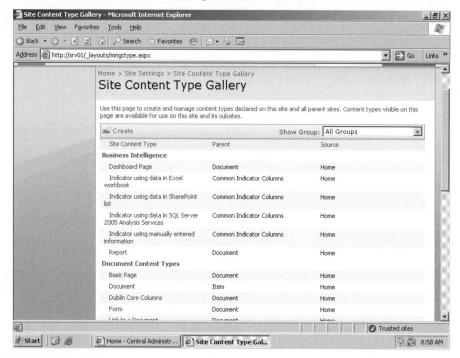

4.   On the New Site Content Type page, give the new content type a name in the Name field and a description in the Description field.

5.   Under Parent Content Type, use Select Parent Content Type From to choose which site content type to use, and then use the Parent Content Type drop-down menu to select the parent content type.

6.   Under Group, select either Existing Group and then use the drop-down menu to choose which group you want to base this content type on, or select New Group and create a custom-made group.

7.   Click OK.

Figure 10.2 shows the selections made on the New Site Content Type page right before step 7. Once you've clicked OK as in step 7, you are taken to the Site Content Type: Partnership Contract page. Stay on this page because the next exercise will begin from this point.

FIGURE 10.2   Creating a new content type

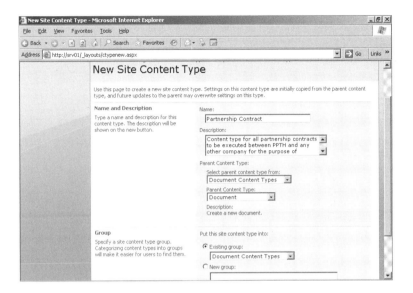

The new content type is now available in a list of site content types. It can now be associated with a particular library and used to create any number of documents based on this content type so that when the legal department needs to draw up a standard partnership contract, it's available to them.

You can also edit the new content type in SharePoint. Exercise 10.5 will walk you through the steps. You'll need to be on the Site Content Type: Partnership Contract page where you left off at the end of Exercise 10.4.

EXERCISE 10.5

Editing Columns in an Existing Content Type

1. On the Site Content Type: Partnership Contract page under Columns, click Add from Existing Type Columns.

2. On the Add Columns to Site Content Type: Partnership Contract page, you can use the Select Columns From drop-down menu to choose the group containing the relevant columns.

3. In the Available Columns box, select one or more column types you want to add, and then click Add to include them in the Columns to Add box.

4. If you want any content types inheriting settings from this one to be updated with the changes you are making here, select Yes; otherwise, select No.

5. Click OK.

In Exercise 10.5 you added a column to this content type based on preexisting columns. To add a new custom-made column, under Columns select Add from New Site Column. To change the order in which columns occur, click Column Order.

Under Settings on the same page, you can select a number of links to modify this content type:

- Name, Description, and Group

- Advanced Settings

- Workflow Settings

- Delete This Site Content Type

- Document Information Panel Settings

- Information Management Policy Settings

- Manage Document Conversion for This Content Type

Modifying the name, description, and group for this content type is a fairly straightforward task. The Advanced Settings selection requires a bit of explanation, but it's also easy to understand once you select it and see the Site Content Type Advanced Settings page, as in Figure 10.3.

FIGURE 10.3   Site Content Type Advanced Settings page

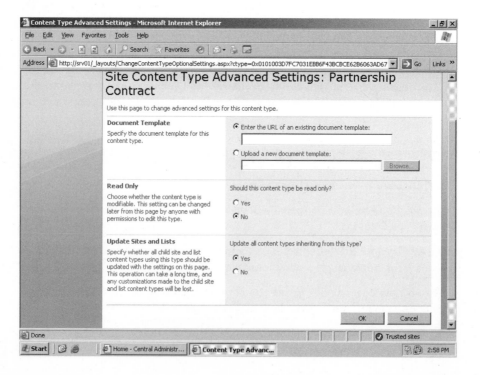

Under Document Template, you can specify the document template for this content type, either by entering the URL to the template or by browsing and uploading a new content type. Read Only lets you decide to allow anyone to modify the content type or to make it read-only. Under Update Sites and Lists, select Yes if you want your changes here to be updated on all content sites inheriting attributes from this one.

The Document Information Panel in SharePoint

When you create or modify a document in a document library based on a content type and check it into the library, a set of columns appear requiring you to save the metadata for the content type. This is the Document Information panel, and the metadata must be saved if you want to retain it prior to the check-in process.

When you select Document Information Panel Settings, you are taken to the Document Information Panel Settings page, as shown in Figure 10.4.

FIGURE 10.4   Document Information Panel Settings page

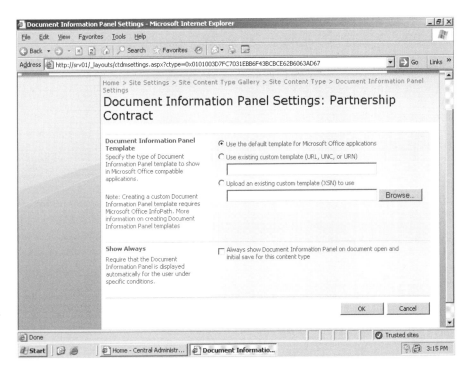

As you can see, under Document Information Panel Template, you can select Use the Default Template for Microsoft Office Applications, which is the default, or you can choose

Use Existing Custom Template and specify the URL, UNC, or URN in the available field or select Upload an Existing Custom Template (XSN) to use and then browse and upload the required template.

Under Show Always, tick the available check box if you want to always show the Document Information panel when the document opens and during the initial saving for this content type.

If you need to have more options available with the Document Information panel, you have the option of creating a customized panel for your use. Exercise 10.6 will show you how to accomplish this task. You will need to be on the Site Content Type: Partnership Contract page to begin this exercise. You will also need to have the InfoPath client application configured for SharePoint in order to successfully complete this exercise.

Using InfoPath with SharePoint won't be covered until Chapter 13, "Using Business Forms and Business Intelligence," so you may not have the tools available to complete Exercise 10.6 at this time. If not, after completing the exercises in Chapter 13, you can come back and complete the exercise.

EXERCISE 10.6

Creating a Customized Document Information Panel

1. On the Site Content Type: Partnership Contract page, select Document Information Panel Settings.

2. On the Document Information Panel Settings: Partnership Contract page under Document Information Panel Template, select Create a New Custom Template.

3. When the InfoPath client application launches in the Data Source Wizard, click Finish.

4. When an InfoPath form opens in Design view, click Horizontal Region to choose all the form fields.

5. Right-click in a blank area of the page, and select Borders and Shading from the context menu.

6. Click the Shading tab, and then select a color from the list.

7. Click OK.

8. Select File ➢ Publish to save your changes.

9. When the Publishing Wizard launches and your Document Information panel is selected by default, click Next.

10. When the next window appears, click Publish.

11. Click Close to close the InfoPath client.

12. If you want the information panel to always appear when the document is open and when you initially save the content type, tick the Always Show Document Information Panel on Document Open and Initial Save for This Content Type check box.

13. Click OK.

This exercise created a fairly modest customized information panel, but as you saw when you went through the process, you have a large number of options available to you.

Working with Word 2007 and SharePoint 2007

Office 2007 allows the use of the new Open XML formats .docx and .docm, which can also be used in conjunction with SharePoint; however, not all organizations have upgraded to the Office 2007 suite yet. Many companies are using Office 2003 or earlier versions, which limits or prevents the ability to interoperate between Office suite software and SharePoint.

If you are using an earlier version of Office such as Office 2000, 2002, XP, or 2003, you still have the option of being able to access .docx and .docm documents. You can download and install the Microsoft Office Compatibility Pack for Word, Excel, and PowerPoint 2007. Once the Compatibility Pack is installed, you can open, edit, and save these Open XML file formats.

Download the Compatibility Pack from http://www.microsoft.com/downloads/ details.aspx?FamilyId=941b3470-3ae9-4aee-8f43-c6bb74cd1466&display- lang=en. If you need assistance installing this software, you can find the instructions at http://support.microsoft.com/kb/923505.

You also have the option of downloading and installing the Word Viewer application, which allows you to open documents created in Word 2003 and earlier without having a full-featured version of Word 2003 installed on your computer. This program interoperates with the Compatibility Pack so that a user with both programs installed on their computer is able to open and view a Word 2007 document.

You can download Word Viewer 2003 from the following location: http:// www.microsoft.com/downloads/details.aspx?FamilyId=95E24C87-8732- 48D5-8689-AB826E7B8FDF&displaylang=en.

If your company uses Word 2003, the program will interoperate with SharePoint 2007, but a necessary prerequisite is to make sure all of the latest updates for Word are applied. Once this is accomplished, you will be able to connect to a SharePoint document library from your desktop and check out and edit a Word document from the library using Word 2003. The process is somewhat different from using Word 2007, so the following exercises will illustrate how to perform the same actions using each version of Word.

Exercise 10.7 will show you how to check out a document from a SharePoint document library, download it to your PC, edit it in Word 2003, and then upload it and check it back in to the document library. Exercise 10.8 will show you the same actions using Word 2007.

EXERCISE 10.7

Accessing a SharePoint Document Library and Editing a Document in Word 2003

1. On the SharePoint site containing the desired document library, click the name of the library in Quick Launch to open it.

2. Click to the right of the document name to open the menu, and then click Check Out.

3. Click to the right of the document name again to open the menu, and select Send To ➢ Download a Copy.

4. Save a copy of the document to the desired location on your local computer.

5. Open the document using Word 2003 on the local computer, make the necessary edits, and then save your work.

6. In the document library, click Upload ➢ Upload Document.

7. Browse to the location of the document you just modified, and select it.

8. On the Upload Document page, tick the Overwrite Existing Files check box if you want the current copy to overwrite the copy in the document library, and then click OK.

9. On the Shared Documents page for the document, click Check In.

This action seems pretty straightforward, but keep in mind that with Word 2007 it's possible to open and edit a document directly in a document library rather than downloading it onto your computer before editing.

EXERCISE 10.8

Accessing a SharePoint Document Library and Editing a Document in Word 2007

1. In the desired document library, click to the right of the document name to open the menu, and then click Check Out.

2. When the confirmation dialog box appears, click OK.

EXERCISE 10.8 *(continued)*

3. On your local computer, open the My Documents\SharePoint Drafts folder; when the dialog box opens asking whether you want to get updates, click Don't Update.

4. Open the document in Word 2007, make the desired changes, and save the document.

5. In the document library, click to the right of the document's name, and in the menu, click Check In.

6. Once SharePoint uploads the document back into the library, verify that the copy of the document in the My Documents\SharePoint Drafts folder on your local computer has been deleted.

As you can see, the process of checking the document out and into the document library is much easier with Word 2007. The process outlined in Exercise 10.8 is necessary only if you want to work with the document offline. As previously mentioned, from your desktop, you could have opened the document directly in the library using Word 2007, edited it, and saved your changes rather than working with it on your local computer.

You can make changes to content located in SharePoint 2007 directly from Word 2007 without ever opening SharePoint. For example, you can add content to SharePoint blogs and wikis. Exercise 10.9 will show you how to add content to a blog from Word 2007. The exercise assumes that the SharePoint blog already exists and that you know the URL to the blog. It also assumes that this is the first time you are connecting to the SharePoint blog directly from Word 2007.

 You will need to have Office 2007 installed on the computer you want to use to add the SharePoint blog entry and be at least somewhat familiar with Word 2007, including the use of the Ribbon.

EXERCISE 10.9

Adding Content to a Blog from Word 2007

1. Open a blank document in Word 2007.

2. Right-click an empty area of the Ribbon, and when the menu opens, click Customize Quick Access Toolbar.

3. When the Customize the Quick Access Toolbar dialog box opens, under Choose Commands From, use the drop-down menu, and click File.

4. In the pane right below the menu, select TBD from the available list, and then click the Add button, moving TBD to the Quick Access Toolbar.

EXERCISE 10.9 *(continued)*

5.   Click the button that appears in the File Menu Options area.

6.   When the Register a Blog Account dialog box appears, click Register Now.

7.   When the New Blog Account dialog box appears, click the drop-down arrow, and click SharePoint in the menu.

8.   In the New Community Server Account dialog box, under User Name, enter your username in the available field, and then enter your password in the Password field.

9.   Enter the URL to your blog in the Blog Post URL field.

10. Under Automatically Upload Picture to My Picture Storage Location, select either Don't Upload Pictures to My Blog Post or Post Images to the Following Location. (If you choose the second option, enter the path to the image in the available field.)

11. Click OK, and when the confirmation dialog box appears, click OK again.

12. In the open Word document, type your blog entry.

13. On the Ribbon, click the Blog Post tab, click Publish, and from the menu that appears, click Publish.

14. If necessary, authenticate to your blog account again using your username and password, and then click OK.

There are quite a number of scenarios involved in blogging from Word 2007, including a number of troubleshooting tips you can find at http://office .microsoft.com/en-us/word/HA101640211033.aspx?pid=CH100626141033.

SharePoint Document Center and Records Center

You've worked with specific document libraries, but document management at the enterprise level is done in the Document Center. The Document Center is a workspace like a team workspace, which means it's a self-contained website dedicated to the task of document management. By default, the top-level portal site comes with a document center.

On the portal site, click Document Center in Quick Launch to gain access. When you do, you'll notice a different Quick Launch menu to the right containing just three items: Documents, Announcements, and Tasks. The primary pane on the web page contains Announcements, Upcoming Tasks, and Relevant Documents web parts, most of which you're familiar with. You cannot add documents to the Relevant Documents list from the primary pane and must click Documents in Quick Launch instead. When you do, you open the Document Center document library, and you can upload documents just as you would in any other library. Once you do, the documents will appear in the Relevant Documents list.

The Document Center is organized around the idea that enterprise-level documents are to be acted on in a collaborative manner. For that reason, the Announcements web part was included so that information regarding additions or changes to these documents could be displayed, and the Tasks web part exists so that any individual or team tasks relative to these documents could be added, assigned, and tracked.

Documents contained here represent policies, procedures, methods, and other types of information that define how your business operates; therefore, they will likely be authored and modified by members of departments such as legal, human resources, and management. The Document Center is perfect for monitoring the interactions of these different stakeholders on critical corporate documentation.

A Records Center manages critical business records on the enterprise level in a manner similar to how a Document Center manages documents. A Records Center does not exist linked from the portal site by default, so if you require this functionality, you will have to create one. The process is the same as creating any other workspace. In View All Site Content, click Create, and under Web Pages on the Create page, click Sites and Workspaces. On the New SharePoint Site page under Template Selection, click the Enterprise tab, and then select Records Center to create it.

Figure 10.5 shows you a newly created Records Center in SharePoint.

Don't worry that these special workspaces are only briefly mentioned here. You'll go into a lot more detail on the Document Center and Records Center as well as the Report Center in Chapter 15, "Working with Content Management." Since they are related to the topic in the current chapter, I wanted you to have them in mind.

FIGURE 10.5 SharePoint Records Center

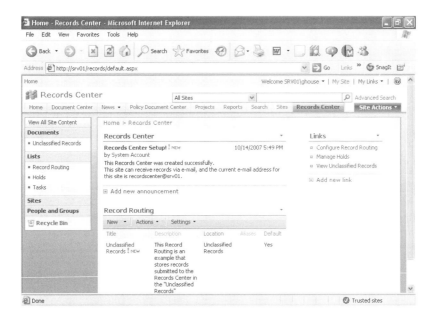

Summary

In this chapter, you learned more specific information about documents and document libraries and were introduced to the different methods of document management, including the following topics:

- You learned about document management planning and the different library and workspace center types that are used for document management.

- You learned about content type management, including more in-depth information about content types, content flow planning, policy management planning, and information rights management (IRM) planning.

- IRM was presented conceptually, including enabling IRM in MOSS 2007, creating IRM permissions policies, and applying an information policy to a library.

- You got the opportunity to get some hands-on experience in creating a new content type, creating a customized Document Information panel, and working with SharePoint directly from within Word, among other tasks.

- Finally, you were given a brief introduction to the Document Center and Records Center.

Exam Essentials

Know how to plan for content management.   Planning the various aspects of content management for documents in libraries in SharePoint is vital to being able to manage how documents are viewed, modified, and saved as well as how you are able to manage different document content types. You will be unable to have a cohesive and organized method of control over your documentation organization-wide unless you first develop an overall management plan.

Understand content types and content type management.   Documentation in SharePoint is managed largely through the use of content types. Associated specific content such as legal, sales, and human resource content with content types allows you to treat each of these special documents differently through the use of policy management features. Applying policies to content types lets you be in charge of how documents are tracked, processed through workflows, archived, and deleted. This is also an important feature for enforcing compliance to company policies and legal requirements for document management.

Have a strong comprehension of information rights management.   Information rights management (IRM) is a method you can use to exercise more complete control over how documents are treated by people who access them in SharePoint. You can decide which groups can view, download, print, or copy any document contained in a library.

Review Questions

1. You are the SharePoint administrator responsible for managing the entire site collection for your company. Peter, one of the corporate administrators, wants to have a particular document library type added but isn't sure which one would suit his needs. He describes what he is looking for as one where content can be accessed by a company-wide audience from any site in the site collection. Which of the following options will best suit Peter's needs?

   A. Document Center library

   B. Portal Site library

   C. Records Repository library

   D. Team Site library

2. You are the administrator for your company's SharePoint site collection. You are giving an in-service training to the department heads on document management to better allow them to control how content is administered on their sites. You are currently describing the role of content types in terms of content management. Of the following options, which do you describe as true for defining content types? (Choose all that apply.)

   A. Workflow type

   B. Policies

   C. Document template type

   D. Library type

3. You are the SharePoint administrator for your corporation. You have been contacted by Gwen, one of the attorneys in your company's legal department. She is concerned about the potential for company employees to be able to download sensitive company documents onto their local computers, print them, or send them to third parties as email attachments. You discuss the matter with her and determine that enabling information rights management (IRM) in SharePoint 2007 would be the best option. You discuss what this would entail with the IT staff, and they outline the work that's required in making IRM available. Of the following options, which are authentic tasks or issues involved in enabling IRM? (Choose all that apply.)

   A. IRM is not enabled by default in MOSS 2007.

   B. IRM is not available unless there is a server available acting as the Rights Management Services server.

   C. You will not be able to enable IRM in MOSS 2007 unless your SharePoint system is part of an Active Directory domain.

   D. You will not be able to enable IRM in MOSS 2007 unless all SharePoint front-end web servers have the RMS 1.0 with SP2 client software installed.

4. You are the SharePoint administrator for your organization. You are meeting with the management committee to discuss what policy to develop for managing the company's business forms. You are currently discussing methods of preparing forms for archiving. The committee wants to make sure that all forms, including both those currently in existence and those yet to be created, will be prepared to be archived without any forms being accidentally passed by. What is your solution to this issue?

   A. Associate the Form Conversion for Archiving policy with a library, and then upload all business forms to that library so that images of the forms will be created that are suitable for archiving.

   B. Add the Archiving Document Library web part to the desired site, and upload all business forms that will need to be archived to that library.

   C. Create a content type for all business forms that will enable you to archive them at a preset expiration date, and then associate that content type to the library you intend to use to contain the company's business forms.

   D. Associate the Form Archiving policy with a particular library, and then upload all business forms to that library, setting their archive bit so that archiving occurs on a scheduled basis.

5. You are the SharePoint administrator for your company. Harry, the head of the human resources department, has a series of documents uploaded in a document library that's intended for viewing by company employees, but he doesn't want the employees to be able to print these documents. You determine that associating an IRM policy to this library would be the solution. When you are setting up IRM for the library, which option must you use to prevent printing?

   A. Tick the Do Not Allow Users to Print Documents check box.

   B. Clear the Allow Users to Print Documents check box.

   C. Select the Do Not Allow Users to Print Documents radio button.

   D. Tick the Do Not Allow Users to Print Documents That Do Not Support IRM check box.

6. You are the SharePoint site collection administrator for your company. You have been tasked by May, the head of the legal department, with creating a content type for all of your company's legal documents. One of May's requirements is that no one without adequate permissions should be allowed to edit any of the attributes of this content type. Of the following selections, which one will allow you to accomplish this task?

   A. On the Site Content Type Advanced Settings page, tick the Do Not Allow Editing check box under Editing.

   B. On the Site Content Type Advanced Settings page under Editing, select No.

   C. On the Site Content Type Advanced Settings page under Read Only, select Yes.

   D. On the Site Content Type Advanced Settings page, tick the Read Only check box under Read Only.

7. You are the SharePoint administrator for your company's site collection. You are in the process of setting up an IRM permissions policy on the document library that contains sensitive research content to make sure no one can print the documents in that library. You've just given the permission policy a title and are about to add a description. Of the following selections, which one most accurately describes the function of the description in an IRM?

   A. The description is optional and is used only to add a definition to the IRM that could easily be determined from the title.

   B. The description is mandatory, and the IRM will fail to function if this field is left empty.

   C. The description is a required field and must be populated so that the keywords it contains are used for policy enforcement.

   D. The description is important because it describes the behavior the policy is supposed to apply to the documents in the library.

8. You are the SharePoint administrator for your company's site collection. You are in the process of setting up an IRM permissions policy on the document library that contains sensitive research content to make sure no one can print the documents in that library. Mary Jane, one of the staff in legal, tells you that the permissions policy should be in effect for only six months and be rescinded after that. Of the following options, which one should you use to end the application of this policy on the document library at the appointed time?

   A. Tick the End Permissions Policy check box, and use the drop-down menus to select a month, day, year, and time to indicate when you want policy permissions to stop being applied.

   B. Tick the Stop Restricting Permission to Documents in This Library On check box, and use the calendar to include the date when you want policy permissions to stop being applied.

   C. Tick the Expiry check box, and use the calendar to include the date when you want policy permissions to stop being applied.

   D. Create an alert in the document library, and configure it to send you an email on the date when you want policy permissions to stop being applied. Then when you receive the email, go back into the document library, and remove the policy.

9. You are the SharePoint site administrator for your organization's site collection. You are in the process of planning the overall content management strategy for the site collection and are currently working on content flow planning with your staff. As a necessary first step to this part of the planning, you are identifying the major locations where content flow can deposit documentation. Of the following options, which ones are valid locations? (Choose all that apply.)

   A. The internal Document Center

   B. The corporate intranet

   C. The customer extranet

   D. The public Internet

10. You are a SharePoint user and member of the Public Relations site in your company's site collection. You have opened a blank Word 2007 document and are going to publish information about the results of your presentation at an industry trade show last night in your SharePoint blog. You follow the appropriate steps in creating the content. Assuming that you won't have to authenticate to your account as a last step in posting to your blog, what should be the necessary final step?

   A. On the Ribbon, click the Blog Post tab, click Publish, and from the menu that appears click Publish again.

   B. On the Ribbon, click the Blog Post tab, click File, and then click Publish in the menu that appears.

   C. On the Ribbon, click the Blog Post tab, click Post Blog, and from the menu that appears click Publish.

   D. On the Ribbon, click the Blog Post tab, click Publish, and from the menu that appears click Post Blog.

11. You are the SharePoint administrator for your company. Robert, the company's CEO, is interested in the various ways that SharePoint 2007 interoperates with other Office 2007 products including Word, particularly in the area of working with the new Open XML formats .docx and .docm. The organization cannot afford to upgrade from Office 2002 en masse and instead is following a multistage upgrade plan. The upgrade process is likely to take at least a year, and Robert wants options that will allow those departments still using Word 2002 to work with documents in MOSS 2007. Of the following options, which are available to meet this requirement? (Choose all that apply.)

   A. Install the Microsoft Office Compatibility Pack for Word, Excel, and PowerPoint 2007.

   B. Install the Microsoft Office Viewer Pack for Word, Excel, and PowerPoint 2007.

   C. Install the Word Viewer application.

   D. Install the Office 2007 Viewer application.

12. You are the administrator for your company's SharePoint site collection. Jonah, the manager of the research and development department, needs to be able to track documents related to a particular product they are developing both in the SharePoint document management system and in print form. The tracking mechanism must also be something that can be identified on hard copies through some sort of electronic scanning. You determine that applying a policy to this content type would be the best option. Of the following options, which policy management feature would be best suited?

   A. Auditing

   B. Barcode

   C. Form conversion

   D. Labeling

13. You are the administrator for your company's SharePoint site collection. Norman, the head of the engineering department, wants to be able to edit documents in his department's SharePoint document library; however, all of their client computers have Word 2003 installed. You inform Norman that his staff will be able to use Word 2003 to edit their documents, but there is one condition that must be met first. Of the following options, which one is the correct condition?

    A. The Microsoft Office Compatibility Pack for Word, Excel, and PowerPoint 2007 will have to be installed on all of the client computers in the department.

    B. The Word 2007 Viewer Pack will have to be installed on all of the client computers in the department.

    C. All of the latest updates must be applied to the operating systems on all of the client computers in the department.

    D. All of the latest updates must be applied to Word 2003 on all of the client computers in the department.

14. You are the administrator for your company's SharePoint site collection. Otto, the head of the robotics department, is trying to determine the best tool for content management on his site. He wants something more robust than a standard document library and was thinking of a workspace. You discuss the features of the Document Center, the Records Center, and the Report Center. He decides that the Records Center will best suit his needs, especially the web parts contained in the Records Center's main pane. Of the following options, which are valid web parts in the Records Center? (Choose all that apply.)

    A. Announcements

    B. Links

    C. Records Routing

    D. Tasks

15. You are the SharePoint administrator for your company. You are in a planning meeting with all of the corporate management officers discussing how content management will be organized in SharePoint. The current issue has to do with how corporate-wide current and past records will be stored and accessed in SharePoint. You propose to use a specific content management container provided by SharePoint that's designed for this task. Of the following selections, which one is the correct choice?

    A. Enterprise Records Repository

    B. Enterprise Records Archive

    C. Corporate Archiving library

    D. Records Archiving library

16. You are the administrator of the SharePoint site collection for your company. Several months ago, you created a new content type for the legal department and have since created several other content types that inherit the characteristics of the original. You've just made a major change to the original content type, and the manager of legal wants you to make sure that all of the inheriting content types reflect those changes. How will you accomplish this task?

A. On the Site Content Type Advanced Settings page in the Inheritance section, tick the Update Sites and List check box.

B. On the Site Content Type Advanced Settings page in the Inheritance section, select Yes under Update Sites and Lists.

C. On the Site Content Type Advanced Settings page in the Update Sites and Lists section, select Yes under Update All Content Types Inheriting from This Type.

D. On the Site Content Type Advanced Settings page in the Update Sites and Lists section, tick Update All Content Types Inheriting from This Type.

17. You are the SharePoint site collection administrator for your company. You are in the process of creating a new content type for the document library on the Projects department's website. You've already selected the parent content type on which this new content type will be based. Now you need to select one of the options for group. Of the following choices, which are valid selections? (Choose all that apply.)

A. Select Current Group to accept the default group selection.

B. Select Existing Group, and use the drop-down menu to choose a specific group.

C. Select New Group, and create a custom group.

D. Select Custom Group, and create a new group.

18. You are the SharePoint site collection administrator for your company. You have created a content type for the marketing department but need to modify the Document Information panel for the content type. On the Site Content Type page for the content type, you click Document Information Panel Settings; on the Document Information Panel Settings page, you are offered several options in order to select a template. Of the following options, which are valid options you can use to choose a Document Information Panel template? (Choose all that apply.)

A. Select Use the Default Template for Microsoft Office Applications.

B. Select Use the Default Template for Microsoft Office SharePoint Server Applications.

C. Select Use Existing Custom Template (URL, UNC, or URN).

D. Select Upload an Existing Custom Template (XSN) to Use.

19. You are the SharePoint administrator for your company. You have been tasked with enabling Windows Rights Management Services (RMS) in MOSS 2007. You consult with the IT staff including the domain administrator to determine the steps required to accomplish this task. One necessary task is the installation of the Windows Rights Management Services client software, and you discover that you don't have the rights to perform this task. Who does?

A. The local administrator for each front-end web server

B. The SharePoint site collection administrator

C. The SSP administrator

D. The domain administrator

20. You are the SharePoint administrator for your organization, and you are in the process of creating a customized Document Information panel for a new content type for the sales department. Wilson, the head of the sales department, has requested that you make the information panel appear whenever the document is open. What is the correct way to accomplish this?

A. Right before you finish creating the customized panel, select Yes under Always Show Document Information Panel on Document Open and Initial Save.

B. Right before you finish creating the customized panel, tick the Show Document Information Panel When Document Is Open check box.

C. Right before you finish creating the customized panel, tick the Always Show Document Information Panel on Document Open and Initial Save for This Content Type check box.

D. Right before you finish creating the customized panel, select Yes Always Show Document Information Panel on Document Open and Initial Save for This Content Type under Document Panel Status.

Answers to Review Questions

1. B. Although a Portal Site library doesn't have the vast scope of a Document Center library, the content is intended to be accessed by a company-wide audience from any site in the site collection. A Records Repository contains numerous libraries focused on different content and is meant to be the central repository for all enterprise content. A Team Site library is too limited in scope since it generally only serves a single, team collaboration site.

2. A, B, and C. A content type can be defined by such attributes as workflow type, policies, and document template type; however, libraries can be configured for multiple content types so they are not one of the attributes used to identify a specific content type.

3. A, B, and D. You must also either specify the location of the RMS server or ensure that it is available as an Active Directory object so its location is defined by default. So although it's an advantage to have SharePoint as part of an Active Directory domain, it's not absolutely necessary.

4. A. The Form Conversion for Archiving policy feature does not directly archive any of your business forms but instead creates an image of a completed form that you can then archive as required. If you associate this policy with a library, the library will generate images of all the forms it contains each time you create a new form so they will be automatically available when you need to archive them. The answers stated in options B, C, and D are bogus.

5. B. Make sure the Allow Users to Print Documents check box is clear. The other answers are bogus.

6. C. The method described in option C is correct. All of the other options are bogus.

7. D. Adding a description for the policy is important because it describes the behavior the policy is supposed to apply to the documents in the library. You may think that once you set a policy or some other configuration setting in SharePoint that you'll never forget what you did and why you did it, but after months or years of administering SharePoint (or anything else), you'll find that you need these reminders. Also, you may not be the SharePoint administrator forever, and your successor will be equally glad that you made such an effort.

8. B. Option B describes the correct procedure. All other options are bogus answers.

9. B, C, and D. Content flow planning recognizes three general locations for corporate content: within specific SharePoint sites, within the corporate records repository, and for public consumption, which can be the corporate intranet, the customer extranet, or the Internet. Content flow planning conceptualizes the flow at the site or site collection level and not at the level of specific workspaces or libraries.

10. A. Option A correctly describes the necessary last step. All other options present bogus answers.

11. A and C. Options A and C are the only valid choices. Options B and D are bogus answers.

12. B. The barcode feature creates a unique identifier value for a given document and then inserts that value as a barcode image in the document. The barcode remains with the document when printed and can be scanned like any other barcode.

13. D. For Word 2003 to be able to edit documents in a SharePoint document library, all of the latest updates for Word must be applied. All of the other answers are either unnecessary or bogus.

14. B and C. Links and Records Routing web parts are included in the Records Center. Announcements and Tasks are included in the Document Center.

15. A. Option A is the correct choice. All of the other options are bogus answers.

16. C. Option C describes the correct procedure. All of the other answers are bogus.

17. B and C. You can select Existing Group and use the drop-down menu to choose which group to use, or you can select New Group and create a custom-made group. The other answers are bogus.

18. A, C, and D. Options A, C, and D are all possible selections on the Document Information Panel Settings page. Option B is a bogus answer.

19. D. Only someone with domain administrator rights can install this software.

20. C. Option C gives the correct procedure. The other options are bogus.

Chapter

11

Working with Microsoft Outlook in SharePoint

MICROSOFT EXAM OBJECTIVES COVERED IN THIS CHAPTER

✓ **Configure Content Management**

- Configure Records Management
- Managing Policies and Compliance

Chapter 10, "Working with Microsoft Documents in SharePoint," spent a bit of time presenting how Microsoft Office Word 2003 and 2007 interoperated with Microsoft Office SharePoint Server (MOSS) 2007. This chapter will go into how you can use Outlook 2003 and 2007 in conjunction with different MOSS 2007 features.

The vast majority of the world uses Microsoft Outlook as its email, calendaring, and contacts manager, both in the corporate environment and in the home. You can now expand the capacities of both Outlook and SharePoint 2007 by using them together to perform a variety of functions such as updating a Tasks list in SharePoint or posting to a SharePoint discussion board directly from Outlook.

A more complete list of Outlook and SharePoint collaboration activities includes adding content to announcements, discussions, and documents within SharePoint from Outlook; synchronizing events and meeting invitations between the calendars in SharePoint and Outlook; creating a meeting workspace in SharePoint by scheduling an event in Outlook; and sending an email to a targeted SharePoint audience.

This chapter will start out exploring how Outlook 2003 and 2007 are used in different ways to interact with SharePoint. Then it will focus on Outlook 2007 and how its specially enhanced features allow for multiple types of collaborative interoperability between these two Office utilities. You'll take a look at email management as a function of document and content management as well as policy compliance. Finally, you'll get a chance to work through a number of Outlook/SharePoint tasks, which will give you experience in enabling many of these features and show you how to take advantage of them to perform business-related activities.

Outlook and SharePoint Interoperations Overview

One of the primary advantages to using Microsoft Office SharePoint Server 2007 is the enhanced set of collaboration tools it possesses. You can use all of the applications offered by the Microsoft Office 2007 suite as well as many other utilities to share documents, create customized group and personal workspaces, and manage project life cycles.

Microsoft Office Outlook 2007 was created to be a fully integrated collaborative component within the larger Office 2007 set of applications; relative to SharePoint, it can be used to provide alerts and notifications about content changes to a targeted group and to share scheduling calendars. That said, Outlook 2003 also possesses many features that interact well with SharePoint 2007.

Working with Outlook 2003 and SharePoint 2007

You learned in Chapter 10, "Working with Microsoft Documents in SharePoint," that you could use Word 2003 to interoperate with MOSS 2007 features, but the level of interactivity was limited when compared to Word 2007. Outlook 2003 has a number of features that will work and play well with SharePoint 2007 without any sort of enhancements, including the ability to send alerts and add content to an email-enabled SharePoint library.

There are several other ways that Outlook 2003 and SharePoint Server 2007 can interact from both the Outlook and SharePoint interfaces.

Working with SharePoint 2007 from Outlook 2003

You can create an appointment in Outlook 2003 and also create a meeting workspace in SharePoint by clicking the Meeting Workspace button. This allows you to configure settings such as the location of the meeting and lets you go to the newly created workspace directly from within Outlook.

You can also create a document workspace in a similar manner from within Outlook. This can be done when you send an email attachment to the library just as you would to another SharePoint user.

Working with Outlook 2003 from SharePoint 2007

When using a Calendar list in SharePoint, you can access Outlook by selecting Actions ➤ Connect to Outlook. This lets you make such selections as Make Items Available Offline and Synchronize Items (referring to items in the SharePoint and Outlook calendars). When you perform these actions, a Windows SharePoint Services folder is added to the list of folders in the left pane in Outlook. The downside is that the items in the folder are read-only, so you won't be able to manipulate any of the calendar items displayed.

You can also use a Contacts list in SharePoint to connect to Outlook; however, just like the Calendar list, the Contacts list you create from SharePoint in Outlook is read-only. To create the Contacts list, select Actions ➤ Connect to Outlook just as you did in the Calendar list. You also have the option of exporting any individual contact from SharePoint to Outlook by selecting Edit ➤ Export Contact and then selecting the specific contact. During this action, you can choose to either open the contact or save it in .vcf format. Rather than this being another read-only option, once the individual contact is saved, you will be able to edit it later.

In a picture library, select Actions ➤ Send To ➤ Microsoft Office Outlook Message if you want to email a graphic to another user from directly within SharePoint. You can perform a similar action in a document library by selecting Edit ➤ Send To and then sending an email recipient a link to a particular document in the body of the email.

Unfortunately, this is the extent of how Outlook 2003 and SharePoint 2007 interact, particularly in terms of the availability of the Connect to Outlook option. You will be unable to access Outlook 2003 from any other SharePoint list or library type.

Working with Outlook 2007 and SharePoint 2007

Although Outlook 2003 will integrate with SharePoint 2007, you've seen that there are severe limitations to how they are able to interact. Outlook 2007 builds on the 2003 features to provide a much wider ability to create connections between Outlook and SharePoint. Some examples include the ability to synchronize data between the contents of a folder in Outlook and a SharePoint document library.

From within a SharePoint list or library, when you click Actions, you have the option of selecting Connect to Outlook. After you click OK in the confirmation dialog box, you are offered a number of options including the Advanced button. When you click the Advanced button, you can perform a number of tasks including changing the name of the default SharePoint folder in the Outlook folder list and choosing not to display this list on other computers you use.

When you move a document from Outlook directly into a SharePoint document library, not only are the document contents transmitted but so is the metadata associated with the document. This includes the following:

- Name
- Changed By
- Checked Out To
- Modified
- Size

As previously mentioned, you can synchronize the contents of a folder in a SharePoint document library with a folder in Outlook so that they contain the same documents and the same versions of each document. Once this is accomplished, you can open the folder in Outlook to access the documents. Right-clicking any document in this folder results in the following menu items being displayed:

- Open
- Print
- Reply
- Forward
- Copy Shortcut
- Mark as Unread
- Find All
- Related Messages
  - Messages from Sender
  - Remove from Offline Copy
- Message Options

As you can see, many of the menu items are what you would expect in an email client, but a few require some explanation.

When you click the Open menu item, you open the document in read-only mode. Once the document is open, you are offered the option of editing it offline. After you have edited and saved the document, you can update your changes to the server once back online.

The Remove from Offline Copy option lets you remove the copy of the document from the folder in Outlook; however, this is not permanent. The next time you synchronize this folder with the folder in the document library, the latest version of the document will be included in the Outlook folder.

You can also right-click the Outlook folder and choose Delete to remove the folder and all its contents. The contents in the SharePoint library will, of course, remain intact.

Unlike Outlook 2003, you can connect a Tasks list in SharePoint to Outlook 2007 by selecting Actions ➢ Connect to Outlook. This option is also available in a SharePoint Calendar list. Additional interoperability features include subscribing to an RSS feed from a SharePoint list or library using Outlook and from the Internet Explorer 7 Favorites list.

You can also configure the Send/Receive options in Outlook to include SharePoint as an email account so that when you open Outlook on your computer and the Send/Receive action automatically begins, emails will be received from and be sent to SharePoint along with any other valid email sources.

Managing Email Content in SharePoint

Although the average home user may not consider their emails to be "official records," anyone who works in a business environment realizes that emails and other electronic forms of communication are company documents in the same way as a hard-copy memo, sales report, inventory sheet, or company network policy form. Not only are electronic communications official corporate documents, but the contents are company property. As such, they fall within the same policies and legal guidelines as any other business document.

For these reasons, email messages must follow the same content management rules in your organization as the rest of your records. This means you must have a plan for email retention, the same way you have a plan for all records retention. The difference is the specific nature of emails. Fortunately, since all the information contained within SharePoint is electronic and digital by its very nature, you can use SharePoint features to manage this communication form.

Usually, when discussing email management as content management, you are actually talking about Exchange Server interoperability with SharePoint 2007 as opposed to working with the Outlook client. So far, we've discussed interoperability of different Office suite products, since SharePoint is part of the overall Microsoft Office application collection. Although Exchange Server 2007 does not fall within that classification, it was still designed (along with most other 2007 Microsoft products) to seamlessly interact with MOSS 2007 features and functionality. This functionality is what makes it possible to manage email content based in Exchange from the SharePoint interface when Exchange is the mail server managing your corporate emails.

 In Chapter 3, "Configuring SharePoint 2007," you learned how to configure incoming and outgoing emails using SharePoint's Central Administration web application. This included connecting to an Exchange server if one was used for email management.

The following sections of the chapter will address email content management when an Exchange server is not being used. Later, you'll have the opportunity to enable different lists and libraries in SharePoint for email functionality. The following will describe using the SharePoint Records Center for email content management.

> The 70-630 exam does not require that you know the details of configuring Exchange Server 2007 features for interoperability with SharePoint 2007.

Managing Email Content Using the Records Center

The Records Center site in SharePoint contains a predetermined set of features that you can use for email content management. A brief tour of the Records Center will help you understand the role of these features in this context.

The SharePoint Records Center has five general areas of functionality: the Information Management Policy feature, the Vault, the Records Collection Programmable Interface, Records Routing, and Hold.

- The *Information Management Policy* feature has three main elements, which should already be familiar to you from Chapter 10, "Working with Microsoft Documents in SharePoint": Auditing, Expiration, and Barcodes. You can manage email records using policy enforcement in the same way as you would any other SharePoint record.

- The *Vault* feature allows you to guarantee the integrity of all your records, including emails, so that you can be sure the content cannot be changed or tampered with once it is contained within the Records Center. This integrity includes making sure the system does not automatically edit or otherwise modify content committed to the vaulting system. The content you upload to the Records Center should always be the same content you will later download and access. If any changes are made to email content, the changes will be expressed by different versions of the content, and the auditing feature will write to a log whenever any content is modified by an authorized user. Users with manager permissions in the Records Center can also add and modify the metadata of each record without changing any of the actual content of the record.

- The *Record Collection Programmable Interface* allows you to configure document management and email management systems to automatically upload content to the Records Center using either the web-based Simple Object Access Protocol (SOAP) or email-based Simple Mail Transfer Protocol (SMTP). This feature is not likely to be covered on the 70-630 exam but is included here for completeness.

- The *Records Routing* feature allows you to determine where any records submitted to the center will be specifically stored based on the type of record involved. This includes any metadata associated with the content, which will be stored separately in XML format as well as in column format.

- The *Hold* feature has an especially important role in terms of policy and legal compliance. Any content in the Records Center that is relevant to a legal proceeding or investigation can be placed on a Hold list. Any content on the Hold list is exempted from any policies you have applied, particularly an expiration policy, so that they will not be inadvertently removed from the system. The content will be "frozen" in place until such time as the legal action is finished and the content can be removed from the list.

Once email content is committed to the Records Center, it is treated in the same manner by the features you've just reviewed as any other record or document. In this sense, you can think of email content in the same way as any other corporate record stored in SharePoint.

 Real World Scenario

Enabling an Announcements List to Receive Email Content

Kevin, the manager of the sales and marketing division for your company, is planning a major reorganization of the departments he oversees including new policies, procedures, and departmental goals. As a result, he will be making frequent announcements on the division portal site that are important for all department heads and staff to receive promptly. Kevin doesn't want to have to log in to SharePoint every time he wants to update the portal site's Announcements list, so he asks whether another option is available. You explain that it's possible to send items to an Announcements list directly from Outlook 2007. Kevin likes the idea and tasks you with enabling the Announcements list on the sales and marketing portal site to receive email content. You explain the various options available when setting up the list, and Kevin tells you he wants any attachments to emails sent to the list saved but doesn't want the original emails saved in the list. He also wants any email invitations saved in the list. You tell him you can either limit who sends emails to the Announcements list based on SharePoint permissions groups or allow anyone to email an announcement. He settles for the former option.

As the SharePoint site collection administrator for your organization, you have the permission to access this portal site and make the necessary modifications. On the portal site, you click the Announcements list title to open the Announcements page. Then you click Settings and List Settings to open the Customize Announcements page. You locate the Communications column and click Incoming E-mail Settings to access the proper controls. You click Yes under Allow This List to Receive E-mail and enter the email address of the list in the available field. You click Yes under Save E-mail Attachments and No under Save Original E-mail. You click Yes under Save Meeting Invitations and click Accept E-mail Messages Based on List Permissions. You finish by clicking OK, and you provide Kevin with the email address of the Announcements list.

Managing Outlook Content with SharePoint

Now that you've had a chance to look over the conceptual information regarding email content management, you can start building on that knowledge by performing the various tasks required in working with both Outlook and SharePoint.

To use Outlook to send email content to SharePoint lists or libraries, the particular lists and libraries you want to use must have email support enabled. Although the process of enabling email support is pretty much the same for all of the different kinds of lists, there are some variations involved. Exercise 11.1 will show you how to enable email support for an Announcements list.

EXERCISE 11.1

Enabling Email Support for an Announcements List

1. On the web page containing the desired Announcements list, click the name of the Announcements list. When the Announcements page opens, select Settings ➢ List Settings.

2. On the Customize Announcements page under Communications, click Incoming E-mail Settings.

3. On the Incoming E-Mail Settings: Announcements page, in the Incoming E-Mail area under Allow This List to Receive E-mail, click Yes.

4. In the E-mail Address field, enter the name of the email address you want SharePoint members to use to send emails to this list.

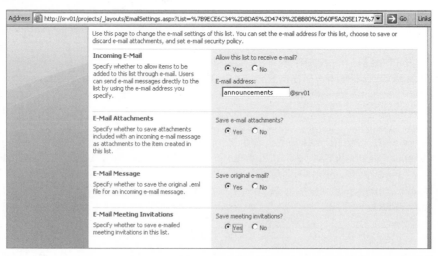

5. Under Save E-mail Attachments, click Yes to save attachments or No to discard email attachments.

EXERCISE 11.1 *(continued)*

6. Under Save Original E-mail, click Yes to save emails in .eml format or No to not save the original.

7. Under Save Meeting Invitations, click Yes to save the invitations or No to discard them.

8. Under E-mail Security Policy, click either Accept E-mail Messages Based on List Permissions or Accept E-mail Messages from Any Sender, depending on your security needs.

9. Click OK to finish.

The process of enabling email support for other lists such as a Calendar or Discussion Board list is so similar to this exercise that additional sample tasks aren't necessary. Exercise 11.2 will show you how to enable email support for a library.

EXERCISE 11.2

Enabling Email Support for a Library

1. Open the library you want to configure for email support, and click Settings. Choose the type of library setting you want, such as Document Library Settings.

2. On the Incoming E-Mail Settings page for the library in the Incoming E-Mail area under Allow This Document Library to Receive E-mail, click Yes.

3. In the E-mail Address field, enter the email address you want SharePoint members to use to send email content to this library.

4. Under Group Attachments in Folders, make one of the following selections:

    Save All Attachments in Root Folder

    Save All Attachments in Folders Grouped by E-mail Subject

    Save All Attachments in Folders Grouped by E-mail Sender

5. Under Overwrite Files with the Same Name, select either Yes to overwrite those files or No if you do not want them overwritten.

6. Under Save Original E-mail, click Yes to save it in .eml format or No to not save the original.

7. Under Save Meeting Invitations, click Yes to save the invitations or No to discard them.

8. Under E-mail Security Policy, click either Accept E-mail Messages Based on List Permissions or Accept E-mail Messages from Any Sender, depending on your security needs.

9. Click OK to finish.

If you select No in step 5 of Exercise 11.2, the following will occur in sequential order if content is sent to the library with the same name as content already existing in the library:

1. The system will add four randomly generated digits to the end of the attachment's name to create a unique name.

2. If action 1 fails, the system will add a globally unique identifier (GUID) to the end of the attachment's name to create a unique name.

3. If action 2 fails, the attachment is discarded.

Once the desired lists and libraries have been email enabled, they are ready to receive content from SharePoint members. Depending on the destination of your email content, members will need to use somewhat different methods.

If a SharePoint user wants to send email content to an Announcements or Calendar list, they will need to send it in the form of an email meeting invitation. If the email content is being sent to a blog or discussion board, the user will need to send the content in the body of the email. If the content is being sent to a library, it must be sent as an email attachment.

The methods of adding content to SharePoint are as easy as sending an email. For instance, all a user needs in order to email a document to an email-enabled document library is the email address of the library. Then the user simply adds the document they want to insert into the library as an attachment to the email and sends the email.

As mentioned earlier in the chapter, once a library or list has been email enabled, to connect to Outlook from within the SharePoint library or list, click Actions ➢ Connect to Outlook.

Another way that SharePoint and Outlook integrate is through the use of SharePoint's Outlook Web Access. Exchange Server 2003 or newer must be managing your corporate emails for you to take advantage of this feature, but when it is enabled, you are able to access Outlook mail directly from a web interface in SharePoint.

You can access the Outlook Web Access feature in SharePoint by using several different Outlook Web Access web parts:

- Calendar

- Contacts

- Inbox

- Mail Folder

- Tasks

Using SharePoint with Exchange 2007, you can also use Outlook Web Access to set up *Windows File Share Integration* so that you can connect to SharePoint document libraries directly from the Outlook Web Access web part interface. The drawback is that you will be able to use only read-only copies of the documents in the library. To edit library documents, you must either connect directly from Outlook 2007 or enter the document library itself.

The previously mentioned Web Access web parts are often configured on an individual's MySite site. For instance, you could access your Outlook Calendar and Tasks lists from your MySite using the Calendar and Tasks list web parts. Both of these web parts should have been included in your MySite by default.

You'll need to enable your MySite for Outlook Web Access support before you can take advantage of this feature. Exercise 11.3 will show you how. Remember, this task will be unsuccessful unless you can access an Exchange server from your SharePoint site.

EXERCISE 11.3

Enabling Outlook Web Access in Your MySite

1. From any site in SharePoint, click the My Site link in the upper-right area of the page.

2. Click the down arrow to the right of the My Calendar title, and then click Modify Shared Web Part from the menu.

3. When the My Calendar Toolbox appears, Under Mail Configuration in the Mail Server Address field, enter the web address of the Exchange Server used to manage your emails.

4. In the Mailbox field, enter your email address.

5. Use the View drop-down menu to select Daily or Weekly to control how you want the calendar to be displayed, as shown here.

6. Click Apply, and then click OK to finish.

Enabling web access in your Tasks list uses virtually the same process, so there won't be a separate exercise covering how this action is performed.

Exercise 11.4 will show you how you can subscribe to a SharePoint RSS feed directly from Outlook. You will need to know the URL to the RSS feed so you can copy and paste it into the appropriate section in Outlook. This means, of course, that the RSS feed must have already been created in SharePoint, and you must have access to Outlook 2007. The exercise assumes you've already copied the URL to the RSS feed and it's available to be pasted.

Remember, you can also subscribe to a SharePoint RSS feed directly from a list or library and from the Favorites list in Internet Explorer 7.

EXERCISE 11.4

Subscribing to an RSS Feed Using Outlook

1. Open the Outlook 2007 client on your computer, and click Tools ≻ Account Settings.

2. Click the RSS Feeds tab, and then click New.

3. When the New RSS Feed dialog box appears, paste the URL of the RSS feed into the appropriate field, and click Add.

4. When the RSS Feed Options dialog box appears, under General in the Feed Name field either give the field a name or accept the default (which is also the channel name).

5. Under Delivery Location, either accept the default location for the feed delivery or click the Change Folder button and specify the location where you want the feed to be delivered.

6. Under Downloads, you can tick the Automatically Download Enclosures for this Feed and/or the Download the Full Article as an .html Attachment to Each Item check boxes.

7. Under Update Limit, tick the available check box if you want to accept the RSS feed provider's recommended update frequency.

8. Click OK.

9. Click Close to close Account Settings.

You'll notice an RSS Feeds folder in the folder list on the left; expanding that folder will display all the feeds for which this folder is the default destination, as you determined in step 5 of Exercise 11.4. In step 5, you could have specified a different folder if you wanted to organize feeds based on topics or sources rather than having all your feeds collected in a single location.

In step 7, if you did not tick the available check box, the RSS feed would update based on how often Outlook's Send/Receive feature is set to update. You could also manually update the feed by clicking the Send/Receive button in Outlook.

Outlook's RSS feed utility is optimized for use with SharePoint RSS feeds rather than outside sources, and many of the features you might use to access feeds in other venues may not be available in Outlook. It is therefore recommended that you restrict your users to accessing feeds provided in SharePoint from their Outlook clients.

Summary

In this chapter, you learned about the interoperations between Outlook email and Share-Point 2007, including the following points:

- The basic interoperation between Outlook 2003 and 2007 and SharePoint 2007
- Looking at emails as a content management issue in SharePoint the way you'd look at forms or documents
- Using a SharePoint Records Center site for email content management
- Using Outlook Web Access web parts

Exam Essentials

Know how to plan for content management.   Planning content management is an important aspect of administering a SharePoint site collection, and email content management is a special case since email communications are an extremely common conduit for information and aren't always thought of as formal corporate documents. You must understand this vital documentation method and how to use features in both Outlook and SharePoint to manage this type of data.

Understand how to configure content management for Outlook.   Both Outlook and Share-Point have specific tools incorporated into their design specifically constructed to allow for both the interoperability of the two Office utilities and the management of email content. Knowing how to configure both the Outlook client and SharePoint content management features is an important part of your administrative role.

Be well versed in policy and compliance management.   Emails are just like any other business documentation and are subject to a number of internal policies, business ethics practices, and legal requirements. You are required to understand how to use SharePoint and Outlook to ensure compliance to all of the records standards that modern corporate practice requires.

Review Questions

1. You are a SharePoint user working in your company's research division. You have been tasked with organizing a presentation to the management team on your latest projects, which includes setting up the meeting and creating a meeting workspace in SharePoint. You have discovered that you can create the meeting workspace directly from your Outlook 2003 client. Of the following options, which is the correct method?

   A. Create an appointment in Outlook 2003, and click the Meeting Workspace button.

   B. Open the Outlook 2003 calendar, create the appointment, and click the Connect to SharePoint Calendar button.

   C. Send meeting invitations to the desired attendees from Outlook 2003, and then click the Meeting Workspace button.

   D. Create an appointment in Outlook 2003, and then send invitations to the attendees and the email-enabled calendar.

2. You are the SharePoint administrator for your organization. You are providing in-service training to all the site owners in the SharePoint site collection on the interoperability of Outlook and SharePoint. You are outlining the similarities and differences in how Outlook 2003 and Outlook 2007 work with MOSS 2007. Of the following options, which one can you perform from both Outlook 2003 and 2007?

   A. After synchronizing content in both SharePoint and Outlook, you can change the default folder in Outlook that contains the SharePoint content.

   B. After synchronizing content in both SharePoint and Outlook, you can enter the default SharePoint folder in Outlook, right-click a document, and select Message Options.

   C. You can create a SharePoint Document Workspace by sending an attachment from Outlook.

   D. You can configure the Send/Receive options in Outlook so that when you initiate a Send/Receive action, any SharePoint content will be transmitted or received along with any other email traffic.

3. You are the SharePoint administrator for your corporation, and you are planning content management for all of the company's emails. You are reviewing all the features in Outlook, Exchange Server, and SharePoint to determine which email content management strategy is the best fit for your organization's needs. Of the following options, which are true for email content management? (Choose all that apply.)

   A. You must use Exchange Server 2007 to enable email content management features within SharePoint 2007.

   B. You can manage email content without an Exchange Server 2007 server present on the network as long as Exchange Server 2003 has been enabled to interoperate with SharePoint.

   C. You can use the features in a SharePoint Records Center to manage email content without an Exchange Server being present on the network.

   D. Incoming and outgoing email support must be configured in SharePoint's Central Administration web application before you can manage email content in SharePoint.

4. You are the SharePoint administrator for your corporation, and the CIO has tasked you with creating an email content management scheme using a SharePoint Records Center site. A necessary part of the task is to make sure that email management systems automatically upload content to the Records Center using either Simple Object Access Protocol (SOAP) or Simple Mail Transfer Protocol (SMTP). Of the following Records Center features, which one will enable you to accomplish your task?

    A. The Information Management Policy feature

    B. The Records Routing feature

    C. The Records Collection Programmable Interface feature

    D. The Vault feature

5. You are the SharePoint administrator for your corporation, and the CIO has tasked you with creating an email content management scheme using a SharePoint Records Center site. You must make sure that different record types are contained within folders designed for each type so that email records can be found easily. You must also make sure that any metadata associated with these records is stored separately in the same site. Using the appropriate SharePoint Records Center feature, which methods can you use to store the email content metadata? (Choose all that apply.)

    A. Metadata can be stored in EML format.

    B. Metadata can be stored in XML format.

    C. Metadata can be stored in column format.

    D. Metadata can be stored in row format.

6. You are the site administrator for your department's SharePoint site. You want to email enable the Announcements list on your site. You are on the Incoming E-Mail Settings: Announcements page. What is the first thing you must do to email enable the list?

    A. In the Incoming E-Mail area under Allow This List to Receive E-mail, click Yes.

    B. In the Receiving E-Mail area under Allow This List to Receive Incoming E-mail, click Yes.

    C. In the Incoming E-mail area, tick the Allow This List to Receive E-mail check box.

    D. In the Receiving E-Mail area, tick the Allow This List to Receive Incoming Email check box.

7. You are the site administrator for your department's SharePoint site. You want to enable email support for your site's document library. You are on the Incoming E-mail Settings page for the library and want to configure how the library treats email attachments. Of the following options, which are available for you to use for email attachments? (Choose all that apply.)

    A. Save All Attachments in Root Folder

    B. Save All Attachments in Folders Grouped by E-mail subject

    C. Save All Attachments in Folders Grouped by E-mail sender

    D. Save All Attachments in Folders Grouped by E-mail Attachment Type

8. You are the site administrator for your department's SharePoint site. You want to enable email support for your site's document library. You are on the Incoming E-mail Settings page for the library and are trying to decide whether you want to have new email content overwrite documents in the library of the same name. You decide not to enable this option. As a result, when content that has the same name as existing documents comes into the library, what actions are likely to occur? (Choose all that apply.)

A. The system will create a new version of the attachment and append the end of the attachment's name with the new version number.

B. The system will add four randomly generated digits to the end of the attachment's name to create a unique name.

C. The system will add a globally unique identifier (GUID) to the end of the attachment's name to create a unique name.

D. The attachment will be discarded.

9. You are the SharePoint site collection administrator for your organization. You are providing in-service training for all the site owners in the site collection, describing how to enable email support for lists and libraries. You are describing how members of their sites can send email content to their various destinations. Of the following selections, which are valid methods? (Choose all that apply.)

A. SharePoint users must send email content to an Announcements or Calendar list as a meeting invitation.

B. SharePoint users must send email content to a blog as an email attachment.

C. SharePoint users must send email content to a document library in the body of the email.

D. SharePoint users must send email content to a discussion board in the body of the email.

10. You are the SharePoint administrator for your organization's site collection. You are planning to enable Outlook Web Access in SharePoint so site owners will be able to use the various Outlook Web Access web parts on their web part pages. As part of your planning, you are determining the necessary requirements for enabling this feature. Of the following options, which one is a necessary prerequisite for enabling Outlook Web Access?

A. Exchange Server 2007 must be managing your corporate emails.

B. Exchange Server 2003 or 2007 must be managing your corporate emails.

C. Exchange Server 2003 or 2007 or a Sendmail server must be managing your corporate emails.

D. Exchange Server 2007 server must be managing your emails in an Active Directory domain structure.

11. You are the SharePoint administrator for your organization. You are planning to deploy Outlook Web Access on the site collection so that members of your company's websites can take advantage of the Web Access web parts on their web part pages. As part of the review of your plan, you inventory the different web parts that can be used with Outlook Web Access. Of the following selections, which are valid Web Access web parts? (Choose all that apply.)

A. Calendar

B. Inbox

C. Outbox

D. Mail Folder

12. You are the SharePoint administrator for your organization. You are planning to deploy Outlook Web Access on the site collection so that members of your company's websites can take advantage of the features available with this technology. One feature you think will be particularly useful is the ability to connect directly to a SharePoint document library from an Outlook Web Access web part interface. Of the following selections, which technology provides this function?

A. SharePoint Outlook Library Integration

B. Windows Outlook Integration

C. Windows File Share Integration

D. Outlook Document Share Integration

13. You are a SharePoint user who wants to have the option of utilizing Outlook Web Access on your MySite. You have learned that after you enable your MySite for Outlook Web Access support, you will be able to use this option on two web parts that are already available on MySite by default. Of the following options, which two web parts can you use?

A. Calendar and Tasks list web parts

B. Announcements and Links list web parts

C. Libraries and Colleagues web parts

D. Memberships and Sites web parts

14. You are a SharePoint user who wants to have the option of utilizing Outlook Web Access on your MySite. You are currently enabling the Calendar list on your MySite for Web Access support and have that web part's toolbox open. Under Mail Configuration, which fields must be configured and how? (Choose all that apply.)

A. In the Exchange Server field, enter the IP address of the Exchange server on your network.

B. Under View, tick the Daily, Weekly, or Monthly check box to set how the Calendar list will display on your MySite.

C. In the Mail Server Address field, enter the web address of the Exchange server used to manage your emails.

D. In the Mailbox field, enter your email address.

15. You are a SharePoint user, and you want to subscribe to a SharePoint RSS feed from your Outlook client. You are unsure as to what prerequisites are necessary and consult with your site collection's administrator. What do you learn needs to be set up before you can subscribe to an RSS feed? (Choose all that apply.)

A. The RSS feed must be created in SharePoint.

B. You must know the IP address of the server providing the RSS feed.

C. You must know the channel name of the feed.

D. You must be using Outlook 2007.

16. You are a SharePoint user, and you have just configured an RSS feed from Outlook. You notice that all of your feeds go into the default RSS Feeds folder in the Outlook folder list. If you wanted to set a feed to be delivered to a different folder, what would you have to do during the configuration process?

    A. Under Delivery Location, type the name of the folder you want the feed to be delivered to and click Add.

    B. Under Delivery Location, click the Change Folder button, and specify the folder where you want the feed to be delivered.

    C. Under Delivery Location, select Change Delivery Location, and specify the folder where you want the feed to be delivered.

    D. Under Delivery Location, tick the Change Folder check box, and type the name of the folder where you want the feed to be delivered.

17. You are a SharePoint user, and you are currently exploring the options in the Document Library on your department's SharePoint site for connecting to your Outlook email client. When you open the Connect to Outlook menu, what options are available to you? (Choose all that apply.)

    A. Make Items Available Offline

    B. Send Items as an Email Attachment

    C. Connect to Multiple Mailboxes

    D. Synchronize Items

18. You are a SharePoint user, and you have connected the Contacts list on your MySite to your Outlook mail client. You want to export a contact from SharePoint to Outlook and then save it. In what format will the contact be saved?

    A. .eml

    B. .vcf

    C. XML

    D. HTML

19. You are a SharePoint user, and you have connected the Contacts list on your MySite to your Outlook mail client. You want to export a contact from SharePoint to Outlook and then save it. What actions must you take to export the contact?

    A. Click File ➢ Export Contact.

    B. Click Actions ➢ Export Contact.

    C. Click List Settings ➢ Export Contact.

    D. Click Edit ➢ Export Contact.

20. You are a SharePoint user, and you previously configured your SharePoint calendar on your MySite to be email enabled. You have just finished synchronizing the items in your Share-Point and Outlook calendars. You go into the SharePoint folder in Outlook to edit one of the Calendar items, but you are unable to do so. What could be the problem?

A. You are attempting to do so from the SharePoint calendar. You must exit that calendar and perform the action directly in Outlook.

B. All items synchronized between the SharePoint and Outlook calendars are read-only in the SharePoint Services folder in Outlook.

C. The most likely problem is that there is a network failure between the SharePoint server and your computer and the items did not synchronize. You will be unable to edit items in the SharePoint Services folder in Outlook until you can synchronize them again.

D. The item you are trying to edit is most likely corrupted. You must delete it and synchronize the calendars again. Once this is done, you'll be able to edit the item.

Answers to Review Questions

1. A. You must create the appointment first in Outlook 2003 and then click the Create a Meeting Workspace button to create the necessary site.

2. C. You can create a SharePoint Document Workspace from Outlook 2003 by sending an attachment. All of the other options presented require that you use Outlook 2007.

3. C and D. You do not need to have an Exchange Server 2003 or 2007 mail server on the network to manage email content. Email content management can be handled using a Records Center site as long as incoming and outgoing email support has been configured in Central Administration.

4. C. The Record Collection Programmable Interface feature allows you to configure document management and email management systems to automatically upload content to the Records Center using either the web-based Simple Object Access Protocol (SOAP) or the email-based Simple Mail Transfer Protocol (SMTP). All of the other features are valid in a Records Center but do not provide the necessary functionality.

5. B and C. Metadata for email and other content in a Records Center can be stored in either XML or column format. EML format is used to save original email content in a list such as an Announcements list. The option for row format is bogus.

6. A. Option A describes the correct action. All of the other answers are bogus.

7. A, B, and C. Options A, B, and C are all valid ways to organize email attachments in an email-enabled library. Option D is a bogus answer.

8. B, C, and D. The actions described in options B, C, and D will occur sequentially, with option B occurring first, option C occurring next if option B fails, and option D occurring third if options B and C fail. Option A is a bogus answer.

9. A and D. Options A and D describe the correct methods of sending email content to an Announcement or Calendar list and to a discussion board. Email content sent to a blog must be sent in the body of the email, and email content sent to a library must be sent as an attachment.

10. B. You can use either Exchange Server 2003 or Exchange Server 2007 server to manage your corporate emails. A Sendmail server is not a valid option, and Active Directory does not have to be available in order to use Outlook Web Access.

11. A, B, and D. The Web Access web parts are Calendar, Contacts, Inbox, Mail Folder, and Tasks. Outbox is a bogus answer.

12. C. Option C is the correct name for this solution. The other options are bogus answers.

13. A. You could access your Outlook Calendar and Tasks lists from your MySite using the Calendar and Tasks list web parts. Both of these web parts should have been included in your MySite by default. All of the other options are bogus answers.

14. C and D. Under Mail Configuration, you must enter the address of the Exchange server in the Mail Server Address field and your email address in the Mailbox field. Instead of using check boxes, use the drop-down arrow under View to select either Daily or Weekly to set how the calendar will be displayed. Option A is bogus.

15. A and D. You must know the URL of the RSS feed but do not need to know any server IP address. You do not need to know the name of the channel feed, since the name is provided by default. This feature is available only when you are using Outlook 2007 and is not supported by earlier versions of Outlook.

16. B. Option B gives the correct procedure. All the other options are bogus answers.

17. A and D. Options A and D are valid selections in the menu when you select Connect to Outlook. The other options are bogus answers.

18. B. When you export a SharePoint contact into Outlook and save it, it is saved in .vcf format. The other options are bogus answers.

19. D. Option D is the only correct answer.

20. B. Items synchronized between SharePoint and Outlook calendars are read-only in the SharePoint Services folder in Outlook and cannot be edited.

Chapter

12

Using Excel Services and Business Intelligence

MICROSOFT EXAM OBJECTIVES COVERED IN THIS CHAPTER:

✓ **Managing Business Intelligence**

- Configure Report Center
- Configure Excel Services

Business intelligence (BI) is an oft sought after, much desired, but frequently misunderstood collection of services offered by Microsoft Office SharePoint Server (MOSS) 2007. Although BI represents a single concept, it is really a collection of services and utilities that interact to deliver an overall presentation of organizational and commercial information gathered under the umbrella of "business intelligence."

Because the concept and practice of BI are both so important and so complicated, this chapter and Chapter 13, "Using Business Forms and Business Intelligence," will be devoted to different aspects of the business intelligence model. As with any new concept, this chapter will begin with an overview of business intelligence as a process and as a group of tools. Since this is an overview, utilities addressed in both chapters will be introduced, but only those specific to this chapter will be presented in detail.

Once the overview is concluded, the chapter proceeds with the Report Center and shows you how it operates to organize all the features that comprise BI. Then we'll move into how Excel Services and Excel Web Access provide specific features for BI and interoperate with the overall collection of tools to seamlessly present the BI "experience." There will likely be a bit of overlap with other BI services as they relate to the other elements involved in BI, but the major points of each feature will be presented in specific sections of this chapter and in Chapter 13, "Using Business Forms and Business Intelligence."

The latter part of this chapter will present a series of exercises that will give you some practice creating and configuring business intelligence tools on your own SharePoint 2007 platform.

Business Intelligence Overview

What is business intelligence? The simplest answer is that business intelligence is a collection of SharePoint 2007 utilities and services designed to organize and present business-critical data to corporate managers, decision makers, and other key individuals and groups within the company. Even more simply put, it's the ability to have the right data presented in the right way to the right people at the right time.

Yes, that sounds like a slogan or an ad of some kind, but it succinctly describes the basic function and purpose of BI. Think of BI as a collection of information streams covering every relevant type of data that could impact critical decision making in your company. If those information streams just sprayed out raw data, it would take time to try to decide which bits and pieces were more important than others and which ones could be discarded completely.

So in addition to BI representing those various streams of data, BI also provides a filtering system so specific data within the streams is brought to the forefront where it can be attended to and acted upon. However, even if data is filtered and prioritized, it still might not be presented in a form that would allow for easy assimilation by the audience.

That's where you also have to think of BI as a series of interactive presentation tools. For instance, this chapter covers Excel Services, which is a method of interoperation between traditional Excel workbooks and SharePoint Server 2007 services. Using Excel Services, you can load, calculate, and display data from an Excel workbook in a SharePoint customized *dashboard*. Information from a single workbook can be presented in several different web parts within a dashboard, each displaying the data in a way relevant to a particular need.

At this point, you may be tempted to think of BI just in terms of the exam objectives listed at the beginning of this chapter, but contained within those objectives are the basic elements that comprise the skeletal structure of BI:

- Dashboards
- Excel Services
- External data sources
- Filter web parts
- Key performance indicators
- The Report Center

Although this chapter will specifically present both the Report Center and Excel Services as they relate to the exam objectives, the other elements will be integrated into the narrative as they apply to the different chapter sections and subjects being presented. That said, a brief introduction to the complete list of elements is in order at this point:

Dashboards   Dashboards are really a feature of the Report Center in SharePoint and function sort of the way the dashboard in your car works relative to the driver. To operate the car, you need relevant information presented to you and styled in such a way that you can understand that information instantly. Imagine if you had to take 10 seconds to figure out how fast you were going in order to adjust your speed as you entered a school zone. Fortunately, the speedometer is designed to let you see and comprehend your velocity almost instantly. The dashboard feature in Report Center does the same because it presents just the relevant information in a way that can be quickly interpreted. Also, like your car's dashboard, it is presented in a modular fashion so you can quickly locate just what you're looking for, just as you know exactly which part of your dashboard displays your speedometer, gas gauge, and so on.

Excel Services   Excel Services is basically an Excel workbook on the server rather than in a spreadsheet application. This service does what the application does—it stores, calculates, and presents data in a spreadsheet format using a web browser interface. The actual presentation of the data is handled by an Excel Web Access web part that you can add to any web part zone. Although the data may be presented in a web interface, all the storage and calculation functions are managed on the server. This results in your overall data store remaining on a secure platform rather than being exposed on the network or the Internet. Also, even though you can present this data in a variety of locations within SharePoint and filter the data in different ways, no data is actually copied or duplicated. The only copy of your spreadsheet information remains on the server, enhancing its security and maintaining a single copy of the information in a central location.

External data sources   SharePoint also has the ability to connect to data sources both within and outside of SharePoint using the external data sources feature and then to collect, filter, and present the data from those different locations in a single, unified interface. It's like taking news feeds from 10 different news agencies and merging the content into a single RSS reader. From the audience's point of view, it's as if they are looking at data originating from a single source. SharePoint can connect to such sources as SAP and Siebel as well as any data sources within SharePoint, and using system connections, you can create a central repository for the collected data in the data connection library of a Report Center. It's the connections that are actually pooled in the library, not the data itself. The data can then be presented in a variety of SharePoint web parts and lists, allowing your users to view and even interact with the data, all from within the SharePoint interface.

Filter web parts   Filter web parts allow you to take the data sources we've mentioned up until now and filter that data so that only relevant portions of the information are presented to your audience. You've seen in previous chapters how lists can be filtered so that you can create multiple information lists from a single master list. This is the same function provided by filter web parts. For example, using this feature, you can present sales figures targeted only for your western regional offices or craft a quarterly financial report for your European branches. There are 10 separate filter web parts that you can use, depending on your needs.

Key performance indicators   Key performance indicators (KPIs) are, as you might imagine, targeted data presentations that describe how a task, project, group, or individual is operating relative to a goal. A KPI is like the gas gauge on your dashboard. It gives you a quick visual indication of just how much fuel you have and, particularly, whether you're running low. You can also think of it as the trip meter function of your odometer, telling you how far you've come and how far you have to go on a road trip from Boise to San Francisco. You are familiar with the Tasks list and how team and individual tasks can be tracked toward completion. KPIs function in the same way, letting teams and managers know just how far work has progressed, whether or not it's on schedule, and whether there is a concern that time lines may not be met.

The Report Center   The Report Center is actually the central framework that most or all of the other business intelligence features are organized within. It also contains document libraries specifically designed for organizing reports, lists, and external data source connections. It is constructed to present the various web parts that allow you to present KPIs, dashboards, Excel Services workbook data, and other BI-specific information. Like the Records Center, the Report Center is created by default when you create a top-level portal site in SharePoint; however, you can create additional Report Centers as needed. Depending on the size of your organization, you may need just the single Report Center, or you may find it more efficient to create additional centers for each office, department, or division in your corporation.

Forms Services and the business data catalog are two critical elements in the business intelligence structure that will be covered in depth in Chapter 13, "Using Business Forms and Business Intelligence."

Business Intelligence and the Report Center

As previously mentioned, the Report Center is the skeletal structure of SharePoint's business intelligence functionality, containing all the elements that comprise BI. This is a good opportunity to take a brief tour of the Report Center and become familiar with how it is organized. To get to the Report Center, go to the top-level portal site, and click Reports in either Quick Launch to your left or on the navigation bar at the top of the page. Figure 12.1 shows you what the default Report Center looks like in SharePoint.

FIGURE 12.1   The Report Center

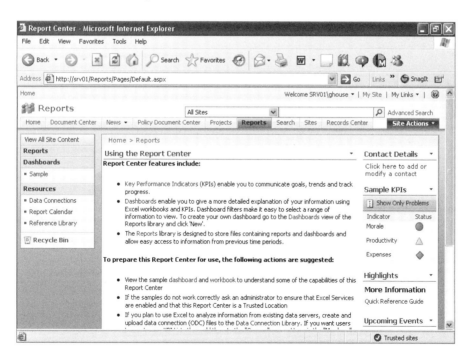

As you can see in the center pane of the Report Center, the available features include key performance indicators, dashboards, and the Reports library. You can access the following from the Quick Launch on the left:

Sample dashboard The sample dashboard contains several different elements: key performance indicators, list items by indicators, goals, values, and status. You can view items in terms of total problems or minimum count in the Indicator column. The items on the lower portion of the dashboard may take a few moments to load, but when they do, you'll see sample items organizing items by user and organization in a tabular format, a pie chart presenting percentages of issues by organization, and a list of percentages by organization. The overall presentation recalls the metaphor of a car's dashboard previously described in this chapter. This sample data originates in Excel workbooks that are filtered for the different displays.

Data connections This list is empty by default, and you'll have to create any desired data connections either by clicking New and then either creating an Office Data Connection file or a Universal Data Connection file or by clicking Upload and uploading the desired file.

Report Calendar This is a standard calendar list that you'll find in other SharePoint site templates, and it contains the usual features and functionality.

Reference Library This is a standard library that you'll find in other SharePoint site templates, and it contains the usual features and functionality that you find in any other library.

On the right side of the main pane you can add contacts under Contact Details, view the sample KPI, access the Quick Reference Guide, and view any upcoming events. Clicking the Sample KPIs list to the right will open the list; when it refreshes, you'll see items appearing in the Goal, Value, and Status columns, just as they were displayed in the main pane of the Report Center. The sample items in the Indicator column are Morale, Productivity, and Expenses, and they give examples of OK Status as a green sphere, Warning Status as a yellow triangle, and Problem as a red diamond.

Contact Details and Upcoming Events are both standard contacts and calendar lists that you've previously encountered. Clicking the Quick Reference Guide link will again open the sample dashboard.

 Real World Scenario

Presenting Business Intelligence Data in a Dashboard

You are the SharePoint administrator for your organization and are currently in a conference with the managers of your company's sales and marketing division. They have launched a promotion for a new software appliance that will enable users of mobile devices to more quickly and efficiently sync their email and personal information management (PIM) data between their personal digital assistants (PDAs) and their messaging servers. They are interested in tracking various customer responses and other information regarding how this product is selling and consumer feedback over the next six months.

You have been tasked with using SharePoint's business intelligence features to graphically display the overall sales of the product, sales by region, customer responses on a scale from totally dissatisfied to totally satisfied, and overall progress of the software development team producing the next version of the product, which is scheduled to be released three months from now.

You determine that creating a dashboard and using Excel Services workbook data presented in various chart and graph formats including KPIs will best fit the stated requirements. The managers want the dashboard in place on the corporate Report Center site in two weeks or less.

After the meeting, you access the Report Center and begin to create the dashboard. You already know which source documents are required because they are all located in the Reports library. On the Report Center main page, you click Dashboards in Quick Launch to begin creating the new dashboard, click New, and then click Dashboard Page. You complete the title, description, and other identifying information required and specify a location for the dashboard. You create a three-column layout to best present the different web parts you'll need to include to meet the required specifications.

After creating the basic dashboard, you connect one of the Excel Web Access web parts to a named item containing the data for the overall sales of the new product. You use several filter web parts to present sales data from the same workbook based on regional sales. You then set up the KPI web part to connect to Tasks list information from the development team's Tasks list so you can present a graphical display of their progress toward releasing the next version of the product. You add another filtered web part and link it to the survey list used for customer feedback. When you are finished, you click Publish to save and publish the new dashboard to the Report Center site.

After testing the new dashboard to make sure it is correctly configured and presenting data as required, you send an email to the sales and marketing division managers notifying them that the dashboard is in place and ready for use.

Business Intelligence and Excel Services

The other major BI element covered in this chapter is Excel Services. Although the Report Center may offer numerous methods of presenting and filtering information, much of that information has a single source: the Excel workbook. As previously mentioned, Excel Services is SharePoint's ability to present spreadsheet workbook data from a single, server-based source to multiple presentation elements including Excel Web Access web parts and KPIs. Excel Services consists of three specific components:

Excel Calculation Services (ECS)   This is the engine that drives Excel Services in SharePoint, including loading workbooks, calculating internal and external data, and maintaining sessions.

Excel Web Access (EWA) This is the specific web part that presents the Excel workbook data and allows users to interact with the server-side data source. It is also the interface that uses DHTML and JavaScript to connect to other BI elements such as dashboards, both on the same page and on different web pages in a site, allowing the same data source to offer different views and presentations depending on the need of the audience.

Excel Web Services (EWS) This is the web service behind Excel Services and can be accessed and used by programmers to build customized web applications based on the Excel workbook format.

Excel Services is available in SharePoint only if you have installed MOSS 2007 Enterprise Edition in your server farm, and all clients must possess the appropriate CALs to use this service. You can access the master Excel Services settings through the Central Administration web application. Click the default SSA for your site collection, such as SharedServices1; then under Excel Services Settings, click Edit Excel Services Settings. Exercise 12.1 will take you through the process of editing Excel Services in Central Administration, starting on the Excel Services Settings page shown in Figure 12.2.

FIGURE 12.2 The Excel Services Settings page

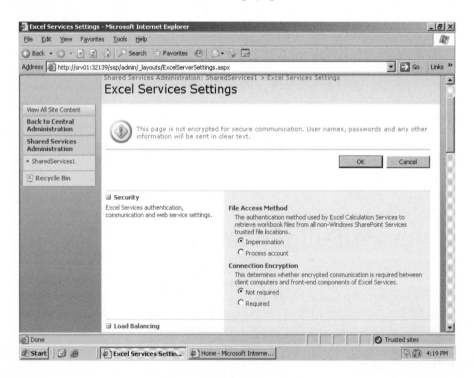

EXERCISE 12.1

Editing Excel Services in Central Administration

1. In the Security section under File Access Method, select either Impersonation or Process Account to choose the authentication method to be used by Excel Calculation Services to retrieve workbook data from trusted file locations outside of SharePoint.

2. In the same section under Connection Encryption, select either Not Required or Required to determine whether communication between client computers and Excel Services servers will be encrypted.

3. In the Load Balancing section under Load Balancing Scheme, choose Workbook URL, Round Robin, or Local to determine which load balancing method you will use across the process of Excel Calculation services.

4. In the same section under Retry Interval, enter a value in seconds in the available field to determine how frequently communications will be reattempted after an initial failed communications session with an Excel Calculation Services server. (The default is 30.)

5. In the Session Management section under Maximum Sessions Per User, enter a value for the number of sessions a particular user can initiate with Excel Services. (The default is 25, and the value –1 indicates no limit.)

6. In the Memory Utilization section under Maximum Private Bytes, enter a value in megabytes in the available field to determine the maximum number of bytes you want allocated to Excel Calculation Services. (The default is –1, which indicates up to 50 percent of the actual physical memory available on the server computer.)

7. In the same section under Memory Cache Threshold, enter a value in megabytes in the available field that is allocated to any inactive objects in Excel Services. (The default value is 90.)

8. In the same section under Maximum Unused Object Age, enter a value in minutes in the available field to indicate the maximum amount of time inactive objects are allowed to remain in cache. (The default value is –1, indicating no maximum limit.)

9. In the Workbook Cache section under Workbook Cache Location, enter the local file system location of the workbook file cache in the available field. If no value is entered in the field, it indicates that a subdirectory of the system temporary directory is the default location of the workbook file cache.

10. In the same section under Maximum Size of Workbook Cache, enter a value in megabytes for the amount of disk space to be allocated to workbooks currently being used by Excel Calculation Services. (The default value is 40960.)

11. In the same section under Caching of Unused Files, tick the available check box to enable caching, or clear the available check box to disable caching. (The check box is ticked by default.)

12. In the External Data section under Connection Lifetime, enter a value in seconds indicating how long a connection should remain open. (The default is 1800, and a value of –1 indicates that the connection never recycles.)

13. In the same section under Unattended Service Account, enter the username and password for any Excel Calculation Services that require access through authentication.

14. Click OK to finish.

Overview of the Business Data Catalog

Before delving deeper into the mysteries of the Report Center and Excel Services, it's important to address a vital aspect of business intelligence and of SharePoint Server 2007—the business data catalog (BDC). The BDC is a new shared service in SharePoint 2007 that allows users to access information from back-end applications within the site collection using the usual Share-Point tools such as web parts, lists, search, and so on. The BDC is not a storage method but rather a cataloging method that keeps track of and allows real-time access to dissimilar data sources as well as defining SharePoint-relevant business applications.

The BDC tracks the various different data sources you need to function productively in commerce and seamlessly offers the data to various presentation interfaces so that the user is completely unaware that they are viewing information from multiple source locations and types. Such source types can include traditional SharePoint data stores such as libraries and lists, Active Directory, internal and external databases, and custom-made applications.

The services provided by BDC are hardly automatic and require one or more subject-matter experts to configure the BDC applications required by SharePoint users. This can be one or several individuals in your organization fulfilling key BDC-related roles:

Administrator   This is a SharePoint administrator, and this role is responsible for importing any specific application definition files required to successfully configure a BDC application. This role is also positioned to deploy any customized business applications so that the information about the application is available to users.

Application definition author   This role requires that the person filling it be familiar with the specifics of an application's API and structure so that the application definition file can be written. This file provides information about the application that users will be connecting to including how the data contained is structured. The role does not require a background in programming but does require that the person have specific knowledge of the application and be familiar with how XML data files are structured as well as having general knowledge of database development.

Business analyst or site manager   Either of these roles can provide expertise regarding the inner workings of a corporation's information systems scheme, especially in matching information systems requirements to SharePoint's data management and presentation abilities.

Developer   This role is responsible for creating any custom-made business applications required to fulfill the business information requirements of the relevant SharePoint users. The developer role will work with application definition authors, business analysts, and site managers to create and define the specifics of a handcrafted BDC application to be used to fulfill needs not provided by any "off-the-shelf" solutions.

I'll cover the BDC and how to configure BDC applications in Chapter 13, "Using Business Forms and Business Intelligence." This overview is offered here because of how basic BDC is to business intelligence as a whole.

Using the Report Center

As you saw earlier, the Report Center is the central interface used to present all your business intelligence information and utilities. Although it comes with a number of sample features, it really won't do you any good until you configure it to display data that is real and relevant to your organization's business needs. You can participate in any number of activities to make the Report Center a highly useful feature in your SharePoint site collection.

Exercise 12.2 starts you off with adding the Report Center to a trusted file location. This is one of the first tasks you must perform, especially if you want to load and access Excel Services workbooks. You will be able to work with Excel Services workbooks only if they are housed in a location trusted by the system. This exercise will show you how to make the Report Center a trusted location in SharePoint.

You must choose from three locations when creating a trusted location: a file share, a SharePoint services location, and a web server address. Before beginning this exercise, determine which location you are going to use.

EXERCISE 12.2

Adding the Report Center to a Trusted File Location

1. Launch the Central Administration web application, and select the SSP for the site collection where you want to create the trusted file location, such as SharedServices1.

2. On the Shared Services Administration home page, under Excel Services Settings, click Trusted File Locations.

3. On the Excel Services Trusted File Locations page, click Add Trusted File Location.

4. On the Excel Services Add Trusted File Location page in the Location area, type the address or path to the trusted location in the Address field.

5. Under Location Type, select Windows SharePoint Services, UNC, or HTTP, depending on the type of location you want to make trusted.

6. Under Trust Children, tick the Children Trusted check box if you want the child libraries and directories under the location to also be trusted.

7. In the Description field, give the trusted location an optional description.

8. In the Session Management area under Session Timeout, input a value in seconds in the available field for the maximum amount of time you want an Excel Calculation Services session to remain open but inactive before it is shut down. (The default is 300, and –1 indicates no timeout.)

9. Under Short Session Timeout, input a value in seconds in the available field that an Excel Web Access session can remain open but inactive before any user intervention should occur or before shutdown. (The default value is 75, and –1 indicates the timeout is disabled.)

10. Under Maximum Request Duration, input a value in seconds in the available field that is the maximum time a single request in a session will occur. (The default value is 300, and –1 results in no duration limit.)

11. In the Workbook Properties area under Maximum Workbook Size, input a value in megabytes in the available field for the maximum size that a workbook can be opened by Excel Calculation Services. (The default value is 10.)

12. Under Maximum Chart Size, input a value in megabytes in the available field for the maximum size of a chart to be opened by Excel Calculation Services. (The default value is 1.)

13. In the Calculation Behavior area under Volatile Function Cache Lifetime, input a value in seconds in the available field for the maximum amount of time a computed value for a volatile function is cached for automatic recalculations. (The default value is 300, and –1 indicates that it is calculated on load.)

14. Under Workbook Calculation Mode, select either File, Manual, Automatic, or Automatic Except Data Tables for the calculation mode to be used by Excel Calculation Services workbooks. (All of the settings override the workbook settings except for File.)

15. In the External Data area under Allow External Data, select either None, Trusted Data Connection Libraries Only, or Trusted Data Connection Libraries and Embedded to determine the data connections from which you will allow information to be processed.

16. Under Warn on Refresh, tick the Refresh Warning Enabled check box if you want a warning displayed before refreshing data from an external location.

17. Under Stop When Refresh on Open Fails, tick the Stopping Open Enabled check box if you want to halt a file from being opened from the external location.

18. Under External Data Cache Lifetime, in the Automatic Refresh (Periodic/On open) and Manual Refresh fields, input a value in seconds for the maximum time that the system can use external data query results. (The default value is 300, and –1 never refreshes the data after the first query.)

19. Under Maximum Concurrent Queries Per Session, input a value in the available field for the maximum number of external data queries that can execute concurrently in a single session. (The default is 5.)

20. In the User-Defined Functions area under Allow User-Defined Functions, tick the User-Defined Functions Allowed check box if you want to allow user-defined functions to be called from workbooks in the trusted location.

21. Click OK when finished.

As you can see, the new trusted location (which in this case is a Windows SharePoint Services location) has been created just as you configured it and now appears on the Excel Services Trusted File Locations page.

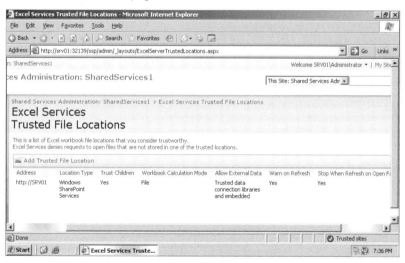

Under Excel Services Settings on the Shared Services Administration page, you can also edit the Excel Services settings you configured in Exercise 12.1 by clicking Edit Excel Services settings. You can also click Trusted Data Connection Libraries to open the Excel Services Trusted Data Connections Libraries page and then click Add Trusted Data Connection Library to add the address and a brief description of a trusted data connection library. The action is quite simple and won't require an exercise to describe it.

Adding a trusted data provider is a little more involved (though not as involved as Exercise 12.2). Exercise 12.3 will take you through the steps.

 Remember, a trusted data provider can be a source internal to SharePoint; external to SharePoint but internal to your local network, such as a database server; or even external to your local network.

EXERCISE 12.3

Adding a Trusted Data Provider

1. On the Shared Services Administration page under Excel Services Settings, click Trusted Data Providers.

2. On the Excel Services Trusted Data Providers page, click Add Trusted Data Provider. (Notice the number of trusted data providers present by default.)

3. On the Excel Services Add Trusted Data Provider page, in the Provider area under Provider ID, type the name of the new trusted data provider in the available field.

4. Under Provider Type, select either OLE DB, ODBC, or ODBC DSN, depending on the desired data provider type.

5. Under Description, type a brief description of the data provider in the available field.

6. Click OK when finished.

As you can see, the new trusted data provider is added to the list on the Excel Services Trusted Data Providers page.

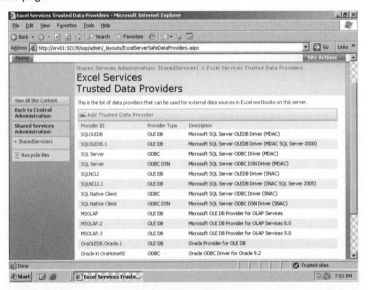

Using Excel Services in the Report Center

It becomes increasingly difficult to separate using the Report Center from accessing and using Excel Services, so the next exercise will show you how to access the sample Excel workbook file that was created when the Report Center was created. You can use this workbook file as the basis for any number of displays in the Report Center and modify the data to experiment with how displayed information is changed. Exercise 12.4 will demonstrate how to edit an Excel workbook in the Report Center's Reports library. For this exercise, you'll need to be on the Report Center's main page.

    You will need Excel 2007 installed on the computer you are going to use in order to perform Exercises 12.4 and 12.5.

EXERCISE 12.4

Editing an Excel Workbook in the Report Center

1. On the Report Center main page, click View All Site Content in Quick Launch.

2. On the All Site Content page, under Document Libraries, click Reports Library.

3. On the Reports Library page, click to the right of SampleWorkbook, and select Edit in Microsoft Office Excel.

4. When the warning dialog box appears, click OK.

5. When the sample workbook opens in Excel, go over the displayed cell range, and then locate and select cell S2.

6. Locate the formula displayed by selecting this cell, and change it to =ROUND(RAND)()*100,6).

7. Copy the formula to each cell in the column by clicking and dragging over all the cells in the column to select them.

8. Repeat the previous step for another column in the workbook, such as Column R.

9. On the Excel Ribbon, select the Data tab, and then click Refresh All.

10. After the values in the selected columns have refreshed, click the Filter and Control down arrow, and deselect Litware, Inc., to prevent this value from displaying.

11. In the Filter Opens dialog box, click OK, and then close the Excel workbook.

12. When you are prompted to save your changes, click Yes.

In the Reports library, if you click the name of the sample workbook, you'll see that the data with four decimal places has been modified based on the edits you completed in the exercise. You will also notice that the values for Litware, Inc., are absent as a result of you filtering that information, so it would not be displayed.

To undo the edits you performed in Exercise 12.4, click to the right of the sample workbook's name in the Reports library, and select Version History. On the Versions Saved for SampleWorkbook.xlsx page, click to the right of the previous version of this document (which should be version 0.1) in the Modified column, and select Restore. The original version of the document will be restored in the Reports library.

Of course, Excel workbook data displayed in the Report Center wouldn't be much good if it were all derived from the sample workbook, so you'll want to know how to publish additional Excel workbooks to the Reports library. Exercise 12.5 will show you how this is done.

 You will need to have a sample Excel 2007 workbook already created to complete Exercise 12.5.

EXERCISE 12.5

Publishing an Excel Workbook to the Reports Library

1. Open the workbook you plan to publish in SharePoint in the Excel 2007 application.

2. Click the Microsoft Office button in the upper left of the application, and select Publish ➤ Excel Services.

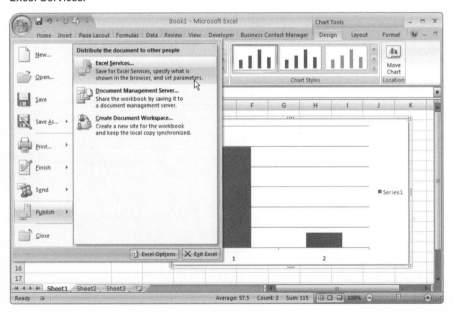

EXERCISE 12.5 *(continued)*

3. When the Save As dialog box appears, click Excel Services Options; on the Show tab, tick any of the available check boxes to make the desired options available in a Web Access web part.

4. Click the Parameters tab, click Add by any named ranges you want SharePoint users to be able to modify in the workbook once it is published, and then click OK.

5. In the Save As dialog box, browse to the Reports library in the Report Center, and then click Save.

 You can upload Excel workbooks to the Reports library just as you can upload any document to any library, but they must still be published before users can interact with the workbook data.

In the Reports library, you can click to the right of an Excel workbook and select the Snapshot in Excel option to view the workbook as a snapshot. A *snapshot* is a restricted view of an Excel workbook that allows a limited amount of information to be displayed on the local computer's desktop. SharePoint users with View Only permissions will see Excel data only in snapshot mode and will be able to view the cell data but not the formulas. This is a method of presenting to the end user only the information that they require while preserving the security of the underlying Excel workbook in the Reports library. Users you plan to restrict to viewing workbook data in a snapshot should be added to SharePoint with View Only permissions.

 See Chapter 5, "Managing Users and Groups," for more information about assigning View Only permissions to SharePoint users.

Using the Snapshot in Excel option, you can see what users with View Only permissions see when they access a workbook to verify that the correct data is being displayed to this group of users and that they do not have access to any data that is restricted to them. Table 12.1 illustrates what data is and isn't visible in a snapshot.

TABLE 12.1   Features Visible and Not Visible in an Excel Snapshot

Visible in a Snapshot	Not Visible in a Snapshot
Cell values	Conditional formatting
Formatting	Connections
Objects	Formulas

TABLE 12.1   Features Visible and Not Visible in an Excel Snapshot *(continued)*

Visible in a Snapshot	Not Visible in a Snapshot
Visible information	Hidden data
	Interactive features
	Private information
	Web-related features

Excel workbook information not only can be displayed in a limited fashion in a snapshot but also can be displayed and filtered in a web part. The Excel Web Access web part is specifically designed to provide filtered views of an Excel workbook on a web part page. In fact, you can display data from the same workbook in two or more web parts in order to present different aspects of that information to your audience.

Using an Excel Web Access web part, you can select specific workbook data and display it in a chart format so that your particular audience is presented with just the right type of information in the most useful way for their purposes. The web part can be added to the Report Center main page or to any web part page in SharePoint. Exercise 12.6 takes you through the necessary steps to accomplish this task. This exercise assumes you'll be using the Report Center.

 See Chapter 8, "Configuring Web Part Pages, Web Parts, and Web Pages," for information about how to add a web part to a web part page.

EXERCISE 12.6

Connecting an Excel Workbook to an Excel Web Access Web Part

1.   On the Report Center main page or any web part page, click Site Actions ➢ Edit Page.

2.   At the desired web part zone, click Add a Web Part.

3.   When the Add Web Parts page opens in a separate window, tick the Excel Web Access check box under Business Data (you may have to expand the All Web Parts list to see this web part), and click Add.

4.   Click the arrow on the Edit button in the Excel Web Access web part title bar, and select Modify Shared Web Part.

5.   In the Excel Web Access web part toolbox, under Workbook Display, click the button to the right of the Workbook field to open the file selection box.

EXERCISE 12.6 *(continued)*

6. On the Select a Link page that opens in a separate window, click Reports Library.

7. When the Reports library selections appear in the Select a Link page, select SampleWork-book, and click OK.

8. In the Excel Web Access toolbox under Toolbar and Title Bar, use the Type of Toolbar drop-down arrow, and select None.

9. Under Toolbar Menu Commands, deselect the four available check boxes.

10. Click Apply, and then click OK.

11. On the Report Center page, click Publish to publish your changes to the site.

 Remember, if the Reports library of the Report Center is not a trusted data source, you will get an error message stating that secure, encrypted communication is required by Excel Services and that the current request does not meet this requirement.

Now that you have the web part connected to the workbook, you can specify the named item or specific information from the workbook so that only that information will be displayed in the web part. A named item can be any of the following:

- A chart
- An Excel table
- A named range
- A PivotTable report

Exercise 12.7 will show you how to select a named item from an Excel Web Access web part and display only the data from the named item in the web part. Use the same web part you added to the web part page in Exercise 12.6.

EXERCISE 12.7

Displaying Named Item Data in an Excel Web Access Web Part

1. On the Report Center main page or any web part page, click Site Actions ➤ Edit Page.

2. Click the arrow on the Edit button in the Excel Web Access web part title bar, select Connections ➤ Get Named Item From, and then select the desired list.

3. When the Configure Connection web page dialog box appears, use the Field Name drop-down menu to select the desired named item, and then click Finish.

EXERCISE 12.7 *(continued)*

4. On the Report Center main page, click Publish to publish your changes to the site.

You will notice that only data from the selected named item is displayed in the Excel Web Access web part. You may have also noticed that in step 2, you could have selected Get Workbook URL From to create a connection between the web part and an Excel workbook. This is an alternative to the steps you took in Exercise 12.6.

Using Business Indicators in the Report Center

The term *business indicators* is a more or less generic way to describe the various methods of presenting corporate performance-related information in SharePoint. This could apply to the methods of displaying data in Excel Services you've already learned about, but it also applies to KPIs and dashboards, which are the two primary subjects of this section of the chapter.

The various types of information display components used by business intelligence including business indicators are web-based and very visually oriented methods of presenting data to your audience in SharePoint. Just about any process related to a business goal can be shown using one or more of the BI indicators. The first one you'll have a look at in this section is the KPI list.

A KPI is really just another SharePoint list that is designed to present information in a particular way. You can configure a KPI to pull data from various sources, including the following:

- Excel workbook
- Manually configured data
- SharePoint lists
- SQL Server Analysis Services 2005

As you can see from the first item in this bullet list, Excel Services has not been left behind in this chapter's previous section but is still with us as a data source. To become more familiar with KPIs, Exercise 12.8 will show you how to modify the data contained in the sample KPI that was created when the Report Center was created. You'll start this exercise on the Report Center main page.

EXERCISE 12.8

Modifying a KPI Using Excel Workbook Data

1. On the Report Center main page, click View All Site Content in Quick Launch.

2. On the All Site Content page under Lists, click Sample KPIs.

3. On the Sample KPIs page, click the down arrow to the right of New, and select Indicator Using Data in Excel Workbook.

4. On the Sample KPIs: New Item page, under Name and Description, type a unique name for the new item in the Name field and an optional description in the Description field.

5. Under Comments, type any helpful comments you want to add to the item in the Comments field.

6. Under Indicator Value in the Workbook URL field, either type the URL to the required workbook or click the Browse button and then double-click the name of the workbook to select it.

7. In the Cell Address for Indicator Value field, click the Select button to choose an Excel cell address for the workbook you previously selected.

8. Under Status Icon, use the Status Icon Rules drop-down menu to select Better Values Are and then either Higher or Lower.

9. Use the "select" button next to the green status icon When Has Met or Exceeded Goal option to determine the value that will indicate this state.

10. Use the "select" button next to the yellow status icon When Has Met or Exceeded Warning option to determine the value that will indicate this state.

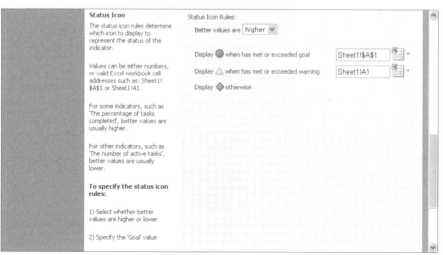

11. Click OK when finished.

Although not absolutely necessary, you can further modify the KPI by expanding the Details Link and Update Rules sections of the Sample KPIs: New Item page. In the Details Link section you can use the Browse button to browse to the URL or UNC of a web page that contains specific information about the KPI. If you do not use this option, the default details page will be used to display details data in the KPI web part. Under Update Rules, you can select either Recalculate the Indicator Value for Every Viewer (the default value) or Manually Update the Value of This Indicator with the Update Values Link on the Status Indicator or on the Status Indicator List Web Part.

To create a KPI list using SharePoint data, you must already have a SharePoint list created and configured with the columns and information you want displayed in the KPI. This requires some planning, so if you want to perform this task, you'll need to create a SharePoint list as a data source, including adding the required column names and column types to contain the necessary properties.

 See Chapter 7, "Configuring and Maintaining Lists and Libraries," for more information about how to create a list in SharePoint.

Rather than modifying the existing sample KPI, Exercise 12.9 will show you how to create a new KPI and display data from your custom-made SharePoint list.

EXERCISE 12.9

Displaying SharePoint List Data in a KPI

1. On the Report Center main page, click View All Site Content in Quick Launch.

2. On the All Site Content page, click Create.

3. On the Create page under Custom Lists, click KPI List.

4. On the New page, under Name and Description, enter the name of the new KPI in the Name field and an optional description in the Description field.

5. Under Navigation, for Display This List on the Quick Launch, select either Yes or No, and click Create.

6. On the new KPI page, click the arrow to the right of New, and select Indicator Using Data in SharePoint List.

7. On the KPI: New Item page, populate the Name, Description, and Comments fields as you did in Exercise 12.8.

8. Under Indicator Value, you can use the Browse button next to the List URL field to browse to the SharePoint list that you will use to supply data to the KPI and then use the drop-down menu for the View field to select the view of the list that displays the number of active issues for the KPI.

9. Rather than selecting the View menu, under Value Calculation, you can select Number of List Items in the View, Percentage of List Items in the View Where, or Calculation Using All List Items in the View.

10. Under To Specify the Indicator Value, use the drop-down arrows and available fields to filter the properties columns necessary to create the desired data presentation.

11. Under Status Icon, configure the available options in the same way you did in the previous exercise, and then click OK.

Although this exercise is substantially similar to Exercise 12.8, there are some significant differences, including a variety of options on how to filter the data, not only based on the view of the selected list but also on typical list filter options. Not only can the information be filtered in the source list, but it can further be filtered in the KPI list.

Up to this point, you've seen how individual web parts or other single elements related to BI have been used to display information. When several of these elements are combined to present data to a specific audience, it's called a *dashboard*. You'll recall the analogy used earlier in this chapter of a car's dashboard. A dashboard in SharePoint is the same thing; it presents information in separate but related ways to produce an overall effect.

You can combine several different web parts, such as an Excel Web Access web part, a Related Links web part, and a KPI web part, or you can combine two or more of the same web part type, such as several KPI web parts, each presenting data differently.

Exercise 12.10 will walk you through the steps of creating a new dashboard using a variety of web parts to display a unified presentation of information. To begin this exercise, you will need to be on the Report Center's main page.

Creating a New Dashboard

1. On the Report Center main page, click Dashboards in Quick Launch.

2. On the Reports Library page, click New ➤ Dashboard Page.

3. On the New Dashboard page under Page Name, create a file name for the dashboard in the File Name field, create a title for the dashboard in the Page Title field, and type an optional description for the dashboard in the Description field.

4. Under Location, use the Document Library drop-down menu to select a location in which to place the dashboard, such as the Reports library.

5. Use the Folder drop-down menu to choose a file folder for the dashboard, such as Top Level Folder.

6.   Under Create Link in Current Navigation bar beneath the Add a Link to Current Navigation Bar? text, click either No or Yes, Use Navigation Heading.

7.   If you chose Yes, Use Navigation Heading, use the drop-down menu to choose a heading such as Dashboards, Reports, or Resources; otherwise, this option is not available.

8.   Under Dashboard Layout, use the Layout menu to select the structure of the dashboard (one, two, or three columns).

9.   Under Key Performance Indicators, select Create a KPI List for Me Automatically, Allow Me to Select an Existing KPI List Later, or Do Not Add a KPI List to This Dashboard. (This exercise will use the first option.)

10.   Click OK.

11.   When you are taken to the new Dashboard page, shown here, click the down arrow to the right of one of the Excel Web Access web parts, and click Modify Shared Web Part.

12.   When the web part's toolbox appears to the right, either connect it to a workbook as you did in Exercise 12.6 or display named item data in the web part as in Exercise 12.7.

13.   Access the other Excel Web Access web part, and repeat the previous step, this time choosing the configuration option you did not choose in the prior step.

14.   Under Key Performance Indicators, click the down arrow to the right of New, and select an option from the menu, such as Indicator Using Data in SharePoint List or Indicator Using Data in Excel Workbook, as illustrated in Exercises 12.8 and 12.9.

15. Click the down arrow to the right of Related Information (also known as Related Links), and click New Link.

16. When the New Link Web Page dialog box appears, use the available tools shown here to create a new link to a web page in SharePoint.

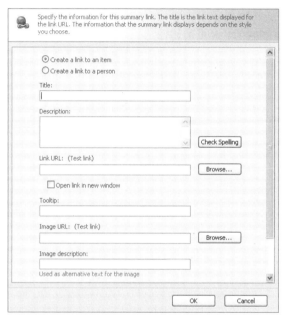

17. Repeat the previous step several times to create a number of links.

18. Click New Group. When the New Group Web Page dialog box appears, give the new group of links a name in the Group Header Name field, and then click OK.

19. Repeat the previous step one or two more times so that you have a few groups under which to organize your links.

20. When you are done, click Publish.

As you can see by building this dashboard, a wide variety of methods and options are available to you. A BI dashboard page can offer an almost limitless variety of methods of presenting and organizing data. With that in mind, you might want to keep the number of elements down to four or five to avoid creating too confusing a display. You can go back and edit your dashboard, close some of the web parts and replace them with others, or open the toolboxes for the web parts and change their properties to see how this changes the dashboard.

Summary

In this chapter, you learned about the general components that make up SharePoint's business intelligence solution, both as a concept and as site and web page elements, including the following:

- The general features of business intelligence, such as dashboards, Excel Services, and key performance indicators
- The role the Report Center plays in business intelligence as the central framework for all the other business intelligence elements
- How Excel Services is used in business intelligence
- A general overview of the business data catalog
- How to assemble various business intelligence elements such as dashboards and KPIs

Exam Essentials

Know the elements of business intelligence.   Learn the various component parts that together make up the SharePoint business intelligence solution, including dashboards, Excel Services, external data sources, filter web parts, key performance indicators, and the Report Center. Understand how each of these elements operates both individually and in concert with the others to provide an overall data presentation.

Understand the role of the Report Center.   Know the individual elements in the Report Center site and how they work together to provide a framework for the overall business intelligence offered by SharePoint. Understand how additional features are added, such as various web parts to make up a dashboard.

Learn the importance of Excel Services in business intelligence.   Understand the workings of Excel Calculation Services, Excel Web Access, and Excel Web Services and how each is used in storing, managing, and presenting data.

Review Questions

1. You are the SharePoint administrator for your organization. You are currently giving an in-service training to new hires in the company on the uses of SharePoint business intelligence (BI) features. You are currently going over the basic elements involved in BI. Of the following options, which are basic BI components? (Choose all that apply.)

   A. Dashboards

   B. Excel Services

   C. Filter web parts

   D. The Reports library

2. You are the SharePoint administrator for your organization. You are accessing the Report Center from your corporation's main portal site for the first time and notice that some sample elements are present, letting you see how they present data. Of the following options, which feature sample data? (Choose all that apply.)

   A. A sample KPI

   B. A sample data connection

   C. A sample workbook

   D. A sample dashboard

3. You are the SharePoint administrator for your company. You are adding a trusted file location in Central Administration so that data contained at that location can be accessed and displayed in various web parts on the corporation's Report Center site. The site you are adding contains several subsites you also want to be trusted. What action do you have to take on the Excel Services Add Trusted File Location page to make sure the site and any child sites are trusted?

   A. Under Trust Subsites, select the Trust All Subsites of This Location radio button.

   B. Under Trust Children, select the Trust All Children of This Location radio button.

   C. Under Trust Children, tick the Children Trusted check box.

   D. Under Trust Subsites, tick the Subsites Trusted check box.

4. You are the SharePoint administrator for your company. You want to deploy the business data catalog services in SharePoint in order to allow users access to information from back-end applications within the site collection. You need to recruit some subject-matter experts to assist you in developing this resource. One of the roles you need to fill requires that the person be familiar with the specifics of the APIs and structure of the applications to be used in the BDC services as well as being familiar with XML data file structures and database development. Of the roles being presented, which one is the most appropriate?

   A. Administrator

   B. Application definition author

   C. Business analyst

   D. Developer

5. You are the SharePoint administrator for your organization, and you've been tasked with adding a database server as a trusted data provider for SharePoint's BI users. The database server is part of the company's infrastructure but not specifically part of SharePoint. When adding the database server, under provider type, what options are available? (Choose all that apply.)

    A. DB2

    B. OLE DB

    C. ODBC

    D. ODBC DSN

6. You want to present information from an Excel workbook regarding year-end sales data to the general employee base, but you want to restrict what information can be seen. You have added general employees to the View Only group and will present the relevant workbook as an Excel snapshot. That way, information such as cell values and formatting will be visible, but restricted data will not. Of the following options, what types of information are not visible in a snapshot to members of the View Only group? (Choose all that apply.)

    A. Objects

    B. Connections

    C. Formulas

    D. Web-related features

7. You are building a KPI in the Report Center to track the progress of the development of the next release of your company's most popular product. The CEO is concerned that the release will be late, giving your competitor's product line the edge. Of the following options, which represent valid information sources you can use to build the KPI? (Choose all that apply.)

    A. Excel workbook

    B. SharePoint libraries

    C. SharePoint lists

    D. Manually configured data

8. You are the SharePoint administrator for your company. You are in the process of editing a dashboard so that an Excel Web Access web part will be connected with an Excel workbook in the Reports library. You have the web part's toolbox open. What do you have to do next to continue with the process?

    A. In the toolbox under Workbooks, use the drop-down menu, and select Reports Library to open the location containing the workbook.

    B. In the toolbox under Workbook Display, tick the Reports Library check box, and then type the URL to the workbook in the available field.

    C. In the toolbox under Workbooks, click the Reports Library link, and when the Reports library opens in a separate window, select the desired workbook.

    D. In the toolbox under Workbook Display, click the button to the right of the Workbook field to open the selection box in a separate window, click Reports Library, and then select the desired workbook.

9. You are the SharePoint administrator for your organization, and you are currently modifying a KPI used by the marketing department to monitor customer responses to their latest promotional campaign. You are currently selecting an indicator value and need to identify the location of the required Excel workbook. Of the following options, which describe valid methods of selecting the necessary workbook? (Choose all that apply.)

A. Type the URL of the workbook in the Workbook URL field.

B. Type the workbook's name in the Search field, and click Search.

C. Use the Indicator Value drop-down menu, and select the location containing the workbook.

D. Click the Browse button, and browse to the workbook's location.

10. You are the SharePoint administrator for your organization. You are in the process of adding a trusted file location. When making this selection, only certain options are available to you when creating the location. Of the following selections, which are valid types of locations? (Choose all that apply.)

A. A file share

B. A network place

C. A SharePoint Services location

D. A web server address

11. You are the SharePoint administrator for your company. You are planning to deploy and use business data catalog services in SharePoint and are doing some research on how this service operates. You discover that you can allow users to access a wide variety of information sources using the BDC. Of the following selections, which represent valid data sources for the BDC? (Choose all that apply.)

A. Active Directory

B. LDAP directories

C. External databases

D. SharePoint libraries

12. You are the new SharePoint administrator for your organization. You have been tasked with configuring Excel Services on the server farm by the CTO so SharePoint's business intelligence solution can be made available for corporate use. You investigate and discover that Excel Services is not available. Of the following options, which are the most likely causes? (Choose all that apply.)

A. The latest version of ASP.NET has not been implemented in the SharePoint deployment.

B. The organization is running Windows SharePoint Services 3.0, which does not include Excel Services.

C. The organization is running SharePoint Server 2007 Standard Edition, which does not include Excel Services.

D. The organization is using Microsoft Office 2003, which cannot make use of Excel Services.

13. You are the SharePoint administrator for a private, nonprofit charitable organization. You are currently setting up a KPI to monitor the progress of fundraising efforts by the regional office. You are using a SharePoint list as the data source and plan to filter the incoming data in order to show the desired results. In setting up data filtering, what options do you have? (Choose all that apply.)

A. You can set up data filtering in the original list.

B. You can set up data filtering in the KPI.

C. You can set up data filtering in the Report Center.

D. You can set up data filtering in Central Administration.

14. You are a SharePoint administrator, and you are currently building a dashboard to provide BI-related data to your company's management team. In creating a dashboard, which of the following statements is most true? (Choose all that apply.)

A. You can create a dashboard using several different KPI web parts.

B. You can create a dashboard using different web parts such as a KPI web part, an Excel Web Access web part, and a Related Links web part.

C. Dashboard creation is limited to only the web parts available when the initial dashboard is created.

D. Dashboard creation is limited to only two of the same type of web part, such as two Excel Web Access web parts, two KPI web parts, and so on.

15. You are the SharePoint administrator for your company, and you are planning to deploy SharePoint's business intelligence solution in your organization as requested by the management team. You are reviewing the procedure for adding trusted data provider and SharePoint and have opened the Excel Services Trusted Data Providers page. This is the first time this page has been accessed since the initial deployment of SharePoint. What do you find when this page opens?

A. The page is populated with numerous instances of trusted data providers such as SQLOLEBD, SQL Server, SQL Native Client, and so on.

B. The page is populated with single instances of trusted data providers such as SQLOLEDB, SQL Server, SQL Native Client, and so on.

C. The page is populated with only the database providers that were initially set up during the SharePoint installation and deployment, which most commonly is a single instance of SQL Server.

D. This page is not populated, and you must manually add each instance of a trusted data provider by clicking Add Trusted Data Provider.

16. You are the SharePoint administrator for your organization, and you are in the process of adding a trusted file location in SharePoint. To do so, you open Central Administration. Where must you go in CA to begin creating the trusted file location?

A. Click the Operations tab, and under Excel Services Settings, click Trusted File Locations.

B. Click the Application Management tab, and under Excel Services Settings, click Trusted File Locations.

C. Click Shared Services Administration, and under Excel Services Settings, click Trusted File Locations.

D. Click the name of the relevant SSP such as SharedServices1, and under Excel Services Settings, click Trusted File Locations.

17. You have just joined the staff of the SharePoint team for your company and are familiarizing yourself with how SharePoint has been deployed. Currently, you are reviewing Excel Services as it's related to how business intelligence is being used, and you are refreshing your knowledge of Excel Services basics. You are particularly interested in the Excel Services component that is designed to be used by developers as the basis for building customized web applications based on the Excel workbook format. Of the following, which Excel Services component fits that description?

A. Excel Calculation Services

B. Excel Web Access

C. Excel Web Services

D. Excel Presentation Services

18. You are the SharePoint administrator for your organization and are in the process of adding an Excel Web Access web part to the Engineering department's portal site so that workbook data containing systems report data can be displayed for the development team's use. You select the desired Excel workbook located in the portal site's document library and click OK, and then you click Apply, OK, and finally Publish to save your changes. Instead of seeing the desired display in the web part, you see an error message stating that secure, encrypted communication is required by Excel Services and the current request does not meet this requirement. What went wrong?

A. You did not use an account with administrator rights to create the connection between the web part and the workbook.

B. The library that contains the workbook is not a trusted data source.

C. You did not encrypt the Excel workbook before you attempted to link it to the web part.

D. You can use Excel Services to connect a web part to a workbook only in the Report Center.

19. You are the SharePoint administrator for your company, and you have just finished performing all the required steps to create a KPI for the QA department. You are reviewing some of the optional settings on the KPI to see whether any of them would enhance the presentation of data. Of the following options, which are valid ways to further modify this web part? (Choose all that apply.)

A. You can expand the Details link section of the KPI.

B. You can use the Browse button to browse to the URL or UNC of a web page that contains information relevant to the KPI.

C. You can expand the Modify Rules section of the KPI.

D. You can select the Recalculate the Indicator Value for Every Viewer option.

20. You are the SharePoint administrator for your company, and you are briefing the management team on the different elements that go into SharePoint's business intelligence solution. You explain that the Report Center is the central structure within which you build BI. Although most of the components can be displayed in other sites, which BI element is really a feature of the Report Center?

A. Dashboards

B. Excel Services

C. Filter web parts

D. Key performance indicators

Answers to Review Questions

1. A, B, and C. The Reports library is only part of one of the main BI features, the Report Center. All of the other answers are correct.

2. A, C, and D. There are no precreated data connections. You must create all the data connections for the Report Center. The Report Center does contain a sample KPI, Excel workbook, and dashboard.

3. C. Answer C is the correct description of how to accomplish this task. The other answers are bogus.

4. B. The role in option B most closely fits the description offered in the question. An administrator is responsible for importing application definition files, a business analyst provides expertise on the inner workings of a corporation's information systems scheme, and a developer creates any customized applications and works with the application definition author.

5. B, C, and D. Option A is an IBM database server type but not a selection available when configuring a trusted data provider. All the other options are valid options.

6. B, C, and D. Objects and visible information can be seen by members of the View Only group in a snapshot. Conditional formatting, connections, formulas, hidden data, interactive features, and web-related features cannot be viewed.

7. A, C, and D. Although SharePoint libraries can't be used as direct information sources for a KPI, you can use SharePoint lists, Excel workbooks, manually configured data, and SQL Server Analysis Services 2005.

8. D. Answer D is the only correct description of how to accomplish the task. The other answers are bogus.

9. A and D. You can use the options described in either option A or D to locate the workbook. Options B and C are incorrect.

10. A, C, and D. Options A, C, and D are the only three valid location types you can use when creating a trusted location. Option B is incorrect.

11. A, C, and D. Option B is a bogus answer. All of the other options are valid data sources that can be accessed by the BDC.

12. B and C. ASP.NET deployment is not related to Excel Services availability, and even if all the company's computers are running Office 2003, that does not affect whether Excel Services is available in SharePoint. Excel Services is available only if MOSS 2007 Enterprise Edition has been installed on the server farm, and so it wouldn't be available with Windows SharePoint Services 3.0 or MOSS 2007 Standard Edition.

13. A and B. You can filter data in any SharePoint list, but you can also create data filters while configuring a KPI. Options C and D are incorrect.

14. A and B. You can create a dashboard using any combination of relevant web parts or even several different instances of the same web part filtering data in different ways. There is no limitation to web part use as suggested in options C and D.

15. A. By default, even if you've added no data providers manually, a collection of data providers is already in place on this page. Options B, C, and D are all incorrect.

16. D. Only option D describes the correct procedure. All the other answers are bogus.

17. C. Excel Calculation Services is the engine that drives Excel Services, and Excel Web Access is the web part–specific component. Excel Presentation Services is bogus.

18. B. The portal site's document library needed to be made a trusted data source prior to attempting to connect the web part to the workbook. If you were able to access the workbook, your account has sufficient rights to create the connection between the web part and the workbook. You do not have to manually encrypt the workbook prior to making the connection, and you are able to connect an Excel Web Access to a workbook in any site in the site collection, not just the Report Center.

19. A, B, and D. There is no Modify Rules section, but instead you can expand the Update Rules section in the KPI web part's toolbox. All the other options are valid.

20. A. Although you can incorporate the other elements of business intelligence in just about any site, dashboards are created and displayed within the Report Center.

Chapter

13

Using Business Forms and Business Intelligence

MICROSOFT EXAM OBJECTIVES COVERED IN THIS CHAPTER:

✓ **Managing Business Intelligence**

  ▪ Configure Business Data Catalog

✓ **Configure Business Forms**

  ▪ Configure Forms Server

  ▪ Manage Data Connection Files

  ▪ Configure Web Service Proxy

  ▪ Manage Form Templates

This chapter picks up where Chapter 12, "Using Excel Services and Business Intelligence," leaves off, so if you haven't read Chapter 12 yet, do so now. Although it's not absolutely imperative for you to have mastered the Chapter 12 material before reading this chapter, several key business intelligence (BI) concepts are introduced there that will directly impact the content of this chapter, and understanding those concepts will better prepare you for mastering what you are about to read here.

This chapter has only two main points of focus; however, they are very important points relative to business intelligence and the 70-630 exam: the business data catalog (BDC) and Forms Services.

You were briefly introduced to the BDC in Chapter 12 just to whet your appetite. In this chapter, you will study the BDC in detail, including the ability of the BDC to access and present information from a wide variety of internal and external data sources without the necessity of writing customized applications. You'll learn how to create a BDC application, how to import an application definition file, how to configure application permissions, and how to do other activities vital to the management of the BDC.

The other central subject of this chapter is managing Forms Services, and particularly how SharePoint interoperates with InfoPath 2007. You'll get an introduction to Forms Services in general and Microsoft's InfoPath services in particular, including how InfoPath works and plays with SharePoint. Topics will include configuring a forms server, creating InfoPath forms, configuring external data sources for forms, and managing business form templates.

As with other chapters, this chapter will finish with a series of exercises allowing you to continue practicing your BI-related skills using the concepts and tools presented in this chapter.

Understanding the Business Data Catalog (BDC)

The business data catalog truly lets the world come to you right inside the SharePoint interface or, more accurately, lets the world's information come to you. As you read in Chapter 12, "Using Excel Services and Business Intelligence," the BDC is a new shared service in SharePoint that allows users to access information from back-end applications within the site collection using the typical SharePoint components. The BDC is not a storage method but rather a cataloging method that keeps track of and allows real-time access to dissimilar data sources as well as defining SharePoint-relevant business applications. Source types can include traditional SharePoint data stores such as libraries and lists as well as external data sources such as Oracle, SAP, and Siebel.

Before the BDC, if you wanted to accomplish all this, you had to write customized web parts that could capture data from these types of sources and display that data in the Share-Point web part. Developers had to learn the APIs for each type of data source, so it wasn't just a matter of using one "off-the-shelf" customization to access them all. This was a tremendously time-consuming activity, and there had to be a significant need for your users to have this data within the SharePoint interface to justify the cost in resources required.

The BDC is now available, but only as part of MOSS 2007 Enterprise Edition. (You Standard Edition people out there are out of luck.) The BDC overcomes the challenges previously placed in the overworked hands of your SharePoint developers by creating XML *application definition files* that provide standard definitions for each information source. Once created, these definition files can be imported into the BDC and access a wide variety of unrelated data sources.

BDC Shared Services can be accessed in Central Administration (where else?), and it includes the following functions:

- Importing the application definition
- Viewing applications
- Viewing entities
- Setting BDC permissions
- Editing the Profile Page template

Writing application definition files is the single most labor-intensive part of providing BDC services. Although the 70-630 exam expects you to know how to configure the various aspects of the BDC within SharePoint, writing individual application definition files is beyond the scope of the exam and thus this book. To learn more about this particular aspect of developing for the BDC, go to the MOSS 2007 software developer kit (SDK) for the BDC at the following URL: `http://msdn2.microsoft.com/en-us/library/ms5444518.aspx`.

As I'm sure you're well aware, the Internet doesn't always keep information in the same place forever. If the previously referenced URL is no longer valid by the time you read this page, go to `http://msdn2.microsoft.com` and search for *integrating enterprise applications*.

To access the BDC settings, go to Central Administration (logged on as an administrator). In Quick Launch, click the relevant SSP, such as SharedServices1, and on the SSP's home page under Business Data Catalog, you will find the links relative to managing the BDC. This is where your BDC configuration activities will take place, including importing a sample application definition file.

The BDC depends on the Office SharePoint Server enterprise site features being activated, which they should be by default. If you believe otherwise or just want to check and make sure, from the portal site, click Site Actions ➤ Site Settings ➤ Modify All Site Settings. On the Site Settings page under Site Administration, click Site Features. On the Site Features page, if the Office SharePoint Server Enterprise Site Features option shows that it is deactivated, click the Activate button. Once the page refreshes, these features will be available.

Configuring a Business Data Catalog Application

Configuring a BDC application involves a number of steps, not the least of which is importing an application definition file. You also need to understand what an *entity* is, assign a user to an application, control entity permissions, and connect a BDC application to a SharePoint web part. The following sections of the book will mix concept and practice as you first gain an understanding of a particular aspect of the BDC and then learn the actions required to configure that aspect.

Importing an Application Definition File into SharePoint

Since you are not required to actually write an application definition file for the following exercises, finding a way to import such a file will require a bit of sleight of hand. You can approach this in one of two ways—you can go through the motions of the import process without really importing anything, or you can create a sample application definition file and import it.

To create a sample application definition file, you don't have to actually write it. Microsoft has done that for you with the AdventureWorks SQL Server 2000 sample site at `http://msdn2.microsoft.com/en-us/library/ms519241.aspx`. Microsoft has provided instructions for everything you'll need to do to create an external database and configure the BDC to be able to access it. I have not written a set of exercises to utilize these resources; however, they are available if you choose to take advantage of them.

One of the resources we will be taking advantage of in this chapter is the sample application definition file found at the following URL: `http://msdn2.microsoft.com/en-us/library/ms497572.aspx`. Simply copy the text of the file, paste it into a text editor such as Notepad on your computer, and save it in XML format. This will be your sample definition file that you'll use when you import an application definition file into SharePoint. Exercise 13.1 will start you off using the BDC, showing you the steps for importing an application definition file. To begin this task, you must be on the SSP home page as described before the "Configuring a Business Data Catalog Application" section.

EXERCISE 13.1

Importing a Sample Application Definition File

1. On the SSP home page under Business Data Catalog, click Import Application Definition.

2. On the Import Application Definition page, click the Browse button next to the Application Definition File field, and browse to the location where you saved your sample application definition file. Then select the file.

3. Under File Type, select either Model or Resource to define the type of application file you are importing.

4. Under Resources to Import, you can tick the Localized Names, Properties, and Permissions check boxes depending on the type of resources you want to import. (All three are ticked by default.)

5. When you are finished, click Import.

6. It will take a few moments for the file to be imported. Then you will be taken to the Application Definition Import Successful page. Click OK. The View Application: AdventureWorksSample page will appear, as shown here.

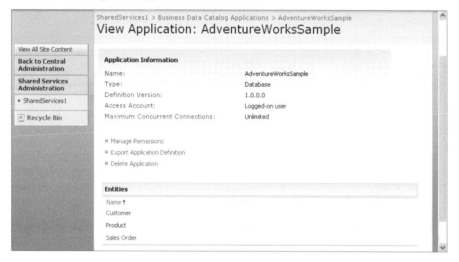

SharedServices1 > Business Data Catalog Applications > AdventureWorksSample

View Application: AdventureWorksSample

View All Site Content
Back to Central Administration
Shared Services Administration
• SharedServices1
Recycle Bin

Application Information

Name:	AdventureWorksSample
Type:	Database
Definition Version:	1.0.0.0
Access Account:	Logged-on user
Maximum Concurrent Connections:	Unlimited

□ Manage Permissions
□ Export Application Definition
□ Delete Application

Entities

Name ↑
Customer
Product
Sales Order

If you don't copy the contents of the sample file from the referenced web page exactly so that it is fully validated XML, you will receive an error message stating that the application definition cannot be imported and referencing the section and line where the error has occurred.

Defining Entities

On the View Application: AdventureWorksSample page you'll notice a box called Entities. Under Name, you'll see three entities: Customer, Product, and Sales Order. An *entity* is the main component of an application definition file and is a business data item that represents some aspect of a company's method of operations. It's easy to see how information about customers, products, and sales orders can fit into this definition.

On the View Applications page under Entities, click to the right of the name of an entity to open the menu, and then click View Entity. Figure 13.1 shows some of the components of the Sales Order entity such as Fields (of Default View) and Relationships. Other components include Actions and Filters (of Finder Method). An application designed to track information regarding a product, sales figures, and customer base would use the data contained in each entity to provide data from the data source being described to SharePoint. Different entities in a definition file can be related. As you can see in this example, the relationships are of the Sales Order entity, which defines how it is related to the Customer entity.

FIGURE 13.1 View Entity: Sales Order page

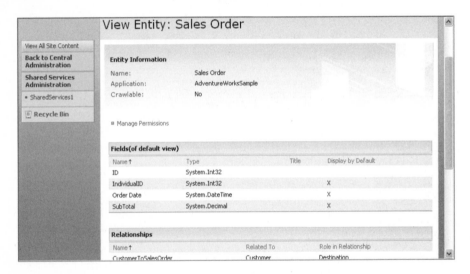

You can also scroll down the page and, under Actions, click the default action for an entity called View Profile. To add an action, in the same section, click Add Action. On the Add Action page, type a name for the new action in the Action Name field, and in the Navigate to the URL field, type the URL to where you want to visit when you click the action's link. To assign a property to a parameter in the URL, click Add Parameter, and then use the Parameter Property drop-down menu to select a property such as SalesOrderID. You can click the Remove button to remove a property as well. If you want to add an icon to represent the new action, click Standard Icon and use the drop-down menu to select an icon, or click The Image at This URL and type the URL to the image you want to use as an icon. Then click OK.

You create and use an action to dynamically parse the URL you added on the Add Action page so that SharePoint users can navigate from a web page in SharePoint to another web location such as a web page in a SAP application. For example, an action defined on a BDC sales order entity can be written to redirect SharePoint users to a web page in a SAP application that supports updates to sales order data. For this to be effective, you will need to add an Actions element to the XML application definition file defining the desired action.

Back on the View Entity page (and in this case, the View Entity: Sales Order page), you can manage user permissions to the Sales Order entity of the application definition file by clicking Manage Permissions. On the Manage Permissions: Sales Order page, in the User/Group Name column, the user who created the definition (in this case SRV01\Administrator) is the only one present. You can add, remove, or modify permissions by clicking one of the following:

Add User/Groups   Click this button to give access to this entity to a user or group.

Remove Selected Users   Tick the check box next to the name of a user or group in the User/Group Name column to remove them from the list.

Modify Permissions of Selected Users   Tick the check box next to the name of a user or group in the User/Group Name column, and click this button to edit their permissions. When done, click Save to finish.

Copy All Permissions to Descendants   Copy all the permissions you created or modified to any descendant entities.

When you choose to modify permissions, you can tick or clear the following check boxes on the Modify Permissions: Sales Order page:

- Edit
- Execute
- Select in Clients
- Set Permissions

You can also add a user or group to an application from the Shared Services Administration: SharedServices1 home page under Business Data Catalog. Click View Applications, and on the Business Data Catalog Applications page, click to the right of the name of the application (AdventureWorksSample in this case). Then select Manage Permissions from the menu. Then click Add User/Groups as described previously.

 Real World Scenario

Importing an Application Definition File for the BDC

You are the SharePoint administrator for your company, and you have configured BDC services for your organization's site collection. Brad, the head of the sales department, wants his staff to be able to access sales order information on a database server of a partner company to display sales order and customer information collected in its database on his department's portal site. You contact Brenda, the database administrator for the partner company, and get the required access including the location of the necessary application definition file you'll need to import. Brenda places the file on her FTP server, and you access and download the file onto your local computer. You open a web browser, launch the Central Administration web application, and then navigate to the required SSP home page.

> Under Business Data Catalog, you click Import Application Definition, and on the Import Application Definition page, you click the Browse button and browse to the location on your local drive where you saved the application definition file. Then you select the file. Under File Type, you select Resource. Under Resources to Import, you tick the required check boxes for Localized Names, Properties, and Permissions and then click Import. You have to wait a few moments while the file is imported; when the process is complete, you are taken to the Application Definition Import Successful page. You click OK to complete the process.

Accessing Business Data in SharePoint

The application definition files you import into SharePoint are used by the BDC to define how the BDC is to access the back-end data source and what queries to execute in order to return information from that source. None of the actual data from the external data source (such as our sample SAP application) is ever imported or transferred into SharePoint in any form. The BDC provides the method of accessing the external data at the external data source and displaying that data inside the SharePoint interface, but at no time does any of that data migrate into SharePoint.

The BDC does act as a conduit of sorts, providing that information to a number of SharePoint standard and custom interfaces including the following:

- Business Data web parts
- SharePoint lists
- SharePoint Search
- User Profile Importer
- Other custom-made solutions

Using Business Data Web Parts

A number of web parts are available in SharePoint by default and are immediately available for use in displaying data provided by BDC services:

- Business Data Actions
- Business Data Items
- Business Data Item Builder
- Business Data List
- Business Data Related List

The full list of Business Data web parts also includes the Excel Web Access, IView, and WSRP Consumer web parts, but the first five are the only ones that are directly related to the BDC.

The next several exercises will show you how to add and modify different Business Data web parts in SharePoint. Exercise 13.2 starts you off with adding a Business Data List web part to a web part page. You can use any web part page for this exercise. For this example, I'll be using the Projects site I created for Chapter 7, "Configuring and Maintaining Lists and Libraries." The exercise assumes you've already added the Business Data List web part to the web part page.

EXERCISE 13.2

Adding a Business Data List Web Part

1. In the Business Data List web part, click the Open the Tool Pane link. (You may have to scroll to the right to see the tool pane when it opens.)

2. Under Business Data List, click the Browse button next to the Type field.

3. When the Business Data Type Picker appears in a separate window, as shown here, select one of the applications in the list, such as AdventureWorksSampleInstance Sales Order, and then click OK.

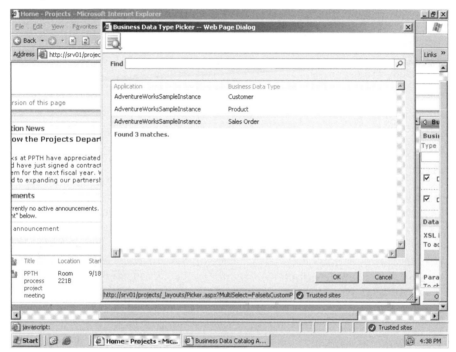

4. Scroll down to the Appearance section in the tool pane, expand the section, and change the text in the Title field to say Sales Orders.

5. Click Apply, and then click OK.

6. Click Exit Edit Mode on the page. (If you added this web part on a portal page, you will have to click Publish.)

If you have not actually configured the BDC to connect to an authentic data source with valid data, you will receive an error message stating Unable to Connect to AdventureWorks-SampleInstance. Although you successfully imported the application definition file, unless you performed the various tasks not included in this chapter—creating a separate database and connecting the BDC to that database—no actual information will be retrieved.

In an actual production environment, you could select a property from the first drop-down list in the Sales Orders web part by selecting the SalesOrderNumber property. You could use the next drop-down menu to the right to select Is Equal To, Starts With, Ends With, or Contains and then click Add Link. Then you would click Retrieve Data to pull in the requested information.

Since this is a list just like any other list in SharePoint, you can create one or more additional views of the list information and filter and sort list data by column.

See Chapter 7, "Configuring and Maintaining Lists and Libraries," for specific information about how to manage lists.

To make searching for business data more effective within SharePoint, you can create a new content source by using the Business Data content source type. You could alternately select a particular business data application to crawl instead and configure crawl rules for which specific content should be reindexed.

See Chapter 9, "Managing SharePoint Navigation and Search," for details about how to configure content sources and crawl schedules.

Once you have created and configured the new content source, searching for information such as specific method types in an application definition file will be much more effective. One issue that you might encounter when you conduct business data searches is that your search results return information not only on entity information but other items such as any documents that may contain the word or part of the word you used in your search string.

If you want to narrow the results to return only information such as order numbers or order dates, you can map a metadata property that you can then use in advanced search queries. Exercise 13.3 will take you through this process. To begin this exercise, go to Central Administration, and in Quick Launch, click the name of the relevant SSP such as SharedServices1.

EXERCISE 13.3

Mapping a Metadata Property

1. On the Shared Services Administration: SharedServices1 page under Search, click Search Settings.

2. On the Configure Search Settings page, click Metadata Property Mappings.

3. On the Metadata Property Mappings page, click New Managed Property.

4. On the New Managed Property page in the mandatory Property Name field, type the name of the specific property, such as SalesOrderNumber.

5. Type an optional description of this property in the Description field.

6. Under The Type of Information in This Property, select Text. (Your other options are Integer, Decimal, Date and Time, and Yes/No.)

7. In the Mappings to Crawled Properties section, select Include Values from All Crawled Properties Mapped, and then click the Add Mapping button.

8. When the Crawled Property selection box opens in a separate window, use the Select a Category drop-down menu, and select Business Data. (If you didn't create a new content source for your business data, no data will be returned in the Select a Crawled Property list in this page.)

9. Select a property field to which you want to create a mapping in the Select a Crawled Property field, and then click OK.

10. On the New Managed Property page, click OK to finish.

The new managed property is now mapped. Remember, you'll have to allow a full crawl after creating the new content type and managed property before you'll see the changes in your search results.

In an actual production situation, you would have likely created a new site in the site collection to present the sales and marketing information being presented in SharePoint through the BDC. In that site, you would create a document library to contain all the documents related to the products, sales reports, and so on, for this project, and then you would add several business data lists to present property information from the remote data source.

You can also add other business data–related web parts to this page to present different information or the same information in different ways. For example, you can add at least one Business Data Related List web part to the page. This web part is actually similar to the Business Data List web part you added and configured in Exercise 13.2. The difference is that it presents child data that has a relationship to the property data you configured to be displayed in the Business Data List web part. Once you add the Business Data Related List web part and click the Browse button next to the Type field, the Business Data Type Picker displays only those items in the list that were previously selected, such as the application you chose in Exercise 13.2. Once you select this item and click OK, you can use the Relationship drop-down menu in the web part's tool pane to select the item related to Sales Order.

The other usual tool pane configuration options are available for you to modify; once you are done, click Apply, and then click OK. After you exit Edit mode, the new information will be available on the page. These actions are similar enough to previous exercises you've performed that they don't need their own exercises; however, you can take some time to create the new site and library as described and then add these web parts to experience creating a SharePoint interface specifically designed to showcase the BDC's features and capacities.

Adding a Business Data Item web part to your page will allow you to display specific items from a list, such as the ones displayed in the Business Data List web parts. Add this web part as usual, and open the tool pane. Use the Browse button next to the Type field to select an entity such as Sales Order, and then use the Browse button next to the Item field. When the Choose Sales Order (in my example) box opens in a separate window, use the Find drop-down menu to select an item such as ID or SalesOrderNumber, type the specific number you want in the search field, and then click the Search button. (Unless you are actually connected to a real data source, no results will be returned.)

Click OK, and in the tool pane, click Apply and OK to finish the process. When the process is complete, you can use this web part to display specific details about the individual item.

Working with Business Forms and InfoPath

Now that you understand the concepts and practices of using the BDC, it's time to move on to the other major section of this chapter and address SharePoint and how to use business-related forms. It's often said that the job is not over until the paperwork is done. The introduction of PCs and the information age promised a "paperless society." We know this is completely untrue; in fact, it seems like there are more forms than ever. Having said all that, SharePoint 2007's document management features and Microsoft's InfoPath 2007 work and play well together and provide you with the ability to create and manage all of your organization's forms with the same level of efficiency as all the other features you've studied up to this point.

Before moving on, there is a significant caveat to be addressed: in order to actually do any of the exercises involved in this section of the chapter, you will need to have Microsoft InfoPath 2007 installed on your computer. As of this writing, you can download an evaluation copy of InfoPath 2007 from `http://www.microsoft.com/downloads/details.aspx?familyid=2D1189BF-D86A-4ACF-9DCC-4D61F500AD6D&displaylang=en`. However, in order to acquire the product key you'll need, you will have to register at TechNet as either an IT professional or developer for Microsoft Office Enterprise 2007. Here's the URL: `http://technet.microsoft.com/en-us/bb736012.aspx`.

On the TechNet page, scroll down to the Additional Trial Software section, and under Office System Products, click Office Enterprise 2007. Then just follow the instructions. Once you've registered and gotten the product key, it might take a while to download the software, depending on your connection speed.

As I previously said, the Internet is a very fluid place, and by the time you read these words, the links posted here might not still be valid. If this one is not, open your favorite search engine, and search for *infopath 2007 trial download*.

 Form developers might also need to install Visual Studio Tools for Office (VSTO) or Visual Studio Tools for Applications (VSTA) to design custom InfoPath forms, but those solutions are beyond the scope of this book and the 70-630 exam.

SharePoint Server 2007 Enterprise Edition comes with InfoPath Forms Services by default, which lets you open and edit forms created with InfoPath. For the purposes of this part of the chapter, you can install InfoPath either on your server or on a client computer. (The latter is recommended.) Installing InfoPath is not a required skill for the 70-630 exam, and like most Microsoft applications, launching the executable and following the wizard should enable you to successfully install the software.

 The trial software you just installed also installs trial versions of the rest of the Office 2007 software suite including Word 2007, Excel 2007, and so on. Although you can take advantage of the new editions of these Office applications, you may also encounter a few surprises, such as trying to open a document and having Word 2007 do it rather than your full-featured version of Word.

What Is InfoPath?

InfoPath is Microsoft's answer to XML-formatted electronic forms development. It's not new. The first version was released with Office 2003, but the current version includes significant improvements. The 2003 version had to be installed on all client computers in order for all users to be able to access and modify InfoPath forms. If any user wanted to do anything with an InfoPath form, they had to have the InfoPath client software installed on their computer.

With the current version of Office, Microsoft developed and deployed a server-side version of InfoPath called InfoPath Forms Services, which runs on MOSS 2007 Enterprise out of the box. This allows users to be able to access InfoPath-based forms via the SharePoint interface without necessarily having the client software installed on their PC or laptop. You can also purchase the separate product, called Forms Server 2007, for use with other platforms.

InfoPath 2007 can natively convert both Word and Excel documents into InfoPath form templates so the user doesn't have to use the InfoPath client to create content to be used as a business form. Forms built in InfoPath can be enabled for use in web pages or embedded in Outlook email messages. InfoPath form templates can be published directly to SharePoint document libraries or to a site collection content type. As you can see, InfoPath Forms Services makes itself right at home in SharePoint and with the other Office suite applications.

Configuring InfoPath Forms Services in Central Administration

Before getting into the nuts and bolts of working with forms and form templates as part of business intelligence, the first order of business is to configure InfoPath Forms Services. As you might have guessed, this is done in Central Administration. Exercise 13.4 will get you started. You can leave the default settings for InfoPath Forms Services as they are if they suit your needs or customize them to fit your business requirements. To begin the exercise, you must be logged into CA as an administrator and be on the Application Management tab.

EXERCISE 13.4

Configuring InfoPath Forms Services

1. On the Application Management tab under InfoPath Forms Services, click Configure Info-Path Forms Services.

2. On the Configure InfoPath Forms Services page, under Browser-Enabled Form Templates, you can tick one or both of the following check boxes: Allow Users to Browser-Enable Form Templates and Render Form Templates That Are Browser-Enabled by Users. (Both check boxes are ticked by default.)

3. Under Data Connection Timeouts, you can set a value in milliseconds for both Default Data Connection Timeout (the value is 10000 by default) and Maximum Data Connection Timeout (the value is 20000 by default).

4. Under Data Connection Response Size, set the maximum size of responses that data connections are allowed to process in kilobytes (1500 by default).

5. Under HTTP Data Connections, tick the Require SSL for HTTP Authentication to Data Sources check box if data connections in browser-enabled form templates require either basic or digest authentication. (The check box is ticked by default.)

6. Under Embedded SQL Authentication, tick the Allow Embedded SQL Authentication check box if forms connecting to databases have SQL username and password information embedded in clear text. (The check box is cleared by default.)

7. Under Authentication to Data Sources (User Form Templates), tick the Allow User Form Templates to Use Authentication Information Contained in Data Connection Files if you want to allow user form templates to use single sign-on application ID authentication information. (The check box is clear by default.)

8. Under Cross-Domain Access for User Form Templates, tick the Allow Cross-Domain Data Access for User Form Templates That Use Connection Settings in a Data Connection File if you want user form templates to be able to access another domain.

9. Under Thresholds, you can specify values for Number of Postbacks per Form Session State (75 by default) and Number of Actions per Postback (200 by default) to specify when to end user sessions or log error messages.

10. Under Form Session State, you can specify a value in minutes for Active Sessions Should Be Terminated After. (1440 is the default value.)

11. You can specify a value in kilobytes for Maximum Size of Form Session State (4096 by default).

12. Select either Session State Service (best for low-bandwidth users) or Form View (reduces database load on server). If you choose the latter, specify a value in kilobytes in the available field. (The default value is 40.)

13. Click OK when you're finished.

You can configure a number of other InfoPath Forms Services in this part of Central Administration, but configuring the web service proxy is an important next step. Enabling the web service proxy for InfoPath will allow you to publish forms and form templates from the browser. This requires a two-part submission process that can result in authentication issues. A proxy resolves the issue of authentication across a multi-tier web service by forwarding web service SOAP messages from the browser-based form. Microsoft's Office Developer Center has a good article on this issue at `http://msdn2.microsoft.com/en-us/library/ms771995.aspx`.

As you can see, enabling browser-based form templates is a great advantage, but not without a "gotcha" or two. Exercise 13.5 will show you how to enable the web service proxy for InfoPath. You should begin this task in Central Administration on the Application Management tab.

EXERCISE 13.5

Managing the Web Service Proxy

1. On the Application Management tab under InfoPath Forms Services, click Manage the Web Service Proxy.

2. On the Manage the Web Service Proxy page, if necessary, click the name of the web application displayed, and click Change Web Application. Then select the required web application, such as SharePoint – 80.

3. Under Enable the Web Service Proxy, tick the Enable check box.

4. Under Enable the Web Service Proxy for User Forms, tick the Enable check box.

5. Click OK.

Short and to the point, but without enabling this service, you are limiting your users as to how and where they are able to publish browser-based forms and form templates within their site collection, and they won't be able to publish to other site collections if desired.

If you click Manage Form Templates under InfoPath Forms Services, you are taken to the Manage Form Templates page. There you can see the form templates available by default, such as CollectSignatures_Sign_1033.xsn. Each was created when SharePoint was initially installed. You can click Upload Form Template to add another template to the list. You can also modify the views of this list by All Forms, Last 20, By Category, and By Status. You can click to the right of any form template and click any of the following menu options, as shown in Figure 13.2:

- Activate to a Site Collection
- Deactivate from a Site Collection
- Quiesce Form Template
- Remove Form

You can also click View Properties, which will show you a list of the properties; however, the only one you can edit is the Category property (which in this case is Workflow).

FIGURE 13.2 Manage Form Templates page

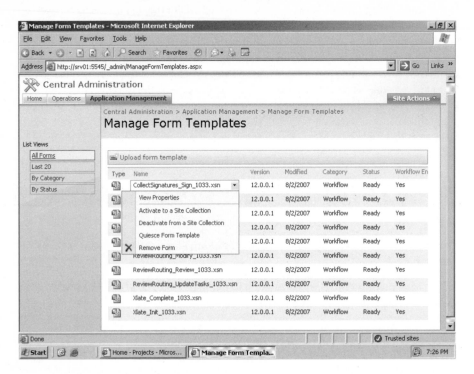

Clicking Upload Form Template under InfoPath Forms Services also lets you perform this action with the same configuration options, including being able to browse for the form template; click Verify to check the template before uploading to see whether it contains errors, warnings, and so on. You can tick Upgrade the Form Template If It Already Exists check box (ticked by default) and select either Allow Existing Browser-Based Form Filling Sessions to Complete Using the Current Version of the Form Template (the default selection) or Terminate Existing Browser-Based Form Filling Sessions. Clicking the Upload button commences the upload process.

You've already worked with data connection files. Clicking Manage Data Connection Files under InfoPath Forms Services will allow you to upload any files to this currently empty list.

If you go to the top-level portal site and click View All Site Content in Quick Launch, on the All Site Content page under Document Libraries you'll see Form Templates. This is a document library specifically designed to contain form documents, as opposed to Word, Excel, or PowerPoint documents. The form templates must be approved by an administrator and be activated to this site collection. Any form templates you want to upload here will have to be activated for the site collection.

You saw this option in the menu shown in Figure 13.2, but none of the form templates in that figure will be available. If you click to the right of any of them and then click Activate to a Site Collection, you'll get the following error message: "This form template cannot be activated or deactivated. It is part of an installed workflow and cannot be accessed directly outside of the workflow." You will need to create a form template that is not part of a workflow.

This is your opportunity to begin using Forms Services by designing a new form using Info-Path 2007. Exercise 13.6 will show you how to get started designing your first form. You will need to be at the computer where you installed InfoPath 2007 to begin this exercise. In this first task with InfoPath, you'll customize a preexisting form template rather than creating a new form.

EXERCISE 13.6

Designing a Form in InfoPath

1. Click Start ➢ All Programs ➢ Microsoft Office ➢ Microsoft Office InfoPath 2007.

2. If the Microsoft Office Activation Wizard opens, click Close.

3. In the Getting Started dialog box under Customize a Sample, select one of the sample forms, such as Sample – Meeting Agenda, and click Design This Form.

4. To modify any of the fields on the form, click the field to open the Text Box Properties dialog box, as shown here.

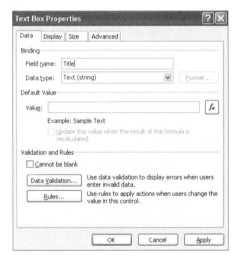

5. On the Data tab, type the designated text in the Field Name field, such as the title of a meeting agenda. You can use the Data Type drop-down menu to choose Text (String) or other data types such as Whole Number (Integer), Decimal (Double), and so on.

6. Use the Display, Size, and Advanced tabs to further modify the presentation and behavior of this text field. Click OK when finished.

7. When the warning dialog box appears stating that this action will cause data loss on any existing forms based on this template, click Yes to continue.

EXERCISE 13.6 *(continued)*

8. Modify any of the other fields as you want using the same steps.

9. To the right, click the arrow next to Design Tasks, and select Clip Art.

10. After the clip art installs, click the drop-down arrow in Search In, and select a collection in which to search for art. Then make whatever selections you desire.

11. When you have finished designing your form, click File ➢ Preview ➢ Form to view a preview of your form.

12. Click Close Preview. When you are ready to publish your form, click File ➢ Save As.

13. When the verification dialog box appears, click OK.

14. Browse to the location on your computer where you want to save the form template, give it a filename, and then click Save.

15. To publish the form template, click File ➢ Publish.

16. When the Publishing Wizard launches, select To a SharePoint Server With or Without InfoPath Forms Services, and click Next.

17. In the available field in the next page, type the location of the SharePoint server, such as http://www.sharepoint.com or //srv01, and then click Next.

18. On the next page under What Do You Want to Create or Modify, select Document Library, and click Next.

EXERCISE 13.6 *(continued)*

---

19. On the next page of the wizard under What Do You Want to Do, select Update the Form Template in an Existing Document Library. Then, in the Document Library to Update list, select Form Templates, and click Next.

20. On the final page of the wizard, review the information, and then click Publish.

21. When the form is successfully published, a notification will appear in the wizard where you can tick the Open This Document Library check box. Then click Close.

22. If prompted, type your administrator account username and password, and click OK.

After the library opens, the form you designed will still need to be uploaded using the same process you would use to upload any document into any document library. Then the newly designed form will be available in the library.

You could also have created a new form library in step 19 by choosing to create a new library for your form rather than publishing it to a preexisting form library. You could do this to organize your forms by type or purpose.

During the publishing process, you could have enabled the form to be filled out in a web browser. Exercise 13.7 shows you how. You'll need to either go back to the form you previously designed or design a new form using InfoPath 2007, save the form, and be ready to publish it.

EXERCISE 13.7

Publishing a Form as Site Content

1. On the open InfoPath form, click File ➢ Publish.

2. When the wizard launches, click Next.

3. In the available field in the next page, type the location of the SharePoint server, such as http://www.sharepoint.com or //srv01, and then click Next.

4. On the next page of the wizard under Site Content Type, select Enable This Form to Be Filled Out by Using a Browser, select Document Library, and then click Next.

5. On the next page, select Create a New Content Type, and click Next.

6. On the next page, browse to the location of the desired form template, enter a name for the template in the available field, and click Next.

7. Select any properties you want to be either promoted or demoted on this page, and click Next.

8. On the final page of the wizard, click Publish.

To use the new content site, you will have to either create a new document library or modify the properties of the library currently containing the form. Exercise 13.8 will show you how to perform the latter.

EXERCISE 13.8

Modifying a Form Template's Library Settings

1. In the Form Templates library, click Settings ➤ Document Library Settings.

2. On the Customize Form Templates page under General Settings, click Advanced Settings.

3. On the Document Library Advanced Settings: Form Templates page, under Content Types select Yes.

4. Under Document Template, type the URL to the template to use as the basis for all new files for the library in the Template URL field.

5. Under Browser-Enabled Documents, select Display as a Web Page so the form can be used in a browser.

6. Under Custom Send To Destination, enter a destination name such as **Special Library** in the Destination Name field, and then enter the URL to that library in the URL field to create a customized destination to which to send the form.

7. Under Folders, select Yes to allow the New Folder command to appear on the New menu or No to prevent this.

8. Under Search, select Yes to allow items in the library to appear in search results or No to prevent this.

9. Click OK when finished.

In step 4 of Exercise 13.7, you could have selected Administrator Approved Form Template (Advanced) if you wanted to publish the form to Central Administration rather than to the Forms Template library. From there, you could go to the Manage Form Templates page, click the arrow to the right of the form, and select Activate to a Site Collection. Then go to the Forms Template library, and upload the administrator-approved form. This gives you a secure central repository for all your business forms and lets you choose which ones to allow or deny to be activated for use in a site collection.

Summary

In this chapter, you learned a great deal about the BDC and about InfoPath Forms Services and InfoPath 2007, including the following points:

- A general review of the BDC including application definition files and entities
- Methods of configuring the BDC including importing a sample application definition file and adding and configuring BDC web parts
- Working with InfoPath Forms Services in SharePoint 2007
- Configuring InfoPath Forms Services including configuring the service and managing the web service proxy
- Installing and working with InfoPath 2007 on the desktop, including designing a new form
- Publishing a form to a form library and enabling a form to be accessible via a web browser

Exam Essentials

Know the characteristics of the business data catalog.   Understand the features offered by the business data catalog and how BDC services work in detail. This includes the roles of the application definition file and entities, how an application definition file is structured, and how to import it into the BDC. You must also know how users can access business data provided by the BDC.

Understand how InfoPath Forms Services works in SharePoint.   Know the specifics of what services InfoPath Forms Services offers in MOSS 2007 Enterprise Edition, including how to configure this service in Central Administration and particularly how to manage the web service proxy.

Know how to use InfoPath 2007.   Understand how to install and use InfoPath 2007 on the desktop, including the basics of designing a form and, more important, the different methods of importing a form into SharePoint and making forms templates available in form document libraries and through web browsers.

Review Questions

1. You are the SharePoint administrator for your organization, and you are giving an in-service training to new IT staff members on SharePoint. Right now, you are covering the basics of the business data catalog and how it can be accessed through the Central Administration web application. Under BDC Shared Services, what functions do you tell your class can be found? (Choose all that apply.)

   A. Import Application Definition

   B. Modify Applications

   C. Modify Entities

   D. Business Data Catalog Permissions

2. You are the SharePoint site administrator for your organization, and you've tasked Sully, one of your staff, with importing an application definition file for the BDC. You provided him with the location of the file and made sure he understood the import process. Later, he comes to you saying that when he tried to import the file, he got an error message stating that the file could not be imported and referencing a section and line in the file. What is the most likely cause of this error?

   A. Sully did not log in to Central Administration with an account with sufficient privileges to import the application definition file.

   B. The XML in the application definition file has an invalid element at the section and line referenced in the error message.

   C. Sully made an error in the file that caused an invalid element to be introduced into the XML source at the section and line referenced in the error message.

   D. Sully forgot to publish the application definition file before importing it.

3. You are the SharePoint administrator for your company. You have imported an application definition file in Central Administration and are reviewing the entity content of the file. On the View Entity page, you click Manage Permissions. By default, in the User/Group Name column, what should you see?

   A. The system group name for the BDC service

   B. The names of the members of the administrators group

   C. The name of the person who imported the application definition file

   D. The name of the person who authored the application definition file

4. You are the SharePoint administrator for your company. You have imported an application definition file in Central Administration and are reviewing the entity content of the file. On the View Entity page, you click Manage Permissions. You select one of the users who has permissions to the entity and decide to modify their permissions. Once you select a user and click Modify Permissions of Selected Users, what options do you have? (Choose all that apply.)

   A. Edit

   B. Execute

   C. Set in Clients

   D. Select Permissions

5. You are the SharePoint administrator for your organization and have just deployed BDC services for the site collection. You are in the process of developing a training program for the company's SharePoint users so they will have some familiarity with the options the BDC provides them in their work. One of the things users will need to know is which elements in SharePoint are able to display data provided by the BDC. Of the following options, which ones can display BDC-provided information? (Choose all that apply.)

   A. Business Data web parts

   B. SharePoint lists

   C. SharePoint libraries

   D. SharePoint Search

6. You are the SharePoint administrator for your organization. You have recently deployed BDC services on the company's site collection and have instituted a system of training for users company-wide to help them understand the advantages of the BDC and how to access BDC-provided data. You get a call from Celia, one of the staff members in the marketing department. She has gone through the training and thinks that adding a Business Data List web part to marketing's portal and configuring it to display data from an external application that contains customer response data would be a great advantage for her team. She is still confused about the basics of adding a Business Data List web part to the portal page. What do you tell her?

   A. You tell Celia that she must open the portal site in Edit mode, navigate to the gallery containing the Business Data List web part, select it, and click Publish to publish it to the portal site.

   B. You tell Celia that she must navigate to the gallery containing the Business Data List web part, open the web part's toolbox, and under Publish use the drop-down list to select the location of the portal site. Then click Apply and OK.

   C. You tell Celia that she must navigate to the gallery containing the Business Data List web part, select the web part, click Export in the gallery toolbar, and browse to the location of the portal site to move the web part there.

   D. You tell Celia that the Business Data List web part is no different from any other web part and that she can just open the portal site in Edit mode, click Add a Web Part on the desired web part zone's title bar, and then proceed with the usual process of locating and adding the web part.

7. You are the SharePoint administrator for your organization, and you have deployed BDC services in the SharePoint system so that users can access external data sources and display the data they contain in the SharePoint interface. You receive a call from Mike in customer support saying that he added a business web part to support's web part page and attempted to configure it but keeps getting an error that says "Unable to connect to BusinessDataInfoInstance." What is the most likely problem?

   A. The connection between the BDC and the remote database was not properly created.

   B. The application definition file was never imported.

   C. The entity data from the relevant application definition file was never published.

   D. The XML in the application definition file contains invalid XML elements.

8. You are the SharePoint administrator for your company, and you have recently deployed BDC services throughout the SharePoint site collection. You are getting calls from some of the users who are using Search to locate relevant data from the information provided by the BDC that their search results pages contain too many items and the results are too indiscriminate. What can you do to make their search results more relevant to BDC data items?

   A. Modify the search parameters to distinguish between application definition file entities and other data types contained in SharePoint.

   B. Create a separate data type for entity data, and configure Search to differentiate between this data type and the other SharePoint data types.

   C. Create a new category in Advanced Search called BDC Entity Data, and map it to the entity data type.

   D. Create a new metadata property mapping and a new managed property using a specific property of an entity in Search.

9. You are the SharePoint administrator for your company. You have recently implemented BDC services for the site collection. You get a call from Randall in sales saying that he just added a Business Data List web part to the sales portal page but is having trouble configuring it to information from the MonthlySalesFigures entity because the entity name isn't displayed in the Business Data Type Picker list. In fact, it displays only the SalesOrder entity, which is already configured to display in another Business Data List web part on the same page. Of the following options, which one is the most likely problem?

   A. Randall didn't realize that you couldn't use two Business Data List web parts on the same page.

   B. Randall accidentally added a Business Data Related List web part to the page, which is designed to display only child data of the entity you configured to display previously in a Business Data List web part.

   C. The data source being accessed via the BDC is down, and the information Randall is trying to access is unavailable.

   D. BDC services is unable to refresh data from the data source, and Randall is able to access only the entity data already in the local cache.

10. You are the SharePoint administrator for your company and are responsible for the site collections in the organization's MOSS 2007 Enterprise Edition deployment. You receive a call from Roz, one of the software developers in research and development. Roz has recently been tasked with developing customized business forms for the corporation but is not familiar with the tools required for this task and is requesting a consult with you and her supervisor Henry. During the consult meeting, you develop a plan for Roz to be able to successfully complete her task including providing her with the required applications for the job. Of the following options, which are valid form development tools? (Choose all that apply.)

   A. Visual Studio Tools for Office

   B. Visual Studio Tools for InfoPath

   C. Visual Studio Tools for Applications

   D. Visual Studio Tools for SharePoint

11. You are a consultant for Docter and Silverman SharePoint Consultants, and you are currently giving a presentation to the executives at the Goodman Merchants Group on the benefits of a SharePoint deployment in their organization. Steve, the marketing manager, is particularly interested in how InfoPath Forms Services runs natively in SharePoint. He sees that being able to work with InfoPath forms in a SharePoint interface without having to add special software packages would be a particular ROI advantage. You explain to Steve that this service does not come "out of the box" with all versions of SharePoint. Of the following selections, which versions of SharePoint come with InfoPath Forms Services by default? (Choose all that apply.)

   A. Windows SharePoint Services 3.0

   B. Microsoft Office SharePoint Server 2003 Enterprise Edition

   C. Microsoft Office SharePoint Server 2007 Standard Edition

   D. Microsoft Office SharePoint Server 2007 Enterprise Edition

12. You are a consultant for Docter and Silverman SharePoint Consultants, and you are currently giving a presentation to the executives at the Goodman Merchants Group on the benefits of a SharePoint deployment in their organization. Goodman Merchants currently is using Share-Point Server 2003 but is considering upgrading to MOSS 2007. They make heavy use of Info-Path 2003 in their company and want to know the benefits of upgrading and any limitations an upgrade would overcome. What do you tell the executives?

   A. Their current SharePoint deployment requires that all desktop computer users who want to access and read InfoPath forms stored in SharePoint must have InfoPath 2003 client software installed on their computers. Upgrading to either MOSS 2007 Standard or Enter-prise Edition will overcome this limitation.

   B. Their current SharePoint deployment requires that all desktop computer users who want to access and read InfoPath forms stored in SharePoint must have InfoPath 2003 client software installed on their computers. Upgrading to MOSS 2007 Enterprise Edition will overcome this limitation.

   C. Their current SharePoint deployment requires that all desktop computer users who want to access and read InfoPath forms stored in SharePoint must have Visual Studio Tools for Office installed on their computers. Upgrading to either MOSS 2007 Standard or Enter-prise Edition will overcome this limitation.

   D. Their current SharePoint deployment requires that all desktop computer users who want to access and read InfoPath forms stored in SharePoint must have Visual Studio Tools for SharePoint installed on their computers. Upgrading to MOSS 2007 Enterprise Edition will overcome this limitation.

13. You are a consultant for Docter and Silverman SharePoint Consultants, and you are currently giving a presentation to the executives at the Goodman Merchants Group on the benefits of a SharePoint deployment in their organization. Jennifer, the head of the development department, is interested in the InfoPath 2007 client software as it relates to SharePoint but is concerned that some of her staff would have a steep learning curve if she incorporated InfoPath into her business plan. What do you say to Jennifer to convince her that the learning curve wouldn't be so great? (Choose all that apply.)

A. InfoPath 2007 can natively convert Word documents into InfoPath form templates.

B. InfoPath 2007 can natively convert Excel documents into InfoPath form templates.

C. InfoPath 2007 can natively convert PowerPoint slides into InfoPath form templates.

D. InfoPath 2007 uses the same design tools as Visio 2007, so the learning curve wouldn't be very great for Jennifer's staff.

14. You are the SharePoint administrator for your company, and you are configuring InfoPath Forms Services in Central Administration so that your users will have the ability to access and work with InfoPath form templates within the SharePoint interface. You are currently configuring the web service proxy; in order to allow this service to display form templates acquired from other site collections to be displayed in a web browser for users on their own sites, what prerequisites must exist before you access the Manage the Web Service Proxy page? (Choose all that apply.)

A. On the Configure InfoPath Forms Services page, you must tick the Enable the Web Service Proxy check box.

B. On the Configure InfoPath Forms Services page, you must tick the Enable the Web Service Proxy for User Forms check box.

C. On the Configure InfoPath Forms Services page, you must tick the Allow Users to Browser-Enable Form Templates check box.

D. On the Configure InfoPath Forms Services page, you must tick the Render Form Templates That Are Browser-Enabled By Users check box.

15. You are the SharePoint administrator for your company. You are in the process of enabling and configuring InfoPath Forms Services in your SharePoint deployment. You want to allow InfoPath forms templates to be displayed in a web browser for your users; however, the data connections require basic authentication for this feature to be usable. On the Configure Info-Path Forms Services page, what action do you perform to allow this?

A. Under Data Connection Response, tick the Require Basic Authentication for HTTP check box.

B. Under Embedded SQL Authentication, tick the Allow Basic Authentication for Users check box.

C. Under HTTP Data Connections, tick the Require SSL for HTTP Authentication to Data Sources check box.

D. Under Authentication to Data Stores, tick the Allow User Form Templates to Use Basic Authentication check box.

16. You are the SharePoint administrator for your corporation. Billy, one of the domain administrators, is interested in whether form templates can be accessed across domains in the organization rather than form template libraries having to contain duplicates of the standard business forms in each SharePoint deployment for each domain. You investigate this option. In your report to Billy, what do you say you've discovered?

    A. There is no method of accessing form templates across domains.

    B. The only method of accessing form templates across domains is to store the templates in the SharePoint deployment at the root domain and then export the templates to SharePoint in the other domains.

    C. You can enable cross-domain data access in Central Administration by configuring the feature on the Web Service Proxy page.

    D. You can enable cross-domain data access in Central Administration by configuring the feature on the Configure InfoPath Forms Services page.

17. You are the SharePoint administrator for your company, and you have configured InfoPath Forms Services in the site collection so that users can access and work with InfoPath-based forms in the SharePoint interface. You get a call from James, the manager of one of the smaller branch offices, saying that his staff is having trouble accessing forms hosted in the forms library on the server at the main office. The response time seems to be quite slow and is making it difficult to develop and maintain the forms for their office. You investigate and determine that the branch office is using an ISDN line to access the Internet and the corporate office because that's the only connection type available in their area. Since they are using a low-bandwidth connection solution, what do you do to improve their performance issues in accessing InfoPath Forms Services on the corporate servers?

    A. In Central Administration on the Configure InfoPath Forms Services page, under Form Session State you select Session State Service (best for low-bandwidth users).

    B. In Central Administration on the Configure InfoPath Forms Services page, under Form Session Access, select Enable Connection Filtering Passthrough to reduce the bandwidth requirements.

    C. In Central Administration on the Configure InfoPath Forms Services page, under Form Session State, select Form View (best for low-bandwidth users), and specify a value in kilobytes of 40 in the available field to reduce the bandwidth requirements for accessing form templates.

    D. Put in a request to IT to develop either a faster connection to the main office or a redundant connection to the main office from the branch office to improve performance.

18. You are the SharePoint administrator for your company, and you have implemented InfoPath Forms Services for your organization. You have enabled the appropriate features on the Configure InfoPath Forms Services page in Central Administration to allow form templates to be viewed in web browsers, but users also want to be able to publish the templates directly from browsers. When they attempt to do so, they receive error messages related to authentication errors. The CIO asks what can be done about this problem, and you decide that you must also enable the web service proxy to resolve this issue. Why will the web service proxy help in this instance?

A. The proxy resolves the issue of authentication across a multi-tier web service by forwarding web service HTTP messages from the browser-based form.

B. The proxy resolves the issue of authentication across a multi-tier web service by forwarding web service SOAP messages from the browser-based form.

C. The proxy resolves the issue of authentication across a multi-tier web service by forwarding web service SSL messages from the browser-based form.

D. The proxy resolves the issue of authentication across a multi-tier web service by forwarding web service XML messages from the browser-based form.

19. You are the SharePoint administrator for your organization. Frank, one of the developers in the content development department, wants to create InfoPath forms and enable them to be filled out in a web browser, but he needs to know the specific process involved. You know you have enabled everything in Central Administration so that InfoPath-based forms can be accessed through browsers. What do you tell Frank he needs to do?

A. You tell Frank he needs to publish the form as site content.

B. You tell Frank he needs to publish the form as an HTML document.

C. You tell Frank he needs to publish the form as an XML document.

D. You tell Frank he needs to publish the form as a preexisting SharePoint document type.

20. Frank, a developer in the content management department, has designed a form that he wants users to be able to fill out in a web browser. You are the SharePoint administrator consulting with Frank and have already given him the initial instructions on how he can accomplish his task. He has enabled the form to be filled out in a browser and selected a document library to house the new form. He then created a new content type for his form. Now that the new content type has been created and he has published it, what next steps could he take? (Choose all that apply.)

A. Frank needs to create a document library for the new content type.

B. Frank needs to modify an existing document library to use the new content type.

C. Frank needs to create a new web part gallery for the new content type.

D. Frank needs to modify an existing web part gallery for the new content type.

Answers to Review Questions

1. A and D. The options available under BDC Shared Services are Import Application Definition, View Applications, View Entities, Business Data Catalog Permissions, and Edit Profile Page Template.

2. B. If the XML is not completely validated, it will throw an error, causing the import operation to fail.

3. C. By default, the only name in the User/Group Name column on the Manage Permissions page for the entity is the person who imported the application definition file. All the other options are bogus.

4. A and B. The options you have are Edit, Execute, Select in Clients, and Set Permissions.

5. A, B, and D. SharePoint libraries don't have the ability to directly display data provided via the BDC. The SharePoint elements that can present such data are Business Data web parts, SharePoint lists, SharePoint Search, and User Profile Importer.

6. D. Although configuring business data web parts may require specific skills, anyone who has added web parts to a web part page in the past can use the identical process to add a Business Data web part.

7. A. The most likely answer is that even though the application definition file was successfully imported, the connection either doesn't exist or was improperly created. If the application definition file was never imported, Mike wouldn't have gotten to the point of being able to configure the web part. Entity data in an application definition file does not need to be published, and if the XML in the application definition file were invalid, it would never have been able to be imported.

8. D. You can use Search settings to configure Search to recognize a new mapped metadata property of application definition file entities so that users using Advanced Search can better define the information they are searching for and get more accurate results relevant to BDC-related data.

9. B. Randall most likely added a Business Data Related List web part, which is specifically designed to present only child data of the entity data already displayed in a Business Data List web part. You can use as many Business Data List web parts on a web part page as you want, so option A is incorrect. If there were a problem with the data source or the BDC, Randall would not have been able to access any entity data at all, so options C and D are incorrect.

10. A and C. Options A and C are valid development tools that will allow Roz to design custom InfoPath forms. Options B and D are completely bogus.

11. D. Only MOSS 2007 Enterprise Edition comes with InfoPath Forms Services on board by default.

12. B. Options A, C, and D are bogus because MOSS 2007 Standard Edition does not have InfoPath Forms Services, which will be required if they do not want to run InfoPath client software on each person's desktop. Visual Studio Tools for Office is not required, and Visual Studio Tools for SharePoint is a bogus answer.

13. A and B. InfoPath 2007 can convert both Word and Excel documents to form templates, so Jennifer's staff can use tools they are familiar with to design forms without having to learn InfoPath 2007 from scratch. InfoPath 2007 does not convert PowerPoint slides into form templates, and option D is completely bogus.

14. C and D. Options A and B are options that you configure on the Web Service Proxy page once the prerequisites have been satisfied and so are incorrect.

15. C. Options A, B, and D are all bogus versions of options available on the Configure InfoPath Forms Services page, but they're not worded to represent that true configuration features. Only option C describes the valid action to accomplish the stated task.

16. D. You can enable cross-domain data access in Central Administration by configuring the feature on the Configure InfoPath Forms Services page under Cross-Domain Access for User Form Templates by ticking the Allow Cross-Domain Data Access for User Form Templates check box.

17. A. Option B is bogus since there is no such category as Form Session Access. The option selected in option C is used to reduce database load on the server and is mutually exclusive to the Session State Service selection, which is used for low-bandwidth users. Although option D may improve performance, it's not a solution that can be implemented within SharePoint.

18. B. The Service Oriented Architecture Protocol (SOAP) is required to exchange XML-based messages over computer networks that ordinarily use HTTP or HTTPS, so option B is the correct answer. All the other options are bogus.

19. A. Frank needs to create a form in InfoPath and publish it as site content. To do this, he needs to enable the form to be filled out in a browser, select the document library where the form will reside, and then create it as a new document type.

20. A and B. Now that the new content type has been created, either an existing document library needs to be modified to use the new content type or a new document needs to be created for the new content type. The options referencing web part galleries are bogus.

Chapter

14

Performing Advanced SharePoint Management

MICROSOFT EXAM OBJECTIVES COVERED IN THIS CHAPTER:

✓ **Manage Administration**

- Manage Central Admin UI
- Manage the Shared Service Provider
- Administrating Moss using STSADM
- Configure Usage Analysis & Reporting

This chapter is definitely the "under the hood" chapter of the book. It addresses aspects of SharePoint management that are more related to the realm of an IT administrator than a SharePoint administrator or site collection manager.

Some parts of this chapter will present information you are already familiar with. The Central Administration web application user interface (UI) should be something you've worked with many times throughout the course of studying SharePoint and moving through the various chapter exercises. As part of using Central Administration, you've also had extensive exposure to the shared services provider (SSP) for our stand-alone SharePoint installation and the features and services available on the shared services administration (SSA) home page.

You will be revisiting those locations, focusing on how they are used to manage SharePoint in general rather than as a means to an end. You'll also have the opportunity to work with some of the options available on those pages that I haven't addressed up until now, such as backup and restore.

`stsadm` should be new to you unless you've had experience with SharePoint outside of what you've done with this book. This is a command-line utility that allows you to perform many administrative tasks directly from the command-line emulator. You'll learn how to perform many common and a few not-so-common administrative tasks using `stsadm`.

Usage analysis and reporting is a common administrator task for just about anyone involved in end user–accessible technology, including system and network administrators. You need to know how the system (in our case, SharePoint) is operating, know when peak and low usage periods are occurring, and, in many other ways, discover how well (or not so well) SharePoint is performing.

The structure of this chapter will not quite follow the Microsoft exam objectives you just read at the start of the chapter but will start by touring Central Administration and managing this user interface. As you progress through the tour, you'll find out just how many of the exam objectives listed for this chapter you've already learned.

Managing the Central Administration User Interface

This section will go over the user interface, but I am presuming you know where to find most features based on both your reading Chapter 3, "Configuring SharePoint 2007," and your experiences visiting the CA interface while performing the exercises in the rest of the book. If you need a refresher before starting this section, you might want to review Chapter 3.

As you'll recall from that chapter, CA is a web application in the same sense that the top-level SharePoint portal site is a web application. It is its own separate site collection within the stand-alone or server farm deployment. Besides the CA home page, which you work with mainly when SharePoint is first installed, the two major tabs are Operations and Application Management.

Although you might be tempted to think of shared services administration as part of CA, it's really a separate location and interface that is merely accessed through CA—usually by clicking the Shared Services Administration link in Quick Launch in CA.

I'll address how to work with shared services administration later in this chapter. Right now, I'll cover parts of CA you haven't visited before and are likely not familiar with, starting by clicking the View All Site Content link in Quick Launch.

All Site Content

You probably think you know what's on this page because you already reviewed this information in Chapter 3, "Configuring SharePoint 2007," but you may notice some changes. Although the All Site Content page may seem virtually the same as the one you can visit off the top-level portal site, some of the items on it are quite different.

Under Document Libraries, you'll notice that just above the familiar Shared Documents library is a library called *HelpFold*, which is the root document library for the SharePoint help system. That's right, whenever you click Help and open a help file in SharePoint, you are accessing a document in this particular library. To gain access to the contents of the library from CA, you have to be logged in with an account that belongs to the Help group, such as an administrator. When you enter the library, you'll notice several items in the Name column:

- Content
- Images
- Lock
- Manifests
- MetaData
- Support

You can view or modify the properties and permissions of each item, but clicking one and drilling down into the directory structure won't produce anything familiar, unless you're a developer (and the 70-630 exam isn't for SharePoint developers). At the heart of the documents in this library is a set of scripts and style sheets that, together, make up the various aspects of the SharePoint help system. The information in this library is indexed so that it's available to SharePoint users who access it through the search feature.

This should be the only item on the All Site Content page that you aren't familiar with and that contains information. Under Lists, you'll see the Administrator Tasks list you first visited in Chapter 3. You'll also see a few other lists that contain no items:

- Content Deployment Jobs
- Content Deployment Paths
- Job Reports
- Migration Profile List

The titles should be fairly self-explanatory, particularly those associated with content deployment and management. You can create lists of different administrative job reports; if you are planning a migration or upgrade, such as you'll learn about in Chapter 16, "Upgrading and Deploying Microsoft Office SharePoint Server 2007," you'll learn to use the latter two lists.

Operations

You have managed a number of features on this tab previously, such as email settings under Topology and Services, antivirus under Security Configuration, and diagnostic logging under Logging and Reporting. We'll take a look at Backup and Restore in a bit. For now, we'll take a tour of what else is here.

Topology and Services

This section of the Operations tab addresses tasks that are specific to server farm management. Although many of your day-to-day tasks in SharePoint aren't configured at this level, you need to be able to administer SharePoint server farms in order to configure and maintain SharePoint as a whole as well as the physical and logical topology that runs SharePoint.

Servers in Farm When the Servers in Farm page loads, the names of the database servers on the farm will be listed on the page, along with which services are running on each server. In my case, there is only one, SRV01, since this is a stand-alone deployment and since the database services are running on the same server as SharePoint. There is also a listing for the mail server managing outgoing emails. You can click a server name to get to the Services on Server page and see what services are running on a server and to either start or stop services on that server. In a multiserver server farm, you can also select a server and server role for that server. In a stand-alone deployment, all the server role selections are unavailable (grayed out) and the role of Single Server or Web Server for small server farms is selected by default. Back on the Servers in Farm page, you can also click the Remove Server link next to a server name to remove the server from the farm.

Services on Server If you clicked the name of a server when you were on the Servers on Farm page, you have already seen this page, which lets you start and stop services on a given server.

Approve/Reject Distribution Groups If you set up a workflow for distribution groups, you can control the approval and rejection process here.

Security Configuration

This section of the Operations tab focuses on those tasks directly related to the security of SharePoint, both as a whole entity and for specific elements such as file types and document management policies.

Service Accounts Use this page to manage Windows services and web applications in the server farm. The Windows Services option is selected by default, and you can select a particular service, such as Document Conversions Launcher Service or Single Sign-on Service, to manage. If you select Web Application Pool, you can use the drop-down menu to choose a Web service such as Windows SharePoint Services web application. You will not need to access this page unless you plan to change the configuration that was designated for these services when SharePoint was originally installed.

Blocked File Types   The name says it all. Use this page to define file formats you do not want users to be able to save or retrieve.

Update Farm Administrator's Group   This one is also pretty obvious. You can use this page to add or remove users from this particular group.

Information Management Policy Configuration   This page lists the available information management policy features that can be used in SharePoint such as labels, auditing, expiration, and barcodes. You can click the name of a policy to enable or disable it.

You will work with information rights management in Chapter 15, "Working with Content Management." You experienced managing antivirus and single sign-on settings in Chapter 3, "Configuring SharePoint 2007."

Logging and Reporting

Although logging and reporting isn't the most thrilling aspect of administering SharePoint, these functions are at the heart of any system manager's job. They provide you with the "nuts-and-bolts" data you need to understand how SharePoint is functioning, to detect trends such as usage loads, and to help troubleshoot any issues that might arise.

You worked with diagnostic logging in Chapter 3, "Configuring SharePoint 2007," so refer to that chapter for information on working with this feature.

Usage Analysis Processing   You can enable usage analysis logging on this page, determine where the logs will be written to by default (C:\Program Files\Common Files\Microsoft Shared\Web Server Extensions\12\Logs), determine the number of log files to create, and enable usage analysis processing including when the processing starts and stops. The default is daily for one hour from 1 to 2 a.m. You can specify the number of files for each web application running in SharePoint. The purpose of these logs is to show you how the SharePoint sites are being used in terms of peak usage, analyzing capacity, and so forth. This information lets you determine when you need to add more web servers to the farm.

Information Management Policy Usage Reports   This page allows you to configure how reports are created for information management policy usage. You can select a particular web application and determine the schedule for generating reports, as well as create reports on demand. There is no default location for such reports, but you can specify a location by inputting one in the Report File Location field and clicking Check URL. You can also choose a report template such as the default or select a custom template and input the URL to that template in the available field.

Upgrade and migration will be covered in Chapter 16, "Upgrading and Deploying Microsoft Office SharePoint Server 2007."

Global Configuration

This area of the Operations tab is used to manage the configuration settings that affect Share-Point at both the server farm level and the site collection level. You will also find controls that let you monitor and modify services running in SharePoint such as timer job status.

Timer Job Status   This is a list page that displays all the automated jobs that run in the server, including which servers the jobs have run on, their status, their progress, and when they were started. Like any list, you can choose a view. The All view is selected by default, but you can also filter the view by service and web application.

Timer Job Definitions   This is also a list page, and it displays the names of each automated job set to run in the server farm including which web application (if any) is set to run and the run schedule, such as minutes, daily, or weekly. Clicking the name of a job will open the job and allow you to disable or enable it.

Master Site Directory Settings   A master site directory is created by default when you install SharePoint and begin adding sites. If you want to establish a new master site directory where all new site collections you create will be collected, use this page to enter the path to the new directory and determine whether you want to enforce site creation metadata such as making no, one, or all site categories mandatory.

Site Directory Links Scan   Use this page to enter the URLs to the site directory views you want to scan for possible broken links. A typical site directory view URL is SRV01/`sitedirectory/` `lists/sitelist/allitems.aspx`. You can also choose to automatically update links, titles, and descriptions during the scan.

Alternate Access Mappings   You can edit public URLs so that the full URL that the public uses, such as `http://www.microsoft.com`, maps to a different link on intranet, Internet, and extranet pages within SharePoint. When any of these web applications receives a request from an external user for an internal URL, the external user can access the page, but the user will see the public URL for the zone.

See `http://technet2.microsoft.com/Office/en-us/library/be9d31d2-` `b9cb-4442-bfc6-2adcdbff8fae1033.mspx?mfr=true` for more information about alternate access mapping.

Quiesce Farm   This page allows you to gradually take the server farm offline by preventing new user sessions for long-running operations. You can specify how long in minutes you want the process to take until the farm is completely offline.

Manage Farm Features   This page allows you to activate or deactivate any SharePoint-wide features such as the data connection library, the Excel Services farm feature, global web parts, and spell checking.

Solution Management   Each custom SharePoint template is deployed as a solution. A discussion of solution management is beyond the scope of this book. For more information, go to `http://msdn2.microsoft.com/en-us/library/bb530301.aspx#WSSDevToolsTechs_` `P2_DeployingWSSSolutions`.

Since Backup and Restore is being treated separately in this chapter, we'll move on to the next area on the Operations page.

Data Configuration

This portion of the Operations tab lets you manage database-related operations relative to SharePoint including identifying the default database server your site collection uses and search operations.

Default Database Server   This page defines the name and location of the default database server. In my stand-alone deployment, the server is SRV01\OfficeServers. You can also define an access account and a password for that account on this page. The fields are left blank if you are using Windows authentication (recommended) but are used to specify SQL authentication.

Data Retrieval Service   This service is enabled by default so that search query requests can be processed. Typical data retrieval services are Windows SharePoint Services, OLEDB, SOAP Passthrough, and XML-URL.

Content Deployment

The Content Deployment section of the Operations tab provides you with the controls you need to manage this SharePoint feature including general content management settings, checking the status of content deployment objects, and defining paths and jobs.

Manage Content Deployment Paths and Jobs   No content deployment paths and jobs are defined by default. Use this page to manage content that you want to deploy from one site collection to another. Define a path between the site collections by clicking New Path ➢ New Job to define the specific job. A path must be created first before a job can be associated with it, and the job defines the particular content you want deployed as well as the schedule of deployment.

Content Deployment Settings   Use this page to determine whether you will accept content deployed from another site collection. (Rejecting incoming deployment jobs is set by default.) If you choose to accept incoming content, you can select the servers you want to manage incoming and outgoing content, whether to require that the content be encrypted, the path to the temp files to be used, and the number of reports to retain per job.

Content Deployment Object Status   Use this page to check the status of content deployment for any individual object by specifying the URL to the object in the available field.

Application Management

You have also spent a fair amount of time on the Application Management tab in Central Administration. In fact, of all the locations in CA, you've worked most often right here. Under SharePoint Site Management, you've already created a site collection and seen how to delete one. You also have learned how to set up quota templates and should be familiar with site collection quotas and locks, site collection administrators, and site collection lists. The Search and External Service Connections have been previously addressed as has workflow management. Shared Services will be covered in the next section of this chapter, and InfoPath and forms services were presented in Chapter 13, "Using Business Forms and Business Intelligence."

Real World Scenario

Managing Services in Central Administration

You are the SharePoint administrator for your company. You have received several phone calls this morning from users in different departments saying they can't access any of their Excel Services workbooks through the Excel Web Access web parts on their local SharePoint sites. This seems to be happening to any user on any site in the collection, and you suspect that Excel Calculation Services may be experiencing a problem. You open the Central Administration web application and click the Operations tab. Under Topology and Services, you click Servers in Farm. On the Servers in Farm page, you locate the name of the server that is listed to be running Excel Calculation Services and click the server's name. On the Services on Server page for that server, you locate Excel Calculation Services in the list, and under Status, you see that the service is Stopped. In the Action column, you click Start to restart this service. After the service is running again, you send out a broadcast email to all the users in the site collection telling them there has been a temporary interruption in Excel Calculation Services but that the service is now available. You also ask any users who are still having problems to call you.

Managing Shared Services

We will begin our review of this section where we left off, on the Application Management tab in Central Administration. As you'll soon discover, you already know the vast majority of the topics in this section of the chapter.

Office SharePoint Server Shared Services

It's easy to confuse management in Central Administration and management in Shared Services because shared services providers are accessed through the CA interface. Nevertheless, Shared Services is a completely different service from any of the features and functions administered through the Operations and Applications Management tabs in CA.

 See Chapter 3, "Configuring SharePoint 2007," for details on shared services administration.

Create or Configure This Farm's Shared Services   Clicking this link takes you to the Manage This Farm's Shared Services page. You'll see the SSP created when we installed our stand-alone server called SharedServices1 (Default) and the two web applications it services,

Central Administration (SharePoint – 32139 [Administration site host]) and the SharePoint site collection (SharePoint – 80). Here you can create a new SSP, change the default SSP (if more than one exists), and restore an SSP that has been backed up. (See Chapter 3, "Configuring SharePoint 2007," for more details.)

Grant or Configure Shared Services Between Farms   This option allows you to use a single SSP to provide services for another farm or allow an SSP from another farm to provide services to yours. In our deployment scenario, these options are unavailable since the single-server deployment does not participate in services between farms.

Check Services Enabled in this Farm   This page allows you to check the services running on the server farm. If you are using a trial version of SharePoint Server 2007, you will see a notice informing you when the trial installation is due to expire.

Configure Session State   This service is enabled by default when the first SSP is created and is required to store any information about specific user session data. You can enable or disable session state here and set the timeout value in minutes.

Shared Services Administration: SharedServices1

Clicking the name of the SSP, such as SharedServices1, will take you to the home page of the SSP. You have been here many times before. Under User Profiles and My Sites, you set up and configured user- and My Sites–related features such as User Profiles and Properties, My Site Settings, and Personalization Site links. You are also familiar with Search and Audiences as well as Excel Services Settings, Business Data Catalog, and Usage Reporting from the previous chapters in this book. To refresh your memory on how Shared Services is managed here, you would need to review most of this text (which isn't a bad idea as you prepare to take the 70-630 exam).

Backup and Restore

Although the backing up and restoring process is familiar to anyone who has managed a server farm or even a small server closet, I can't stress enough that this is a vital set of skills to acquire and possess. All your skills in configuring and managing SharePoint site collections and services won't do much good if the system goes down or is corrupted and you either have never performed a backup or haven't a clue how to perform a restore.

You've gone through a rather grand tour so far in this chapter but haven't really gotten your hands dirty. It's time to change that with Exercise 14.1, where you'll learn how to perform a backup. For this exercise, you'll need to be logged into Central Administration with administrator rights and be on the Operations tab.

For Exercise 14.1 you will want to select a relatively small amount of data to back up so you don't need a lot of space or require a lot of time. You'll also need to prepare a shared folder on another computer on the network where you can back up your data.

EXERCISE 14.1

Performing a Backup

1. Under Backup and Restore, click Perform a Backup.

2. On the Perform a Backup – Step 1 of 2: Select a Component to Backup page, tick any of the check boxes next to any of the displayed components you want to back up. (To back up everything, tick the Farm check box.)

3. Click Continue to Backup Options.

4. On the Start Backup – Step 2 of 2: Select Backup Options page, under Backup Content, either accept the default (which you selected in the previous step) or click the down arrow and click Change Backup Component.

5. Under Type of Backup, select either Full or Differential. (Choose Full if this is your first backup.)

6. Under Backup File Location, type the path to back up to in the Backup Location field, such as **\\server\backup**. You'll notice the Estimated Disk Space Required notation below indicating how much space you'll need at the backup site to successfully accomplish this task.

7. Click OK.

You are taken to the Backup and Restore Status page, which periodically refreshes to show the progress of the backup, as you can see here.

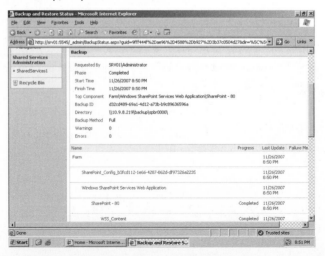

If you click Backup History, you'll see all the prior backups that have been performed. (Right now, you'll see only the current backup.) Use the breadcrumb link to take you back to the Operations tab in CA.

Now it's time to reverse the process by using your backup to perform a restore. As you saw, the backup was a relative "piece of cake," and the restore should go just as smoothly. Exercise 14.2 will show you how to perform the restore operation.

EXERCISE 14.2

Restoring from a Backup

1. On the Operations tab in CA under Backup and Restore, click Restore from Backup.

2. On the Restore from Backup – Step 1 of 4: Select Backup Location page, the path to the backup file you specified in the previous exercise should already be populating the Backup Location field. If not, enter it here, and click OK.

3. On the Restore from Backup – Step 2 of 4: Select Backup to Restore page, select the type of backup you want to perform. (Since you have performed only one backup, there will be only one option.)

4. Click Continue Restore Process.

5. On the Restore from Backup – Step 3 of 4: Select Component to Restore page, tick the check boxes next to the components you want to restore. (In our example, select only the components you originally backed up.)

6. Click Continue Restore Process.

7. On the Restore from Backup – Step 4 of 4: Select Restore Options page, accept the selection under Restore Component. Under Restore Options, select Same Configuration.

8. When you receive a warning dialog stating that this selection will overwrite the files on the server, click OK. The options under New Names will become unavailable when you make this selection.

9. Click OK.

The Backup and Restore Status page will appear, periodically refreshing to show the progress of the restore process until it's completed. Once the restore process has concluded, you can click View History to see both the backup and restore jobs listed.

Using *stsadm*

Welcome to the command line. There's a tendency to think of Microsoft products as highly GUI-driven in terms of management, which is true, but the command-line interface hasn't been ignored. The fact that this is a requirement for the exam says that it's most likely a requirement for the job. With that in mind, get ready to click Start ➢ Run, and then type **cmd** in the Run box and have some fun.

As previously mentioned, the vast majority of administrative tasks you can perform with stsadm can also be performed in Central Administration. The advantage of administration on the command line is flexibility and "scriptability," which GUIs typically don't offer.

Open a command-line emulator on the server hosting SharePoint, and type **stsadm** at the prompt. You should receive a message stating stsadm is not recognized as an internal or external command, operable program, or batch file. The reason for that has to do where stsadm.exe is located. The path to the executable is C:\program files\common files\microsoft shared\web server extensions\12\bin. That's quite a pain to have to type in at a command prompt each time you want to use this utility. There are several ways around this issue, and Exercise 14.3 will show you my preferred method. You'll need to perform this task on the actual server computer where you want to run the command. Many of you may be old hands at creating system variables, but I wrote this next exercise for those of you who aren't.

You must be a member of the local administrators group to use stsadm.exe.

EXERCISE 14.3

Creating an Environment Variable

1. At the Windows Server 2003 computer hosting your SharePoint installation, click Start ➢ Control Panel ➢ System.

2. When the System Properties dialog box opens, click the Advanced tab.

3. On the Advanced tab, click Environment Variables.

4. In the Environment Variables dialog box under System Variables, click New.

5. When the New System Variable box appears, type a name for the new variable in the Variable Name field. (I typed **hive**, but you can use another name.)

6. In the Variable Value field, enter the path to stsadm.exe, which is C:\program files\ common files\microsoft shared\web server extensions\12\bin, and click OK.

7. Click OK in the Environment Variables dialog box, and click OK again in the System Properties box.

8. Open a command emulator, and at the C:\> prompt, type **cd %hive%**. Then press Enter.

9. When the full path to the directory containing stsadm.exe is displayed, type **stsadm -help**, and press Enter to verify you can execute this utility.

10. When done, type **exit**, and press Enter to close the command emulator.

Figure 14.1 shows you the specific path that leads to the directory containing `stsadm.exe` as an environment variable after you add it.

FIGURE 14.1   Adding an Environment Variable

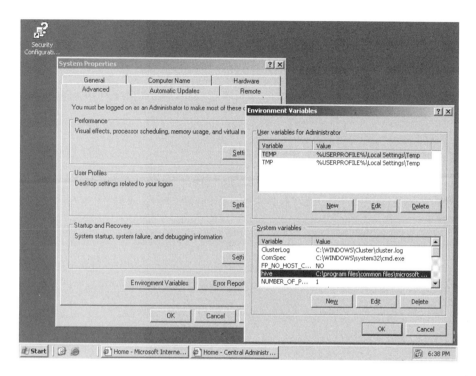

Now, to use the `stsadm` command, just open a command window, change directories to %hive%, and use this executable for any administrative tasks you require. Even after you have become familiar with the `stsadm` utility, you may need help remembering the commands, which is one of the reasons I had you run the `stsadm -help` command. The output will help you remember the more common commands and switches.

If you remember part of the name of a command, such as web, you can type **stsadm | find "web"** and press Enter to see any output containing the word *web*. The list returned will be significantly shorter than what you get from `help`.

Teaching you to become fluent on the command line is well beyond the scope of this book. Although the following information shows you `stsadm`-specific commands, you will have to learn the common DOS commands to navigate the file structure and perform typical tasks.

Basic SharePoint Administration with *stsadm*

Earlier in this chapter, you performed a backup and restore process in Central Administration. Now you'll have the opportunity take a look at the same set of actions on the command line using stsadm. To begin, open a command emulator, and at the prompt, type **%hive%**. Then press Enter.

To perform a full backup of a particular directory, the syntax is as follows:

```
stsadm -o backup -directory \\server\backup -backupmethod full
```

That command would perform a server farm–level backup. To perform a backup of an individual site, use this:

```
Stsadm -o backup -url http://servername/pages/sitename -filename
➡backup.stsadm \\servername\directory
```

Once you execute the command, the backup will occur, and you'll see the progress in the command window. When it is finished, to view the backup history from the command line, type the following:

```
Stsadm -o backuphistory -directory \\servername\directory
```

You should get the backup ID of the specific backup, which you'll need to perform the restore process. To restore the site you just backed up, type the following:

```
Stsadm -o restore -showtree -backupid type_long_hexidecimal_value_of_the_
backup_id -directory
➡\\servername\directory -quiet
```

The -showtree option will display the directories being restored.

In Exercise 14.2 you restored the SharePoint – 80 web application. To perform the same operation using stsadm, you would type this:

```
Stsadm -o restore -backupid type_long_hexidecimal_value_of_the_backup_id -
directory
➡\\servername\directory -item "SharePoint - 80" -restoremethod overwrite
```

Since the name of the item to be restored contains spaces, you'll need to enclose the name in quotation marks. You'll also see that, just as you did in Exercise 14.2, your restore method is to overwrite the files on the server with the backup files.

As you may have noticed, stsadm is not an interactive tool. You must type the operation and all of the parameters in one operation and then execute the operation by pressing Enter, as opposed to filling in missing parameters while the operation is running. The -o switch is used in all the prior examples and is required to identify any operation you want to run, such as backup, backup history, and restore. Typing stsadm and the name of the operation without the -o parameter will not execute the operation. To find out what syntax is required for any particular operation, type the operation with no parameters, and the output will give you a list of what stsadm requires for that operation.

Day-to-day administration using `stsadm` isn't particularly complex once you get used to the command syntax. Although the majority of the content of this book has presented Share-Point administration tasks using GUI tools, it can be as easy or even easier to perform many of the same tasks on the command line.

For more backup and restore scenarios, Microsoft has a support page on its site that is very helpful: `http://support.microsoft.com/kb/889236`.

Using *stsadm* to Administer Site Collections, Sites, and Web Pages

Some of the most common SharePoint tasks are creating and administering sites and subsites. Of course, something is only truly "easy" when you know how to do it, so you should do a bit of research before diving in and creating a new site in SharePoint with `stsadm`. As previously mentioned, using the `-help` switch with the `stsadm` command will provide output on the general commands and switches that `stsadm` expects. Using `stsadm-help <operation>` will give you information on the requirements for the named operation. Open a command window, use the environment variable you created in Exercise 14.3, and execute the following:

```
C:\>stsadm -help createsite
```

The resulting output will show you the valid parameters that will be accepted by the `createsite` operation:

```
-o createsite
-url <url>
-ownerlogin <DOMAIN\name>
-owneremail <someone@example.com>
[-ownername <display name>]
[-lcid <language>]
[-sitetemplate <site template>]
[-title <site title>]
[-description <site description>]
[-quota <quota template>]
```

If you are creating sites only occasionally, such as adding a site to the site collection for a new branch office, you will likely use this command on a regular but not frequent basis. On the other hand, if you have to create a site every time a new hire is added to the company, this task would get tiring fast. The following is a way to automate the creation of individual user sites by writing a script:

```
stsadm -o createsite -url http://localhost/users/%1 -ownerlogin
➥wiredwriter\%1 -owneremail %1@wiredwriter.net -sitetemplate
➥usersite.stp -title "User site for %1" -description "User site for %1" -quota
"300 MB"
```

The domain name is expressed as wiredwriter and wiredwriter.net in the previous example, but when you use it, you'll want to substitute the domain name relevant to your environment. If you compare the sample script to the list of createsite operation variables presented in the prior code, you'll see how each parameter is used in writing an actual command.

When you create this as a script, write the command syntax in a plain-text editor such as Notepad, and then save it with a .cmd suffix, as in createusersite.cmd. Then, every time you want to create a new site for an individual user, you can execute this command followed by the person's username, such as the following:

```
createusersite.cmd jpyles
```

As you can see, creating a script once and then running the script by typing a single line of text is a lot easier than doing all of that typing for every user site you want to make. If you want to use this basic command structure to create web pages instead of sites, substitute the term createweb for createsite. (stsadm uses the term web to indicate a website.)

You can use the deletesite and deleteweb operations to delete SharePoint sites and web pages, respectively. You can also rename an existing web page by using the following command:

```
stsadm -o renameweb -url http://srv01/oldname -newname newname
```

Substitute the name of the relevant localhost for srv01, and while -newname is the name of the command parameter, substitute the actual new name for the web page for the second instance of newname in the sample command.

As sites and site collections change, you may tire of having to go to the Site Directory page to view the changes. You can use the stsadm command to create a scheduled task that lists the site collections available and writes the list to an XML file by using the following commands:

```
stsadm -o enumsites -url http://localhost
c:\inetpub\wwwroot\excludedsite\sites.xml
```

The XML file being written to must be written to a directory published with IIS, but not under SharePoint administrative management. The purpose of writing to an XML file is to make the information available to be presented in a custom Data View web part. Once the web part is added to the desired web part page and configured to display the content of the XML file, it will constantly display the most updated information about SharePoint site collections.

You will need to use SharePoint Designer 2007 to add the Data View web part to the desired web part page since it is not available by default. Then the web part will need to be pointed to the URL that describes the location of the XML file.

Getting More *stsadm* Help

It isn't practical to cover every possible stsadm command available. That would take a chapter in itself (at least). Fortunately, a number of resources are available from Microsoft that you can access online for further study and practice. Now that you have access to stsadm on your SharePoint stand-alone server deployment, you'll be able to continue practicing with it using the following resources:

- A number of handy scripting commands are available on Mark Arend's blog: `http://blogs.msdn.com/markarend/archive/2007/11/08/scripting-stsadm-commands.aspx`.

- TechNet has a general page on the `stsadm` utility: `http://technet2.microsoft.com/Office/en-us/library/188f006d-aa66-4784-a65b-a31822aa13f71033.mspx?mfr=true`.

- Microsoft's Office site contains a comprehensive list of `stsadm` command operations and switches at the following URL: `http://office.microsoft.com/en-us/winsharepointadmin/HA011608431033.aspx`.

If you were to search the Web, you'd come across a number of blogs hosted by individuals who have taken `stsadm` to the next level and extended the utility to provide customized commands. Although these are extremely innovative and useful, you will not be tested on `stsadm` customizations in the 70-630 exam, so those resources are not included here.

Summary

In this chapter, you learned a number of methods of SharePoint administration including the following points:

- You took a general tour of the Central Administration interface and reviewed options that you have already become familiar with as well as newer ones.

- You reviewed the Operations tab in CA including the various sections it contains and what each of the options in those sections can perform.

- You did the same for the Application Management tab as well as Shared Services.

- You performed a backup and restore operation of the SharePoint – 80 web application.

- You became familiar with the `stsadm` command-line utility, discovered how to locate and launch it, and learned which actions it can accomplish.

Exam Essentials

Know how to manage the Central Administration user interface.   Understand what options are available in Central Administration and where to find those options, including on the All Site Content page and on the Operations and Application Management tabs on the site.

Comprehend how the shared service provider is managed.   Know how to access the default shared service provider for your server farm; what options are available in Shared Services that allow you to manage SharePoint-wide features; and how to create, delete, and restore a shared service provider.

Be knowledgeable about the *stsadm* utility.   Know what `stsadm` is, how to locate it, how to launch it, and how to perform common administrative tasks on the command line with `stsadm.exe`.

Be able to configure Usage Analysis and Reporting.   Be aware of where to locate this option in Central Administration and how to configure and use this tool.

Review Questions

1. You are the SharePoint administrator for your company. You suspect that one of the nightly automated jobs you configured to be performed in SharePoint's Central Administration has stopped. You just want to see a list of jobs without options to configure those jobs. You launch the CA web application and log in as administrator. Where can you go to see whether this automated job is running?

    A. Click the Operations tab, and under Global Configuration, click Timer Job Definitions.

    B. Click the Operations tab, and under Global Configuration, click Timer Job Status.

    C. Click the Application Management tab, and under SharePoint Site Management, click Automated Job Definitions.

    D. Click the Application Management tab, and under SharePoint Site Management, click Automated Job Status.

2. You are the SharePoint administrator for your organization. When you originally created your SharePoint server farm, you created a default SSP for the company's site collection. Now Jeff, the CTO, has tasked you with creating a separate server farm for the western regional offices but wants that new server farm to have the same features and options as the current farm. You determine that allowing both server farms to share the same SSP would be the best solution. What do you do to configure this option?

    A. On the Operations tab, under Topology and Services, click Services on Farm to share the current SSP with a new server farm.

    B. On the Operations tab under Shared Services Provider, click Manage Farm Features to access the current SSP and share it with a new server farm.

    C. On the Application Management tab under Office SharePoint Server Shared Services, click Create or Configure This Farm's Shared Services in order to share the SSP with another server farm.

    D. On the Shared Services Administration page for the SSP, click Create or Configure This Farm's Shared Services in order to share the SSP with another server farm.

3. You are the SharePoint administrator for your company. You have just completed a backup of the web application for your organization's site collection and are reviewing the status of the backup on the Backup and Restore Status page. You see the value 10.9.8.219\backup\spbr0000\. What does this value signify?

    A. The directory to which the SharePoint web application was backed up

    B. The backup ID of the SharePoint web application backup file

    C. The top component you backed up

    D. The location of the SharePoint files for the web application you backed up

4. You are the SharePoint administrator for your company, and you want to use the `stsadm.exe` command-line utility to perform various administrative tasks rather than going through the GUI in Central Administration. You are in the process of creating an environment variable so that you can more easily launch `stsadm.exe` from the command prompt. You have opened the Environment Variables dialog box from the System Properties box on your server. Where must you create the proper variable to accomplish your task?

A. Create the variable in User variables for the administrator.

B. Create the variable in Administrator Variables for the server.

C. Create the variable in Administrative Variables.

D. Create the variable in System Variables.

5. You are the SharePoint administrator for your company, and you want to perform a backup process of an individual site for the sales department as a web application. You are at the command prompt now. Of the following selections, which one is the correct syntax for performing a full backup of the web application?

A. `stsadm -o backup -directory \\server\backup -backupmethod full`

B. `stsadm -o backup -url http://servername/pages/sitename -filename`
`backup.stsadm \\servername\directory -backupmethod full`

C. `stsadm -o backup -directory http://servername/pages/sitename -filename`
`backup.stsadm \\servername\directory -backupmethod full`

D. `stsadm -o backup -url \\server\backup -filename backup.stsadm`
`\\servername\directory -backupmethod full`

6. You are the SharePoint administrator for your company, and you have been tasked by Diana, the CIO, with performing more administrative tasks for SharePoint from the command line rather than the GUI. She believes that the `stsadm.exe` utility is very powerful and will make you more efficient at performing particular SharePoint management duties. You are not completely familiar with `stsadm` and decide to explore the tool. Logged in as administrator, you type **stsadm.exe** and press Enter. You receive an error message stating `stsadm` is not recognized as an internal or external command, operable program, or batch file. What went wrong?

A. You are logged into SharePoint from a remote computer and must type **stsadm.exe -r** to launch the utility remotely.

B. You executed the command incorrectly. Using the `.exe` extension will produce an error. The correct command to launch the utility is `stsadm`.

C. The command is case sensitive, and you must type **STSADM.EXE** to launch the utility.

D. The `stsadm.exe` utility is not in your variable path. You must either add it to the path or create an environment variable so you can launch the utility.

7. You are the SharePoint administrator for your company, and you are using an environment variable to make it easier to launch the `stsadm.exe` utility at the command prompt. You switch to the variable you've created, and your prompt suddenly is displaying a very long path name ending in `\bin`. What happened?

    A. Nothing. When you created the variable and then used it, you quickly switched to the directory containing `stsadm`, which is `C:\program files\common files\microsoft shared\web server extensions\12\bin`. That path will be displayed as part of the command prompt.

    B. You mapped the incorrect environment variable. The prompt should appear as just `C:\>`.

    C. You used the `cd variable_name` command and should type in just the variable name and then launch `stsadm.exe`.

    D. You accidentally mapped a user variable rather than a system variable, and this is the result.

8. You are the new SharePoint administrator for your company, and you are going through the Central Administration web application to review how SharePoint administration is configured. You are on the All Site Content page and have clicked HelpFold under Document Libraries. This is the root library for SharePoint's help files system, and you are scanning the different files present. The library is set up for the default view. Of the following options, which are valid column names in this library? (Choose all that apply.)

    A. Lock

    B. Presentation

    C. MetaData

    D. Support

9. You are the new SharePoint administrator for your company, and you are going through the Central Administration web application to review how SharePoint administration is configured. You are on the Operations tab and are reviewing the options located in the Topology and Services section. The site collection is deployed using a stand-alone SharePoint server installation, and you want to see the running services. Which options can you click in this section that will let you see the services? (Choose all that apply.)

    A. Services on Farm

    B. Services on Server

    C. Service Accounts

    D. Services Reports

10. You are the SharePoint administrator for your organization, and you've been tasked by Scott, your supervisor, with generating an immediate information management policy usage report. It's a Friday just before a long holiday weekend, and he is concerned that there is an issue with this system and wants it either tracked down before the weekend starts or verified that there is no issue. You log in to Central Administration as a supervisor and attempt to manually generate a report and have it write to the log's default location. Of the following options, which one is the most correct?

    A. There is no on-demand method for generating an information management policy usage log, and you must change the schedule so that it will generate a report just a few minutes in the future to the default location and then review the log report.

    B. You use the on-demand process for generating a report and navigate to the default location of the log to review it.

    C. There is no method for on-demand report generation and no default location for the log, so you must set the schedule to generate a report five minutes later and quickly define a path to where you want the log file to write.

    D. Although there is an on-demand method of generating a report, there is no default location for writing log reports, so you must define this location before using the on-demand feature.

11. You are the SharePoint administrator for your organization, and you are planning to perform some administrative tasks on the SharePoint server farm that require taking it offline. You have sent out a broadcast email notice to all users informing them of when the system will be taken offline and for approximately how long. You also plan to perform this maintenance during "off-hours" when the system has relatively few users, but you know there will still be some users who will want to access the system. Rather than cut them off abruptly, you plan to gradually take the system offline by preventing new user sessions for long-running operations. How do you go about this?

    A. In Central Administration on the Application Management tab under SharePoint Site Management, click Manage Farm Features.

    B. In Central Administration on the Operations tab under Global Configuration, click Quiesce Farm.

    C. In Central Administration on the Application Management tab under Global Configuration, click Manage Farm Operations.

    D. In Central Administration on the Operations tab under SharePoint Site Management, click Quiet Server Farm.

12. You are the SharePoint administrator for a company running a small site collection. This site collection is managed on a stand-alone server deployment hosting both SharePoint and database services on a single server computer. Mary, the new CEO for your company, wants a separate SQL server to manage database services and has heard that SQL authentication is more secure than Windows authentication for allowing queries to the database. As part of complying with the CEO's requirements, you will need to configure an access account and password to specify SQL authentication to the new SQL server. Where do you perform this action?

   A. In Central Administration on the Operations tab under Data Configuration, click Default Database Server.

   B. In Central Administration on the Operations tab under Data Configuration, click Database Server Services.

   C. In Central Administration on the Application Management tab under Data Deployment, Click Database Deployment Services.

   D. In Central Administration on the Application Management tab under Data Deployment, click Database Object Status.

13. You are the SharePoint administrator for your company. You've come into the office over the weekend to perform some maintenance tasks for Shared Services during a time when few to no users will be accessing the system. You need to perform a wide variety of Shared Services tasks that must be accessed from different locations in Central Administration. Most of these are accessed by clicking the name of the SSP in Quick Launch from the CA main page, but some must be accessed from the Application Management tab in CA. Of the following options, which are accessed from the Application Management tab under Office SharePoint Server Shared Services? (Choose all that apply.)

   A. User Profiles

   B. Check Services Enabled in This Farm

   C. Configure Setting State

   D. Excel Services Settings

14. You are the SharePoint administrator for your company, and you have tasked PJ, a member of your staff, with configuring the nightly differential backup of the SharePoint web applications. As the web applications grow with use, PJ has become concerned that the size of the applications will eventually exceed the storage capacity of the backup location. PJ already knows the fixed capacity of the backup location for the web applications. How can he know the size of any given web application before the backup operation is performed?

   A. On the Perform a Backup – Step 1 of 2: Select a Component to Backup page, when PJ selects the backup components, an automatic counter displays the size required to back up those components.

   B. On the Perform a Backup – Step 1 of 2: Select a Component to Backup page, each SharePoint component displayed on the page has its estimated size shown in the Size column.

   C. On the Start Backup – Step 2 of 2: Select Backup Options page, the estimated size of the selections you made on the previous page are displayed next to the Type of Backup selection section.

   D. On the Start Backup – Step 2 of 2: Select Backup Options page, the estimated size of the selections you made on the previous page are displayed below the Backup Location field.

15. You are the SharePoint administrator for your company, and you have tasked PJ, a member of your staff, with managing the backup and restore processes for SharePoint. One of the web application components in SharePoint has become corrupted, and PJ is responsible for restoring those components from the most recent backup. He has begun the restore process and has just selected the type of backup he will be performing. What is his next step?

   A. PJ must tick the check boxes for just the components he wants to restore on the Restore from Backup – Step 3 of 4: Select Component to Restore page.

   B. PJ must tick the Restore Previously Backed Up Components check box on the Restore from Backup – Step 3 of 4: Select Component to Restore page.

   C. PJ must click Continue Restore Process on the Restore from Backup – Step 3 of 4: Select Component to Restore page.

   D. PJ must specify the URL to the web application files he wants to restore in the available field on the Restore from Backup – Step 3 of 4: Select Component to Restore page.

16. You are the SharePoint administrator for your company, and you are currently working with the `stsadm` utility performing various administrative tasks. You need to perform a task with the word web as part of the command but can't quite recall the exact syntax of the command. How would you go about tracking this information down on the command line using `stsadm`?

   A. Type `stsadm -help "web"`.

   B. Type `stsadm -? "web"`.

   C. Type `stsadm | grep "web"`.

   D. Type `stsadm | find "web"`.

17. You are the SharePoint administrator for your company, and you have created an environmental variable so that you can more easily use the `stsadm.exe` utility without having to input a long path at the command line each time you want to execute this tool. You have named this variable getstsadm. At the `C:\>` prompt, how do you involve this variable so that it takes you to the proper directory to allow you to use `stsadm.exe`?

   A. Type `cd "getstsadm"` including the quotation marks.

   B. Type `cd getstsadm`.

   C. Type `cd %getstsadm%`.

   D. Type `"cd %getstsadm%"` including the quotation marks.

18. You are the SharePoint administrator for your company, and you are providing an in-service training for your staff on advanced SharePoint administration. You are currently discussing the `stsadm.exe` utility including its capacities and limitations. A member of your staff has been having problems performing the tasks he usually does in the GUI on the command line and is especially interested in this subject. Of the following selections, which are true for `stsadm.exe`? (Choose all that apply.)

   A. You can perform scripting tasks using `stsadm.exe`.

   B. You must be a member of the domain administrators group to use `stsadm.exe`.

   C. You can perform backup and restore operations using `stsadm.exe`.

   D. `stsadm.exe` is an interactive tool that will prompt you for parameters during the operation.

19. You are the SharePoint administrator for your company, and you are providing an in-service training for your staff on advanced SharePoint administration. You are currently presenting information about Central Administration and especially about unique lists on the All Site Content page of CA. Of the following options, which are list items in the CA All Site Contents page? (Choose all that apply.)

A. Content Deployment Jobs

B. Content Deployment Paths

C. Job Reports

D. Support Reports

20. You are the SharePoint administrator for your company, and you are currently performing administrative tasks in the Central Administration web application. You are currently on the Servers on Farm page and plan on reviewing some information about running services and performing a few maintenance tasks. Of the following selections, what can you expect to see or do on this page? (Choose all that apply.)

A. You can expect to see the names of database servers on the farm.

B. You can expect to see the names of the web application servers on the farm.

C. You can expect to see the server role selections available for servers on the server farm.

D. You can expect to see the name of the mail server managing incoming emails for the server farm.

Answers to Review Questions

1. B. Option A is incorrect because that option allows you to see not only the names of each automated job but also their run schedules and lets you enable and disable jobs. Options C and D are bogus.

2. C. Options A, B, and D are all bogus answers. Only option C describes the valid process for initiating this task.

3. A. The value indicates the IP address, the directory, and the name of the backup file, showing where the SharePoint component you backed up is located. The backup ID is a long, hexadecimal string; the top component would indicate the name of the web application; and the source location of the web application is not listed on this page.

4. D. Option A exists in the Environment Variables dialog box but will not let you create a mapping to the desired location of stsadm.exe from the command prompt by inputting a variable. Options B and C are bogus.

5. B. Option A is the correct syntax for backing up a directory but not a single site as a web application. Options C and D are bogus syntax examples and will do nothing but yield error messages.

6. D. It is true that you cannot launch the stsadm.exe utility from a remote computer and must be at the server computer where you want to work, but using the -r switch will not let you work remotely, as suggested in option A. You can launch the utility using either stsadm or stsadm.exe, and the command is not case sensitive, so options B and C are bogus.

7. A. When you create a system variable and then change directories using that variable name, it quickly takes you to the location of stsadm.exe so you can launch the utility. The path name is very long, and option A displays the correct path. You must use the cd variable_ name command, such as cd %hive%, in order to quickly switch to the proper directory for this utility. This is a system variable, so option D is bogus.

8. A, C, and D. The valid column names for the default view of this library are Content, Images, Lock, Manifests, MetaData, and Support. Presentation is a bogus answer.

9. A and B. You can view running services on the server farm (including a stand-alone server) either in Services on Farm by clicking the name of the server or by opening Services on Server directly under Topology and Services. Service Accounts is on the Operations tab but under Security Configuration and is used to manage Windows services and applications such as the Document Conversions Launcher Service or Single Sign-on. Services Reports is a bogus answer.

10. D. Only option D describes the correct configuration and features of the Information Management Policy Usage Reports page. Options A, B, and C are all bogus.

11. B. Options A, C, and D are all bogus answers. Only option B describes the correct process of gradually shutting down the server farm.

12. A. Options B, C, and D are all bogus answers. Only option A describes the correct process.

13. B and C. Check Services Enabled in This Farm and Configure Settings State are two Shared Services features accessed from the Application Management tab in Central Administration. User Profiles and Excel Services Settings are accessed from the home page of the individual SSP servicing the server farm.

14. D. Options A, B, and C are all bogus. Only option D describes how to determine the estimated size of the selected files before performing the backup.

15. A. On the Restore from Backup – Step 3 of 4: Select Component to Restore page, the directory structure tree for all the SharePoint clients is displayed with check boxes beside each component. PJ must tick only the check boxes next to the components he wants to restore before clicking Continue Restore Process. All the other options are bogus.

16. Answer D. The -help and -? switches are general "help" switches and will return a large amount of information about the stsadm command but will not work by adding web to the end. Piping to grep (using |) may work on the Unix or Linux box but generally not in Windows. Option D is the only one that presents the correct command.

17. C. The %getstsadm% environment variable is just a shortcut method to get to the correct directory. Typing **cd %getstsadm%** with the percent signs before and after is like issuing the cd command and specifying the actual path. The solutions given in options A, B, and D are bogus and will result in error messages.

18. A and C. You can write batch files and scripts in stsadm.exe, and you must be a member of the local administrators (rather than domain administrators) group to use this utility. You can perform backup and restore operations with this tool, but it is not an interactive tool that prompts you for parameters during the operation. You must type in all the operations and parameters at once and then execute the command.

19. A, B and C. Valid list items on the CA All Site Content page are Content Deployment Jobs, Content Deployment Paths, Job Reports, and Migration Profile List. Support Reports is a bogus answer.

20. A, B, and C. You can expect to see the name of the mail server managing outgoing emails for the server farm, not incoming emails. All the other answers are correct.

Chapter

15

Working with Content Management

MICROSOFT EXAM OBJECTIVES COVERED IN THIS CHAPTER:

✓ **Configure Content Management**

- Configure Records Management
- Configure Web Content Management
- Managing Policies and Compliance
- Configure Workflows

Chapter 10, "Working with Microsoft Documents in Share-Point," and Chapter 11, "Working with Microsoft Outlook in SharePoint," addressed the area of content management as it related to Microsoft Word and Microsoft Outlook. This chapter will throw a much wider net over the concept and present content management as an overall function of all information management in SharePoint 2007.

Although the chapters mentioned in the previous paragraph addressed a significant amount of detail on document and records management, we'll start with the basics of those subjects, particularly in terms of how the SharePoint Records Center site functions as the main content repository tool. We will drill down into how you can use the Records Center to perform a number of detailed tasks such as making it available from document libraries in the site collection and enabling content auditing.

The main focus of this chapter will be on the features and functions of web content management. Although this may seem to be only one part of the overall content management objective for the 70-630 exam, it is in fact a major player in the content management arena. This is because virtually all content within SharePoint can be thought of as "web content" given that SharePoint's primary interface is through a web browser.

As part of discussing the various aspects of content management in general, we'll revisit policies, compliance, and workflows in the different sections of this chapter as you learn to envision SharePoint content management principles as an overarching concept.

Reviewing SharePoint Records Management

SharePoint content management functions are handled primarily through a specialized site called the Records Center. You can think of the Records Center as the central repository for all your important corporate data, not just in terms of storage but in terms of total life-cycle management, from creation to versioning to archiving to obsolescence and deletion. The Records Center features that are brought into play to achieve this level of information oversight include Information Management Policy, Records Routing, Hold, Vault, and Record Collection Programmable Interface.

Chapter 11, "Working with Microsoft Outlook in SharePoint," defined each of the Records Center terms and their uses.

Records management planning should be mapped out from records creation through expiration, as should an archiving and retention plan. The plan will define which records you intend to upload into the Records Center, which content types will be employed, how records will be routed to the Records Center, and the roles and responsibilities of the SharePoint members who will be assigned to the records management function in your company.

If you plan to use a single Records Center for all your corporation's content management requirements, you should not need to create a new site. A Records Center site was created as part of the top-level portal site when you first installed SharePoint, as shown in Figure 15.1.

FIGURE 15.1   Records Center site

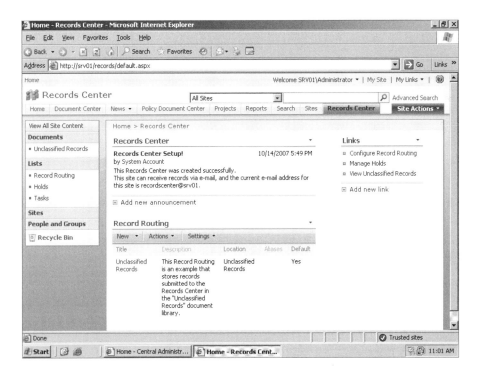

By default, the Records Center has one document center for unclassified records and three lists: Record Routing, Holds, and Tasks, as shown in the Quick Launch menu on the site. You will need to perform a number of required functions using the prompts available in different web parts in the site's main pane. Under Records Center, you can click Records Center Setup to configure the center. The Links list web part also contains a number of task links such as Configure Record Routing, Manage Holds, and View Unclassified Records. We'll go through the Records Center and related pages in detail in this chapter to enable content management in your SharePoint site collection.

Although you primarily configure the Records Center from within its own site, you must set up certain features from inside the SharePoint Central Administration web application. Earlier in the chapter, you read that you can enable a Records Center to be accessible from all of the document libraries within the SharePoint site collection. You must enable this feature from within Central Administration.

Also, although it is possible to have more than one Records Center available in your site collection, you can enable only a single Records Center to be accessible from all the document libraries within a single server farm. This means it is virtually mandatory to have only one central location for corporate content management per SharePoint 2007 installation. Once this feature is enabled, you can send content to the Records Center from a document library by clicking Edit and then Send To in the library. Unless you've created additional document libraries in the Records Center, any documents sent to that site will be uploaded to the Unclassified Documents library by default.

Fortunately, documents are not transmitted from document libraries to the Records Center without a method of organization. If you have not created one for the Records Center, any document sent to the Unclassified Documents library will be contained in a folder marked with the date and time it was created. Within the folder are both the actual document file and a Properties folder associated with the file. The filename is appended at the end with a random series of letters and numbers in order to create a unique identifier for the file. If a copy of the same file (with the same filename) is subsequently uploaded into the Records Center, a different set of alphanumeric characters will be appended to that file's name, creating a separate identifier, even if the content of both files is identical.

Working with the Records Center

It will be easier to understand the different functions and features of the Records Center by actually working with it and setting the site up to manage content within SharePoint. The following set of exercises is designed to do just that. Since I previously mentioned how to allow the site collection document libraries to send content to the Records Center, Exercise 15.1 will show you how to do this.

EXERCISE 15.1

Configuring a Records Center to Be an External Service Connection in Central Administration

1. Launch the Central Administration web application, and click the Application Management tab.

2. On the Application Management page under External Service Connections, click Records Center.

3. On the Configure Connection to Records Center page, click Connect to a Records Center.

4. In the URL field, type or paste in the URL to the Records Center web service to which you want to create a connection (such as `http://servername/portalname/_vti_bin/officialfile.asmx`).

5. In the Display Name field, type the name you want to appear in the document libraries' Send To menus.

6. Click OK to finish.

Step 4 in this exercise is a crucial step. You are not inputting the URL of the Records Center, such as `http://servername/records/default.aspx`, but rather the name of the Records Center web service. This URL should consist of the server name, the path to the Records Center (records in this case), and then `_vti_bin/officialfile.asmx`. Unless this specific path is included, the desired feature will fail to function.

To test the success of your actions, go to a document library in your site collection, click to the right of any document name, and select Send To ➤ Records Center from the menu.

On the Records Center site, the Records Center web part is actually an Announcements list web part. If you click the Records Center Setup link, you'll be taken to an announcement that states the Records Center was successfully created, states that it can receive records via email, and states the email address for the Records Center, which in my case is `recordscenter@srv01`. Like any list item, it can be edited or deleted. You can also add more items to this Announcements list.

Your first task in the Records Center is to create different document libraries for each document or content type you plan to store and manage on this site. In Quick Launch, click Documents to get to the All Site Content page. As you can see in Figure 15.2, four document libraries are created in the Records Center by default:

- The Hold Reports library is a repository of reports for documents placed on a hold.

- Missing Properties includes an entry point that allows you to add any missing metadata for files in the Records Center.

- Records Pending Submission is a "holding cell" for files submitted to the Records Center but that are missing required metadata (which can be added in the Missing Properties library).

- Unclassified Records, as you learned previously, is the default destination for any files sent to the Records Center.

To send files to other destinations in the Records Center, you first must create the desired libraries and then add the appropriate entries in Record Routing. You have had plenty of experience creating document libraries and other libraries in previous chapters of this book, so you won't need to go through any exercises to take you through the steps. Before moving on in this chapter, take some time to add some libraries in your Records Center. You can add document, form, wiki, picture, data connection, report, and slide libraries as you see fit. The libraries you create will be the basis for a number of exercises to follow.

In my example, I've created a document library for secure records, a report library, and a picture library. Your selections may be different but will likely be sufficient to follow the subsequent exercises.

FIGURE 15.2 Records Center's All Site Content page

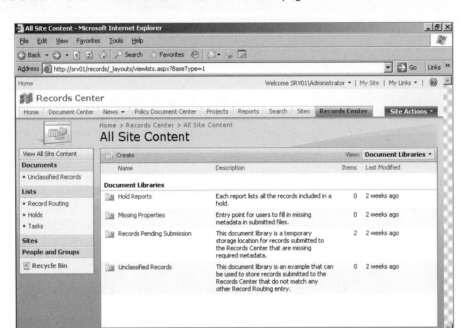

Now that you have created some sample libraries, the next task is to create entries for them in Records Routing. Exercise 15.2 will take you through this process. Use any of the libraries you created. This example will use the new document library on my Records Center site.

EXERCISE 15.2

Creating a Records Routing Entry for a Library

1. On the Records Center main page, click New ➤ New Item in the Records Routing web part toolbar.

2. Type the name of the records routing entry for the library in the required Title field, and give it an optional description in the Description field.

3. In the required Location field, type the name of the library, such as **Secure Library**.

4. In the Aliases field, enter any other names by which this library is called, separating the names with a forward slash (/).

5.   Tick the Default check box if you want this library to be the default location for all documents that do not match any other records routing descriptions; otherwise, leave the check box clear.

6.   Click OK.

The new entry will appear in the Records Routing web part on the main Records Center page.

Since the Unclassified Records library is the default repository location for any unspecified records sent to the Records Center, you will not likely tick the Default check box in step 5 for this or any other routing entry you create, unless you want to change the default. You would then have to edit the routing entry for the Unclassified Records library to remove the tick from the Default check box.

    To edit a Records Routing entry, just click to the right of its name in the Record Routing web part, and select Edit Item from the menu.

For records to be routed to the proper destination, the document library must also be configured for the correct content type or types for the designated documents. If not, then all documents sent to the Records Center will still be routed to the Unclassified Records library. Make sure the document library you are sending documents from and the documents themselves are configured to be the content type that will be received by the new document library.

In addition to sending documents from a document library in the site collection to a specific document library in the Records Center using the Send To menu option, you can also upload documents to Records Center libraries in the same way you can from any other library in the site collection.

Also, like any other list, you can create views, add, or remove columns, as well as configure the list to send you an alert when certain conditions change, such as when list items are added, modified, or deleted.

You can take a few minutes and repeat Exercise 15.2 to add routing records for your other document libraries. You cannot create a routing record for a picture library because only libraries under Documents are subject to this feature.

The content management features you learned to use in Chapter 10, "Working with Microsoft Documents in SharePoint," and Chapter 11, "Working with Microsoft Outlook in SharePoint," can be applied to the libraries in the Records Center. In addition to enabling libraries for one or multiple content types, you can apply information management policy settings and workflows, enable incoming emails, and perform every other function you would ordinarily use with a document library in SharePoint. Combining all these features and abilities in the Records Center will complete your ability to use it for the content management "nerve center" of your company's SharePoint site collection.

Also, the Report Center in the Records Center is its own specialized site designed for managing your organization's reporting environment. I covered the material associated with the Report Center in detail in Chapter 12, "Using Excel Services and Business Intelligence," and Chapter 13, "Using Business Forms and Business Intelligence," when reviewing business intelligence, so there won't be any additional information or exercises involving this workspace. Refer to those chapters if you need a refresher on this site type.

There's another site collection–level task that you can perform to enhance content management in SharePoint. You already know how to use information management policies to configure auditing for a particular library; however, you can also configure the auditing feature over the entire site collection. Exercise 15.3 will show you how to do this. You will need to be at the top-level portal site to begin this exercise, and you will need to be logged in with an account that has site collection administrative rights.

EXERCISE 15.3

Configuring Site Collection Auditing

1. On the top-level portal site, click Site Actions ➢ Site Settings ➢ Modify All Site Settings.

2. On the Site Settings page under Site Collection Administration, select Site Collection Audit Settings.

3. On the Configure Audit Settings page under Documents and Items, beneath Specify the Events to Audit, you can tick any of the following check boxes:

   Opening or Downloading Documents, Viewing Items in Lists, or Viewing Item Properties

   Editing Items

   Checking Out or Checking In Items

   Moving or Copying Items to Another Location in the Site

   Deleting or Restoring Items

4. Under Lists, Libraries, and Sites, beneath Specify the Events to Audit, you can tick any of the following check boxes:

   Editing Content Types and Columns

   Searching Site Content

   Editing Users and Permissions

5. Click OK when finished.

6. On the Site Settings page under Site Collection Administration, click Audit Log Reports.

7. Click any of the options on the View Auditing Reports page to see the results of the auditing features you enabled. (You may have to wait some time before enough activity has occurred to result in significant log entries.)

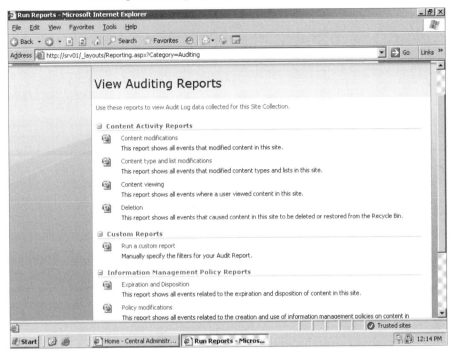

8. After you've reviewed the desired report, click the Back button on your browser, and then click Home to return to the top-level portal site.

Working with Web Content Management

Web content management (WCM) is the collection of SharePoint features that allows user members in the SharePoint site collection to modify and manage how information is published on SharePoint websites. This function was previously relegated to the Microsoft Content Management Server 2002 (MCMS), but in the interests of expanding the scope of usability and end user collaboration, the features were integrated into Microsoft Office SharePoint Server (MOSS) 2007.

WCM is most commonly applied to some type of web publishing function such as creating and applying a custom master page, managing layout pages, and publishing a site in multiple languages.

Working with WCM and Design Elements

You've already practiced a wide variety of WCM procedures every time you worked through an exercise involving creating or modifying a site, list, or library. Workflow and applying an information management policy such as labeling are also considered part of the WCM collection of features, although labels in this instance are most appropriately applied to content published in more than one language.

I'll briefly review these design elements before showing how they are incorporated in WCM:

Master pages The master page defines the framework of the web page. It contains the elements you want all of your web pages in the site to have in common, and it provides a single location where you can control all the design elements. Typically, a SharePoint site uses a single site master page; however, very large websites can use more than one. One reason to use more than one master page is if you want the sites for different departments or divisions in your organization to be presented differently; another reason is if you want to brand each of your products in a unique fashion.

 You were introduced to these design element types in Chapter 8, "Configuring Web Part Pages, Web Parts, and Web Pages."

Content pages Each content page in SharePoint consists of text, images, and other content stored as an entry in a pages library. Each item in a pages library represents an individual web page. The pages library is just like the master pages or any other library, and because of that, content pages are subject to auditing, versioning, workflow, the checkout and check-in process, and content approval, just like any other library object. Although all pages in a site are in a single pages library, specialized sites such as intranet portal sites and Internet presence sites consist of a tree of sites, each with its own separate pages library. Creating and editing web pages in SharePoint is done either by using the SharePoint web interface or by converting a document into an HTML page.

Layout pages This is a web page type that defines the layout for a content page. When you open a SharePoint web page in a browser, the layout page for that web page is combined with the master page for the site or portion of the site. After that, the contents of the page are supplied to the field controls on the layout page. The layout page must be designed for a particular content type since the field controls vary among content types. For instance, an Article Page content type would have several field controls that include a Page Content field control to hold the contents of the Page Content column and a Page Image field control to hold the image displayed on the page as a result of being linked to its location in a picture library.

Field controls Field controls are actually a part of page layouts and are simple Microsoft ASP.NET 2.0 controls that are bound to WSS data contained on the page. They have a small amount of code to display the two modes of the controls: one for render time and one for edit time. Windows SharePoint Services (WSS) 3.0 and MOSS 2007 provide several default field controls that you can use in your pages. All field controls that you use in a SharePoint Server 2007 site are derived from a base class in WSS 3.0 called `FormComponent`. You can use any of the default field controls or write a field control by deriving from the `BaseRichField` class to suit your own specific needs.

Before continuing, it will be necessary to create a publishing portal in SharePoint. The publishing portal is the most common site used for WCM since it is the site collection's "public face" so to speak. It contains all the information specifically created for a wide audience such as the corporation's intranet or your company's public Internet site. A publishing portal isn't created at the same level as the top-level portal site or a subsite in the site collection; instead, it must be made in the SharePoint Central Administration web application. In essence, you are creating a new web application when you create this new portal. Exercise 15.4 will let you see how this works.

EXERCISE 15.4

Creating a Publishing Portal Site in Central Administration

1. Launch the Central Administration web application, and then click the Application Management tab.

2. On the Application Management page under SharePoint Site Management, click Create Site Collection.

3. On the Create Site Collection page under Web Application, click the arrow to the right of the currently displayed web application, and then click Change Web Application.

4. Select the SharePoint-80 web application (the URL for mine is `http://srv01/`).

5. Under Title and Description, give your new publishing portal site a name in the Title field and an optional description in the Description field.

6. In the Web Site Address area under URL, use the drop-down menu to select /sites/, and then add a name to the URL extension, such as **publishing**.

7. In the Template Selection area under Select a Template, click the Publishing tab, and then select Publishing Portal.

8. In the Primary Site Collection Administrator area, type the name of the valid SharePoint user you want to be the main administrator for this site collection in the User Name field, and click the Check Names button to verify the name.

9. In the Secondary Site Collection Administrator area, perform the same actions you did in step 8 using a different user's name.

10. In the Quota Template area, use the Select a Quota Template drop-down menu to select a quota template type.

EXERCISE 15.4 *(continued)*

11. Click OK when finished.

12. When the Top-Level Site Successfully Created appears, click the link for the publishing portal site.

It will also be helpful to add this portal site to your browser's favorites list so you can return to it without always having to remember the URL.

As you can see in Figure 15.3, the default appearance of a publishing portal is very different from the sites and workspaces you've created in SharePoint up to this point.

FIGURE 15.3   A publishing portal

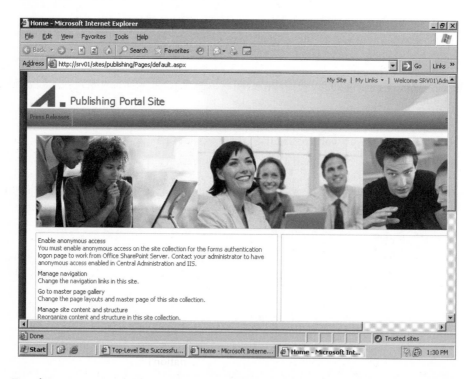

Few features are available on this site by default; therefore, what you want, you'll have to add. Since this is a top-level portal site, any changes you make will have to go through an approval process by default. The user who created this site collection is an approver by default, but the primary site administrator is not. If you want other users to belong to the approvers group, click the Add Users to the Approvers and Members Groups link on the main page. Then, on the People and Groups: All Groups page, click Approvers to add any valid Share-Point users you want to this group.

Chapter 5, "Managing Users and Groups," showed you how to manage SharePoint users and groups.

If this is to be an Internet site, you will have to allow anonymous users to have access. To do so, click the Enable Anonymous Access link on the main page, and then configure permissions to allow anonymous users to access part of or the entire publishing portal site.

Earlier, you reviewed information on what a master page and layout pages are in SharePoint. WCM features include creating and modifying these pages and changing from one page to another. Exercise 15.5 will take you through the steps of creating a new custom-made master page.

Many of the WCM activities require the use of Microsoft Office SharePoint Designer 2007. Unless you have this application installed on the computer you want to use to perform these tasks, you will not be able to complete the following exercises.

EXERCISE 15.5

Creating a New Page Layout

1. On the Publishing Portal main page, click Go to Master Page Gallery.

2. On the Master Page Gallery page, click New ➢ Page Layout.

3. On the New Page Layout page in the Associated Content Type area, under Content Type Group, use the drop-down menu to select the content type group you want to use for the new page layout.

4. Under Content Type Name, use the drop-down menu to select a content type (such as Welcome Page).

    You can also click Create a New Site content type to create an entirely new content type.

5. In the Page Layout Title and Description area, use the URL, Title, and Description fields to type in the URL to the content type, the name of the content type, and an optional description, respectively.

6. In the Variation Labels area, if available, select any variation label in the Available Labels field, and click the Add button to add them to the Labels for Layout field.

7. Click OK to finish.

Once you are returned to the Master Page Gallery, you can select the new page and, in the menu, select Edit in Microsoft Office SharePoint Designer. Check out the new page if you are prompted to do so. Then you can edit the page in Designer and, when finished, save your changes, close the page, and check the page back in to the Master Page Gallery.

You can create a new, custom-made master page for the publishing portal, but you will need to begin the task from SharePoint Designer. Exercise 15.6 will show you this process.

EXERCISE 15.6

Creating a Custom-Made Master Page

1. Launch SharePoint Designer 2007, click File ➤ Open Site, and then enter the URL to the portal site where you want to create the new master page.

2. Under site name, select _catalogs, and then select MasterPage (Master Page Gallery).

3. In the list, right-click the name of one of the available master page templates, and then select Copy.

4. Select the _catalogs field by placing the cursor inside the field, and then paste the master page template you copied in the previous step.

5. Rename the template in the _catalogs field to CustomPublish.Master, and then double-click the name to open the page in Designer.

6. Use Designer to edit the master page in whatever way you desire, and then save your work.

7. To publish the newly created master page, in the Master Page Gallery, select the name of the new master page (CustomPublish.Master in this case), and then click Check In.

8. In the Check In dialog box, select Publish a Major Version, and then click OK.

9. When the confirm dialog box appears, click Yes.

10. When you are returned to the Master Page Gallery, select the name of the new master page, click Approve/Reject, and then approve the master page.

To use the new master page on the publishing portal site, you will need to change the default master page for the site. You can do this from the portal site by clicking Site Actions ➤ Site Settings ➤ Modify All Site Settings. On the Site Settings page under Look and Feel, click Master Page. On the Site Master Page Settings page under Specify a Master Page to Be Used By This Site and All Sites That Inherit from It, use the drop-down arrow to select the name of the new master page. Under System Master Page, you can make the same selection if you also want the new master page to be applied to the system. Click OK, and then click Publishing Portal Site to return to the portal's main page so you can review your work.

The site master page defines the look and feel of the published pages in the site, whereas the system master page defines the look and feel of the system pages. System pages include such pages as the home page for the Master Page Gallery and the settings pages.

You may not think of it as such, but the structure of the site collection is itself a design element. SharePoint makes it possible to actually move a site within the site collection while preserving all the links so that links to the moved web content are not broken. Exercise 15.7 will show you how to do this. This task requires that you create at least two subsites beneath the publishing portal site you created in Exercise 15.4 so you have sites available to move.

EXERCISE 15.7

Moving a Site in a Site Collection

1. On the publishing portal site, click Site Actions ➢ Manage Content and Structure.

2. On the Site Content and Structure page, in the menu on the left, click to the right of the page or item you want to move, and then select Move from the menu.

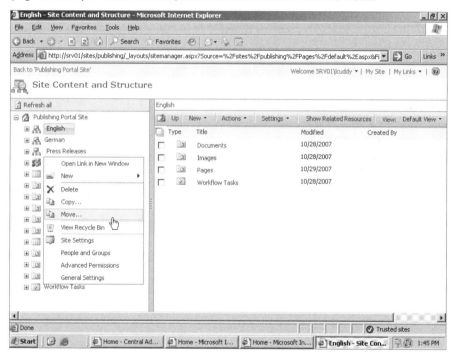

3. When the Move Web Page dialog box appears, select the page where you want the item moved to, and then click OK. (The move operation may take a few seconds.)

Once the move operation is complete, go to the site where you moved the page or item to verify that it is in the proper location.

 **Real World Scenario**

Configuring a Records Center for Content Management

You are the SharePoint administrator for your site. Ian, the CIO, has tasked you with enabling the corporate site collection for the content management of all enterprise documents and forms. You have determined that the Records Center located one level down from the organization's main top-level portal site would be ideally suited for the task. Ian outlines the features and capacities he wants to see the Records Center perform, including having the ability to receive documents directly from any document library in the site collection. Further, Ian wants records to be routed to different libraries in the Records Center based on content type.

As a necessary first step in accomplishing these goals, you must configure the Records Center to act as an external service connection for the site collection. To do this, you launch Share-Point's Central Administration web application and click the Application Management tab. Under External Service Connections, you click Connect to a Records Center, and when that web page loads, you enter the URL to the Records Center web service in the available field. Finally, you enter the name of the Records Center in the Display Name field, and click OK to finish your work.

Working with WCM and Variations

Besides working with the various design elements on a publishing portal, another major WCM realm is in the area of Variations. The site Variations feature is vital for enterprise-level corporations that work with multinational clients and thus communicate in multiple languages. Part of what this means is that you may be offering different business documents in several different languages. However, what if you need to publish entire websites, all containing the same content but in different languages?

Consider the publishing portal we just finished creating. Let's say this is an Internet-facing site collection designed for your European customers and potential customers. You need to present the content in several different languages besides English including Spanish, French, and German. What are you supposed to do?

SharePoint 2007's Variations feature is designed to answer that question. The feature allows you to create a website hierarchy so that you can present site content in several different languages based on who is visiting the site and the language configured to be used on the visitor's computer.

The Variations feature doesn't actually translate each and every web page on your site automatically but rather creates a special workflow that allows you to process the necessary content so that teams will be assigned to translate pages into different languages by using approval workflows. The Variations feature organizes the locations of these translated pages so that they can be selected and viewed by visitors based on their language requirements.

Returning to the publishing portal site collection we previously created, we can enable the Variations feature for that site to allow you to begin the process of presenting site content in at least one other language besides English. Exercise 15.8 will get you started with this task.

EXERCISE 15.8

Enabling Variations on a Publishing Portal Site

1. On the publishing portal site main page, click the Set Up Multilingual Support link. (You can also start on the Site Settings page under Site Collection Administration by clicking Variations.)

2. On the Variation Settings page under Variation Home, in the Location field, either type or browse to the specific part of the site you want to configure for variation. To indicate the entire site collection starting at the top-level site, enter a forward-slash (/), as shown here.

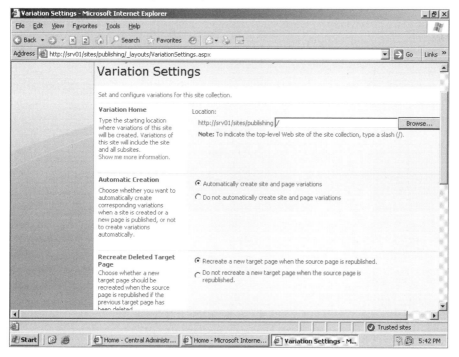

3. Under Automatic Creation, select either Automatically Create Site and Page Variations or Do Not Automatically Create Site and Page Variations, depending on whether you want the system to create variation pages or you want to create them manually.

4. Under Recreate Deleted Target Page, select either Recreate a New Target Page When the Source Page Is Republished or Do Not Recreate a New Target Page When the Source Page Is Republished, depending on whether you want this process to be system or manually controlled.

5. Under Update Target Page Web Parts, select either Update Web Part Changes to Target Pages When Variation Source Page Update Is Propagated or Do Not Update Web Part Changes to Target Pages When Variation Source Page Update Is Propagated, depending on whether you want an automatic or a manual process to have control.

6. Under Notification, tick the Send E-mail Notification to Owners When a New Site or Page Is Created or a Page Is Updated By the Variation System box if you have an automated system in place and want to be notified when the system makes a change.

7. Under Resources, select either Reference Existing Resources or Copy Resources, depending on whether you want the Variations system to use the same resources as the original web page or you want the system to copy resources from an alternate location.

8. Click OK.

The Variations source main page is not the same as the main page for the publishing portal site. In my example, here are the relative URLs:

- `http://srv01/sites/publishing/Pages/default.aspx` is the original portal site.

- `http://srv01/sites/publishing/EN/Pages/default.aspx` is the source site (English).

You will need to re-create the English source site in the "image" of the original publishing portal site after it is created. If you do this after you've created one or more variation sites labeled for other languages, the changes will be reflected on those pages automatically.

Now that you've enabled the publishing portal site for the Variations feature, you still have more work to do. The next step is to create a specific information management policy for each language you want to use. The specific policy feature required here is labeling. You'll need to create a separate label for each desired language.

For the purpose of the following example, we'll create a label for only one language (English), but you will need to repeat the exercise as many times as necessary to add any other language labels. Don't worry—you won't need to understand or write in another language to complete the exercise. Exercise 15.9 will show you how to create a language label in the Variations system. You will need to go to the Site Settings page for the publications portal site to begin the exercise. Also, the first language label you will create will be English since this will be the basis for establishing the language label hierarchy.

Creating a Language Label for the Variations System

1. On the Site Settings page of the Publications Portal site under Site Collection Administration, click Variation Labels.

2. On the Variation Labels page, click New Label.

EXERCISE 15.9 *(continued)*

3. On the Create Variation Label page in the Label and Description area, type **EN** (for English) in the Label Name field, and type an optional description of the label in the Description field.

4. In the Display Name area in the Display Name field, type **English**.

5. Using the Locale drop-down menu, select English (United States).

6. Under Hierarchy Creation, select the scope of the source hierarchy you want to be copied, such as Publishing Sites and All Pages.

7. In the Source Variation area under Source Hierarchy, tick the Set This Variation to Be the Source Variation box (since this is the source language), and when the confirmation box appears, click OK.

8. Use the drop-down menu in the same area to select the publishing site template you want to use.

9. Click OK.

WARNING   Once the source variation has been selected, it cannot be changed, so make sure you want this particular language to be the source. Also, after you start creating a hierarchy, the publishing site template cannot be changed. You will see a warning to this effect on the Variation Labels page.

Now that you've created a label for the source language, you will need to create additional labels for other languages. In our next example, you'll create a label for German. The steps are the same as in the previous exercise. The only differences are that the two-letter language code for German you'll specify in step 3 is DE. You can set the display name in step 4 as German, and in step 5, you use the drop-down menu to select German (Germany). The settings in the Source Variation area will be unavailable since they were already set when you configured the previous label.

Now you are ready to create the Variation Labels hierarchy. This is a very simple but somewhat time-consuming process. (It takes longer to create a hierarchy than it does to create a site.) On the Variation Labels page, click Create Hierarchies. The process will take a few minutes, but when it's done and you're returned to the page, you'll see Yes indicated in the Hierarchy Is Created column next to each language label you've created. You can still add more languages and have them added to the hierarchy as needed.

Now, when a visitor browses to the publishing portal site, SharePoint will detect the language preferences set in the visitor's browser and direct the visitor to the appropriate site. Of course, both the English and German site content has to be created. You can also manually select the language you want in the Quick Launch menu on the top-level site.

Ideally, when you create a new web page in the source website, you initiate an approval workflow process to manage the translation of that source page. The workflow launches after you are done creating the source site page and when you check it back into the system. The translation task is assigned to the designated personnel and managed just like any other task in SharePoint. Once the translation task is completed, it must be approved (or rejected) by a member of the approvers group before it can go into production.

Exercise 15.10 will show you how the translation workflow operation works by helping you add a new web page to the source publishing portal site. You will need to have at least one SharePoint user account available that is authorized as an approver and another user who can be assigned the translation task.

EXERCISE 15.10

Creating a New Web Page in a Source Site

1. On the main page of the publishing portal, click Site Actions ➤ Create Page.

2. On the Create Page page in the Title field, give the new web page a name such as **Corporate Information** and an optional description in the Description field.

3. Under Page Layout, select the page layout type in the available field, such as (Article Page) Article Page with Body Only.

4. Click Create.

5. When the new web page appears under Page Content, click Click Here to Add New Content.

6. In the rich-text editor that opens, use the various text-editing tools to create content for this page. When finished, select Check In in the Page drop-down menu.

7. Choose the Major Version option, and add an optional description in the Description field.

8. Click OK.

9. Click Start to launch the approval workflow.

10. When the page loads, click Approve.

11. On the Approval page, click Approve.

12. Click the German link in Quick Launch.

13. Click the name of the newly created web page under German.

At this point, members of the team responsible for translating this content into German will be notified either by email if email notification is set up or by having this task assigned to their tasks list. The page is still checked out until they complete the translation and submit it for a second workflow approval process. Once it's approved, the translated page can be checked in and published and can become accessible to the intended audience.

Summary

In this chapter, you learned about a variety of different aspects of content management in SharePoint, including the following points:

- A detailed account of the SharePoint content management features available in the Records Center site

- How to configure a Records Center from the SharePoint Central Administration interface

- Web content management as it pertains to SharePoint web page and website design elements

- How to apply variations in web content management in order to present site content in multiple languages

- How to restructure a website or site collection by moving elements, including actual sites

Exam Essentials

Know how to plan for content management.   Know how to plan and implement content management by understanding and configuring the various features in the Records Center site. This includes giving all sites in the site collection access to the Records Center and enabling them to send documents to the Records Center from any document library in the site collection.

Understand the process of applying policies and compliance to content.   Understand the details of applying information management policies to content and how this practice affects your ability to control what happens to a document throughout its life cycle.

Be well versed in the different aspects of web content management (WCM).   This includes how to create, modify, and reassign the different design elements that affect how a web page or site is displayed. This also includes how sites and site collections are structured and how to move a web page or website within a site collection.

Be knowledgeable of how WCM is applied in the area of language variation management.
This includes managing language content in web pages and websites so that they can be presented to audiences in different languages based on the audience language preference. You need to know how to create source sites, construct site hierarchies, and manage content translation through approval workflows.

Review Questions

1. You are the SharePoint administrator for your company. You have been tasked with configuring the Records Center for your site collection to be used for overall content management. Your CIO wants you to make sure that all the document libraries on every SharePoint site can send content to libraries in the Records Center. You go into Central Administration to set this up. On the Configure Connection to Records Center page, in the field to be used to identify the URL of the Records Center, what extension must the URL have?

   A. .ampx

   B. .asmx

   C. .aspx

   D. .vmx

2. You are the SharePoint administrator for your company. You have been tasked with configuring the Records Center for your site collection to be used for overall content management. You have finished setting up the Records Center and are reviewing the features it offers including the default libraries that are created when the Records Center is created. Of the following options, which are valid default libraries in the Records Center? (Choose all that apply.)

   A. Hold Reports

   B. Missing Properties

   C. Records Pending Submission

   D. Classified Records

3. You are the SharePoint administrator for your company. You have been tasked with configuring the Records Center for your site collection to be used for overall content management. You have finished setting up the additional libraries for the Records Center and are now creating Records Routing entries for the libraries. You want a newly created library called the Pending Documents library to be the default location for all documents sent to the Records Center that do not match any of the other routing entries, but the option is unavailable. Of the following choices, which one is the most likely cause of the problem?

   A. You haven't set up the Records Center in Central Administration to be an external service connection for the libraries in the site collection.

   B. You must first deselect this option in the default Records Pending Submission library.

   C. You must first deselect this option in the default Unclassified Records library.

   D. You are logged in as a site administrator and must be logged in as a server farm administrator to have access to this option.

4. You are the SharePoint administrator for your organization. Sheila, the CTO for the company, has assigned you to enable content auditing for the entire site collection rather than just at the library level. How do you initiate this process?

   A. Go to Central Administration, click the Application Management tab, and under Site Administration click Site Collection Auditing.

   B. Go to Central Administration, click the Application Management tab, and under Site Collection Administration click Auditing.

   C. From the top-level portal page, navigate to the Site Settings page, and under Site Collection Settings click Auditing.

   D. From the top-level portal page, navigate to the Site Settings page, and under Site Collection Administration click Site Collection Audit Settings.

5. You are the SharePoint administrator for your corporation, and you are currently configuring auditing for the entire site collection. As part of the configuration process, you are specifying the events you want to have audited under Documents and Items. Of the following options, which are valid audit events? (Choose all that apply.)

   A. Viewing items in spreadsheet mode

   B. Editing items

   C. Checking out or checking in items

   D. Deleting or restoring items

6. You are the SharePoint administrator for your company's site collection. As part of your plan to implement web content management in the site collection, you are to create a publishing portal site. To do this, you have to go to Central Administration. On the Create Site Collection page under Web Application, what is your first step?

   A. Click to the right of the current web application, and select Change Web Application ➤ SharePoint-8080 web application.

   B. Click to the right of the current web application, and select Change Web Application ➤ SharePoint-80 web application.

   C. Click to the right of the current web application, click Edit, and then edit the available field, changing it from 8080 to 80.

   D. Accept the current web application.

7. You are the SharePoint administrator for your company's site collection. As part of your plan to implement web content management in the site collection, you are to create a publishing portal site. To create a publishing portal, you must make specific selections. Of the following options, which one represents the correct choices?

   A. In the Template Selection area under Select a Template, click the Collaboration tab, and then select Publishing.

   B. In the Template Selection area under Select a Template, click the Publication tab, and then select Publishing Portal.

   C. In the Template Selection area under Select a Template, click the Publishing tab, and then select Publishing Portal.

   D. In the Template Selection area under Select a Template, click the Publishing Portal tab, and then select Publishing.

8. You are the SharePoint administrator for your company, and you have just created a publishing portal site to be used for web content management (WCM). You have edited some of the content on the page and want to publish the changes so your manager or the department heads can see them, but you are instead prompted to begin another process. What is the problem?

    A. You are prompted to perform a checkout before making any changes. Although you can enter Edit mode, add web parts, and make other changes, if you neglected to check the web page out first, those changes won't be saved.

    B. You are prompted to begin an approval workflow. By default, any changes you make on a top-level portal must go through an approval workflow before being published.

    C. You are prompted to check in a draft version prior to publishing. By default, portal sites must first be viewed in draft mode before they can be published.

    D. You are prompted for your administrator username and password before publishing your changes.

9. You are the SharePoint administrator for your company. You have created a publishing portal site to be used for web content management. None of the default page layouts for the site meet the requirements of the management team, and you've been tasked with creating a new page layout according to their specifications. To begin this process, what steps must you take?

    A. On the Master Page Gallery page, click New ➢ Page Layout.

    B. On the Layout Page Gallery page, click New ➢ Page Layout.

    C. On the Master Page Gallery page, click New ➢ New Page Layout.

    D. On the Master Page Gallery page, click Open ➢ SharePoint Designer 2007, and then open a new Page Layout template in Designer.

10. You are the SharePoint administrator for your company. You have created a publishing portal site to be used for web content management. None of the default page layouts for the site meet the requirements, so you start the process of creating a new, custom-made page layout. You have gone through most of the creation process. What do you need to do to finish?

    A. In the Variation Labels area, select any variation label in the Available Labels field, click the Add button to add the label to the Labels for Layout field, and then click OK.

    B. In the Page Layout Title and Description area, use the URL, Title, and Description fields to type in the URL to the content type, the name of the content type, and an optional description, and then click OK.

    C. In the Master Page Gallery, select the new page layout, and in the menu select Check In ➢ Publish.

    D. In the Master Page Gallery, select the new page layout, and in the menu select Edit in Microsoft Office SharePoint Designer.

11. You are the SharePoint administrator for your company. You have created a publishing portal site to be used for web content management. The current master page for the site doesn't meet the requirements, so you initiate the process of creating a new master page. What are your first steps?

    A. On the Master Page Gallery page, click New ➢ Master Page.

    B. On the Master Page Gallery page, click New ➢ Create Master Page.

    C. Launch SharePoint Designer 2007, click File ➢ Open Site, and enter the URL to the portal site where you want to create the new master page.

    D. Launch SharePoint Designer 2007, and click File ➢ New ➢ Create New Master Page.

12. You are the SharePoint administrator for your company. You have created a publishing portal site to be used for web content management. The current master page for the site doesn't meet the requirements, so you have created a new, custom-made master page. To use the new master page, you must change the default master page for the desired site. What steps must you take to start this process?

  A. On the portal site, click Site Actions ➢ Site Settings ➢ Modify All Site Settings, and on the Site Settings page under Look and Feel, click Master Page.

  B. On the portal site, click Site Actions ➢ Site Settings ➢ Modify All Site Settings, and on the Site Settings page under Site Administration, click Master Page.

  C. On the portal site, click Site Actions ➢ Site Settings ➢ Modify All Site Settings, and on the Site Settings page under Galleries, click Master Page.

  D. On the portal site, click Site Actions ➢ Site Settings ➢ Modify All Site Settings, and on the Site Settings page under Site Design, click Master Page.

13. You are the SharePoint administrator for your company. You have created a publishing portal site to be used for web content management. The current master page for the site doesn't meet the requirements, so you have created a new, custom-made master page. You want to apply this page to pages such as the home page for the Master Page Gallery and the Settings pages. On the Site Master Page Settings page, what must you do?

  A. Specify the new master page as the site master page.

  B. Specify the new master page as the system master page.

  C. Specify the new master page as the home master page.

  D. Specify the new master page as the primary master page.

14. You are the SharePoint administrator for your organization. You have created a publishing portal to manage the web content management for the site collection. You need to move some of the pages in the publishing portal to make it easier to navigate the site's structure. What must you do to start this process?

  A. On the publishing portal site, click Site Actions ➢ Site Settings ➢ Modify All Site Settings, and under Site Administration, click Manage Content and Structure.

  B. On the publishing portal site, click Site Actions ➢ Site Settings ➢ Modify All Site Settings, and under Site Administration, click Site Content and Structure.

  C. On the publishing portal site, click Site Actions ➢ Site Structure and Content.

  D. On the publishing portal site, click Site Actions ➢ Manage Content and Structure.

15. You are the SharePoint administrator for your organization. You have created an Internet-facing publishing portal site collection for your multinational customers and now need to enable multilanguage support for the site. Of the following options, which correctly describe how to begin this process? (Choose all that apply.)

  A. On the publishing portal site main page, click the Set Up Multilingual Support link.

  B. On the publishing portal site main page, click the Enable Variations link.

  C. On the publishing portal site main page, click Site Actions ➢ Site Settings ➢ Modify All Site Settings, and on the Site Settings page under Site Collection Administration, click Multilingual Support.

  D. On the publishing portal site main page, click Site Actions ➢ Site Settings ➢ Modify All Site Settings, and on the Site Settings page under Site Collection Administration, click Variations.

16. You are the SharePoint administrator for your organization. You have created an Internet-facing publishing portal site collection for your multinational customers and now need to enable multilanguage support for the site. You have the option of specifying which pages on the site you want the Variations feature applied to, or you can specify the entire site. Of the following options, which one correctly describes how to specify that you want Variations to apply to the entire site?

A. On the Variation Settings page in the Location field, enter the URL for the publishing portal top-level page.

B. On the Variation Settings page in the Location field, enter a forward slash (/).

C. On the Variation Settings page in the Location field, enter a backward slash (\).

D. On the Variation Settings page in the Location field, enter the word **root**.

17. You are the SharePoint administrator for your organization. You have created an Internet-facing publishing portal site collection for your multinational customers and now need to enable multilanguage support for the site. You are in the process of enabling Variations, and you want to make sure the site owners are notified when a new site or new web page is created in the publishing portal so they can ensure the translations to those pages are made. How can you accomplish this task?

A. On the Variation Settings page, select Send E-mail Notification to Owners When a New Site or Page Is Created or a Page Is Updated by the Variation System.

B. On the Variation Settings page, tick the Send E-mail Notification to Owners When a New Site or Page Is Created or a Page Is Updated By the Variation System check box.

C. On the Variation Settings page under Notifications, enter the email addresses of the site owners separated by semicolons in the available field.

D. On the Variation Settings page under Notifications, enter the usernames of the site owners in the available field, and then click the Check Names button.

18. You are the SharePoint administrator for your organization. You have created an Internet-facing publishing portal site collection for your multinational customers and have enabled it for multilingual support using the SharePoint Variations feature. Now you need to create labels for each language you want to support. You plan to add only German at this time. Of the following selections, which one most accurately describes what you need to do?

A. You need to create a label for German.

B. You need to create a label for Deutsch.

C. You need to create labels for both English and German.

D. You need to create labels for both English (United States) and German (Germany).

19. You are the SharePoint administrator for your organization. You have created an Internet-facing publishing portal site collection for your multinational customers and have enabled it for multilingual support using the SharePoint Variations feature. Now you need to create labels for each language you want to support. Your company is planning to provide services to the European market, but the management team isn't sure yet which languages should be supported. Considering this, which of the following options is the best?

    A. You will need to add labels for all the languages to be supported before setting up the hierarchy since no labels can be added afterward.

    B. Once the labels have been created, they cannot be added to, subtracted from, or changed, so the decision as to which languages are to be supported must be finalized prior to creating labels.

    C. After you've created a hierarchy, you can still add more languages; however, once you've specified a source language, the source language cannot be changed.

    D. Once the labels have been created, you can edit the labels if you need to change the languages supported, but you will need to open the labels in SharePoint Designer.

20. You are the SharePoint administrator for your corporation. You have enabled the publishing portal site in the site collection for multilanguage support and created labels for English, German, and French. You have also added several web pages to the portal called About Us, Contact Us, and Our Products. When you go to test the translations by clicking the links for the various languages, you see them all displayed in English. What is the most likely cause of this problem?

    A. The pages designated for German and French have not yet been translated into those languages.

    B. The links to the German and French sites are broken, and the default action is to redirect to the source page written in English.

    C. The German and French web pages have not been checked into the system and are published only in draft mode.

    D. You have to manually edit the links in the Quick Launch menu to point to the pages created by the Variations feature.

Answers to Review Questions

1.   B. Rather than the usual .aspx extension used by all SharePoint sites, you must use the .asmx extension, which points to the Records Center web service. Options A and D are bogus answers.

2.   A, B, and C. Option D would be correct if it said Unclassified Records.

3.   C. The Unclassified Records library is the default location for any documents sent to the Records Center that don't match any of the other routing entries. To enable another library to take on that role, you must first deselect that option in Unclassified Records.

4.   D. Only option D is correct. All of the other answers are bogus.

5.   B, C, and D. Other valid events are opening or downloading documents, viewing items in lists, viewing item properties, and moving or copying items to another location in the site. Option A is a bogus answer.

6.   B. The currently displayed web application is the one for Central Administration. You must change it to SharePoint-80 to create the new site collection as part of the larger SharePoint site collections available as a publicly accessible portal. All of the other options are bogus answers.

7.   C. Only option C describes the correct steps. The other options are bogus answers.

8.   B. Any changes you make to a top-level portal site must go through an approval workflow by default. For this to be successful, at least one SharePoint user must be assigned to the approvers group, and only users in that group can either approve or reject your changes.

9.   A. Option A gives the correct set of steps to begin the process of creating a new page layout. The other answers are bogus.

10.   D. After you are done with the initial creation of the page layout, you still need to edit it in SharePoint Designer, save the changes when done, and check the page back into the Master Page Gallery.

11.   C. You must start the process in SharePoint Designer 2007, and you must first specify the site where you want the master page created.

12.   A. Only option A describes the correct sequence of steps. The other options present bogus answers.

13.   B. A system master page defines the look and feel of the system pages including the home page for the Master Page Gallery and the Settings pages. A site master page defines the look and feel of the published pages in the site. Options C and D are bogus.

14.   D. Only option D describes the correct set of steps. All the other options are bogus answers.

15.   A and D. You can enable multilanguage support from either the main page of the publishing portal or from the Site Settings page as indicated in options A and D. Options B and C are bogus answers.

16.   B. Only option B correctly describes how to specify that you want Variations to apply to the entire site. All the other options are bogus answers.

17. B. Option B correctly describes the steps required to accomplish this task. The other options are bogus answers.

18. D. You need to create a label for the source language and well as the language you want to add. Also, the languages have nation-specific references.

19. C. Once you specify a source language such as English by creating a label, that choice cannot be changed. However, even after creating the hierarchy, you are free to add as many other language labels as are supported in SharePoint.

20. A. Although you can configure the Variations feature to automatically create pages for the languages you have made labels for, those pages still need to go through a translation workflow where the content is translated into those languages. Otherwise, the content will be displayed in English.

Chapter
16

Upgrading and Deploying Microsoft Office SharePoint Server 2007

MICROSOFT EXAM OBJECTIVES COVERED IN THIS CHAPTER:

✓ **Deploy/Upgrade Microsoft Office SharePoint Server 2007**

  ▪ Manage CMS Assessment

  ▪ Configure Shared Services

  ▪ Manage Business Intelligence tools

  ▪ Manage Portal and Site Migration

  ▪ Finalize Upgrades

You might think this chapter is badly placed in the book. After all, it's addressing the concept and practice of deploying Microsoft Office SharePoint Server (MOSS) 2007 (which you've already done) and upgrading from SharePoint Server 2003 to MOSS 2007. Why not feature the "upgrading" chapter closer to the beginning of the book?

There are a couple of simple answers to this question. First, you really need to know that you want to upgrade from 2003 to 2007, and for that, you need to understand what SharePoint 2007 offers and how it operates in detail. After all, if you are going to upgrade SharePoint for your corporate environment, you are going to be the person who will have to administer it. How can you make a competent upgrade decision unless you know what you're getting into?

The other simple answer has to do with selling the upgrade to the decision makers and stakeholders of your company. In the lab environment you've been using throughout this book, you are the only decision maker involved, but in the real world, the decision to use any product such as SharePoint is largely based on business needs rather than technical needs. To justify the cost of the upgrade in terms of time, money, and effort, you have to establish the return on investment for "the powers that be" in your organization, and you can't do that unless you know what you're talking about. You can't know what you're talking about unless you have a detailed understanding of both your current SharePoint product and the product to which you are proposing to upgrade.

Thus, here we are, at the last chapter of this book, talking about upgrading and deploying to SharePoint Server 2007 and all that it entails. So, what does it entail? Is it really worth the effort?

To some degree, you first need to consider what MOSS 2007 offers that SharePoint Server 2003 doesn't. Chapter 1, "Getting Started with Microsoft Office SharePoint Server 2007," and Chapter 2, "Installing and Deploying SharePoint 2007," should have answered those questions. You can also get a high-level overview of MOSS 2007 and its benefits for an organization at Microsoft's Office website: `http://office.microsoft.com/en-us/sharepointserver/default.aspx`.

Another really helpful article aimed at the IT professional who needs to understand what MOSS 2007 offers, called "What's New for IT Professionals in Office SharePoint Server 2007," is at `http://technet2.microsoft.com/Office/en-us/library/527763c3-90a5-4d3b-9781-fc9580314a2d1033.mspx?mfr=true`.

The real work begins in deciding a migration path, and I'll cover several in this chapter. Choosing a method of upgrading SharePoint depends both on the parameters defined by your network and server infrastructure and on your corporation's business requirements, so a great deal of this chapter will be focused on this area.

Content Management Server (CMS) 2002 works hand-in-hand with SharePoint Server 2003 to provide services such as navigation, summary links, and scheduled deployments. These services are now fully integrated in MOSS 2007, which allows end users to perform tasks related to these services that formerly required subject-matter experts to conduct. Since you will likely want the CMS configuration in 2003 to be preserved in the upgrade deployment, you will need to assess these services so that once the upgrade has been completed, there will be little or no delay in users being able to access services.

The same can be said for shared services and business intelligence tools and features. A clean, first-time install of SharePoint 2007 might have seemed a bit daunting to you when you were approaching it at the beginning of this book, but you had a blank slate to work with and you could write on it anything you desired. Here, you have to take an already fully configured and working system and migrate it to a newer version of the platform while preserving all the functionality you (or a predecessor) built into the original system.

This final chapter begins with you taking a look at where you are, where you want to go, and the best path available for you to get from origin to destination.

Planning a SharePoint 2003 to SharePoint 2007 Migration

Although the utilities built into SharePoint Server 2007 make migrating from 2003 a fairly straightforward task, it's still one you shouldn't take lightly. Procedurally, the migration isn't very involved, but after you've spent months or years setting up an enterprise-level SharePoint 2003 environment, you still want to be particularly careful that when all is said and done, you don't irretrievably lose portions of your data and configuration. As you've seen in many of the chapters you've already read (assuming you took my advice and are reading through this book in a linear fashion), the first step is developing a strategic plan.

Developing a Migration Plan

The first part of your plan involves knowing what you're working with. In the case of SharePoint Portal Server 2003, there are only two options, so it's pretty simple:

- Microsoft Office SharePoint Server 2007 with Standard Edition Client Access Licenses (CALs)

- Microsoft Office SharePoint Server 2007 with Enterprise Edition Client Access Licenses (CALs)

Our working MOSS 2007 deployment for this book has been the Enterprise Edition, but if you'll recall when you first went through the installation process, you had the option to install either the Standard Edition or the Enterprise Edition. The upgrade options are the same.

If you are running Windows SharePoint Services (WSS) 2.0, you can migrate to Windows SharePoint Services 3.0. There is an option to migrate from WSS 2.0 to MOSS 2007; however, it's an advanced option that must use `stsadm` site transfers.

Determining the Migration Readiness of SharePoint Portal Server 2003

Before you can do anything, you need to determine whether your current SharePoint 2003 site structure is prepared for the migration. Most likely, the site structure won't be ready by chance, and you'll need to perform tasks during the assessment process in order to make sure the migration goes smoothly. You must investigate several areas to ensure that your 2003 sites migrate correctly to SharePoint 2007.

The first major hurdle is to determine whether any portion of your site collection has been modified or customized in any way. The most common utility used to customize SharePoint 2003 is FrontPage 2003. Any site or portion of a site that has been so modified will not be "understood" by the SharePoint 2007 migration tool and will retain any "look-and-feel" elements that were created by FrontPage. The good news is that after the migration, you can return each modified site to the look and feel you'd expect in SharePoint 2007. The bad news is twofold: first, you must do so on a site-by-site basis so it will be time-consuming, and second, in returning the look and feel as described, you will likely overwrite any of the modifications that FrontPage originally performed.

This issue doesn't exist just at the site level. Any customized web parts you added in 2003 will also not be able to migrate correctly to 2007 for the same reason. Because creating customized web parts is a fairly common practice, you will likely have to face this issue; in fact, you'll likely discover that some of the "off-the-shelf" web parts that came with 2003 will also suffer migration problems. There's no workaround here. After the migration is done, you'll need to test every web part in your site collection to see whether it retained its functionality.

You will also need to check any other customizations that were performed in 2003 such as themes, customized branding, any added extensions, and other programmatic tweaks. It is likely that these will have been overwritten during the migration process and will not function correctly.

As you can see, migration is not without its risks. Although the process will certainly have better results if you are migrating a completely "out-of-the-box" version of SharePoint 2003 to 2007, even then the results aren't guaranteed. For that reason, it would be better to test the migration process first in a lab scenario before applying it to your production environment.

Testing the Migration in the Lab

You, the reader, are ideally positioned to understand this portion of the chapter because you have been working in and have become familiar with a SharePoint lab environment. By now, you should be well acquainted with creating, testing, breaking, and fixing various scenarios in SharePoint. Creating a lab environment for migration testing is just a bit different, though.

In essence, you will need to create a small, mirror image of your production SharePoint 2003 environment. Although it doesn't have to contain the scope of your corporate SharePoint platform, it must contain all the individual elements that you want to survive the migration process. This means that if you have customized some of your websites using FrontPage, you'll need to duplicate those customizations on sites in the test model. The same goes for customized web parts, themes, and so on. In fact, given that even "standard" web parts are prone to breaking during migration, your test platform should contain examples of every web part in your production platform.

In addition to creating your test SharePoint 2003 environment and migrating it to 2007, you must also make it available to a team of subject-matter experts who will represent the end users. Although it wouldn't be very productive to have all the company employees both doing their actual work in the production environment and duplicating their actions on the test platform, you can select representatives to simulate all the typical tasks end users are expected to perform and see how the test environment responds. This is better than just performing the testing yourself since you can't hope to know every detail of every task that people in the company perform in SharePoint on a daily basis. If you're lucky, you'll work in an environment that has a Quality Assurance or other testing department that is trained for such a function.

In preparation for the migration, and particularly once you've created your test environment and subject testing has begun, it is critical that you do not perform any modifications on the production SharePoint platform. SharePoint 2003 must become completely static as far as any changes in design and functionality are concerned, and the test environment must mirror that static state so that you know the data resulting from the testing will truly represent what you can expect when you perform the actual migration on the production SharePoint environment.

Migrating Database Services

I'm tempted to say "there aren't any issues with migrating database services" and just move on, but since SharePoint 2003 and 2007 must access database services pre- and post-migration, you need to know (and are perhaps relieved) that you aren't required to migrate your Microsoft SQL Server database just because you are migrating SharePoint. SharePoint 2007 supports database services provided by Microsoft SQL Server 2000 SP3a or newer, so you can continue to use whatever version of SQL Server under 2007 that you were using with 2003 as long as it meets this requirement.

Of course, ambitious database server administrators might see this as an opportunity to upgrade their hardware and/or software platform, but ideally the CIO or CTO will make those decisions based on financial and administrative costs as well as overall impact on productivity. Migrating SharePoint and SQL Server at the same time might result in a longer service downtime, and performing a migration of two critical systems at the same time increases the opportunity for something to go wrong.

Performing Premigration Tasks

As part of the overall migration planning, you will need to perform some tasks in order to make sure SharePoint 2003 is ready for the migration. Certainly, you'll want to perform these tasks first in your migration test environment so that you'll be more completely familiar with how these procedures are performed and so that you can work out any of the bugs in the process while you are "flying with a safety net." Some of these tasks will be familiar to you because you performed them in the exercises in Chapter 2, "Installing and Deploying SharePoint 2007."

Verifying Migration Prerequisites

The following are the four prerequisites to performing a 2003 to 2007 upgrade migration:

- All the web and application server computers you plan to use must be running some version of Microsoft Windows Server 2003 SP1, including the following:
  - Standard
  - Enterprise
  - Datacenter
  - Web Edition
- Microsoft .NET Framework 3.0 must be installed on all your server computers.
- Microsoft ASP.NET 2.0 must be enabled on all your server computers.
- SharePoint Portal Server 2003 must have SP2 applied.

In Chapter 2, refer to Exercise 2.1, "Installing and Configuring IIS," and Exercise 2.2, "Enabling ASP.NET 2.0," to address these prerequisites. You can find information about how to download and install .NET Framework 3.0 at the following location: `http://www.microsoft.com/downloads/details.aspx?FamilyID=10CC340B-F857-4A14-83F5-25634C3BF043&displaylang=en`.

Performing a Complete Backup

This probably goes without saying, but to be safe I'll say it anyway. Before performing any major maintenance task and certainly before performing a platform upgrade migration, you must perform a complete backup of all affected systems. In this case, that means performing a complete backup of your current SharePoint 2003 environment.

See Chapter 14, "Performing Advanced SharePoint Management," to review standard SharePoint backup and restore procedures. Of course the procedures in Chapter 14 only apply to backup and restore for MOSS 2007, not SharePoint Server 2003.

The complete backup is part of your rollback plan and acts as a fail safe so that you can restore your 2003 production environment should anything go wrong with the migration. You will test your backup and rollback process on your test lab SharePoint 2003 environment before ever touching your production system because you will want to make sure the rollback process is working as required, even if your test lab migration from 2003 to 2007 goes without a hitch. Using the SharePoint 2003 backup utility will generate the necessary backup, but make sure all your databases, site definitions, customized websites, and so forth, are backed up before proceeding with the migration in both your lab and production environments.

After performing the backup in your test environment, perform a complete restore, and then completely test the lab platform to make sure that all the features and elements in Share-Point 2003 work the same way after the restore process.

Running a Preupgrade Scan

Microsoft has developed preupgrade scan tools for a number of its software systems, including Windows Server 2003, so that you can scan your current system and receive a list of any outstanding issues that may inhibit a smooth upgrade migration before actually beginning the upgrade. SharePoint 2007 contains such a tool, but to use it to scan SharePoint 2003 you have to install SharePoint 2007 first. This seems like a catch-22 situation, but there's a way around it; in fact, you have it in your hands.

To run the scan utility on SharePoint 2003, you need only two files contained in SharePoint 2007: `prescan.exe` and `preupgradescanconfig.xml`. Both files are in your current lab installation in the following directory: `C:\program files\common files\microsoft shared\web server extensions\12\bin`.

Just select Start ≻ Run, paste this path in the Run box, and click OK. When the directory opens, copy the two files to a location where you can find them again when you need them. If you were a SharePoint administrator in a production environment, you could install a trial copy of SharePoint Server 2007 on a computer and extract the files as I've just described, without having to actually install 2007 on a 2003 machine in order to run the preupgrade scan tool. When you are ready to run the scan in SharePoint 2003, copy the two files onto the 2003 machine, and run `prescan.exe`.

You might have to run this utility more than once. In the first scan, you may find issues you need to address. Once you've performed the corrective actions, run the scan again to make sure everything shows as resolved. This is a command-line utility, so if you want to scan all your websites under 2003, you'll need to use the `/all` switch after the `prescan` command, as in the following example:

```
C:\prescan tool folder>prescan /c preupgradescanconfig.xml /all
```

You can also specify a particular site by using the `/v` URL switch. If you use no switch at all, the utility will scan all sites by default.

Determining an Upgrade Migration Path

There is usually more than one road to any destination, and this is true for migration paths from SharePoint 2003 to 2007. Which one you pick depends on a variety of factors, and as you go through the following sections, you'll see how each path is defined and the reasons you would choose one path over the others.

In-Place Upgrade

An *in-place upgrade* is the simplest and most straightforward upgrade migration path. It assumes that there are no complications involved in your move from SharePoint 2003 to 2007 and that you want to upgrade your entire SharePoint environment in one fell swoop. This is an "all-or-nothing" deployment scheme, which means that when the company employees all go home on Friday night, they will have just finished their work in a SharePoint Portal Server 2003 environment, and when they report to work on the following Monday morning, they'll begin their work in a Microsoft Office SharePoint Server 2007 environment.

The bright side to this option is that all your work is done, and now it's just a matter of administering the MOSS 2007 environment for your corporate users. Procedurally, performing the upgrade is as simple as inserting the MOSS 2007 media disc into the relevant servers and launching the upgrade tool. The migration process sweeps through every SharePoint site and replaces all the 2003 look-and-feel elements, web parts, and other components with 2007 counterparts, leaving your data (ideally) intact.

The dark side is that it probably will never be that simple. If something goes wrong with the migration, the scope of what goes wrong could be vast, affecting your site collection (or collections) as a whole. This could include all your content-bearing containers including libraries, lists, documents, and items. Also, even if the migration goes flawlessly, there will always be some users who either have forgotten what they were supposed to learn in the upgrade training or didn't attend specific parts of the training. In either case, the support calls will come rolling in from people seemingly baffled by the change in the interface and functionality of the new environment.

 Microsoft recommends using an in-place upgrade only for small, single-server SharePoint deployments or only in a testing environment and to use the gradual upgrade path for all production environments.

Gradual Upgrade Migration

The *gradual upgrade* migration path is more complex than an in-place upgrade, but it has a number of built-in safety factors that will allow you to stair-step the upgrade process. This path requires that you install MOSS 2007 on the same system that hosts SharePoint 2003. Each platform relies upon its own content databases, so nothing is changed in each environment until you decide to institute a change. Once in place, you then can migrate one site or one group of sites at a time from 2003 to 2007, leaving the remainder of sites on the 2003 platform.

This process allows your SharePoint users to get used to the change one group at a time. For instance, let's say you migrate the sales department's site from 2003 to 2007, leaving the sites operated by all of the other departments untouched. The sales department becomes your pilot project of sorts, allowing you to determine the impact of migration for the entire corporation based on this one department. You can use this experience to work out the kinks in the process and then move on to the next site and then the next. If something goes wrong with a migration, you just need to roll back a single site rather than the entire SharePoint environment. Whatever support calls that come in will be limited to a single department rather than coming from all areas of the corporation.

The downside is that it takes a lot longer. The length of the migration time depends on how frequently you initiate migrations (one a day, one a week, and so forth), how many sites you migrate at any given point (one site, two sites, ten sites, and so forth), and the overall size of the environment. A SharePoint environment containing a single site collection consisting of 10 sites will go faster than one containing 10 site collections with each collection containing 100 sites.

In terms of the actual process involved, when content for a particular site has been called, the content database accessed will depend on whether that site has been migrated. The URL or FQDN of the site doesn't change before or after migration, but the migration process translates HTTP service requests, allowing the correct content to be accessed.

Database Migration

I mentioned previously that you wouldn't have to perform a database upgrade migration just because you were performing a SharePoint migration, but I also said it could be a viable option. This isn't a usual upgrade scenario, and Microsoft doesn't formally present it as a SharePoint upgrade option at all. It's considered an advanced option and one that you would utilize only if you were going to perform a hardware upgrade or upgrade your SQL Server software. In the latter case, you'd perform an in-place upgrade of the SQL Server system, say from 2000 to 2005. That said, it is unlikely that you, as a SharePoint administrator, would be asked to participate in a database upgrade migration and very unlikely that you will encounter any questions on the 70-630 exam on this subject.

Managing CMS in a SharePoint Upgrade Migration

This is a major area in this section of the exam objectives and rightfully so. Performing a CMS assessment prior to upgrade is required before initiating the actual migration. As you read earlier in this chapter, SharePoint 2003 works with CMS 2002 to provide services such as navigation, summary links, and scheduled deployments. These services are all integrated into MOSS 2007, so there is no need for a separate CMS deployment once the migration is done. However, there is a great need to perform an assessment (somewhat like the preupgrade scan on SharePoint 2003) to identify all the relevant information, programming, and components in the CMS application so that you can determine your upgrade migration strategy.

Microsoft published an online article called "Assessing and Analyzing Your MCMS 2002 Application for Migration" in May 2006 that describes all the details involved in performing the assessment. You can access the article at the following URL: `http://msdn2.microsoft.com/en-us/library/aa480227.aspx`.

The article includes an overview of the assessment process, how to install the CMS assessment tool, all the prerequisites for installing and running the tool, and how to interpret the report results. You can download the CMS assessment tool `.exe` file from this site: `http://www.microsoft.com/downloads/details.aspx?familyid=360d0e83-fa70-4c24-bcd6-426cafbcc627&displaylang=en`.

Managing Business Intelligence in a SharePoint Upgrade Migration

In SharePoint Portal Server 2003, the concept and practice of business intelligence wasn't an integrated service but was presented through a collection of onboard and third-party solutions. For instance, SharePoint 2003 administrators who wanted to offer business intelligence features in the SharePoint environment relied heavily on Microsoft Office Web Parts and Components, also referred to as Office Web Components (OWC). OWC is a collection of web parts, web part pages, templates, and other services that interoperate with both Office 2003 and WSS 2.0 services. OWC utilizes ActiveX controls to provide chart, data source control, PivotTable, and spreadsheet services in the SharePoint environment to take advantage of the features offered by the Office 2003 suite of applications and present information in a business intelligence (BI) type of setting.

 To review information about business intelligence in SharePoint 2007, see Chapter 12, "Using Excel Services and Business Intelligence," and Chapter 13, "Using Business Forms and Business Intelligence."

MOSS 2007 includes integrated BI solutions consisting of a larger variety of more evolved components, and as a result, OWC has been phased out. Although this is good news in terms of offering SharePoint users a more effective BI option, it presents difficulties when you have been using OWC functionality to provide BI presentations and now are at the threshold of an upgrade migration to SharePoint 2007 that uses an entirely different approach to BI. What happens to the customizations and particularly the data you previously configured?

There are two basic options: keep using OWC, or abandon your original BI solution and re-create it using SharePoint 2007 BI options.

Yes, OWC is no longer being supported, but you can still use the required web parts by extracting the CAB files from your 2003 installation and moving them to your 2007 platform once the upgrade is completed. These are the three required CAB files:

- `Microsoft.sharepoint.solutions.greatplains.cab`
- `Microsoft.sharepoint.webparts.quickquote.cab`
- `Microsoft.office.dataparts.cab`

They are located at the following path: `C:\Program Files\Common Files\Microsoft Shared\Web Server Extensions\60\wppacks`. Once you locate the referenced CAB files, you will need to use the `stsadm.exe` utility to add them to your SharePoint 2007 installation. The following is the command syntax required:

```
stsadm.exe -o addwppack -filename "c:\program files\common
files\microsoft shared\web server
extensions\60\wppacks\microsoft.office.dataparts.cab" -globalinstall
```

You can learn more about these `.cab` files at the following blog: `http://msmvps.com/blogs/shane/archive/2006/09/02/How-to-manually-install-the-Office-Web-Parts-in-SharePoint-v3.aspx`. You can find more useful information here: `http://support.microsoft.com/Default.aspx?id=929320`.

Managing Shared Services in a SharePoint Upgrade Migration

The shared services architecture in SharePoint 2007 is markedly different than it was in 2003, and although these changes have allowed more flexibility and ease of use in sharing resources, the fact that the changes are so significant presents upgrade issues. Microsoft provides two viable solutions for managing the upgrade of shared services from 2003 to 2007:

- Perform a gradual upgrade with shared services by upgrading the parent portal first.
- Perform a gradual upgrade with shared services by upgrading a child portal first.

Performing a gradual upgrade of shared services by upgrading the parent portal is the recommended option. This process has five basic steps:

1. Upgrading the parent portal

2. Upgrading the personal site host

3. Upgrading MySites

4. Upgrading team sites

5. Upgrading child portals

Performing a gradual upgrade of shared services by upgrading child portals first has four basic steps:

1. Creating a new SharePoint Server 2007 environment

2. Upgrading the personal site host and personal sites in SharePoint Portal Server 2003 and attaching them to the new shared services provider

3. Upgrading team site host and team sites and attaching them to the new shared services provider

4. Upgrading child portals and attaching them to the new shared services provider

Each of the steps in these two approaches is a separate, multistep task, and you'll have the opportunity to perform them later in the chapter. Since both of the shared services migration plans are based on performing a gradual upgrade migration, you'll learn how to perform the basics of both the in-place and gradual migration processes before addressing these more complicated solutions.

Performing an Upgrade Migration

Before getting into the nuts and bolts of actually upgrading SharePoint Portal Server 2003 to MOSS 2007, you should realize (if you haven't already) that the only way to perform these exercises is to have a SharePoint Server 2003 environment already in place so that you can work through the actions required to upgrade it to SharePoint Server 2007. Since there are two basic paths (in-place and gradual), you will need to have either two separate 2003 environments or a single environment that you will upgrade and then restore from a backup to its original state and upgrade again using the second option. On top of that, you will need to repeat the gradual upgrade steps twice more to practice the exercises involved in upgrading shared services.

Of course, the easiest (and least expensive...the full version costs $5,619) way to acquire your own copy of SharePoint 2003 is to download and install a trial version. As of this writing, you can still locate the trial software at the following location: `http://www.microsoft.com/downloads/details.aspx?FamilyID=16006564-4575-4463-920D-C920B4AEAE64&displaylang=en`. You can find more general information about downloading and installing SharePoint Portal Server 2003 at the following location: `http://www.microsoft.com/products/info/product.aspx?view=22&pcid=2f7ba03d-1762-4ae9-b059-23aa198c08fb&type=ovr`.

It is beyond the scope of this book to provide a set of exercises and instructions on how to install and configure SharePoint 2003 to have it available in order to upgrade it to SharePoint 2007, but by now, the experience you've had installing and configuring MOSS 2007 will have likely given you the required skills. Unfortunately, there are no simulators or other types of software that would allow you to enact the migration process in a more artificial environment, so to get the full experience, you'll have to create the full experience. Of course, you don't have to go overboard. Just install the out-of-the-box SharePoint 2003 deployment, create a couple of portal sites, and call it good.

 I'm not going to say it's OK to simply read along with the exercises, studying the steps but not performing the tasks; however, I can't say that not performing the exercises will automatically mean you won't be successful when you take the 70-630 exam. Part of it is a matter of conscience, part of it is how well you understand both the material and how you learn, and part of it is simply being aware that doing something helps you learn a task more effectively than just reading about how to do it.

Performing an In-Place Upgrade Migration

Exercise 16.1 starts you out with upgrading a SharePoint Server 2003 environment to a Share-Point Server 2007 environment using an in-place upgrade migration. To actually perform the migration, you'll need to have a SharePoint 2003 environment available to you plus the Share-Point 2007 installation files available on an optical disc. The task assumes this is a stand-alone server installation of 2003 both because that has been our standard model throughout this book and because it is the most reasonable deployment for student and lab purposes.

This will be a rather lengthy exercise, at least in terms of the number of steps, so give yourself plenty of time to complete the process. Also, you will want to have performed all of the required preupgrade steps discussed earlier in this chapter before actually launching into the exercise. In addition, you will need to have the product key for the SharePoint 2007 application software handy at the beginning of the exercise. This exercise skips the preinstallation scan process, but you can perform this task if desired.

EXERCISE 16.1

Performing an In-Place Upgrade from SharePoint 2003 to SharePoint 2007

1. Insert the SharePoint Server 2007 installation media into the optical drive of the server computer running SharePoint Server 2003, and when prompted, launch Setup.exe.

2. When the Enter your Product Key page appears, enter the product key, and click Continue.

3. When the License Terms page appears, tick the I Accept the Terms of This Agreement check box, and click Continue.

4. On the next page of the upgrade wizard on the Upgrade tab, select Yes, Perform an Automated In-Place Upgrade, as shown here.

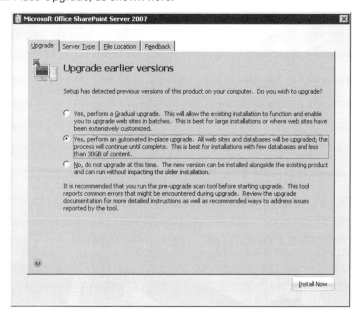

5. On the Server Type tab, select Complete – Install All Components.

6. On the File Location tab, either accept the default location for the installation files or click the Browse button and browse to a customized location on the server. (If you intend to use the server as a search server, you can either accept the second default installation path or click the Browse button to select a different path.)

7. Click Install Now.

8. After the installation process is complete, when the Completion page appears, verify that the Run the SharePoint Products and Technologies Configuration Wizard Now check box is ticked, and click Close. (If you didn't run the preupgrade utility previously, you might be prompted to do so now.)

9. When the Welcome to SharePoint Products and Technologies Wizard launches, click Next.

10. When the warning dialog box appears stating that various services may need to be restarted, click Yes.

11. When the Language Template Packs notification dialog box appears, click OK.

12. On the Configure SharePoint Central Administration Web Application page, accept the port number assigned by default and the NTLM authentication option, and click Next.

EXERCISE 16.1 *(continued)*

13. On the Completing the SharePoint Products and Technologies Configuration Wizard page, click Next.

14. While the SharePoint products and technologies are configuring, if a dialog box appears notifying you that you must install new binary files for all the servers in your server farm, click OK.

15. When the Configuration Successful page appears, click Finish.

16. The Upgrade Running page will open and prompt you for your username and password. Enter your administrator username and password, and click OK to open the page.

17. When the upgrade process completes, click Continue to open the home page of the Central Administration web application.

The upgrade process is now complete, and you are operating within a SharePoint Server 2007 environment. At this point, you would ordinarily begin to perform various site management tasks that were outlined in Chapter 3, "Configuring SharePoint 2007," but in this case, it's just a job well done. As you went through the upgrade process, you most likely noticed that many of the steps you followed were the same as when you initially installed SharePoint 2007 on your stand-alone server in Chapter 2, "Installing and Deploying SharePoint 2007."

Performing a Gradual Upgrade Migration

As stated earlier in this chapter, the gradual upgrade migration option allows you to run both SharePoint Server 2003 and SharePoint Server 2007 side by side on the same web and application servers in your server farm. In the case of a stand-alone installation, both versions of SharePoint run on the same server computer.

This process allows you to select which sites or groups of sites you want to migrate first, second, third, and so on. If for some reason you decide not to migrate all your sites to SharePoint 2007, those sites not selected will continue to run under SharePoint 2003. This also means that the SharePoint 2003 sites will continue to access services through the 2003 shared services provider, while the SharePoint 2007 sites will access services through the 2007 shared services provider.

There is more preparation involved in getting your SharePoint 2003 deployment ready for migration. Chief among these tasks is to create alternate domain URLs for each of your sites (which can be quite time-consuming depending on how many sites you have created). What this means in practice is that if the URL for a given site is as follows:

```
http://srv01/sites/projects.aspx
```

then you will need to create a temporary URL for the "old" or unupgraded site, like this:

```
http://srv01/sites/projects_old.aspx
```

During the upgrade process, you'll be asked to input a temporary URL for the site being upgraded; use the `projects_old.aspx` address. The existing URL will be "taken over" by the upgraded site, so from the SharePoint user's point of view they have access to their upgraded site at the same address they've always used. The site redirect will send users to the upgraded site, which now is accessing the correct content database for SharePoint 2007.

When you have upgraded all of your sites, you will then delete all the redirections, all the previous version sites, and all the temporary URLs.

Exercise 16.2 will walk you through the steps of performing a gradual upgrade migration of SharePoint 2003 to SharePoint 2007. For much of the exercise, the steps involved will be the same or similar to those you followed in Exercise 16.1. To begin, you must have SharePoint Portal Server 2003 running on a server computer and the SharePoint 2007 installation disc and product key handy. All the conditions and assumptions that were valid for Exercise 16.1 apply for Exercise 16.2 as well.

EXERCISE 16.2

Performing a Gradual Upgrade from SharePoint 2003 to SharePoint 2007

1. Insert the SharePoint Server 2007 installation media into the optical drive of the server computer running SharePoint Server 2003, and when prompted, launch Setup.exe.

2. When the Enter Your Product Key page appears, enter the product key, and click Continue.

3. When the License Terms page appears, tick the I Accept the Terms of This Agreement check box, and click Continue.

4. On the next page of the upgrade wizard on the Upgrade tab, select Yes, Perform a Gradual Upgrade.

5. On the Server Type tab, select Complete – Install All Components.

6. On the File Location tab, either accept the default location for the installation files or click the Browse button and browse to a customized location on the server. (If you intend to use the server as a search server, you can either accept the second default installation path or click the Browse button to select a different path.)

7. Click Install Now.

8. After the installation process is complete, when the Completion page appears, verify that the Run the SharePoint Products and Technologies Configuration Wizard Now check box is ticked, and click Close. (If you didn't run the preupgrade utility previously, you might be prompted to do so now.)

9. When the Welcome to SharePoint Products and Technologies Wizard launches, click Next.

10. When the warning dialog box appears stating that various services may need to be restarted, click Yes.

EXERCISE 16.2 *(continued)*

11. When the Language Template Packs notification dialog box appears, click OK.

12. On the Configure SharePoint Central Administration Web Application page, accept the port number assigned by default and the NTLM authentication option, and click Next.

13. On the Completing the SharePoint Products and Technologies Configuration Wizard page, click Next.

14. While the SharePoint products and technologies are configuring, if a dialog box appears notifying you that you must install new binary files for all the servers in your server farm, click OK.

15. When the Configuration Successful page appears, click Finish.

16. The Upgrade Running page will open and prompt you for your username and password. Enter your administrator username and password, and click OK to open the page.

17. When the upgrade process completes, click Continue to open the home page of the Central Administration web application.

Except for the selection in step 4, the process is the same as an in-place upgrade, but once the Central Administration web application becomes available, the real task begins. Thus far, none of your sites has been upgraded, and in fact, they are all waiting to be upgraded. Exercise 16.3 will begin where Exercise 16.2 left off—in Central Administration.

Exercises 16.1 and 16.2 both performed installations that specified stand-alone server installs and did not address the option to either create a server farm or notify the system that you would create a server farm later using the Connect to a Server Farm page. You also did not go through the process of selecting a database server and database name on the Specify Configuration Database Settings page.

EXERCISE 16.3

Selecting a Web Application for a Gradual Upgrade

1. In the Central Administration web application, click the Operations tab.

2. On the Operations tab under Upgrade and Migration, click Site Content Upgrade Status.

3. On the Site Content Upgrade Status page, choose the URL of the site you want to upgrade from the list, and click Begin Upgrade next to the name of the desired site.

4. On the Set Target Web Application page, in the Web Application to Upgrade section, verify that the correct web application is displayed in the Updating Web Application list. (If not, click the down arrow to open the list, and select the correct web application.)

5. Under New URL for Original Content, type a new port number for the site in the Port field, and if necessary, add a port header in the Port Header field.

6. Under Application Pool for New Web Application, select either Use Existing Application Pool or Create New Application Pool. (It is recommended that you either use an application pool you previously created for the upgrade or create a new application pool in this step.)

7. If you selected Create New Application Pool in step 6, under Select a Security Account for This Application Pool, select Predefined and use the drop-down menu to select a security account, or select Configurable and use the available fields to input a username and password for this security account.

8. Under Reset Internet Information Services, select either Restart IIS Automatically or Restart IIS Manually.

9. Under Security Configuration, select either Negotiate (Kerberos) or NTLM.

10. Under Content Databases, select either Automatic Database Name Selection or Manually Set Database Names.

11. Under SSP Database Settings, type the SSP database name in the SSP Database Name field, and type the search database name in the Search Database Name field. (These are the names of the database used to host the upgraded audience, user profile, and search configuration data.)

12. Under Index Server, use the Index Server drop-down menu to select an index server. (The path displayed by default for the path of the index file location can be accepted.)

13. Click OK to finish.

If you selected any of the "manual" options in this exercise, additional options would have appeared requiring you to input additional data. After you click OK, an Operation in Progress page will appear. Once the web application has been successfully upgraded, you will be taken to the Site Collection Upgrade page.

When you upgraded the web application, you didn't actually upgrade any sites, but rather the web application hosting the sites. For instance, all the sites in my site collection, such as my portal site, the Projects site, and so forth, are all hosted on the SharePoint – 80 web application. If that application were running in SharePoint 2003 and I upgraded it to SharePoint 2003, my next step would be to either upgrade another web application (such as Central Administration) or begin to upgrade sites hosted in the web application. Exercise 16.4 will go through the steps of selecting and upgrading a site collection hosted by the now-upgraded web application.

On the Site Collection Upgrade page, you will see a list of the site collections available in your SharePoint environment, including the root site collection. If you intend to upgrade any of these site collections, you must upgrade the root site collection first. In Exercise 16.4, you will choose a site collection and upgrade it from SharePoint 2003 to SharePoint 2007.

EXERCISE 16.4

Performing a Gradual Upgrade on a Site Collection

1. On the Site Collection Upgrade page, tick the check box next to the root site collection. (You can also choose one or more sites under the root site collection.)

2. Click Upgrade Sites.

3. On the Sites Selected for Upgrade page, verify that the information displayed is correct, including the number of site collections to be upgraded, the amount of storage the site collections originally used, and the names of the originating and target databases, and then click Upgrade Sites.

4. When the Upgrade Running page opens, the upgrade process will run for some time depending on the number and size of the selected site collections and their database. When the upgrade is finished, you can click the Home tab to return to the main page in Central Administration.

At this point, you can visit the upgraded sites; however, the 2003 version of the portal site still exists, and you can visit it at the temporary URL you previously selected.

 Real World Scenario

Preparing a Test Server for an Upgrade from SharePoint 2003 to SharePoint 2007

You are the SharePoint administrator for the Wallaby Way Corporation, a wholesale distributor of dental office equipment. For the past three years, you have administered Wallaby Way's Share-Point Portal Server 2003 environment very successfully. Peter Sherman, Wallaby Way's CEO, has been favorably impressed by the ROI the company has enjoyed as a result of the SharePoint deployment, and he is ready to consider upgrading to Microsoft Office SharePoint Server 2007. He has tasked Hunter, the CTO, to work with you to develop an upgrade plan. As part of developing the plan, you and Hunter determine that performing an in-place upgrade migration in a testing environment is necessary.

Hunter secures a test server for you to use. Your first job is to make sure it meets all the prerequisites for the upgrade test including all the software and operating system requirements. You install Windows Server 2003 Enterprise Edition on the computer and apply all the latest service packs and patches. Next, you go through the list of software that needs to be installed and configured.

You are not going to install SharePoint 2003 until your next meeting with Hunter, but you want the server ready for the installation and upgrade once he gives final approval. To prepare the server for a stand-alone SharePoint installation, you install and configure IIS services through Administrative Tools on the server. Next you install version 3.0 of the .NET Framework and enable ASP.NET 2.0 in the IIS Manager. The server is now ready for the SharePoint 2003 installation and, subsequently, for the upgrade migration to SharePoint 2007.

Performing a Gradual Upgrade with Shared Services

Now that you've performed both basic upgrade migration types, it's time to see how the gradual upgrade process can be used to manage a shared services upgrade. As previously discussed, you can select from two overall processes, and each process involves more than one exercise. The following sections will take you through these tasks.

Performing a Gradual Upgrade with Shared Services by Upgrading the Parent Portal First

Some of the steps involved in these exercises will be something like "perform a gradual upgrade of the parent portal." Since you have already performed these exercises, the steps involved in these tasks won't be repeated. I'll just put an instruction in place, and you will need to return to the earlier exercise in this chapter to review the steps. This includes any preliminary work you need to do to prepare the 2003 environment for upgrade, such as installing any language template packs if needed, reviewing log files, preparing web applications, and so on.

Upgrading the Parent Portal

The first task is to upgrade the parent portal, which will require that you repeat Exercises 16.2, 16.3, and 16.4. In Exercise 16.4, in step 1, tick the check box next to the parent portal site, which should be the root, and then complete the exercise.

Upgrading the Personal Site Host

This task is usually redundant since in most SharePoint Server 2003 deployments, the personal site host is the parent portal. The only time it would be different is if you set up a personal site host in its own server farm in Central Administration. If this is the case, you would repeat Exercise 16.4, specifying this site.

Upgrading MySites

Since MySites runs on a separate web application and represents a completely different site collection (or collection of site collections in some cases), you will need to perform Exercises 16.2, 16.3, and 16.4, repeating Exercise 16.4 if necessary if there are a large number of sites and site collections involved.

Upgrading Team Sites

Team sites are usually hosted on the same server farm as the rest of the site collections, but occasionally they're not. If they're not, you'll need to repeat Exercises 16.2, 16.3, and 16.4.

Otherwise, you will need to perform only the steps in Exercise 16.4 to upgrade all the team sites in your site collection.

 Remember, in our lab deployment, we are working with a simple SharePoint deployment, so a minimal amount of administrative cost is required to perform these tasks. In a large and complex production environment, you could find yourself performing many of the possible variations presented in order to complete the migration.

Upgrading Child Portals

Although a simple SharePoint deployment might contain only one portal site and various child or subsites, a large and complex environment could contain a number of child portal sites, such as one child portal for every nationwide office in an enterprise-level, international organization.

Basically, the previous four tasks were performed for the parent portal and any sites and site collections that operated beneath that portal. Now you will repeat those tasks as necessary for each child portal managed in your SharePoint 2003 environment. As far as our stand-alone server lab deployment goes, your job is done, but in the real world, it might be only the beginning.

Performing a Gradual Upgrade with Shared Services by Upgrading a Child Portal First

The second method of performing a gradual upgrade for shared services is by upgrading a child portal before the parent. In this case, you will be performing the same tasks you did in the previous section, but in a different order. They involve the same three exercises that have previously been referenced, so there is no new material. The order of the required tasks is as follows:

1. Upgrade personal site host and personal sites.
2. Upgrade team sites.
3. Upgrade child portals.

At what point you upgrade any MySites is up to you, but it's recommended that you upgrade all your MySites at the same time so that all your users will be able to access their upgraded MySites across the board.

For more information on upgrading from SharePoint 2003 to SharePoint 2007, visit the following Microsoft sites:

Upgrading to Office SharePoint Server 2007 `http://technet2.microsoft.com/Office/en-us/library/a44147be-3658-4bf0-ae39-0fca0794c01b1033.mspx?mfr=true`

Chapter overview: Perform a gradual upgrade in a shared services environment `http://technet2.microsoft.com/Office/en-us/library/21dd7a46-8433-4115-8004-850a6c8a1a891033.mspx?mfr=true`

Perform a gradual upgrade with shared services (upgrading the parent portal first) `http://technet2.microsoft.com/Office/en-us/library/13c54c47-f931-4cd2-ad7f-1bdea4d628da1033.mspx?mfr=true`

Perform a gradual upgrade with shared services (upgrading a child portal first) `http://technet2.microsoft.com/Office/en-us/library/4361b71b-7a69-4ea5-b064-f266705e4f331033.mspx?mfr=true`

Summary

In this chapter, you learned a great deal of information about the various aspects of upgrading and deploying from SharePoint Portal Server 2003 to SharePoint Server 2007, including the following points:

- Developing a migration plan for your SharePoint 2003 environment that determines your environment's readiness for migration, developing a migration testing lab, and understanding migrating database services

- Performing premigration tasks including verifying that you have met the prerequisites of the correct server platform versions, performing a complete backup of your environment, and running a preupgrade scan of the system

- Deciding which upgrade migration path to select such as an in-place or gradual upgrade as well as planning for CMS, business intelligence, and shared services migration

- Performing both in-place and gradual upgrades

- Performing a gradual upgrade for shared services by either upgrading the parent portal first or upgrading a child portal first

Exam Essentials

Be able to manage portal and site readiness for migration. Know how to prepare your SharePoint 2003 environment for migration including performing any premigration scans and other tasks and testing to verify that it is ready for migration to 2007.

Know how to perform different migration methods. Understand how to perform both in-place and gradual upgrade migrations, including managing the complexities involved in the gradual upgrade process.

Be able to assess the requirements for upgrading CMS and business intelligence. Know how CMS and business intelligence is performed in SharePoint 2003, how migration will affect those processes, and how to provide those services with SharePoint 2007 components.

Configure shared services migration. Be well-versed in the different methods of upgrading shared services using different models of the gradual upgrade migration process.

Review Questions

1. You are the SharePoint administrator for your company. You are in the process of planning an upgrade from SharePoint 2003 to SharePoint Server 2007 and are assessing the readiness of your current deployment for migration. You are currently assessing the impact the migration will have on all the services now being provided by Content Management Server (CMS) 2002 in SharePoint so that you can determine what you will have to re-create once the migration has been completed. In your current environment, what services does CMS manage? (Choose all that apply.)

   A. MySites

   B. Navigation

   C. Scheduled deployments

   D. Summary links

2. You are the SharePoint administrator for your company. You are in the process of planning an upgrade from SharePoint 2003 to SharePoint Server 2007 and are assessing the readiness of your current deployment for migration. You are currently reviewing the necessary prerequisites for the migration including the necessary server platforms to support the upgrade. Of the following, which server platforms will support the migration from SharePoint 2003 to SharePoint 2007? (Choose all that apply.)

   A. Windows Server 2000 SP3 Standard Edition

   B. Windows Server 2003 SP1 Standard Edition

   C. Windows Server 2003 SP1 Datacenter Edition

   D. Windows Server 2003 SP1 Web Edition

3. You are the SharePoint administrator for your company. You are in the process of planning an upgrade from SharePoint 2003 to SharePoint Server 2007 and are assessing the readiness of your current deployment for migration. You want to run a preinstallation scan of your SharePoint 2003 environment and see what outstanding issues exist in your current deployment. The CTO has advised you not to install SharePoint Server 2007 on any of your 2003 machines but instead to extract the necessary files from a test machine running SharePoint 2007, install the files on SharePoint 2003, and run the scan. You know the files that are required. In SharePoint Server 2007, what is the location where you will find the necessary files?

   A. `C:\program files\common files\microsoft shared\application server extensions\10\bin`

   B. `C:\program files\common files\microsoft shared\application server extensions\12\bin`

   C. `C:\program files\common files\microsoft shared\web server extensions\10\bin`

   D. `C:\program files\common files\microsoft shared\web server extensions\12\bin`

4. You are the SharePoint administrator for your company. You are in the process of planning an upgrade from SharePoint 2003 to SharePoint Server 2007 and are assessing the readiness of your current deployment for migration. You are considering the type of migration path to take and are consulting with the IT staff to develop a plan that would best meet the requirements of your organization's SharePoint environment. You work for a small business using a stand-alone server deployment and administer approximately 25 sites. Many of your web parts have been customized, and you have used FrontPage 2003 to modify three of the sites in the site collection. Jim, one of the IT techs, has done some research and presents Microsoft's official recommendation for an upgrade path of a production environment such as yours. Of the following options, what is Jim's answer?

A. An in-place upgrade is the Microsoft-recommended procedure because of the small size and limited number of sites in the SharePoint deployment.

B. An in-place upgrade is technically reasonable, but Microsoft recommends using this method only for testing purposes and to use the gradual upgrade method for all production environments.

C. An in-place upgrade is technically unreasonable according to Microsoft because it is designed to be used only in testing environments. Jim says that the gradual upgrade method is the only recommended option.

D. Jim says that the Microsoft-recommended method for your SharePoint environment is a gradual upgrade migration because each site in a production environment must be upgraded separately to avoid losing any specialized web part and web page customizations.

5. You are the SharePoint administrator for your company. You are in the process of planning an upgrade from SharePoint 2003 to SharePoint Server 2007 and are assessing the readiness of your current deployment for migration. You manage a large set of site collections for a multinational corporation and have determined that a gradual upgrade migration path is the best option. You are giving your team a high-level briefing on this procedure since none of them have performed a large-scale SharePoint 2003 to 2007 upgrade before. Of the following, which statements are most true about a gradual upgrade? (Choose all that apply.)

A. SharePoint Server 2007 replaces SharePoint Portal Server 2003 on each web server as sites and site collections are upgraded.

B. SharePoint Server 2007 and SharePoint Portal Server 2003 coexist on the servers during the entire upgrade migration process.

C. As individual sites are upgraded from 2003 to 2007, they acquire new URLs that must be mapped so users can access the upgraded sites.

D. After an individual site is upgraded, user requests are automatically redirected to the upgraded site when they use the URL originally used by the 2003 version of the site.

6. You are the SharePoint administrator for your company, and you are currently planning an upgrade migration of your SharePoint Portal Server 2003 environment to SharePoint Server 2007. You make heavy use of OWC components and various third-party solutions to provide business intelligence functionality in your SharePoint 2003 environment. You are considering how to provide the same features for your users after the migration to SharePoint 2007. Of particular interest are features specifically provided by OWC. Which of the following are specifically provided by OWC? (Choose all that apply.)

A. ActiveX controls

B. Charts

C. Data source control

D. PivotTables

7. You are the SharePoint administrator for your company, and you are currently planning an upgrade migration of your SharePoint Portal Server 2003 environment to SharePoint Server 2007. You make heavy use of OWC components and various third-party solutions to provide business intelligence functionality in your SharePoint 2003 environment. Although SharePoint 2007 provides a wide variety of business intelligence utilities, there are some unique configurations in OWC that you still want to utilize after the migration. Of the following, what option can you use to preserve the specific OWC components? (Choose all that apply.)

A. Extract the necessary CAB files for OWC from SharePoint 2003, and install them on SharePoint 2007 after the upgrade is complete.

B. Add the path `C:\Program Files\Common Files\Microsoft Shared\Web Server Extensions\60\wppacks` in SharePoint 2007, and then import the necessary CAB files from 2003 to the `wppacks` folder in 2007.

C. Run the command `stsadm.exe -o addwppack -filename -hostname2003 - hostname2007` to move the necessary CAB files to run OWC components from the SharePoint 2003 installation to SharePoint 2007.

D. OWC is not supported in SharePoint 2007, and any customizations that depend on OWC in 2003 will be lost after the upgrade. Any desired functionality will need to be re-created in 2007 using its BI tools once the upgrade is complete.

8. You are the SharePoint administrator for your company, and you are currently planning an upgrade migration of your SharePoint Portal Server 2003 environment to SharePoint Server 2007. You are planning a method for migrating shared services from SharePoint 2003 to SharePoint 2007. There is a significant difference in how shared services operates on either platform, so the migration method to correctly make sure the upgrade is successful is very specific. Of the upgrade migration options presented, which can you use to successfully migrate shared services? (Choose all that apply.)

A. Perform a gradual upgrade by upgrading the parent portal first.

B. Perform a gradual upgrade by upgrading the team sites first.

C. Perform a gradual upgrade by upgrading the child portals first.

D. Perform a gradual upgrade by upgrading the personal host site first.

9. You are the SharePoint administrator for your company, and you are currently planning an upgrade migration of your SharePoint Portal Server 2003 environment to SharePoint Server 2007. You are planning a method for migrating shared services from SharePoint 2003 to SharePoint 2007. There is a significant difference in how the shared services feature operates on either platform, so the migration method to correctly make sure the upgrade is successful is very specific. You have determined that performing a gradual upgrade of shared services by upgrading child portals first is the best option for your environment. Of the following options, which represent the basic required steps in this process? (Choose all that apply.)

A. Creating a new SharePoint Server 2007 environment

B. Upgrading child portals and attaching them to the new shared services provider

C. Upgrading MySites and attaching them to the new shared services provider

D. Upgrading the personal site host and attaching it to the new shared services provider

10. You are the SharePoint administrator for your organization, and you are about to begin the upgrade migration process from SharePoint 2003 to SharePoint 2007 in a testing environment to make sure the upgrade migration will go as you have planned. You want to perform a pre-upgrade scan of the current system to see whether any outstanding issues must be resolved prior to beginning the upgrade. Darla, one of your staff, has asked at what points during the process the scan could be initiated. What do you tell her?

A. The preupgrade scan can be performed only prior to beginning the in-place upgrade migration process.

B. The preupgrade scan can be performed before beginning the in-place upgrade migration process and after the installation, at the point where you are launching the SharePoint Products and Technologies Configuration Wizard.

C. The preupgrade scan can be performed before beginning the in-place upgrade migration process and just after running the SharePoint Products and Technologies Configuration Wizard.

D. The preupgrade scan can be performed only after launching `Setup.exe` on the SharePoint 2007 installation disc and entering the product key.

11. You are the SharePoint administrator for your organization, and you are about to begin the upgrade migration process from SharePoint 2003 to SharePoint 2007 in a testing environment to make sure the upgrade migration will go as you have planned. You perform the in-place upgrade in your testing environment on a stand-alone server, and everything seems to go well. When you actually perform the upgrade in your production environment, you will be upgrading a much larger environment for your enterprise-level organization. You anticipate that additional steps will be involved in the upgrade of your production environment. Of the following selections, which are the likely steps you'll encounter that you didn't go through during the test migration? (Choose all that apply.)

A. On the Connect to a Server Farm page, you'll be asked whether you want to create a server farm or wait until a later time.

B. On the Connect to Web Applications page, you will be asked which web applications you want to upgrade.

C. On the Specify Configuration Database Settings page, you will be asked to specify a database server and database name.

D. On the SSP Database Settings page, you will be asked to choose an administrator account name and password for access to the SSP database.

12. You are the SharePoint administrator for your organization, and you are about to begin the upgrade migration process from SharePoint 2003 to SharePoint 2007 in a testing environment to make sure the upgrade migration will go as you have planned. After you begin running the SharePoint Products and Technologies Configuration Wizard, some dialog boxes come up one after the other requiring you to respond. Of the following options, which dialog boxes appear, and what should you do?

A. A dialog box appears notifying you that an authentication method has not yet been set and that the system is insecure until a method has been selected. Click OK.

B. The Language Template Packs notification dialog box appears. Click OK.

C. The warning dialog box appears stating that various services may need to be restarted. Click Yes.

D. A dialog box appears notifying you that you must install new binary files for all servers in your server farm. Click OK.

13. You are the SharePoint administrator for your company. You have successfully completed the upgrade migration process from SharePoint 2003 to SharePoint 2007 in a test environment and are almost ready to perform a gradual upgrade migration in your production environment. Since you will be upgrading a few sites at a time, there is one crucial prerequisite task you must perform because 2003 and 2007 SharePoint sites will be coexisting. Of the following options, which one is the required task?

A. Create temporary URLs for the upgraded 2007 sites.

B. Create temporary URLs for the "unupgraded" 2003 sites.

C. Create a temporary web application for the upgraded 2007 site collection.

D. Create a temporary web application for the "unupgraded" 2003 site collection.

14. You are the SharePoint administrator for your company. You have successfully completed the upgrade migration process from SharePoint 2003 to SharePoint 2007 in a test environment and are ready to perform a gradual upgrade migration in your production environment. You have scheduled the migration to begin after the end of business on Friday and will progress through the upgrade, gradually moving sites from 2003 to 2007 over the next several weeks. You get a frantic phone call from Dory, one of the users in accounting, late on Friday afternoon saying that she is still in the middle of a project that requires she be able to access accounting's site to update resource files. She is concerned that the upgrade will cause a data loss that will in turn cause her project to suffer a serious delay. You assure Dory that all data has been backed up and can be recovered if the upgrade of accounting's site should cause any problems, but she still wants to know whether the 2003 version of accounting's site can be accessed in any way after the upgrade migration. What do you tell her?

A. You tell Dory that once the migration of accounting's site is done, it completely replaces the 2003 version, and although all her data should also be safely migrated, if it isn't, the data files can still be recovered from the backup.

B. You tell Dory that once the migration of accounting's site is done, it completely replaces the 2003 version; you also tell her that you have backed up all of the original content databases for the 2003 sites, and the original accounting site can be restored from the database backup if necessary.

C. You tell Dory that the 2003 version of accounting's site can still be accessed using the original URL and that all of the upgraded sites use new URLs that are to be provided to all SharePoint users as sites are upgraded.

D. You tell Dory that the 2003 version of accounting's site can still be accessed using a temporary URL that you can provide her with if necessary.

15. You are the SharePoint administrator for your company. You have successfully completed an in-place upgrade migration process from SharePoint 2003 to SharePoint 2007 in a test environment and are ready to perform a gradual upgrade migration in your production environment. You insert the SharePoint 2007 installation disc and launch the `Setup.exe` file. You progress through the required steps and notice that the process of performing the initial parts of the gradual upgrade seem quite similar to the in-place upgrade. Between launching `Setup.exe` and SharePoint Products and Technologies, what differences do you notice? (Choose all that apply.)

A. On the Upgrade tab, you notice you have to select Yes, Perform a Gradual Upgrade.

B. On the Server tab, you notice that you must select Complete – Install All Components.

C. On the File Location tab, you notice that you are offered the option to browse to a different directory from the default for the installation files.

D. On the Authentication tab, you notice you are offered the option of selecting Kerberos or NTLM.

16. You are the SharePoint administrator for your company. You have successfully completed an in-place upgrade migration process from SharePoint 2003 to SharePoint 2007 in a test environment and are ready to perform a gradual upgrade migration in your production environment. You have finished the initial installation phase of the upgrade and have moved on to the upgrade of a web application. You plan to select the SharePoint – 80 web application that hosts your SharePoint site collections. Where must this action be performed?

A. In Central Administration on the home page

B. In Central Administration on the Operations tab

C. In Central Administration on the Application Management tab

D. On the home page for the default shared services provider

17. You are the SharePoint administrator for your company. You have successfully completed an in-place upgrade migration process from SharePoint 2003 to SharePoint 2007 in a test environment and are ready to perform a gradual upgrade migration in your production environment. You have finished the initial installation phase of the upgrade and have moved on to the upgrade of a web application. You plan to upgrade the SharePoint – 80 web application that hosts your SharePoint site collections. During the upgrade, you must identify more than one database to update. Of the following choices, which are valid database types you must address in the web application upgrade process? (Choose all that apply.)

A. Content database

B. SQL database

C. Search database

D. SSP database

18. You are the SharePoint administrator for your company. You have successfully completed an in-place upgrade migration process from SharePoint 2003 to SharePoint 2007 in a test environment and are ready to perform a gradual upgrade migration in your production environment. You are at the part of the process where you must begin selecting site collections to upgrade. What is the first site collection that you must select, even if you select others to be upgraded at the same time?

A. The root site collection

B. The MySite site collection

C. The first web application site collection

D. The child portal site collection

19. You are the SharePoint administrator for your company. You have successfully completed an in-place upgrade migration process from SharePoint 2003 to SharePoint 2007 in a test environment and are ready to perform a gradual upgrade migration in your production environment. You are currently upgrading shared services using a gradual upgrade by upgrading the parent portal first method. You are about to upgrade the team sites and find that it is necessary to not just select these sites for upgrade but to perform all of the initial upgrade steps starting with relaunching Setup.exe and upgrading a web application. What circumstance required this?

A. The team sites are hosted under a child portal.

B. The team sites are hosted in MySites.

C. The team sites use a separate server farm.

D. The team sites use a separate personal site host.

20. You are the SharePoint administrator for your company. You have successfully completed an in-place upgrade migration process from SharePoint 2003 to SharePoint 2007 in a test environment and are ready to perform a gradual upgrade migration in your production environment. You are currently upgrading a web application and are at the part of the process where you need to select an application pool. You decide to select Create a New Application Pool. Of the following options, which ones are valid selections as next steps? (Choose all that apply.)

A. You can select Predefined and use the drop-down menu to select a security account.

B. You can select Configurable and use the drop-down menu to select a security account.

C. You can select Configurable and use the available fields to input a username and password for a security account.

D. You can select Predefined and use the available fields to input a username and password for a security account.

Answers to Review Questions

1. B, C, and D. CMS 2002 manages the features described in options B, C, and D. Option A is incorrect.

2. B, C, and D. All versions of Windows Server 2003 SP1 will support the migration including Standard Edition, Enterprise Edition, Datacenter Edition, and Web Edition. No version of Windows Server 2000 will support migration.

3. D. Option D displays the correct path to find the necessary files. The other options are bogus.

4. B. Although it is technically feasible to perform an in-place upgrade on a small SharePoint 2003 deployment, Microsoft recommends using this method only in a test environment.

5. B and D. Option A is false and option B is correct because both SharePoint 2003 and SharePoint 2007 installations coexist throughout the entire lifetime of the gradual upgrade process. Option C is false and option D is correct because upgraded sites take over the original URLs used by their 2003 versions and user requests are automatically redirected to the upgraded content. The 2003 versions continue to exist and can be accessed by temporary URLs that you must configure.

6. B, C, and D. Option A is incorrect because OWC uses ActiveX controls to provide charts, data source control, and PivotTables. OWC does not provide ActiveX controls as a service or feature.

7. A. You can extract the necessary CAB files from `C:\Program Files\Common Files\Microsoft Shared\Web Server Extensions\60\wppacks` on SharePoint 2003 and install those files in SharePoint 2007 to continue to use the required OWC components after the upgrade. You do not need to add that path to 2007, so option B is false. Option C is false because it does not reference the correct `stsadm.exe` command to add the CAB files to 2007, and option D is false because although OWC is not supported, you can still use OWC in 2007. Only option A is correct.

8. A and C. The only two valid methods of performing the shared services upgrade are those described in options A and C. Options B and D are bogus.

9. A, B, and D. Option C is not a required basic step in this process because the MySites upgrade can be included at any point in the gradual upgrade process that involves upgrading child portals first. The correct basic steps are creating a new SharePoint Server 2007 environment, upgrading the personal site host and personal sites in SharePoint Portal Server 2003 and attaching them to the new shared services provider, and upgrading child portals and attaching them to the new shared services provider.

10. B. You can run the scan either before starting the upgrade or just before running the SharePoint Products and Technologies Configuration Wizard. Option A is incorrect because it doesn't include both options. Options C and D are bogus.

11. A and C. The pages described in options A and C will be encountered in a large enterprise-level upgrade migration that will require a server farm and external database server. Options B and D are bogus.

12. B, C, and D. Option A is bogus since you already determined an authentication method before you got to this point in the upgrade process. All other options represent dialog boxes you will encounter and the correct responses.

13. B. You must create alternate domain URLs for each of the 2003 sites. During the migration process, you will be asked to input a temporary URL for each site being upgraded because the existing URL for the site will be "taken over" by the 2007 upgrade site. Options A, C, and D are bogus.

14. D. Even after a site is upgraded, it still exists and can be accessed using a temporary URL you configure for the site during the upgrade. The temporary URLs and the older sites can be deleted after all the sites have been upgraded to SharePoint 2007 and tested to make sure they are working properly.

15. A. Of the selections presented, only option A is different from the options you are offered in an in-place upgrade. Options B and C are offered in both methods, and option D is a bogus option since there is no Authentication tab and authentication is offered on a different page of the upgrade wizard.

16. B. The wizard that takes you through the process of upgrading a web application begins on the Operations tab of the Central Administration web application. All the other options are bogus.

17. A, C, and D. You must specify names for the content, search, and SSP databases during the web application upgrade. The option for the SQL database is bogus.

18. A. You must select the root site collection to be upgraded first, even if you select other site collections beneath the root to be upgraded at the same time. The other options are bogus.

19. C. You should have to go through these additional steps only if you have your team sites hosted on a separate server farm than the other sites. This is done only when you are administering an unusually large number of team sites. Both the parent portal and all child portals will likely contain team sites, so option A is false. Team sites aren't hosted under MySites, so option B is false. The personal site host is usually also the parent portal site, so option D is false.

20. A and C. A and C are the only two valid options. Options B and D are bogus.

Appendix

About the Companion CD

IN THIS APPENDIX:

✓ What you'll find on the CD

✓ System requirements

✓ Using the CD

✓ Troubleshooting

What You'll Find on the CD

The following sections are arranged by category and provide a summary of the software and other goodies you'll find on the CD. If you need help with installing the items provided on the CD, refer to the installation instructions in the "Using the CD" section of this appendix.

Some programs on the CD might fall into one of these categories:

Shareware programs are fully functional, free, trial versions of copyrighted programs. If you like particular programs, register with their authors for a nominal fee and receive licenses, enhanced versions, and technical support.

Freeware programs are free, copyrighted games, applications, and utilities. You can copy them to as many computers as you like—for free—but they offer no technical support.

GNU software is governed by its own license, which is included inside the folder of the GNU software. There are no restrictions on distribution of GNU software. See the GNU license at the root of the CD for more details.

Trial, demo, or *evaluation* versions of software are usually limited either by time or functionality (such as not letting you save a project after you create it).

Sybex Test Engine

For Windows

The CD contains the Sybex Test Engine, which includes all of the Assessment Test and Chapter Review questions in electronic format, as well as two bonus exams located only on the CD.

PDF of the Book

For Windows

We have included an electronic version of the text in .pdf format. You can view the electronic version of the book with Adobe Reader.

Adobe Reader

For Windows

We've also included a copy of Adobe Reader, so you can view PDF files that accompany the book's content. For more information on Adobe Reader or to check for a newer version, visit Adobe's website at http://www.adobe.com/products/reader/.

Electronic Flashcards

For PC, Pocket PC and Palm

These handy electronic flashcards are just what they sound like. One side contains a question or fill in the blank, and the other side shows the answer.

System Requirements

Make sure that your computer meets the minimum system requirements shown in the following list. If your computer doesn't match up to most of these requirements, you may have problems using the software and files on the companion CD. For the latest and greatest information, please refer to the ReadMe file located at the root of the CD-ROM.

- A PC running Microsoft Windows 98, Windows 2000, Windows NT4 (with SP4 or later), Windows Me, Windows XP, or Windows Vista

- An Internet connection

- A CD-ROM drive

Using the CD

To install the items from the CD to your hard drive, follow these steps:

1. Insert the CD into your computer's CD-ROM drive. The license agreement appears.

 Windows users: The interface won't launch if you have Autorun disabled. In that case, click Start ➤ Run (for Windows Vista, Start ➤ All Programs ➤ Accessories ➤ Run). In the dialog box that appears, type **D:\Start.exe**. (Replace **D** with the proper letter if your CD drive uses a different letter. If you don't know the letter, see how your CD drive is listed under My Computer.) Click OK.

2. Read through the license agreement, and then click the Accept button if you want to use the CD.

The CD interface appears. The interface allows you to access the content with just one or two clicks.

Troubleshooting

Wiley has attempted to provide programs that work on most computers with the minimum system requirements. Alas, your computer may differ, and some programs may not work properly for some reason.

The two likeliest problems are that you don't have enough memory (RAM) for the programs you want to use, or you have other programs running that are affecting installation or running of a program. If you get an error message such as "Not enough memory" or "Setup cannot continue," try one or more of the following suggestions and then try using the software again:

Turn off any antivirus software running on your computer. Installation programs sometimes mimic virus activity and may make your computer incorrectly believe that it's being infected by a virus.

Close all running programs. The more programs you have running, the less memory is available to other programs. Installation programs typically update files and programs; so if you keep other programs running, installation may not work properly.

Have your local computer store add more RAM to your computer. This is, admittedly, a drastic and somewhat expensive step. However, adding more memory can really help the speed of your computer and allow more programs to run at the same time.

Customer Care

If you have trouble with the book's companion CD-ROM, please call the Wiley Product Technical Support phone number at (800) 762-2974. Outside the United States, call +1(317) 572-3994. You can also contact Wiley Product Technical Support at http://sybex.custhelp.com. John Wiley & Sons will provide technical support only for installation and other general quality control items. For technical support on the applications themselves, consult the program's vendor or author.

To place additional orders or to request information about other Wiley products, please call (877) 762-2974.

Glossary

Active Directory   A directory service environment for Microsoft Windows that contains information about Active Directory objects such as users, groups, and organizational units and allows administrators to assign enterprise-wide policies.

Antivirus protection   A software solution that scans computer systems and their contents for viruses and other malware. You can configure antivirus protection in SharePoint to scan documents and perform other functions.

Application Definition file   An XML-formatted information file that provides standard definitions for each information source and that can be imported into SharePoint.

Application portal site   This type of portal site can be deployed for either internal or external customers; however, its structure is different because of the nature of the information presented. Application portals often include digital dashboards and other features for viewing and manipulating data related to the portal's purpose. The information presented in an application portal site usually comes from diverse sources, such as databases or other SharePoint sites.

ASP.NET 2.0   A free technology that allows programmers to create dynamic web applications. ASP.NET can be used to create anything from small, personal websites to large, enterprise-class web applications.

ASP.NET forms   Enables SharePoint to work with identity management systems that implement the Membership Provider interface.

Automatic site change adjustment   Automatically changes the site navigation links, correctly updating and renaming them when you change the structure of your website.

Breadcrumb navigation   Displays a dynamically generated set of links at the top of web pages to show users their current position in the site hierarchy.

Business data catalog (BDC)   A SharePoint shared service that accesses data from numerous back-end applications that exist outside of SharePoint Server and combines that information into a single report or profile.

Business intelligence (BI)   A collection of SharePoint 2007 utilities and services designed to organize and present business-critical data to corporate managers, decision makers, and other key individuals and groups within the company in the form of a chart, spreadsheet, or other organized forms for the purpose of analysis.

Cascading Style Sheets (CSS)   This is a style sheet language that is applied to an HTML page to provide styling to web pages.

Central Administration interface   A SharePoint web interface that allows you to apply administrative management of SharePoint services including mail, workflow, and Excel Services.

Collaboration site template   Collection of site templates that is available to help your business by providing a platform for sharing information and allowing collaborative efforts by teams working together on common documents and resources. The default site templates in the collaboration category are Team Site, Blank Site, Document Workspace, Wiki Site, and Blog.

COM+ An enterprise-level development environment for creating component-based, distributed applications. It is based on Microsoft's Component Object Model (COM).

Content approval The method by which site members with approver permissions control the publication of content.

Content flow The movement of documents from one location to another inside and outside the SharePoint site collection depending on the needs of the content creators and consumers.

Content Management Server (CMS) 2002 A necessary co-worker with SharePoint Portal Server 2003 that provides services such as navigation, summary links, and scheduled deployments. These services are fully integrated components of MOSS 2007, and CMS services are no longer required.

Content pages Each content page in SharePoint consists of text, images, and other content stored as an entry in a Pages library.

Content sources Used to crawl content in your site collections or on related external sites or business data applications.

Crawl rules Used to avoid crawling irrelevant content by excluding one or more URLs from being crawled.

Crawler impact rules Enable administrators to manage the impact your crawler has on the servers being crawled.

Current navigation Used to determine whether a site has unique navigation settings or inherits navigation from the parent site.

Customization The modification of the theme, style, branding, layout, and other visible elements of a site collection. Often the customization of your company's web presence site is different from the corporate intranet site. Partner and customer extranet site collections might also have their own, unique appearances.

Dashboard A feature integrated into the Report Center that allows you to organize a collection of dissimilar web parts and data sources such as KPIs and charts to display multiple streams of data in different ways for the purpose of presenting a set of graphic indicators of business-critical data.

Data filters Using filters, you can display only a subset of a data collection, designing the presentation for specific audiences that need to see only the information relevant to them.

Default content access account The account used by default when crawling content sources.

Diagnostic logging A SharePoint feature that allows you to use a number of troubleshooting tools on your server including event messages, trace logs, user-mode error messages, and Customer Experience Improvement Program events.

Directory Management Service A SharePoint service you can set up with incoming email configuration to allow the creation of distribution lists in SharePoint.

Discussion boards   A type of list in SharePoint that allows users to have interactive discussions in a text format.

Document Center site template   One of the default site templates native to MOSS 2007; it provides document management for large-scale companies with functions including checkout and check-in for editing, versioning, auditing, and support for various document formats.

Document Information Panel   The set of columns containing metadata for a document type being checked into a document library.

Document libraries   Containers in SharePoint for collections of documents.

Document management   A system to control the flow of documents including how they are created, reviewed, published, retained, and disposed.

Email settings   Configuration settings in SharePoint enabling collaboration with Microsoft Office Outlook and Exchange Server.

Entity   A main component of an application definition file and a business data item that represents some aspect of a company's method of operations.

Event throttling   A process you configure in SharePoint diagnostic logging that allows you to determine the level of critical events to have recorded in various logs for different event categories.

Excel Calculation Services (ECS)   The engine that drives Excel Services within SharePoint, loading workbooks, calculating data, and maintaining sessions.

Excel Services   The SharePoint service that allows for the storage, presentation, and manipulation of Excel workbook data stored on a secure server to be presented to SharePoint users in its totality or filtered for a specific presentation.

External data connections   Links to external data sources outside of SharePoint such as SAP and Siebel that can integrate information into SharePoint and be displayed in lists, libraries, and web parts.

External data sources   Data sources both within and outside of SharePoint that SharePoint can connect to and then collect, filter, and present within the SharePoint interface. Data sources can include SAP and Siebel.

Field controls   A part of page layouts that are simple Microsoft ASP.NET 2.0 controls bound to WSS data contained on the page. They have a small amount of code to display the two modes of the controls: one for render time and one for edit time.

Filter web parts   Web parts that specifically filter information received from various data sources so that only the relevant portions of the data are presented to SharePoint users.

Global navigation   Used to determine the navigation scheme for the parent site that will also be the navigation for subsites if the subsites are set to inherit navigation from the parent.

Governance   The rules and processes you want to establish for your site.

Gradual upgrade   An upgrade migration path from SharePoint 2003 to SharePoint 2007 that involves upgrading only a few sites or site collections to 2007 at one time rather than all sites or site collections being upgraded all at once.

HelpFold   The root document library for the SharePoint help file system.

Hierarchical portal site   A portal site structure designed along organizational lines. This can be a reflection of the company's official organizational chart or defined by different company processes or functions.

Hold   A library in the Records Center designed to contain documents that must be exempt from information management policies so that they will remain available pursuant to a policy or legal action.

Index   A service that indexes contents and properties of files on local and remote computers and provides rapid access to files through flexible querying language.

Information Management Policy   Allows you to control different content types for the purposes of tracking location and changes and managing document behaviors such as expiration. This feature is used in a Records Center to manage email and other records with features such as auditing, barcodes, and expiration elements.

Information rights management (IRM)   Works with Windows Rights Management to allow you to control how SharePoint documents can be used offline, such as allowing or preventing printing.

In-place upgrade   An upgrade migration path from SharePoint 2003 to SharePoint 2007 that involves a single upgrade action for the entire SharePoint platform.

Kerberos   A computer network authentication protocol that allows individuals communicating over an insecure network to prove their identity to one another in a secure manner.

Key performance indicators (KPIs)   Specialized lists and web parts in SharePoint that let you visually track progress made toward specific business goals.

Keywords   Sometimes called *keyword phrases*, the words users type into a search box when constructing a query.

Layout pages   A web page type that defines the layout for a content page.

Lists   Containers in SharePoint for collections of lists including links.

Master page   Defines the framework of the web page. It contains the elements that you want all your web pages in the site to have in common, and it provides a single location where you can control all the design elements.

My Site   A personal site within SharePoint that provides the user with a central location to store and manage their documents, graphics, links, and contacts. It is composed of both public and private areas and allows the user to collaborate with other users in the site collection directly from their My Site.

.NET Framework   Microsoft's managed code programming model for building applications.

NTLM (NT LAN Manager)   A Microsoft authentication protocol used with the SMB protocol. MS-CHAP is similar and is used for authentication with Microsoft remote access protocols.

Office InfoPath 2007   An information-gathering program included in the 2007 release of Microsoft Office that you can use to create and deploy electronic forms solutions to gather information efficiently and reliably.

Office Project Server 2007   A Microsoft Server product used to manage and coordinate work ranging from one-time projects to complex programs across the entire life cycle of a project. It is designed to be accessible by its client applications, Microsoft Office Project Professional 2007, and Microsoft Office Project Web Access.

Office SharePoint Designer 2007   SharePoint's primary design tool; it allows you to create a new master page or modify page layouts utilizing Cascading Style Sheets (CSS) technology so you can make changes across your entire MOSS site collection.

Office Web Components (OWC)   A collection of web parts, web part pages, templates, and other services that utilizes ActiveX controls to provide chart, data source control, PivotTable, and spreadsheet services in the SharePoint environment to take advantage of the features offered by the Office 2003 suite of applications and present information in a business intelligence type of setting.

Personal site   The heart of the user's My Site; it contains all the content relevant to the user including document libraries, picture libraries, and links. Anyone can use their personal site to collaborate with other users, but there's also a private home page only the user can access by default. This site functions as the user's My Site home page. Each user who has a personal site is the administrator of the site and can create and edit other pages, change the default layout or customize the page to personal taste, and change site settings.

Personalization   Individual customization. You can configure content filters that present only the information and features targeted to specific audiences based on their roles or interests.

Personalization site   Owned by the SharePoint administrator and used to disseminate targeted data to My Site users. For instance, if you wanted to publish a link to the HR department's Company Network Use Policy document to all SharePoint My Site users, you would use the personalization site to do so. Once published to My Sites, users cannot modify or remove the link.

Picture libraries   Containers in SharePoint for collections of pictures and other types of graphics.

POP (Post Office Protocol) 3 service   A standard mail protocol used to deliver mail from a mail server to a client mail program such as Microsoft Office Outlook.

Profile Services   Used to connect to user-profile data sources such as Active Directory or LDAP and import user properties into SharePoint user profiles.

Public profile page   The My Site page visible to anyone with access to the SharePoint site collection. Users can publish whatever information about themselves they want to be publicly available. The public profile page is also known as the My Site Public Page and is the public view of each user's User Profile and My Site. Anyone can access a user's public profile by clicking any link to a user within a portal site or site collection, including links in search results.

Query   A service used by search to crawl content in a database or index and produce a results list.

Quota template   Allows you to limit the amount of data stored on any individual site. You can set a quota using a default quota template or configure a customized quota template.

Record Collection Programmable Interface   A Records Center feature that lets you configure document and email management systems to automatically upload content into the Records Center based on either the SOAP or SMTP protocol.

Records Center site template   The main utility within SharePoint for managing the maintenance and retention of business records, providing a records collection interface, records routing, records vault capacities, and information policy management tools.

Records management   The process by which an organization determines what types of information are records, how to manage them through their retention periods, and how to ultimately destroy or archive them.

Records Pending Submission   A library in the Records Center designed to contain any documents sent that are missing the required metadata associated with the documents.

Records Routing   A Records Center feature that lets you route different records to specific libraries in the Records Center based on content type.

Report Center   The central framework site that organizes all the other components that make up business intelligence.

Rollup portal site   Ignores the hierarchical structure of the company and presents information for the organization as a whole. Subsites are not structured by teams, departments, or divisions, but they can be mapped to divisional portals. The overall goal is to allow resources, information, and subject-matter experts to be accessible to all levels of the corporation.

Scheduling   The ability to determine when users want content to appear; SharePoint users can do this only if they create content that uses major or minor versioning.

Securable object   In SharePoint, securable objects can include lists, libraries, sites, documents, or other SharePoint elements. Each of these levels can have access rights separately configured.

Self-Service Site Creation   Setting that enables you to allow anyone besides the SharePoint administrator to create and manage sites. Once you've enabled this, you can delegate the creation of SharePoint sites to other SharePoint users. This service also lets you create sites and site collections from the Site Directory.

Server role types The function a server plays in a server farm or other system based on the service or services it provides. Examples of different server roles are application servers, file and print servers, DNS servers, and domain controllers.

Shared Services Providers (SSPs) The logical environment that contains all the particular services that you want to make available across your web applications and SharePoint sites including Excel Calculation Services, Index Services, Search Services, and Web Services.

Simple Mail Transfer Protocol (SMTP) The standard protocol used to transfer email messages between mail servers.

Single sign-on (SSO) Allows SharePoint users to access external data sources without having to authenticate multiple times after signing on in SharePoint.

Site Directory Your site toolbox, allowing you as the SharePoint administrator to access, view, and manage all the sites in the site collection associated with the current portal site. You can view the portal's structure, view individual sites, and add, delete, approve, and reject sites.

Site map A collection of links leading to every web page on a website. The links are usually organized by category.

Site templates The building blocks for creating SharePoint sites and site collection. Specific templates come equipped with particular types of elements suited for providing a specific functionality.

SMTP See Simple Mail Transfer Protocol (SMTP).

SQL Server 2000 Desktop Engine (Windows) A free, redistributable database engine that is fully compatible with SQL Server. MSDE 2000 is designed primarily to provide a low-cost option for developers who need a database server that can be easily distributed and installed.

SSO encryption-key server Generates and stores the encryption key used to encrypt and decrypt credentials that are stored in the SSO database.

stsadm The command-line utility used to perform administrative tasks in SharePoint that are otherwise performed in the Central Administration web application.

Surveys A feature in SharePoint that collects responses from users on various subjects.

Top Sites A Content Query Tool part designed to display a dynamic set of items based on a query that you build by using a web browser. You use the query to specify which items are displayed, and you can set presentation options to determine how those items are displayed on the finished page.

User profile database A special database in SharePoint that contains information, meta-data, and properties for all SharePoint users.

Vault A Records Center feature that lets you guarantee the integrity of all records stored within it. Any record downloaded from the vault is assured to contain the same content as when the record was originally uploaded to the vault.

Versioning   The method by which successive iterations of a document are numbered and saved.

Web presence portal site   A Publications site usually designed with a tightly controlled theme, branding, and appearance and contains the data, services, and links you want to publicly offer and represent your company. Although many of the appearance elements remain stable over time, public sites are often very dynamic as to specific content in order to keep customers, partners, shareholders, and everyone else informed about and attracted to the company.

Windows authentication   The standard IIS Windows authentication methods are supported: Anonymous, Basic, Certificates, Digest, Kerberos (Integrated Windows), and NTLM (Integrated Windows).

Windows File Share Integration   An Outlook Web Access feature that lets you directly connect a SharePoint library to an Outlook Web Access web part interface.

Windows SharePoint Services (WSS)   Built on Microsoft Windows Server 2003, provides a foundation platform for building web-based business applications that can flex and scale easily to meet the changing and growing needs of your business.

WMSDE   See SQL Server 2000 Desktop Engine (Windows).

Workflows   Implement business processes on documents, web pages, and list items including routing a document for review, tracking an issue through its various stages of resolution, or guiding a contract through an approval process.

Workspaces   A special site template designed for specific tasks such as meetings or document management.

XML (Extensible Markup Language)   A W3C specification for a markup language specifically designed for creating web documents using customized tags.

Index

Note to the Reader: Throughout this index **boldfaced** page numbers indicate primary discussions of a topic. *Italicized* page numbers indicate illustrations.

N

Wiley Publishing, Inc. End-User License Agreement

READ THIS. You should carefully read these terms and conditions before opening the software packet(s) included with this book "Book". This is a license agreement "Agreement" between you and Wiley Publishing, Inc. "WPI".

By opening the accompanying software packet(s), you acknowledge that you have read and accept the following terms and conditions. If you do not agree and do not want to be bound by such terms and conditions, promptly return the Book and the unopened software packet(s) to the place you obtained them for a full refund.

1. License Grant. WPI grants to you (either an individual or entity) a nonexclusive license to use one copy of the enclosed software program(s) (collectively, the "Software," solely for your own personal or business purposes on a single computer (whether a standard computer or a workstation component of a multi-user network). The Software is in use on a computer when it is loaded into temporary memory (RAM) or installed into permanent memory (hard disk, CD-ROM, or other storage device). WPI reserves all rights not expressly granted herein.

2. Ownership. WPI is the owner of all right, title, and interest, including copyright, in and to the compilation of the Software recorded on the physical packet included with this Book "Software Media". Copyright to the individual programs recorded on the Software Media is owned by the author or other authorized copyright owner of each program. Ownership of the Software and all proprietary rights relating thereto remain with WPI and its licensers.

3. Restrictions On Use and Transfer.

(a) You may only (i) make one copy of the Software for backup or archival purposes, or (ii) transfer the Software to a single hard disk, provided that you keep the original for backup or archival purposes. You may not (i) rent or lease the Software, (ii) copy or reproduce the Software through a LAN or other network system or through any computer subscriber system or bulletin-board system, or (iii) modify, adapt, or create derivative works based on the Software.

(b) You may not reverse engineer, decompile, or disassemble the Software. You may transfer the Software and user documentation on a permanent basis, provided that the transferee agrees to accept the terms and conditions of this Agreement and you retain no copies. If the Software is an update or has been updated, any transfer must include the most recent update and all prior versions.

4. Restrictions on Use of Individual Programs. You must follow the individual requirements and restrictions detailed for each individual program in the About the CD-ROM appendix of this Book or on the Software Media. These limitations are also contained in the individual license agreements recorded on the Software Media. These limitations may include a requirement that after using the program for a specified period of time, the user must pay a registration fee or discontinue use. By opening the Software packet(s), you will be agreeing to abide by the licenses and restrictions for these individual programs that are detailed in the About the CD-ROM appendix and/or on the Software Media. None of the material on this Software Media or listed in this Book may ever be redistributed, in original or modified form, for commercial purposes.

5. Limited Warranty.

(a) WPI warrants that the Software and Software Media are free from defects in materials and workmanship under normal use for a period of sixty (60) days from the date of purchase of this Book. If WPI receives notification within the warranty period of defects in materials or workmanship, WPI will replace the defective Software Media.

(b) WPI AND THE AUTHOR(S) OF THE BOOK DISCLAIM ALL OTHER WARRANTIES, EXPRESS OR IMPLIED, INCLUDING WITHOUT LIMITATION IMPLIED WARRANTIES OF MERCHANTABILITY AND FITNESS FOR A PARTICULAR PURPOSE, WITH RESPECT TO THE SOFTWARE, THE PROGRAMS, THE SOURCE CODE CONTAINED THEREIN, AND/OR THE TECHNIQUES DESCRIBED IN THIS BOOK. WPI DOES NOT WARRANT THAT THE FUNCTIONS CONTAINED IN THE SOFTWARE WILL MEET YOUR REQUIREMENTS OR THAT THE OPERATION OF THE SOFTWARE WILL BE ERROR FREE.

(c) This limited warranty gives you specific legal rights, and you may have other rights that vary from jurisdiction to jurisdiction.

6. Remedies.

(a) WPI's entire liability and your exclusive remedy for defects in materials and workmanship shall be limited to replacement of the Software Media, which may be returned to WPI with a copy of your receipt at the following address: Software Media Fulfillment Department, Attn.: *MCTS: Microsoft Office SharePoint Server 2007 Configuration Study Guide (Exam 70-630)*, Wiley Publishing, Inc., 10475 Crosspoint Blvd., Indianapolis, IN 46256, or call 1-800-762-2974. Please allow four to six weeks for delivery. This Limited Warranty is void if failure of the Software Media has resulted from accident, abuse, or misapplication. Any replacement Software Media will be warranted for the remainder of the original warranty period or thirty (30) days, whichever is longer.

(b) In no event shall WPI or the author be liable for any damages whatsoever (including without limitation damages for loss of business profits, business interruption, loss of business information, or any other pecuniary loss) arising from the use of or inability to use the Book or the Software, even if WPI has been advised of the possibility of such damages.

(c) Because some jurisdictions do not allow the exclusion or limitation of liability for consequential or incidental damages, the above limitation or exclusion may not apply to you.

7. U.S. Government Restricted Rights. Use, duplication, or disclosure of the Software for or on behalf of the United States of America, its agencies and/or instrumentalities "U.S. Government" is subject to restrictions as stated in paragraph (c)(1)(ii) of the Rights in Technical Data and Computer Software clause of DFARS 252.227-7013, or subparagraphs (c) (1) and (2) of the Commercial Computer Software - Restricted Rights clause at FAR 52.227-19, and in similar clauses in the NASA FAR supplement, as applicable.

8. General. This Agreement constitutes the entire understanding of the parties and revokes and supersedes all prior agreements, oral or written, between them and may not be modified or amended except in a writing signed by both parties hereto that specifically refers to this Agreement. This Agreement shall take precedence over any other documents that may be in conflict herewith. If any one or more provisions contained in this Agreement are held by any court or tribunal to be invalid, illegal, or otherwise unenforceable, each and every other provision shall remain in full force and effect.

Microsoft Office SharePoint Server 2007 — Configuring Book/CD Package on the Market!

Get ready for your MCTS: Microsoft Office SharePoint Server 2007 — Configuring certification with the most comprehensive and challenging sample tests anywhere!

The Sybex Test Engine features:

- All the review questions, as covered in each chapter of the book.

- Challenging questions representative of those you'll find on the real exam.

- Two full-length bonus exams available only on the CD.

- An Assessment Test to narrow your focus to certain objective groups.

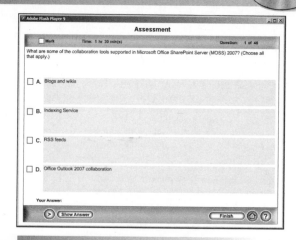

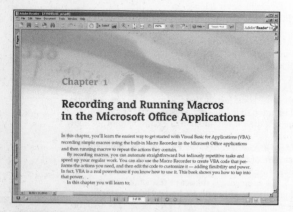

Search through the complete book in PDF!

- Access the entire *MCTS: Microsoft Office SharePoint Server 2007 Configuration Study Guide (70-630)* complete with figures and tables, in electronic format.

- Search the *MCTS: Microsoft Office SharePoint Server 2007 Configuration Study Guide (70-630)* chapters to find information on any topic in seconds.

Use the Electronic Flashcards for PCs or Palm devices to jog your memory and prep last-minute for the exam!

- Reinforce your understanding of key concepts with these hardcore flashcard-style questions.

- Download the Flashcards to your Palm device and go on the road. Now you can study for the Microsoft Office SharePoint Server 2007, Configuring (70-630) exam any time, anywhere.

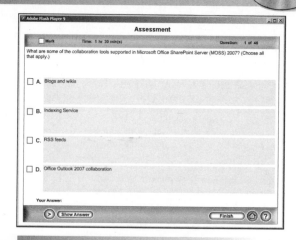